CU00960278

A
CENSUS OF IRELAND

CIRCA 1659

COIMISIÚN LÁIMHSCRÍBHINNÍ NA hÉIREANN

A
CENSUS OF IRELAND

CIRCA 1659

WITH ESSENTIAL MATERIALS
FROM THE
POLL MONEY ORDINANCES
1660–1661

EDITED BY

SÉAMUS PENDER, MA

LECTURER IN HISTORY, UNIVERSITY COLLEGE, CORK

WITH A NEW INTRODUCTION BY

WILLIAM J SMYTH

PROFESSOR OF GEOGRAPHY, UNIVERSITY COLLEGE, CORK

DUBLIN
IRISH MANUSCRIPTS COMMISSION
2002

ACKNOWLEDGEMENTS

I am indebted to many colleagues for insights relating to the limitations of the
'1659 Census'. My particular thanks to John Andrews, Paddy Corish, Paddy Duffy,
Bill McAfee, Kenneth Nicholls and Philip Robinson for commenting on earlier drafts
of all or part of this paper. I wish to acknowledge the helpful comments of participants
at seminars given at the Institute of Irish Studies, Queens University Belfast; the
Department of History, Trinity College Dublin; and a British Society for Population
Studies meeting in Dublin. I also wish to thank University College Cork for providing
support, through the Arts Faculty Fund, for this project. Thanks to Orla O'Sullivan
and Michael Murphy respectively for their careful typing and cartography.
I also wish to express my gratitude to Wendy Dunbar for her patience,
design work and production.

May, 2002 Willam J.Smyth.

© Irish Manuscripts Commission, 2002
© Government of Ireland, 2002

Printed by ColourBooks Ltd, Dublin
Cover design by Dunbar Design

ISBN 1 874280 15 0

WRESTLING WITH PETTY'S GHOST

THE ORIGINS, NATURE AND RELEVANCE OF THE
SO-CALLED '1659 CENSUS'

INTRODUCTION AND SUMMARY:

After three decades of significant economic development and massive immigration, during which the island was gradually integrated into the wider Atlantic economy, Ireland's population in 1640 may have stood at close on two million. By 1653, it was probably reduced to around 1.3 million – that is, by about one-third. A man close to the action at this time, William Petty, suggested a reduction of that order in Ireland's population. However, the precise nature of, and the regional variations in, these population transformations are unclear. What is clear is that the new radical Commonwealth government quickly set in motion a series of acts of settlement and a number of associated property surveys. Both the acts and surveys provided the framework (outside of the already planted areas) for the massive transfer and redistribution of property units to a new Protestant elite and for the consequent reconstruction of such properties in both town and countryside by a new energetic landlord class. At the end of the Commonwealth period and in part to ingratiate themselves with the soon-to-be restored Charles II, the Cromwellian members of the Commonwealth Convention in Ireland also agreed to the imposition of a *poll tax* that would partly defray the expenses of the large army that was then garrisoned on the island. Early in the reign of Charles II, and under the stimulus of the tireless Sir William Petty, the poll tax was replaced by a tax on all fireplaces – known subsequently as the hearth tax.[1]

The conquest and settlement of Ireland in the mid-seventeenth century has, therefore, provided the historian, the historical geographer and anthropologist with a wide range of surveys and related materials that can yield insights into the nature

---

1. For a general introduction to these themes, see W.J. Smyth, 'Society and settlement in seventeenth century Ireland: the evidence of the '1659 Census'', in W.J. Smyth and K. Whelan (eds), *Common Ground: Essays on the historical geography of Ireland* (Cork, 1988), pp. 55–83.

and reconstruction of society and settlement at this time. However, unlike nine-teenth-century state documents, the reliability, comprehensiveness, and meaning of the seventeenth-century materials are still far from clear. To redistribute land from the old owners to the new Cromwellians, a survey by local juries in each barony in each of twenty-seven counties was carried out in 1654, giving a narrative descrip-tion of each property, its relative location and estimated valuation, and occasional-ly uneven and often incidental details about land use, settlement, and leasing patterns. This survey has come to be known as the Civil Survey. Unfortunately, only fourteen of all or part of the county volumes of the Civil Survey have survived. After the Civil Survey in 1654, all confiscated properties were mapped at parish and barony scales, providing clear details of the lie of property and denominational boundaries but again offering highly uneven and ambiguous insights into the lay-out of settlement, roads, and infrastructural items generally. This mapped survey, planned and administered by William Petty, complete with its terriers that give additional information in relation to property owners and settlements, came to be known as the Down Survey. The survival rate of the parish maps of the Down Survey varies both within and between counties.

As argued below, Sir William Petty was also instrumental in conserving for us the records of the 1660–61 poll taxes. Pender (and before him Hardinge) interpreted these as a population census – hence the title of Pender's edition of the manuscript returns, *A Census of Ireland c. 1659*. This 'census' appears to be the most compre-hensive and most accessible of all such documents that have come down to us from the mid-seventeenth century; yet it has received little attention – no doubt because it is generally perceived as an incomplete, highly flawed, and very ambiguous doc-ument. And it should be remembered that the above surveys and the poll-tax – now known as the '1659 Census' – were carried out in a 'frontier' Atlantic country undergoing probably the deepest social, political and economic transformations that it had ever experienced.

The objectives of this preface are twofold. Firstly, the origins and nature of the '1659 Census' and Petty's role in its construction are examined. Secondly, the prac-tical relevance of this document to ongoing research on 17th century Ireland is briefly analysed and outlined through a series of maps. At the outset and by way of summary I will make the following observations:

1   The '1659 Census' is an abstract of poll-tax returns for 1660/61.

2   The 'Census' is a better, more consistent and more important source of infomation on mid-seventeenth century Ireland than has been allowed for in the existing literature.

3   We can now arrive at a much clearer idea of the strengths and deficiencies
    of the returns at all geographical levels and can also identify some of the
    reasons for county and baronial variations in the quality of the returns.

4   There are still outstanding problems of interpretation about the degree of
    reliability of the data-source which can only be clarified by detailed local
    and regional studies.

5   We can now more precisely situate this 'Census' in the context of William
    Petty's overall work objectives of the 1660s and can establish most of the
    methods and reasons why he engineered the abstraction of the poll-tax
    returns in the first instance.

6   By way of a series of examples and island-wide maps, the relevance of the
    'Census' to on-going scholarly research on 17th century Ireland is
    demonstrated.

I

CENSUS OR POLL-TAX?

WHILE SEARCHING FOR DOWN SURVEY MAPS at Lansdowne House in the spring
of 1864, W.H. Hardinge discovered what he later described as "copies of
.... townland census returns of the inhabitants of Ireland" in a wooden box containing manuscripts of "Sir Wm. Petty's Survey of Ireland, and other documents
relating to Ireland".[2] Arranged geographically by counties, baronies, parishes and
townlands and by cities, parishes and streets, these returns begin with a column
dealing with 'Numbers of People' per townland, or street. The next column headed 'Tituladoes Names' lists persons holding titles of honour whether lords, knights,
esquires or gentlemen or titles of office, profession, or calling whether mayor, alderman, doctors, lawyers or merchants. The final column distinguishes the number of
people classified as 'Eng/English and Scotts' as opposed to 'Irish'. At the end of each
baronial entry, the returns also identify the principal *Irish* family names and their
number for each barony.

Hardinge considered the returns to be "carefully and contemporaneously prepared

---

2. W.H. Hardinge, 'Observations on the earliest known manuscript returns of the people of Ireland',
in *R.I.A. Trans.*, 24 (1864), pp. 317–28.

transcripts of original official returns, compiled at the close of the Commonwealth period".[3] By examining specific names in the list of 'tituladoes', Hardinge arrived at the conclusion that the original returns had been compiled no later than the close of 1659 and was of the opinion "that these Census returns were made up during the period of Petty's [Down] Survey by Petty between December 1654 and 1659".[4] In his invaluable edition of these returns for publication by the Irish Manuscripts Commission, Pender saw "no reason to depart from Hardinge's statement that we are dealing with a census return (unfortunately incomplete) of the people of Ireland".[5] Pender further notes a comment of the Marquess of Lansdowne, Petty's biographer, who suggested that the returns "might well have been collected between 1655–1659 and then fair-copied by Petty's clerks for his own use".[6] Pender examined one of the three surviving Poll-Tax returns for County Tyrone – that for the parish of Termonmcgork – and argues that "this return as printed bears not the slightest resemblance to our returns: it has no tituladoes and lists of principal Irish and English names: there is no division of the inhabitants into English and Irish and the parish total does not appear".[7] The Poll-Money Ordinances of 1660 and 1661 were also examined by Pender but these did not convince him that the returns he was editing were poll-money returns: "Nowhere in the Ordinances does any reference occur as to a distinction between the Irish and English inhabitants of the county".[8] To Pender, this omission was the principal obstacle in attempting to identify the 'Census' returns as poll-money returns.

On the other hand, Pender, in his introduction, did include R.C. Simington's argument in favour of seeing the returns as an "abstract of ye people in Ireland that payed poll money 1660". Simington pointed out that poll-tax was levied in Ireland in pursuance of an Ordinance of the General Convention 24 April 1660 which directed that "all persons of the rank and degrees therein mentioned should pay the respective sums of money appointed viz. that every person above the age of 15 years of either sex under the degree or quality of a Yeoman or Farmer or Yeoman or Farmer's wife or widdow shall pay twelve pence".[9] In an ascending scale, the sum payable by gentlemen, esquires and knights and so on are specified.

A second Ordinance dated March 1661 doubled the tax (now referred to

3. Hardinge, *op. cit.*, p. 320.
4. Hardinge, *op. cit.*, p. 321.
5. S. Pender (ed.), *A Census of Ireland circa 1659 with supplementary materials from the poll money ordinances 1660–61*, (originally published, Dublin 1939). See this volume below.
6. Pender, *op. cit.*, this volume.
7. Pender, *op. cit.*, this volume.
8. Pender, *op. cit.*, this volume.
9. Pender, *op. cit.*, this volume.

specifically as 'Pole-Money') on those above 15 years of age and imposed much stiffer levels of taxation on persons of higher ranks and degrees. To Simington, therefore, these Ordinances "and the machinery provided for the collection of the Poll-money tax" supplied sufficient evidence as to the true source of origin of the so-called Census returns:

> Able and discreet Protestants [almost certainly assisted by parish constables] appointed by County Commissioners named in the Ordinances, were "to enquire of all and every person within the respective places limited to their care, of each sex, of and above the age of 15 years, of their ranks, qualities and degrees and of the dwelling and abiding place of such persons. These particulars, when obtained were to be furnished to the County Commissioners who, in turn, were to deliver to the High Collector in each county, "one estreat indented" comprising the names of the persons assigned to levy the sums rated on the inhabitants of every barony, *as well as the names of the persons chargeable*.[10]

To Simington then, the poll-tax records could provide a mass of data relating to the number, role, quality, degree and dwelling places of the people above the age of fifteen years which could then be abstracted probably at the baronial but possibly at a higher level in the form represented by the Survey 'Census' returns.

One of the strongest arguments advanced by Simington relates to the Trinity College manuscript 'An Estimate of the Pole-Money' found in a collection of papers relating to King Charles II's revenue for the second half of the seventeenth century (Table I, see pages x–xi).

Divided into provinces, sums of money are distinctly returned against each city or county with four columns captioned respectively: 'the first single Pole: the second single Pole: the first double Pole: the second double Pole'. In the so-called '1659 Census', population returns only exist for three baronies, Duleek, Ratoath and Skreen in County Meath. In 'An Estimate of the Pole-Money', the entry on the side of the first column under Co. Meath states '3 baronies only viz. Duleek, Skreen and Rathoath'. The missing returns for nine baronies in Co. Meath would, therefore, appear to be explained as would the absence of returns for counties Mayo, Cavan and Tyrone [but not counties Galway and Wicklow] since no returns are entered in either of the first two columns for any of these three counties. The date of '[1]660' on the back of the volume of manuscript returns for Co. Leitrim is, therefore, seen

10. Pender, *op. cit.*, this volume.

	C. JULY 1660 THE FIRST SINGLE POLE	C. SEPT. 1660 THE SECOND SINGLE POLE	C. MAY 1661 THE FIRST DOUBLE POLE	C. JULY 1661 THE SECOND DOUBLE POLE
	£	£	£	£

PROVINCE OF CONNAUGHT

Co. of Galway and Town of Galway	1871-03-00 [Lost?]	–	3010-08-00 [Not used]	2200-04-00
Co. of Mayo	–	–	–	–
Co. of Sligo	505-10-00	–	900-00-00	938-00-00
Co. of Roscommon	844-07-00	–	1218-10-00	1050-10-00
Co. of Leitrim	303-16-00	–	575-16-00	526-06-00
Town of Athlone –		126-02-00	94-06-00	

PROVINCE OF ULSTER

Co. of Antrim	894-09-00	–	1529-14-00	1475-00-00
Co. of Downe	960-14-00	–	1500-06-00	1466-04-00
Co. of Armagh	509-16-00	–	910-10-00	–
Co. of Monaghan	302-04-03	–	597-02-00	566-04-00
Co. of Cavan	–	–	798-02-00 [Why Not Used?]	566-08-00
Co. of Fermanagh	580-06-00	–	614-18-00	648-08-00
Co. of Tyrone	–	–	–	–
Co. of Donegal	229-09-00 [Not used]	–	876-04-00 [Used by Petty?]	822-06-00
Co. & City of London Derry	684-12-00	–	1546-18-00	1271-06-00
Town of Carrickfergus	106-00-00	–	166-06-00	113-16-00

Note: Comments inside square brackets are my own and relate to key questions as to which returns Petty used or did not use.

TABLE I –

Trinity College Mss entitled 'An Estimate of the Pole-Money' (Abbott's Catalogue, No. 808)

	C. JULY 1660 THE FIRST SINGLE POLE	C. SEPT. 1660 THE SECOND SINGLE POLE	C. MAY 1661 THE FIRST DOUBLE POLE	C. JULY 1661 THE SECOND DOUBLE POLE
	£	£	£	£

PROVINCE OF LEINSTER

City of Dublin	1181-09-00	–	–	1594-10-00
Co. of Dublin	1009-04-00	–	–	1577-18-00
Co. of Meath	639-10-00	–	–	2531-18-00

(* 3 Baronies only viz. Duleek, Skreen and Rathoath)

Co. of Westmeath	890-04-00	–	1257-00-00	

(Note: The barony of Moygish and Brawny for the 1st double poll not returned)

Co. of Louth	563-10-00	–	–	1009-10-00
Co. of Kildare	983-15-00	–	–	–
Co. of Wicklow	299-01-00	–	–	578-18-00
[Why not used?]				
Co. of Wexford	983-09-00	–	–	1771-10-00
Co. of Caherlagh	374-18-00	–	–	47-00-00

(Barony of Caherlagh only returned in 2nd double poll)

Kings Co. (Offaly)	566-10-00	–	–	855-12-00
Queens Co. (Laois)	734-07-00	–	–	969-04-00
Co. of Kilkenny and city of Kilkenny	1241-08-00	–	–	–
Town of Drogheda	No return	–	112-08-00	238-16-00
Co. of Longford	338-16-00	–	–	438-14-00

PROVINCE OF MUNSTER

Co. of Cork	No Account	–	6835-06-00	8392-04-00
City of Cork	3969-04-00	–	621-44-00	571-10-00
Co. of Tipperary	No Account	–	3551-02-00	3165-16-00

(*Towns of Cashel, Fethard, & Carrick 1st Poll £115-18-00)

Co. of Waterford	679-14-00	–	1173-08-00	1096-08-00
City of Waterford	138-04-00	–	226-06-00	–
Co. of Kerry	489-10-00	–	855-14-00	500-14-00
Co. of Limerick	1513-14-00	–	1995-04-00	1451-02-00
City of Limerick	233-02-00	–	453-02-00	402-16-00
Co. of Clare	**	–	1702-16-00	–

(** Not signed 1st Poll £1304-13-00)

TABLE I – (Continued)

as pertinent by Simington. For him, the so-called '1659 Census' is a Poll-tax return for 1660.

As Simington further argues, William Petty was quite familiar with the poll-tax. Perhaps the most important reference is in *The Political Anatomy of Ireland* where Petty notes that "the number of them of all degrees who paide poll-money, *Anno 1661*, was about 360,000".[11] Although Simington does not refer to it, the latter figure may be even more important for the 'small and rather neat figures' of county population totals which Petty added on to the front of each county manuscript volume included quite a number of errors. The correct total is 379,628 but Petty's own total would probably have come to 357,035. It should be also noted that Petty's influential *A Treatise of Taxes and Contributions* (written in early 1662) included chapters on poll-money and hearth money taxes where he stresses the clear advantages of hearth tax "as the easiest and clearest, and fittest to ground Revenue upon: it being easier to tell the number of hearths *which remove not as Heads or Polls do*".[12] It could be argued, therefore, that Petty may have originally intended to use these poll-tax returns to estimate total populations (as he actually did for Dublin City where his great friend John Graunt notes that the estimate of about 30,000 ... "agrees, with that which I have heard the Books of Poll-Money ... have exhibited as the number of inhabitants of that city").[13] The introduction of the hearth tax in 1662 may have made redundant the further use of the poll-tax abstracts for population estimates. To Simington, the authorship of the format of the returns would seem definitely indicated by the Anglo-Spanish term *Tituladoes*, Petty's own word, "and the specific inclusion of details as the number of 'Irish' and 'English'/'English and Scotts' also suggested the hand of Petty" who had continually sought information of this kind for Ireland in 1641, c. 1653 and presumably for 1660/61.[14]

Pilsworth adds further support to Simington's arguments. Noting that sheriffs, mayors and aldermen held office *not* over say the calendar year of 1659 but from Michaelmas day 1659 to the following Michaelmas, he confirms that the Sheriffs of Dublin and Drogheda as returned in the 'Census' were, therefore, in office during most of 1660. Using other biographical evidence, he clearly indicates that at least "a portion of returns" were collected in the early summer of 1660 and specifically between the publication of the Ordinances on 24 April and the completion of the

11. W. Petty, *The Political Anatomy of Ireland*, first published in 1691, reprinted by C.H. Hull (ed.) in *The Economic Writings of Sir William Petty* (Cambridge, 1899).
12. W. Petty, *A Treatise of Taxes and Contributions* first published in 1662, reprinted in C. H. Hull, *op. cit.*
13. Graunt's estimate is noted by Hull, op. cit., p. 399.
14. R.C. Simington, 'A "Census" of Ireland c.1659' – the term "Titulado" ' in *Anal. Hib.*, 12 (1943), pp. 177–8.

collection on 1 July 1660.[15] The Ordinances also exempted members of Trinity College, ordained ministers, their wives or such children as are resident and living in their families unmarried, 'hospitalmen' and 'people living upon alms'. Pilsworth stresses that there is not a single mention of any clergyman (including bishops) in any of the lists of tituladoes – presumably because such clergymen were not taxed and, therefore, could not have appeared in the poll-tax lists. Finally, Pilsworth notes the very rare entry on page 444 for the barony of Garrycastle in the Kings County: "besides Shropshire adventurers wch pd 02l (A similar entry is returned on p. 276 for Co. Limerick – 'John Jurin, Aduenturer 10li' [10$^{s?}$ wJS]) which strongly supports the view that the returns had something to do with the payment of tax. To Pilsworth, "the lists before us appear to coincide both as regards the period of time and the exceptions with the known conditions of poll-tax and when taken in conjunction with the cogent arguments adduced by Mr Simington it seems to be proved convincingly that they do in fact represent a summarised form of the Poll-Tax Returns for 1660".[16] However, the difference in poll-tax amounts paid by Limerick's Jurin as compared to the Shropshire adventurers may signal that the returns for this King's County barony may be for 1661 and not 1660.

Scattered through the 'Census' are other indications of it being a Poll-tax. The entries for the City of Drogheda are particularly interesting in the hierarchical layout of the qualifications of the different populations in the city:

> Esquires, and Esquiresses &c
> Gentlemen, and Gentlewomen
> Yeomen and their wives, &c,
> Labourers, and their wives, &c,
> Souldiers and their wives, (p. 475),

thus clearly replicating the different taxation levels outlined in the Ordinances. The town of Charlemont in Co. Armagh exhibits a more truncated version of the same (p. 39). The frequent references elsewhere to 'soldiers and their wives' also emphasises quite clearly that married females are certainly included in the returns. City references to 'alien' and 'foreigner' also indicate a concern with the Ordinance classification as all 'foreigners' were required to pay double their respective taxation levies. Those named as tituladoes also incorporates *all* the Ordinance taxation gradations in the upper echelons of society. Likewise, the reference in 'O'Neyland' barony in Co. Armagh that 'the servants Names are not written in ye Booke' (p. 40) and for the barony of Athlone, Co. Roscommon, that 'the Servants Names in this

15. N.J. Pilsworth, 'Census or poll-tax' in *R.S.A.I. Jn.* (1943), pp. 22–4.
16. Pilsworth, *op. cit.*, p. 23.

Barrony are not set down' (p. 592) points, amongst other things, to another major taxation grouping.

And even if deficient by the order of 50–55 per cent, the hearth money records of the mid 1660s – the records of the tax on hearths or fireplaces initiated in 1662 to replace the poll-tax – also clearly, if indirectly, confirm that the poll-tax is a partial list [i.e. of adults] and not a *full* census of all the population. Likewise, an analysis of surviving individual poll tax returns for three Tyrone parishes (1660) and for Clonmel (1661) confirms that the overall sex ratio in these poll tax returns is quite even and that, apart from children, and even allowing for early age of marriage, both single adult females and most single adult males who were not working as servants or otherwise employed were *excluded* in these returns.

Simington and Pilsworth, therefore, were correct in seeing the returns as abstracts from the 1660 poll tax. Pender's reluctance to accept these arguments stemmed in part from his reliance on Hardinge's prior arguments. As we have seen, Pender did examine one of the surviving poll tax returns for County Tyrone – that of the parish of Termonmcgurk – but argued that this return bore not the slightest resemblance to what he called the '1659 Census' returns. The original returns, he argued, had no listing of 'Tituladoes', no division of inhabitants into English and Irish, and no listing of principal Irish or English names. However, it is clear that the 'Tituladoes' – the highest taxpayers – could easily be identified from the original parish returns of the poll tax lists; it is equally clear that Irish and English family names could have been identified from the detailed listing of both Christian names and surnames. Pender's examination of the Poll-Money Ordinance of 1660 thus did not convince him that the returns he was editing and which he called the '1659 Census' could emanate from this source. Pender clearly did not allow for either Petty's great organizational skills or his penetrating mind, which could plan for specific details regarding both the gentry and the ethnic status of taxpayers to be abstracted from the original poll tax returns.

In conclusion, Pender and Hardinge's arguments must now be set aside. First, the central date for the so-called census is not 1659 but 1660. Second, the returns as published are not a census but an abstract of adults taxed mainly in the poll tax of 1660. Third, the surviving original poll tax parish records (see Section III below) confirm that the full population can be estimated by using a multiplier of the order of 2.8 – 3.0. Fourth, returns clearly are missing for identifiable counties and baronies and for a not yet fully identified series of parishes within individual counties. Fifth, internal inconsistencies in the returns as between counties and baronies – although not a major issue – still need to be ironed out (see Section III below). In summary, the realization of the nature, provenance, and date of the returns allows the scholar to make careful yet powerful inferences about Irish settlement and society in the 1660s.

II

HOW AND WHY PETTY CONSTRUCTED 'THE 1659 CENSUS'

ONE OF PETTY'S CENTRAL AMBITIONS when coming to Ireland was to take an active part in the government's survey of forfeited lands. He was given control of this major mapping enterprise late in 1654 and with the production of the Down Survey early in 1656, one of the most original, comprehensive and accurate surveys ever attempted of any country had been achieved. As Goblet wrote, Ireland then became the best mapped country in the western world.[17] In one bold stroke, Petty had significantly advanced the objectives of the Baconian school of natural philosophy and reformist programmes generally in the production of this comprehensive mapping 'narrative' of a specific geographical region. The Civil and Down Surveys of 1654/56 came to constitute Ireland's Domesday Books and their entrepreneur was William Petty.

But Petty had wider ambitions. Parallel to the satisfaction of the government contract as to the surveying of the forfeited land, Petty had from the beginning strategically seen this mapping project as a means by which he could eventually construct what we can justifiably call his *Atlas of Ireland*. As Goblet in his brilliant reconstruction notes, Petty instructed his key cartographers led by his loyal cousin John Pettie and the tireless and skilful Thomas Taylor to not only reproduce a set of cadastral type maps similar to the Down Survey itself but more significantly to begin work on the barony and county maps for 'A Geographical Description of Ireland' or *Hiberniae Regnum*.[18] In February of 1661 he instructed his cousin that

17. Y.M. Goblet, *La transformation de la géographie politique de l'Irlande au XVIIeme siécle dans les cartes et essais anthropogéographiques de Sir William Petty,* (Paris, 1930); see also Goblet's introduction to *A topographical index of the parishes and townlands of Ireland* (Dublin, Irish Manuscripts Commission 1932), originally published in Paris (1930) as *Les noms de lieux Irlandais dans l'oeuvre géographique de Sir William Petty.*
18. See J.H. Andrews's introduction to *Hiberniae Delineatio* by Sir William Petty (1685) and *A Geographical Description of ye Kingdom of Ireland* by Sir William Petty and F.R. Lamb (c.1689), Shannon, Ireland, 1969.

a "description of each map" should be included in the book of intended county and provincial maps.[19]

By March of 1661 Petty suggests that he also intends this strategy for a new set of barony maps. The barony was always the central unit of administration, enumeration and mapping for Petty. Writing on 19 March 1661, he tells his cousin: "Now that you have beaten up your drum and have hands enough, let there be made a general catalogue of all ye baronies in each county, of ye parishes in each baronie, and all ye small denominations in each parish as they appear in any of your '53' or '54' civil surveys or in our own admeasurements whether ye land be forfeited or not ...... there be descriptions of each barony in ye Civil Survey. Have your eye out for a pretty youth or a man who can write clearly shorthand, read Latine etc. These lists I would make use to order of ye maps within mentioned".[20] These barony maps – now in the Bibilotheque Nationale in Paris – are quite different from the Down Survey barony maps. They are not cadastral in theme but geographical in scope and seek to represent a *synthesis* of geographical materials at the baronial scale. And the crucial point here as the above quotations suggest, Petty intended to match the images of these baronies, counties and provincial maps in his 'Atlas' with parallel narrative descriptions and statistics of each territory so as to provide a comprehensive view of Ireland and all its parts, firstly to influence English administrators and secondly for a larger international audience. Nothing short of a synthesis of Ireland's geography was on Petty's mind i.e. 'the new Geography we expect of that Island [Ireland]'.[21]

The early stirrings of his now famous book – *The Political Anatomy of Ireland* (actually completed in 1671 but not published until after his death in 1691) – were also fertilising in the late 1650s and early 1660s. The polymath scientist Petty had been a Professor of Anatomy and Music and had experimented with a whole range of new inventions including the double-bottomed boat but fundamentally Petty's intellectual concerns were centered on the better management or government of the state. John Keynes describes him as 'the father of modern economics' or perhaps we should say 'political economy'.[22] One of the most impressive things about Petty is his comparative method and range. Hence his need to gather data not only on English and Irish cities, populations, imports-exports, government institutions but

19. Letter of 5 February 1661 from William Petty to John Pettie "his cousin and agent in Ireland", Petty manuscripts, Letters, Vol.6, No.14, Department of Manuscripts, British Library, London.
20. Letter of 19 March 1661 from William Petty to John Pettie, Petty manuscripts, Vol.6, No.25, Department of Manuscripts, British Library, London.
21. See the Preface of Petty's *A Treatise on Taxes and Contributions* in Hull, *op. cit.*, p. 6.
22. John Keynes, as referenced by his brother Geoffrey Keynes in *A bibliography of Sir William Petty FRS and of Observations on the Books of Mortality by John Graunt FRS*, Oxford, 1971, Preface, vii.

also the equivalent data for France, Italy, the Netherlands, America, wherever. As a founder member of the Royal Society and a mover in various other intellectual circles, he was well-read in the most advanced ideas of this time. He was well aware of the burgeoning geographical literature and also aware of the now blossoming trade in atlases – whether those of Mercator, Ortelius or Saxton. His objective was to put Ireland on the world map.

Petty's friendship with John Graunt, their intimate discussions – especially in the first half of 1661 – about the content of the latter's observations on the London Bills of Mortality (first published in April 1662) and especially its concluding section on the application of population statistics to state policy are all pertinent to Petty's drive to utilise and abstract the poll-tax returns. In October 1662, Petty wrote to Lord Brouncker of the Royal Society of London: 'When I first landed here [middle of 1661?] some matter presented itself whereupon to make *observation(s) upon Ireland* [my italics] not unlike those which Mr Graunt made upon the London Bills of Mortality, I have done so much uppon it, as hath cost me a few pounds – but not so much as is worth more than a bare mention'.[23] Geoffrey Keynes and C.H. Hull[24] both assume that Petty is here referring to his gathering of materials on the Dublin Bills of Mortality. But Petty is clear if typically cagey about his project: it is 'matter' relevant to making *observations upon Ireland* that he refers to. And the likely 'matter' is the poll-money material and the 'few pounds' relate to the cost of their abstraction by Petty's clerks. With the help of the poll-tax, he wished to write a geography of Ireland – 'of its numbers, weight and measures' – just like Graunt's observations regarding London. Petty was in the Irish Parliament when the Committee enquiring into the poll-monies reported to the House in July of 1661.[25] On the same day, Petty was appointed to another Parliamentary Committee which shared a number of common members with the poll-tax Committee. Petty, therefore, was very well informed about the nature of the poll-taxes and recognised very quickly their potential for realising his burning ambition 'to compute the people and their occupations'. Hardinge's claim (see Pender's introduction) that he could not find any payment of money to the persons employed in making out 'the details of the 1659 Census' is justified. What he did not know is that Petty had spent a three figure sum to pay for the clerks and paper used to abstract the poll-tax returns for his own policy-driven and publishing concerns.

It may also be worth noting that on the same day that Petty wrote to Brouncker,

23. Letter of Sir William Petty to Lord Brouncker, 29 October 1662, Letter No.3162, Royal Society of London Library, London.
24. G. Keynes, *op. cit.*, Preface, x; Hull, *op. cit.*, p. 480.
25. Journal of House of Commons, July, 1661, pp. 422–43.

he also wrote to Sir Robert Moray of the Royal Society: 'I have forborne to give you my scheme about ye *Survey* [my italics]until I might have an occasion to be at ye place myself [i.e. London] for I would not have such a design either baffled or abused'.[26] The 'Survey' in this case could be his mapping enterprises following on from the Down Survey (which he always called 'the Map' or the 'Grand Map') but in the context of that day's letter-writing, it is more likely that he is referring to his poll-tax abstracts which were to be treasured by Petty and eventually stored in a wooden oak chest which is still marked 'Sir William Petty's MSS relating to the *Survey of Ireland*. And just as in later life Petty was to claim authorship of Graunt's *Observations*, so at the close of his life Petty does seem to imply that the poll-tax materials were a unique product of his own survey work. It is, therefore, not surprising that Hardinge, Landsdowne and indeed Pender were misled by the use of the term 'Survey'.

However, there is little doubt but that the destinies of the maps of *Hiberniae Regnum* and the poll-tax abstracts were inter-linked – even to the extent of the use of paper strips from the barony maps to bind the poll-tax volumes together and more particularly in the clear, consistent overlap between the key scribes for the two projects. It is also clear that the corrections made to the work of the clerks abstracting the poll-tax are made by the same hand as a key Down Survey scribe – most likely John Pettie. And in the end William Petty himself brackets all these 'Survey' materials together in his will and stores them in the same wooden chests.[27]

Thus in the later 1650s and more particularly in the early 1660s, after he succeeded in having the trusted John Pettie appointed as Deputy Surveyor General (1660–1667) of the Court of Exchequer at Dublin Castle and Thomas Taylor in turn appointed as John Pettie's chief assistant, Petty instructed these two key lieutenants and collaborators to obtain a vast range of often classified statistical data from the government archives. Petty's friends in high places – Dr Robert Wood (one of the Accountants General of the Customs and Excise), Sir Allen Broderick (Surveyor General) and Sir Robert Southwell – opened many doors for Pettie, Taylor and their clerks as they sought to meet the usually focused, always curious and often insatiable demands of the master 'statistician' and political scientist Sir William Petty (knighted by Charles II on 13 April 1661). As Hardinge notes: "No

---

26. Letter from Sir William Petty to Sir Robert Moray, 22 October 1662, Letter No.3160, Royal Society of London Library, London.
27. The details of Petty's will are contained in the Petty papers, Box T, No.40, Department of Manuscripts, British Library, London. Also in Appendix H of W.H. Hardinge's 'On Manuscript Mapped and Other Townland Surveys in Ireland from 1640 to 1688', in *R.I.A.. Trans.*, XXII, pp. 110–15.

one connected with Ireland had a fairer opportunity of gratifying his taste in whatever custody the original record might have been, than the Doctor [Petty]".[28] All
the evidence suggests that Petty was gathering material for a number of projects
including a major work of geographical synthesis.

It is easy, therefore, to imagine Petty sitting at his desk in New Buildings in
Dublin's Castle Street laying out the column headings for his abstract books of 'ye
population' from the 'pole-money' books. In the first column the names of the
parishes are returned and in the second the 'places' or 'denominations' which we
would now designate as townlands. England had had a *Notarum Villarum* from the
13th century. Petty was now going to lay the foundations for the same kind of settlement register for Ireland. And for this, a key geographical scale of his Down
Survey maps – that of the parish – is critical. The parish remained a central unit of
management, enumeration and assessment for Petty. He was often to argue that the
parish should be the basic unit for a census and always insisted on getting at actual
numbers rather than estimations or conjectures as to numbers. Time and time
again he insisted on the need for the provision of *printed* headlines for population
enumeration at the parish level. And his radical attempts at the standardisation of
parish distributions in England and Ireland did get beyond the drawing board.[29]

The poll-tax records also provide a vast amount of information on townlands and
their seventeenth century pronunciation in English. Although Petty had little
knowledge of the Irish language, he had attempted to understand the meaning of
some key placename terms; he had toyed with the idea of eradicating these 'uncouth
and unintelligible' names and replacing them with 'new names'. Early in 1661 Petty
had asked John Pettie to make a comprehensive index of Irish placenames from "the
Civil, Down, Grosse/Stafford surveys, from *poll-books*, hearth books, excise bookes
with their English names or names in English and also establish what new name
each present proprietor used".[30] In the end Petty decided that his best strategy was
a thorough anglicisation of Irish names. The listing of the names in the '1659
Census' is, therefore, of fundamental importance to Irish placename scholars today.
It provides a critical single benchmark across most of the island of the phonetic rendering of townland names in the mid-seventeenth century.

Next comes the crucial column on *Number of People*. Petty required his clerks to
reduce the poll-tax estreats or returns to their essence i.e. number of tax-payers per
townland and parish or per street and parish while also providing at the critical

28. W.H. Hardinge, 'Manuscript Returns', *op. cit.*, p. 323.
29. See, for example, Petty's *A Treatise of Taxes and Contributions*, London, 1662, pp. 23–5.
30. Letter from William Petty to John Pettie, March, 1661, Petty manuscripts, Vol. 6, Department
of Manuscripts, British Library, London.

barony level the total number of 'taxpayers'/'people' for that barony. This task of abstraction was probably carried out between the latter end of 1661 and the middle of 1662. It was a massive undertaking to abstract this material for the whole country – and while not remotely in the same league in physical or organisational demands, it nevertheless matches in vision and detail the earlier Down Survey. Petty did not have an actual Census to use to help write his geographical descriptions or economic analyses. But he had the imagination and organisational skills to construct the nearest thing to a Census out of the poll-tax records. Through this laborious abstraction, townland by townland, parish by parish, barony by barony, Petty came close to realising one of his central goals – the provision of statistical data on Ireland's [adult] population at a variety of scales from the townland/street, parish, barony to the four provinces and the island as a whole. So Petty was getting his General Register of the inhabitants of the country just as he had advocated and sought to construct a Land Registry as well as Registry of Commodities.[31] Petty's philosophical background and practical orientation geared him to seek for calculations of and the number and distribution of people over the whole island so as to be better able to both measure the wealth of the country and manage its political and economic affairs.

Petty was also getting closer to identifying the number, distribution and ethnic status of the elites. The next column is called by the distinctive Petty title of 'tituladoes', already used in Petty's *A Treatise of Taxes*, written in early 1662 and published in April of that year. In March of 1661, Petty instructed his cousin John – how that he had a larger working staff of 10 clerks – to make a general catalogue "of all proprietors, Protestant and Papist as they stand in any of ye Surveys to be arranged according to provinces, counties, parishes and denominations".[32] The poll-tax abstracts provided further detailed information for all these levels. And it is clear that Petty sought precise information as to the actual townland residence of the 'tituladoes'. There is quite a number of instances of double-checking of locations in this column for County Carlow, County Cork, Kings County and County Wexford. For example, it would appear that John Pettie corrected the Carlow entry for Symon Kavenagh, whose townland residence is corrected to Lissalican and not as originally designated at Balliline.

Finally comes the most controversial column of all, that of the 'English/Scotts' and 'Irish'. Throughout most of his whole adult life, Petty remains obsessed with

31. See, for example, Box A, Letter 24, 1661 with regard to Petty's scheme for the use of surveys and for registers to be set up, Department of Manuscripts, British Library, London.
32. Letter from William Petty to John Pettie, March, 1661, Petty manuscripts, Vol. 6, Department of Manuscripts, British Library, London.

this question – regularly seeking details as to the ratio of Irish to English/Scotts in
1641, in 1660 and in 1685. This was not an idle speculative question. For Petty
the ratio of Irish to English/Scots related crucially to the balance of demographic
power within the island and bore particularly on the safety of the British population. The long shadow of 1641 hung heavily over his shoulder. Petty was especially fearful in the immediate post-Restoration period – and more especially with the
ascent to power of James II – of an Irish Catholic overthrow of the established
Protestant order. Not surprisingly it is Petty himself who completes many of the
county totals for this column in the original manuscript.

It was the same column which most baffled Hardinge and Pender. How could
such an ethnic classification emerge from the seemingly innocent poll-tax returns?
They had not reckoned on Petty's passion for numbers, precision, definitions and
the century's need for classification. However, it still remains a mystery as to what
instructions Petty issued to his collaborators and clerks to help them make their ethnic classifications on the basis of the available lists of Christian and surnames.

What is now clearer, however, is how Petty managed the numerical summaries for
English/Scotts and Irish and more particularly how the astonishingly rich, comprehensive listing of 'principal Irish [family] names [and] their Numbers' are provided
at the end of each barony. When I visited Bowood House in April 1988, I inspect-
ed the original manuscript volumes of the so called 'Census'. As Pender notes, the
scribe involved with the County of Cork (but not the City) and County Kerry was
more careless in writing style. In addition, it appears that this scribe was not following the proper instructions for the barony summary of principal Irish family
names. For the towns of Bandon, Youghal and Mallow and for the baronies of
Kinsale, Kerrycurrihy and Kinalmeaky corrections and additions had to be made to
all the key family lists. Some of these additions are pinned to the back of the relevant original manuscript pages. It is clear that the scribe's original cut off point for
including family names was too sharp. For example, for the barony of Kinalmeaky,
the original listing ran from 'O Cullane, 13' to 'McDonagh, 20'. The additional
names from 'O Boigid (8)' to 'McDonnell (8)' were subsequently added to the list
(p. 207). Alternatively, the Cork County volume was the first volume to be
abstracted and Petty may have been experimenting with the detailed cut off point
for family name lists. Either way, it appears that this scribe is not used or retained
for the rest of the project as all other counties are produced by two key scribes who
also played pivotal roles in designing the Down Survey and later barony maps. And
whatever the sequence of counties as completed – whether Cork was first or later –
these baronial amendments provided essential clues as to how the ethnic columns
were first arrived at. It strongly appears that Petty's clerks were required to identify

all Irish family names for each townland and parish. The absolute total for the Irish in a barony was arrived at cumulatively in this way. The figure for the Irish was then likely subtracted from the 'Number of people' to give the figure for the English column. Or alternatively, as with County Fermanagh, the 'English/Scotts' column was also completed, townland by townland, just like that for the 'Irish'.

And so by early 1663 Petty was poised to complete his 'Geographical Description of the Kingdom of Ireland' with maps and texts for each barony, county and province. In the manuscript summary of his own writings, Petty notes 'the Grand Map of Ireland' and the 'Books of Baronies' for the year 1663. The latter entry refers in the first instance to the barony maps now held in Paris but may also include narrative descriptions and statistics for each barony. In 1722 in a catalogue of Petty's descendant's Library – that of the Earl of Shelbourne – it is interesting that the oak-box containing 'Sir William Petty's MSS Survey of Ireland' is also said to contain a 'book in paper cover of 80 pages' which begins with 'Cork County 62032', then 'Londonderry, Sligo' and on to the last entry on 'Armagh County'.[33] Does this book of 80 pages represent the now lost(?) notes of Petty, he having made further tabulations and calculations from the original county volumes? What is clear is that Petty himself is responsible for the county totals carried out on the front cover of each MSS volume and it is also clear that he worked on some of the barony totals – including those for Kilkenny and Roscommon. And in his famous private register of materials abstracted from government sources, Folio 30 refers to an "Abstract of ye people in Ireland that payd poll money 1660".[34]

As events transpired Petty's dream of an Atlas/Geographical Description of Ireland was never fully realised. By July of 1663 Petty is writing that "we are all whipped by scorpions in the Court of Pleas; everyman is at his wits end about the defence of his estate".[35] Over the next number of years, Petty becomes embroiled in a series of lawsuits, in public affairs and in the management of his own estates. His vast energies are deflected away from his mapping and statistical projects. But he did manage to gain sufficient leisure to write his *Political Anatomy of Ireland*. This latter work includes a number of tantalising references to population numbers, occupational distributions, age structure and number of married females. As Karl Pearson notes, it must be from sources such as the poll-tax returns that Petty derived quite an amount but by no means all of the statistics used in the *Anatomy* and elsewhere.[36]

---

33. 'Catalogue of the Earl of Shelbourne's books September 28 1722', in Petty Manuscripts, K.30, Department of Manuscripts, British Library, London.
34. 'Copy of the Fly-leaf Subjects in Dr. Petty's Register 1655–1670', Appendix F of Hardinge, 'Surveys', *op. cit.*, p. 105.
35. Letter (25) of 31 July, 1663, Royal Society of London Library, London.
36. Karl Pearson's letter to Lord Lansdowne, December, 1921, Petty materials, Box L (12), Department of Manuscripts, British Library, London.

Indeed, when he returned to these matters in the 1680s, Petty's unpublished manuscripts have information on number of esquires and other taxation categories which indicate that he is likely to have made occupational summaries from the poll-tax book. As usual, Petty does not reveal his sources. He was still not going to have his scheme for the 'Survey baffled or abused'. Yet it may well be that parts of the *Political Anatomy of Ireland* were originally written for his 'Geographical Description of the Kingdom of Ireland'.

At the latter end of his days, Petty returned to the 'Atlas' project and comparative materials on poll-taxes for Ireland, England and France. His interest in poll-monies was sufficiently revived for him to again advocate to the government the usefulness of the poll-tax as a surrogate for a Census.[37] He cut his losses on the 'Geographical Description of Ireland' and sent the county and provincial maps to be printed as well as the first modern single map of Ireland as a whole, made famous with the publication of *Hiberniae Delineatio* in 1685. But narrative descriptions, population abstracts or explanatory texts were not included. The skeletal, layered volumes of the '1659 Census' with their yellowing vellum pages were to keep their silence until Hardinge opened that famous oak-box in the spring of 1864.

III

THE STRENGTHS AND WEAKNESSES
OF THE '1659 CENSUS' AS A DATA SOURCE

ONE OF THE ADDITIONAL REASONS why Petty, perhaps, eventually left his poll-tax abstracts behind him for some time – he clearly returned to them in the 1680s – was his knowledge, as evident in his 1662 *Treatise on Taxes*, of weaknesses in this kind of data-source. After the mid 1660s, he regarded the hearth-money records of houses or 'smoakes' as more reliable indicators of population trends. This latter preference is a little ironic in that it was Petty himself who was partially instrumental in convincing Charles II's administration to substitute the hearth-money for the poll-tax, "it being easier to tell the number of hearths which remove not as Heads or Polls do".[38] Petty was well aware that evasions were frequent in poll-tax collection and knew that the poll-tax constituted a relatively insecure basis for accurately estimating a country's population.

37. Petty manuscripts, Box C, Letters 35/36, Department of Manuscripts, British Library, London: See also No.54, Vol. 13 of Petty letters/materials.
38. Petty, *Treatise on Taxes*, *op. cit.*, p. 94.

It is widely accepted that tax returns are inadequate aids to population study. The 1660 poll-tax is no exception – it fairly bristles with difficulties. Amongst others, Butlin, Cullen and Corish have drawn attention to difficulties with the returns in relation to inaccuracies and deficiencies, examples of underestimations and problems about knowing who was being counted in the first instance.[39] A whole series of questions, therefore, arise from the returns. How comprehensive and consistent are the returns for different parishes, baronies and counties? Who is actually being counted under the heading 'Numbers of People'? How can one determine levels of under-estimation and, most problematic, what is the unknown proportion who manage to escape taxation altogether? How uniform are the levels of evasion across different parts of the country? What does the list of 'tituladoes' really mean and how representative is it for each barony and county? And finally, what do the 'English'/'Scotts' and 'Irish' columns mean and how reliable is this classification in the first case?

To begin with, no returns have survived for counties Cavan, Tyrone, Galway, Mayo and Wicklow. As we have seen, returns have only survived for three baronies in County Meath. Returns for the four baronies of Duhallow, Fermoy, Imokilly and Muskerry are missing for County Cork as are returns for parts of the baronies of Condons and Clangibbon and Barrymore. In addition, some of the returns for specific towns and villages are missing: for County Tipperary alone, returns for Carrick-on-Suir, Cashel, Clonmel and Fethard are missing while in a number of other cases specific urban populations – those of Clonakilty, Lisburn, Lurgan and Antrim town – are submerged in overall parish/district/barony totals.

Detailed local studies are required to determine the number of cases where returns for quite a number of civil parishes are missing. At least seven parishes – Ballynakill, Calry, Kilcolman, Killaspughrone, Kilmacowen, Killoran and Tawnagh – are missing for County Sligo. Muckno and Tehallen in County Monaghan, the parishes of Christchurch and St Nicholas Without in the City of Dublin and Monkstown in County Waterford are missing. A small number of parish totals seem absent too in, for example, counties Louth, Londonderry and Wexford. The actual number of missing returns at townland level will probably never be fully known.

This picture of missing returns is further complicated by significant variations in the range of administrative divisions used in making the returns. The dominant pattern over about two-thirds of the country (see Figure 1) is a clearly graded series

39. R.A. Butlin, 'The population of Dublin in the late seventeenth century', *Irish Geography*, V, No.2 (1965), pp. 51–66; L.M. Cullen, 'Population trends in seventeenth century Ireland', *Economic and Social Review*, VI, No.2 (Jan, 1975), pp. 150–3; P.J. Corish, *A New History of Ireland, III: 1534–1691* (Oxford, 1976), p. 357.

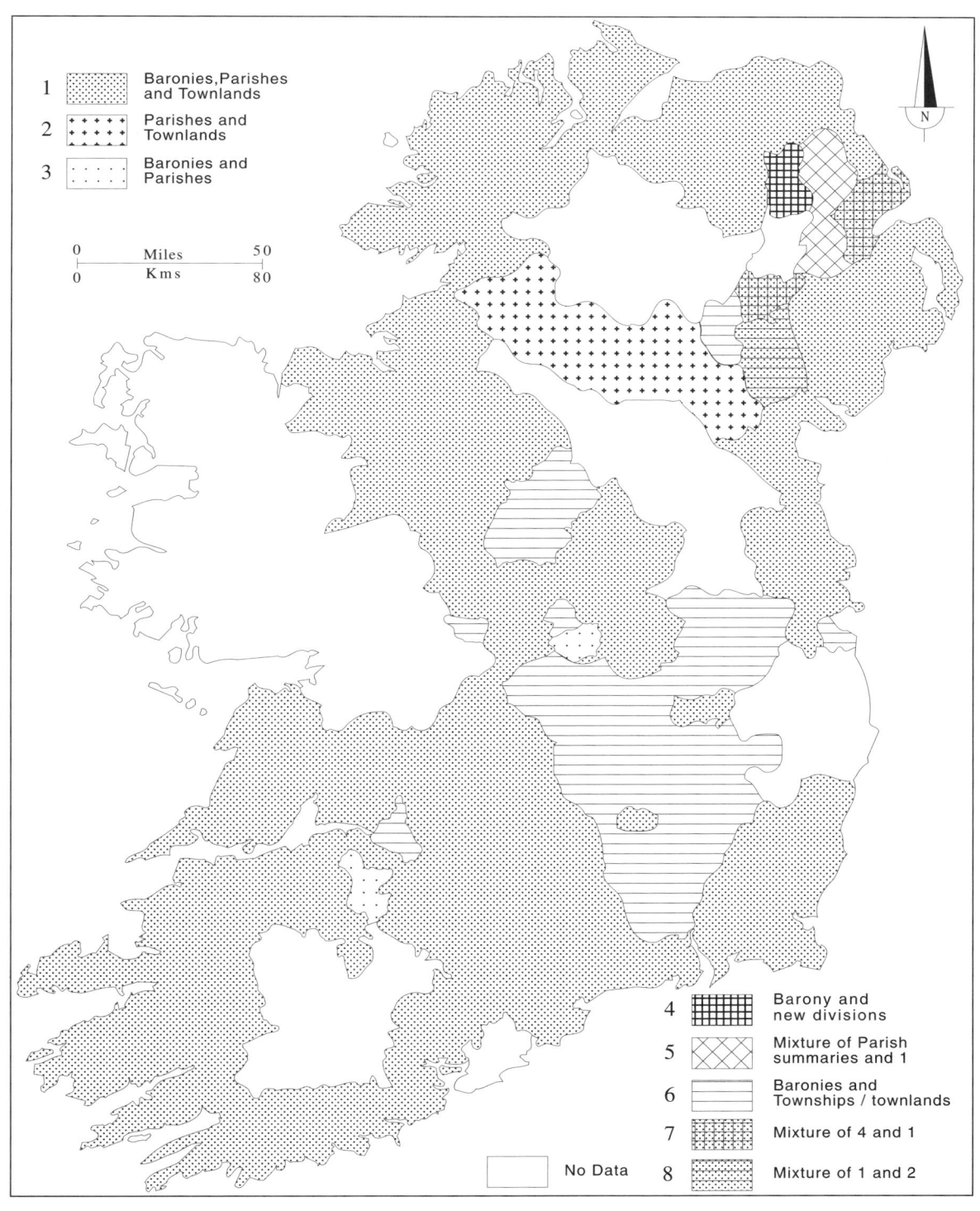

FIGURE 1

Combination of areal units used in making the 1660 poll-tax abstracts per barony

of returns by townland, parish and barony. Returns for counties Kilkenny, Carlow, Laois (Queens), Kildare, Longford, much of Armagh, parts of Monaghan, and Offaly (Kings) and one barony each in Counties Dublin, Limerick and Roscommon omit parish entries altogether. In Fermanagh and most of Monaghan returns are by parishes and townlands with baronies excluded while in Coshma in County Limerick and Ballycowan in Offaly the returns are at the barony and parish levels and townlands are excluded. County Antrim has the most uneven arrangement of returns; the baronies of Cary, Dunluce, Glenarm and Kilconway have the standard parish-townland format, the barony of Belfast is by street and townlands only, the barony of Massareene is a mixture of parish summaries and the standard format while the baronies of Antrim and Toome utilise, for the most part, areal units other than those of parishes and townlands. It is, therefore, an impossible task to establish the full extent of the missing parish returns, but it could be hypothesised that the more irregular and unorthodox the basic unit of enumeration, the more problematic the nature of the returns.

   To clarify the quality of returns at the 'denomination/place/townland' scale will require detailed and careful study at the individual parish and barony level by local scholars. As a preliminary probe, I compared the early hearth-money returns and Civil Survey denominations with the 'places/townlands' used in the 1660 poll-tax. For some old medieval counties such as Kilkenny, these are practically identical. Correlation between townlands used in both kinds of taxations are reasonably close for County Armagh, allowing for the fact that two large parishes in Oneiland barony are only returned in summary form in 1660. In contrast and where one can establish a pattern, there seems to be significant divergences in the counties of Antrim, Monaghan and south-east Londonderry. For example, there appears to be a 50 per cent reduction in the number of townlands returning population in the 1660 poll-tax for the barony of Loughinsholin as compared with the units of taxation for the 1663 hearth returns. In the barony of Farney in Monaghan, 83 townland denominations are returned for 1660 as compared with 144 townlands in 1663/64 hearth tax. In County Monaghan there appears to be an overall deficiency of about 20 per cent in the 1660 townlands. In County Wexford, there is a major divergence between the percentage number of townlands enumerated in '1659' for the more Gaelic/northern/more recently planted baronies of Ballaghkeen (47.3%), Gorey (28.8%) and Scarawalsh (35.5%) when compared with the total number of townlands returned in the Wexford Civil Survey. This contrasts very sharply with the four southern baronies where 83 per cent of the 1654 Civil Survey townlands return populations in 1660. There appear, therefore, to be holes in the data which do not always match with the realities on the ground. On the other hand, the weakness of the north Wexford poll-tax returns may reflect both the continuing severe effects of war and plague, as well as the extent of surviving woodland in this region. The task of establishing missing returns at the townland and parish level is a long and tedious one and requires detailed work at the local level: in short a thousand local studies!

Apart from the problem of missing returns for areal units at a variety of scales from county through barony to parish and townland, there are also the central problems of determining both levels of understimation and levels of evasion in the areas in which returns are actually made. The second government Poll-Tax Ordinance for March 1661 identifies the insolvencies and deficiencies of the two former polls (the first single and the second single) as arising mainly from "the removal of many of the under-tenants and meaner sort of people out of the town and villages wherein they did inhabit at the time of the making up of estreats or lists of inhabitants of such towns and villages so that the collectors of the said counties and baronies could neither find them or their distress to make payment of the summe or summes charged on them on the said estreats".[40]   In June of 1661 a Parliamentary Committee was established to compare the returns of the first single (mid 1660) and first double (May 1661) and then make recommendations as to how best to have the arrears of the double poll paid with greater efficiency. Yet by July 1661, "their lordships have now at length the Return of the whole double Poll-money raised by the last Ordinance of the late General Convention; and whereas it was supposed, that the same should have amounted to £80,000 it appears now to be but £43,000 or thereabouts."[41]   In short the actual return was only about half of the expected return. And this despite the Parliament's best efforts to take special care "that no Persons whatsoever do escape paying their full Proportions that so the Poll amount to double, if not more what the first did".[42]   This parliamentary drive for better returns included comparing estreats of the first single with the first double poll and by making diligent enquiry as to "what persons have escaped paying the double Poll by changing of their Habitations or by other Subterfuges".[43]

It is, therefore, abundantly clear that there was a high level of evasion in the 1660 poll-tax.   Collectors obviously encountered difficulties in the raw, fluid, post-war/post-famine situation where levels of local mobility were often still very high. This is especially the case in parts of Ulster and its borderlands where the civil surveyors often note "no improvements or habitations, only creaghts which can be

40. See Poll-Money Ordinances, this volume.
41. Journal of the House of Commons, July, 1661, pp. 422–3.
42. *Ibid.*, p. 442.
43. *Ibid.*, p. 443.
44. R.C. Simington (ed.), *The Civil Survey A.D. 1654–56*, iii, Cos. Donegal, Derry and Tyrone (Dublin, 1938).

removed at the owner's pleasure".[44]   Similar conditions prevailed in parts of Connaught and the Leinster and Munster uplands. Likewise, it is clear from comparing the actual monetary returns of the poll-tax per population units that cities also presented particular difficulties for collectors. "Changing habitations and other subterfuges" were as likely to be a feature of the tax evasion in crowded city streets and lanes as in the open countryside. It may also be significant that the ordinance for the cities recognised that the taxation classes had to be more flexible, leaving further room for underestimation and evasion.[45] In the broader context, the poll-tax was seen to be an oppressive, unpopular and inefficient system of taxation. There was, therefore, local resistance to the payment – resistance often supported by local magistrates and landlords whose relationships with the central state may not have been so harmonious. This may have been particularly the situation for some of the tightly-organised Scots Presbyterian communities who were coming increasingly under severe establishment pressures as the Anglican Restoration elites moved into top gear.

In attempting to get a precarious foothold in this bogland of uncertainties, the 1660 county poll-tax population totals (i.e. the '1659 Census') were tested against the county hearth tax receipts for 1672, 1676 and subsequent years.[46] Clearly intervening population growth generally and a significant new wave of immigration mainly into the north-eastern counties will affect these results. Nevertheless, the first striking feature of this exercise is the highly significant correlations between the '1659 Census' totals and the hearth-tax returns and, especially between the '1659 Census' and the returns for 1672 as well as very strong correlations even with the much later 1706 and 1712 county hearth-tax figures. Likewise, highly significant correlations exist between the 1660 returns and the equivalent 1696 poll-tax returns at the barony level. At the same time, rather revealing inter-baronial variations within counties are also suggested by this probe. Despite, therefore, all the difficulties raised above about the poll-tax returns, there is a strong consistent relationship between the county figures for 1660 and the earliest and indeed later hearth-tax and poll-tax returns. One is, therefore, in a position to say that we can place far more reliance on the 1660 returns than some commentators have suggested. Certainly one can depend on a comparative analysis of the returns across baronies and counties.

Secondly, and equally important, testing the 1660 poll-tax returns against the later hearth-tax and poll-tax returns, while recognising likely regional variations in

45. See Poll-Money Ordinances, this volume.
46. D. Dickson, Có Gráda and S. Daultrey, 'Hearth tax, household size and Irish population change 1672–1821', *R.I.A. Proc.*, Vol. 82c (1982), pp. 125–81, especially pp. 156–62 and appendices pp.177–80.

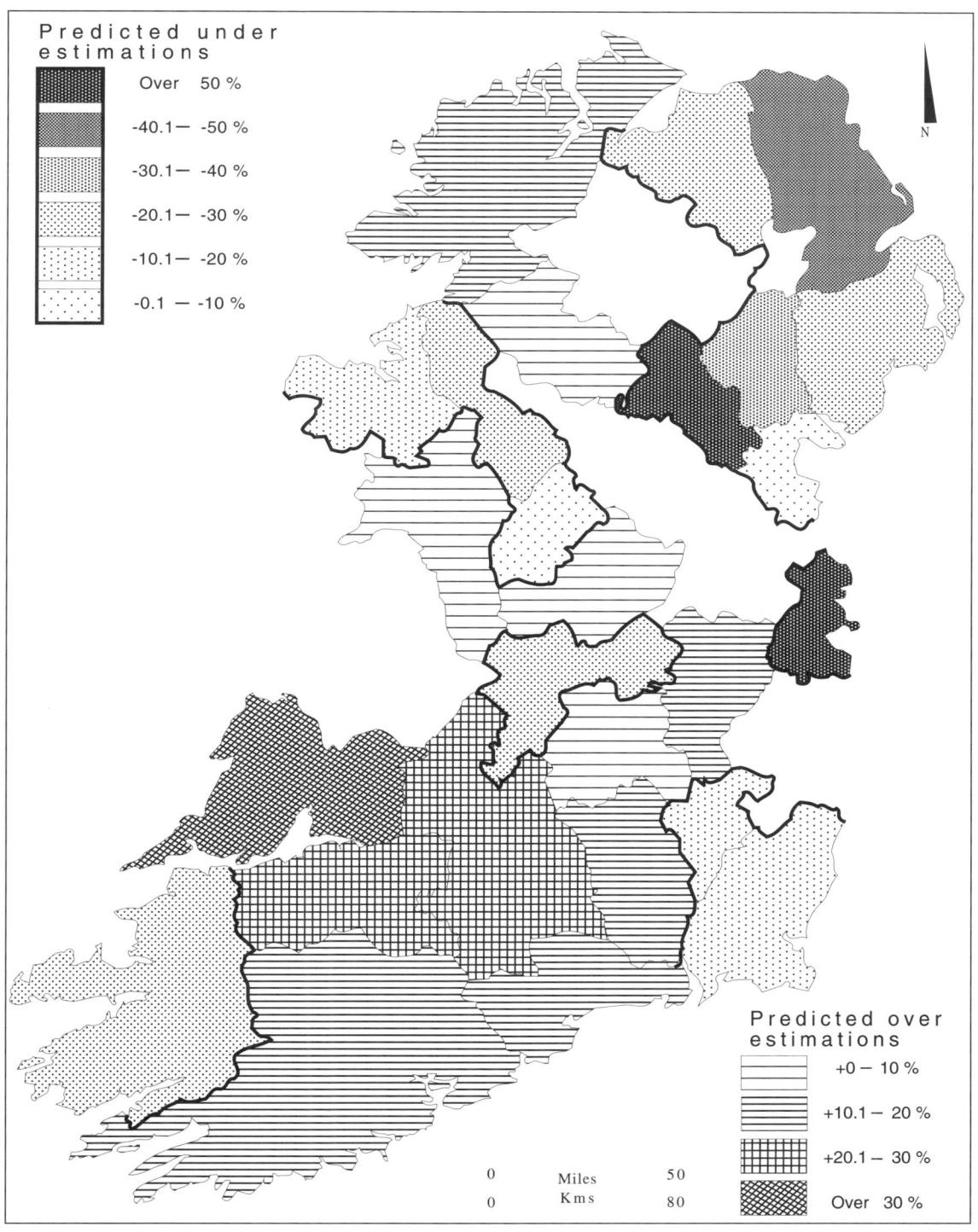

FIGURE 2
Predicted levels of underestimation and overestimation of county population totals in 1660 (using 1672 hearth-tax receipts as the independent variable)

population changes in the intervening years, also suggests where some of the biggest problems in the 1660 poll-tax returns may be located. Arising from these tests, and most particularly the relationship between the '1659 Census' and the 1672 hearth-tax receipts, there are strong suggestions of deficiencies in the following counties and cities: City and County of Dublin, Monaghan, Antrim, Armagh, Leitrim, Londonderry, Kerry, Sligo and Down with Carlow, Wexford, and Kings (Offaly) showing probably smaller deficiencies. Donegal, Louth, Fermanagh, Longford, Roscommon and Westmeath occupy a stable middle ground position. At the other end of the scale, Waterford, Kilkenny, Kildare, Cork, Limerick, Tipperary, and Clare reveal a higher number of tax-payers in 1660 than would have been predicted from the 1672 hearth-tax receipts (see Figure 2). Some of these results may relate to deficiencies in the 1672 database and more particularly to population shifts – especially immigration to Dublin and the north-east – in the intervening short period. Yet there are still very strong indications of inadequate returns for the northern half of the island (apart that is for Fermanagh and much of Donegal) while the south and south-west (with the particular exception of County Kerry) reveals very robust returns indeed in 1660.

One of the most interesting features is the overall similarity in the evidence emerging from a comparison of the TCD poll-money estimate with both the '1659 Census' itself and the later returns of the 1672 and 1676 hearth-tax receipts. There is strong empirical evidence to support at least some of these predicted patterns of underestimation or evasion in the '1659 Census'. County Sligo's deficiencies are explained for the most part by the missing returns for at least seven parishes. Monaghan's problems are partly explained by missing returns for two parishes and an overall deficiency of about one-fifth in the number of townlands returning populations in 1660. Counties Down and particularly Antrim raise a number of problems, not least in terms of the quality of the distinctions made as between 'Irish' and 'English/Scotts' populations. In addition, it would appear that the 1660 returns for the baronies of Antrim, Toome and Belfast are somewhat defective, while those for Massareene may also be affected. County Londonderry is particularly influenced by significant reductions in the number of townlands deemed to be populated in 1660 as compared with the much larger number of hearth-tax units. There are also very inconsistent relationships between 1660 and 1663 townland returns here. The Kerry figures – while possibly reflecting rapid population growth in the 1660s – point to probable deficiencies in the returns for the southernmost Gaelic baronies of Dunkerron, Glanerought and Iveragh and even some problems with the northern baronies. The position of the City and County of Dublin – while clearly reflecting the rapid rise to dominance of the capital in the immediate post-Restoration

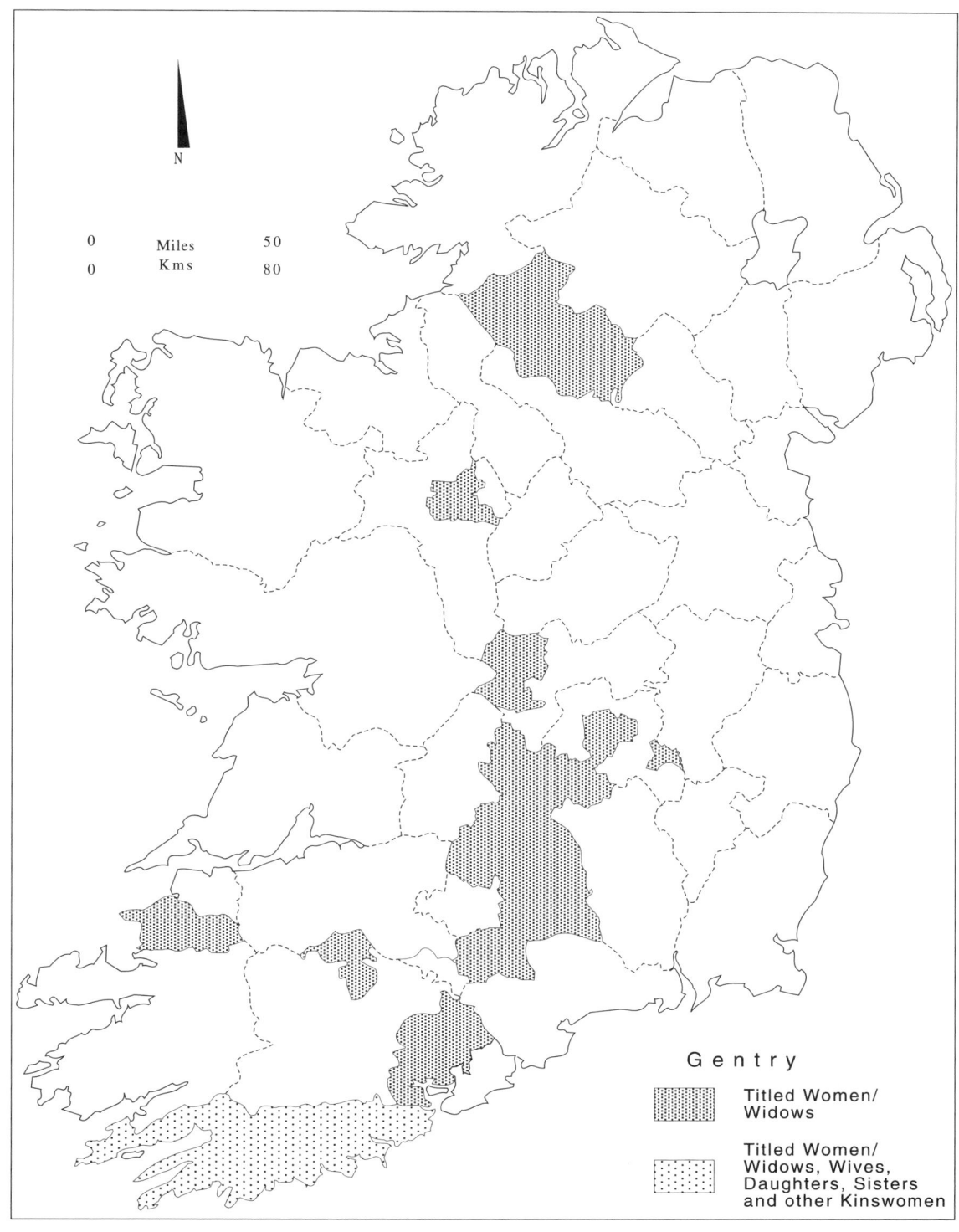

FIGURE 3
Distribution of gentry women in the 1660 poll-tax returns

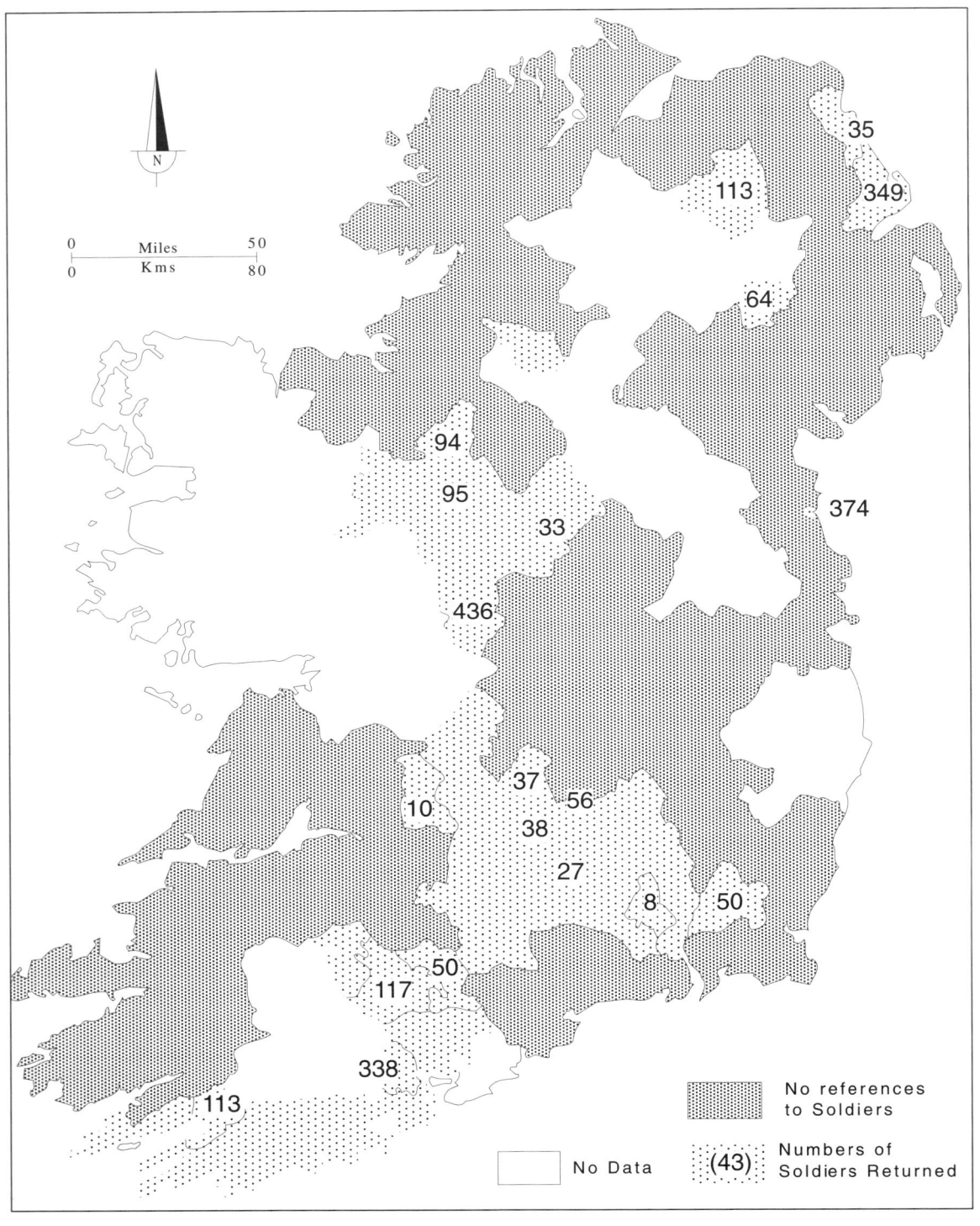

FIGURE 4
Distribution of soldiers returned in the 1660 poll-tax

period – is affected by missing returns for two inner city parishes. Taken in conjunction with Butlin's careful analysis of the early hearth-money records, a return nearer to 12,000 rather than 8,000 adults seems more realistic.[47] The surviving hearth-money returns also support evidence of some underestimation in County Dublin, particularly for places like the Liberities of Donore on the burgeoning outskirts of the capital.

The positive divergence at the other end of the country – i.e. for Munster outside of Kerry – is more difficult to explain. The apparent non-existence of the first single poll-tax returns for counties Tipperary and Cork raises questions as to what actual data Petty's clerks used for these counties. County Clare could also be included in this question as well, although the TCD estimate suggests that the county's first poll 'not signed' yielded 76.6 per cent of what was officially returned for Clare in the first double poll. The returns for the County of Cork (but not the City) are exceptional in the extent to which wives, daughters, sometimes other kinswomen, widows and high ranking females generally are named in the list of 'tituladoes'. Only four baronies of south-east Tipperary and three baronies each in Offaly (Kings) and Laois return any tax-paying women – in these instances mostly widows – as 'tituladoes' (Figure 3). Counties Cork and Tipperary are also striking in the detailed returns made of soldiers and their wives – the only other units with similar coverage are Roscommon, Drogheda and Carrickfergus, as well as the towns of New Ross, Charlemont and Magherafelt. Longford and Kilkenny towns also provide some details in the military domain. Only about 2,000 of a total of 13,700 soldiers in 1660/61 are actually returned in the poll-tax lists.[48] A great majority of soldiers are, therefore, not included in the '1659' returns (Figure 4).

It is worth noting that the new ordinances for the poll-tax of 1661 differ in a number of significant respects from those of 1660. For 1661, there is a clear specification that "every Widdow [shall pay] respectfully according to her Husband's degree; that every Heir Male and Female of what age soever shall pay, according to their respective degrees, qualities and estates as if he,/she, or they, were of full age".[49] The 1661 Ordinance is also more specific about the amount of poll-tax paid by handi-craftsmen, carmen and carriers, inn-holders and shopkeepers not [living] in Corporations. Most interesting is the very last clause which specifies ... "that every other person or persons ... *as well as soldiers* (my italics ...) shall pay two shillings".[50] Soldiers are not specified as a class in the first ordinance of 1660. Given that the

47. Butlin, *op. cit.*, p. 55.
48. S. Egan, *Finance and Government in Ireland 1660–85*, unpublished Ph.D. thesis (T.C.D., 1983).
49. See Poll-Money Ordinances, this volume.
50. *Ibid.*

FIGURE 5

Relative distribution of 'sons of gentry' in 1660 poll-tax returns

first poll-tax was aimed at "defraying the publick charge and particularly towards the supply of the Army", this omission may not be too surprising. The likely outcome, however, of the first ordinance was at least uncertainties as to whether soldiers should be taxed or not. The second ordinance, in contrast, is quite emphatic on this point.

Likewise, the second ordinance breaks new ground in the taxation of heirs. It is striking that in the return for 'tituladoes', the Munster counties – again with the notable exception of Kerry – almost invariably return the sons of gentry. The only other counties where this pattern is made explicit are Counties Meath (part of), Wexford, Dublin, most of counties Fermanagh, Roscommon, Donegal, Kildare, the baronies of Bargy in Wexford, Ardee and Ferrard in Louth, Glenarm in Antrim and Iveagh, Ards and Lecale in Down. The major region with no returns in relation to the sons of the gentry stretches north of a line from mid-Louth through Longford and north Roscommon. A second belt includes the midland counties through to north Wexford. Apart from the barony of Magunihy, Kerry stands out as a weak zone in Munster (Figure 5).

The cumulative evidence, therefore, points to the possibility that Petty may have used the first double poll-money abstracts of 1661 for part or all of the counties of Cork and Tipperary. In this context, it is also worth observing that Petty in the *Political Anatomy of Ireland* notes that "the number of all them of all degrees, who paide poll-money, *Anno 1661* [my italics] was about 360,000".[51] Petty was, therefore, in command of the 1661 as well as the 1660 details. Apart from Cork and Tipperary, one must also ask questions about the high quality of the returns for Athlone, Drogheda and counties Clare, Roscommon and Donegal. There is more than a possibility we are not only not dealing with a 'Census of 1659' but not dealing with a poll-tax for the year *1660* alone. It may well be that Petty used the most available county or barony estreats and that some of these were of 1661 vintage. Alternatively, there may have been different assumptions made by commissioners in different counties or baronies as to the full implications of the ordinances for their jurisdictions. And in County Cork, do the exceptional returns for gentry women very simply reflect an early stage in the implementation of Petty's still experimental instructions as to how the abstracts should be made and standardised by his clerks? I increasingly get the feeling that County Cork was the first county attempted in the whole abstracting process.

It should also be recollected that the 1661 Parliamentary Committee set up to investigate the poll-tax returns insisted on a double checking or review of estreats by the relevant local authority. Interestingly, County Tipperary is the only county

51. W. Petty, *op. cit.*, (See ref. 11 above).

where additions are clearly made "upon the revieu" (p. 308) to the townland totals at the end of some barony tables. There is also some indication of double checking in County Laois (Queens) as well. In County Tipperary, additions to original totals range from 3.4 per cent of the barony totals in Slieveardagh, 7.7 per cent in Middlethird, 8.7 per cent in two parishes in Owney and Arra and, perhaps, as high as 13.2 per cent in Upper Ormond. Initially, I was tempted to suggest that the tighter administration of the poll-tax in Tipperary was a function of its location amongst the more normanised, long-established administrative regions of the south and south-east as opposed to the more Gaelic, western/north-western and more often recently planted baronies where county administrations were more recent creations. The apparent strengths in the returns for not only Tipperary but Kilkenny, Limerick, Cork, Kildare, Meath (part of), Westmeath and south Wexford seemed to support this view. Yet the quality of the returns for Longford, Fermanagh and most if not all Donegal challenge this kind of simple assertion. Indeed, one could equally argue – given the parallels between the 1660/61 poll-tax in Ireland and the perpetuation of 14th century poll-tax models in England's taxation history over three centuries – that the incoming Protestant settler/collectors were at least as familiar with these models of taxation as were the locals.[52]

On reflection the 'review' of Tipperary figures is more likely a product of the promptings of the Parliamentary Committee and so further suggests 1661 returns for at least some baronies in Tipperary. And as we have seen Tipperary is part of a wider southern belt of counties revealing the most robust poll-tax returns. It could well be that both better gentry returns especially inclusive of sons and in fewer instances, daughters, sisters and wives and the inclusion of soldiers may be pointers to a more comprehensive system of taxation. What is certain is that there are small but significant barony and county variations in Petty's returns in relation to such categories as soldiers, females, sons and heirs. There are, therefore, regional variations in the actual composition of the adult populations being assessed and/or abstracted and strong suggestions that some counties or baronies contain a higher percentage of the total adult population than other counties or baronies where certain class categories are not included.

The ordinances specify that all adults of and above 15 years of age of either sex were taxed according to their status. Due to the destruction of the Four Courts's records in 1922, no poll-tax returns survive which directly correspond to the 1660 abstracts. For County Tyrone (a county which it appears made no returns to the Central Exchequer for *any* of the poll-monies) detailed returns, person by person, townland by townland, have survived for four parishes, Donaghkedy and Urney in

52. M.W. Beresford, *Lay Subsidies and Poll Taxes* (Cantebury, 1963), pp. 19–29.

the barony of Strabane, Termonmcgork in the barony of Omagh and Aughelow in the barony of Dungannon.[53] There is also one 1661 poll-tax return for the town of Clonmel which is indeed fortunate as there have been suggestions of significant differences in the quality and nature of urban *vis-à-vis* rural returns as well as between 1660 and 1661 returns.[54]

The Tyrone parishes reveal what appears to be an almost routine pattern of entries dominated by the husband and wife in all classes whether servant, labourer, farmer or gentry. Between these widely-spaced parishes, there are striking variations in the ratio of servants and labourers to farmers. A much higher proportion of yeomen farmers in Donaghkeady and Urney (39%) as compared with Aughelow (26%) and Termonmcgork (24%) is clearly reflected in the much higher proportion of single servants returned as living in Donaghkeady and Urney (12%) as compared with 5.6 per cent in Aughelow and only 1 per cent returned in Termonmcgork. The returns, therefore, reflect in part the different social structures of the four parishes but they also clearly indicate – as Carleton confirms – the evasion of higher tax payments by farmers claiming labourer or servant status, especially in the poorer parishes.[55] The overall sex ratio in these four major Tyrone parishes is quite even, while slightly favouring the male in areas with large proportions of servants living in. Even allowing for a very early age of marriage, it is also quite clear that *single* adult females and indeed most single adult males who are not servants are *excluded* in all these returns. Indeed in Termonmcgork 404 out of the 409 people taxed were married couples. One gets the strong impression that the highly problematic job for the collector of assessing all those aged 15 and over was avoided by the consistent and strategic taxation of married couples and *single employed* persons only. What is most interesting is that returns from the three different baronies, while reflecting local situations, are so similar and consistent in form so as to point to a much wider frame of reference. The comparisons of these returns and the late 14th century poll-tax records for England strongly suggests that a medieval pattern of poll-tax classification and administration was still partially operative as a controlling model in County Tyrone (and, one assumes, elsewhere in Ireland).

The Clonmel poll-tax reveals a more complex picture of status groups and household structures although it must be allowed that 1661 ordinances were – as we have seen – far more specific in relation to the taxation of widows, heirs, soldiers and indeed all occupational groups. While also reflecting the central dominance of both

53. S.T. Carleton, *Heads and hearths: the Hearth Money Rolls and Poll Tax Returns for County Antrim 1660–69* (Belfast, PRONI, 1991).
54. The manuscript of the Clonmel 1661 poll-money return is held in the South Tipperary County Museum, Clonmel.
55. Carleton, *op. cit.*, p. 176.

male and female heads of households (especially in the lower status areas of the towns), the proportion of single servants living in Clonmel is far higher (29%) than the Tyrone parishes, thus increasing somewhat the single male and female categories. Other females – kinswomen, spinsters, widows and single 'labouring women' – are also more strongly represented. In a few of the wealthier households, sons and daughters (as heirs?) are returned as paying, but this is still a very rare feature. The overall sex ratio is balanced with women somewhat under-represented in the higher status of streets (because of the higher proportion of male servants there) and over-represented in some poorer areas which contain a higher proportion of independent, single and widowed females.

A further interesting point from the Clonmel returns is that levels of exemptions and 'official' tax avoidance can be calculated. A total of 10 per cent of the householders were formally exempted and many of these are from the poorer Irishtown area. It also appears that three per cent of the population on the list did not pay their poll-tax although not in the exempted class. It is, therefore, worth noting that since the '1659' population abstracts were almost certainly computed from these estreats, those *listed* who either were later exempted from paying their tax or failed to pay the tax are still probably included in Petty's population returns. The Tyrone parishes are much less forthcoming on this issue but there is a hint in the Donaghkeady and Urney returns that c. 9 per cent were exempted from or did not involve themselves in paying the tax.

There still remains the problem of estimating those who avoided getting on the poll-tax lists in the first place and, therefore, could not be accounted for in Petty's abstracts. Carleton's comparison of the household names on the poll-tax records for these four widely dispersed Tyrone parishes with their equivalent hearth-money records three years later is highly instructive as to actual poll-tax evasions and deficiencies. He states that "roughly half the householders paying hearth-tax in 1664 had evaded the poll tax just over three years earlier".[56] Together with the unknown number who managed to evade both taxes, Carleton rightly argues that there is a deficiency of well over 50 per cent in the poll-tax returns for these four parishes.

A parallel examination of the Clonmel poll-tax household names with the 1666 hearth-money records for this county town reinforces Carleton's conclusions on Tyrone. As many as 41 per cent of the 1661 household names in Clonmel are not listed in the hearth-tax records five years later. Equally 58 per cent of 1666 hearth-tax householders are not known in the 1661 poll-tax returns. Clonmel's population had grown in the immediate post-Restoration period. But, even allowing for such

---

56. *Ibid.*, p. 177.

an increase and recognising that there were again households who were excluded from or evaded both taxation lists, the Clonmel evidence confirms that at the very least poll-tax returns constituted only about half of the eligible tax-paying house-holders in that town.

It should be stated that in both the Tyrone and Clonmel examples we are dealing with communities which did not fulfil the requirements of the ordinances as to the submission of estreats and payment of poll-tax to the central administration. They also constitute a very small sample of the total number of parishes who made the poll-tax returns. But, in the absence of any other evidence of this type, and on the basis of these particular returns we have to move forward assuming a level of eva-sion of the order of 40 per cent – 50 per cent. And, as in the equivalent English studies of poll-taxation returns, we also have to assume that these levels of tax eva-sion were fairly evenly distributed across the country.[57] Certainly there does not appear to be a significant difference between levels of evasion in the four rural Tyrone parishes and urban Clonmel.

To arrive at a revised figure for the total adult population of Ireland in 1660/61 we have to combine both an estimate of the population deficit arising from missing returns at all geographical scales _and_ a further estimate of the overall level of evasion island-wide. Given the missing returns for two of the five counties and the parish deficiencies already identified, it is estimated that the probable adult population returns of the Province of Connaught would have been of the order of 63,500. County Galway's missing adult population is estimated to be c. 27,600 and Mayo c. 10,600. While it is estimated that Ulster's adult population returns are deficient by perhaps one-third, the revised figures require a more thorough evaluation of all the _missing_ returns than is possible to do so for this paper. The provisional adult population totals for counties Tyrone and Cavan are set at 11,500 and 8,800 respec-tively. As we have seen, there appears to be a number of missing or defective returns for Counties Antrim, Armagh, Londonderry and Down with Donegal and particu-larly Fermanagh returning the most reliable results. The revised provincial tax-pay-ing total is of the order of 105,000 adults. The actual amount of the missing population is still in doubt but what is clear is that Ulster's adult population, includ-ing 'Irish' and 'English/Scotts' proportions, was significantly greater than the exist-ing '1659 Census' would indicate.[58]

It is estimated that c. 82 per cent of Leinster's tax-paying population is actually returned in 1660. A revised County Meath total would give a probable adult

57. M.W. Beresford, _op. cit.,_ pp. 19–29.
58. See also W. Macaffee and V. Morgan 'Population in Ulster 1667–1760' in P. Roebuck (ed.), _Plantation to Partition: Essays in Ulster history,_ Belfast, 1981, pp. 46–8 for discussion on this point.

population of c. 28,900 and that of Wicklow c. 9,300. The only other major change necessitated is to account for the missing parish populations in the City and County of Dublin while minor transformations are necessary for a small number of parish revisions in Louth, Carlow, Offaly, Kilkenny and Wexford, so as to bring the estimated provincial total to c. 157,300. Munster's tax-paying populations is estimated to be effectively correct at 157,109 with under-returning in County Kerry and in the missing figures for the four towns in South Tipperary probably balanced against the very robust returns for the Munster counties as a whole.

Based, therefore, on estimates for additional tax-payers from the missing counties, baronies, parishes and townlands it is suggested that Connaught with 13.2 per cent, Munster (32.5%), Ulster (21.7%) and Leinster (32.6%) share in a revised tax-paying population figure of about 483,000. The observant Petty had estimated County Cork's parishes and [adult] population as constituting one-eight of the island total, that is 62,032 multiplied by eight giving an island total of 490,000![59] In addition, there is still the unknown number of individuals who avoided/evaded paying the poll-tax across the whole country. My original multiplier for the '1659 Census' was 2.5. In the light of the new evidence in relation to levels of evasion, Louis Cullen's multiplier of 3.0 now looks the more sensible one thus giving a probable total population for Ireland in 1660/1661 of the order of 1,449,000 or c. 1.5m.[60] However, my original caveat that any poll-tax constitutes a relatively insecure basis for accurately estimating a county's population remains in force!

IV

USING 'THE CENSUS' RETURNS

FOR THE PURPOSES OF THE REMAINDER OF THIS PAPER, many of the problems associated with the poll-tax can be circumvented by avoiding absolute totals and concentrating attention on a series of inter-baronial comparisons. A number of strategies have been adopted to fill in the gaps on the map for those counties with no 1660 poll-tax returns. Tyrone and Wicklow have hearth money returns for the 1660s which allow for a reasonable interpolation of 1660 densities at the barony level. Counties Cavan, Galway and Mayo – with no solid population figures until

59. Petty's statistical notes on Ireland including his scheme for 'the use of surveys made in last 7 years (1654–1661) for a Registry of Lands, Commodities and Inhabitants', Petty manuscripts, Box C, Vol.4, Department of Manuscripts, British Library, London.
60. W.J. Smyth, *Common Ground*, *op. cit.*; L.M. Cullen, 'Seventeenth century Ireland', *op. cit.*, p. 153.

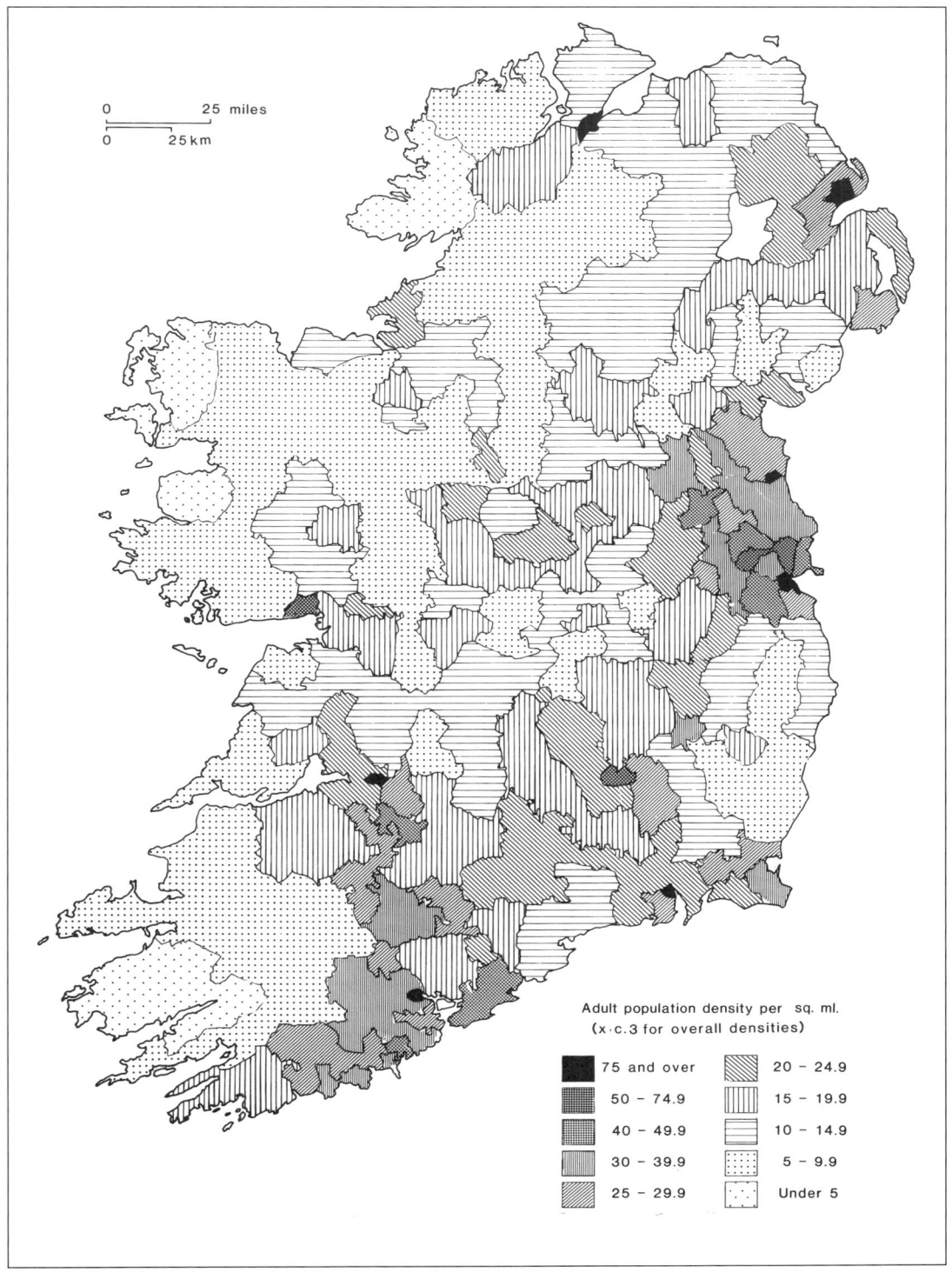

Adult population density per sq. ml.
(x·c.3 for overall densities)

■ 75 and over	▨ 20 – 24.9
▦ 50 – 74.9	▥ 15 – 19.9
▤ 40 – 49.9	▤ 10 – 14.9
▤ 30 – 39.9	⠒ 5 – 9.9
▨ 25 – 29.9	⠄ Under 5

FIGURE 6
Adult population distribution in 1660

the nineteenth century – present far greater difficulties. In this context, estimated county populations – based on computer projections from the 1672 hearth-tax receipts – have been redistributed amongst the relevant baronies in proportion to the percentage number of denominations returned for each barony in the Books of Survey and Distribution. While allowing for the greater antiquity of the townland network, a comparison of the 1660 barony returns with their respective townland densities for the adjacent counties of Clare and Roscommon suggests that such an exercise is reasonably predictive (±5.0%) of 1660 population distributions. Use of denominational proportions from the Books of Survey and Distribution would appear to understate the population densities of the more accessible 'modernising' baronies while overstating those for the less urbanised, remoter territories. In short, the townland densities antedate the shifts in population consequent upon rapid economic developments in the late sixteenth and especially in the first half of seventeenth century Ireland. The estimates are, therefore, further modified to take account of the urban populations of specific baronies. The patterns suggested for the missing baronies in counties Cork and Meath are more robust and are based on evidence from the Civil Survey, Books of Survey and Distribution and other taxation details from the 1660s.

The mid-seventeenth century population patterns are dominated by a number of maritime regions, each interwoven with its own distinctive array of outside connections (Fig. 6). The Pale region – with a salient westwards into Westmeath – stands out as the zone of highest population densities. Dominated by the needs of the expanding capital of Dublin (and those of England beyond), this mixed-farming/tillage region of north Leinster was full of market towns, mills, castles, stone-houses, weirs, roads and bridges – in short a well-furnished economic region. County Meath's status in this region is well documented, its market-towns and diversified agricultural economy of commercial grain, sheep and cow/cattle production focused on the port city of Drogheda. Indeed, rural population densities are often twice as high as they were either before or after the Famine.

Between the Midland bogs and the hills and woods of the Wexford/Wicklow borderlands, the Upper Liffey and Barrow valleys form a bridgehead into a second region of population concentration along the riverine lowlands of the south-east. Here, under the longstanding patronage of the Butler lordship and pivoting around the port-city of Waterford, substantial rural communities and solid inland towns had crystallised along the navigable waterways of the Nore, Suir and Barrow. County Kilkenny is the anchor county here, its tillage economy specialising in rotations of winter and spring grain. On the western side, south Tipperary had also a sheep and cattle economy while the 'martlands' of Carlow and north Wexford signal the prevalence of cattle in this commercialising mixed-farming region. The remainder of Wexford was also a tillage land specialising in summer corn while the southern halves of Laois and Kildare were also active in mixed-farming/arable enterprises.

The power of the Munster province is further revealed by the port-dominated regions of Cork and Limerick. The sea-enriched baronies on each side of Cork harbour under-pinned the agricultural surpluses – especially of grain – that found their way to the growing city of Cork and the still vibrant ports of Kinsale and Youghal. Figure 6 also identifies the labour-intensive granary lands of 'Roches country' in mid-Cork. The wider Cork hinterland – now geared to dairying and cattle production for the growing Atlantic economy – is linked by Kilmallock to the Limerick port region. This core area has affected the fortunes and populations of south and east Clare – indeed Clare as a whole benefited from its sandwich location between the late medieval 'city-states' of Galway and Limerick. Gernon's description of Limerick villages with their haggards stacked with corn captures the density of life in these lime-rich Munster lowlands.[61]

The city of Galway, looking out to the Atlantic and Iberia, shows up as more isolated, a weaker (and weakening) axis of population concentration in the west. On the other hand, the solidity of the settlements of mid and south Galway should not be overlooked. The map underestimates the power of the land stretching northwards from Ballinrobe through to the Moy valley and curving eastwards to embrace the relatively well-developed coastal hinterland of Sligo. The early seventeenth century spread of both new and refurbished market foundations highlights the penetration of commercial forces into this remoter region.

The most striking changes from the late medieval pattern of population concentrations emerges in the north-east. An embryonic core of planter settlement and economic power is already consolidating in a triangular region between north Down, Armagh city and Coleraine. Arable, mixed-farming, and pastoral zones had emerged in this area where a new urban network had cemented economic and cultural links with Scotland and northern England. A secondary core is emerging around the city of Derry and east Donegal with salients of further development indicated along the Bann valley, fanning south-westwards through the Monaghan corridor into the hearthlands of counties Cavan and Fermanagh.

Between the most densely populated maritime regions and the areas of sparsest and least stratified populations, a number of transitional areas can be identified. County Wexford exhibits an enduring trinity of regional qualities. There is the fragmented, crowded tillage lands of Bargy and Forth described in harvest time as

61. Smyth, *op. cit.*

looking like "a well-cultivated garden".[62] There is the mixed-farming middle zone with its moated sites and placenames pointing to its marchland hybrid character. North Wexford in turn, forms part of a pastoral wooded region incorporating much of Wicklow and the adjacent borderlands of Carlow and Kildare – resilient Gaelic territories then undergoing successful planter colonisation. The less disturbed grazing heartland of *na Déise* in west Waterford emerges clearly. Equally emphatic is the woodland/bogland core of the Gaelic and Gaelicised midlands. To the west its borderlands extend into north Tipperary and the southern flanks of County Westmeath. The pastoral areas of north Clare, north Galway and much of Roscommon and Leitrim appear as areas of similar status. Finally, a wide crescent of territory with moderate to low population densities – in lands which yielded "very little grane without much stores of manure and labour"[63] – curves from south Down across the broken drumlin country of south Ulster and swings northwards again to embrace part of Derry and all of Inishowen.

The far west emerges as distinctive in the mid-seventeenth as it did in the mid-nineteenth century but for different reasons. Its areas with the greatest densities on Freeman's pre-Famine population maps are often the least densely settled parts of mid-seventeenth century Ireland. Much of Kerry (with a core in the Iveragh peninsula), and Mayo, west Clare and west Galway were then the least populated parts of the moist Atlantic peripheries of north-west Europe. The Sligo-Galway-Roscommon and Longford-Leitrim-Cavan borderlands, west Donegal and its inland extension into the Sperrins of Tyrone also belong to this world. Jones Hughes has noted that most of these areas "only experienced close and permanent settlement by farming people at a very late date" and those late colonisers were probably evicted from adjoining more desirable regions.[64] As the seventeenth century evidence confirms, the great centres of enduring rural cultures in Ireland were not in these far western lands.

The poll-tax listing of the most important Irish family names for each barony allows for the mapping of the relative distribution of Gaelic and Old English names. It also permits the exploration of relationships between population densities, social structures and cultural backgrounds. Apart from the north-east, Figure 7 confirms the correspondence between the zones of highest population density and the areas

62. R.C. Simington (ed.), *The Civil Survey, AD. 1654–56, ix, County Wexford* (Dublin, 1940), p. x.
63. Down Survey barony and parish maps, Cos. Down, Armagh and Tyrone, P.R.O.N.I., D.597; R.C. Simington (ed.), *The Civil Survey A.D. 1654–56; iii, Cos. Donegal, Derry and Tyrone* (Dublin, 1938).
64. T. Jones Hughes, 'Society and settlement in nineteenth century Ireland', in *Ir. Geogr.*, 5, 2, (1965), pp.79-96. See also T. Jones Hughes 'The large farm in nineteenth century Ireland', in A. Gailey and D. Ó hÓgáin, (eds.), *Gold under the furze* (Dublin, 1982), pp. 93–100.

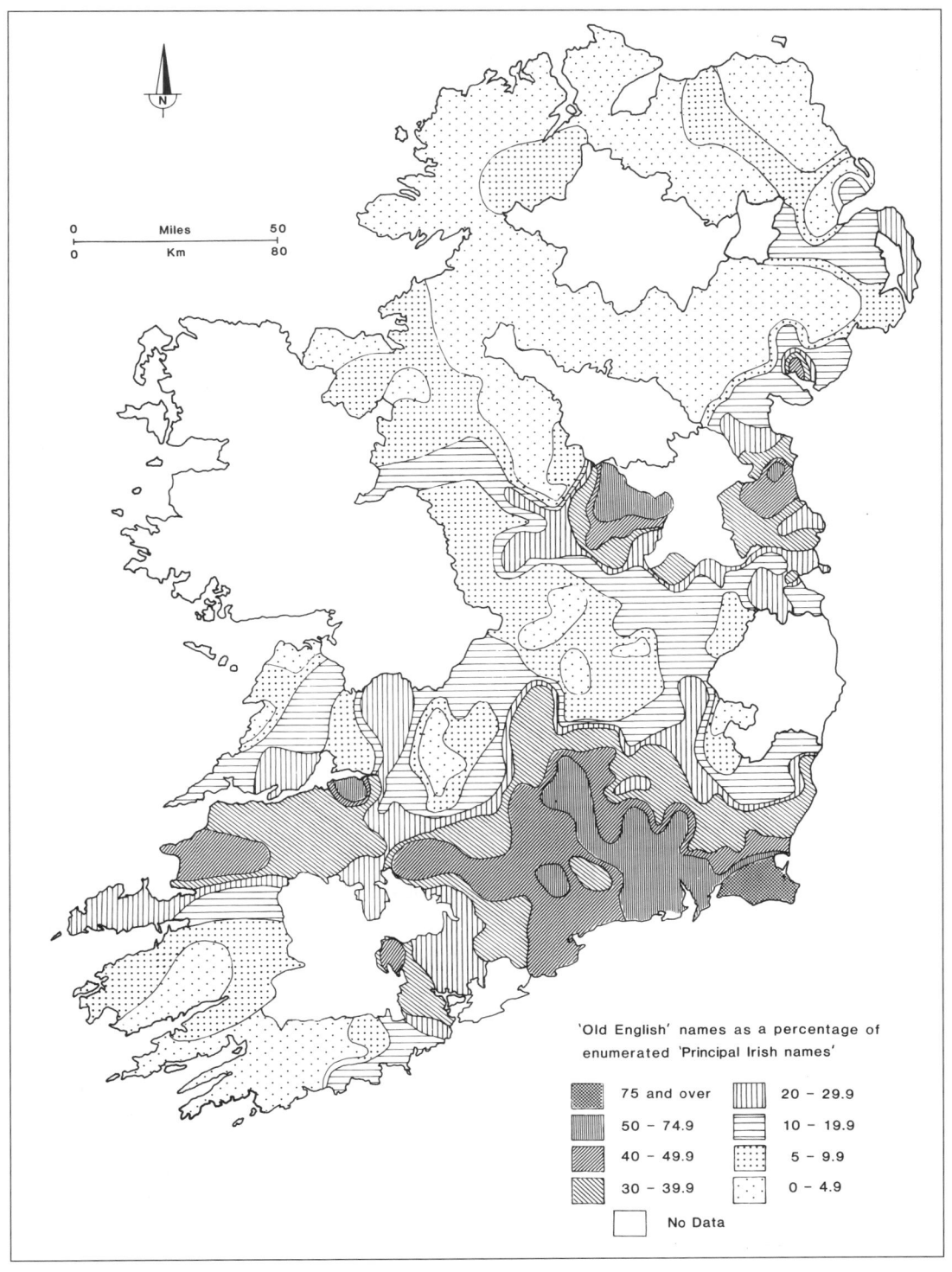

'Old English' names as a percentage of
enumerated 'Principal Irish names'

	75 and over		20 – 29.9
	50 – 74.9		10 – 19.9
	40 – 49.9		5 – 9.9
	30 – 39.9		0 – 4.9
	No Data		

FIGURE 7
Relative distribution of Old English as returned in the 1660 poll-tax abstracts

of enduring Anglo Norman *and* mixed Norman-Gaelic settlement. The Old English Pale area emerges again but in this case apparently more Boyne-valley based. As with the big farms of the nineteenth century, the strength of the population with Gaelic names over much of Louth, south Meath, Dublin and particularly Kildare is striking. The mid-seventeenth century evidence also establishes the spread of medieval settlement and culture in south-east Ireland. Outside of the north-west, the south-west and the hills of Tipperary, Figure 7 emphasises the strength of Norman naming patterns over Munster. But, what the map does not reveal is the infinitely subtle gradations in the rendering of the same Anglo-Norman names as they work their way inland and westwards into such Gaelicised lands as north Kerry, not to speak of the naming and cultural permutations that characterise Connaught.

The strength of the Gaelic tradition so close to Cork city is a feature of Figure 7. Indeed the Gaelic heartland of the south-west is as clear and as extensive in 1660 as it was in 1260. The introverted Gaelic heartland of Laois-Offaly and its border-lands stands out as does the weak Norman imprint in the wetter lands of north-east Connaught, north Longford and all of Ulster, outside of east Down and Antrim. The map confirms the hybrid areas in Irish culture where the most coveted lands were fought over by Norman and Gael and where the deepest levels of assimilation between the two traditions emerged. East and north Cork, north Kerry, most of Limerick, much of mid-Tipperary and Laois belong to this 'middle nation' as do all the lands bordering the north Leinster core of Anglo-Norman settlement. Figure 7 also suggests the regional diversity, demographic power and resilience of these Old English worlds in the first half of seventeenth century Ireland. Flexible in lifestyle and language, the Old English were still skilful enough to hold on to and indeed expand their control of key properties and positions until the traumas of the Civil War and the Cromwellian settlement stripped them of the material bases for their distinctive culture and ideology.

One of the great attractions of the 1660 poll-tax is the emergence for the first time in Irish history of a picture of the population structure at the townland level. The poll-tax figures thus allows us to probe more deeply into the patterns of settlement and social stratification at this, the most intimate of scales, while also indicating the relevance of parochial, baronial and county structures in a study of the settlement and social hierarchy. Combined with an analysis of materials from counties Kilkenny, Limerick and Meath, a detailed survey of all the available mid-seventeenth century evidence for County Tipperary suggests a three-fold classification of 1660 townland population returns. It can be demonstrated that in 1660 at least three-quarters of County Tipperary's townlands with an adult population of 40 or over (i.e. a total population of 120 and over) did contain *nucleated* settlements in the mid-seventeenth century. It has also been established that such settlements housed more complex social structures – comprising servant, artisan, farming and service populations as well as lay and/or ecclesiastical elites. It is more difficult to make as clear a statement about the settlement characteristics of townlands with adult populations of 20-39 (total 60–110) but at least half of these townlands in County Tipperary then hosted nucleated or agglomerated settlement. With some exceptions, townlands with less than twenty and particularly less than ten adults were clearly not as diversified in social and institutional structures – irrespective of whether their settlement form was clustered or scattered. Correlation of settlement details from the excellent Down Survey parish maps for the barony of Crannagh in County Kilkenny with the 1660 poll-tax returns confirms the above patterns. It is also worth noting that three-quarters of the nucleated settlements identified by O'Connor in his work on the Civil Survey for County Limerick, and whose populations can be confirmed in 1660, reveal adult populations in excess of 40.[65]

The following analysis is, therefore, based on the twin assumptions that the bigger the townland population returns, the greater the possibility of a more stratified population and the greater the likelihood that at least some of that population lived in a more 'nucleated' as opposed to a more scattered form of settlement. It should also be pointed out that whenever the poll-tax returns only one population figure for two or more named townlands, it is assumed for the purposes of this analysis that more than one settlement is involved. Using these assumptions, the strategy here is to provide general clues to island-wide variations in social and settlement hierarchies. Detailed local studies are necessary to further examine all the intricacies of society and settlement on the ground.

Figure 8 indicates the relative distribution of townlands returning 40 adults or more, i.e., a total townland population of c.120 in 1660. County Tipperary, for example, exhibits three distinct patterns of townland population size. In the southeastern baronies of the county, well over 20 per cent of the total number of townlands had populations in excess of 120. Here in the best and historically the most secure land in the county, with a good communications network by road and river to Waterford port, a dense network of substantial market towns and a compact 'manorialised' property structure were dominated in 1641 by individual landowners of Anglo-Norman descent. These lorded over a zone of commercialised mixed-farming specialising in wheat, barley and sheep production. South-east Tipperary was, therefore, on the edge of a wider belt of high farming and a developed settlement and social hierarchy which had matured in a time of feudalised centralisation

---

65. See T. McErlean, 'The Irish townland system of landscape organisation' in T. Reeves-Smyth and F. Hamond (ed.), *Landscape archeology in Ireland* (Oxford, 1983), pp.315–9.

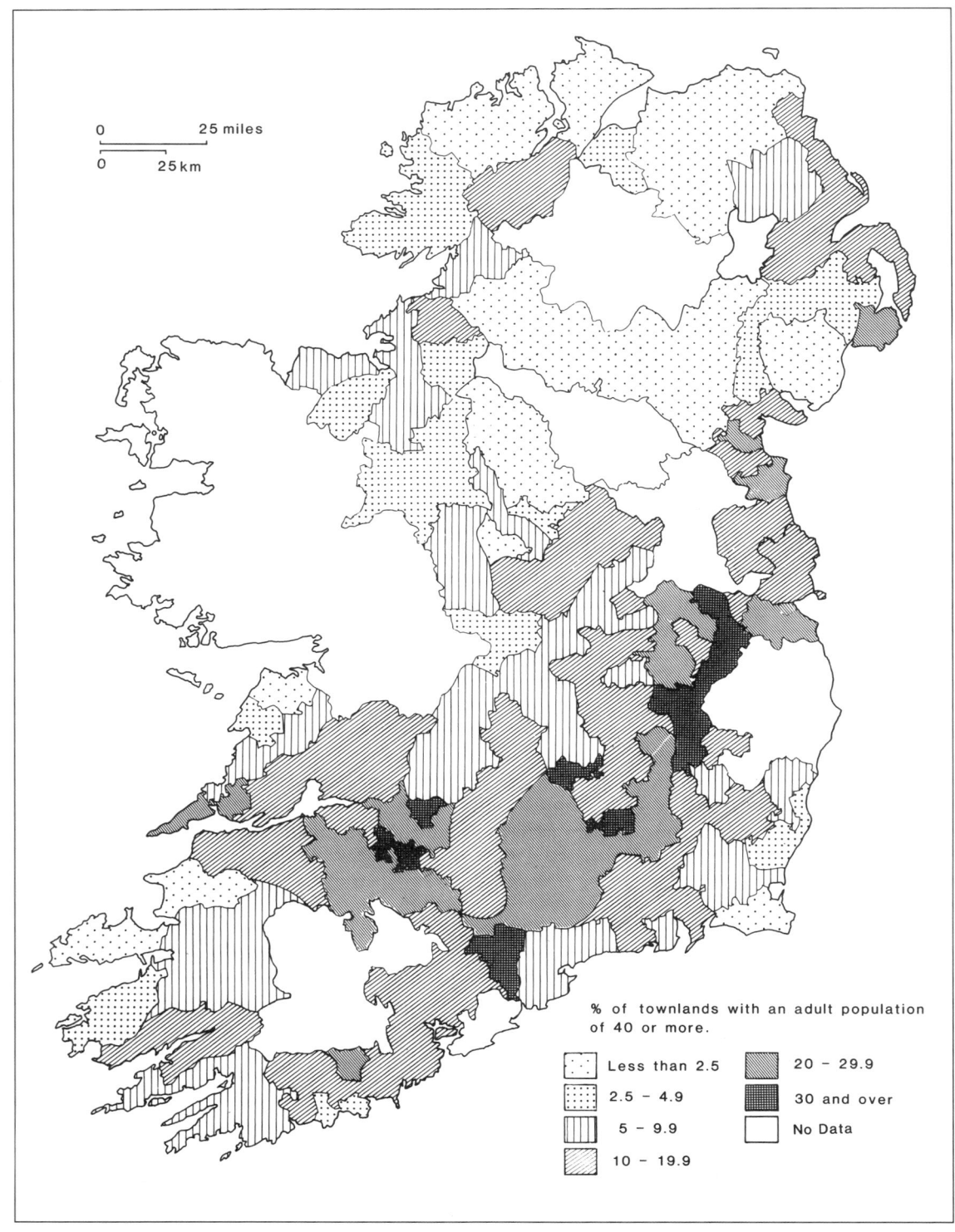

% of townlands with an adult population
of 40 or more.

Less than 2.5		20 – 29.9	
2.5 – 4.9		30 and over	
5 – 9.9		No Data	
10 – 19.9			

FIGURE 8
Townlands in 1660 with an adult population of forty or more

– where a 'manorial' village economy, substantial farmers, markets, mills, fairs and towns, were long-standing features of the society. The central heartland of Kilkenny county was party to this world as were the rich tillage lands of the Barrow and the village-studded lands of east County Kildare and south County Dublin. This was the nuclear area of large settlements, often still set amongst open fields long nurtured by "the industrious hand of the laborious husbandman".[66] A core area in south and mid County Louth was equally an essentially medieval landscape of villages and associated farm clusters. Graham's work would suggest that the Boyne valley could also be interpreted as another great spine of settlement nucleation. This, therefore, was not only a society of gentry, farmers and merchants but also of labourers, ploughmen, husbandmen, cowmen, horseboys, smiths and weavers and even its smaller towns had their malsters, millers, tanners, butchers and innkeepers.[67] This nuclear area of Leinster is further revealed by a consideration of the distribution of townlands with over 20 adults (60 people or more). In south Kildare and north Carlow, over 60 per cent of all townlands contain such levels of population concentration and there is a broad belt of territory stretching from west Dublin beyond north Kildare and on into the southern parts of Laois and most of Kilkenny where well over 50 per cent of townlands are in this category – as they are in most of County Louth. This Leinster core-region is, therefore, outstanding in settlement terms in 1660.

On the south-western flanks of County Tipperary, west Waterford also has a strong pattern of villages and towns – an older nucleated pattern here is strongly augmented by new English planters and immigrant craftsmen in the iron-working settlements and the refurbished towns. North Cork and much of east Limerick were also studded with a hierarchy of towns and villages. O'Connor has given a conservative estimate of 65 nucleated villages for County Limerick.[68] Given its great density of tower houses and their often adjacent house clusters, one is not too surprised to find that east and mid Limerick emerges with one of the most elaborate settlement hierarchies in the whole country full of what the Civil Survey describes as *Irish Townes*. Plantation processes clearly intensified this settlement hierarchy. Outliers of these high density settlement patterns included the diverse regions of peninsular Moyarta in Clare, coastal Imokilly and inland Kinalmeaky in County Cork.

---

66. Down Survey parish maps for Crannagh barony, Co. Kilkenny, N.L.I., MS 720.
67. W.J. Smyth, 'The dynamic quality of Irish "village" life – a reassessment' in *Hommes et Terres du Nord*, 1988; J. Burtchaell, 'The South Kilkenny farm villages', in Smyth and Whelan (eds.), *Common Ground, op. cit.*, pp. 110–23.
68. P.J. O'Connor, *Exploring Limerick's past: an historical geography of urban development in county and city* (Limerick, 1987), p. 23.

At the other end of Tipperary, in the lakeland-midland baronies of Owney and
Arra and the two Ormonds, a weak nucleated settlement pattern is evident in this
region long dominated by Gaelic lords. This mosaic of lowland, bogland, woodland and hills was on the margins of a commercialised economy in the seventeenth
– as in the nineteenth – century. Remoteness, the lack of an urban hierarchy, the
fragmentation of landownership patterns in a more Gaelic world, the dominance of
a pastoral economy in what is often "small oats and cow country", and the scattering of a wide range of institutional foci (churches, castles and mills) in different
townlands within single parishes – all had combined to produce a more dispersed,
less stratified and less populous settlement pattern.[69] Under ten per cent of these
denominations held populations in excess of 120. The dispersal of population here
often involved the scattering of communities within and between townlands in
small clusters of two, three or four houses. The Gaelic or Gaelicised lands of *na
Déise*, west Cork, south and mid Kerry also reflect similar processes. Northwards
from the Ormond lowlands in Tipperary, a wide belt of equivalent settlement and
population structures dominate the wet midlands on each side of the Shannon with
an even more emphatic levelling off in townland populations in Garrycastle
(Offaly), north Roscommon, south Sligo and south Donegal. Apart from coastal
and southern Galway and a relatively narrow strip through central and coastal
Mayo, it is likely that similar patterns prevail over the rest of Connaught – as they
clearly did in north-west Clare. On the other hand, many of these same baronies
emerge with over 30 per cent of townlands with adult populations in excess of 20.
For example, the status of Rathvilly and Forth in Carlow and Scarawalsh and Bantry
in Wexford – significantly located on the borders of the rich south Leinster spine of
nucleation – is seen to be strongly enhanced at this level as are the other parts of
Munster named above. Likewise, the southern halves of Longford and Roscommon
emerge as areas with quite a number of lower order settlements as do the baronies
of Beara in Cork, Tireragh in Sligo and Tirhugh in Donegal. The boost in the settlement structures of these coastal baronies reflects the importance of the sea for
fishing, coastal trading and enhancing the productivity of the coastal lands in general. The recent upsurge in iron-works and forges produced an additional widespread boost to local settlement structures.

County Tipperary has a third important region of moderate population densities
where from 10 to 19 per cent of townland populations exceed 120 and where over
40 per cent exceed 60. This middle bandolier of settlement is in a zone of mixed
ecology containing much good land but also some hill, wood and bogland. It is also
a zone of old and newly-emerging towns where mixed-farming, a mixed settlement

69. W.J. Smyth in W. Nolan (ed.), *Tipperary: History and Society*, (Dublin, 1985), pp. 104–38.

structure and a mixed ethnic heritage are evident. Much of County Meath appears
to belong to this hybrid zone as well. Here a very mixed farming economy sustained
over 90 manorial villages, 45 castle-hamlets (or 'fortified clusters' as Graham calls
them), over 50 non-fortified farm clusters as well as a substantial number of solid
independent farmsteads.[70] Figure 8 suggests that parts of north Kerry and west
Limerick, the southern half of County Clare, some baronies in south and north
Kilkenny, much of Laois and indeed all the baronies bordering the dominant core
of settlement along the Barrow and the Liffey are characterised by similar mixtures
of settlement. The Down Survey parish maps for the barony of Crannagh in
County Kilkenny reveal the complex array of nucleated settlement items that characterise this plateau-interfluve country west of Kilkenny city.[71] The axis of a mod-
erately well developed settlement hierarchy also extends westward through County
Westmeath and northward to the Cooley peninsula. Further north a combination
of medieval and planter settlement boosts the settlement structures of parts of east
Antrim and east Donegal. The old settled baronies of Ards and Lecale are also on
the edges of this wider settlement region whose rhythms and lifestyles seem to
belong more to a south-eastern than a north-western culture world. All the evidence from the late sixteenth and early seventeenth centuries suggests a greater integration of these hybrid zones with the revitalised (if short-lived) centres of Old
English power.

   A dialectic between the cultures of the northern and southern halves of Ireland is
also suggested by the seventeenth century settlement evidence. Stretching north of
one of the oldest and most persistent territorial divides in Ireland, the poll-tax evidence identifies this final settlement region which stretches north of a line from the
Cooley peninsula to the Cavan-Meath borders, through mid-Longford and mid-
Roscommon to reach the sea around Clew Bay. Exclusive of the few coastal foci discussed already, this region was profoundly characterised in 1660 by a scattering of
settlements and societies. The few glimpses we get of the local rural societies also
suggest a much less stratified population – it was a society of farmers, labourers,
herders, shepherds, carpenters and rabbit catchers. The historic absence of a nucleated settlement tradition is much starker in this zone of rapid and recent urbanisa-
tion.

   This essentially Gaelic, pastoral, and subsistence world sustained the most integrated territorial hierarchies in Ireland until the turn of the seventeenth century –
stretching seamlessly from the greater and lesser lordship through the ballybetagh to

70. B.J. Graham, 'Anglo-Norman settlement in County Meath' in *R.I.A. Proc.*, 75C, 11(1975),
pp.223–48; Down Survey barony and parish maps for Co. Eastmeath, N.L.I., MS 715.
71. Down Survey parish maps for Co. Kilkenny, N.L.I., MS 720.

the ballyboe or its equivalent at the base. As Duffy and MacErlean have illustrated, these kin-centred structures were broken only by the plantations of Ulster.[72] Then, these corporate sept estates – with partible inheritance and the regular redistribution of townlands as central features – were stripped down and recombined into the indivisible, commercially-oriented, "manorial" estates of the new landowners. A private property system was now married to old territorial frameworks.

The surviving Civil and Down Surveys for Ulster baronies regularly stress that "a few creaghts [cabins] are scattered about ye said parish" and in some instances note that a parish contains no buildings but "removable creaghts" for "the Irish inhabitants always lived in creaghts which they remove from place to place to enrich the small plots of arable for tillage" (Orior, Armagh).[73] The barony description for Orior is also instructive: "The soil is good for breeding cattle and corn and steeds but not for sheep and there is but a small part thereof that yields any kinds of grane and not without good store of industry and labour because the land is very strong, the unforfeited part is in the plain and is much better land". In the drumlin country of the parish of Creggan in the Fews, this description notes that "the Curroghs" (meadowlands) encircle "the small hills wherein natives live".

The relatively sparsely distributed residences (some few of stone) of the local lords had been important foci for larger settlements here. Yet, in this region which had never experienced a deep integration into a feudalised European economy (as much of the south and east had), it is striking how sacred places – parish or diocesan centres, monasteries, nunneries or abbeys – acted as the gathering points for peoples and settlements in this northern region where church land was more extensive and less subject to secular control than elsewhere.[74] On a broader front, Figure 7 cannot reveal the rather different forces making for nucleation further south. In the Pale area and in north and mid-Leinster generally, the roots of a richer village culture may have been older, deeper and more strongly based on a tillage economy. The patterns of nucleation in the tower-house studded lands of south-west Leinster, all of Munster and south Galway may have been more complex, in some cases more recent, and almost certainly had more to do with the growth of a commercialised stock-rearing/arable economy in the later medieval period.

The poll-tax allows us to both identify and locate the most prestigious people in

72. P.J. Duffy, 'The territorial organisation of Gaelic landownership and its transformation in Co. Monaghan 1591–1640' in *Ir. Geog.*, 14 (1980), pp. 1–26; McErlean, op. cit.; see also P.J. Duffy, 'The evolution of estate properties in South Ulster 1600–1900', in Smyth and Whelan (eds), op. cit., pp. 84–109.
73. Down Survey parish maps for Co. Armagh, P.R.O.N.I., D.597.
74. P. Robinson, *The plantation of Ulster* (Dublin, 1984), pp. 109–28. See also R. Gillespie, *Colonial Ulster – the settlement of East Ulster 1600–1641*, (Cork, 1985).

the island – the so-called 'tituladoes' – and to explore the relationship between these resident elites and the development of patterns of colonisation and settlement hierarchies. As a crude measure of the distribution of the wealthiest and most powerful people – and hence the most stratified and privileged societies and landscapes of the country – the proportion of 'tituladoes' per adult population in each barony was assessed. Two great belts of 'gentrified' territories emerge; on the one hand the lands west of the Shannon (comprising most of Roscommon, most emphatically all of County Clare and also including, one assumes, much of Mayo and Galway) and the rich lands of north- and mid-Leinster on the other. In Clare and Connaught, the juxtaposition of many old Gaelic and Norman families, other old English and Gaelic merchant investors (from the cities of Limerick and Galway) and an increasing number of pre- and post-Cromwellian New English landholders and lessees was to endow this western region with a distinctive and densely concentrated ruling class.

The second region of 'gentry' concentration connects south Roscommon with County Westmeath, widens out into a belt of powerful people in the Pale region and stretches south along the Barrow corridor deep into Carlow. This region (together with east Galway) may well be the area where the greatest continuities in landownership patterns helped sustain older settlements and social hierarchies for much longer than we have imagined. Certainly this was the region with the most elaborate village and urban structures in the mid-seventeenth century. Much of the rest of south Leinster and east and south Munster is also characterised by a moderate concentration of resident gentry, whereas the more Gaelic regions of *na Déise*, south Kerry and west Limerick reveal a weaker aristocratic layer. Likewise, apart from east Down, and a mixture of old and new landlords in east Donegal and parts of Fermanagh, this recurring northern world from County Sligo across to County Louth appears least top heavy in terms of a gentry and substantial rural middle class in this zone of weaker settlement hierarchies. However, since this region was also likely to be the zone of greatest tax evasion, this interpretation will require further refinement.

We are on safer ground when analysing the ethnic background of the 'tituladoes'. The most telling statement emerging from the poll-taxes is the strength of the new planter elite in the northern half of the island. Apart from Inishowen and the baronies of south Down, the country that lies north of a line from mid-Roscommon to mid-Louth was emphatically a region of Scottish and English elites. The depth, extent and rapidity in the transformation of the power structures of this region leaps from Figure 9 emphasising the cultural cleavages which followed on from this abrupt ascendancy by a new ruling class. The older society had lost its patrons and

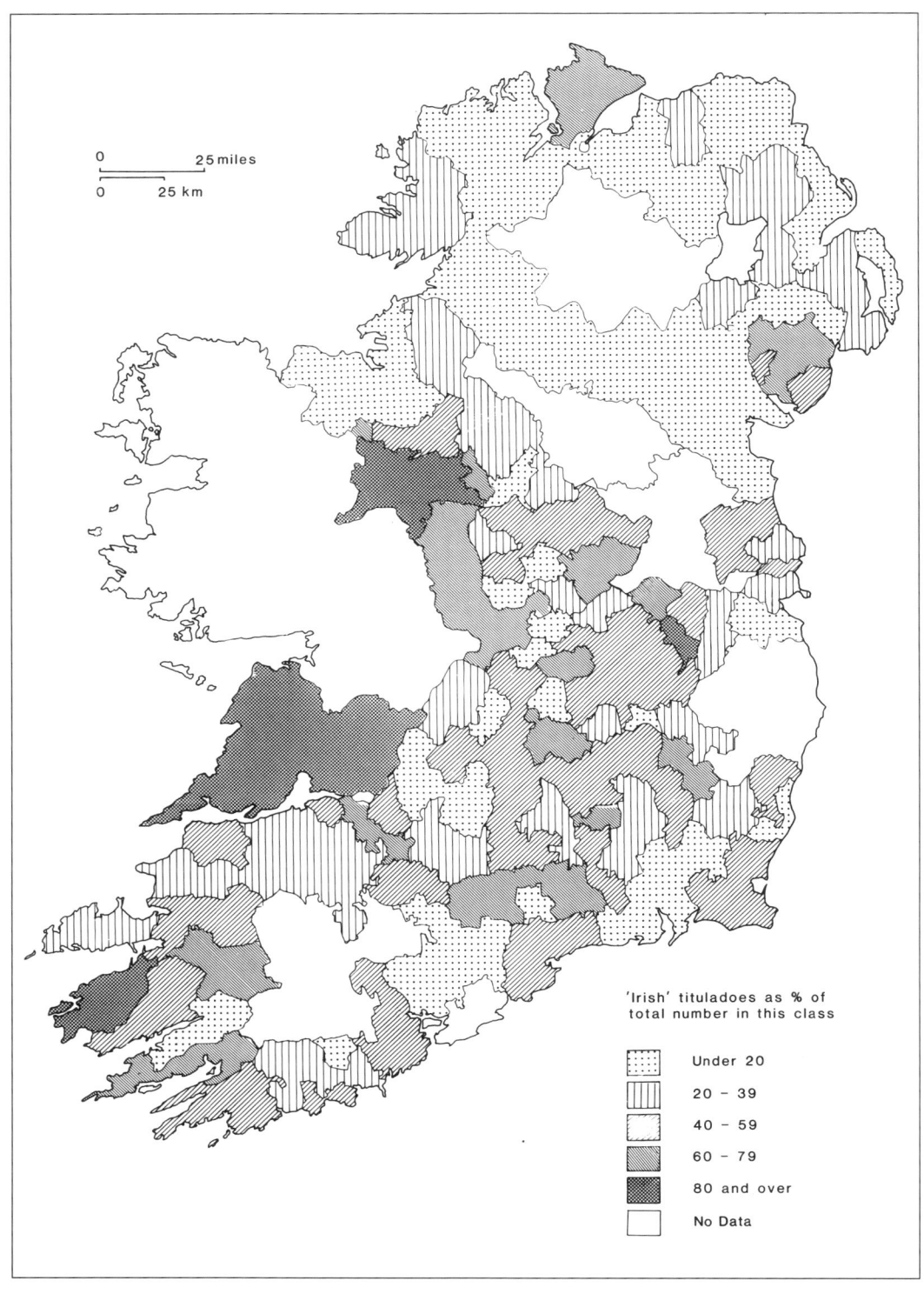

FIGURE 9
'Irish' *tituladoes* in 1660 as a proportion of the total enumerated for this taxation class

leaders – and Petty's county maps for this northern region in *Hiberniae Delineatio* (1685) starkly revealed the residual and scrappy character of the surviving Irish lands. The poll-tax references to the officer rank of so many of the new elite emphasises the militarised nature of this conquered world. So do the early seventeenth century town maps which mirror intimately the subjugation of lands where the Normans had never penetrated.

Figure 9 reveals the sharpness of the cultural and political frontier between this settler region and the rest of Connaught. Only the barony of Boyle acts as a buffer between the planted areas of Sligo-Leitrim and the outstanding density of old elites stretching south from Roscommon to Clare. Yet, even in Clare, there is a small planter class along the Shannon estuary baronies – developers of both new towns and new economies. The most striking feature of the rest of Munster and Leinster is the mosaic-like distribution of different ethnic elites. There are localised power structures, social hierarchies and related landscape expressions in these provinces which makes generalisation difficult. One can identify, however, an axis of New English control from south County Dublin through Wicklow into north Wexford (the core of the officially designated 'New Pale') which extends westwards in a narrow salient into the Laois midlands. A second axis of New English control emerges in the immediate hinterland of Waterford city. East Cork (excluding Imokilly), Kinalmeaky and Carbery, not surprisingly in view of the Munster plantation, reveal a strong planter elite. But the overall pattern for both County Cork and the wider Limerick hinterland is a fragmented one. MacCarthy Morrogh's emphasis on the intermixed, fretted and piecemeal character of the English settlement in Munster is supported by this map.[75] The remainder of Munster and Leinster emerges as a battleground of interests – areas where often the planters' more narrow political ascendancy is matched by both the residual class power and greater population size of the older society. Members of the latter society still held on to powerful hinge positions in urban and rural social hierarchies and ensured that the relative success of the new landlord-inspired economy would both depend on and be mediated by them.[76] This process has been illustrated elsewhere for County Tipperary; over the southern half of the island, therefore, surviving territorial and social structures were often orchestrated to deflect the full brunt of colonial rule. The dominance of old or new elites also had a bearing on the extent to which settler immigration was a significant feature in their respective regions and towns.

The 1660 poll-tax documents this process of settler immigration. Figure 10

75. M. MacCarthy Morrogh, *The Munster plantation: English migration to southern Ireland 1583–1641* (Oxford, 1986).
76. T. Jones Hughes, 'The origin and growth of towns in Ireland' in *University Review*, 2, 7 (1960), pp. 8–15. See also Smyth, 'Tipperary', *op. cit.*, pp. 136–8.

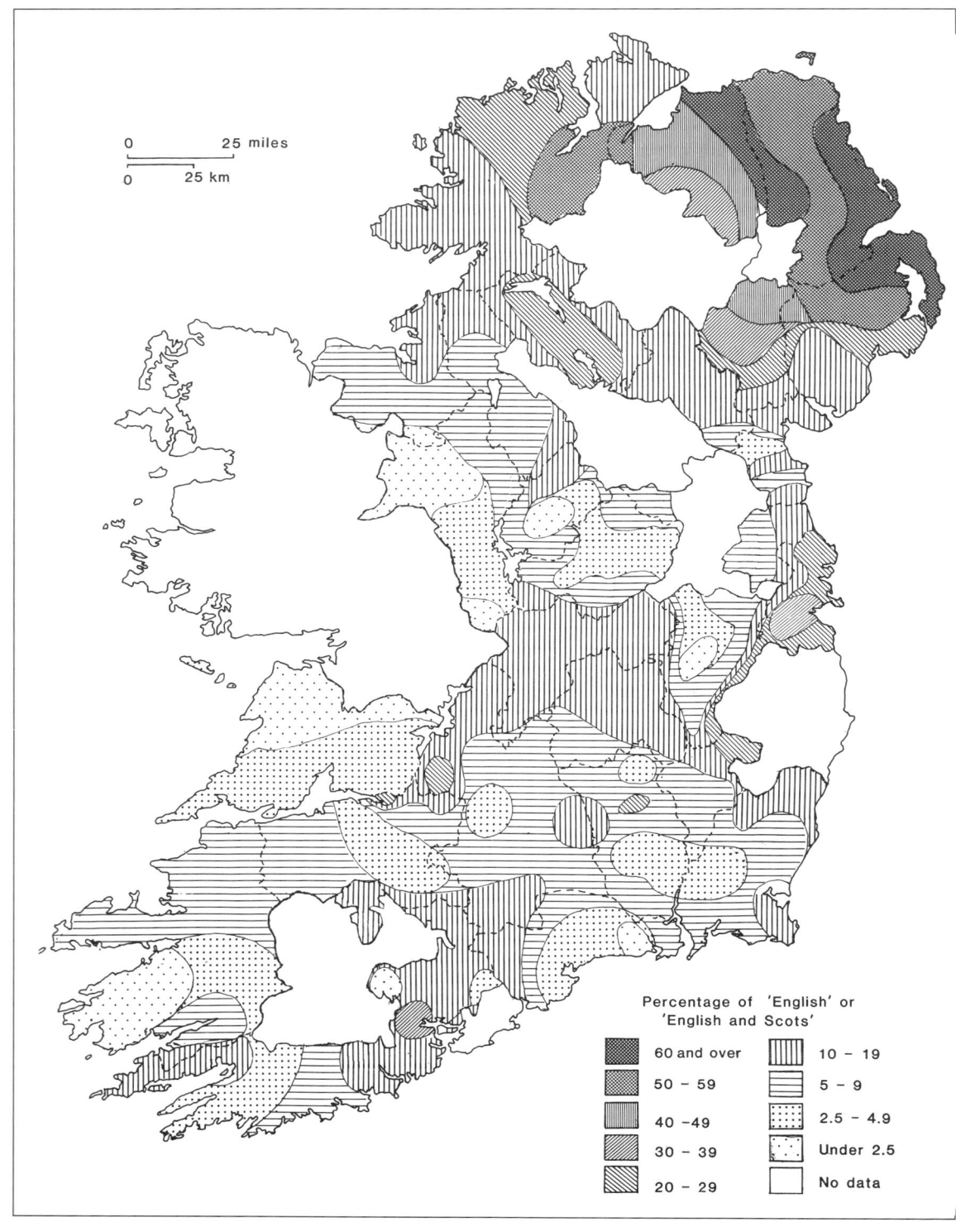

FIGURE 10
Distribution of 'English' and 'English and Scots' in 1660

incorporates a minimal adjustment of the returns to give a more realistic distribution of the ethnic groups in the north-western region and summarises at the barony scale the level of immigrant penetration and consolidation in Antrim, most of Down, north Armagh, much of the county of Londonderry, east Donegal and a core around the lakes of Fermanagh. It highlights the cutting edge of a south-westward moving frontier as it spilled over into the less densely populated edges of Connaught and the north-west midlands generally. This advancing front was running up against an old Gaelic world and in the process deflected some of the older populations further south into Omeath in the Cooley peninsula to the east, and onto the Galway-Clare borderlands and the islands to the west. New frontier nucleations had emerged as in the Scotch planter town of St Johnstown in County Longford and in pockets elsewhere as in Carrigallan and Manorhamilton in County Leitrim. This map assumes that the missing populations are divided proportionately between Planter and Gael but there is a strong possibility that the strength of the tightly knit Scotch-Presbyterian communities is still underestimated.

The poll-tax assists us in identifying the core areas of polarisation in the newly planted territories (while also pointing to the possibilities for colonising previously unsettled, if extensively used, townland units). The poll-tax evidence allows one to identify the townlands occupied by English/Scottish populations only. Consequently, a kind of segregation/dislocation index can be calculated which further refines our view of the hearthland of the colony. This core of planter settlement pivots around three inter-locked areas – east Londonderry, coastal and mid-Antrim (information is missing at this level for south Antrim) and north and central Armagh where 18 to 28 per cent of all townlands enumerated appear to be the sole preserve of the settlers. A domain area with eight to twelve per cent of townlands segregated can be identified for the remainder of north-east Ulster with secondary cores of equal strength emerging in east Donegal and Fermanagh. The fringe of this extension of Scottish and English cultures into the north, that is where less than six per cent of the townlands are segregated, can be identified for Inishowen, west Donegal, south Armagh and part of mid-Down. Overall, County Down is quite striking in its admixture of populations and the densely populated lands of Ards and Lecale register no segregated townlands. Its rich variegated societies and landscapes appear to have had more assimilative powers than much of the rest of Ulster. Further south along the Connaught-Leinster borderlands, settler expansion was less compact and more individualistic in nature and for the most part represented the infilling of settlement within already populated townlands – 'outliers' in what must have been a hostile world.

The second most powerful core of planter settlement pivoted around the Pale region and Dublin city – a cockpit of diverging interests where Irish, Old English and a variety of settler elements congregated around the richest prizes. Apart from a strategic northern coastal salient, planter settlement had only limited success in the rich heartlands of north Leinster. But, to the south and west a new wide band of a significant minority population was well established, reaching right across Laois, Offaly and the edges of north Tipperary to reach the Shannon at Limerick and on the other flank curving southwards to colonise the west-Wicklow, north-Wexford borderlands. This too was an enduring settlement which laid down a whole range of new nucleations on the edges of north Munster at Cloghjordan, Borrisokane and Birr and on the edges of the midlands generally through Castlecomer in Kilkenny to Dunlavin in County Wicklow and Gorey in Wexford.

    Thirdly, there was a south-western core of settlement, pivoting round Cork City and the Munster plantation precincts. However, the barony-based map obscures the expansion of settlers south-westwards – as they followed the fish along the coasts of west Cork and south Kerry. The integration of this south Munster region into a wider economic context is symbolised by the inland frontier town of Bandon – an outlier of the West Country woollen industry and a pivot for future colonisation westwards.[77] Unlike the other two settler regions, however, this Munster plantation – with the exception of the wider west Cork area – was initiated in an already long settled well-developed region. In addition, much of this gentry rather than soldier-led colonisation was begun in an earlier period when religious-political affiliations were not as deep or as divisive as they were to become in mid-seventeenth century Ireland. It would appear that the shock of 1641 and longer term processes of assimilation were to absorb much of the fringes of this southern settler area into the old body politic – and nowhere more emphatically than in that most assimilative of counties, Limerick. But much of this lay in the future. South-west Munster, given its mixed heritage, was to underpin the most innovative and wealthiest overseas English settlement anywhere in the seventeenth century.

    The most enduring colonial contributions and populations were, however, in the towns – and towns were, as always, the central instruments of imperial expansion and control. The poll-tax allows us to make a more than tentative identification of the distribution and size of these urban settlements while also providing a picture of the ethnic composition of the urban populations. Dublin's primacy is one obvious feature of Figure 11 – a position of dominance which had been, for the most part, achieved by a possible five-fold increase in population between c. 1600 and

77. D. Dickson, An economic history of the Cork region in the eighteenth century, unpublished Ph.D. thesis, T.C.D., 1977; see also N. Canny, 'Migration and opportunity: Britain, Ireland and the New World' in *Ir. Econ. Soc. Hist.*, 12 (1985), pp. 7–32.

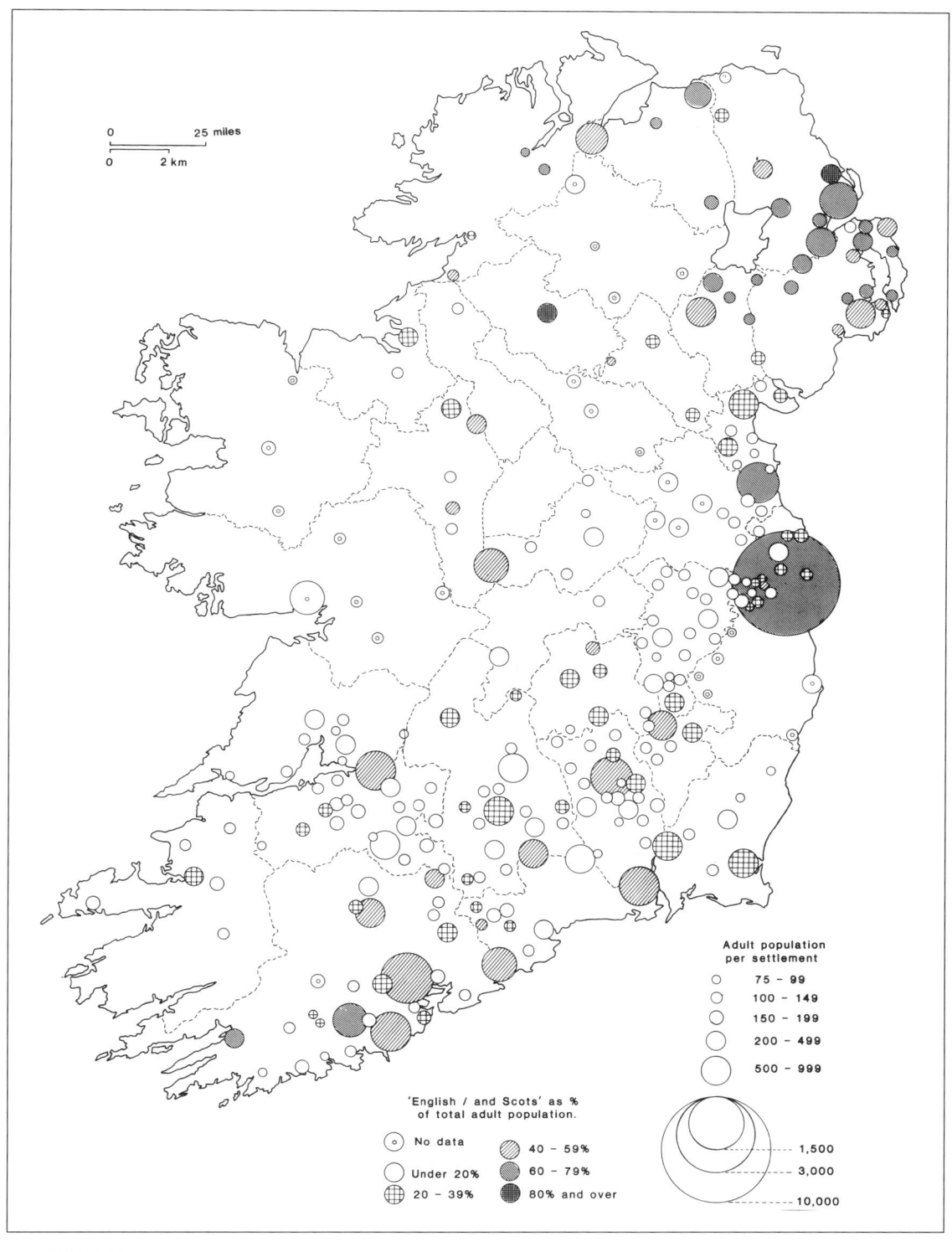

FIGURE 11

Distribution and ethnic composition of nucleated settlements with an
adult population of seventy-five and over in 1660

1660. Its primacy is also suggested by its list of 'tituladoes' (624) which is as large as the elites of all the other Irish cities and towns put together. Then, as today, it was the dominant governmental, legal, military, financial, industrial, commercial and educational centre – full of lords, judges, attorneys, merchants, army officers, distillers, clothiers, clerks and innkeepers. Cork had achieved second place in the urban hierarchy by 1660, outstripping Galway and Limerick which ranked second and third in the 1600s. Cork too, with the expulsion of its old merchant families outside its walls, had a large new elite population (144) especially active in its dominant role as the import centre of south Munster. Waterford, Limerick (and Galway?) were of almost equal rank and population and all retained a significant minority of the old merchant families. Drogheda, Carrickfergus, Youghal, Kinsale and the growing city of Derry were also important port centres with a substantial number of wealthy taxpayers. Kilkenny was the most significant inland city with its own complex economic structures, supporting as it did a wide range of shops, services and small industries. Figure 11 therefore reveals three types of regions with different urban structures and lifestyles – areas with an elaborate urban hierarchy in the east, the south and increasingly in the north-east; areas with a still developing urban hierarchy running through the midlands and on the borders of the feudalised world generally; and thirdly the remoter areas where urban settlement hierarchies and ways of living were still only in their infancy.

The most telling aspect of Figure 11 is not only the primacy of Dublin and the larger port-cities but also the conquest of Dublin and indeed the conquest of all the large port-cities and county towns by immigrant peoples and elites. The Cromwellian settlement was not only to make for massive property transfers in the countryside; more significantly Cromwellian policy and independent economic processes saw the radical acceleration of planter command of urban properties, agricultural surpluses, external trade and a whole range of political and administrative offices based in the cities and towns.[78] Underpinning this urban ascendancy were the officers, the soldiers and the elaborate garrison fortifications which had been grafted on to the walls of these old cities and towns. Although, the poll-tax is markedly deficient in its enumeration of all garrisons, it is still impressive how often the enumerated military rulers turn up in the cities and bigger towns. Even more striking still, running through this strategic middle belt of the country – from Carrickfergus, Magherafelt and Charlemont, through Boyle, Roscommon and the great garrison pivot at Athlone, and on to Thurles, Mallow, Cork, Kinsale and Bantry – the soldiers' barracks is a prominent and sometimes an overwhelming

---

78. T. Barnard, *Cromwellian Ireland: English government and reform in Ireland, 1649–60*, (Oxford, 1975).

element in the urban setting. In Roscommon, the civilian population, for the most part local, is almost outnumbered by the English soldiers of the garrison.

Such control made for a radical restructuring of the social geography of cities and towns. The medieval city of Kilkenny provides a dramatic example of this. In the core of the city, in the High Street and elsewhere, over 72 per cent of the population was of planter stock. In the ring of urban settlement around the core, 40 per cent of the population were settlers, while in the outlying liberties of the city 24 per cent were 'outsiders'. Similarly, the core of Cork city had been lost yet Shandon was still 72 per cent Irish. A core-domain-periphery structure characterised even the largest cities. Expanding Irishtowns characterised the urban scene everywhere. The deep divisions of the post-Cromwellian society were most sharply chiselled into the narrow confines of the urban fabric.

A second major feature of Figure 11 is the almost exclusive dominance of the planter population in these often newly planned urban centres in Ulster. Apart from the newly created towns which must have been literally outstanding features of this hitherto rural world, the surviving secular centres and more especially the diocesan towns such as Clogher, Dromore, Kilmore and Raphoe were now solidly in the hands of the planter. Only in some older towns of east Down (Downpatrick, Strangford, Kilclief and Ardglass) and in the more outlying cities of Armagh and Derry was a substantial Gaelic population represented within the towns. There are equally vivid contrasts between the wealth of the strong comfortable planter towns at the core – not only Larne and Belfast but also Antrim, Ballymena and Lisburn – with their bigger houses and developing markets, fairs and communications networks – and the rudimentary and isolated frontier towns like Enniskillen where over 80 per cent of the population was of planter stock. Here and likewise in fortified Monaghan, Carrickmacross, Ballyshannon and Lifford the poll-taxes and the early town maps highlight the sharpness of the clash between the planter townsmen and the remnants of the rural order. Beyond this region, the towns with a 20 to 40 per cent planter population highlight the great buffer zone stretching from south Down across to Sligo and Roscommon. Figure 11 also illustrates the strength of planter settlement in the episcopal, county, and new planter towns elsewhere in the country. Everywhere, too, the poll-tax notes the powerful role of the resident landlord in patronising these centres of administration and trade.

Thirdly, Figure 11 reveals a more hidden urban Ireland where the often walled, sometimes small but always socially and morphologically complex borough towns of the south and east still retain an overwhelming proportion of older towndwellers. East Limerick is typical of this resilient urban world of Munster – Cork County's urban ethnic mix reflects a more exposed settlement history. In Leinster – and particularly along the western edges of Wexford, in Kilkenny, Kildare, Meath and Westmeath – an older corporate tradition of urban living also survived.

And so another lesson emerges from the poll-tax pages – these old and battered towns had weathered the storms of the medieval period and were in place to bene-fit from the upswing in the economy from the sixteenth century onwards. Clearly, it was these elaborate and enduring urban societies which helped sustain the popu-lation densities and more complex rural settlement hierarchies outlined above. Figure 11, therefore, provides a dramatic illustration of the coexistence on the island of very different urban cultures.

CONCLUSIONS:

In the last analysis, the 1660 poll-tax evidence stresses how much of the foundations of modern Ireland had been laid down and firmly put in place by the mid-seven-teenth century. It was, as Andrews had pointed out,[79] a ragged framework where old worlds, transitional worlds and literally new worlds co-existed within and between even two or three adjacent streets or parishes. Sharp polarities are evident in many places and at many levels, not least where the Scottish borderers along the Fermanagh frontier faced "the men of Connaught". On the other hand, the mosa-ic-like qualities of so many patterns points to the tensions and creativities that sprang from new encounters. And so a whole series of retreating, stable, embryon-ic and transitional culture regions are identified – regions of devastation and despair, regions of sustained continuities and hope, regions of powerful intrusions and enterprise and regions with hybrid, ambivalent qualities.

After 1660, the forces of massive economic and demographic growth, the deep-ening of external political control and the profound island-wide impact of what Jones Hughes has termed landlordism[80] were to transform, if again unevenly, these seventeenth century patterns and lifestyles. The poll-tax evidence is, therefore, of immense significance to the study of seventeenth century Irish life and its later transformations. Once its limitations are exposed (and this is still an on-going exer-cise) and other sources of evidence are used in conjunction with it, the poll-tax is enormously fruitful in unravelling the stratas and stresses, territorial and societal, that made up later medieval/early modern Ireland. It also helps us to reclaim and enlarge our vision of seventeenth century Ireland and, through that, our vision of ourselves.

79. J.H. Andrews, 'Land and people, c.1685', chapter xviii in *A New History of Ireland, III, op. cit.*, p. 477.
80. T. Jones Hughes, 'Landlordism in the Mullet of Mayo' in *Ir. Geogr.* 4, 1 (1959), pp. 16–34; *ibid.*, 'Landholding and settlement in the Cooley peninsula of Louth' in *Ir. Geogr.*, 4, 3 (1961), pp. 145–74' and *ibid.*, 'Society and settlement', pp. 79–96.

INTRODUCTION

BY
SÉAMUS PENDER
(1 9 3 9)

INTRODUCTION

In a paper read before the Royal Irish Academy in 1864, and afterwards published in volume 24 of the Transactions of that body,[1] W. H. Hardinge announced his discovery of what has since been known as The Census of Ireland (1659). He had been searching among the papers of the Marquess of Lansdowne for Down Survey Baronial Maps and alighted on the Census during the course of his search. The manuscripts were at that time in the Muniment Room, Lansdowne House, London. Hardinge obtained permission to have them transferred to Dublin and deposited in the Landed Estates Record Office. He had copies made of them before returning them to their owner. The copies are now in the Library of the Royal Irish Academy; the originals are in the Muniment Room of the Marquess of Lansdowne, Bowood. They comprise returns for Antrim, Armagh, Derry, Donegal, Down, Fermanagh, and Monaghan, in Ulster; Clare, Cork City, Cork County [incomplete], Kerry, Limerick City, Limerick County, Tipperary, Waterford [City and County], in Munster; Carlow, Dublin City, Dublin County, Kildare, Kilkenny, King's County, Longford, Louth, Meath [incomplete], Queen's County, Westmeath, Wexford, in Leinster; and Leitrim, Roscommon, and Sligo, in Connacht. The volumes are of paper and measure 12″ × 15″. They are all in a well-preserved condition, the script throughout being clear, neat and legible, with the exception of the Cork County volume. This particular volume has been written in a very careless manner, indeed; the scribe paid absolutely no attention to the correct distribution of minims or to differentiating between the letters *u* and *n*. Each of the thirty volumes of the collection is tied together with strips of vellum, apparently cut from a legal document of some kind. On one of the strips tying the Leitrim volume the words *thousand, six hundred and sixty* may be read. Hardinge[2] read this as the date 1660. According to a hand-list of the collection, drawn up in 1864 by Hardinge and now preserved among the Miscellaneous Petty Papers at Bowood, the volume containing the Cork County returns was in two separate portions at the time of its discovery. The two portions, evidently on Hardinge's instructions, were united. When I examined the volume in November of the present year I found folio 80 to be very discoloured and stained, indicating that it had formed the outer folio of the second portion.

The outer folio of the (original) Carlow volume has a now almost illegible pencilled note, in Hardinge's hand, relating to extracts from the Carlow Hearth Money Rolls and ending as follows: " . . . . I am of opinion that these Census Returns were made up during the period of Petty's Survey by Petty (because no other person could compile it) between December 1654 and the year 1659." Folio 1 *verso* of the Longford volume has also a note by Hardinge: " T.R. proprietor by C. S. 1653 "; this refers to the Thomas Robinson of folio 2, [see Text]. The late Marquess of Lansdowne inserted some observations in the Kerry volume to the effect that Patrick, Lord Kerry, mentioned as a Titulado on folio 7, died in 1660, " which is, therefore, the latest possible date of the Census Return. The returns are not copies, as they are in different hands.

---

[1] Observations by W. H. Hardinge, M.R.I.A., on the earliest known Manuscript Census Returns of the People of Ireland, *Trans., R.I.A., vol.* 24 (*Polite Literature and Antiquities*), p. 317.
[2] *Op. cit.*, p. 320.

They were probably made by Petty's Surveyors on the spot ; nobody else would have been in a position to collect the figures." Those observations were amplified by his Lordship in a letter written in February, 1936, to the Secretary of the Commission, when the publication of the Census was under consideration. I quote the relevant extracts : " I should have thought that if the date of the MS. is after 1655 the probabilities were that it was made by Petty's Surveyors, who were for the next 3 or 4 years at work in every county in Ireland, and would have had exceptional facilities which probably no one else had at the time for compiling a (rough) Census of this kind. It need not, indeed, have been all the work of any single year. It might well have been collected between 1655–1659 and then fair-copied by Petty's clerks for his own use (he was always striving after a complete Census return both for Ireland and England, *vide* my Petty Papers). This would account for there being no mention of it anywhere and for the unique copy being in Petty's hands. He would not have published it because he was looking for something better and more detailed (with Government assistance). I do not agree with Hardinge that Petty did not ' secure ' the Census till after the writing of the Political Anatomy or the Dublin Observations (1683). I know Petty's hand pretty well, and the small and rather neat figures which he has added on the front of each volume of the Census are almost certainly in his earlier script before he practically lost his sight, c. 1670." In addition to writing the county totals on the outer folio of each volume Petty also inserted page totals, barony totals (by pages) and county totals (by baronies). The page totals have been omitted by me.

As was to be expected, the transcript in the Royal Irish Academy was availed of by many writers on Irish county and municipal history. Gilbert prints the returns for Dublin City in the Calendar of Ancient Records of Dublin (vol. iv, p. 560) ; Shirley as Appendix III to his History of Monaghan prints the returns for that county ; O'Rorke in his History of Sligo gives the returns for Sligo (vol. 2, app. II) ; Walsh in " Fingal and its Churches " gives extracts relating to Fingal ; Frost in his History of Clare prints the names of the Tituladoes of county Clare, and Canon Burke in his History of Clonmel the Tituladoes for the Barony of Iffa and Offa, county Tipperary. Wood in his Guide to the Records deposited in the Public Record Office of Ireland (1919) refers[3] to the " so-called Census of 1659 (really a Poll-Tax) in Royal Irish Academy." As such of the original Poll-Tax Rolls 1660–61 as were in the Public Record Office perished in 1922 it is not possible now to compare the two sets of returns. However, Lord Belmore in his " History of two Ulster Manors " prints (p. 305) under the title of " Subsidy Roll 1666 " one of the original Poll Tax returns—" A Return of the Parish of Termon McGoork for the Second Poll Money." This return, as printed, bears not the slightest resemblance to our returns ; it has no Tituladoes or Lists of Principal Irish and English Names ; there is no division of the inhabitants into English and Irish, and the Parish total does not appear. I, at any rate, see no reason to depart from Hardinge's statement that we are here dealing with a Census Return (unfortunately incomplete) of the people of Ireland.

I am indebted to Mr. R. C. Simington, the learned Editor of the *Civil Survey*, for drawing my attention to the existence of copies of the Poll Money Ordinances of 1660 and 1661 in Marsh's Library. Through the courtesy of Mr. Newport B. White, M.A., Librarian, they are printed below, as an appendix. An Examination of them has not convinced me that the Returns here published are Poll Money Returns.

[3] P. 133, s.v. *Poll Tax Rolls.*

Nowhere in the Ordinances does any reference occur to a distinction between the Irish and English inhabitants of the country. This it is that forms the principal obstacle in attempting to identify the Census Returns as Poll-Money Returns. In informing me of the existence of the Poll Money Ordinances Mr. Simington wrote as follows : " Some four or five months prior to the English Act, Poll-tax was levied in Ireland in pursuance of an Ordinance of the General Convention dated April 24, 1660. It directed that all persons of the ranks and degrees therein mentioned should pay the respective sums of money appointed, viz., 'that every person above the age of fifteen years of either sex . . . under the degree or quality of a yeoman, or farmer yeoman, or farmer's wife or widdow shall pay twelve pence '. [*See* Ordinance I *in Appendix*, S.P.]. The sums payable by gentlemen, esquires, knights, barons, earls, and so on, are then specified in an ascending scale. A second Ordinance, [No. II *in Appendix*, S.P.] passed by the same Convention, dated March 1, 1660 [=1661], doubled the Tax referred to specifically as ' Pole-money '—on those above 15 years of age, and imposed much higher levies on persons of particular ranks and degrees. It is from these Ordinances and the machinery they provided for the collection of the Poll-money tax, that a definite conclusion may be drawn as to the true source of origin of the hitherto called Census Returns. ' Able and discreet Protestants ' appointed by County Commissioners, named in the Ordinances, were ' to enquire of all and every person within the respective places limited to their care, of each sex, of and above the age of 15 years ', of their ranks, qualities and degrees, and of the dwelling and abiding places of such persons." These particulars, when obtained, were to be furnished to the County Commissioners who, in turn, were to deliver to the High Collector, in each county, " one estreat indented " comprising the names of the persons assigned to levy the sums rated on the inhabitants of every barony, as well as the names of the persons chargeable. Out of the Poll-money, the various Commissioners were authorised to deduct the fees and expenses of the collectors and clerks.

" Mr. Hardinge, who was Keeper of the Landed Estates Record Office, does not disclose, in his well-known paper, whether he had considered the Poll-tax proceedings before declaring his conclusions to the Royal Irish Academy. In this connection a valuable statement has been furnished by Mr. James F. Morrissey, the present Assistant Deputy Keeper of the Record Office : ' In the volume of Hardinge Tracts in the Record Office Library, referring to the originals of the Petty MS. the following note was made by the late Mr. Mills :—" Some of them were (unknown to him) in Hardinge's own custody." ' On the Précis printed by Hardinge of the ' Census Returns ' by Provinces and Counties Mr. Mills made this further note : ' Had Hardinge turned to Petty's Register in his custody (fol. 30d) which he refers to in another paper he would have seen better the meaning of these figures and Petty's reference in the Index to same would have explained the origin of them as the Poll Tax money of 1660, not an imaginary census.' Petty's Register, and such of the original Poll Tax Returns 1660-61 as were in the Record Office, perished in 1922. Hardinge in his paper prints as Appendix F to his paper on ' Surveys in Ireland 1640 to 1688 ' ' A copy of the Fly Leaf Subjects or Referential Index to a volume endorsed Dr. Petty's Register 1655, *a* 1670.' On Fol. 30 was ' An abstract of ye people in Ireland that payd Poll Money 1660.'

" There is extant, however, in Trinity College library a MS. entitled ' An Estimate of the Pole Money,' Abbott's Catalogue, No. 808. It is with a collection of papers relating to the King's revenue in the 17th century, but it is undated and unsigned.

Divided into provinces, sums of money are distinctly returned against each city or county within four columns captioned respectively : ' The first single Pole : The second single pole : The first double Pole : The second double Pole.' Here light is thrown quite definitely on the missing Returns for part of one county. Hardinge stated that there were ' no census returns for five entire counties, namely Cavan, Galway, Mayo, Tyrone and Wicklow ; and none for four baronies in the county of Cork and for nine baronies in the county of Meath.' At this last-named county there is the following note, explanatory of the amount entered in the first column of the Estimate. ' 3 baronies only, viz., Duleek, Skreen, and Ratoath.' These are the three baronies for which the Returns are available in the Royal Irish Academy, and the missing nine baronies would appear to be thus explained. As regards Mayo, Cavan and Tyrone, it is observed that no figures are entered in either of the first two columns of the Estimate. The second Ordinance of 1660 (1) refers, indeed, to the ' insolvencies and deficiencies ' of the ' two former polls ' [? 1660 *and* 1659, S.P.]. In August, 1662, a Proclamation by the Lord Lieutenant and Council (State Papers I. 1660-1662, pp. 580-82) announced that several collectors of the first and second Poll-moneys ' had not accounted in the Exchequer ' and that certain commissioners had not returned to the Vice-Treasurer, Receiver General, etc., ' the estreats of the said poll moneys as they should have done.' Explanation for all the missing Returns is latent here, as well as the years to which the ' Estimate of the Pole Money ' relates.

" From 'internal evidence' Hardinge had fixed A.D. 1659 as the date of the MSS. he had discovered : ' I find that Sir Charles Coote created in September, 1660, Earl of Mountrath, is returned as a Tituladoe in the county of Dublin by the name of Sir Charles Coote, Bart.' This shows conclusively that Hardinge had overlooked the Poll tax proceedings which were in operation some four months before Coote was made Earl of Mountrath. He was nearer the correct year when he wrote : ' One solitary date presented itself in the course of my examination—the year 1660 occurs on the concealed side of a parchment slip employed to unite together the leaves of the county Leitrim volume.' [Hardinge was wrong in reading the date 1660 ; *see* Page .i. above, S.P.]. That his research had failed to locate the source of origin of the valuable MSS. he had found is again evidenced by the statement ' I have searched in vain for any payment of public money to the persons employed in making out the enumeration returns." It has been shown that the cost of collection—the payment of the clerks employed—was to be defrayed by the various county Commissioners out of the moneys raised.

" In fairness to Hardinge it should be stated that it is not until the year 1695 is reached that the Statute Book reveals the imposition of a Poll tax. The Ordinances were the acts of the Convention of Estates summoned during the transition period and a few months prior to the Restoration of Charles II in May, 1660.

" Petty makes numerous references to the Irish Poll tax in his writings : ' The number of them of all degrees who paid Poll-money, Anno 1661, was about 360,000.' (The political Anatomy of Ireland—1691—Hull's edn, p. 143. Vol. 1). Again : " The Convention and Parliament which made the Acts of Settlement gave the King 2 Pole-Moneys, £20,000 for particular uses, £120,000 as a supplement to the year's value.' (A Treatise of Ireland, 1687 : Conclusions : Vol. II, p. 600). The first figure approximates to that given in the Estimate of the Pole Money already quoted, viz., £20,992. Discussing the relative mortality figures for Dublin and London, Petty says :

' It will follow that the number of inhabitants of Dublin be about 30,000, viz. about one fifteenth part of those in and about London which agrees with that number which I have heard the Books of Poll-Money, raised but little before the time of this Bill have exhibited as the number of inhabitants of that city ' (Appendix, p. 399, Vol. II, Graunt's Observations, A.D. 1665).

" It is clear that the Poll-tax records were well known to Petty and it may be concluded that in his striving to establish population numbers the information they afforded would be eagerly sought by him for translation into statistical form. Here was provided a mass of data relative to the number, rank, quality, degree and abiding places of people above the age of 15 years. The authorship of the format of the Returns would seem definitely indicated by the textual word Tituladoes, Petty's own word ; the provision of particulars as to the number of persons in the racial classifications specified also indicates the hand of Petty, whose desire for knowledge of this kind had been manifested by his question : ' How many Irish, English and Scotch were in this country in 1641 and how many in 1653.' At the end of the Commonwealth period, the relative numbers would have had much more significance for Petty, and their prominence is not surprising."

In the above statement Mr. Simington has gathered together the arguments in favour of the " Poll-Tax theory." My own point of view is that the Returns here printed are not Poll Tax Returns, and I have stated above my reasons for regarding them as a form of Census. A definite conclusion could not be reached without a detailed examination of the Returns themselves. Such an examination is outside the scope of this Introduction.

The term " Titulado," which appears throughout the returns, is best explained as referring to the principal person or persons of standing in any particular locality ; such a person could have been of either sex, a nobleman, baronet, gentleman, esquire, military officer, or adventurer ; that from other sources we learn of a particular Titulado being also a landowner need not surprise us : the landowner is normally the person of standing in a district. Still, it must not be forgotten that " Titulado " and " Land-owner " are not necessarily synonymous terms.[4]

Hardinge's Paper, to which I have referred in the opening paragraph of this Intro-duction, contains a full and lucid description of the Census, together with a critical examination of its contents. With the permission of the Council of the Royal Irish Academy I now give the following extracts from it, adding in some cases additional information of my own.

According to Hardinge, " These manuscripts are copies of—as yet undiscovered— or it may be lost—townland census returns of the inhabitants of Ireland. They are arranged geographically in counties, baronies, parishes, and townlands ; and in cities, parishes and streets. In addition to mere numbers, the returns supply the names of the principal or distinguished occupiers of townlands and streets under the Anglo-Spanish compound designation of Tituladoes. In setting down the numbers on each inhabited townland and in each street, the proportions of English, Irish, and Scotch, are expressed. It would appear, and the fact is probable and significant, that there were no Scotch inhabitants in Munster [*but see the Tables below* : *Agha Parish, barony of Lower Ormond, county Tipperary*] or Connaught, as none are set down in the census

---

[4] The New English Dictionary defines *Titulado* as *a man of title.*

returns for these provinces ; and those of that nation returned in Ulster are undistinguished from the English, for the reason, as I conceive, that the English and Scotch element so liberally introduced there at the time of the Plantation by King JAMES THE FIRST, had subsequently become so merged by family alliances, that any truthful division of the races was impossible at the period of taking the census.

" The returns also supply important and interesting baronial and city lists of the names and numbers of the principal Irish ; as, for example, in the barony of Rathdown and county of Dublin, it is stated that there were 28 principal Irish families of the name of Birne, 12 of Cavenagh, 10 of Callen and Cullen, 29 of Doyle, 8 of Farrell, 12 of Kelly, 7 of Moore, 12 of Murphy, 6 of Neale, 6 of Nowland, 11 of Toole, and 11 of Walsh, making in all 12 principal Irish families, consisting of 152 persons. These persons are included in the gross townland numbers of Irish in that barony, amounting to 265—the repetition being intended to preserve to posterity the names of such of the Irish race as at the time were considered the most distinguished.

" These returns have, unhappily, in their long exile suffered some spoliation, and that too, in all likelihood, for no better purpose than from time to time to aid the kitchen maids in kindling their masters' fires. There are no census returns for five entire counties, namely, Cavan, Galway, Mayo, Tyrone, and Wicklow ; and none for four baronies in the county of Cork, and for nine baronies in the county of Meath. Judging from the character of the paper and its water marks, and from the manufacture, appearance, orthography, and writing of the books and their contents, I consider them to be carefully and contemporaneously prepared transcripts of original official returns, compiled at the close of the Commonwealth period. One solitary date presented itself in the course of my examination, the year 1660 occurs on the concealed side of a parchment slip employed to unite together the leaves of the county Leitrim volume.

" The exact date of the original census survey from which the copy was taken may be readily fixed by the internal evidence abundantly supplied in the transcript. I have compared the names of the Tituladoes appearing in the transcript, and the townlands returned as their respective places of residence, with the names of the Commonwealth tenants of corresponding townlands and counties in the years 1657, 1658, and 1659, and have found complete and convincing identity in numerous instances. I found many persons described in the transcript as mayors, sheriffs, and aldermen of cities, who were collectively so in those years, and not afterwards.[5]   I find that Sir CHARLES COOTE, created in September, 1660, Earl of Mountrath, is returned as a Tituladoe in the county of Dublin by the name of Sir CHARLES COOTE, Bart. In the census transcript of same county Sir ADAM LOFTUS, Knt., ADAM LOFTUS, Esq., and ROBERT LOFTUS, gentleman, are returned as Tituladoes on the lands of Rathfarnham ; NICHOLAS Lord Viscount BARNWALL, HENRY BARNWALL, Esq., FRANCIS BARNWALL, Esq., and MATTHEW BARNWALL, Esq., are returned as Tituladoes on the lands of Turvey ; WILLIAM Lord Baron of HOWTH, PETER WYNNE, gentleman, and WILLIAM FITZWILLIAM, gentleman, are returned as Tituladoes in the house at Howth ; and CHARLES Earl of CAVAN, OLIVER LAMBERT, Esq., WALTER LAMBERT, Esq., and

---

[5] *E.g.*, Sheriff Pausy and Sheriff Crabb of Limerick : Robert Passy and John Crab,Sheriffs of Limerick, 1659 (Fitzgerald and McGregor's History of Limerick, vol. 2, App., p. xiv) ; Mayor Houghton of Waterford : John Houghton, Mayor of Waterford, 1659 (Smith's History of Waterford, p. 160) ; Sheriff Price of Dublin : John Price, Sheriff, 1659 (Gilbert, Calendar of Ancient Records of Dublin, vol. iv, p. 167) ; *et multi alii* [S.P.].

EDWARD TAYLOR, gentleman, are returned as Tituladoes on the lands of Tartayne. No doubt Ulster King-at-Arms can readily assign an exact period within which these illustrious groups of individuals were contemporaneous. Mixed up with others in these census returns I find the familiar Commonwealth leaders' names of EDWARD LUDLOW as Tituladoe on the lands of Monktowne ; MICHAEL JONES on the lands of Balgriffin ; and MILES CORBETT, Sen., and MILES CORBETT, Jun., on the lands of Malahide. By these latter Tituladoes alone I will demonstrate the date of the original census, which must have been at the very time these CORBETTS occupied these lands. It is historically known that MILES CORBETT was one of the regicides who sat in judgment upon the unfortunate King CHARLES. He was soon afterwards sent over to Ireland as one of the Commissioners of the Parliament of England for the affairs of this country. And it appears,[6] by an order of OLIVER CROMWELL, given at Whitehall, the 27th March, 1658, addressed to the Lord Deputy and Council of Ireland, that a lease was directed to be passed for a term of years to MILES CORBETT, Esq., Chief Baron of the Exchequer there, of the castle and town of Malahide, containing 605 Irish plantation acres of land, valued at six shillings per acre, reserving such yearly rent and contribution as to the Lord Deputy and Council should appear meet. The lease thus conceded to CORBETT was immediately passed to him, as his name appears in charge, and for the first time, upon the Commonwealth rental of the county of Dublin of the year 1659, with an annual rent of £50 for said 605 acres, described as the lands of Malahide and Nutstowne. These lands were taken away from JOHN TALBOT an ancestor of LORD TALBOT DE MALAHIDE. CORBETT continued his tenancy until about the 29th of September of the year 1659, when the records of that date evidence commotion, and symptoms of approaching retreat from Ireland of the leaders of the Cromwellian party.

" In exemplification of this fact, as well as of MILES CORBETT's period of possession of the TALBOT family seat, I find an order,[7] signed by CORBETT himself and others of the Council already adverted to, which recites, ' that forasmuch as there was lately paid quarterly to the Right Honourable MILES CORBETT, Esq., Serjeant-at-Law, as Chief Baron of the Exchequer, the sum of £66 4s. 4½d., *and for that expectation hath been for settling the Courts, and it not being intended to continue the payment thereof any longer than until 29th September, 1659, without special instructions of Parliament,* said sum of money was directed to be paid out of the Treasury to said CORBETT to that date ; " and for this sum the said CORBETT passed a receipt at foot of the order to the Receiver and Paymaster-General at the Treasury.

" CHARLES THE SECOND was restored to his throne early in 1660, from which time the name of MILES CORBETT disappears from all Crown rentals and other records ; and I find by a subsidy roll of the barony of Coolock and county of Dublin for the year 1661, that JOHN TALBOT was again residing and rated for that tax at his family mansion of Malahide. It is manifest from these evidences and transactions that the original census survey returns were compiled some time between the 27th of March, 1658, when OLIVER CROMWELL's order required possession of the lands of Malahide to be given to MILES CORBETT, and the close of the year 1659, when the Privy Council signed their last warrant of payment of his salary. It is historically authenticated that at this very time negotiations for the restoration of King CHARLES THE SECOND were all but successfully accomplished, and therefore the necessity for the hasty retreat of notorious Cromwellians.

[6] Landed Estates Record Office, lib. 17, fol. 145, press 14, shelf F.
[7] Landed Estates Record Office, Warrants, press 154, shelf D.

" The copy of the original census survey, discovered at Lansdowne House is attributable, judging from all its characteristics, to a closely contemporaneous period with that original itself. I have looked in vain for any payment of public money to the persons employed in making out the enumeration returns. The failure, however, cannot be regarded as evidence of non-payment, as the wages of the operators may have been dispensed through the medium of the collectors of the several well-organized Precincts into which the entire kingdom was in the year 1653 first divided. It has been suggested that the returns were the work of the hearth money collectors by approximation from the rolls of their accounts ; but this could not be so, as the enumeration papers contain a detail of townlands, people, and other matter far in excess of these rolls, and of a nature that was foreign to them ; besides the hearth money tax was a royal, not a Commonwealth impost,—its imposition ceased upon the death of the first CHARLES, and was not revived until the accession of the last. And from a kindred subsidy roll I have already supplied evidence of the place of residence of JOHN TALBOT in 1661. The census returns of 1659 show this place to have been in the tenancy of another person, which is in itself a proof that the hearth money record was not the origin of these returns.

" Dr. WILLIAM PETTY's published and unpublished writings prove him to have been an industrious and eminent statistician ; many of his works are based upon such data, and it is not surprising that he should have possessed the copy of the census found amongst the library collections of his lineal descendant. No one connected with Ireland had a fairer opportunity of gratifying his taste, in whatever custody the original record might have been, than the Doctor. That PETTY must have known of the existence of this record is clear, from a manuscript found in the same box, with the copy of it, entitled ' An Index to the Political Anatomy of Ireland, dated 1686.' In a portion of that compilation he assumes the form of dialogue, and asks two very important and pertinent questions, namely, ' How many Irish, English, and Scotch were in this country in 1641, and how many in 1653 ? ' He thus attests his desire to possess for each of these years the very same heads of information that his copy of the enumeration returns supplied him with for the year 1659. The importance of the information is manifest ; the year 1641 was the commencement of the ill-judged and unfortunate civil war in Ireland, and in that year her population, were it possible for Petty to ascertain it, would have exhibited a greater amount of inhabitants than, in all probability, the country at any time previously maintained. The year 1653 represents the time of the complete subjugation of the country, after twelve troublous years of bloodshed, famine, and pestilence ; a census, were such then taken, would have exhibited, in contrast to the other, the smallest amount of Ireland's population at any time. So reduced was that population in Connaught, that I believe it to have been all but annihilated.

" It is important to ascertain certainly, or by approved approximation process, the number of the inhabitants of this country in 1659, when the census returns in question were taken. In consequence of the absence of five entire counties and thirteen baronies, already adverted to, the number certain cannot be arrived at, and I must be satisfied with the result approximate. The process employed to arrive at the numbers of the inhabitants of these as yet undiscovered district census returns is based upon the principle of proportion, calculated by the number of inhabitants of neighbouring counties and baronies corresponding, or nearly so, in areas with the missing districts."

By a series of approximations Hardinge calculated the population of Ireland in 1659 to have been 500,091. He deduced " that in the year 1659 there were no Scotch settlers in the provinces of Munster or Connaught,[8] and but seven in the province of Leinster ; " that the relative proportions of English, Scotch and Irish were : " in Leinster 5½ Irish to 1 English and Scotch ; in Ulster 1½ Irish to 1 English and Scotch ; in Leinster [sic ! leg. Munster] 10 Irish to 1 English ; in Connaught 10 Irish to 1 English ; and in the kingdom the proportions were 5 to 1." But the figures he gives would make the proportion for all Ireland 27 to 4, or almost 7 to 1.

" These returns," continues Hardinge, " exhibit the only known actual numbering of the people of Ireland antecedently to 1821. Thom, in his very comprehensive and useful Almanac,[9] gives nine periodic census results before that year. That of 1672 represents the entire population at 1,320,000 ; but these figures cannot be relied upon, as they are but approximate results, based upon the number of hearths that were rated and registered for taxation purposes under Act of Parliament, and are not the result of an actual enumeration of the inhabitants. If the population of this country was 1,320,000 in 1672, as stated, it requires no straining of the imagination to conclude that the progressive increase must have been far greater than the Almanac admits it to have been at each of the indicated years down to and including the year of 1814, when the approximate period of calculation ends. On the other hand, if 500,091, returned as the gross population by the census returns of 1659, be accepted as the basis of the calculation, I am much deceived, if, upon admitted population increase principles, the numbers arrived at by the published enumeration returns of 1821, namely, 6,821,827, will not be very closely approximated to.

" It will not surprise me if it yet turns out that the complaints made by Adventurers and Soldiers of the evasion of many persons falling within the rule to transplant into Connaught and Clare, and the consequent continuance of these persons on the lands distributed to the Adventurers and Soldiers, were the originating causes of the census of 1659. This census, as I have already explained, distinguishes races of inhabitants, and their exact numbers, on each townland, a knowledge that would enable the Government to decide upon the justice or injustice of such non-transplantation complaints."

Some two months subsequent to reading the Paper on the Census of 1659 Hardinge communicated to the Academy an account of an unpublished Essay on Ireland by Petty.[10] He stated that he had found the Essay among the Lansdowne Collection. In the course of a detailed search of the Petty papers at Bowood I failed to find any copy of this Essay of Petty's. The late Marquess of Lansdowne queried it as missing in a handlist drawn up by him. I need not then apologise for quoting,[11] almost in extenso, Hardinge's paper, particularly as portions of it are relevant to our Census. Speaking of the Essay, Hardinge says :

" The document is invested with a character peculiarly its own, and is very illustrative of the uncommon genius of the Author. It opens ambiguously, developes its subject cautiously, and concludes by an attempt, when the subject is at last announced, mathematically to demonstrate the practical advantages the application of the alarming experiment proposed would have upon Ireland and the Empire.

[8] In this he erred ; see the Tipperary Returns in the Table below [S.P.].
[9] For 1865, p. 779.
[10] On an Unpublished Essay on Ireland, by Sir W. Petty, A.D. 1687 (Trans., R.I.A., vol. 24, p. 371).
[11] With the permission of the Council of the Royal Irish Academy.

" The Essay commences with a brief heading, a Latin metrical address, and a dedication. This triple combination may be regarded as a superscription upon an envelope, which conceals within it ' lettres cachet,' whose nature is only revealed when the mystic seal is broken.

" The heading is unpretending, and is thus expressed, ' The Elements of Ireland, and of its Religion and Policy, by Sir WILLIAM PETTY, Fellow of yᵉ Royal Society, 1687.' The metrical lines are selected from various parts of VIRGIL. The theft, however, may readily be forgiven in consideration of the ingenuity displayed in their adaptation to PETTY's design of but faintly foreshadowing the nature of the subject to be propounded and proved. These lines are forced and inelegant, if not ungrammatical ; but, as their number is only seven, they may be permitted to speak for themselves ; they are as follows :—

> " Ut parêre greges, armenta, atq' arva coiono ;
> Ut variæ gentes uniri fœdere certo
> Possint, edoceo, poniq' horrentia martis
> Arma : favete precor, Dîi qui posuistis et illa ;
> Surgite jam superi ! vastisq' incumbite cœptis ;
> Ut populi coeant, quingentos qui, supra et, annos
> Discrepuere, unum et fiant tua Regna, Jacobe."

" I have ventured, by a free translation, to turn them into English verse, thus :—

> " I teach the husbandman to tend
> Flocks, herds and fields, with sure increase ;
> And how, when diff'ring races blend
> In faithful league, war's woes will cease.
> Grant, ye high gods, who laid aside
> In distant times contentious arms,
> My mighty plan be not denied
> Propitious rest from like alarms :
> Cast centuries of direful hate
> Into oblivion's mystic flames,
> And from the ashes raise ONE state,
> Blest 'neath thy fost'ring sway, O James !

" The next move of the Author—his Dedication—does not enlighten the reader further in reference to what is coming ; it is so brief, that it seems best to cite it in full also, as follows :—

" ' To the King's most excellent Majesty :

" ' When I find out puzling and perplexed matters that may be brought to tearms of number, weight, and measure, and consequently may be made demonstrable ; and when I find things of vast and general concernment, which may be discussed in a few words, I willingly engage upon such undertakings, especially when they tend to your Majesty's glory and greatness and the happiness of your people, being one of them myself, and

" 'Your Majesty's most humble,

" ' Faithful, and obedᵗ Servant,

" ' WM. PETTY.'

" From the foregoing introductory specimens of the Essay manuscript, no one could imagine what the Author was about to communicate. He admits that he delighted, ' in political pastimes and paradoxes ; ' and this Essay verifies that description of himself. Imperceptibly he leads his followers by the hand through circuitous routes, until suddenly they find themselves placed on the summit of an eminence, from whence to view nature's landscape in mute, it may be in magnificent subjection at their feet.

" At this very point of PETTY's Essay we have now arrived—the seal of the mysterious envelope is broken, and we are presented with ' les lettres cachet,' in a preface, which solves all that before was enigmatical, and without disguise communicates the secret to his readers, in the following language :—

" ' Some have imagined, there being about 1,300,000 people in Ireland, that to bring 1,000,000 of them into England, and to leave the other 300,000 for herds-men and dairy-women behind, and to quitt all other trades in Ireland but that of cattle only, would effect the settlement, improvement, and union above propounded ; but against this method there lies this gross and obvious objection, viz. that the transporting of a million of people will cost a million of pounds ; that the housing and other goods in Ireland which will be lost thereby are worth two millions more ; nor is it safe to estimate other damages and expenses consequent on this undertaking, at less than one million more, in all at £4,000,000 of expense and damage.

" ' To which objection there is a gross answer, which is, that by bringing 1,000,000 people into England, where are 7 already, the King's Revenue of Customs, Excise, and Hearths, will rise from 7 to 8, that is, to two hundred thousand pounds per annum, which increase, at 20 years' purchase, is above £4,000,000, and more than the loss above mentioned. Now, when the King's Revenue shall naturally and spontaneously increase, it is rationally to be supposed that the people's wealth may increase 20 times as much, the Public Revenue being, almost by a law of nature, $\frac{1}{20}$ part of the people's expense.

" ' Wherefore, suspending any further answer to the said gross objection, we proceed to say, That the transplantation, and new cattle trade above propounded, will produce the effects hereafter mentioned, viz.' . . . .

" PETTY then subdivides his subject, for examination, into the following thirteen heads or sections, viz. :—

" ' 1st. The political anatomy of Ireland.
" ' 2nd. The commotions and bruilleries which happened there from anno 1641 to anno 1666.
" ' 3rd. The foreign trade of that nation anno 1685.
" ' 4th. The proportion between the English and Irish both in number and weight.
" ' 5th. Several decays in Ireland between the years 1683 and 1687.
" ' 6th. The waxing and waning of the King's revenue there in the said five years, with the causes thereof.
" ' 7th. That estates in Ireland may be improved from 2 to 3 with a perpetual settlement of the same, and rooting up all the causes of discords which have infested that country for above 500 years.
" ' 8th. That therewith the revenue of the Church of England, and of particular landlords there, may increase from 3 to 4.

" ' 9th. And the King's revenue from 4 to 5 without being a senciable burden to the people, and so as the King may have £6,000,000 for every 4th year, supposed to be war.

" ' 10th. How fears and jealousies concerning religion, even the Test, may vanish of themselves.

" ' 11th. How the King's subjects may be doubled in 20 years, and also united.

" ' 12th. That the King of England's territories and people may in weight and substance be little inferior to those of France, by a safe and sufficient liberty of conscience perpetuated.

" ' 13th. That there may be a real *Mare Clausum* begun in Ireland ; and that the King hath a more natural right to sovereignty within the same than any of his circumjacent neighbours.'

" The Essay continues with a separate treatise on each of the above heads to the 10th, inclusive. Treatises on the remaining three heads are wanting ; in consequence, I am persuaded, of the illness and death of the Author. Sir WILLIAM PETTY died either within the year 1687, expressed at the opening preface to the manuscript, or early in the next following year, as probate of his last will and testament was issued out of the Prerogative Court of Ireland to his widow, Lady ELIZABETH PETTY, on the 2nd April, 1688.

" In this very remarkable Essay, Sir WILLIAM PETTY admits that in 1687 the population of this country was 1,300,000. This statement, I consider and submit, proves the accuracy of the result of the census of 1659, in reference to which I recently had the honour of reading a paper before this Academy. That census, in round numbers, returns the population at 900,000, which in a period of 28 years, to 1687, is by PETTY admittedly augmented by only 50 per cent.[12] This rate of percentage is sustained by our modern census returns from 1820 to 1840, which show an increase of 33 per cent. in 20 years, or a close approximation to 50 per cent. in 28 years. It cannot be truly said that the period from 1659 to 1687 was less favourable to the increase of the human family in Ireland than the period from 1820 to 1840—It was infinitely more so. Within the latter years there were two cholera visitations, as well as other disturbing causes ; while from 1650 to 1683 there were unvarying healthful and abundant seasons ; and superadded to these blessings there remains the undeniable fact, that in 1659 the country had just emerged from deadly strife and desolation to a condition of peace and prosperity. The Restoration of King CHARLES THE SECOND, and the effects of the Acts of Settlement and Explanation, continued this happy state of things, while the ordinary population increase was made extraordinary by the return of numerous families who had been voluntarily and involuntarily exiled from their native land, and by the rush of adventurers and soldiers, their families and dependents, to take possession of their then recently acquired landed, and other possessions."

The following tables show in summary how the Census Returns of 1659 classify the population under the heads of English (E), Scottish (S), and Irish (Ir). Unfor-

---

[12] There is a discrepancy here. In his paper on the Census Hardinge had estimated the total population of the country in 1659 at 500,091 ; see above, p. ix, and volume 24 of the Royal Irish Academy Transactions, pp. 325–326. [S.P.].

tunately those classed as English and those classed as Scottish are not separately
enumerated :—[13]

PROVINCE OF ULSTER.   E = English ; S = Scotch ; Ir = Irish.

County	Barony	Races	Total
ANTRIM	Antrim	620 E ; 841 Ir	1461
	Glenarm	721 ES ; 743 Ir	1464
	Massereene	1007 E ; 1358 Ir	2365
	Toome	730 E ; 778 Ir	1508
	Belfast	2027 E ; 1825 Ir	3852
	Dunluce, Cary and Kilconway	1138 E ; 2940 Ir	4078
	Carrickfergus Town	831 E ; 480 Ir	1311
ARMAGH	Armagh	450 ES ; 891 Ir	1341
	Tiranny	108 ES ; 546 Ir	654
	Orior	193 ES ; 694 Ir	887
	Fewes, Lower and Upper	373 ES ; 858 Ir	1231
	Oneilland	1269 ES ; 1366 Ir	2635
DONEGAL	Tirhugh	244 ES ; 1474 Ir	1718
	Boylagh and Banagh	285 ES ; 1556 Ir	1841
	Raphoe	1825 ES ; 1330 Ir	3155
	Kilmacrenan	605 ES ; 1551 Ir	2156
	Inishowen	453 ES ; 2678 Ir	3131
DOWN	Lecale	1071 ES ; 1631 Ir	2702
	Upper Iveagh	448 ES ; 2149 Ir	2597
	Lower ,,	1352 ES ; 1381 Ir	2733
	Newry	166 ES ; 785 Ir	951
	Kinelarty and Dufferin	693 ES ; 763 Ir	1456
	Castlereagh	1363 ES ; 950 Ir	2313
	Ards	1447 ES ; 984 Ir	2431
FERMANAGH	[Baronies are not given]	1800 ES ; 5302 Ir	7102
LONDONDERRY	City	572 ES ; 480 Ir	1052
	Tirkeeran	640 ES ; 979 Ir	1619
	Keenaght	1012 ES ; 1215 Ir	2227
	Loughinsholin	655 ES ; 1431 Ir	2086
	Coleraine (Town and Barony)	1549 ES ; 1201 Ir	2750
MONAGHAN	[Baronies are not given]	434 E ; 3649 Ir	4083

[13] Dr. Eoin MacNeill writes, in the course of a communication, " The classification under the headings of English, Scottish and Irish in the Census of 1659 is not trustworthy. It would seem to show that in the county of Antrim one barony alone, that of Glenarm, contained any Scottish, and that in the other baronies the proportion of English to Irish was about 7 to 9. No Scottish are enumerated in the county of Monaghan. I do not think that anyone acquainted with the general evidence will attach any value to the classification thus exemplified. Outside of Ulster, the only Scottish inhabitants numbered in the Census appear to be limited to one parish in Leinster and one parish in Munster. No distinction is made between English and Welsh, though, if I am not mistaken, there is evidence that many Welsh settled in Ireland under the Tudor régime and under Cromwell's régime. On the other hand, I think that the Sean-Ghaill (commonly called in English the Anglo-Normans, but comprising no small proportion of Welsh, Flemings, and probably many French) are classed as Irish in this Census. This opinion is confirmed by the enumeration of the inhabitants of Bargy, co. Wexford, ' 126 English, 1353 Irish and Old English.' The explanation here must be found in the Flemish-English dialect which was spoken in the baronies of Bargy and Forth until recent times."

PROVINCE OF MUNSTER.

County	Barony	Races		Total
CLARE	Bunratty	144 E ;	4204 Ir	4348
	Tulla	106 E ;	3903 Ir	4009
	Inchiquin	34 E ;	1961 Ir	1995
	Island	58 E ;	1593 Ir	1651
	Clonderalaw	32 E ;	1144 Ir	1176
	Corcomroe	5 E ;	1034 Ir	1039
	Moyarta	31 E ;	993 Ir	1024
	Burren	7 E ;	816 Ir	823
	Ibrickan	23 E ;	826 Ir	849
CORK	City and Liberties	1607 E ;	3219 Ir	4826
	Kinsale	580 E ;	760 Ir	1340
	Bandon	542 E ;	304 Ir	846
	Youghal	469 E ;	642 Ir	1111
	Mallow	789 E ;	234 Ir	555
	Kinalea	234 E ;	2460 Ir	2694
	Kerrycurrihy	168 E ;	852 Ir	1020
	Kinalmeaky	264 E ;	1628 Ir	1892
	Ibawn and Barrymore [leg. *Barryroe*]	104 E ;	1604 Ir	1708
	Liberties of Kinsale	244 E ;	613 Ir	857
	Courceys	62 E ;	405 Ir	467
	Kilbrittain	198 E ;	1699 Ir	1897
	Carbery East	422 E ;	4999 Ir	5421
	,, West	236 E ;	4811 Ir	5047
	Beare and Bantry	233 E ;	1321 Ir	1554
	Barretts	49 E ;	1954 Ir	2003
	Kinnatalloon [*Imperfect*].			
	Barrymore	500 E ;	3953 Ir	4453
	Orrery and Kilmore	338 E ;	2847 Ir	3185
KERRY	Trughanacmy	215 E ;	2168 Ir	2383
	Clanmaurice	86 E ;	1040 Ir	1126
	Iraghticonnor	81 E ;	1139 Ir	1220
	Corkaguiny	97 E ;	1086 Ir	1183
	Magunihy	42 E ;	1122 Ir	1164
	Glanarought	31 E ;	505 Ir	536
	Dunkerron	2 E ;	355 Ir	357
	Iveragh	12 E ;	409 Ir	421
LIMERICK	City and Liberties	819 E ;	2286 Ir	3105
	Small County	120 E ;	2950 Ir	3070
	Coshlea	133 E ;	2775 Ir	2908
	Clanwilliam	159 E ;	1590 Ir	1749
	Connello	431 E ;	7545 Ir	7976
	Kenry	35 E ;	1092 Ir	1127
	Owney	62 E ;	391 Ir	453
	Coonagh	75 E ;	1034 Ir	1109
	Pubblebrien	24 E ;	655 Ir	679
	Coshma	70 E ;	2121 Ir	2191
	Killmallock town and liberties	610 E ;	73 Ir	537

County	Barony	Races	Total
TIPPERARY	Slieveardagh	307 E ; 2101 Ir	2408
	Lower Ormond	341 ES ; 2731 Ir	3072
		[ES in Agha Parish]	
	Kilnamanagh	86 E ; 1749 Ir	1835
	Middlethird	134 E ; 3778 Ir	3912
	Iffa and Offa	223 E ; 4729 Ir	4952
	Eliogarty and Ikerrin	326 E ; 4339 Ir	4665
	Upper Ormond	92 E ; 1631 Ir	1723
	Owney and Arra	235 E ; 989 Ir	1224
	Clanwilliam	180 E ; 2713 Ir	2893
WATERFORD	Decies	129 E ; 3574 Ir	3703
	Coshmore and Coshbride	355 E ; 2180 Ir	2535
	Glenahiry	56 E ; 665 Ir	721
	Upperthird	65 E ; 1909 Ir	1974
	Middlethird	31 E ; 1484 Ir	1515
	Gaultier	76 E ; 1115 Ir	1191
	City and Liberties	637 E ; 1010 Ir	1647

PROVINCE OF LEINSTER.

County	Barony	Races	Total
CARLOW	Carlow Borough	271 E ; 289 Ir	560
	,, Barony	124 E ; 833 Ir	957
	Rathvilly	176 E ; 719 Ir	815
	Forth	46 E ; 558 Ir	604
	Idrone and St. Mullin's	136 E ; 2282 Ir	2418
DUBLIN	City and Liberties	6459 E ; 2321 Ir	8780
	Newcastle and Uppercross	1635 E ; 3043 Ir	4678
	Rathdown	244 E ; 908 Ir	1152
	Nethercross	318 E ; 1473 Ir	1791
	Balrothery	518 E ; 1990 Ir	2508
	Coolock	419 E ; 1425 Ir	1844
	Castleknock	189 E ; 885 Ir	1074
KILDARE	Offaly	51 E ; 2187 Ir	2238
	Naas	110 E ; 1563 Ir	1673
	Clane	32 E ; 760 Ir	792
	Connell	20 E ; 912 Ir	932
	Salt	180 E ; 1772 Ir	1952
	Reban and Narragh	1317 E ; 1516 Ir	1653
	Kilkea and Moone	142 E ; 1327 Ir	1469
	Ikeathy	50 E ; 1122 Ir	1172
	Carbury	40 E ; 1503 Ir	1543
	Kilcullen	34 E ; 367 Ir	401

County	Barony	Races	Total
KILKENNY	Galmoy	128 E ; 1446 Ir	1574
	Gowran	311 E ; 3543 Ir	3854
	Iverk	99 E ; 1358 Ir	1455
	Ida Igrin Ibercon	79 E ; 1867 Ir	1946
	Knocktopher	61 E ; 1301 Ir	1362
	Fassadinin	53 E ; 1688 Ir	1741
	Kells	50 E ; 1150 Ir	1200
	Shillelogher	75 E ; 1190 Ir	1265
	Crannagh	79 E ; 1778 Ir	1857
	Callan Town	83 E ; 339 Ir	422
	,, Liberties	3 E ; 26 Ir	29
	City and Liberties	421 E ; 1301 Ir	1722
KING'S COUNTY	Philipstown	186 E ; 1007 Ir	1193
	Coolestown	62 E ; 428 Ir	490
	Ballyboy	91 E ; 484 Ir	575
	Ballycowan	132 E ; 562 Ir	694
	Geashill	139 E ; 591 Ir	730
	Warrenstown	73 E ; 357 Ir	430
	Clonlisk	109 E ; 972 Ir	1081
	Garrycastle	158 E ; 960 Ir	1118
	Kilcoursey	40 E ; 316 Ir	356
	Eglish	54 E ; 376 Ir	430
	Ballybritt	181 E ; 1032 Ir	1213
LONGFORD	Rathcline	83 E ; 849 Ir	932
	Shrule	42 E ; 694 Ir	736
	Ardagh	19 E ; 971 Ir	990
	Longford	67 E ; 396 Ir	463
	Granard	66 ES ; 1416 Ir	1482
		[7 *Scotch in St. John's town*]	
	Moydow	4 E ; 785 Ir	789
LOUTH	Louth	39 E ; 1019 Ir	1058
	Dundalk	327 E ; 2209 Ir	2536
	Ferrard	115 E ; 1675 Ir	1790
	Ardee	356 E ; 2345 Ir	2701
	Drogheda City and Liberties	958 E ; 647 Ir	1605
MEATH	Duleek	616 E ; 3303 Ir	3919
[*Imperfect*]	Skreen	127 E ; 1621 Ir	1748
	Ratoath	128 E ; 1479 Ir	1607
QUEEN'S COUNTY	Ossory	350 E ; 2663 Ir	3013
	Upper Ossory	92 E ; 619 Ir	711
	Maryborough	231 E ; 1638 Ir	1869
	Cullenagh	164 E ; 1174 Ir	1338
	Slievemargy	112 E ; 954 Ir	1066
	Ballyadams	104 E ; 592 Ir	696
	Portnahinch	101 E ; 728 Ir	829
	Stradbally	89 E ; 709 Ir	798
	Tinnahinch	153 E ; 642 Ir	795

County	Barony	Races	Total
WESTMEATH	Demifoure	109 E ; 1224 Ir	1333
	Moycoish	48 E ; 1086 Ir	1134
	Corkaree	44 E ; 847 Ir	891
	Moyashel and Magheradernon	37 E ; 970 Ir	1007
	Fartullagh	41 E ; 678 Ir	719
	Moycashel	132 E ; 1347 Ir	1479
	Rathconrath	75 E ; 1751 Ir	1826
	Farbill	11 E ; 776 Ir	787
	Clonlonan	123 E ; 917 Ir	1040
	Kilkenny	75 E ; 1272 Ir	1347
	Delvin	52 E ; 1057 Ir	1109
WEXFORD	Town and Liberties	340 E ; 562 Ir	902
	New Ross ,, ,, ,,	241 E ; 377 Ir	618
	Enniscorthy ,, ,, ,,	67 E ; 322 Ir	389
	Forth	178 E ; 1667 Ir	1845
	Bargy	126 E ; 1353 Ir and Old English	1479
	Shelmaliere	163 E ; 1650 Ir	1813
	Shelburne	101 E ; 1893 Ir	1994
	Bantry	56 E ; 1347 Ir	1403
	Ballaghkeen	122 E ; 1219 Ir	1341
	Gorey	107 E ; 687 Ir	794
	Scarawalsh	131 E ; 971 Ir	1102

PROVINCE OF CONNACHT.

County	Barony	Races	Total
LEITRIM	Leitrim, Mohill and Carrigallen	207 E ; 2139 Ir	2346
	Drumahaire and Rosclogher	112 E ; 1817 Ir	1929
ROSCOMMON	Roscommon	46 E ; 1974 Ir	2020
	Ballintober	160 E ; 2593 Ir	2753
	Boyle	218 E ; 2110 Ir	2328
	Ballymoe	18 E ; 551 Ir	569
	Moycarn	3 E ; 469 Ir	472
	Athlone	160 E ; 3466 Ir	3626
	,, Borough	544 E ; 531 Ir	1075
SLIGO	Carbury	211 E ; 1187 Ir	1394
	Leyny	76 E ; 1105 Ir	1181
	Corran	76 E ; 1031 Ir	1107
	Coolavin	00 E ; 307 Ir	307
	Tireragh	86 E ; 1409 Ir	1495
	Tirerrill	89 E ; 1300 Ir	1389

An examination of the foregoing tables furnishes us with interesting information. The general numerical superiority of the native race is at once evident.   Where English or English and Scotch are in a majority the presence of a town may immediately be noted.   In Ulster the Scotch appear to have been widespread, with the exception of the entire county of Monaghan and the greater part of Antrim ; the barony of Glenarm, alone, in this latter county is returned as having a Scotch element.   Outside of Ulster, we find mention of them in Agha Parish, barony of Lower Ormond, Tipperary, and in St. Johnstown, barony of Granard, Longford.   Alone amongst the baronies, Coolavin, Sligo, boasts of having no English within its borders.   In the barony of Bargy in Wexford a curious division of the races appears ; on the one side we have English, and on the other Irish and Old English.   It must be strongly emphasised, however, that in any use that may be made of these returns for the purpose of estimating the constituent elements of the population as regards countries of origin, the greatest caution, as Dr. Eoin MacNeill has intimated to me (*vide* Page xiii *supra*), is necessary. The enumerators do not appear to have worked everywhere on the same basis of classification or to have attached the same meanings to the terms of classification, ' Irish,' ' English,' ' Old English,' ' Scotch.'   For example, the use of the term ' Old English ' might be taken to imply that where the term ' English ' is used, it denotes an element of recent introduction.   Such interpretation is seen to be invalid, when we recognise that the ' Old English ' of this Census are found only in the single barony of Bargy, which is in Co. Wexford.   The terms ' English ' and ' Old English ' were current in writings of the period, distinguishing recent settlers and strangers, regarded as English, from the descendants of those who came from England and other countries and settled in Ireland in the course of the Anglo-Norman invasion.   The corresponding terms ' Nua-Ghaill ' and ' Sean-Ghaill ' are found in Irish writings.   In the Census of 1659, this terminology leaves a doubt whether the ' Old English ' element, outside of the barony of Bargy, is classed under ' Irish ' or under ' English,' a doubt to be resolved only by a study of the details.   In the Civil Survey, which preceded this Census by a few years and which must have been well known to those who had official direction of this Census, we find a classification under two heads, ' English Protestants ' and ' Irish Papists,' natives of Scotland settled in Ulster a generation earlier being described as ' English Protestants,' while members of the ' Old English ' families, Burkes, Butlers, Powers. Fitzgeralds, etc., are classed as ' Irish Papists.'   How far the same classification was in the minds of the enumerators of 1659, or of any of them, is matter for investigation.   An equal difficulty arises from the use of the term ' Scotch ' in this Census. In the county of Antrim, for example, the only barony in which it recognises a Scotch element is the barony of Glenarm, though there is abundant historical evidence that the Scottish element predominated in other parts of the county.   In the Civil Survey, it is clear that the religion, and not the regional origin, of the inhabitants, was the basis of classification.   In the cases of the baronies of Bargy and Glenarm it seems likely that language was the deciding factor in 1659.   The barony of Bargy retained until quite recent times a peculiar dialect of English, or of Flemish and English, derived probably from ' little England beyond Wales,' Strongbow's earldom of Pembroke. The barony of Glenarm was largely peopled by families of Hebridean stock, whose language was Gaelic, under the lordship of the MacDonnells, earls of Antrim.   In many other parts of that county, from the time of James I., the bulk of the rural population was Lowland Scottish in origin, religion and dialect.   These peculiarities, positive and negative, suffice to show that the ethnic classifications of this Census are not to be taken at ' face value.'

To the local historian must be left the elucidation of these and kindred points. The text has been reproduced exactly as Petty's clerks transcribed it. Evident errors have not been corrected, and any words or phrases added by me have been enclosed in square brackets. The Index is of the persons and places as they appear in the text, not as they ought to have appeared. My transcript was made in the first instance from the Royal Irish Academy copy. I afterwards was enabled to collate it with the original.

My best thanks are due to Rev. Timothy Corcoran, S.J., D.Litt., Professor of Education, University College, Dublin, and Mr. J. F. Morrissey, Assistant Deputy Keeper of Public Records ; to the Marquess of Lansdowne and his mother the Marchioness for the facilities afforded me during the time I was engaged in the work of collation at Bowood ; to the Council of the Royal Irish Academy who granted me leave of absence to proceed there ; and to Mr. Hollrow, Chief Clerk at Bowood, who went to the utmost pains to see that I worked under conditions of comfort and seclusion as delightful as they are rare.

SÉAMUS PENDER.

December, 1936.

COUNTY OF ANTRIM   1311

AND TOWNE OF CARICKFERGUS   4078
                                         ———
                                         5389.

COUNTY OF ANTRIM

BARONY OF ANTRIM

Parishes	Places	Number of People	Tituladoes Names	English	Irish
Moylmey		459	James Adaire gent, John Boyd gent, Francis Shane gent, John Crawford gent, William Shaw gent.	218	241
Antrim		301	Sr John Clotworthy K^t, Sr John Skeffington Bart., James Collvill Esqr.	167	134
Kert		176	Teige Ô Hara Esqr, Henry O Hara gent.	064	112
Kells and Conyer		245		091	154
Braid		280		080	200

Principall Irish Names & Scotch [and] Their Numb'.

Adire, 7 ; Armstrong, 5 ; McAlester, 6 ; Blair, 9 ; Boyd, 7 ; Browne, 6 ; McCormick, 6 ; Crawford, 7 ; McCullough, 6 ; Donnell, 7 ; Farguson, 6 ; Graham, 7 ; Hunter, 6 ; Ô Hara, 9 ; Ô Heveran, 5 ; Johnson, 8 ; McIlroy, 5 ; McKye, 11 ; McKinstry, 5 ; Kenedy, 6 ; Loggan, 5 ; Millar, 6 ; Mountgomery, 5 ; McMullen, 5 ; Moore, 7 ; O Neill &c, 6 ; Read, 9 ; Russell, 7 ; Taggard, 9 ; Wallace, 6.

(*folio* 1, *verso*).   Barony of Antrim : Eng, 620 ; Irish, 841 ; Totall of Eng & Irish, 1461.

BARONY OF GLENARME

Parishes	Places	Number of People	Tituladoes Names	Eng & Scotts	Irish
Kilvowghter	Actescall	010		002	008
	Lishdrinnbard	002		002	000
	Drummindonachy	013		007	006
	Killvowghter	006		000	006
	Mulachbuy	003		002	001
	Belledardairne	006		006	000
	Tavanagrasane &c	011		007	004
	Drummho	007		007	000
	Lellis	013		011	002
	Ballyhemptone	012		012	000
	Bellikeill	009		009	000
Larne	Inwer	211		182	029

Parishes	Places	Number of People	Tituladoes Names	Eng & Scotts	Irish
	Monalorane	011		011	000
	Ballybolly	012		010	002
	Bellicragie	017		017	000
	Grinland	009		009	000
	Blackcabe	006		006	000
(folio 3).	Coran and Drumalos	013		011	002
	Portpier	006		000	006
Carncastell	Carncastell P'ish ⎫ Bellymulock towne ⎭	015		012	003
	Killiglene	011		001	010
	Drummaine	009		009	000
	Bellibober	019		019	000
	Drains	017		010	007
	Droach	010		007	003
	Carin-finock	008	John Shawe gent	008	000
	Bellivilline	014		010	004
	Holmger	010		008	002
	Tarnamoney	014		000	014
	Bellyhankett	011	William Fenton gent	009	002
	Sallache	018		017	001
	Bellygelly	018	James Shaw Esqr and John Shaw Esqr his sonn	012	006
	Cockermaine	022		018	004
(folio 4).	Belligane	015		013	002
	Belliruder	014		014	000
	Belligilbert	013		013	000
	Lisney	017		017	000
	Drumingreack	018		017	001
	Mynes	008		008	000
Tegmacrewa.	Glenarme	073	John Donnoldson Esq.	042	031
	Browy	004		000	004
	Broghbowy	008		000	008
	Bellimackvea	024		000	024
	Duntrage	016		000	016
	Anhagash	017		000	017
	Onclochy	004		000	004
	Tully	047		014	033
	Demaines	012	Randall Buthells gent.	011	001
	Glenclives & Stradhill	086	James Donoldson gent	026	060
(folio 5) Ardclins.	Carmulach	010		010	000
	Lunnary	029		013	016
	Ovanh	013		000	013
	Rinfad	007		005	002
	Drumnasoll Bellivillgan & ⎫ Lochane ⎭	010		000	010

Parishes	Places	Number of People	Tituladoes Names	Eng & Scotts	Irish
	Galldwelly & Ancllynes	015		000	015
	Kirismurphy	023		000	023
	Glenariff	049		000	049
Lays	Glasmuline	026		000	026
	Forriff	026		000	026
	Ridbay and ye places neir adioyning therunto	031	William Stuartt gent, Allexander Hall gent.	012	019
	Ardinonan Court McMartin Faculty and Feig	027		012	015
	Cloches Carnneheag, Eshery and Fall McRelly	051		002	049
(folio 6).	Garnacrayse	021		000	021
	Lubitavish, Tirkally and Bellybrecke	022		000	022
	Glencorpe	021		000	021
	Layd	011		002	009
	Anhahery	014		000	014
	Glendune	074	Neall og McAully gent, Mortagh McAully gent.	004	070
	Souldiers and their wifes in Learn and Glenarm.	035		035	000

Principall Irish Names & som Scotch [and] Their Numbs.

Agnew, 6 ; McAully, 42 ; McAlester, 6 ; Boyd, 14 ; McBritany, 9 ; McCurry, 4 ; Craford, 10 ; McCallin, 8 ; McDarragh, 7 ; & McDonald, 9 ; McGoune, 5 ; McGill, 37 ; Hunter, 8 ; McIver, 7 ; McKillop, 7 ; Loske, 12 ; Moungomery, 10 ; O Mulvena, 8 ; O Mony &c, 9 ; O Murphy & O Murchy, 10 ; McVeagh, 8 ; Young, 10 ; Woodsy, 12.

(folio 6 verso). The Number of People in the Barony of Glencarne according to the severall pages : Eng, 721 ; Irish, 743 ; totall Eng & Irish, 1464.

(folio 7). **BARONY OF MASSAREENE**

Parishes	Places	Numb' of People	Tituladoes Names	English &c	Irish
Lisnegarvie	Lisnegarvie	357	Edward Viscount Conway, George Rawden Esqr, William Close gent, Marina Roma gent, Hugh Smyth gent, Bryan Magee gent, Denis Magee gent, Oliver Taylor gent.	217	140

Parishes	Places	Numb' of People	Tituladoes Names	English &c	Irish
	Knockmore	068		050	018
	Causey	017		011	006
	Ballymacosse	100	Ensigne Ralph Smyth gent	058	042
Ballinderry	— — —	305		121	184
Magharemesk	— — —	168	Henry Spencer Esq	027	141
Aghagaleng	— — —	117	Francis Courtney gent	031	086
(fol. 8) Maghragall	Mogherlisrirke	014		006	008
	Mullacarton	027	Edward Breers gent	026	001
	Inelargee	010		006	004
	Murusk and Dendrumssella }	024		011	013
	Knocknerea and Maghragall }	026		011	015
	Knocknedaunagh	017		000	017
	Maior Rawdens Tennants &c }	087	William Betts gent, Mathew Betts gent	053	034
Aghelee	— — —	071		026	045
Glenavie	Towneland of Glenavie }	062	John Fortescew Esqʳ	052	010
	Ballyminimor	014		006	008
	Tullinebanicke	012		010	002
	Ballymatty	010		007	003
(fol. 9)	Ballynecoymore	012		006	006
	Patt Mave	012		003	009
	Crew	006		000	006
	Karnkillie	009		004	005
	Ballymaffrickett	011		002	009
	Achadallagin	011	Feulke Gwilliams gent	003	008
	Ballynakally	012		000	012
	Ballyvanan	009		000	009
	Phe More	014		000	014
	The Tunie Quarters	008		004	004
Tullyrusk	Tullyrusk	019		000	019
	Boodoro	032		004	028
	Dondrod	048		020	028
	Knock-kairne	027		012	015
	Ballynecoybegg	008	James Line gent	006	002
(fol. 10). Camline	Ballydonothie	073	Thomas Gilcrist gent Christopher Clements gent	026	047
	BallymᶜCravin	008		000	008
	Ballytramrie	055		030	025
	Ballyshinachie	020		000	020
	Ach-ne-derach	014		000	014
	Ballyvallan	006		002	004
	Linnegarre	034		008	026

Parishes	Places	Numb' of People	Tituladoes Names	English &c	Irish
Muckamore Masareene	Camline Church land	004		002	002
	Ballygartgarr'	013		004	009
	Muckamore	070		031	039
	Masareene towne	061		032	028
	Division of Kill Makevatt. }	083	Captn Hercules Langford gent	022	061
	Killileagh	180		057	123

Principall Irish Names [and] Their Numb.

McBride, 5 ; McCanne, 8 ; McCormick, 6 ; McConnell, 9 ; Donelson, 6 ; McGill &c, 7 ; McGee, 9 ; Hanon, 8 ; McKee, 7 ; O Neall &c, 5 ; Lynsie, 10 ; Lowry, 15 ; Magee, 8 ; Smyth, 14 ; Welsh, 8 ; Wilson (Scotch), 11 ; White, 9.

(*folio* 10 *verso*). Barony : Masareene ; Eng, 1007 ; Irish, 1358 ; Totall of Eng & Irish, 2365.

(*fol.* 11). **BARONY OF TOOME**

Parishes	Places	Number of People	Tituladoes Names	English	Irish
	The Lyne of Mountereredy	461	Cormuck Ô Steille gent Thomas Dobbin gent Bryan Ô Steille James Hamilton gent William MaColloch gent Leu^t Coll Walter Stuartt Esq.	215	246
	Divission of Fivagh	231	Doct^r Daniell O Sheill gent Leu^t Dalway Clements gent	096	135
Query if this bee a P'ish	Largie	287	Richard Bickerstaffe Esqr	140	147
Query if this be a Parish	Graunge	116	Cornelius Divelin gent	041	075
Query if this be a Parish	Ballymenagh	226	William Adaire Esqr	116	110
Query if this be a Parish	Galgorme	187	Robert Colwill Esqr William Houstan gent	122	065

Principall Irish Names [and] Their Numbers.

Brownes not all Irish, 12 ; McBride, 9 ; McCullogh, 5 ; Cunningham, Query whither Irish, 6 ; Magrogan, 5 ; Lorenan, 7 ; Martin, 7 ; Mullan, 7 ; Millar, 7 ; Ô Quin, 6 ; Steill and Ô Steill, 8.

(*folio* 11 *verso*). Bar of Toome : Eng, 730 ; Irish, 778 ; Totall of Eng and Irish, 1508.

(folio 12)

BARONY OF BELFAST

Parishes	Places	Number of People	Tituladoes Names	English	Irish
	Towne and Quart^rs of Belfast		The R^t Honorable The Marquess of Antrim, Peter Polewheele gent, John Appellwhite gent, Allexander McDonell gent, Donnell McDonnell gent, The Ri^t Honno^ble The Earle of Donnegall, Mathew Harrison gent, James South gent, Samuell Bluett gent ; Gilbert		
	Belfast Towne	589	Wye gent, John Begg gent, Richard Cannon gent, Capt. Francis Meeke Esqr, John Leathes gent, George Martin gent, Thomas Warring gent, Hugh Deake gent, John Ridgby gent, George McCartey gent, William Warreing gent, William Stuckley gent, John Clugston gent.	366	223
(folio 13)	Belonging to Belfast The towne lands of Edendery, Ballysilly and Lagainele	066		043	023
	The towne lands of Balloghan ; the old parke, and part of Listillyard	024		013	011
	The towne lands of Cloghcastle, New parke and Skeggan Earle	038		020	018
(folio 14). Vide page 15	West Quart^r of Carrickfergus	354	Richard Callcatt gent	155	199
	Mogheremorne	509		288	221
Quere if these	Ballylmey	023		011	012
be parishes	Foure townes of Carngrany	095		060	035
Query of					
Carngrany	Balygeilogh and Brusly	026		005	021
and the	Ballytalcat	002		002	000
rest be	Ballyrobert	032		006	026
parishes	Carnee	012		006	006
	Balyling Balyhon and Balywalter	006		004	002
	Ballylmey	177	Anthony Horsman gent	079	098

Parishes	Places	Number of People	Tituladoes Names	English	Irish
(*folio* 15)	East Division off Carrickfergus	094	Richard Dob Esqr	062	032
Quere if a parish	Ballyhill of ye same division	041	Allexsander Dallway gent	024	017
Quere if this be a P'ish	Crosmary of ye same divission	001		001	000
Quere if this be a P'ish	Kilroote of ye same divission	075		041	034
	Divission of Castle Norton	292	Arthur Upton Esqr	117	175
	The Quarter of Bally-nure (Quere if this be a p'ish)	169		076	093
	Iland of Magee	035	James McCollo Gent	019	016
	Balliamford in ye said Iland	039		039	000
Quere if any of these be parishes All these are in the sd Iland of Magee	Belicronen beg	014		014	000
	Belidoun	155	Richard Webster gent	043	112
	Ramphinell	027		010	017
	Belitober	017		011	006
	Belipreor-mor	051		015	036
(*folio* 16)	Mylone		George Ogilvie gent		
Quere if these be parishes	Dunmurry and the Fall	388	Thomas Walcott gent, Francis Daviss gent, William Lasley gent, Edward Renolds gent	241	147
	Broad Iland Division	216	John Edmonston gent, Archbald Edmonston Esqr, Leut-Coll James Wallis Esqr	077	139
	Divission of Derivolgie Killotin Towneland	023		023	000
	Lambegge People	202	Thomas Ritkaby gent, Rich: Beers gent, John Waringe gent	155	047
	Castlerobin	050		013	037
	Magrileaue	040	Michaell Harrison Esqr	018	022

Principall Irish Names [and] Their Numbs.

Agnew, 9 ; Bell, 10 ; Burnes, 6 ; Browne, 12 ; Beggs, 8 ; McCalmont, 6 ; Campbell, 15 ; McCartney, 7 ; Christian, 7 ; McClealand, 7 ; McCreery, 7 ; McCullough, 10 ; Craige, 7 ; Cowan & McCowan, 12 ; Donell and McDonell, 10 ; Donelson, 6 ; Eccles, 7 ; Fulton, 8 ; McGee, 11 ; Graham, 6 ; Hill, 10 ; Kenedy, 12 ; Loggan, 6 ; Martin, 23 ; Moore, 10 ; Miller, 12 ; McNeely, 8 ; Read, 11 ; White, 8.

(*folio* 16 *verso*). Barony : Belfast ; Eng, 2027 ; Irish, 1825 ; Totall of Eng and Irish, 3852.

(*folio* 17)   **BARONYES OF DUNLUCE**[1] **CARRY**[2] **AND KILCONRIE**[3]

Parishes	Places	Number of People	Tituladoes Names	Eng	Irish
Dunluce	Ballynalurgan	14		00	14
	Ballybogie	16		00	16
	Ballyhirgan	10		00	10
	Beirvardon	07		00	07
	Ballyhuntsly	11		00	11
	Ballyclogh	47		26	21
	Ballytibert	17	Thomas Eggart gent	13	04
	Ballylikin	12		11	01
	Ballynesse	08		04	04
	Ballylikin	06		06	00
	Lissenduffe	17	Robert Shrewbridge gent	09	08
	Buishmills	27		08	19
	Gortneway	10		03	07
	Gortnagaple	06		02	04
	Standulon	06		—	06
	Cregenbany	04		00	04
(*folio* 18).	Ferenlesrie	04		00	04
	Priestland	06		06	00
	Pristland	12		04	08
	Dunluce	46		15	31
	Cloney	10		02	08
	Glentaske	08		04	04
	Leike	12		00	12
	Ballyhom	18		00	18
	Ballymacree	06		05	01
	Ballymagery	21		03	18
	Ballykill	11		00	11
	Ballycraige	13		02	11
Ballywillin	Toberdornan	14	Robert Harvie gent	05	09
	Knockentotan	07		00	07
	Carnally	07		06	01
	Crosreagh	07		04	03
	Ballywillin Uper Cloghcour }	11		09	02
(*folio* 19)	Cloghcare	10		03	07
	Portrush	19		00	19
	Carnglasse	14	Arch : McPhetrish gent	08	06
	Ballywatt	06		04	02
	Outall	05		00	05
	Ravalaght	08		06	02
	Ballyvrog	15		06	09
	Killmoyle	05		03	02

[1] *Donluce,* folio **24** ;   [2] ***Carie,*** folios **20**-43 ;   [3] *Kilconrye,* folio **37**.

Parishes	Places	Number of People	Tituladoes Names	Eng	Irish
	Ballywatt	04		00	04
	Carnglasse	03		03	00
	Ballyvat	03		02	01
Dirikichan	Ballydimdy	08		04	04
	Island Howagh	07		00	07
	Ballynarisse	06		02	06
	Ballyhibistock	13		06	07
	Carncogie	22		16	06
	Maghereboy	12		05	07
(folio 20) Dirikichan	Cull	06		03	03
	Carnaff	12		00	12
	Knockanvallan	16		00	16
	Lissconan	16		02	14
	Knockanboy	06		00	06
	Knockanboy	06		00	06
	Stronn	06		00	06
	Ballyratachan	15		12	03
	Deroogg	32		07	25
	Aughnicrosie	06		05	01
	Carncologht	09		07	02
	Carncologhbegg	08		06	02
	Inishgran	08		08	00
	Ballynafeigh	04		00	04
	Mafragee	13		04	09
	Drumcrotagh	02		00	02
	Carnfeigh	10		00	10
	Tullyban	02		00	02
(folio 21). Dirikichan	Kerucloghan	08		02	06
	Carnanboy	03		00	03
	Liverie	13		05	08
	Drumbruan	04		04	00
	Manister	04		00	04
	Mosside	06		00	06
	Kerulelues	06		00	06
	Kittell	06		00	06
	Killmacomoge	06		00	06
	Kerucloghan	09		02	07
	Killmoyle	08		00	08
	Keruriagh	13		00	13
	Lismurirty	12		02	10
	Carnkerm	07		00	07
(folio 22). Billy	Ballynarish	12		10	02
	Lower Ballylagh	18		00	18
	Upper Ballylagh	14		02	12
	Clountish	10		04	06
	Ballylaghbeg	06		00	06

Parishes	Places	Number of People	Tituladoes Names	Eng	Irish
	Cavanmor	12		00	12
	Glyb	04		02	02
	Cullramony	21		03	18
	Mullindeber	05		00	05
	Ballyhomlin	09		00	09
	Egarie	10		10	00
	Ballynesse	13		07	06
	Orphahum	10		00	10
	Magherentenrie	08		03	05
	Clossre	09		00	09
(folio 23)	Carmumone	07		04	03
	Stradvally	11		07	04
	Loghlesh	08		05	03
	Glassenerin	06		00	06
	Carnbor	06		00	06
	Deverick	11		07	04
	Toberdony	15		00	15
	Ballymukfin	10		06	04
	Urbbreagh	10		02	08
	Clochergall	22		04	18
	Maghereboy	24		05	19
	Killcubin	17		06	11
	Carnkerk	20		06	14
	Ballintalor	10		00	10
	Duaghmore	13		00	13
	Ballyny	08		00	08
(folio 24)	Ardeohtraght	08		00	08
	Carnssid	11		00	11
	Ballyalaghtie	06		02	04
	Ballymoy	13		00	13
	Lisarlues	13		03	10
	Tondon	08		00	08
	Carncolpe	06		02	04
	Altimacarinik	09		00	09
	Feach	20		03	17
	Cubrasheskan	11		00	11
	Crogballyno	10		05	05
	Templasragh	07		07	00
	Ballnastrad	05		00	05
	Carnanreagh	10		00	10
	Parke	07		00	07
	Clegenagh	17		00	17
	Lameneghmor	12		04	08
(folio 25)	Lisvallynagroghmor	07		06	01
	Lisvallynagroghbeg	10		00	10
	Upper Lisnagunog	08		05	03

Parishes	Places	Number of People	Tituladoes Names	Eng	Irish
	Lower Lisnagunog	07		00	07
	Drumnagassen	05		03	02
	Crnachbeg	17		00	17
	Toberkirk	08		04	04
	Stradkillin	13		00	13
	Ballynkea	18		00	18
	Illand Macallen	03		00	03
	Cregnamadey	08		00	08
	Ballyoglag	11		00	11
	Moycreg	18		07	11
	Moycregloer & Moycreg	22		00	22
(folio 26)	Maghereboy loer	07		00	07
	Maghereboy upper	06		00	06
	Ballantoy	51	Arch : Stuartt gent	20	31
	Ballynastrad	13		00	13
	Knocksochie	08		00	08
	Lagevarie	13		00	13
	Maghereher	11		00	11
	Maghrichastle	15		00	15
	Creganivie	06		00	06
	Clocher	05		00	05
	Glastachie	15		00	15
(folio 27). Belle-mone	Tonn and demanes	149	Robert Stewart gent John Stewart gent	040	109
	Bellebrak	014		008	006
	Benvelane	006		003	003
	Knekell	005		002	003
	Bellecormick	007		007	000
	Minegaben	004		003	001
	Bellepatrick	006		002	004
	Drumnewalaght	006		006	000
	Drummnert	009	Alexander Stewart gent	005	004
	Gare	004		002	002
	Dunevernan	009		009	000
	Mulaghmore	004		004	000
	Semecok	002		002	000
	Drochindulk	400		002	002
	Ballemenagh and Carrereagh	022		017	005
(folio 28)	Carnenane	11		11	00
	Coldow and Antethomasbuy	07		003	04
	Drenescheills	16		13	03
	Glenloagh	08		00	08
	Craigatimper	06		06	00
	Gilevanner	08		06	02

Parishes	Places	Number of People	Tituladoes Names	Eng	Irish
	Bellebolan	06		03	03
	Tap and Kilnaceel	08		03	05
	Litrim	01		00	01
	Culramone	07		03	04
	Brekogh	06		02	04
	Farnelesre	04		00	04
	Scronokum	14	Archbald Hutchone gent	05	09
	Bellerobin	05		04	01
	Bellecubedell	16		11	05
	Carnognele	13		03	10
(folio 29)	Kirkhills	10		09	01
	Taghephud	05		05	00
	Ballegen	17		10	07
	Colreseskan	04		04	00
	Cokrome	05		03	02
	Artegoran	13		08	05
	Drumahegles	06		06	00
	Ardmalphine	09		06	03
	Seacon	03		03	00
	Seconmore	11		00	11
	Seacon and Bellevatik	04		04	00
	Seaconbeg	04		04	00
	Kilmoyle	09		07	02
	Tallaghgore	35	James Commune gent	22	13
			James Hammilton gent		
	Cloghcur	05		04	01
	Coldach	06		06	00
(folio 30)	Bellenacre	06		02	04
	Taghephad cros	06		05	01
	Bellenacre more	08		08	00
	Bellenavatik	10		10	00
	Bellegaben	07		06	01
	Bandurok	06		01	05
	Drumreagh	05		00	05
	Glesdall	07		07	00
	Drumaheske	06		04	02
	Bellenacre	05		03	02
	Gnogh	18		07	11
	Drumske	11		06	05
	Bellenamone	06		04	02
	Pollentnue	07		00	07
	Clache	07		07	00
	Carnetele	05		02	03
(folio 31). Logh-geell	Bellenagabuk	24		00	24
	Disker	04		00	04
	Drumraken	09		00	09

Parishes	Places	Number of People	Tituladoes Names	Eng	Irish
	Corke	07		00	07
	Knockgallen	06		00	06
	CernKearich	07		00	07
	Bellebraden	08		00	08
	Altemeden	02		00	02
	Knoknabrenen	07		00	07
	Alterichard	06		00	06
	Machrecone	07		00	07
	Sciane	10		00	10
	Tilltene	03		00	03
	Ordok	06		00	06
	Ballebreagh	06		00	06
	Clontephenan	06		00	06
	Machreboy	06		00	06
(folio 32)	Bellecragagh	11		00	11
	Belletagart	11		00	11
	Cowlbane	05		00	05
	Drumdolagh	07		00	07
	Castell q^r	06		00	06
	Tornegro	06		00	06
	Lisnusk	05		00	05
	Lawaghbeg	07	William McPhatricks gent	04	03
	Tapernagola	06		00	06
	Belleportrie	06		00	06
	Balleteeme	04		02	02
Kilraghties	Knokanephren	06		06	00
	Magheroan	07		00	07
	Corngeragh	06		00	06
	Hilnageeve	11		00	11
(folio 33)	Lagaglire	07		00	07
	Artepherall	05		05	00
	Loghaber	05		00	05
	Magrabny	06		00	06
	Kilrachts	04		03	01
	Drumcerne	05		05	00
	Ilanmore	04		00	04
	Ganubie	06		06	00
	Leisbwie	03		00	03
Donache, Clogh, and Killagane	Glenlesle	05		05	00
	Bellecaigh	16		09	07
	Ogles	02		00	02
	Carnebeg	03		00	03
	Carnemore	04		04	00
	Drumdermond	02		02	00
(folio 34). Donache, Clogh, and Killage	Bellereagh	09		05	04
	Tillemewe	07		05	02
	Gilleree	07		07	00

Parishes	Places	Number of People	Tituladoes Names	Eng	Irish
	Iuschast	02		00	02
	Bellehanderland	04		02	02
	Frusus	24		13	11
	Cargnee	07		00	07
	Craigdunleif	15		00	15
	Cortrowan	06		00	06
	Inschgraught	04		00	04
	Lognemanok	11		00	11
	Tulleketoch	04		00	04
	Crmgfad	02		00	02
	Linneralachan	07		05	02
	Hinfla	04		00	04
	Drumboght	12		04	08
(folio 35). Donache, Clogh, and Killagane	Farme Gusok	09		03	06
	Clogh	02		00	02
	Drumbare	02		02	00
	Glenlyll	04		04	00
	Belloboge	15		05	10
	Tullekose	09		06	03
	Loghadvarinsch	02		02	00
	Drumdowan	06		00	06
	Ballig	13		11	02
	Ardvorneis	02		02	00
	Bellelub	09		00	09
	Lisdimderik	03		03	00
	Rosedernat	18		14	04
	Umerbane	03		03	00
	Maghraboy	04		00	04
(folio 36). Finboy	Belle McCallrent	22		10	12
	Dunloy	14		00	14
	Gallorogh	14		10	04
	Unsknogh	10		04	06
	Gareduff	12		00	12
	Caltephachan	19		00	19
	Slavanagh	08		00	08
	Mulone	15		00	15
	Dra	07		00	07
	Loer Knokan	14		13	01
	Upper Knok	05		00	05
	Loer Correreagh	06		00	06
	Upper Correreagh	09		07	02
	Loer Dermulee	10		07	03
	Upper Dermulee	11		09	02
(folio 37)	Loer Munekeman	12		07	05
	Upper Monek	08		04	04
	Risknaschian	04		00	04

Parishes	Places	Number of People	Tituladoes Names	Eng	Irish
	Hellenes	10		oo	10
	Diskerteavne	10	Donold McClay gent	oo	10
	Ardeloman	o8		o8	oo
	Logchichan	o7		oo	o7
	Schannache	o7		oo	o7
	Madekeell	11		o8	o3
	Carteferte	o8	John Galland Esqr	o6	o2
	Oden	19		o8	11
	Bellenagarve	20		o8	12
Roscearken	Antecor	13		oo	13
	Ballachen	13		o4	o9
	Kilcrene	o8		o1	o7
	Doremune	22		oo	22
(folio 38). Ros-charken	Killedonek	11		oo	11
	Derene	o3		oo	o3
	Killegnen, Drumiter and, Domanene	o9	Caven Steill gent	o1	o8
	Glenbuk	10		oo	10
	Gortrig	15		oo	15
	Ballelismgor	11		oo	11
	Balledonele	o9		oo	o9
	Tallalagh	11		oo	11
	Dereene	o7		o3	o4
	Ticherone	10		oo	10
	Drumcoane	10		oo	10
	Drumak	11		oo	11
	Carrowbard	12		oo	12
	Carnephertan	o2		oo	o2
	Moneteik	o7		oo	o7
	Maghrabuy	o8		oo	o8
	Ballecolmore	10		oo	10
(folio 39). Calfach-terny	Part of Ballelagh	16	George Gordon Esqr	o4	12
	Costrim	o6		oo	o6
	Tornamurie	o5		oo	o5
	Carmillagh	o3		oo	o3
	Knocklesky	o2		oo	o2
	Knockeigan	o3		oo	o3
	Laghedaghten	o3		oo	o3
	Tercor	o2		oo	o2
	Achishelag	o4		oo	o4
	Lochan	o3		oo	o3
	Aghenholly	o4		oo	o4
	Ru McAdam	o4		oo	o4
	Tor	16		oo	16
	Ballyechin	14	Daniell McGee gent	oo	14
	20 Acres	o5		oo	o5

B

Parishes	Places	Number of People	Tituladoes Names	Eng	Irish
	Dunekellber	01		00	01
(folio 40)	Crivagh	05		00	05
	Dunard	12		00	12
	Twornaron	18		05	13
	Ballyreagh	06		00	06
	Ballyboy	06		00	06
	Mollindiume	06		00	06
	Rodin	07		00	07
	Down	07		00	07
	Culnowpog	06		00	06
	Glenmakin	14		00	14
	Magherelogh	10		00	10
	Drumnakill	08		00	08
	Magheretemple	11		00	11
	Loskid	08		00	08
	Ballyverie	04		00	04
	Brekney	05		00	05
(folio 41)	Drumnakitt	06		00	06
	Drumnacaman	04		00	04
	Duncarbitt	19		00	19
	Bonemargie	03		00	03
Ramoan	Corvally	08		00	08
	Agheleck	06		00	06
	Killirobert	02		00	02
	Ballyvilly	02		02	00
	Drumniy	04		00	04
	Drumgnoly	04		00	04
	Ballycastle	43	Leut Daniell McNeall gent	07	36
	Drumonts	02		02	00
	Brommore	11		00	11
	Brumbeg	04		00	04
	Drumniwillin	04		04	00
	Moyergitt	06		00	06
	Upper Moyergitt	09		00	09
(folio 42)	Culkeney	09		00	09
	Carnetilagh	07		00	07
	Carnsamson	02		02	00
	Movally	10		08	02
	Church	02		02	00
	Gortamady	04		00	04
	Kircony	07	Brice Dunlape gent	04	03
	Clarr	04		00	04
	Drumnamargie	04		00	04
	Carnduff	04		04	00
	Carnemoan	06		04	02
	Cregenboy	06		00	06

Parishes	Places	Number of People	Tituladoes Names	Eng	Irish
	Cloghdunmurre	08		00	08
	Kepcastle	06		00	06
	Magremor	06		04	02
	Toberbilly	04		00	04
	Ballylige	05		00	05
(folio 43). Armoy	Torninrobert	15	Robert Kenedy gent	00	15
	Ballybreagh	06		00	06
	Mogaver	11		05	06
	Killcroce	ɔ8		00	08
	Torilaverty	06		00	06
	Alcrosagh	08		00	08
	Crumage	03		00	03
	Torreagh	06		00	06
	Brum	18		00	18
	Shruangalmor	06		00	06
	Tulicor	05		00	05
	Gortmilles	06		00	06
	Moninalegh	06		00	06
	Knockanes	05		03	02
	Ballyany	09		00	09
	Ballycaver	04		00	04
	Bunshenclony	05		00	05
	Mullaghdou	04		00	04
	Mullaghdow-Gorther	06			06
	Parke	05			05
The Iland of Rathry					
	Ballymore	19	James Boyd gent	04	15
	Ballynafirgan	12			12
	Ballycary	06			06
	Repatrick	12			12
	Ballywilly	15	Alexander Johnston gent	03	12
	Rovever	11			11

Principall Irish Names & their Number.

McAlester, 30 ; McAula, 09 ; Bryan, 06 ; Browne, 16 ; O Boyle, 11 ; McBryd, 06 ; Black, 10 ; Boyd & O Boyd, 20 ; Conoghye, 19 ; McConnell, 16 ; McCormick, 27 ; McCollum, 13 ; McCampbell &c, 36 ; McCahan &c, 10 ; McCooke, 10 ; McCurdy, 34 ; O Conogher, 08 ; McCurry, 12 ; McKay or McCay, 37 ; McCaw, 09 ; McDonell &c, 10 ; McDowgall, 06 ; McGoune, 15 ; McGilaspie, 08 ; McGillon, 13 ; McGloughlen, 13 ; McHenry &c, 20 ; McIlchrist, 10 ; McIlimchell, 07 ; McGee, 08 ; McIlroill, 07 ; McIlan &c, 09 ; McKeghan, 15 ; Kelly, 13 ; Kenedy, 18 ; McKinlay, 13 ; Killpatrick, 08 ; Loggan, 10 ; O Lovertie, 07 ; Lin & Line, 07 ; Martin, 08 ; Murry, 08 ; Moore, 31 ; Murphy, 20 ; Millan & Mullin, 55 ; McMichell, 11 ; Mullegan, 07 ; Miller, 16 ; O Money, 08 ; M Naughten, 10 ; McNeill, 49 ; & Steill, 12 ; Smyth & McSmyth, 27 ; Stuart & McStuart, 60 ; McTayler, 06 ; McTayer, 06.

(folio 43 verso). The Number of People in the Baronyes of Dunluce Carey & Kilconway :
Eng, 1138 ; Irish, 2940 ; Totall of Eng & Irish, 4078.

(folio 44 verso).   The Number of People in the County of Antrim & in each Barony &c.

Baronyes	Page	Eng	Irish	Eng & Irish
Antrim	1	0620	0841	1461
Glencarne	6	0721	0743	1464
Masareene	10	1007	1358	2365
Toome	11	0730	0778	1508
Belfast	16	2027	1825	3852
Dunluce Carey and Kilconway	43	1138	2940	4078
The Totall		6243	8485	14728

TOWNE AND COUNTY OF CARRIKFERGUS

(folio 1).   **CARRIKFERGUS**

Towne, County and parish of Carrikfergus	Number of People	Tituladoes Names	Eng	Irish
The Garrison Souldiers being three foot companies in the said towne and their wifes	349	Capt Charles Twigg Esq, Richard Baker Ensigne gent, Capt Leut Harraway gent, Ensigne William Breerton gent, Coll John Gorges Esqr, Capt. Leut. Beniamin Barrington gent, Ensigne Richard Elliott gent,	337	012
Towne	315	John Davies Esqr, Hercules Davies, and Henry Davies gent his sonns, John Dalway gent, Roger Lyndon Esqr, John Murtin Esqr deceased, James Dobbin gent, Mathew Johnson gent, William Dobbin gent, John Orpin gent, Edmond Davies gent, Robert Welsh gent, John Byrt gent, John Bulworthy gent,	218	097
(folio 2)		James Sparke gent, John Harris gent, John Wadman gent, Anthony Hull gent, Bryan Smyth Esqr, Peter Taylor gent, Samuell Treherne gent, Rice Powell gent, John Tooley gentle, Thomas Dobbin gent, William Thomson gent, Thomas McClellan gent, Thomas Ô Kane gent, Soloman Faith gent, John Redworth gent, Michaell Kerr gent, John Whitehead gent, Robert Savidge gent, Richard Westbrooke gent, William Hill gent, Richard Edwards gent, Charles Plukenet gent, Edward Graunt gent, Andrew Willoughby gent, Edmond Yeo gent, Theophylus Taylor gent, John Groce gent.		

Towne, County and parish of Carrikfergus	Number of People	Tituladoes Names	Eng	Irish
Scotsh Quarter and east Suburbs	176		096	080
Irish Quarter	105	Michaell Savidge gent	037	068
North East Quarter	113		056	057
North Quarter	144	John Preston gent	038	106
West Quarter	109	John Kune gent, Richard Johnson gent, Ralph Hillman gent decayed, Joseph Johnson gent.	049	060
The Number of all the inhabants in the said towne is besides souldiers are	962		494	468

(*folio* 1). Principal Irish Names [and] Their Numb.

Boyd, 5 ; Boale, 6 ; McCullagh, 8 ; Davies, 6 ; O Donnell, 4 ; Kune, 5 ; Loggan, 7 ; Magee, 6 ; Meane, 6 ; Ô Merran, 5 ; Martin, 4 ; Smyth, 4 ; Savidge, 4.

(*folio* 2 *verso*). The Number of People in the towne & liberties of Carikfergus : Eng, 0831 ; Irish, 480 ; Totall of Eng & Irish, 1311.

ARDMAGH BURROUGH

(*folio* 1) Ardmagh County	Towneland	Number of People	Tituladoes Names	Eng & Scotts	Irish
Ardm agh Burrough		409	Thomas Chambers Esqr, Henry Fetherston, Thomas Sanders, Thomas Arrall, Owen Mathewes, James Gurry, Evid : Shelton, Henry Parkinson, Charles Chappell, —— Ratsfore, Marke Middleton, Thomas Lawfore, Henry Lesquire, John King, and Samuell Theaker, gentlemen.	186	223

ARDMAGH BARRONY

	Townelands				
	Grene more and Corklea	012			012
	Aghomagoongan	010			010
	Dondrome	009			009
	Darkly	008			008
	Tuliglish and Rathcarbry	023			023
	Dunlahirck and Crosmore	010			010
(*folio* 2)	Tollenemollagg	06			06
	Dromdirigg	10			10
	Cargaghlatergane and Crossdamedd }	12			12
	Lorgallea	12			12
	Leggan	10			10
	Counyhy	14			14
	Deryhinnett	09			09
	Dromgrinnagh	10			10
	Cavangurvan & Drominun }	15			15
	Dromcantery	07			07
	Farrinnyn Illoy	11			11
	Mauellin	08			08
	Rillrevey	10			10
	Tanlatt	10			10
	Roan and Dromhurt	08			08
(*folio* 3)	Maghery Killcrany	06			06
	Killcrive-o-tra	08			08
	Killcrive-i-tra	10			10
	Drombruchis	10			10
	Brutully	16			16

Parrishes	Townelands	Number of People	Tituladoes Names	Eng & Scotts	Irish
	Derinlea	08			08
	Lissogally	10			10
	Cormeenc Tollickall-oidde and Bromgarr	33			33
	Aroll	14			14
	Baltoeagh	10			10
	Dericha	12			12
	Crerim	10			10
	Magravidd	10	James Maxwell gent	3	7
	Moonooney	13	Francis Stafford gent	4	9
	Trea and Balliaughy	12	Nicholas Severs gent	4	8
(folio 4).	Aghirefinny	06			06
	Breckhanriagh	08			08
	Tonagh and Cullentragh	13			13
	Lisdromard	13		02	11
	Crewroe	05	Nathaniell Sichsheuerall gent	05	—
	Teryearly	14		14	—
	Ballirey and Amaghboy	14		11	03
	Ballyhonemore	11		05	06
	Ballyhereland	02		—	02
	Farin McKaughly	12		07	05
	Ballyhonbegg	23		11	12
	Ballyards	18		13	05
	Aghivilly	02		—	02
	Lisbono	08		06	02
	Aghercrooill	26		22	04
	Kenedus	18		10	08
(folio 5).	Ballirath	13		07	06
	Nauin	04		04	—
	Ballybroly	11		10	01
	Tirinanargill	02		—	02
	Ballybromy	17		017	—
	Tirath	015		002	013
	Bally McIllmury	14			14
	Listanvolly	14		04	10
Ardmagh Cassan	Drombee, Ballimatram-otra, Ballimatramitra, Tullencull	20	Samuell Powell Esqr	10	10
	Blackwaterstowne	38		28	10
	Mullatagin & Dromcullin	13		05	08
	Mullintra & Mullenary	12		10	02
(folio 6)	Killmore	06		—	06
	Ballycullen	04		—	04
	Teriskean	08	Edmond oge McVagh gent	—	08
	Lisadine	17		—	17

Parishes	Townelands	Number of People	Tituladoes Names	Eng & Scotts	Irish
	Terra	20		—	20
	Tallagaran	04		—	04
	Clouchfin	06		—	06
	Ballytridane	10		—	10
	2 Sessues of Crane	08		—	08
	Ballygasoone	06		06	—
	Anachlay	08		08	—
	Cnockawny	07		07	—
	Tullaghgolgan	06		06	—
	Allistaker	10		02	08
	Killalin	04		—	04
	Teregarife				
(*folio* 7).	Dromsill	013		010	003
	Gragmore	023		011	012

Principall Irish Names [and] Their Number.

McCarran, 6 ; Ô Carbry, 4 ; Ô Cromy, 5 ; Ô Donelly, 10 ; Ô Dally, 4 ; Ô Diuin & Diuen, 6 ; O Fenighan (4), Ô Finaghan (3), 7 ; McGirr, 5 ; McGooregan, 7 ; McGeough, 4 ; Ô Hugh, 13 ; Ô Hagan & Ô Haggan, 6 ; McIlmurry, 4 ; Kenedy, 4 ; Ô Kenan and Ô Kennan, 7 ; Ô Kelly, 4 ; Martin, 4 ; Ô Mulkerane, 4 ; Ô Murry & O Morry, 6 ; O Rouerty, 7 ; McSherry (4), Ô Sharry (3), 7 ; McWard, 4.

(*folio* 7 *verso*). Barrony of Ardmagh : Eng & Scotts, 450 ; Irish, 891 ; 1341 totall.

(*folio* 8). Ardmagh County **TARRANNEY BARRONY**

Parishes	Townelands	Number of People	Tituladoes Names	Eng & Scotts	Irish
	Argonnell and Feduffe	08	Edward Rowley gent	02	06
	Upper Tullybracke	08		03	05
	Coolekill	13		02	11
	Malen	11		—	11
	Tolighis	05		02	03
	Rawviner	02		—	02
	Lislany	05		—	05
	Patreliske	07		—	07
	Killebritt	08		—	08
	Cavandugen	10		—	10
	Degerry	10		06	04
	Mullinary	08		04	04

Parrishes	Townelands	Number of People	Tituladoes Names	Eng & Scotts	Irish
	Portnelegan	o8		—	o8
	Knockcineligh	o7		—	o7
	Caricklane	11		—	11
	Knocbane	o6		—	o6
	Tolihiogohen & Creviseren	16		—	16
(*folio* 9).	Caranagh	o20		—	20
	Crosband	o6		—	o6
	Liskaroell	10		—	10
	Dromnehanly	o2		—	o2
	Carrickgarvan	o4		—	o4
	Rughaglan	14		—	14
	Drombanuell & Tirucre	18		—	18
	Dromelan	o4		—.	o4
	Mahsade				
	Crossrewagh				
	Furgett				
	Lorcony				
	Crossnamoyle				
	Tullyheren				
	Brackly & Boly				
	Ye 2 Rates				
(*folio* 10).	Dromneherry				
	Skery				
	Derry Dorke				
	Corfeghan				
	Unsogh	o7		—	o7
	Glasdromen	o1		—	o1
	Drumgoves	o8		—	o8
	Upper Crossdally	o4		—	o4
	Lower Crossdally	o5		—	o5
	Braughfye	14		—	14
	Ballynametry	o4		—	o4
	Lifhagh	o7		—	o7
	Mucklagh	o6		o6	oo
	Lisbane	o2		—	o2
	Gortmulegg	o6		o6	—
	Tynan	24		17	o7
	Quoy	11		o2	o9
(*folio* 11).	Cortynan	o8	Will Culwell and George Speare gent	o8	—
	Tolyo Saran	o5	Jo : Young gent	o5	—
	Upper Sandrades	o8	Thomas Ferberne gent	o7	o1
	Anagmoine & Anagilare	o9		o9	—
	Ashjuly	16		o2	14
	Evenderry	o9		oo	o9
	Tollynesken	o5		—	o5

Parrishes	Townelands	Number of People	Tituladoes Names	Eng & Scotts	Irish
	Tollymoore	02		—	02
	Maydowne	05		—	05
	Caricknesse	11		—	11
	Tollymoores—2	16		—	16
	Cor & Ashtargh	29		—	29
	Clunteceran	16		—	16
	Ashymaratt	16		—	16
	Tury	07		05	02
(folio 12)	Anagrage	05		05	—
	Gromgulfe	12		04	08
	Clunscarty	05		05	—
	Cavanbaylaghy	09		—	09
	Cullkeren	02		—	02
	Cnapagh	04	Robert Neisbett gent	04	—
	Foher and Palannagh	14		—	14
	Knocknee and Anagnanagh	12		—	12
	Cabragh	02		02	—
	Mullaketerry	01		—	01
	Colliarne & Gillnamadooe	25		—	25
	2 Dromsallens and Killbrotty	27		—	27
(folio 13).	Lisneside, Drombroske & Derrynasey	25		—	25
	Eglis, Mulliturmaly, Logan and Laraghlankell	27		—	27
	Argornett	02	Maur : Thompson gent	02	—

Principall Irish Names [and] Their Number.

Ô Bryne, 5 ; Ô Corr (8), Ô Carr (4), 12 ; Ô Donely, 8 ; Ô Gormely, 7 ; Ô Hugh, 32 ; Ô Hary, 5 ; McIlmorry, 9 ; McKee, 6 ; Ô Kenan, 6 ; Ô Lapan, 9 ; Ô Moone & Ô Mone, 5 ; Ô Mury & Ô Murry, 6 ; Ô Neile, 10 ; McQuoid & McQuod, 7 ; Ô Quine, 5 ; Ô Ronaghan, 5 ; Ô Toole, 6.

(folio 13 verso). Barrony of Tarranny : Eng & Scotts, 108 ; Irish, 546 ; 0654 totall

(folio 14) **ORYER BARRONY**

Parrishes	Townelands	Number of People	Tituladoes Names	Eng & Scotts	Irish
Dunashye	Ballymoore	107	The Earle of Middlesex. Toby: Points and Henry St John Esqrs Francis Ruare, and Francis Richardson, gentlemen	72	35

Parrishes	Townelands	Number of People	Tituladoes Names	Eng & Scotts	Irish
	Parke	06		02	04
	Tullylien	10		08	02
	Drumalegg	06		06	—
	Tannamachan	04		04	—
	Mullaglasse	11		11	—
	Augliske	06		06	—
	Lisban	05		05	—
	Moycluntye	06		—	06
	Modoge	12		04	08
	Bullyshealmoore	09		—	09
	Tulykin	06		—	06
	Crenbegg	06		04	02
	Crevemore	12		02	10
	Cargans	10		—	10
	Torryhugan	10		—	10
(folio 15)	Aughatarahan	10		06	04
	Edernagh	08		—	08
	Ballyreagh	10		—	10
	Ye halfe towne of Carickbrack }	06		—	06
	Deamon	10		—	10
	Carcoum	08		—	08
	Tueliske	08		—	08
	Clare	12		06	06
	Halfe a qr of Dunmaner	02		02	—
	Moymakulen Ballyshaelbeg }	11		11	—
	Caberagh	08		—	08
	Lisvicke	06		—	06
	Brusagh	10		—	10
	Cornettsrill	10		—	10
	Cordrine	10		04	06
(folio 16) Kilsleeve	Mullheade	20		20	00
	Carricksticken	16		—	16
	Carickbradagh	18		—	18
	Lisloe	12		—	12
Loughgilly	Syan	08		—	08
	Carickcorke	06		—	06
	Sanro	06		—	06
	Mullaghbane	09		—	09
	Tanrymoliree	15		—	15
	Cargin	07		—	07
	Corneare	16		—	16
	Killcaran	08		—	08
	Maytowne	08		—	08

Parishes	Townelands	Number of People	Tituladoes Names	Eng & Scotts	Irish
	Kedymoore	06		—	06
	Tollyhiryne	06		—	06
	Ballygorman	06		—	06
(folio 17)	Lisnebye	05		—	05
	Lisdeane	08		—	08
	Dromhirmy	08		—	08
	Aghnelocree	10		—	10
	Tollye	05		—	05
	Dromilly	06		—	06
	Mayvicullen	10		—	10
	Coron	06		—	06
	Mullaghmoore	05		—	05
	Dromilt	06		—	06
	Bollony	04		—	04
	Sturgan	20		—	20
	Ballymucragan	04		—	04
	Duffernagh	14		—	14
	Tullyhagee	10		—	10
	Leisse	11		—	11
	Lisdromgallin	08		02	06
(folio 18).	Leasfekill	06		—	06
	Drominter	10		—	10
	Ballytemple	06		—	06
	Foghillotragh	13		—	13
	Ballymakermott	12		—	12
	Clontigory	08		—	08
	Corumsogath	16		—	16
	Kilnamodagh	06		06	—
	Drombanagher	04		01	03
	Lissomen	06		06	—
	Knockduff	03		03	—
	Seers	06		—	06
	Halfe Kill-Managhan	06		02	04
	Agheneclowagh	04		—	04
	Derymoore	08		—	08
	Crosre	08		—	08
	Karickbrakan	08		—	08
(folio 19).	Koggall	04		—	04
	Cortloughan	08		—	08
	Bullocke	06		—	06
	Cloughgarvan	06		—	06
	Tossmarye	08		—	08
	Glassdromin	05		—	05
	Derimulligin	07		—	07
	Lasty	08		—	08
	Coraughes	09		—	09

Parrishes	Townelands	Number of People	Tituladoes Names	Eng & Scotts	Irish
	Cloghenagh	02		000	02
	Ashynew	04		—	04
	Clarekill	10		—	10
	Korekinagullagh	08		—	08
	Cloughgoenew	10		—	10

Principall Irish Names [and] Their Number.

McCawell (6), McCawle (4), 10 ; O Donelly, 7 ; McDowell, 6 ; McDonnell, 4 ; Ô Finan, 5 ; McGormly, 5 ; McGwill, 6 ; Ô Hanlen & Ô Hanlon, 13 ; McIlterny, 6 ; McIlcreve, 4 ; Ô Mulcreve, 5 ; Ô Murphy, 44 ; Magee, 5 ; McNally, 5 ; McParlan, 5 ; Ô Sheall, 6.

(*folio* 19 *verso*).   Barrony of Orryer : Eng & Scotts, 193 ;   Irish, 694 ;   0887, totall.

(*folio* 20)   **UPPER FEWES**

Parrishes	Townelands	Number of People	Tituladoes Names	Eng & Scotts	Irish
Creagan	Glasdroman & Dunrevy	22		07	15
	Comonagh	12		—	12
	Clarenagh	09		—	09
	Creganduff	06		—	06
	Ballynaghy	10		—	10
	Droumvale	12		—	12
	Cregan	10		—	10
	Corliss	09		—	09
	Cornacary	09		—	09
	Drulogher	06		—	06
	Clonlatescale	07		—	07
	Ballynarea	16		—	16
	Dorssy & Fyniskin	17		05	12
	Drumbee	11		—	11
	Clare & Cablane	46	Lt Thomas Ball & Tho : Proctor gents.	20	26
	Tullyvallane & Culehannagh }	37	Patrick Groumy O Coune gent	—	37
	Lissarra	06		—	06
	Legmoylen	14		—	14
(*folio* 21)	Lurgen Cullenboy	15		—	15
	Clonligg	10		—	10

Parrishes	Townelands	Number of People	Tituladoes Names	Eng & Scotts	Irish
	Shetrym	13		—	13
	Enaghmar	02		—	02
	Drumill	08		—	08
	Numrican	17		—	17
	Cloghog	16		—	16
	Carnaly	09		—	09
	Camly	18		—	18
	Ballintemple	030		—	30
	Cnockevanane	19		—	19
	Aghecorke	15		—	15
	Cavenkill	17		—	17
	Uttleakean	02		—	02
	Ardmaghbreg	16		—	16
	Tonergee	10		—	10
	Tollenagin	05		—	05
	Lisnadell	10		10	—
	Killyfody	16		—	16
	Balleoyre	12		—	12
(folio 22)	Broghan	08		—	008
	Droumconnell	16		16	—
	Ennisslare alius Monpotog }	07		07	00
	Ballemanran	21		16	05
	Lettmacollen	04		04	00
	Droumga	10		10	—
	Kyllyne	12		10	02
	Killnecapell Baltetowne }	05		05	—
	Uttleck	04		04	—
	Droumbeemore	08		—	08
	Droumbeebegg	18		10	08
	Edamnapagh	03		03	—
	Conlone	13		—	13
	Folly	16		—	16
	Bally McNabe	06		—	06
	Seygahane	06		04	02

LOWER FEWES BARRONY

Parrishes	Townelands	Number of People	Tituladoes Names	Eng & Scotts	Irish
(folio 23).	2 Ballileans	18		08	10
	Cladibegg	18		—	18
	Damonly	14		—	14
	Cladymore	21		—	21
	Kilmakne	14		—	14
	Carne	12		—	12

C

Parishes	Townelands	Number of People	Tituladoes Names	Eng & Scotts	Irish
	Cavan	11		—	11
	Dromnecy	18		—	18
	The Lower halfe towne of Lurgaboy	02		—	02
	Ballymakeally	16		—	16
	Droumaty	10		—	10
	Moylurge	11	John Earph Esqr	09	02
	Mullakbrak	10		10	—
	Monalan	17	Hance Hamelton Esqr and Francis Hamelton gent	17	—
	Cory	06		—	06
(folio 24)	Ballynury	21	John Grundle gent	—	21
	Ballygrumbonagh	09	Peerce Joanes gent	07	02
	Rillordan	08		08	—
	Droumenis	06		04	02
	Droumforgus	02		02	—
	Garragh	02		—	02
	Droumnegloy	12		—	12
	Magredogery	09		02	07
	Derenenagh	09		09	—
	Dromen	07	John Reemes gent	07	—
	Dromargan	14		02	12
	Magantrim	08		08	—
	Mullagbane & Droumnecross	08		08	—
	Corenecrue & Dromensalla	12		07	05
	Derereane	12		06	06
	Dromsavagh	06		02	04
	Lanylea	10		08	02
(folio 25).	Upper Creagan	10		10	—
	Lower Creagan	06		04	02
	Lisdromcorr	13		07	06
	Corovagh	11		10	01
Pt of Kilclinoy	Maghernevery	08		04	04
	Kilbrackes	15		—	15
	Brackly	09		09	—
	Balliandargh	11		—	11
	Lower Cullmalish	13		13	—
	Lisnegatt	10		00	10
	Cordromon	09	William Hanny gent	—	09
	½ towne of Edneranany	04		—	04
	Corrohomacke	08		—	08
	Derynesmulen	04		—	04

Parishes	Townelands	Number of People	Tituladoes Names	Eng & Scotts	Irish
Ye other pt of Loghgilly (folio 26).	Bryandrum	08	Sr George Achyson Barrtt	04	04
	Ballyany	03		03	—
	Carickleane	15		15	—
	Loarierose	09		09	—
	Dromgoyne	12		10	02
	Derylett	08		08	—
	Dromlary	06		04	02
	Derykeeghane	10		08	02

Principall Irish Names [and] Their Number.

McArdell (4), McCardell (5), 9 ; McCane, 10 ; Ô Coune, 12 ; McDonnell, 9 ; Ô Gorman, 6 ; McGill, 5 ; McGrory, 8 ; Ô Heherty, 6 ; McIlroy, 5 ; McIlvalluly, 6 ; McKeyne (4), McKeene (15), 19 ; Ô Kelly, 6 ; O Kelloghane & Ô Kealloghane, 6 ; Murphy, 7 ; Ô Neile, 12 ; McParlan, 6 ; Ô Quine, 7 ; Ô Raaverty, 5 ; McShane, 12 ; McShery, 5 ; Ô Toner, 6 ; Ô Toole, 6.

(folio 26 verso). Barrony of Upper & Lower Fewes : Eng & Scotts, 373 ; Irish, 858 ; 1231, totall.

(folio 27) **O NEYLAND BARRONY**

Parishes	Townelands	Number of People	Tituladoes Names	Eng & Scotts	Irish
Killmoore and Mullabreeke &c	Ballynehinch	015		07	08
	Mullawdroy	09		07	02
	Mullalelish	24		10	14
	Ballybreagh	27		—	27
	Derryhill	26		—	26
	Lower Quarter of Mulledroy	14		—	14
	Ballylockin	27		—	27
	Leggacurry	99	Edward Richardson Esqr	066	33
	Rockmacleny	02		—	02
	Shuish	08		04	04
	Corcrivye	15		13	02
	Luskoeburrow	28		19	09
	Crewcall	02		02	—
	Towlagurdin	05	William Archer gent	03	02
	Mullyletra	11		09	02
	Shessough Molinter	01		—	01

Parishes	Townelands	Number of People	Tituladoes Names	Eng & Scotts	Irish
(*folio* 28)	Drumard	21		015	06
	Clandroute	14		14	—
	Dromart	06		06	—
	Bottlehill	01		01	—
	Ballintagart	27		27	—
	Aughioryer	35		06	29
	Canan	01		01	—
	Killmoore	03		03	—
	Monney	07		06	01
	Gluntiologan	02		02	—
	Grynan	02		02	—
	Cuicon	04		04	—
	Annaheugh	10		06	04
	Killmakenty	06		—	06
	Ballyhagan	11		11	—
	Raonelan	08		—	08
	Dunginan	03		03	—
	Amaboe	12		04	08
(*folio* 29)	Tullymoore	12		—	12
	Carraghshanagh	25		—	25
	Ballytrue	05		05	—
	Lurgan Cott	04		04	—
	Derry Corr	22		—	022
	Marlecowmoore	06	Turlagh Ô Donely gent	—	06
	Marlecowbegg	07		07	—
	Tymoore	12		09	03
	Shancrakin	28		—	28
	Drumart	18		—	18
	Drumnamoider	16		—	16
	Tafnachmoore	04		—	04
	Drumnamader	07		04	03
	Murorkan	08		—	08
	Tafnaghmoore	12		04	08
(*folio* 30)	**ONEYLAND CONES**[1]				
	Bollymurhan	20		10	10
	Droumaratally	14		08	06
	Aghebrahoge	12		10	02
	Dromshew	10		08	02
	Mehann	07	Mr Amlett Ô Boyns gent	03	04
	Kill McMurtagh	17		17	—
	Mulaghtian	15		04	11

[1] This is the heading of folios 30, 31, 32, 33 ; folios 34, 35, 36 have *O Neyland*.

Parrishes	Townelands	Number of People	Tituladoes Names	Eng & Scotts	Irish
	Annagh	07		—	07
	Clonagh	12		—	12
	Tannagh	22		18	04
	Balliorane	07		—	07
	Garvaghie	03		—	03
	Solshan	11		—	11
	Corcullen Traghbeg	04		02	02
	Corcullen Traghmore	07		07	—
	Baltilom	06		06	—
(folio 31)	Ballynagone	04		—	04
	Deryhanvill	16		—	16
	Corbrackoge	06		—	06
	Ballynagoneotragh	04		02	02
	Droumcree	02		02	—
	Droumfuse	04		04	—
	Killmagins	04		—	04
	Droumnalduff	06		—	06
	Anaghkearagh	06		—	06
	Droumynagh	08		06	02
	Droumallis	10		—	10
	Derycarane	05		—	05
	Muckerie	02		—	02
	Faymore	08		—	08
	Droumnavin	04		—	04
	Bragh	13	Mr Waldronn gent	01	12
	Ballymagone	12		—	12
(folio 32).	Anghgore	04		—	04
	Raa	07		00	07
	Kingarrow	04		—	04
	Corr	08		—	08
	Ballyfodrim	04		—	04
	Farrow	06		06	—
	Tirmakeele	08		—	08
	Droumhirff	02		02	00
	Roghan	06		—	06
	Kinagollenbegg	08		—	08
	Kinagollenmore	10		—	10
	Unsenagh	02		—	02
	Diriletiue	10		—	10
Taghtirahan	Counemakate	08		—	08
	Derikeavan	05		—	05
	Mahergrane	07	Captn Hartt gent	01	06
	Conegill	06		06	00
	Aaygaradie	04		02	02
(folio 33)	Droumanan	09		03	06
	Teggie	18		—	18

Parrishes	Townelands	Number of People	Tituladoes Names	Eng & Scotts	Irish
	Eflis	18		—	18
	Bragh	o6		—	o6
	Droumanffie	o4		oo	o4
	Kinaneile	o4		o4	
	Clountilen	o2	Mr Bickerton gent	o2	—
	Derileare	16		—	16
	Derinraa	o6		—	o6
	Ballimeniririe	o4		—	o4
	Deriane	o4		—	o4
	Derilee	o6		—	o6
	Glanconcurk	o4		—	o4
	Clouncorow	o2		—	o2
	Srabry	o2		—	o2
Loughgall[1]	Lebolyegliss	10		10	—
	Drumelly	17	Walter Cope & Francis Chambers gent	12	o5
(folio 34).	Ballygassy Tullyardallis	11		o9	o2
	Loghgale	26		19	o7
	Balitorn	o7		o7	—
	Lesefielde	o6		o2	o4
	Lisneny	o7		o7	—
	Droumhirff	o8		o6	o2
	Mallaghbane	14	John Ellish gent	o2	12
	Molaghnasyby	22		o4	18
	Drumnashu	25		19	o6
	Ardress	12		—	12
	Anicmore	14		—	14
	Clenmaine	10		10	—
	Cleauenedonn	11		o9	o2
	Agherlogher	14		12	o2
	Cossana	o8		o8	—
	Coragh	17		o3	14
	Ballymagrue	17		o7	10
(folio 35)	Derynegrea	12		o4	o8
	Anichsamery	11		11	—
	Turkhary	o7		o7	—
	Roderamgreny	o4		—	o4
	Droumartt	o6		o2	o4
	Ardrey	o8		o2	o6
	Ballanick	12		12	—
	Grynon	12		—	12
	Anagh Cromph	10		o8	o2
	Bollybrononn	o6		—	o6

[1] *Loghgall,* folios 34, **35,** 36.

Parishes	Townelands	Number of People	Tituladoes Names	Eng & Scotts	Irish
	Droumogher	08		—	08
	Killmague	09		09	—
	Droumnabegg	04		—	04
	Dromodmore	09		07	02
	Killuney	04	Robert Greia gent	00	04
	Anagcliere	04		—	04
	Muloghlograngh	13			13
(folio 36)	Deryne Scopp and Alturk	17		—	17
Killamon and Clankell p^te	Clanmore and Clountly clee	10		—	10
	Molaghnakilla	06			06
	Deremagoine	08	Owne Ô Cullen gent	04	04
	Kineriss	08		04	04
	Deryscabopp	02		—	02
	Copney	08		—	08
	Derycary	08		—	08
	Tulerin	25		—	25

(folio 37)

CLANBRASSELL

Parishes	Number of People	Tituladoes Names	Eng & Scotts	Irish
Shankell	344	Sr William Bromloe Knight, Fulke Martin Esqr, Will Draper, William Jones, Alexander Gill, Richard Bromloe, John Realy, John Burne, John Barnes, Cuth: Harrison & Wrighton Taylor and Lawrence Swarbricke gent.	242	1 2
	396	George Blacer Esqr Richard Smith gentleman, Valentine Blacker Esqr, Miles Boulsfeld, Robert Lackworth, and William Stewart, gentlemen.	251	145

CHARLEMOUNT

Townelands	Number of People		Eng & Scotts	Irish
	117	William Lord Canfeild Barr^tt	057	60
Souldiers & their wiues	064		060	004
Yeomen & their wiues	026		019	007

Townelands	Number of People		Eng & Scotts	Irish
College lands	017	John Browne gent	004	013
Ter McChenan	002		—	02
Lisbost	008	Mr Swan gent	002	006

The Principall Irish Names of Neyland Barrony & ye underwritten towne [and] Their Number.

Makatye, 6 ; Ô Carr & O Corr, 6 ; O Connellane, 16 ; O Cullen, 10 ; McCann, 28 ; McCawell, 12 ; Ô Donely (5), O Donelly (8), 13 ; Ô Denelin, 8 ; Ô Duyne, 6 ; McDonell, 6 ; O Ferrall, 7 ; McGin & McGinne, 7 ; O Hanlon, 5 ; O Hugh, 11 ; McIlcrivy, 5 ; McKelly, 6 ; O Kenan, 7 ; O Keny & Ô Kenny, 5 ; O Kergan & Ô Kurgan, 7 ; Ô Lurkane, 5 ; Ô Mulan & Ô Mullan, 17 ; Ô Marly, 8 ; Makellcree, 7 ; Ô Neale (5), Ô Neile (14), 19 ; Ô Quine, 6 ; O Roverty, 8 ; McVagh, 6.

The seruants Names are not written in ye Booke.

(folio 37 verso).   Barrony of Oneyland :   Eng & Scotts, 1269 ;   Irish, 1366 ;   2635, totall.

Barronies	Pages	Eng & Scotts	Irish	Totall
Ardmagh	07	450	891	1341
Tarranny	13	108	546	0654
Orryer	19	193	694	0887
Upper & Lower Fewes	26	373	858	1231
Oneyland &c	37	1269	1366	2635
		2393	4355	6748

COUNTY OF DONEGALL 12001

(*folio* 1). Donegall County.   **TIRHUGH BARRONY**

Parrishes	Townelands	Number of People	Tituladoes Names	Eng & Scotts	Irish
Killbarron	Ballishannon	134	Thomas Lord Folliot of Ballishanon Michall Houtsone gentleman and Charles Dunsterfield gent.	063	071
	2 Belliboes of Kircally	006		—	006
	Q^r of Ashiroe	007		—	007
	6 Belliboes of Bally McAward	027	John Folliot Esqr and Anthony Folliot gent	005	022
	Q^r of Killdony	010		004	006
	½ Q^r of Crieac	024		002	022
	Killbarron Q^r	023		002	021
	Q^r of Cullebegg	013		—	013
	Q^r of Cassell	008			008
	Q^r of Killcarbry	064		019	045
	4 Q^r of forecoss Q^r of Casslehard	005			005
	Q^r of Callinahorne	014			014
olio 2)	Q^r of Tobea	008			008
	Q^r of Garvanagh	12			12
	Q^r of Corlea	23			23
	3 Qrs. of Ballinamanagh	182		31	151
Enish McSaint	Q^r of Bundrous	22			22
	Qr. of Ardfarna	26			26
	Qr. of Rashmore	22			22
	½ Qr. of Raglasse	03			03
	Q^r of Finner	04		02	02
	Q^r of Kilborlagh	19			19
	Q^r of Donmak	21			21
	Quarter of Donoghmore	49			49
	Qr. of Crivagh	34		06	28
	Two Balliboes of Poolnosoni	06		00	06
(*folio* 3)	½ Q^r of Ballihany	04			04
Drumhome	Qr. of Ballininterbray	28			28
	Q^r of Ballimagroerty	26		03	23
	Drumore	18			18
	Q^r of Glassboly	14			14
	Qr. of Lorgan	13			13
	Qr. of Killinaquill	25		02	23
	Qr of Ballinechan	18			18
	Morvagh	05			05
	Quarter of Drumlaumhill	13		04	09
	Drumeross qr	09			09
	Tolis Modan Q^r	10		06	04

Parrishes	Townelands	Number of People	Tituladoes Names	Eng & Scotts	Irish
folio 4)	Twelue Balliboes of Rassnalagh	44		02	42
	Donegall Towne	095	Captn Henry Brook Esqr	24	71
	Carrignegan Qr. land	035			35
	Clare Loghesk Qr. Land	54			54
	Ye Balliboe of Goulduffe	10			10
	Ye Balliboe of Clarlisgrugan	06			06
	Tawininvilly	29			29
	Y^e 6 Balliboes of Magheryhy	26	Capt. Thomas Stewart Esqr	08	18
	Drumgananagh Qr	03			03
	Tully Qr	35		13	22
	Lackan Qr Land	34			34
	Ye Qr of Rosses	49		04	45
	Ballyrodes Qr.	22		04	18
(*folio* 5).	Ballinagunnenagh ½ Qr	010	George Knox gent	03	07
	Rosslie Qr	06		—	06
	Ye 2 Quarters of Tulligallan and Ranenie	44		12	32
	Carrig Qr	23		02	21
	Rattunny Qr. Land	14			14
	Treman Qr.	29			29
	Ballmakilly qr	29		06	23
	Ye 2 Balliboes of Killgoell	07		07	—
	Ye 2 Balliboes of Drumcumlisk	06			06
	Ballydermott qr	09			09
Carne	Ye Sessiogh of Mirikagh	06			06
(*folio* 6)	Ye Sessiogh of Aghnakene	08		02	06
	Ye Sessiogh of Cannow	03			03
	Ye Sessiogh of Fincastle	04			04
	Ye Sessiogh of Carrickrosy	14			14
	Ye 3 Sessioghes of Petigoe	11			11
	Ye 3 Sessioghes of Oghafaye	06		06	—
	Ye 3 Sessioghes of Couet Barkeoge	12			12
	Ye 3 Sessioghes of Aghean Lagh, Drumcruin barfill	07		02	05
	Ye Sessiogh of Carne	09			09
	Ye Sessiogh of Kilty	10			10
(*folio* 7)	Ye 2 Sessioghes of Dromouerick	12			12
	Ye Sessiogh of Ballimanrary	04			04
	Ye 2 Sessiogh of Teeuenowe & Drumnogarden	14			14
	Ye Sessiogh of Aghnabile	06			06
	Ye Sessiogh of Lettercorne	06			06

Parrishes	Townelands	Number of People	Tituladoes Names	Eng & Scotts	Irish
	Ye Sessiogh of Crologh	o4			o4
	Ye Sessiogh of Tanelagh	o8			o8
	Ye Sessiogh of Banow	o6			o6

Principall Irish Names [and] Their Number

McAnulty, o9 ; Ô Boyle, 11 ; Ô Breenan, o7 ; Ô Connelly, o7 ; Ô Cassady, o6 ; Ô Connor, o9 ; Ô Cleery, o9 ; Ô Cullen, o8 ; Ô Donnell, 11 ; McFlarty, o9 ; Ô Gollogher, 26 ; McGargill, o7 ; McGowan, 10 ; McGillmartyn, o6 ; McGragh, 14 ; McGrean, o6 ; McKee, o7 ; O Kelly, o7 ; McAloone, o6 ; O Murray, 18 ; Monaghan, o6 ; Ô Toolan, o6 ; Ô Mealy, o7

(folio 7 verso). Barrony of Tirhugh : Eng & Scotts, 244 ; Irish, 1474 ; 1718, totall.

(folio 8)   **THE BARRONY OF BOYLAGH & BANAGH**

Parrishes	Townelands	Number of People	Tituladoes Names	Eng & Scotts	Irish
Killamarde	Belliweell Qr.	17	Tho Ld Viscount Stormont	o2	15
	Drumgun	o6			o6
	Drumarke	o9			o9
	Altaduffe	15			15
	Drumchan	14		o7	o7
	½ Quarter of Killkighan	14	William Lawson gent	o2	12
	Dowan Qr, Drumclan	15		o6	o9
	Bellidett	11			11
	Drumclan	12		o6	o6
	Mullens	13		o2	11
	Drumruske Qr	21		o4	17
	Drumgornan	o7			o7
	Drumrusk	16		o4	12
	Lecrum Qr, Clarteskan	12		o9	o3
	Clarteskan	o6			o6
(folio 9)	Orbeg	o8			o8
	Orrmore	11			11
	Aghatillo	11			11
	Logheaske Qr	18		o9	o9
	Drumeniagh	o3		o3	ooo
	Logheaske	o2		—	o2
	Grenian	19		o2	17
Inver	Qr of —— ——	23	Andrew Nesbit & James Nisbit gent	o4	19

Parrishes	Townelands	Number of People	Tituladoes Names	Eng & Scotts	Irish
	Drumranny	04		02	02
	Killingrodann ½ Qr	013	Andrew Nisbit gent	08	05
	Monyallagher Bellboe	04		—	04
	Castlegory Qr	25		08	17
	Inver halfe Qr	15	Francis Haris gent	06	09
	Bonyglan Qr	29		—	29
(folio 10).	Lettermore Qr	42			42
	Drumconnor Qr	26		05	21
	Tamnitullen Qr	28	William Cunynghame and George Cunynghame gent	07	21
	Drumbegg Balliboe	02	Charles Murry gent	—	02
	Dromcoe Qr	33		11	22
	Craigdarum Qr	31		12	19
	Rancle Qr	27		15	12
	Disert Belliboe	04			04
	Drumlerty Qr	17			17
	Drumlest Belliboe	04			04
Killagtie	Castle Muray Qr	29	Sr Robert Murray Knt of Glenmir Archibald Pearsane John Greeg & James Crightone gentlemen	14	15
	Carrickross 3 Balliboes	07			07
(folio 11)	Bellecroy Qr	15		05	10
Killaghtie.	Bellysaggart	08		04	04
	Bellioderlane ½ Qr	17		—	17
	Beillibo Donnell, two Belliboes	09		02	07
	Bellinagone, three Belliboes	07		000	07
	Drumreny ½ Qr	15		15	000
	Castletowne three Belliboes	08		06	02
	Ballvocks	19		—	19
	Coragh feeaghan, one Belliboe	07		—	07
	Ahan one Qr	35		10	25
	Killaghtee ½ Qr	12		05	07
	Duncanally three Belliboes	04		04	—
(folio 12)	Drumaghly one Belliboe	04		—	04
	Belliloghan one quarter	09		09	—
	Carnemore	08		08	—
	Croghcastlemeran ½ qr	13		—	13
Killebeggs	Fentraugh Qr	040	James Hamilton gent	03	37
	Lazy Sallagh Qr	16		10	06
	Belliara Qr	08	Allexr Cunyngham & Andrew Cunyngham gents	03	05
	Dremenow Qr	10		—	10
	Glenlee belleboe	04		—	04

Parrishes	Townelands	Number of People	Tituladoes Names	Eng & Scotts	Irish
	Ye ould towne of Kille-beggs	31		11	20
	Minihughan Belleboe	07			07
	Drumbert belliboe	08		02	06
(folio 13)	Killebeggs Corp'acon	31		010	21
	Conlone	12		—	12
	Stragore two Belliboes	06		—	06
	Carnemore Qr	31		010	21
	Carricktullagh	09		003	06
	Killterny	09			09
	Glengeske	03			03
	Drumbarren	05			05
	Doughell	11			11
	Killrien	08			08
	Doris	07			07
	Duchell	14			14
	Karnyford	16			16
Killcarr	Killcarr ½ Qr	14			14
	Boggagh ½ Qr	09			09
(folio 14)	Direlad ½ Qr	07			07
	Itralile Belliboe	04			04
	Belliduffe Qr	25			25
	Senaghan ½ Qr	13			13
	Taunagh ½ Qr	10			10
	Macruss Qr	12		04	08
	Largimore Qr	34	Andrew Nisbitt gent	07	27
	Glencolmikill 5 Qrs	108	John Montray gent	03	105
Enishkiell, Templecron, & Letter McAward	Castlegollan	25			25
	Kinkony Qr	20			20
	Shrathnadaragh	10			10
	Ballirustin Qr	12			12
	Bealeanamore Qr	08			08
	Iregtogke	02			02
(folio 15)	Tulliard	08			08
	Letterilly	09			09
	Gortnesallagh	07			07
	Mase	04	Teage Ô Boyle gent		04
	Mulvagh & Samagh Qr	28			28
	Dawrush Qr	30			30
	Srudoragh Qr	24			24
	Durian	08			08
	Mullenweager	04			04
	Sraneglogh	22		02	20
	Loghrass fiue qrs	57	Torlagh Ô Boyle gent		57
	Seanchan	06			06
	Kinnoghtie	46			46

Parishes	Townelands	Number of People	Tituladoes Names	Eng & Scotts	Irish
(*folio* 16)	Leconnell	10	Francis Gattery gent	01	10
	Clogher	18			17
	Archane	15			15
	Crosskenny	03			03
	Drumboghill qr	24			24
Ye Capitall of Letter McAward	Corr qr	10	Gory McAward gent		10
	Cross qr	14			14
	Tum qr	13			13
	Cullbe qr	15			15
	Ye 4 qrs of Craugh & Termon & all ye p'sh of Templecrone	54			54

Principall Irish Names.

McAtire, 6 ; McAnulty, 8 ; McAward, 11 ; Ô Brislane, 8 ; Ô Boyle, 41 ; Ô Birne, 9 ; Ô Cannan, 8 ; Ô Conigan, 10 ; Ô Conaghan & Ô Conighan, 11 ; Ô Carney, 10 ; McCollin, 13 ; Ô Cassady, 9 ; Ô Connally, 6 ; Ô Cuningham (5), Cuningham (4), 9 ; O Donell, 20 ; Ô Doghertye, 14 ; McDeve, 6 ; McGillaspick, 8 ; Ô Gallogher, 51 ; McGlaghlin, 14 ; O Kenady, 6 ; McKillker, 7 ; Ô Kelly, 9 ; McKee, 8 ; Ô Kenny, 6 ; Ô Mullghill, 6 ; Ô Mullmoghery, 6 ; Ô Murrey, 11 ; McNelus & McNellus, 9 ; Scott, 10 ; Ô Shearing, 11 ; McSwyne, 7.

(*folio* 16 *verso*).   Barrony of Boylagh & Banagh : Eng & Scotts, 285 ; Irish, 1556 ; 1841 totall.

(*folio* 17)   **RAPHO BARRONY**

Parishes	Townelands	Number of People	Tituladoes Names	Eng & Scotts	Irish
Ray	Dowish Qr.	27	Robert Galbraith Esq	14	13
	Lishmogery Qr	05		04	01
	Galdinagh Qr	15	Archibald Thomsone, John and Anthony his sonns gents	09	06
	Cowlglee Qr	06	John Stewart Esqʳ and Robert Stewart gent	05	01
	Moncloynt Qr	06	Anthony Kenady Esqʳ	05	01
	Mondowy Qr	08	James Stewart gent	05	03

Parrishes	Townelands	Number of People	Tituladoes Names	Eng & Scotts	Irish
	Drumoghell Qr.	10	John Stewart and Francis Stewart his sonn gent	09	01
	Drumbarne qr	12	Mathew Stewart gent	06	06
	Glybb land	02		02	—
	Killevery Qr.	11		11	—
	Mumimore qr	09		05	04
	Bellilane qr	12	William Stewart Esq	10	02
	Bellileven qr	07		04	03
	Veagh Qr	06		—	06
	Monyhaghly Qr	06		05	01
	Belliaghan Qr	013	James Cuningham Esqr & John his sonn Esqr	09	04
(folio 18)	Magheribeg Qr	08		08	00
	Drien Qr.	08		06	02
	Magherimore Qr.	46		38	08
	Ray Qr.	07	William Lennox gent	07	—
	Gracky Qr	14		07	07
	Corky Qr	09	James Calhoune Esqr	06	03
	Gortomore Qr.	08		04	04
	Rowsky Qr.	09		02	07
	Lish Clamarty Qr.	07		06	01
	Labedesh Qr	13		07	06
	Carrik bellidowy qr	05		05	—
Stranorlane	Corgarron Qr	06	Thomas Dutton Esqr	03	03
	Corlecky	20			20
	Galboly Qr	22			22
	Shirroy Qr	22			22
	Letter Killy ½ qr	09			09
(folio 19)	Bellkergan	09	Conn Ô Donnell gent		09
	Altepast qr	16			16
	Aghevay ½ qr	09			09
	2 Belliboes of Letterbricke	04		03	01
	Bellibonibany	02			02
	Bellibonitem	03			03
	Drombo Craigan qr & Caprietrame	27	Edward Torltone gent	13	14
	Drwish qr	14			14
	Liskeran	05		04	01
	Coraghoncoyan	10		06	04
	Ballimafay	07		06	01
	Stranorlan	13	Peter Bensone gent	09	04
	Downwyly	08		06	02
	Tivickamoy	06			06
	Tirkallane ½ qr	05		04	01
	Gortinliter	07		07	00
(folio 20)	Knockfaire qr	03		—	03

D

Parrishes	Townelands	Number of People	Tituladoes Names	Eng & Scotts	Irish
Leck	Ardmaran qr	04		—	04
	Lergee qr	22		09	013
	Listillane qr	14		13	01
	Aghliharde & Tavinyviny qr	17		12	05
	Drumardagh qr	10		06	04
	Maghrybuy qr	15		13	02
	Rossbreake & Drumore qr	07		05	02
	Largibreake, two belliboes	04		02	02
	Ferranogh qr	10		03	07
	Cullen qr	13			13
	Lishmonaghan qr	04			04
	Rahan qr	07		02	05
	Corr qr	09		08	01
(folio 21)	Crue two Belliboes	08		03	05
	Rossbreake qr	08		04	04
	Tromer qr	04		02	02
	Coronogh five Belliboes	07		02	05
	Leck Qr	13	James Lecky & Walter Colhoune gents.	09	04
	Crew 2 Belliboes	03		03	—
	Balliconnell	04		04	—
	Cronaglack Qr	10			10
	Killamasly Qr	05			05
	Drominagh Qr	08			08
	Rowghan qr	08		03	05
	Trickendy qr	09		03	06
	Rareagh qr	07			07
	Letterleag qr	10			10
Taghboine	Mongarlin qr	09	Charles Earle of Leitchfield L^d of ye mannor of Mongarlin	06	03
(folio 22)	Maymore Qr	21	Mathew Lindsay gentleman	14	07
	Ratine Qr	12		04	08
	Drumenan qr l^d	08	James Lindsay gent	06	02
	Craghedon qr L^d	15		09	06
	Momein qr Land	09		03	06
	Ballilenan qr l^d	12		06	06
	Letterquill qr. land	11		07	04
	Tullerapp qr. land	16		04	12
	Fadeglass qr land	10		06	04
	Drumore qr land	14		14	—
	Carshanogh qr	15		06	09
	Castle qr land	18	William Noble gent	13	05
	Moness qr land	10		04	06
	St Johnstowne qr Land	37		19	18

Parrishes	Townelands	Number of People	Tituladoes Names	Eng & Scotts	Irish
	Trintogh qr land	12		02	10
	Ardagh qr land	03			03
(*folio* 23)	Carrowkill qr land	10		02	08
	Clashegowan qr	15		09	06
	Tamogh & Cloghfin qr	24		16	08
	Ye Church qr land	25	Thomas Bruce gent	19	06
	Lustikill qr land	20		15	05
	Cross qr land	15		07	08
	Castle qr land	11		11	—
	Drumlogher qr land	08		04	04
	Corcomon qr land	06		04	02
	Ye qr land called Mont-glass & clum	14		10	04
	Letrim qr land	07		06	01
	Bogay glebse	06		03	03
	Gortlush qr land	05		05	—
	Portlogh qr land	09		07	02
(*folio* 24) Tagh-boyne.	Gortry qr land	12		12	—
	Ballihaskan qr	07		—	07
	Col McIltraine qr land	26		015	11
	Ruskie qr land	17		12	05
	Drumellen qr land	07		04	03
	Tulleanan qr land	07		04	03
	Bellibeglimore qr land	11		09	02
	Bellibiglibeg qr land	11		07	04
	Ruchen qr land	10		03	07
	Drumboy qr ld	15		09	06
	Munegrevan Qr land	09		07	02
	Monfad qr land	51	William Cuninghame Esqr	35	16
	Plaister qr land	24	William Cuninghame gent	19	05
	Ardy Qr land	15		12	03
(*folio* 25) Tagh-boine	Moyle qr land	26	Robert Boyle gent	16	10
	Dacustrewes qr ld	13		02	11
	Carskowie qr land	18		11	07
	Culdrum qr land	30		24	06
	Gortinleaue qr ld	13		13	—
Killa Taghboine	Carikene qr land	35		23	12
	Altoghadare qr Land	17		13	04
	Dunmoire qr land	25		10	15
Rapho	Cloghroy	09			09
	Callen	13			13
	Lettermore	14			14
	Drumcheen	13			13
	Trentibuy	12			12
	ArdeKelly	14			14
	Castletorris	10		10	

Parishes	Townelands	Number of People	Tituladoes Names	Eng & Scotts	Irish
	Cornigellagh	16		08	08
(folio 26)	Tillidonnell	21	Capt[n] John Nisbitt Esq[r]	17	04
	Drumgumerlan	16		10	06
	Conavay	19		17	02
	Agagalty	12		04	08
	Machricorren	13		05	08
	Killmure	27	Capt[n] Francis Hamilton gent	18	09
	Findrum	13		06	07
	Carrikebreake	16		10	06
	Rusky Qr	21		15	06
	Magheriehee	12		06	06
	Cullachymore	12		05	07
	Balliholly	13		06	07
	Machrisolus	14		14	—
	Cullachybegg	18	George Buchanan gent	16	02
	Gorteguigly	16		13	03
	Boggagh & Stranorlaghan	35	Archibald Spruell & John Spruell gents	28	07
(folio 27)	Fendorke	10		10	—
	Glen McQuin	27		19	08
	Ardemecke	05		05	—
	Asmoyen	23		21	02
	Tallidemy	33		28	05
	Beltony	07		—	07
	Culladerry	32		26	06
	Lesnorcullen	06		06	—
	Figar	07		07	—
	Killtowell	13		07	06
	Rapho towne	104	William Wigtone gent	80	24
Donoghmore	Belliarell qr	106	John Kingsmill Esq[r]	56	50
	6 Sessioghs of Bellmicar	13		09	04
	Drumneviss	08		04	04
	Bellibune qr	47	William Crafford gent	24	23
(folio 28)	Drumban qr	36	William Younge gent	23	13
	Lebellicastle qr	36		30	06
	Art quarter	25		16	09
	Magherireagh	20	James Sime and John Sime his sonn gents	18	02
	4 Sessioghs of Cloghfyn	08	Robert Hamilton gent	05	03
	Magherishanvally	22		16	06
	Donoghmore	19	William Squire Esq[r]	12	07
	Castlefine town	29	William Warran Esq[r]	22	07
	Cavan qr	24	John Hamilton Esq[r]	12	12
	Carnone qr	41		27	14
	Corren 4 Sessioghs	09		—	09
	Corshendunyman	06	John Mountgomery gent	04	02

Parishes	Townelands	Number of People	Tituladoes Names	Eng & Scotts	Irish
	Killkadan	04		04	
	Killigadan	42	Allexᵣ Knox & Ralph Mauffield gents	22	20
(folio 29)	Lightikerelan	14	Thomas Fairfax Esqᵣ	14	
	Imlagh qr Craggan	31		26	05
	Cormagrath 3 Sessioghes	13		—	13
	Cuny	31		04	27
Lifford	Lifford corporac'on	68	Charles Burten & Hugh Barclay gents	44	24
	North side of Croghan qr	42	Richard Perkins & Gustavus Hamilton Esqrs	18	24
	South Side of Croghan	37		20	17
	Belliboggan qr	32		21	11
	Bellilast	03		02	01
	Shanon and Drumleer	35	John Hamilton gent	15	20
	Moyne qr	37		23	14
(folio 30)	2 qrs of Clonlee	53		09	44
	Argory qr	35		22	13
	Moynster qr	21		19	02

Principall Irish Names

Browne, 09 ; Ô Boyle, 07 ; McCormick, 07 ; Cunyngham, 27 ; McCallin, 07 ; McClintock, 08 ; McCarter, 07 ; McConnell, 11 ; Ô Doghertye, 16 ; Ô Donnell, 10 ; McDevet, 08 ; O Gollogher, 19 ; O Kervallan, 10 ; McKinlay, 06 ; O Kenady (3), Kenady (10), 13 ; O Kelly, 12 ; McKee, 10 ; Ô Karran, 07 ; Ô Kenny, 06 ; Ô Lowry, 07 ; Porter, 08 ; Ô Pattan, 07 ; Smith, 18 ; White, 07;

(folio 30 verso). Barrony of Rapho : Eng & Scotts, 1825 ; Irish, 1330 ; 3155, total.

(folio 31) **KILL McCRENAN BARRONY**

Parishes	Townelands	Number of People	Tituladoes Names	Eng & Scotts	Irish
Mevagh		07	John Fleeming Esqᵣ	04	03
	Ravross ½ qr	06	Dauid Stewart gent	02	04
	Aghlettiff ½ qr	06		04	02
	Tullogh ½ qr	08		00	08
	Diuelan qr	10			10
	Iland bray ½ qr	10			10

Parrishes	Townelands	Number of People	Tituladoes Names	Eng & Scotts	Irish
	Magherisosky qr	14	Gabriell Ultagh gent		14
	Largireagh ½ qr	05			05
	Magheribeg qr	08			08
	Downyne ½ qr	08			08
	Derricassan ½ qr	07			07
	Magheriarny	07			07
	Downdowan ½ qr	06			06
	Mellimore qr	12			12
	Drin ½ qr	05	William Dutton Esqʳ	05	
	Glencragh ½ qr	07			07
(folio 32)	Glenmanagh ½ qr	09			09
	Glengrillgrenny ½ qr	11			11
	Magherimagangan ½ qr	06		04	02
	Wmlagh ½ qr	07		05	02
	Bellioghogan qr	08			08
	Finwer and Downemore qr	06	Michaell Harry Esqʳ and Dauid Cather gent	05	01
	Glenree qr	08			08
	Aghyocor and Creery qr	07			07
	Mevagh Qr	04			04
Conwall	Letterkenny town	73	Alexᵈʳ Cuningham, James Cuningham, his sonn, Alexᵈʳ Ewing, Levinis Sempill, Gillbert MᶜIlwee, Peter Colhoune, William Jamisone, Walter Buchanan, Will Andersone and John Colhoune gents	49	24
(folio 33) Conwell	Lisnanane qr	04		02	02
	Carrongboggagh qr	05		03	02
	Gortleg qr	06	John Baxter gent	06	—
	Bellireehan qr	05		—	05
	Glencarre qr	05		03	02
	Salarigrean ½ qr	01		—	01
	Bellimacoole qr	08		06	02
	Towell Mᶜ Adegan qr	09		05	04
	Tulligey	07		06	01
	Dowen qr	06		—	06
	Boharill ½ qr	04		02	02
	Gortnevarne qr	10		07	03
	Elistran & Drumny qr & ½ qr	12		—	12
	Cowleboy qr	10		06	04
(folio 34) Conwell	Killilasty ½ qr	02			02
	Drunwire qr	08			08

Parrishes	Townelands	Number of People	Tituladoes Names	Eng & Scotts	Irish
	Treyntagh qr	06			06
	Clunkeny qr	08			08
	Carrick qr	05			05
	Killogs qr	04			04
	Drumcaveny ½ qr	03			03
	Polland 6 Belliboes	07			07
	Stakernagh 6 Belliboes	05			05
	Carbry qr	05			05
	Killicling qr	05			05
	Glanleragh qr	09			09
	Derrira qr	12			12
	Cragth qr	11			11
	Killpeag ½ qr	05			05
(*folio* 35) Conwall	Drumaine ½ qr	05		—	05
Killigarvan	Ramullan qr	23		17	06
	Kreeury qr	27		19	08
	Glencross qr	06		06	—
	Balligalachan qr	12		04	08
	Killigarvan qr	13		09	04
	Drumhalagh qr	12		—	12
	Ochterlin qr	10	Captn John Kinlar Esqr	01	09
	Creeve qr	15			15
Auchnish	Castleshenachan ½ qr	07	Thomas Groves gent	04	03
	Castleshanaghan qr	09		09	—
	Ardrumond qr	07		07	—
	Kerucastle qr	07	Dauid Dunbare Esqr	06	01
	Killdonnell qr	06		05	01
(*folio* 36)	Kerugall qr	06		02	04
	Glenlary qr	08		04	04
	Gortvaigh qr	09		03	06
	Auchnish qr l^d	10		—	10
	Ramelton qr	26	Thomas Stewart Esqr	19	07
	Croghan qr	08	James Delapp gent	05	03
	Bellilinmore	13		06	07
	Ray Qr	16	Major Knox Esqr	04	12
	Drumherife ½ qr	08		04	04
	Glenala ½ qr	07		—	07
	Achengady ½ qr	05		05	—
Gartan	Killmore qr	04	James Knox gent	04	—
	Losset qr	06			06
	Kerrowtrans qr	05			05
	Kerrowreagh	07			07
(*folio* 37).	Dirreveagh qr	06			06
	Glendon qr	12			12
	BalliM^cQuin & Corbara	08			08
	Kerrowport qr	08			08
Clauderhurka	Mullro qr	24			24

Parrishes	Townelands	Number of People	Tituladoes Names	Eng & Scotts	Irish
	Largibreake qr	16			16
	Cloghernagh qr	14			14
	Kestimore ½ qr	08			08
	Sessiogh qr	19			19
	Breghimoy ½ qr	13			13
	Ye other ½ qr of Breghimoy	15			15
	Pollegill qr	15			15
	Cleggin qr	15			15
(*folio* 38) Clan-dehurka	Muntermilan	16		—	16
	Massinass qr	10		06	04
	Floonmass qr	20		—	20
	Ballimore ½ qr	08	Alex^dr Stewart Esqr	06	02
	Ye other ½ of Ballimore	09		—	09
	Dircastle qr	10			10
	Arries qr	16		04	12
	Rinisligo qr	10		08	02
	Magherierorty	10		02	08
	Creeslagh qr	09		02	07
	Killoghcaran qr	11			11
	Drinmacarrow ½ qr	06			06
	Garverry	07			07
	Skeagh qr	11			11
	Kill McKallow qr	04		02	02
(*folio* 39) Clon-dehurka	Clandehurka qr	17		—	17
	Portainlian qr	13		—	13
	Castledoe qr & ½ qr	56		45	11
Ray	Belliconnell & Bellimass	32	Olphert Wybrune gent	01	31
	Irrervoymore qr	18			18
	Irrervoybeg ½ qr	03			03
	Ray qr	06	Ambross Ô Crean gent		06
	Mogora qr	14			14
	Carranfanan qr	13	Michaell Harrisone gent	01	12
Tolloghobegly	Tolloghobegly qr	15			15
	Cassill ½ qr	09			09
	Downeley 3 Belliboes	09			09
	Downley 1 Belliboe	03			03
(*folio* 40) Tulloghobegly	Carrowblagh qr	12			12
	Ardies qr	21			21
	Glassiagh two Belliboes	06			06
	Killulty qr	22			22
	Killdrum qr	22			22
	Ilanderry	03			03
	Baltinee ½ qr	05			05
Tully	Fergory qr & Clonkin	07	John Braedin & John his sonn gents	04	03
	Ardehely qr	07			**07**

Parrishes	Townelands	Number of People	Tituladoes Names	Eng & Scotts	Irish
	Cratullagh qr	07			07
	Saginduffe qr	06		04	02
	Karrowkill & Rany	09	Robert Algoe gent	08	01
	Gorrelly ½ qr	07		05	02
	Duntrumen ½ qr	05			05
(folio 41)	Downmore	04		02	02
	Gartevain ½ qr	06			06
	Gortwerne ½ qr	04			04
	Tirehoming qr	04		04	—
	Clagin qr	06		04	02
	Garrowgolly ½ qr	03		—	03
	Rubbeshim third	02			02
	Drumbarne qr	06		02	04
	Senagham qr	06		04	02
	Belligay qr & ye third of Dromloghen	03		03	—
	Gondidally qr	07		07	—
	2 thirds of Dromcloghan	06			06
	Belliconally qr	07		07	—
	Bellikeny qr	07		04	03
	Carne seauen Belliboes	06		04	02
(folio 42)	Clowny qr	09		06	03
	Glenmore qr	04		04	—
	Glenbeg qr	04		04	—
	Drumonaghan qr	05		03	02
	Claragh ½ qr	03		—	03
	Tully qr	06	John Cunynghame gent	04	02
	Tully beg ½ qr	06		04	02
	two thirds of Muls qr	04		04	—
	Ye other third of Monell	03		—	03
	Clouny more qr	06		06	—
	Belliare tenn Belliboes	07		03	04
	½ qr of Belliare Gleabe	03			03
	Mullogh upp two belliboes	03			03
(folio 43) Agha-nunshen	Bogay Qr	12	James Erskin Esqr & Henry Wray gent	11	01
	Cornigill qr	07		07	—
	Magherienan qr	11		11	—
	Aghanunshen qr	06		04	02
	Listames qr	10		04	06
	Bellimolly & Eighters 15 Belliboes	12		06	06
Clandevadocke	Runducharick & Mimagh 2 qrs	08	John Campbell gent	08	—
	Bellihirin 2 qrs	10	Collin Campell gent	04	06
	Bellihurke qr	07		04	03
	Leatemore qr	06			06

Parishes	Townelands	Number of People	Tituladoes Names	Eng & Scotts	Irish
	Glinsh qr	05			05
	Daughmore qr	07			07
	Gortnatra ½ qr	05			05
(*folio* 44) Clandavadocke	Leddan qr & ye ½ of Gortnatra	06	Donell McSwyne gent	02	04
	Tullinadale, Kindruin and Fallanes third	06	Thomas Wallace gent	03	03
	Bellirusky 5 thirds	07		—	07
	Bellihirnan & ye ½ qr of Fanwally	11		04	07
	Tone qr & ye ½ of Fanulty	06			06
	Magheridramen qr	06			06
	Magheridramen Culladerry	05			05
	Arrihirin more qr	09			09
	Arrihirminabeo qr	06			06
	Dowagh beg ½ qr	05			05
	Dowagh Knopin ½ qr	06			06
	Glen Fanet qr	07			07
(*folio* 45) Clandevadocke	Corry third	06		—	06
	Bellimagarghy qr	08		02	06
	Ye upper ½ qr of Bellimagh	06		—	06
	Ye lower ½ of Bellimagh	06		—	06
	Aghindrinagh qr	07		01	06
	Magherihober qr	06	Patrick Campbell gent	05	01
	Carnekeile qr	04			04
	Croghan qr & Tanugh Bellibo	06	Henry Paton gent	02	04
	Moras qr	07		07	—
	Rossnakill qr & Taunagh Bellibo	07		07	
	Cloghfyne ½ qr	06			06
	Cranrus and Corin bellagh ½ qr	08	Robert Campbell gent	08	
	BelliMcKnocker and ye ½ qr of Drumeny	06	Dauid Mortimer gent	02	04
(*folio* 46) Clandevadock	Knockbrack ½ qr	05			05
	Magheriardan qr	07			07
	Carrin qr	04			04
	Belliclan McCallin qr	08			08
	Drumfadd qr	06			06
	Bellimagowne Lower ½ qr	06		04	02
	Ye upper ½ qr of Bellimagown	04		04	
	Carlane ½ qr	06			06
	ye other ½ qr of Carlane	06			06

Parishes	Townelands	Number of People	Tituladoes Names	Eng & Scotts	Irish
	Gortnotrogh qr	11			11
	Bumptin qr	05		02	03
	Carrow garow qr	08			08
	Largibreak qr	10			10
(folio 47) Kill	Gortmocallmore quarter	06		—	06
McCrennan	Kill McCrenan two quarters	15	William Vas gent	09	06
	Gort McCall begg qr	10		08	02
	Court qr	05		03	02
	Portline qr	06		06	—
	Bellscanlan and Ardahy three ½ qrs	13			13
	Tawny qr	06			06
	Ray qr	06		02	04
	Carowniconona qr	08			08
	Carownysall ½ qr	04			04
	Gouldrum ½ qr	06			06
	Fane ½ qr	05			05
	Barnes ½ qr	06			06
	Craford qr	06	Adam McClelland gent	03	03
	Carnnany qr	09		05	04
	Wood qr	10			10
(folio 48) Kill	Cowle ½ qr	06			06
McCrenan	Gollan qr	08			08
	Drumobedan ½ qr	06			06
	Letter qr	06			06
	Soker qr	07		02	05
	Stradonnell qr	08			08
	Carcarow qr	08			08
	Curren and Bren letter 2 qrs	14			14
	Clankelly ½ qr	04			04
	Tirargus ½ qr	04			04
	Stragrady ½ qr	06			06
	Belligennan ½ qr	04			04
	Laggan hury qr	09			09
	Edanbarnan 6 Belliboes	09			09
	Edancarran two Belliboes	04			04
	Castlegay qr	06		06	—
	Ballyheran qr	05		05	—

Principall Irish Names.

McAward, 06 ; Ô Boyle, 15 ; Ô Brillaghan, 08 ; Ô Canan, 09 ; Ô Cullan (6) & Cullin (8), 14 ; Ô Colhoune (7), Ô Colloune (4), 11 ; Ô Donnell, 27 ; Ô Diver, 07 ; Ô Divet, 10 ; Ô Dowy, 06 ; Ô Dogherty, 34 ; Ô Fary (8), Ô Ferry (5), 13 ; Ô Friell, 07 ; Ô Ferill, 09 ; McFaden, 07 ; Ô Gollogher, 52 ; McGinnelly, 21 ; McGee, 11 ; Ô Harkan, 05 ; McIlbreedy, 13 ; McIlchole, 11 ; McIlbreed, 05 ; McKerran, 07 ; O Mulvog, 05 ; McPadin, 13 ; McSwyne, 39 ; Ô Sheall, 06 ; Wltagh, 06.

(folio 48 verso). Barrony of KillMcCrennan : Eng & Scotts, 605 ; Irish, 1551 ; 2156, totall.

Parrishes	Townelands	Number of People	Tituladoes Names	Eng & Scotts	Irish
Movill	Cluncro qr	050	George Cary Esqr & George Cary his sonn gent	22	28
	Balliarchus qr	27		11	16
	Drung qr	37		14	23
	Ruskey ½ qr	17		06	11
	Creehenan qr	16		06	10
	Cabrie qr	23		17	06
	Carrow Keele qr	29		06	23
	Trumatee 2 trines	16		—	16
	Tullinynavan qr	31		08	23
	Clare qr	27		—	27
	Bellirattan qr	21		08	13
	Bellilan qr	33		—	33
	Carrownowff qr	14		12	02
	Cully qr	17		04	13
	Tiriruan qr	06		—	06
	Cluncro qr	05		01	04
	Bellinanely qr	21		07	14
	Collidue qr	26	Robert Fleming gent	02	24
(*folio* 50)	Bradna glin qr	29			29
	Carngarow qr	04			04
	Bellibrack qr	08		02	06
	Drumavire qr	16			16
	Eleven Belliboes of Green Castle	25	Henry Newtowne & James Newtowne gents	06	19
	Seaven Belliboes of Fardrum & Bellichan	23			23
	6 Belliboes of Bellim^{c}Carto'	23			23
	Crehue qr	08	Hugh Boy Ô Dogherty & Shane O Dogherty his sonn gentlemen		08
	Carrowtressan qr	10			10
	Shroove qr	22			22
	Glanigoveny qr	12			12
	Meaneletterbaille qr	16	Brian Og McGlaghlin gent		16
	Masagleen qr	16	Donnell McGlaghlin gent		16
	Bellimagaraghy	08			08
	Carrowmanagh Two Triens	10			10
	Bellibrin one Trine	10			10
(*folio* 51)	Leckemy one trine	12			12
Desertegine	Lislin qr	15			15
	Monelubane qr	14			14
	Leaon qr	11			11

Parishes	Townelands	Number of People	Tituladoes Names	Eng & Scotts	Irish
	Monagh qr	12			12
	Ledereg qr	15	Rory Ô Doghertye gent		15
	Toneduffe qr	72			72
	Gortiaragan qr	14	Phelomy Ô Dogherty gent		14
Culdaffe.	Bellicarran qr	29	George Butler, George & William his sonns Esqrs		29
	Glangadd qr	40			40
	Bellichan qr	31	Owen McDevet gent		31
	Bellichan ½ qr	08			08
	Culldaffe Gleab	10			10
	Teir McCrowra qr	18			18
(folio 52) Culldaff.	Bellicarry qr	20			20
	BelliMcGargie	09			09
	Drimbilly third	04			04
	Cashell qr	21	John Nighton gent	02	19
	Carrowmore qr	22	Donell McAllin gent		22
	one third of Waskill	05			05
	Two thirds of Waskill	12			12
	Augaglasan ½ qr	15			15
	3 Belliboes of Worth	06			06
	Fiue Belliboes of Worth	05			05
	Leitrim two Belliboes	08			08
	Cregcorr qr	06			06
	Culldaffe qr	02			02
	Munidaragh qr	23			23
(folio 53) Culdaff.	Dromlie third	02			02
	Dristernan 2 thirds	08			08
	Aughatibert qr	11			11
	Kindroit third	05			05
Templemore	Castle Hill Qr	15		07	08
	Bellimony Qr	14		00	14
	Drumgone Qr	14		02	12
	Molevee Qr	11		01	10
	Bohillin more qr	17		13	04
	Bohillin beg qr	12		07	05
	Tullet qr	10		03	07
	Castle Cooke qr	11		04	07
	Moneff qr	11			11
	Carne mady qr	18			18
	Skeog Qr	16	Bassill Brooke gent	06	10
(folio 54)	Lisfarien ½ qr	07		07	00
	Carrowreagh qr	12		09	03
	Bonamany qr	21		10	11
	Castle qr in ye Insh	09		04	05
	Moriss qr wth 3 bell' Glacke	13	Andrew Stewart gent	08	05
	Grange qr	12	George Swetenham gent	02	10

Parrishes	Townelands	Number of People	Tituladoes Names	Eng & Scotts	Irish
	Belli McKilly qr	14		03	11
	Carrickiny qr	11		07	04
	Bellet qr	08		05	03
	Bellinacarnagh qr	09	Archibald **Stewart** gent	05	04
	Cullin ½ qr	05		05	—
	Belldramven qr	18		08	10
	Magh beg qr	15		04	11
	Dundrien qr	11		08	03
	Drumsegart qr	13		07	06
(*folio* 55)	Soppag qr	07		07	—
	Dereven qr	13		04	09
	Muffe qr	16		08	08
	Cragg qr	21		17	04
	Gortcormagan	09		—	09
	Carne Moyle qr	20		02	18
	Eskehen qr	15		—	15
	Drimskellan qr	21	William **Backer** Senir gent	09	12
	Ardmore qr	19		04	15
	Ardcrum qr	17		05	12
	Trimata 3 parts	12		—	12
	Ture qr	12	Jerimiah **Griffith** & William **Griffith** gents	02	10
	Aught qr	22			22
	Mintallaghes	09			09
Clonca	Ardmalin qr	12	Cahair Ô **Dogherty** gent		12
(*folio* 56)	Brigh qr	21	Thomas Ô **Dogherty** gent		21
	Belligorman ½ qr	10			10
	Conlurt qr	14	Rory Ô **Dogherty** gent		14
	Kenagh ½ qr & ye upper ¼ qr of Cullurt	19			19
	Bellikenny qr	15			15
	Kenogh ½ qr	05			05
	Tully one trien	05	Edmond Moder Mc**Laughlin** & Hugh his sonn gentlemen		05
	Bellidogh qr, ½ qr of Granny, Carrowbate one Belliboe, Drunge one Trian	16			16
	Killin one trian	10			10
	Belliknawsie qr	21			21
	Ballagh qr	06			06
(*folio* 57)	Ballileaghan qr	15			15
	Norire qr	13			13
	Carrowmore qr	18			18
	Drum Carbitt qr	21			21

Parrishes	Townelands	Number of People	Tituladoes Names	Eng & Scotts	Irish
	Belliraghan ½ qr	16			16
	Templemore qr	14			14
	Drumovill qr	17			17
	Carrow Temple qr	18			18
	Laracrill qr	16			16
	Dunrosse qr	21			21
	Dunogranan one Trien	12			12
	Dristreman one Trien	04			04
	Menedaragh ⅓ of a qr	10	Donnell Ballagh McGlaghlin gent		10
	Grellagh 2 qrs	06			06
(folio 58) Donagh.	Carrowmore qr	33	Gerauld ô Doghertye & Cahair Ô Doghertye gents		33
	Carrow bleagh qr	20			20
	Cashell qr	17			17
	Belliblosky qr	14	Robert Cary gent	02	12
	Carrowreagh qr	20			20
	Magheridrumon qr & ⅓ of Tullenary	30			30
	Carrick coddan	28		03	25
	Donogh 3 qrs	55			55
	Altosheen Qr	11			11
	Carne ½ qr	05			05
	Carne ½ qr	05			05
	Glassalte qr	21			21
	Clun McKee qr	14			14
Clanmany	Lenan Qr	15	Mr Arthur Lening & Donnell ô Dogherty gents	01	14
	Irish Managh qr	09			09
(folio 59) Clonmany.	Lettr Qr	14			14
	Downaff qr	13			13
	Rosmach qr	17	Conn Ô Dogherty gent		17
	Crossconnell qr	10			10
	Downally	31			31
	Cleagh qr	06			06
	Rusky Qr	15			15
	Strad Qr	25			25
	Altically qr	13			13
	Monecloyne qr	18			18
	Ardagh ½ qr	06			06
	Annagh qr	14			14
	Downchgullen ½ qr	08			08
	Tullinebcatilly	06			06
	Belli McMurty qr	10			10
	Rasedg qr	10			10
	Belli Mcguihen qr	09			09

Parrishes	Townelands	Number of People	Tituladoes Names	Eng & Scotts	Irish
	Figart qr	08			08
	Carrick braky qr	06			06
	Lagacury qr	13			13
	Carrowreagh qr	10			10
(*folio* 60)Fahen	Luddan	17		—	17
	Gransaghan, Trelegie	24		14	10
	Bellimacary	09		—	09
	Ardaramon	28		10	18
	Tonner ô Gee	10			10
	Tullyduck	28		02	26
	Aghalay	17			17
	Bellimagan	14			14
	Sledru	20			20
	Bellinary	11		02	09
	Monywory	21	Comon Ô Sheale & Japhry his sonn gents	—	21
	Tuliarvill	31	Henry Vaughan Esqr	03	28
	Duntacsone	16			16
	Connogh	17			17
	Fefenagh	13			13
	Muff	14			14
	Bellinee	22		04	18
(*folio* 61)	Tully wony	32		12	20
	Garvery	17		06	11
	Kill McKillvenny	18		14	04
	Carnashinagh	15		05	10
	Tubban Caragh	25		12	13
	Crislaghmore	09		08	01
	Crislaghkiell	03		—	03
	Fahen Castle	11		02	09
	Litter	29		08	21
	Carrenshewo	26	Phillip Hill gent	04	22
	Carrow Mulling	26		05	21
	Lishfanan	13		09	04

Principall Irish Names

Ô Barr, 07 ; Ô Brillaghan, 23 ; Ô Boyle, 08 ; Ô Cally, 22 ; McCallin 15, ô Callane & O Cullane 12, 27 ; Ô Conagill, 09 ; Ô Carran 16, Ô Currin 03, 19 ; O Carny, 10 ; McCollgan, 30 ; McConway, 06 ; Ô Callaghan, 08 ; Ô Doghertye, 203 ; Ô Doy, 06 ; Ô Deuer, 08 ; McDevet, 27 ; Ô Donell, 20 ; ô Dermond, 35 ; O Deveny, 09 ; O Farran, 14 ; McGlaghlin, 76 ; Ô Granny, 06 ; McGillneske, 08 ; Ô Gollogher, 12 ; Ô Herrall, 08 ; Ô Hegerty, 23 ; Ô Harkan, 21 ; Ô Knawsie, 09 ; Ô Kelly, 11 ; McKay, 06 ; Ô Lunshaghan, 22 ; McLaughlin, 63 ; Ô Luog, 09 ; Ô Mrisane, 07 ; Ô Moran, 06 ; Ô Mulloy, 07 ; McMurray, 08 ; O Muney, 08 ; Porter, 11 ; Ô Quigley, 25 ; Ô Rodan, 13 ; Ô Sheale, 08 ; Ô Towlan, 14 ; McVagh, 06.

(*folio* 61 *verso*). Barrony of Enishowen : Eng & Scotts, 453 ; Irish, 2678 ; 3131 totall.

Barronies	Pages	Eng & Scotts	Irish	Totall
Tirhugh	07	244	1474	1718
Boylagh & Banagh	16	285	1556	1841
Rapho	30	1825	1330	3155
Kill MᶜCrenan	48	0605	1551	2156
Enishowen	61	0453	2678	3131
		3412	8589	12001

E

COUNTY OF DOWNE 15183

(*folio* 1).   **BARONY OF LECALE**
County of Down

Parrishes	Townlands	Number of people	Tituladoes Names	English & Scotts	Irish
Downe	Downe towne	308	Earl of Ardglasse Oliver Cromewell John Napper	146	162
	Ballentogher	23		10	13
	Rinybane	33		2	31
	Walthestowne	44	Patrick Russell gent	2	42
	Coyle & Lishboye	27		14	13
	Mille quarter of Coyle	06		1	5
	Saule and Ballysugagh	29	James Hamilton gent	12	17
	Saule	05		04	01
	Ballysugagh	14		03	11
	Carrow boye	12		00	12
	Ballywoodans	16		00	16
	Ballynegarricke	11		00	11
	Ballynary	22		00	22
	Whitehills	08		00	08
	Shroull	06		04	02
	Clogher	14	Thomas Lindsay gent	10	04
	Ballywarrett	14		07	07
	Russells quarter	3		00	03
	Ballydugan	11		02	09
	The Mille quarter	17		08	09
	Dromyvillans	11	Cromwell West gent	04	07
	Cranlcys quarter	14		06	08
	Woodgremgies	31		00	31
	Magerlagan	07		04	03
	Cargaghnobregg	13		07	06
(*folio* 2)	Tollomury	04		00	04
	Ballyrolly	17		09	08
	Ballybeell	17		06	11
	Lishnemale	14		06	08
	Tobercorran	27		05	22
	Ballydonnell	15		00	15
	Ballygalbegg	13		02	11
	Quarter Colmack	17		03	04
	Ballydonety	09		05	04
	Grange Came	10		07	03
	Ballyshrow	17		02	15
	Ballymotts and Saule Quarter }	15		05	10
	Boncastles	06		02	04
	Ballybaines	15		05	10
Ballee	Loghmoney	11		00	11
	The quarter of Quaronekea	12		00	12
	Ballywalter	09		00	09

Parishes	Townelands	Number of people	Tituladoes Names	English & Scotts	Irish
	Stockestowne	07		00	07
	Slewnegridell West	01		00	01
	Deline	04		02	02
	Inglish Ballynagrosse	06		00	06
	Irish Ballynagrasse	04		01	03
	Ballyalton	08		04	04
	Ballyrenan	04		04	00
	Ballytruston·	09		06	03
(folio 3)	Ballymaire	04		01	03
	Ballycrutell	06		05	01
	Ballysalagh	12		08	04
	Upper Ballybranagh	11		05	06
	Lower Ballybranagh	10		00	10
	Ballee and Spitell quarter	13		06	07
	Kilderes Crowe	08		05	03
	Jordans Crowe	11		06	05
	Ballyhosett	19	John Woole gent	14	05
	Ballyclende	11		07	04
Bright	Bright	25	William Hamilton Esqr	19	06
	Ballydewganes	06		03	03
	Castle Creen	05		04	01
	Ballygallagh	10		00	10
	Iland Bane	02		00	02
	Erganagh	12		08	04
	Kiltaghlines	14		09	05
	of the same	07		07	00
	Comanston	25		05	20
	Ballygellem	10		05	05
	Callegalaghan	14		00	14
	Kilbreed	14		08	06
	Ballyligge	26		06	20
	Grangewals	23		06	17
(folio 4).	Ballyvigges	31		14	17
Killmeagan	Dondrome	72	Michaell Smith gent	38	34
	Murleagh	30		23	07
	Water Eske	26		09	17
	Monealean	28		12	16
	Machery Sall	09		05	04
	Moneycaragh	19		12	07
	Ballybannen	24		17	07
	Ballylagh	16		00	16
	Achlishnefin	11		00	11
Rathmullen &	Rathmullen	41		27	14
Tireleagh	Killogh	21		11	10
	Ballywaston	30		11	19
	Ballylucas	09		07	02

Parrishes	Townelands	Number of People	Tituladoes Names	English & Scotts	Irish
	Bally Plunt	21		11	10
	Ballyneiboe	11		03	08
	St Johnstowne	32		03	29
Toreleagh	Clarmaghrog	13		05	08
	Glinell	20		11	09
	Lower Iland Mucke	17		08	09
	Upper Iland Mucke	16		02	14
	Carricknabb	08		08	00
	Ballykinloe	24	John Gibbones gent	10	14
	Croyle ye quarter	18		00	18
	Janestowne	12		08	04
	Lishnemoghan	15		05	10
(folio 5) Dunsford	Sheepland begg and New-towne }	28	James Lesley	14	14
	Sheepland mor	15		07	08
	Ballyidocks	17		07	10
	Dunsford	30	Daniell Gowne alius Smith	02	28
	Kingvoid	13		06	07
	Ballyhornan	21		02	19
	Ardtoall	21		04	17
Ardglass	Ardglass & Ringfad	34		17	17
	Collemgrange	09		04	05
	Bishop Court	38		31	07
	Corbally	11		08	03
	Ballybegg	10		10	00
Killcliff	Killcliff towne	45	Nicholas Fitzsymons and Henry his sonn gent	017	28
	Ruffyglass	18		10	08
	Carrowe Shake & Carrowe Annis }	11		02	09
	Tollofoill West	02		00	02
	Tollofoallan	06		00	06
(folio 6) Killclife.	Lisban towne	08		06	02
	Rosse	18		13	05
Inch	Inch	13		04	09
	Ballyrenan	31		06	25
	Downelly	15		07	08
	Ballynecreigg	14		000	14
	Maghramoney	11		02	09
	Fane broage	06		04	02
	Bally McNegally	31		29	02
	Terniman	10		08	02
	Anacloye	54		08	46
Ballyculter	Castleward	44	Barnard Ward & Nicholas Ward Esqrs Cromwell Ward gent	18	26
	Carrowcassie	08		00	08

Parrishes	Townelands	Number of people	Tituladoes Names	English & Scotts	Irish
	Andlystowne	21		02	19
	Strangfoard towne	96	Andrew Grahine	51	45
			George Hull gent		
	Ballyculter	31		22	09
	Tolloneratty	08		00	08
	Ferry Quarter	24		19	05
	Kilardes	10		02	08
(folio 7)	Carricke McCavell	07		—	07
	Ballylinagh	08		—	08
	Castlemoghan	08		—	08
	Carrowtagart	05		—	05
	Ballenstleane	05		—	05
	Loghkillands	12		—	12
	Rachalpe	37		10	27
	Carrowcanland	06		02	04

Principall Irish Names

McBruine, 07 ; McBryde, 07 ; McCrerie, 07 ; Coun, 06 ; Ô Killin, 07 ; Ô Kelly, 12 ; Ô Kenan, 06 ; Ô Murphy, 11 ; Moore, 08 ; McNuske, 08 ; McMullan & McMullen, 11 ; McMellen, 07 ; McTagart, 06.

(folio 7 verso).   County of Downe : Barrony of Lecale : Eng & Scotts, 1071 ; Irish, 1631 ; 2702 Tottall.

(folio 8)   **UPPER IVEAGH BARONY**

Parrishes	Townelands	Number of People	Tituladoes Names	English & Scotts	Irish
Kilbrony	Rosse Trevor	53	Marcus Treuor Esqr John Raynalds Henry Ovinton gent	28	25
	Kilbrony quarter	11		00	11
	Dromreagh ½ towne	08		00	08
	Levollyreagh ½ towne	09		02	07
	Knockebearagh	21		00	21
	Ballyagholly	11			11
	Tanyvea quarter	06			06
	Ballytue	11			11
	Ballylurgan	23			23
	Ballyedmond	17			17

Parrishes	Townelands	Number of People	Tituladoes Names	English & Scotts	Irish
	Ballyran	15		02	13
	Ballynedan	05	Barnard Ward Esqʳ	03	02
Aghedericke	Clonknaverly	26		08	18
	Loghbrickland	40		23	17
	Grynan	07		05	02
	Lishratyerny	14		04	10
	Seuchall	24		02	22
	Ballytagart	18		10	08
	Lishnegunall	12		08	04
	Loghdein	17	John Smith gent	07	10
(folio 9).	Shesagh of Bally Mᶜ Eratiemore	08		00	08
	Dromsalagh	30		18	12
	Creevy	08		07	01
	Glaskerbegg	06		06	00
	Ballygone	15		13	02
	Colnecavell	17		07	10
	Legganamig	24		11	13
	Lishnegade	11		03	08
	Druma Chara	21		16	05
	Cassgem	17		03	14
	Ballisciagh	20		00	20
	Glasskemore	18		00	18
	Derry Drumucke	23		13	10
	Drumore Breege	13		09	04
Mlaghern	Tollymore	09	Barnard Magines Coun Magines gent	03	06
	Carne Cawell	04		02	02
	Couroge qr	06		02	04
	Caruagh qr	04		03	01
	Ballyginie	13		11	02
	Drennige	08		06	02
	Ballyloghlin	12		04	08
(folio 10)	Murlagh ½ towne	02		00	02
Dromgagh	Rathryland	53	Arthur Lesquire gent	18	35
	Dromgagh halfe towne and Carwey ½ towne	16		00	16
	Ballykeell	07			07
	Lurgancughan	12			12
	Drumgungagh	12			12
	Dromlogh	10			10
	Barnemyne	18			18
	Tollyquillin	08			08
Pᵗ of Sea patrick	Tollyconagh	17		09	08
	Ballyivy	18		08	10
	Lisnaree	13		11	02

Parrishes	Townelands	Number of People	Tituladoes Names	English & Scotts	Irish
	Duchory	10		08	02
	Tollyear	17		16	01
	Ballyvally	22		20	02
	Ballydowne	16		—	16
	Edenderie	16		03	13
Clonallan	Carrychnossan	18			18
	Croune	09			09
	Cullyn	14			14
	Bawne	09			09
(folio 11)	Edentrymby	14		00	14
	Ballaghnecoglly	10			10
	Moyo	08			08
	Aghnegone	02			02
	Corroggs	06			06
	Aghnemibragll	13		02	11
	Downagee	02			02
	Milbowne	02			02
	Narowe Water	09		06	03
	Dromor	04		02	02
	Ring McIlroy	03		—	03
	Conallan	18		04	14
	Ballyrosse	02		—	02
	Clotefleyes	04			04
	Ballydeslan	26		02	24
Donoghmore	Berecra	07	John Cambbell gent	02	05
	Tollemor	24		02	22
	Killeshanan	20		02	18
	Ringban	10		05	05
	Ringe Imulbeece	10		—	10
	Anaghban	17		03	14
	Lurgmare	19		01	18
	The three halfe townes of Knockenenarney, Bally-logh, and Corgery	24		—	24
(folio 12)	The halfe towne of Cargaghy	12		—	12
Donaghmore.	Ballyblegg	04		—	04
	The other three halfe townes of Knockenen-arney Ballylogh and Corgery	17		02	15
	Ballyharnetty begg	11			11
	Ballyharnaty mor	12	Edmond McBryan gent	00	12
	Mune More ½ towne	16		00	16
	Moneydrombrist	05		00	05
	Aghy Cauin ½ Towne	10		00	10
	Tolleny Cross	04		04	—

Parrishes	Townelands	Number of People	Tituladoes Names	English & Scotts	Irish
	Tollenemary	07		03	04
	Cargaghban	08		00	08
Anaghclon	Lisard brin	19		00	19
	Tollymtenvolly	18		00	18
	The Glabe	07		00	07
	A qr of Lisneslickan	07		00	07
	A qr of Lisneslickan & a qr of Ballynefearn	10		00	10
	The halfe towne of Ballyfearn	09		00	09
	A qr of Ballynegross	03		00	03
(folio 13)	Ballynefoy and a qr of Ballynegross	27		05	22
	Ballynany	13		04	09
	Cleay	14		08	06
	Cappy	16		04	12
	Dereylogh a qr	08		05	03
	one qr of Ballynegross	03		03	—
Garvaghy	Killconemie	15		—	15
	Corbalye	10		—	10
	Shamerad	08		03	05
	Balilye	10		04	06
	Rilleni	09		07	02
	Knocknegaren	08		—	08
	Castlevenan	11		04	07
	Ballilie	11		02	09
	Tolliorie	08			08
Dromaragh	Dery	16		00	16
	Crosgue	16		02	14
	Greanee	18		—	18
	Meybrick	06		00	06
	Finsh	14		—	14
(folio 14)	Moneyneban	14			14
	Drimborredon	14			14
	Brosgar	04			04
	Finish	02			02
Drumballrony	Bolly McGillbrick Upper halfe towne	12			12
	Lower halfe of ye said towne	12			12
	Edingarye	12			12
	Imdelld	04			04
	Grullagh ½ towne	06			06
	Ballynemognagh	16			16
	Kneknapen	06			06
	Lisnenaghough	06			06
	See Fyn	06			06
	Terekelly	08		04	04

Parrishes	Townelands	Number of People	Tituladoes Names	English & Scotts	Irish
	Tyrfergus ½ towne	06			06
	Dromak ½ towne	04			04
	Drumgrernagh	04			04
	Drumrenagh	08			08
	Mourgarr	04			04
	Lisenusky	12			12
(folio 15)	Adnughanshegagh	12			12
	Tyrgerye	10			10
	Lackin	10			10
	Castletowne	18			18
Killingan	Collerkill	13	Phellomy McGinis Phellomy McCartan gent	00	13
	Castell Wellden	02			02
	Dandrer	06			06
	Glenvaragorahan	16			16
	Sloueneskid	16			16
	Bally Will	18			18
Clonduffe	Upper Iveagh	04			04
	Ballygorgarmore	16			16
	Ballgorgonbegg	06		02	04
	Lissomcy Vigan	08			08
	Drumneskaugh	06			06
	Cauan halfe towne	04			04
	Mulaghmore	10			10
	Cloyomoicke	12			12
(folio 16)	Carrocallin	10			10
	Lettenin	14			14
	Ballymagheree	10			10
	Ballyaghyan	10			10
	Ballynanagh	10			10
	Goward	10			10
	Slangg	08			08
	Ballykell ½ towne	10			10
	Ballymill ½ towne	04			04
	Leamgske ½ towne	08			08
	Ballycosson	04			04
	Illen Moyle	13			13
	Cabragh	02			02
	Kinkeele ½ towne	01			01
	Ballinegapke	03			03
	Brumbanife ½ towne	08			08
	Lood ½ towne	02		00	02
Kilcowe	Newcastle	28	Tobias Norrice Esqr	10	18
	Ballyaghbegg	12			12
	Tollybranegan	18			18
(folio 17)	Ballyheffery	05		03	02

Parishes	Townelands	Number of People	Tituladoes Names	English & Scotts	Irish
	Ballynteir	04			04
	Burnbane	07			07
	Monyscalpe	10			10
	Dromeny	14			14
	Slevnelargay	05			05
	Fosenybane	12			12
	Feofenyagh	14			14
	Lettullan	10			10
	Tollyrie	04			04
	Ardough	08			08
	Ballynemoney	10			10
	Tollensue	16			16
	Aughcullan	18			18
	Burnireagh	07			07
Drumgollan	Slanebally West	04			04
	Pt McRian	12			12
	Nunis lane	16			16
	Donoghdonell	10			10
	Dicovott	20			20
(folio 18)	Dromlee	06		02	04
	Ballymagnily	12			12
	Bakeaderry	16			16
	Lettrym	19		02	17
	Legananu	16			16
	Denra	08			08
	Benry	04			04
	Clavahery	08		000	08
	Bally McGrean	08			08
	Dorry Nelle	16			16
	Ballyward	10			10
	Magermay	08			08
	Pt Droman	07			07
	Garvegary	08			08
	Cloghskelta	16			16
Kilemeagn	Clarkill	13	Phellomy Magines, Phellomy McCartan gents		13
	Clonnarirhin	16			16
	Castle Wellden and Dundren	08			08
	Slevmuskre	16			16
	Ballyvollwill	18		02	16

Principall Irish Names [and] their Number.

Boy & McIleboy, 20 ; McBryne, 12 ; McBrin, 10 ; McConnell, 09 ; McIlepatricke, 10 ; Ô Kelly, 17 ; Ô Fegan, 24 ; Ô Heire, 21 ; McMurphy, 31 ; O Morgan, 23

(folio 18 verso). Barrony of Upper Iveagh : Eng & Scotts, 448 ; Irish, 2149 ; 2597 Totall.

(*folio* 19)　　　　　　**LOWER EVAGH BARONY**

Parishes	Townelands	Number of People	Tituladoes Names	Eng & Scotts	Irish
Macherally	Corbett	13		09	04
	Tulliraine	17		13	04
	Drumoth	13		10	03
	Kilmacrane	15		13	02
	Macherally	19		12	07
	Ballycrosse	28		19	09
	Mullatornegah	19		09	10
	Tollehennan	22		06	16
	Ballymony	12		07	05
	Tannathmore	14		09	05
Drummore	Cowgillaghe	25		09	16
	Ilanderry	18	Allex[r] Waddell gent	16	02
	Greenog	13		06	07
	Ballynoris	19	Francis Hall gent	12	07
	Grenan	18		10	08
	Drumskea	23	John Verner gent	17	06
	Edenardry	09		07	02
	Quilly	28	Cristopher Marshall gent	19	09
	Ballyvicnekelly	08		04	04
	Larganbane	18		04	14
(*folio* 20)	Ballysallogh	13		11	02
	Dromiller	14		12	02
	Tollandony	25		16	09
	Keele	29		—	29
	Skoage	30		10	20
	Kinmmallin	18		02	16
	Bally M[c]Cormack	18		06	12
	Vickonmollagh	30		21	09
	Drumnaknockan	16		00	16
	Growle	08		04	04
	Drumlagh	32		13	19
	Edentrillicke	30		03	27
	Magherabegg	33		28	05
	Listillicarran	20		17	03
	Drumbrony	29		18	11
	Drumna Iadowan	10		06	04
	Tuliglish	12		08	04
	Eord	10		06	04
	E Anigon	19		14	05
(*folio* 21)	Kiliscolban	17		08	09
	Lisnereward	04		00	04
	Ballyanny	18		07	11
	Tolle M[c]Anratty Kilfarran	06		04	02
	Derry maccomuskie	10		08	02

Parrishes	Townelands	Number of People	Tituladoes Names	Eng & Scotts	Irish
	Drummore towne	178		130	48
Part of Sea Patrick	halfe towne of Ballyloch	13	Daniell Monro	04	09
	½ Lisnefuthy	12		00	12
	½ towne of Ballykeil	14		10	04
	½ towne of Drummunagally	08		06	02
	½ towne Kilpick	05		04	01
	qr of B : Mony	05		04	01
	Drumnovoddry	08	John Boide	06	02
	BallyKelly	08		02	06
Pt of Gorvachy	Gorvacky towne	16		12	04
(folio 22) Pt of Garvachy	Tilleniske	19		12	07
	Enoch	21		04	17
	Carnitt	14		00	14
	Phenanny	17		00	17
Donnaclony	Ballygonigon	07		06	01
	Donnaclony	06		04	02
	Megonan	10		06	04
	Ballybrogatt	11		02	09
	Anaghnoan	23	William Warren Esqr	09	14
	Mahernac	14		04	10
	Tolleherim	13		04	09
	Corkrery	14		00	14
	Lurgan teaury	10		06	04
	Edengreny	13		10	03
Tollelistes	Drumaran	14		00	14
	Laughan	16	Captn Barett Esqr	00	16
	Cooselaraderke	12		08	04
	Knocknajor	14		04	10
	B : McNally	12		00	12
(folio 23)	The towne of Drumnost Ancly and Menalon	12		08	04
	Ballygarricke	14		00	14
	B : Dugan	14		00	14
	B : Lerry	13		04	09
	Keerinan	18		00	18
	Mullebracke	12		00	12
	Clare	18		00	18
Pt of Drumarah	Drumindony	17	John Vance	11	06
	Mullagdrinn	14			14
	Derry	16			16
	Begny	06			06
	Moydalgan	12		10	02
	Drumara	04			04
	Artanagh	16			16
	Aghnoskea	02		02	—
	Levallyleagh	06		04	02

Parishes	Townelands	Number of People	Tituladoes Names	Eng & Scotts	Irish
(folio 24). Crumlin Arrabilt and Pt of Blaris	Hils borrow town	165	Arthur Hill Esqr, William and Conway his sonns, Arthur Parsons gent.	96	69
	Ballykeele	058		25	33
	Camereagh	027		10	17
	Carnebane	50		42	08
	Dromotehough	12		10	02
	Drumnesantly	19		12	07
	Crumlin	08		04	04
	Aghodonvarran	14		10	04
	Clogher	09		02	07
	Mease	28	Carroll Bolton Esqr	07	·21
	Agalresk	12		03	09
	Magheregary	09	John Costell gent	07	02
	Culcovy	33		26	07
	Aughnecloghe qarter	12		10	02
	Edentilly Colloghe	06		00	06
(folio 25)	Ballybrin	09		05	04
	Maghereconlish	24		04	20
	Ballylintagh	24		02	22
	Cobragh	23		11	12
	Ballyhumtagh	21		08	13
	Tullynore	08		00	08
	Bauernon	23		14	09
	Maghredorun	16	James Renolls gent	10	06
	Ballyuorphy	22		13	09
	Caperkendorrogh	20		04	16
	Bally Murphy	28		12	16
	Corgigreg	16		06	10
	Bally Keellogherne	13		13	00
	Aghnelecke	19		15	04
	Cargicrevy	26		08	18
	Tunghblane	13		06	07
	Lessodine	16		13	03
	Corcreeny	27		09	18
(folio 26) Magharalin	Ballymagin	18	William Burly Theophilus Burly gents	12	06
	Ballynagmeane	19		09	10
	Tullenggrosse	16		10	06
	Drumlin	26		16	10
	Ballymackinteare	20		18	02
	Tony Eranny	02		00	02
	Tollyamcor	04		00	04
	Ballykeele	09		06	03

Parrishes	Townelands	Number of People	Tituladoes Names	Eng & Scotts	Irish
	Lisnegsewer	08		04	04
	Ballylynny	18	James Manson gent	08	10
	Drummunteferry	04		02	02
	Bally McKanollan	08		04	04
	Corcossocke	06		02	04
	Drommor	04	Andrew Wyke gent	04	00
	Ballackanall	02		02	00
	Derry Drummust	04		04	—
	Balumigan	04		04	—
	Clare	05		05	—
	Magharalinch	09	Symond Bateman	09	—
	Aukyluscaly	04		04	—
	Gurtingmony	06		02	04
(folio 27).	The Sessiagh of Kilmonyoge	10		00	10
	Drumbane	10		02	08
	Moyrough	36		32	04
	Feany	04		04	00
	Denmore	06		00	06
	Drumbree	13		03	10
	Reaske	09		08	01
	Baliknoske	22		08	14
	Lurgan Veele	18		07	11
	Ballygowone	18		14	04
	Bottyre	08		00	08
	Tollyard	08		00	08
	Bally McBrenan	17		00	17
	Bally McGarchan	15		03	12
	Geagrelagh and Traghlomny }	10		00	10

Principall Irish Names [and] Their Number

McBrinn, 20 ; McCollogh, 12 ; McCormack, 10 ; Ô Kelly, 08 ; Martin, 08 ; Magee, 11 ; O Neale, 09 ; Ô Lawry, 15.

(folio 27 verso). Barrony of Lower Eveagh : Eng & Scotts, 1352 ; Irish, 1381 ; 2733 total.

(folio 28). **THE BARRONY OF YE NEWRY**

Parrishes	Townelands	Number of People	Tituladoes Names	Eng[1]	Irish
Newry	The towne of Newry	174	Nicholas Bagnall, Richard Rice, Wm Hatfield, and Robert Fenwicke Esqrs, Ensigne Hyatt gent.	66	108

[1] *Eng & Scotts*, folio 31.

F

Parrishes	Townelands	Number of People	Tituladoes Names	Eng	Irish
Newry Lord-ship	Ballincrag and Crine	13	Michaell Garvy gent	02	11
	Corcrighagh & Lizard boy	20		02	18
	Lisduffe ½ towne & Carrogboy ½ towne	10		02	08
	Cloghanrawer halfe towne	08		00	08
	Cormine ½ towne	03		03	00
	Damolly ½ towne	08		00	08
	Damolly ½ towne Cloghanrawer ½ towne	14			14
	Toremore	18			18
	Loghorne	13		05	08
	Kanachan two townes	23			23
(folio 29)	Upper Ballyholand	14		—	14
	Grenan and Donlegh ½ towne	20			20
	Lisduffe ½ towne & Cormyn ½ towne	10		05	05
	Drumcassellowen	10		02	08
	Cornehough	02			02
	Ceo : Bane	07			07
	Derrillackoghe and the ½ towne called Tempell-gurine	11			11
	Benaghe	13			13
	Dizarts	14			14
	Finer and halfe Finer	12			12
	Croreiaghe	08			08
	Savellmore	12			12
	Lower Ballyholand	12			12
	Savellbegg Sheepstowne & ½ Sheepstowne	21			21
(folio 30)	Grange	06			06
	Sheine	16			16
	Castleneggan	10			10
	Ardarra & ½ Finer & halfe Corrobegg	19			19
	The ½ of Ryan	06			06
	Edenmore	15			15
Kilkeele	Glasdromine	10		10	—
	Mullurtan ½ and ye other ½ waste	08	Savadge Leech gent	06	02
	Analong qr	04		—	04
	Monydoroghmore & Monydoroghbegg one towne and quarter	15	Arthur Monipenny gent	11	04
	Bally McMartin	06		03	03

Parrishes	Townelands	Number of People	Tituladoes Names	Eng	Irish
(folio 31)	Bally M^creamore waste	—			
	Bally McVeabegg alius Brecknogh	19		06	13
	Carricknagh waste	—			
	Ballykeele and Derrye	17		04	13
	Maghreagh	12		—	12
	Kilkeele alius Magre Murphy	14		12	02
	Driogg ½ towne and ye other halfe waste	04		03	01
	Granfield	06	Richard Huston gent	03	03
	Grange ½ towne	12		—	12
	Lorgencomy ½ towne	05		05	—
	Downaiull halfe	06		02	04
	Ballyardle	06		—	06
	Ballymagart ½	20		04	16
	Downnan halfe	09		02	07
	Ballymageogh	06			06
	Ballyrogan	08			08
	Aghnahury	13			13
	Ballyrann	15			15
	Lisnashallagh & ½ Drominmor	15			15
(folio 32).	Drominmor halfe towne	12			12
	Banagh and Lisnagarran	22			22
	Corcrichagh and Drominleen	15			15
	Ballygowen	04			04
	Bally McTeerfy	20		02	18
	Lettrim	08			08
	Moyadd and Anticall	12			12
	Aghrim	03			03
	Tullyfrane	06		03	03
	Clown Lochan	13			13
	Tinduffe	06			06
	Lisnecree	16	Patricke Modder O Howen gent		16
	Aghyall	12		03	09
	Dromcroe	12			12
	Aghnatooby	08			08
	Green Castle	10			10

Principall Irish Names [and] Their Number
Ô Doran, 20 ; Ô Feggan, 08 ; Garvy, 07 ; McIlroy, 08 ; Ô Quinne, 10 ; Slowan, 08 ; White, 08,

(folio 32 verso). Barrony of Newry : Eng & Scotts, 166 ; Irish, 785 ; 0951 total.

     KINALERTY¹ AND DUFFRANE BARRONIES

Parrishes	Townelands	Number of People	Tituladoes Names	Eng & Scotts	Irish
Killeleagh	Killeleagh Castle	34	Richᵈ Loughbee, James Hamiltone, Mʳ Sᵗ John, James Hamilton.	24	10
	Killeleagh Corporacōn	175	John Robinsone, Archballd Hamiltone, Dauid Williamsone, Dauid Pollock.	126	49
	Moulloch	16		09	07
	Clantoch	39		14	25
	B : Trim	13		10	03
	Ardigon	33		24	09
	Talleviry	53		39	14
	B : MᶜCarren	05		05	—
	Randuffrane	08		02	06
	B : MᶜCrambell	02		02	—
	Ralph Cunigham	12		10	02
	Mamore	05		03	02
	Toytowne	07		06	01
	Kirkland	04		04	—
	Lissduffe	04		02	02
(*folio* 34)	Clay	13		11	02
	Tack Mill	05		03	02
	B : Allgan	26		18	08
	B : Willin	23		18	05
	Dereboy	33		10	23
	B : Gossgoran	16		08	08
	Tollechine	22	James Waile Esqʳ	17	05
	Lissnagh	22	Allexʳ Sloane gent	11	11
	Tolle MᶜKnowes	08		08	00
Killinchy	B : Bregoch	13	Capt. James Moore Esqʳ	03	10
	Kinchady and Tollimore	09		07	02
	Carrireagh	04		02	02
	B : Marran	09	John Stewart gent	06	03
	Killinikin	07	Allexʳ Stewart gent	04	03
	B : Dorne	10		04	06
	Carick Rusky	06		06	—
	Killinchy	22		07	15
(*folio* 35).	Ballow	21		14	07
	B : MᶜChassan	17		04	13
	B : MᶜCrelly	30		24	06
	Carrigullen	09		09	00
Dromkayes	Dromkey towne	18	Archbald Wardlaw gent	06	12

¹ *Kinallerty*, folio 36.

Parrishes	Townelands	Number of People	Tituladoes Names	Eng & Scotts	Irish
	Clareoch	11	James Meslvyne gent	05	06
	Knockstickan	14		10	04
	Cloch 3 qrs	02		02	00
	Dunardeley	08		05	03
	Clochrom	12		07	05
	Dromin q[r]	12		08	04
	Dunturk	08		04	04
	Dromrod	09	Richard Sauadge gent	03	06
	Screbltowne	10		00	10
	Drumononach	08		00	08
Lochon Iland	Murvagh, Cloagagh	12	Edmond Sauage gent	06	06
(*folio* 36)	Macherluan	12		00	12
	Feconatt	17		02	15
	Reshoner	09	John Sauage gent	07	02
	Farnfade	20	John Rainalds gent	14	06
	Drumgollan	12		04	08
	Lochin Iland	24		17	07
	Chrecyduffe	09		07	02
	Nachan ½ towne	07		06	01
	Nachan	13		08	05
	Artaunack	18		12	06
	Caunndarach	25		06	19
	Drumetikelly	19	Edward Mulckamp Esq[r]	11	08
	Lochneboy	20		12	08
	Castlenavan	18		09	09
	Dunenew	19	Rich[d] Meriman gent	10	09
Magher-haulett Maghere-drole P[t] of Kilmore& P[t] of Anagh-ellt (*folio* 37).	Crivitenasse	14		00	14
	Glassdrumon	12		00	12
	B : Coin	07		05	02
	Magherknock	11		09	02
	Ballymaran-Itragh	13		00	13
	Dunbegg	14		00	14
	Clontinegollin	15		00	15
	Burin	10		00	10
	Bally kein Itragh	22		00	22
	Drumgouly	14		00	14
	B Maran Itragh	12		—	12
	Maghertempane	12		—	12
	Macheredroll	04		—	04
	B : Machaghanotragh	13		—	13
	Dremnesse	13		—	13
	Dromsnaite	08		—	08
	Edendarue	09		—	09

Parrishes	Townelands	Number of People	Tituladoes Names	Eng & Scotts	Irish
(*folio* 38)	Dowmore	12		04	08
	Genvise	04		—	04
	Drinkiragh	12		—	12
	Drummachlist	10	James Whatope gent	08	02
	Rademane	15	Walter Johnstoune gent	03	12
	Tullenetree	13		02	11
	Drumtitonor	07		05	02
	In the other pt Drumtitoner }	12		00	12
	Raleagh ½ towne	12		00	12
	In ye other ½ town	07		00	07
	Comber	12		00	12
	B : Laan Itragh	26		02	24
	Ballynehinch	05		00	05
	Bally McGlane Itragh	05		00	05

Principall Irish Names [and] Their Number

     Ô Kelly, 011 ; Smith, 14 ; McKee, 12 ; Ô Rogan, 011 ; O Bern, 012 ; Ô Lowry, 009.

(*folio* 38 *verso*).   Barrony of Kinalertye & Duffrane : Eng & Scotts, 693 ; Irish, 763 ; 1456 total.

(*folio* 39).   **CASTELLREAGH BARRONY**

Parrishes	Townelands	Number of People	Tituladoes Names	Eng & Scotts	Irish
Cumber	Cumber	116	Robert Monro & James Montgomerre Esqrs, John Griffith gent.	67	49
	Cullentragh	005		02	03
	Ballycattock	28	Hugh Sauage gent	17	11
	Carnesure	08		02	06
	Ballynuoll	14		04	10
	Maghrescows	29		14	15
	Ballygowne	07		05	02
	Mullagh	13		02	11
	Bally Keele	18		10	08
	Lisleene	10		02	08

Parrishes	Townelands	Number of People	Tituladoes Names	Eng & Scotts	Irish
	Monerar	14		02	12
	Granshagh	08		07	01
	Ballebeane	10	Alexdr McDowell gent	03	07
	Tullyhubbert	18		10	08
	Crosnecrevy	14		08	06
	ClonteneKelly	12		12	00
(folio 40).	Ballycrelly	26	Hugh Dundasse gent	15	11
	Edenslat	02		02	00
	Tullegarvin	15	John Keish gent	08	07
	Ballyhenry	04		04	00
	Ballyalton	02		02	—
	Killinether	03		03	—
	Castlenevary	04		04	—
	Ballyriccart	18		12	06
	Rincrevy	19		11	08
	Cherryvally	05		00	05
	Ballyhenry lessor	11		06	05
	Ballyhennod	19		11	08
	Ballymaghiff	32		07	25.
	Ballystockart	16		09	07
	Ballyloghan	08	Fergus Kennedy gent	06	02
	BallyKillighan	11		06	05
	Ballymalady	07	Hugh Montgomery gent	07	00
	Ballralboghly	16		10	06
(folio 41). Comber	BallyWilliam	05		04	01
	Ballyrush	19		14	05
	Ballymageaghan	04		04	00
Dindonnall	Castlebegg	06		06	00
	Ballyrennie	12		04	08
	B: Lishbredan	14	John Ross gent	07	07
	Ballycren	05		02	03
	Carri Reagh	11		09	02
	Dunlady	06		04	02
	Ballyregane	09		07	02
	B: McSca	15		09	06
	Church qr	09		06	03
	B: Bine	07		05	02
	B: Russell	08		06	02
Hollywood.	Ballyrobert	09		06	03
	Craigitade	09		09	—
(folio 42). Holywood	Ballydauy	08		08	00
	Ballygrony	07		05	02
	B: Cultra	09		04	05
	B: Managh	09		02	07
	B: Keell	05		03	02
	Holywood	20		18	02

Parishes	Townelands	Number of People	Tituladoes Names	Eng & Scotts	Irish
	Knocknegony	11		11	00
	B : Meaghan	09		03	06
	Strone towne	15		13	02
	Killine	05		05	—
	B : Cloghan	08		05	03
	B : haghamore	08		03	05
	Holywood	15		08	07
Blaris and Bredaghs	daghs	06		02	04
	Lishnor	06		05	01
	Dunreach	20		18	02
	Large Moore	10		07	03
	Mr Brinfs Parke	02		02	00
(folio 43).	Lishnetronk	12		08	04
	B : Millton	09	Joseph Strond Esqr	06	03
	Plantasion	07		05	02
	Tollencross	04		04	00
	Lisnagarvy Brige	12		06	06
	Ballydullaghan	10		08	02
	Ballylenoghan	11		11	00
	Knockbraken	04		02	02
	Bredagh	13		08	05
	Galivally	07		04	03
	BallyMcCarrett	23		16	07
	Ballenefay	18		14	04
	Bally McConnoghy	19	William Beares gent	13	06
Knock	Tolletarnan	10		08	02
	Portgrib	02		02	—
	Ballyneherick	11		07	04
	Castlereagh	13		11	02
	Knock	03		03	00
(folio 44).	Castellreagh	06		00	06
	Carnymuck	07		04	03
	Bellycloghan	04		02	02
	Lisnesharragh	03		02	01
	Craigogh	04		000	04
	Bronell	20		06	14
	Lisnebrene	19		15	04
	Keshboy	06		06	00
Tollenekill & Kilmood	Ballymartine	15		04	11
	Lishbane	17		08	09
	Ringneill	18		14	04
	Tolinkill	08		06	02
	Ballyglohorne	12	James Dalyell & James Dalyell gent	08	04
	Castelspie	12		09	03
	B : Draine	09		05	04

Parishes	Townelands	Number of People	Tituladoes Names	Eng & Scotts	Irish
(folio 45). Kilmood	Ballybondon	10		06	04
	Tolleneghee	11		08	03
	Lisbarnagh	12		10	02
	Ballygraffan	06		04	02
	Kilmood	04		02	02
	B : Monestrogh	09		07	02
	Drumhirk	12		02	10
Drumbo	Dunkilmick ½ towne	08		08	00
	Tolle Arde	10		10	00
	Drombo	32		28	04
	Clantinically	13		09	04
	Caroduff	12		11	01
	Knockbreckan	14		08	06
	Millagh	19		13	06
	Ligecory	04		00	04
	Cargicray	10		08	02
	Drynan	06		02	04
(folio 46).	Criuihckavrick	10		10	—
	Crossane	07		05	02
	Lisnestrean	18		15	03
	Clogher	07	James McGill gent	05	02
	Lismad	07		07	—
	Bellelessan and Edenderry	20	George Montgomerie Esqr	10	10
	Ballecarne	14		08	06
	Leverog	05		04	01
	B : Nebrean	29		23	06
	Carngarran	20		16	04
	Ballynegarrick	08		05	03
	Carr	09		—	09
	Ballycrwan	16		14	02
	Ballybound Elvaly	12		06	06
	B : nehatty and B : dullochan	06		04	02
	Drumcra	04		04	—
(folio 47). Killileagh and Killinsy	Kaffry	20		04	16
	Aghin Darragh	12		04	08
	Drumen or the Lower Aghindarragh	12		06	06
	Carrickmanan	20	Ever Oge Ô Nealle gent	02	18
	Drumreagh	20		12	08
	Ballygowne	07		07	—
	Ravarra	12		—	12
	Killinchy in ye Woods	14	Wm Sauadge gent	08	06
	Ballycloghan	17		15	02
	Ravarra	19		—	19

Parishes	Townelands	Number of People	Tituladoes Names	Eng & Scotts	Irish
Kilmore	Kilmore	64		39	25
	Crevysarwonan	28		04	24
	Clowneglare	28	James Hamilton gent	18	10
	Barnemaghery	20		06	14
	Listooder	12		03	09
	Crevyarigan	13		03	10
	Drumgiven	20	Dauid Kenedy	14	06
(folio 48)	Cahard	22		02	20
	Ballydeine	18	Wm Fairley Esqr	18	—
Tawnaghnym	Tawnaghmore	12		01	11
	Laggegewan	13	Neale Roe Ô Kelly gent	01	12
	Crevyloghgarr	10			10
	Lisswyne	11	Coline Maxwell Esqr Gawen Hammilton gent.	04	07
	BallyMcCassin	18			18
	Lisbane	12		04	08
	Killenny	02			02
	Carrickmaddorog	20		20	
	Bresagh	12		08	04
	Tollevastikinagh	13		09	04
	BallyMcAraveny	11		08	03
	Arsdalgan	05		04	01
	Lessans	13		10	03
	Glasdroman	19		04	15
	Drumma cunnell	09		08	01
	Ballyagherty	12		08	04
(folio 49).	Carricknesessanagh	11			11
	Ballyburckan	06		02	04
	Lisdownan	15		03	12
	Lisnesallagh	02		02	
	Killimeure	06		02	04
	Oghley	12		08	04
	Bumlig	13		13	
	Carricknewagh	15		12	03
Drumbegg Pt	Ballyaghlisk	09		07	02
	Dunkinmuck	20		18	02
	Drumbegg	13	James Maxwell gent.	11	02
	Tulligoune	08		06	02
	Ballyskeogh	18		14	04

Principall Irish Names [and] their Number

McDowell, 15 ; Browne, 15 ; McCome, 08 ; McCormick, 07 ; Ô Kelly, 15 ; McKie, 10 ; McMurry & O Murry, 20 ; McMullen, 15 ; Martine, 14 ; Smith, 11.

(folio 49 verso). Barony of Castlereagh : Eng & Scotts, 1363 ; Irish 950 ; 2313 to :

ARDS BARRONY

Parrishes	Townelands	Number of People	Tituladoes Names	Eng & Scotts	Irish
Ballyphillip	Tollemally	14		10	04
	Tollebeerd	10		04	06
	Bally McNemee	11		09	02
	Ballyruslelly	07		05	02
	Ballygarvagan	13		09	04
	Ballyblack	04		01	03
	Ardkighan	02			02
	Derry	04		02	02
	Ballycam	06		05	01
	Porteferry	75	Archibald Moore gent	50	25
Slanes	Slanes	07		01	06
	Lismore and Ballyspuige	11	Robert Ross gent	07	04
	Dowy	09		07	02
	Loghduff and Ardmennan	18		13	05
	Cloghy and Tolletramman	13		08	05
(*folio* 51)	Drumarden	06		02	04
	Balladam	03		03	
Arkin	Arkin	20	John Sauadge Esqr James Sauadge gent	11	09
	Dunevally	10		02	08
	Ballyward	10		09	01
	Lisbane	12		11	01
	Cookstowne	10			10
	Ballycranbeg	06		02	04
	Ballygelagh	19			19
	Ballycranmore	17		02	15
	Kirkestown	20	Hugh Coghran Esqr	08	12
Ardwhin	Ardwhin	32	Robert Ward Esqr	17	15
	Johnstown	07		01	06
	Ballywhyte	11			11
	Thomastown	07		05	02
	Ballyriddelly	06		06	
	Ballewallen	16		06	10
(*folio* 52). Ard-ivhin	Ballywaddan	03		02	01
	Ballyhenry	08		01	07
	Ballyherly	10		03	07
	Bally McNish	06		06	
	Ballymurphy	28	Hugh Sauadge Esqr	14	14
Woltar	Ballyquintine & Tollecarnan }	22	Robert Maxwell & Coline Maxwell his sonn gents	12	10
	Ballyidock	12		04	08
	Towsilly	12		07	05
	Taragh	09		06	03
	Kintagh and Carrowdressagh	04			04

Parrishes	Townelands	Number of People	Tituladoes Names	Eng & Scotts	Irish
	Ballymartire	017		02	15
	Ballefeneragh	08		05	03
	Ballegalgat	15	Patrick Sauadge and Patr : Sauadge gents	05	10
	Ballyculler	14			14
(folio 53) Bally-	Karny	26		17	09
trustan	Craigirodon	06		06	
	Ballyward	13			13
	Ballefoner	17		14	03
	Ballytrustan	05		04	01
	Ballynicoll	08		06	02
	Granagh	11			11
	Corrog	03			03
	Ballyvranegan	08		02	06
Ballyhalber	Roddins	08	Hugh Wallace gent	06	02
	Ballyhamline	11		08	03
	Ballyhilbert	22		12	10
	Ballyesbrough	19		10	09
	Glassery	15		12	03
	Ballygraffan	06		04	02
	Rowbane	09	William Hamilton gent	09	
	Ballyfrenge	09		04	05
(folio 54) Balle-	Portevoggy	11	Thomas Boyde gent	09	02
halbert.	Rowreagh	15		05	10
	Kirkcubbine	09		08	01
	Granshagh	13		11	02
	Fisher Quarter	10		05	05
Ballywalter	Ballyuggin	10		07	03
	Ballyackwart	07		05	02
	Ballyobikin	17	James Wallace gent	13	04
	Carrowboysty	04		04	
	Whyte church	18	John Moore gent	13	05
	Ballyferis	21		10	11
	Dunover	14		05	09
	Ganivy	16		12	04
	BallyMᶜGowne	10	John Hamilton gent	10	
	Ballylimp	09		08	01
	Inshargy and Ballymullen	21	John Bailly Esqʳ Alexʳ Bailly gent	11	10
(folio 55).	Ballygargan & Nuns quarter	18	Edward Bailly gent	14	04
	Ballywalter Village	68		48	20
Gray Abbay	Gray Abbay	29	William Montgomery Esqʳ	11	18
	Ilands	05		03	02
	Ballymurcock	09	George Austine gent	07	02
	Ballyboly	08		04	04
	Ballygrangee	08		02	06

Parishes	Townelands	Number of People	Tituladoes Names	Eng & Scotts	Irish
	Ballyblack	07		05	02
	Tullecavone	06	John Peacock gent	06	
	Ballybryan	09		06	03
	Killivolgan	06		04	02
	Blackabbay	10	Wm Buchanan gent	08	02
	Callinaterny	03		03	
	Templecrone	11		06	05
	Ballycastle	16		11	05
(folio 56). Don-nadee	Donnadee Village	146	Roger Crymble, Robert Brearely, Henry Cresans, Archibald Mullen & William Browne gents	83	63
	Ballyanwy	05		04	01
	Kilbright	07		06	01
	Ballydonnan	06		05	01
	Ballymoney	08		04	04
	Slewanstowne	05		03	02
	Carnyhill	04		02	02
	Ballyraer	09		08	01
	Drumfad	16	John Cunynghame gent	11	05
	Ballyhosker	11		08	03
	Ballyrolly	08		06	02
	Ballyfrenis	10		07	03
	Granshagh	02		02	
	Iland Hill	08		02	06
	Ballybutle	12		10	02
(folio 57).	Bally McShrew	20		14	06
	Ballycoplan	31	Thomss Nevin gent	19	12
	Killaghy	28		15	13
	Ballycreboy	19	Patrick Montgomery and Hugh Montgomery gent	12	07
	Ballyvester	18		13	05
	Carrowreagh	05		04	01
	Balleno	05			05
	Ballenocross	10		10	
	Ballywilliam	09	Patrick Moore gent	03	06
Bangor	Bangor Corporačon	97		62	35
	Portavo, Ballyfutherly, and Coplan Iles	} 38	Robert Ross and James Ross gent	22	16
	Ballymanan Itragh	16		12	04
	Ballow	10	George Ross gent	06	04
(folio 58).	Orlog and Carrowreagh	05		05	
	Ballymanan utragh	18		14	04
	Bally McConnell	09		02	07
	Ballymanan utragh	07		02	05
	Bally McCormick	07		04	03

Parishes	Townelands	Number of People	Tituladoes Names	Eng & Scotts	Irish
	Ballyholme	o8		o4	o4
	Groomsport	33		25	o8
	Ballycroghan	o5		o2	o3
	Bally Neghee	10		o9	o1
	Ballygreny	17		o7	10
	Granshagh	22		13	o9
	Ballerie	o7		o4	o3
	Ballow next Bangor	11		o6	o5
	Rafgill	18	William Barclay gent	o6	12
(*folio* 59).	Lisbane	o9		o9	
	Ballyvernon	23		11	12
	Killaire and Carnelea	15		13	o2
	Ballylidie	10		o5	o5
	Ballysallagh minor	17	Robert Cunynghame gent	o12	o5
	Ballygilbert	o7		o6	o1
	Ballysallagh Major	24		16	o8
	Ballemullen	36	William Crawfurd gent	27	o9
	Ballygrott and Bally—skelly	20	Robert Hamilton gent.	14	60
Newtowne	Newtowne Corporacōn	146	Hugh Lord Viscount Mont-gomery oᵗ Ards, Hugh Shaw, Hugh Mont-gomery, Charles Camp-bell & William Shaw gents.	87	o59
	Cunyngburne	o7		o4	o3
	Ballyblack	13		o6	o7
(*folio* 60).	Ballywitticock	10	John Shaw Esqʳ	o5	o5
	Ballerea	10		o4	o6
	Drumchay	o9	Thomas Nevin gent	o3	o6
	Loghrescow	14		o8	o6
	Movilla	15	William Montgomery gent	10	o5
	Ballyhonney	o5	Hugh McGill gent	o4	o1
	Drumhirk	15		11	o4
	Couleck	o8		o8	
	Milecross alius Tomegardy	15		10	o5
	Ballyhary	o4		o4	
	Ballybairnes	o2		o1	o1
	Ballyskeagh	13	John Moneypeany and Hugh Montgomery gent	11	o2
	Ballymoney	o4		o4	
	Carrickgantelan	o6		o4	o2
	Killerny	o4	Dauid Kennedy gent	o4	
(*folio* 61).	Ballyvogan	o4		o2	o2
	Gnonegranes	10		o6	o4

Parrishes	Townelands	Number of People	Tituladoes Names	Eng & Scotts	Irish
	Ballymagwoghan	03		01	02
	Ballequillan	08		06	02
	Scrabo	07		04	03

Principall Irish Names [and] Their Number

McCormick, 14 ; Clerk, 18 ; McConnell, 09 ; Browne, 19 ; Carr & Ô Carr, 07 ; McDowell, 15 ; Ô Gilmor, 11 ; Gowne, 07 ; McKie, 14 ; McMullen, 15 ; Moore, 23 ; Martine, 08,

(*folio* 61 *verso*).   Barrony of Ards : Eng & Scotts, 1447 ; Irish, 984 ; 2431 total.

Barronies	Pages	Eng & Scotts	Irish	Totall of Eng Scotts & Irish
Lecale	7	1071	1631	2702
Upper Iveagh	18	0448	2149	2597
Lower Iveagh	27	1352	1381	2733
Newry	32	0166	0785	0951
Kinalerty & Duffrane	38	0693	0763	1456
Castlereagh	49	1363	0950	2313
Ards	61	1447	0984	2431
		6540	8643	15183

FARMANAGH COUNTY 7102

(folio 1), Parishes	Places	Numb's of Persons	Tituladoes Names	English	Irish
1. Clownish	Killey	10	Con MᶜColl MᶜMahon gent	—	10
	Lissenegosenagh	11		—	11
	Corredulagh	8		—	8
	Lis MᶜShelly	10		—	10
	Clothnemore	9	Manus MᶜColleny gentle	—	9
	Annaghmartin	4		—	4
	Mullenehunshevan	6			6
	Mullaghglas	17		—	17
	Tatetemore	29		—	29
	Annaghgolgen	11		o	11
	Anaghsamer	11		—	11
	Lissaraly	15		—	15
	Corroney	19		—	19
	Colesona	21		o	21
	Crebagh	5		—	5
	Drumacrulin	12		—	12
	Tategormegan	8		—	8
	Knockballymore	14	William Davis Esqʳ Morgan Davis gent	9	5
(folio 2)	Claghmoran	9	James Gabbryth Esqʳ	3	6
	Tulley	12		—	12
	Tulley	9		—	9
	Mullimane	4		—	4
	Mullinemane	2		—	2
	Cortrasna	16		—	16
	Mullabane	8		—	8
	Uttan	4	James Wagh gent Walter Wagh	4	—
	Killinferduff	8		—	8
	Gorten	7			7
	Lisluskea	4		2	2
	Drumcrue	3	Thomas Bradshaw gent	3	—
	Starlostran	10			10
	Dredcree	4			4
	Galnolly	4			4
	Clufiell	13			13
	Maharanelick	7		5	2
	Gartmor	4	John Slack gentle	3	1
	Maherinillicke	3		3	—
	Drumhorne	5			5
	Drumbonish	5			5
	Shannock	8	Gilbert Eckles gent		8
(folio 3).	Anninare	12	William Ross gentle Robert Ross gent	5	7
	Anaghcullan	5	Walter Stewart Esqʳ	5	—
	Anaghard	3		—	3

Parishes	Places	Numb's of Persons	Tituladoes Names	English	Irish
	Trimconoris	8		4	4
	Anaghilly	4		2	2
	Ittircashil	2		2	—
	Poyteighagh	4			4
	Gartondarragh	7	James Arnot Esqʳ		7
	Crommagh	10		2	8
	Gortenure	4			4
	Ashdrumsie	19			19
	Mullagheloghey	4			4
	Aghencule	30			30
	Cornegeye	8			8
	Killurit	3			3
	Drumbellin	4			4
	Tenetigarmon	6	Robert Stokes gent	4	2
	Agharnsky	5	James Arnolt gent	3	2
	Rosbrick	10			10
(folio 4).	Dorringe	6			6
	Clonegany	5			5
	Clontenorin	36	John Wishert Esqʳ Francis Hambleton gentle	5	31
	Batedicesmore	12	Jobe Atkins gent Thomas Maines gent	5	7
	Lisnemaltate	4		4	—
	Ballirunore	4			4
	Killinelifbane	12			12
	Tategirr	8			8
2. Aghaveigh	— —	3	Hugh Rowley Esqʳ	1	2
	Letra	13	John Fulton gent	5	8
	Carrowkeel	20			20
	Rathnetely	22		2	20
	Mullagh	29			29
	Aghnecloye	17	Hugh McMahon gent		17
	Aghevey	12			12
	Owenbryden	11			11
	Cavannegarvan	10	Cormack Kittagh gent		10
	Skeoge	6			6
	Lissobvan	6		2	4
(folio 5).	Drumhee	4		2	2
	Drumstegarren	20		6	14
	Tomislan	7		3	4
	Aghnecloygh	7		2	5
	Tirivry	6		6	00
	Boyaghall	12		9	3
	Kilkirin	8		3	5
	Killaittry	2		—	2
	Rathkeylan	17	John Nesbitt gent	5	12

Parishes	Places	Numb's of Persons	Tituladoes Names	English	Irish
	Fodragh	14		—	14
	Skeagh	13		—	13
	Drumloan	15		4	11
	Corran	10		2	8
	Gartynedy	8		—	8
	Drumbada	13		8	5
	Tatetrasna	12		—	12
	Clyhunagh	14		—	14
	Knockargan	03		3	00
	Coolgohill	11		—	11
	Coolrakilly	18		—	18
	Ardunlion	10		2	8
(folio 6)	Lissebane	18			18
	Billy	4			4
	Tullanegoon	11			11
	Gortin	10			10
	Tullarcagh	12	Art McMahon gent		12
3. Devonish	Koltos	8	Sr John Hume Kt & Bart Dame Mary Hume Dowager	3	5
	Ballyhose	6		2	4
	Drumbory	24	Henry Langford gent	3	21
	Fanagrain	4	William Hambleton gent	4	00
	Tully	2		2	00
	Robian	6			6
	Belligonnagh	5			5
	Magherynagenan	7		7	
	Belligonnaght	6		6	
	Mulligillyholme	6		6	
	Ardvenehan	7	Robert Luderdale gentle	3	4
	Brocho	5		5	0
(folio 7)	Agherim	6	Patrick Hume gent	4	2
	Dromra	5		4	1
	Magherynagiran	4	Robert Weire gent John Herbert Herbert gent	4	—
	Mullagilliholme	4		4	—
	Tullikelher	6	David Johnston gent John Johnston gent	3	3
	Crott	7		7	—
	Lissoneire	2		—	2
	Drumleish	2		—	2
	Drumbeggan	6		6	—
	Tullicrivy	3	John Hambilton Esqr	3	—
	Tulliscanlon	6	Gabriell Cathcart gent	3	3
	Drumaduller	4		4	—
	Agassillis	5	Allexsander Cathcart gent	4	1

Parishes	Places	Numb's of Persons	Tituladoes Names	English	Irish
	Drumadown	11	Thomas Sumerwell gent	9	2
			Robert Catchcart gent		
	Drumrisk	4	John Paterson gent	2	2
	Coringreagh	6	John Wilkes gent	4	2
	Dromcose	4		2	2
(folio 8)	Ruskey	2			2
	Knocknerny	4			4
	Enahan	3		3[1]	—
	Drumagh	2		2	—
	Levelly	9		7	2
	Sranaseugh	4		4	—
	Casibcon	22	Adam Cathcart Esqr Adam Cathcart agent to Lodewick Hamilton Esqr	16	6
	Symeriartagh	3		1	2
	Kiltagh	6		6	—
	Drumary	11			11
	Drumcroehan	5			5
	Knockmore	9			9
	Carriggfarmer	8			8
	Rosneurmor	6			6
	Aghakiran	15	Cohanagh McGuire gent		15
	Bonenubber	16			16
	Drumgarum	13			13
	Stramore	7			7
	Goblisk	17			17
	Ballicashedy	3			3
	Anagh	6			6
(folio 9)	Cloghbelly	9			9
	Stragh	8			8
	Trory	17			17
	Carige	7			7
	Ring	3			3
	Drumcor and Kill McCormack	6		2	4
	Derrigore	5		5	—
	Stratanacho	8			8
	Rosnenure	3			3
	Tonaghmore	10			10
	Corhullagh	14		6	8
	Carranmore and Aghmuldony	9		3	6
	Off ye Garrison	14		12	2
	Ferlagh	5	Alexander Weire gent	3	2

[1] This column is headed *English & Scotch* from folio 8 to end of volume

Parishes	Places	Numb's of Persons	Tituladoes Names	English	Irish
(folio 10). 4. Bohue	Monahan	4	Robert Weire gent	2	2
	Ahaherize	10	John Cormick gent		10
	Lagnagramore	4			4
	Lagnegebegg	2			2
	Langanvy	10	Pat McDonell oge McGwyre gent		10
	Aghanlaike	9			9
	Leaskea	4			4
	Trely	9			9
	Gartgahell	4		4	
	Truimly	14			14
	Drumerke	8			8
	Agharrin	7			7
	Cordarogag	6			6
	Rayfadd	6			6
	Mackenagh	4			4
	Clunaly	11	Tirlagh Merriggh McGuire gent		11
	Kildrome	10			10
	Drumdaw	9			9
5. Rossory	Culkye	5		5	—
	Gratedrehett	3		3	
	Roscarne	6		5	1
	Larragh	12		—	12
(folio 11).	Gransha	3			3
	Lamkill	8		8	—
	Drumkean	6		4	2
	Drumlaghan	3		3	—
	Mullacreogh	7		7	—
	Moyglass	10		8	2
	Brochus	7		5	2
	Cloghan	5		5	—
	Derrileckey	2		2	—
	Drumskew and Mullanaca	6		4	2
	Vinmerew	2		2	—
	Lenahan	3		3	—
	Rotonagh	4		4	—
	Rossorry	16		14	2
	Ebgarr	5		2	3
	Drumlyan	8		8	—
	Drumsillagh	5		4	1
	Shaeame	8		8	—
	Granskragh	3		3	—
	Portmush	5		4	1
	Drummee	10	Ralph Warick gent	4	6

Parishes	Places	Numb's of Persons	Tituladoes Names	English	Irish
	Rigg	3		2	1
	Drummee	17		15	2
(*folio* 12). 6. Cleenish			The Right Honble the Countesse of Huntington for her estate in this p'ish for the mannor of Lisgoole		
	Skeagh and Drunscrull	14	Patrick Humes Esqr Allexander Humes gent	12	2
	Derrylan	5		4	1
	Derriskob.	6		4	2
	Coolermont	8		—	8
	Maybron	15		7	8
	Mulligarry	10		9	1
	Moy	16		8	8
	Leam	9		7	2
	Temple M^cfrean	11		7	4
	Ballystrohary	9		4	5
	Belcow	18		—	18
	Mulliar	10		—	10
	Strahavy	8		2	6
	Temple Nesceren	16		—	16
	Mullaghdon	4		—	4
	Tint	8		4	4
	Clayme	11			11
	Mullicomd	6			6
	CarryKeran and Rahallan	10			10
	Gartacork	9			9
(*folio* 13). Clenish	Drunikin	4			4
	Corteskin	15	Conla Ô Cassidy gent Phillip o Cassydy gent		15
	Crinagh	7			7
	Killifelam	6			6
	Coshros	6			6
	Cavan	11			11
	Kilcrin	10			10
	Carronaley	12			12
	Mullatust	4			4
	Druman	6			6
	Moolet	10			10
	Listrilick	10			10
	Derrileke	6		4	2
	Boheway	6			6
	Cluntwill	6			6
	Gartadread	5		5	
	Largan dorrogh	2		2	

Parishes	Places	Numb's of Persons	Tituladoes Names	English	Irish
	Rahallan	8			8
	Killonabrakaogh	2			2
	Cardonagh	6		4	2
	Kilordrunly	5	Ensigne Robert Johnston gent	4	1
	Drumada	15			15
(folio 14).	Clune	3			3
	Beco	14		2	12
	Dirrihony	4			4
	Ederalash	2			2
	Fahart	4		2	2
	Mulibeill	2		2	—
	Lisula	2		2	—
	Derriharne	6			6
	Derriholagh	4			4
	Corrard	6		5	1
	Hally McManus	4		2	2
	Sheshiagh	6			6
	Kilt	4			4
	Colitee	4			4
	Tonamalaw	2			2
	Drumcraynyh	2			2
	Cleenish	6			6
	Ardtonagh	4			4
	Chentrick	2			2
	Tonyheig	9			9
	Dirrinh	2			2
	Rosdony	7			7
	Drumbarty	4			4
	Rosrenwoly	6			6
(folio 15).	Ferininielan	6		4	2
	Cleenish	5		5	—
	Riamalanay	3		3	—
	Mullasker	2		2	—
	Oximan	3		2	1
7. Killasher.	Cavanreragh	4	Thomas Magwire gent	2	2
	Lunge	6			6
	Culentrage	3			3
	Cliuragh	5			5
	Gortetowell	2			2
	Lyminmily	10			10
	Killasher	4			4
	Aghunihavy	2			2
	Cnockigihin	12			12
	Gortyne	10			10
	Clunidarragh	2			2

Parishes	Places	Numb's of Persons	Tituladoes Names	English	Irish
	Calkell	10			10
	Gurtmaconnell	9			9
	Gurtincrunagh	8			8
	Legmarvyvirkevir	6			6
	Carne	10			10
	Coryaragh	12			12
(folio 16).	Lisdare	5			5
	Lisblahick	2			2
	Lisdeurick	6			6
	Tallyhona	12			12
	Crockbrack	3			3
	Trian	2			2
	Dromeoyne	8			8
	Croyhryin	7			7
	Kelimanmay	6			6
	Agheteerourky	9			9
	Tully-yvan	5			5
	Lismuly	3			3
	Dromlaghin	4			4
	Duhaty	10			10
	Dromduff	6			6
	Edenmore	4			4
	Tattinmonur	8			8
(folio 17). 8. Agha-hurcher.	Legogheken	31		4	27
	Kenaghane	8		5	3
	Collarone	15		6	9
	Kartkine-beaotk	20			20
	Dromcroe	15		3	12
	Lyra	7		2	5
	Fany	3		3	—
	Lirneskeahill	8		5	3
	Coswask	7		5	2
	Rosgad	2			2
	Killypady	10			10
	Derrymunne	11			11
	Iniscolline	7			7
	Corgoobe	5			5
	Innisleag	6			6
	Ennisroske and Corcra	8			8
	Drombad	4			4
	Clonris	6			6
	Money McKyn	9			9
	Kinmor	10			10
(folio 18) Agha-hurchur.	Dery	13		3	10
	Lisneskea	48	Sr William Belfour Kt Charles Belfour Esqr Phillipp Browning gent	33	15

Parishes	Places	Numb's of Persons	Tituladoes Names	English	Irish
	Crochane	15		5	10
	Clun McFelem	2		—	2
	Killicutton	5		5	—
	Ferene skollogg	7		4	3
	Ferenne connoghy	7		—	7
	Macknagh	16		10	6
	Aghamor	13		8	5
	Carrurry	6		—	6
	Lislost	9	Barthlomew Belfour gent	7	2
	Lisnaskea	7		3	4
	Gartgarran	6			6
	Aughamore	11			11
	Coolbegg	6		4	2
	Kilmore and	4			4
	Dunbarrow	6			6
	of the Droles	7			7
	Corrileene	7			7
(folio 19).	Agharalow	11			11
	Mullagh-kippin	10		5	5
	Mullagh-kippin	2			2
	Drumcraugh	3		2	1
	Druinmack	13		3	10
	Mullinaskartey	6		6	—
	Garnohill	2		2	—
	Drombrocus	8	Cornett John Leonard gent	5	3
	Lister-derry	13	Robert Hamilton gent	13	—
	Listagole	8		—	8
	Drombrocus	8		6	2
	Tattenderry	12		8	4
	Killi-shanwally	5		5	—
	Lisduff	5		3	2
	Lislea	8		7	1
	Killiologhy	8		—	8
	Tullagh	09	Francis Straton gent	4	5
	Kilmore	11		8	3
(folio 20)	Kilmillen	11		7	4
	Killenamullaga and Dunmear	18		3	15
	Duimgoun	11		8	3
	Corrard and Corrigan	21		9	12
	Drumleck	24			24
	Garvoohill	2			2
	Corrilongford	9			9
	Dyrryquhillen	7			7
	Owensherrey	8			8
	Killerbran	10			10

Parishes	Places	Numb's of Persons	Tituladoes Names	English	Irish
	Derrylunan	18			18
	Coltram	4			4
	Tullyvarne	7			7
	Claragh	4			4
	Tullivonen	10			10
	Tyrana	8			8
	Monygebagham	9			9
	Tattinlee	5			5
	Tattimorlin	4	Cahair Ô Dougherty gent		4
(folio 21).	Tatenfeccle	4			4
	Rafinten	12		8	4
	Tullinageeran	10		5	5
	Carrilopollin	5			5
	Derrycuillen	8			8
	Grogath	7			7
	Cunen	8			8
	Camwerll	11			11
	Tattina	10			10
	Achacramfield	8			8
	Tyreaghan	8			8
	Lamkhill	5			5
	Aghageaghter	16			16
	Clean	5			5
	Tollinagarnavan	6			6
	Killybricke	8			8
	Derrilumman	9			9
	Kilarbren	7			7
	Derrycullin	4			4
	Grogagh	4			4
	Corin	6			6
(folio 22).	Aughageaghter	12			12
	Clean	4			4
	Tatene	3			3
	Tullymore	3			3
9. Enniskeane	Mullaghsilogagh	5		2	3
	Cluntelton	33			33
	Drombreane	6			6
	Dromcorr	7			7
	Dromnemeale	19		2	17
	Lorgaclabey	2			2
	Tulleyvoile	11	Andrew Galbreath gent Robert Galbreath gent		11
	Cuffe Jaudaghan	12			12
	Tulleyvoile	4			4
	Leame	11			11
	Imrowe	14			14

Parishes	Places	Numb's of Persons	Tituladoes Names	English	Irish
	Culecranha	10			10
	Glangrevonan	9			9
	Brackagh	2			2
	Kille Kollow	10			10
	Brogher	6			6
	Dromdergg	10		6	4
(folio 23).	Fala	6			6
	Sankoe	11			11
	Tircalton	7			7
	Killee	11			11
	Cloghtogall	3			3
	Mully Knochow	8	Henry West gent	5	3
	Eddenmore	15		00	15
	Tempo	10	Richard Courtes gent	2	8
	Downe	15			15
	Ardgroehan	3			3
	Carrowne	4			4
	Rathoran	13			13
	Letterbelly	28	Edmond Mc Conn^r Magwyre gent		28
	Garvorey	10		6	4
	Killevilley	3			3
	Mullyneskegh	2			2
	Carrow Mcmeaue	3		1	2
	Killenure	2			2
(folio 24).	Dromyea	6		5	1
	Rathkillan	3		3	—
	Aughoe	3		3	—
	Cavenleik	7		3	4
	Upper Drumclay	2			2
	Munnenoe	2			2
	Direkighan	10		10	—
	Killynan	3		—	3
	Rossevolan	5		3	2
	Gartgonnell	9		7	2
	Dromard	2			2
	Direvore	6			6
	InnisKeane	9			9
	Cornegrad	8	Thomas Picken gent	4	4
Magherycoolmony	Crevenish	13	Henry Bleuer Hassett Esqr		13
	Rosecade	6		2	4
	Litterkeane	14		4	10
	Corranland	12			12
	P^t of Corranlary	26			26
(folio 25). Maghery- coolemoney.	Kilmore	19		2	17
	Fararall	8		8	—

Parishes	Places	Numb's of Persons	Tituladoes Names	English	Irish
	Drumader	4		—	4
	Drumard	8		6	2
	Ballmant	10		02	8
	Crumlin	16			16
	Drom McLarye	4			4
	Aghegrehan	9			9
	Drumkerhin	4			4
	Crolane	7			07
	Gortnegullin	8			8
	Clunkey	8			8
	Burra	14			14
	Drommore	12			12
	Formill	7			7
	Clunniweale	6		4	2
	Tullyhoman	6			6
	Cholahcah	3	Richard Notley gent	3	—
	Lawrey	4	Phillipp Ozenbrooke gent	4	—
	Mullahnagrott	8		2	6
(folio 26).	Ballyconnelly	12		6	6
	Eddennanny	7		—	7
	Muckrush	14		2	12
	Clumilly	4		—	4
	Banoghbegg	8		2	6
	Aghhuehanagh	15		2	13
	Aghaleag	8			8
	Drumkeen	8			8
	Eddenclay	20			20
	Tirry Winney	9			9
	Litterboy	10			10
	Edernah	17			17
	Drumerin	4			4
	Glangarn	2			2
	Coolelangfeild	6		6	—
	Brinan	10			10
	Drumginvie	4			4
	Mullagh Ferny	14			14
	Drumsawny	25			25
	Drumcoose	4			4
	Colaghty	10			10
(folio 27)	Tynny McSpiritt	12			12
	Mullaghmore	8			8
	Cronam	9			9
	Strandarro	10			10
	Drumcume	5		5	—
	Agherruny	4		4	—
	Fargrum	4		2	2

Parishes	Places	Numb's of Persons	Tituladoes Names	English	Irish
	Ordress	9		03	06
	Drumconny	9			9
	Tulligimgin	8		6	2
	Kiltorney	4			4
	Tullicolerick	2	John Johnston gent	2	
	Kilterny	2	Henry Robinson gent	2	
	Tullinigin	2	Thomas Umphrey gent	2	
	Coolumphill	2	John Armstrong gent	2	
	of the Cash	2		2	
	Drumrane	2		02	
(*folio* 28). Drumully		53	Roderick Mansell gent Humphrey Coole gent	31	22
	Kell McBrack	6		6	—
	Derrycoba	4			4
	Killyharnan	3			3
	Fengch	4		2	2
	Clenelty	9			9
	Agharuske	5			5
	Legma Cafferey	4		4	
	Milladuff	4		3	I
	Bellaghey	5		2	3
	Dromleagh	5			5
	Donebarry	5			5
	Drumsasrey	8			8
	Mullahorne	5			5
	Leteigrene	3			3
	Drumrayne	2			2
	Drumgoll	8			8
	Mulleahen	8			8
	Lettergreine	7			7
	Lesaghnegrogh	12	Allexander Lowry gent	3	9
	Crum	8	Abraham Cereighton gentl	3	5
(*folio* 29). Dumully.	Dery McRoe	5		I	4
	Killeard	10			10
	Port	12			12
	Derreclocoy	9		5	4
	Derryada	10			10
	Knockebowady	10			10
	Drumcae	8			8
	Ruske	7			7
	Clevagh	4			4
	Lanscardan	9			9
	Brainsh	6			6
	Quillan	4			4
	Gortganaher	7		7	—
	Drumloas	4		3	I

Parishes	Places	Numb's of Persons	Tituladoes Names	English	Irish
	Corcecheard	2			2
	Gob	4		2	2
	Bunn	4		4	—
	Killecran	4		2	2
	Carleten	11	Gabriell Goodfellow gent	2	9
	Drumgollan	5		5	—
(folio 30).	Quillan	5		5	—
	Aghnemeh	9		6	3
	Drumkolagh	6		5	1
	Lettrim	4		4	—
	Corresmore	5			5
	Cleenke	11			11
	Manernagart	7	Bartholemew Drops gent	7	
	Ballyvoyla	5	Simon Pressly gent	3	2
	Garttmervin	4			4
	Hargrem	4		3	1
	Drummagh	4		4	—
	Rathnohill	5		2	3
	Hargrem	2		2	—
	Drumbalick	7			7
	Bogavosaught	3			3
	Killnecran	5			5
	Killnekirke	10			10
	Arthonagh	5			5
	Knockmakihan	3			3
	Mullanagonn	6		3	3
(folio 31).	Killrute	2		2	—
	Cluncaron	4		4	—
	Mullenevanhoe	3		3	—
	Ramnahare	5		3	2
	Loghgalgrin	2		2	—
	Clunmullan	12			12
	Drumlowan	6			6
	Drumverlebegg	5			5
	Munlaghglas	7			7
	Carrow	31	Nicholas Willoughby Esqr	12	19
	Clencolugg	14	John Madeslon gent	0	14
	Lysnadorke	6			6
	Tore	6			6
	Anagh	5		5	—
	Drumonolly	6			6
	Clunsannagh	9		7	2
	Edergoll	9		9	—
	Drumcorbe	5		3	2
	Cornalahan	12		7	5
	Galloone	6		4	2

Parishes	Places	Numb's of Persons	Tituladoes Names	English	Irish
(folio 32).	Kinnanebir	6	John Andrewes gentle	2	4
	Targin	20	Robert Elliott gent	6	14
	Drumgollan	12		—	12
	Donagh	8	Edward Coates gent	5	3
	Lisnayranagh	4		2	2
	Pategew	3		3	—
	Tonaghboy	16		—	16
	Bullecullan	6	Arthur Graham Esqr	3	3
	Ballagh	16			16
	Boreill	4			4
	Killemore	5		5	
	Corinanclea	5		3	2
	Carrowmore	17	Tirlogh McMahon gent		17
	Knockbey	2			2
	Kernymore	22	John Maguire gent		22
	Listebridy	4		2	2
	Pategare	2		2	—
	Slady	4		3	1
	Donagh	2		2	—
	Killte kemore	10			10
	Heffogory	5			5
(folio 33). Derri-bruske	Derrisbroske	12	Nicholas Mountgomery gent	4	8
	Killenslee	10		2	8
	Tonyreagh	3			3
	Fay	6			6
	Drumreny	5		2	3
	Gollagh	6			6
	Tullyharne	9	Henry Parkins gent	4	5
	Glasmullagh	3		3	—
	Killallagh	6		2	4
	Ballyreagh	16	Patt McGuire gent		16
	Largie	17	Conner Maguire gent		17
	Killnymady	17			17
	Mullity-Thomas	16		6	10
Derrivollan	Castlecoole	10	John Corry gent / James Corry gent	5	5
	Lackaghboy	5			5
	Shankill	5			5
	Gortmaslan	8			8
	Derryhillagh	8			8
	Fedan	2			2
	Laveighey	6			6
(folio 34).	Ballytarson	7		2	5
	Derryclavan and Cloghcorr	19		3	16
	Farnaugh	2		2	—

H

Parishes	Places	Numb's of Persons	Tituladoes Names	English	Irish
	Glissmullagh	2			2
	Killyvanan	2			2
	Taylagh	2		2	
	Derryvollan	14	James King gent	2	12
	Derrybegg	5			5
	Carivan, Ardybegg, & Slee	17		2	15
	Aghey	2			2
	Drumcruen	2			2
	Tatemacahell	16			16
	Tateguire	6		6	
	Cooleboocke	9			9
	Killterman	5			5
	Kavan Kilmore	16	Cuconagh Ô Hone gent		16
	Leason	2			2
	Agharinagh	6			6
	Mann˅ Archdall	2	William Archdall Esq˅	2	
(folio 35). Derry-vollan.	Bonywiner	22		2	20
	Mileaker	4			4
	Clunkeine	11		2	9
	Crevemshahi	3			3
	Lisnarrogue	9		3	6
	Drumerkiere	2		2	—
	Moynahan	7		3	4
	Latenstowne	8			8
	Rahall	13			13
	Dirochon	6			6
	Keiran	5			5
	Teid	4			4
	Drumbolcan	10			10
	Drumdofe	8		6	2
	Monahie	6		4	2
	Ahen	5		2	3
	Tylly-clee	7			7
	Belli Mᶜategartt	2		2	
	Mollis	2		2	
	Duerogg	4	Miles Hollowwood gent	4	
(folio 36)	Rossquire	6	Edward Humphery gent	2	4
	Legenameltog	4		4	—
	Downan	5		3	2
	Drumcorry	2		—	2
	LissKritten	7		5	2
	Drumcrane	4		4	—
	Drumsheane	9		7	2
	Rosguire	5		3	2
	Ardagh	4		4	—

Parishes	Places	Numb's of Persons	Tituladoes Names	English	Irish
	Monahan	6		—	6
	Drumsaren	4		4	—
	Rosskrun	8		6	2
	Decudd	11		9	2
	Mullanossagh	2		2	—
	Lowthertwone	9		8	1
	Cullen	2		2	—
	Ballenadolagh	6	William Irwin gent	4	2
	Boghan	6		4	2
	Drumuntanbegg	2		2	—
	Dringe	7		7	—
	Drumslush	6		6	—
	Rosclare	3	Thomas Steevenson gent	3	—
	Drummauld	3	Edward Bampton and his sonne gent	3	—
(folio 37) Magherycross	of the Coule	3	James Goodfellow gent	2	1
	Sidater	7		7	—
	Killguttnebegg	2		2	—
	Salliry	4		4	
	Cluncarry	2		2	
	Leternemeney	8	John Symerell gent	4	4
	Drumbulkan	6		5	1
	Agheneburne	6		6	
	Drummurry	5		2	3
	Killemitell	9			9
	Beagh	6			6
	Tullyrane	9			9
	Drumslowe	6			6
	Drumsloe	5			5
	Coe	9			9
	Drumcrinn	5		5	
	Clenagher	4			4
	Balledoolagh	18			18
	Mullaghmeene	10		8	2
(folio 38).	Fernagh	4		4	—
	Drumkeene	8		8	—
	Knocknenavell	6		6	—
	Gatolaghan	8		6	2
	Drumcullen	11		8	3
	Drumconish	5		5	
	Farnan	15		8	7
	Newporton	8		3	5
	Drumreney	4		4	
Ennis McSaint	Drombodarigh	3		2	1
	Corcle	2			2
	Brologh	11			11

Parishes	Places	Numb's of Persons	Tituladoes Names	English	Irish
	Greaghneing	3			3
	Rostare	8			8
	Calltin	6			6
	Langhill	5			5
	Tollaghmore	5			5
	Faslon	12			12
	Conaugh	10			10
	Cormecke	4			4
	Kariggmore	21			21
(*folio* 39)	Minrin	6			6
	Garvan	5		4	1
	Tonagh	7		4	3
	Derrygonelly	7		5	2
	Tolenedale	7	George Hulson gent	2	5
	Glanwalley	12		5	7
	Bleny	16		10	6
	Raheltan	5			5
	Mogelnegne	11			11
	Derynegnan	4			4
	Slavan	4			4
	Ardgeartt	16			16
	Terenavey	6			6
	Drumbudd	6			6
	Bollast	4			4
	Drummera	11	Capt. William Cosby Esqr Francis Archdall gent	8	3
	Carranro	9		4	5
	Partnecloduffe	7			7
	Drumriske	8		2	6
	Beagh	16	William Dunbarr gent	7	9
	Downe	8		2	6
(*folio* 40).	Gurtneale	9			9
	Carranro	4		4	
	Boheneny	4		4	
	Tehenagh	4		4	
	Aghomolan	2		2	
	Drumenagh	4		4	
	Tully	4		2	2
Templecarne	Bellecke	5	Edward Bleverhassett Esqr Gilbert Parker gent Phillip Husnell gent	3	2
	Rathmore	8		—	8
	Belleck	6		4	2
	Lackaghdoy	9		2	7
	Graffoe	5			5
	Drummniler	8	Phillip Bleverhassett gent		8

Parishes	Places	Numb's of Persons	Tituladoes Names	English	Irish
	Mogherymonagh	10		8	2
	Leeter	6		4	2
	Aughablany	4		—	4
	Tony Winy	8		2	6
	Rossarbell	4			4
	Derry colue	6			6
	Rossbegg	7		3	4
	Voughternan	6		5	1
(folio 41).[1]	Tunynoran	10		6	4
	Derryrona	2		—	2
	Rossmore	2		2	—
	Lawry	6	Walter Johnston gent	3	3
Kilnawly.	Callonhill	17	John Browne gent	12	5
	Aghibule	8			8
	Corradawer	8			8
	Cloghan	4			4
	Gorttnevalley	5			5
	Corrogabees	5			5
	Cortrasna	6			6
	Gortecorke	8			8
	Gortery	2			2
	Gortened	4			4
	Aghadissartt	2			2
	Gorttmoylan	6			6
	Kilnekelly	14		5	9
	Killskick	3			3
	Kilmacken	6			6
	Kinrush	8			8
	Mullenecogh	3	William Morton gent	3	
(folio 42)[1]	Hackigh	11		6	5
	Fermoyle	4			4
	Tonymore	7			7
	Drumonully	19			19
	Derryvore	5	Thomas Henlowe gent	2	3
	Drumborry	11		3	8
	Gortecorgon	4	Coll Barton Esqr	4	—
	Derrycannon	5	William Rosse gent	3	2
			Hugh Rosse gent		
	Derr cree	2		oo	2
	Drummany begg	3		3	—
	Prasna	2		2	—
	Drumkeilan	10		3	7
	Drumlaght	11		2	9
	Drumdericke	3		—	3

[1] See also *Principal Names*, below.

Parishes	Places	Numb's of Persons	Tituladoes Names	English	Irish
	Drumconner	4		3	1
	Derrybricke	3			3
	Drumully	6			6
	Dresternan	14		3	11
	Ter McCarsy	6			6
	Terryrooe	7			7
	Crosstonera	8			8
(folio 43).[1] Kil-mawly	Cornelecke	7			7
	Portoran	12		2	10
	Aghakillamady	10			10
	Fachanacloghan	10			10
	Mullineyny	4			4
	Clowfeene	11			11
	Cam	17			17
	Fachanacloghy	6			6
	Ramoane	4			4
	Patecale	10			10
	Fay-Carttan	8			8
	Killoghy or Killoggy	4			4
	Stramnatt	10			10
	Colldragh	12			12
	Mullislogh	6			6
	Teermoonan	5			5
	Corrykelly	4			4
	Corardryne	5		—	5
	Dervay Cloggan	5		0	5
(folio 44)[1]	Cooraheen	5		—	5
	Corre	4			4
	Dromherryff	5			5
	Tonyhomas	4			4
	Drumherriff	2			2
	Shanra	2			2
	Corne Cree	2			2
	Cora	8			8
	Kenaghan	9			9
	Drumbennis	2			2
	Moontagh	17			17
	Cleanliffe	4			4
	Corracoose	4			4
	Creaghue Faddina	4			4
	Dromkannan	12			12
	Crommor	6			6
	Killogogh	4			4

[1] See also *Principal Names*, below.

Parishes	Places	Numb's of Persons	Tituladoes Names	English	Irish
	Dromhacken	4			4
	Drombrocus	4			4
	Derrycolaght	11			11
(*folio* 45)[1]	Clunnersen	4			4
	Terevalley	6			6
	Cluntimoylan	14			14
	Killybracken	3			3
	Mullagharne	2			2
Enniskillen	Enniskillen	210	John Pagett gent, John Dane gent, Jason Hassart gent, David Rynd gent, William Helyott gent, Leut Mordykay Abbott gent, Ensigne William Webster gent, Harah Caldwell gent.	176	34

[1] See also *Principal Names*, below.

(*folio* 41). Principall Irish Names in the parishes of Clownish Aghaveigh Devonish [and] their numbers.

Ô Banan, 3 ; Ô Brady, 3 ; Ô Bryan & Ô Brein, 4 ; McCaffery, 2 ; McO Coen, 4 ; McCabe, 6 ; O Corrony (6) & Ô Corroney (2), 8 ; Ô Connelly, 13 ; Ô Clerican, 3 ; Ô Cashedy, 17 ; Ô Cogley, 4 ; Ô Corrican, 4 ; Ô Clerigan, 2 ; Ô Clenican, 2 ; McCarran, 3 ; McCaffery, 19 ; Crery & McCrery, 7 ; McDonell, 10 ; O Dyoddan, 5 ; MacGuire, 50 ; Ô Higgan, 4 ; Ô Hoen etc, 4 ; Ô Hollahan, 7 ; O Hultigan, 12 ; Killpatrick, 3 ; McKilroy, 3 ; McKilmartin, 6 ; McKernan, 4 ; Ô Murchey, 8 ; McManus, 17 ; McMahon, 30 ; Ô Mulligan, 18 ; O Keley, 5.

Principle Names of English & Scotts & their Number.
Armstrong, 4 ; Catchcartt, 8 ; Ellyott & Ellot, 12 ; Johnston, 11.

(*folio* 42)   Principall Irish Names in the Parishes of Bohue Rossory Clenish and Killasher [and] their numbs

Ô Brislan, 5 ; Ô Cormick, 10 ; McCormick, 5 ; Ô Coshedy, 13 ; McDonell, 4 ; Ô Dolan, 4 ; Ô Flannagan, 4 ; Ô Fee, 9 ; McGuire & Maguire, 26 ; McGee, 4 ; McGowen, 6 ; McHugh, 19 ; McKenny, 6 ; O Lunnin, 7 ; McLynnan, 11 ; McMaryne, 4 ; McMurchey, 3 ; McMurphey, 3 ; MacManus, 30 ; Ô Mullican, 5 ; Moore, 4 : McSculloge, 5.

Principall English & Scotts & Numb's.
Armstrong, 9 ; Johnston, 4 ; Nixson, 6.

(*folio* 43)   Principall Irish Names in the P'ishes of Aghaharcher Enniskeane and Magherycoolmony [and] their numbs

McBryan, 15 ; McCaffery, 35 ; McCabe, 13 ; Ô Cassydy, 11 ; Ô Connelly, 5 ; Ô Clerikan, 8 ; Ô Cormick, 5 ; Ô Corrigan, 3 ; McCallan, 5 ; McCarvey, 7 ; McDonell, 8 ; Ô Donell, 3 ; Ô Dogherty, 7 ; McGilosker &c, 5 ; Ô Gowen, 7 ; McGee, 8 ; McGilroy, 16 ; McGillmartin, 3 ; McGillcuskell, 5; McGragh & McGra, 8 ; McGuire & Maguire, 46 ; Ô Hoone, 8 ; Ô Harron, 5 ; Ô Kenan, 6 ; Ô Kelly, 4 ; McKelly, 2 ; Ô Kenan, 6 ; McMorchey, 5 ; McMurphey, 8 ; McManus, 38 ; Ô Muldowne, 8 ; Ô Morris, 4 ; Ô Managhan, 14 ; Ô Reley, 6 ; McRorkan, 5 ; Ô Sheale, 6 ; Ô Sheanan, 7 ; McTeggart, 6 ; Ô Torney, 5.

Some Principall Scotts and English and their Numbs
Armstrong, 15 ; Belfore, 3 ; Johnston, 16 ; Ellyott and Ellet, 5 ; Nixson, 5.

(*folio* 44).   Principall Irish Names in the Parishes of Drumully, Terribruske, Derryvollan, Magherycross, & Ennis McSaint

Attegartt, 5 ; Ô Banan, 7 ; McCosker, 5 ; Ô Clerican & Ô Corrygan, 7 ; McCabe, 6; McCaffery, 23 ; McCormick, 5 ; Ô Cassady, 10 ; McCarran, 4 ; McCanna, 4 ; McDermott, 9 ; McDunn, 6 ; McDonell, 23 ; McDunagan, 5 ; McDonaghey, 8 ; Ô Durinng, 5 ; Ô Flanagan, 18 ; Ô Fee, 4 ; Gillgon & Gillgun, 11 ; McGragh, 5 ; McGee, 3 ; McGilroy, 3 ; McGillmartin, 3 ; McGuire (12), & Maguire (41), 53 ; Ô Gowen, 7 ; Ô Howen, 6 ; Ô Hone, 12 ; Ô Kelly, 9 ; Ô Kernan, 5 ; Ô Lynnan, 8 ; McManus, 8 ; McMurchey, 8 ; Ô Mullpatrick, 11 ; McMahon, 8 ; Ô Meehan, 4 ; Moore, 5 ; Ô Morrish, 7 ; Ô Monaghen, 3 ; Ô Really, 6 ; McRory, 5 ; Ô Sheerin, 6 ; Ô Tressy, 7 ; McWynny, 6.

Some principall English & Scotts Names & their Numb's

Armstrong, 19 ; Crozier, 6 ; Ellyott, 11 ; Ellot, 4 ; Graham, 21 ; Irwin, 8 ; Johnston, 13 ; Mountgomery, 4 ; Nixson, 3 ; Noble, 6 ; Scott, 7.

(*folio* 45).   Principall Irish Names in the Parishes of Templecarne, Kilmawly, and towne of Enniskillen [and] their numb's.

McCaffery, 4 ; Ô Cassydy, 10 ; McCorry, 34 ; M^c & Ma Cawly, 11 ; Ô Drum, 7 ; McDromma (4), & Ô Dromma (5), 9 ; McGuire (8), & Maguire (34), 42 ; McManus, 13 ; McMarten, 5 ; McMorphey, 5 ; Ô Really & Ô Rely, 6 ; M^c A Vynny, 9.

(*folio* 45 *verso*).   The Number of People in ye County of Fermannagh

Eng &c	Irish	totall of Eng & Irish
1800	5302	7102.

LONDONDERRY CITTY AND COUNTY

$$
\begin{array}{r}
1052 \\
8682 \\
\hline
9734
\end{array}
$$

(folio 1). Londonderry Citty and suburbs and yᵉ pᵗᵉ of the Liberties lyeing on ye North side of ye Riuer of Loghfoyle

Parrishes	Streets	Number of People	Tituladoes Names	Eng & Scotts	Irish
Templemore					
	Siluer Streete	052	Coll George Gorges, Samuell Hill Esqʳ, Henry Osborne, and John Plunkett gents, John MᶜKenny, John Burnside, and James Lenox Marchants	034	018
	Diamond Streete	14	James Hobson, John Craig and Thomas Moncreife Marchant	10	04
	Without Ship Gate	4	— — — — —	4	000
	Pᵗ of Siluer streete	37	Robert Truman, Henry Osborne, John Gifford, Robert Houston and Samuell Norman, gentlemen, Thomas Bourke Esqʳ Robert Carter collector of ye Costomehouse	22	15
	The back of Siluer Streete	32	— — — — —	23	9
	Pᵗᵉ of ye Diamond	23	Thomas Cole Esqʳ & Henry Finch Esqʳ Geruis Squire gentleman George Squire & Robert Morison Marchants	18	05
	Pᵗᵉ of Butchers Streete	036	John Gamble Marchant	027	009
(folio 2).	Without Butchers gate	65		31	34
	Pᵗᵉ of ye Diamond	15	James Fisher & James Wilson Marchᵗ	11	4
	Pᵗᵉ of Ferrygate Streete	26	Symon Pitt Esqʳ & William Fowler Mchᵗ	18	8
	Pᵗᵉ of Pump Streete	38	Hugh Thomson gent	22	16
	Pᵗᵉ of Ferrygate Streete	44	John Hanford & Robert Lawson Esqʳˢ Peter Lawson, and Nathaniell Drew gentlemen William Rodgers and James Rodgers Merchants	35	9
	At Ferry gate	7		2	5
	Without Ferry Gate	119	Henry Conway Esqʳ, Will Gardner and Henry Gardner marchants	75	44
	Pᵗᵉ of ye Diamond	20	John White and Hugh Edwards Marchᵗˢ	14	06
	Pᵗᵉ of Bishop Gates Streete	26		13	13
	The lane to ye Ould church	8		4	4

Parishes	Streets	Number of People	Tituladoes Names	Eng & Scotts	Irish
(folio 3).	Pte of Bishop Gate Streete	84	Luke Esqr Maior of Derry, Sr Baptist Staples Barronnett, John Reiues gent, John Godbold and William Hepburne Esqrs, Henry Symkins, John Campsie and James Wilkins Marchants, Mathew Draper marcht	58	26
	Pte of Pomp Streete	124	James Nesmith, Henry Neile and John Denny Marchants	058	066
	Elogh qr land	12	Peter Benson gentl	04	08
	Ballynegallagh qr	16		—	16
	Cragan ½ qr	15		03	12
	Ye fiue Ballyboes of Leruske	28		05	23
	Ballymagroty qr	34	Will Latham gent	09	25
	Cosquin qr	19		08	11
	Termonpakagh Qr land	17		11	06
	Mullenan qr	19		12	07
(folio 4)	Killea ½ qr	24		07	17
	Ballyoughrie qr	07		04	03
	Ballygoane ½ qr	12		06	06
	Shantallon Qr	27		16	11
	Ballyneshelloge qr land	12		06	06
	Ballingard qr	11		02	09
	Ballygarwell	25		—	25

Principall Irish Names.

Ô Doghertye, 05 ; McLaughlin, 04 ; Whyte, 03.

(folio 4 verso). Londonderry Cittye : Eng & Scotts, 572 ; Irish, 480 ; 1052, totall.

(folio 5).
Londonderry County

TERKERIN BARRONY

Parishes	Townelands	Number of People	Tituladoes Names	Eng & Scotts	Irish
Clandermont	4 Townelands of Cloune and Gobmaskeale	087	John Eluin late Maior of Derry Alexdr Thomkins gent	053	034
	Corucle	05		04	01
	Colkeragh	18		11	07
	6 Enogh	18		07	11

Parishes	Townelands	Number of People	Tituladoes Names	Eng & Scotts	Irish
	Granchoghs	12		—	12
	2 Cayes	17		12	05
	Ballyowen	43		21	22
	Altongelton	11		05	06
	Lishaghmore and ¾ of Cromkill	11		06	05
	¼ Cromkill	03		—	03
	Ballymady and Mullylane	15		11	04
	Drumacoran and Bogagh	21		17	04
(folio 6).	Cloghore	05		05	—
	Terkefenny	010		004	006
	Killymallock & Colrefrie	14		06	08
	Craig	09		07	02
	Dromnagor	08		08	—
	Tachrina	06		06	—
	Lower Tully	11		08	03
	Upper Tully	18		14	04
	Rosenecalagh	04		02	02
	Gortowne	08		08	—
	Towne of New Buildings	44		24	20
	Prehen	06		—	06
	— —	05		—	05
	Lishackmore	07		02	05
	Gortenue	04		—	04
(folio 7). Clondermont.	Knockbrack and Ardkill	14		12	02
	Clonkean	14		10	04
	Lismakerrell	03		—	03
	Gorticae	06		05	01
	Tebracon	06		—	06
	Ederreaghs	13		06	07
	Gortnasles	11		—	11
	Gorticrosse	18		15	03
	Fincarne	06		03	03
	Drumnahoes	09		04	05
	Killamoreeceneclogh	17	Thomas Skipton gent	10	07
	Macknaneskie	03		000	03
	Tullyallyes	16		06	10
	Gortigranagh & Famully	10		08	02
(folio 8).	Lisglass and Letteraine	010		004	006
	Lisdahan and ½ Shean	12		08	04
	Monaghmore	05		02	03
	Monaghbegg	08		—	08

Parrishes	Townelands	Number of People	Tituladoes Names	Eng & Scotts	Irish
Faughanvale	Tullymoan and Carrickhugh	13		07	06
	Listveile and 2 Carnuffs	21		08	13
	Termacoy and Barnakelly	20		02	18
	Colekenaght	04		04	—
	Coolaght	19		15	04
	Killater	13		06	07
	Faughanvale	43	Lᵗ Coll: Alexʳ Staples Esqʳ Robert Staples gentleman	15	28
(folio 9).	Tullyverry	12		12	—
	Glasteelemore & Gallaghaloonagh	15		13	02
	Glastelle beg & Glastmullan	11		08	03
	Cargan and Gortlack	06		06	—
	Dunguillian	04		04	—
	Magherymore	15		11	04
	½ Cragan	04		03	01
	Lamfield beg & Terebrislan	19	Henry Finch Junʳ gent	06	13
	Lamfield more	02		02	—
	Drumaneny	13		02	11
	Dunybroore	22		05	17
(folio 10).	Killylanes	16	John Ash gent	07	08
	Tullanee	009		—	009
	Moigh	47	John Kilner Esqʳ Paul Brasier gent	32	15
	Colafeny	06		04	02
	Templemoyle	07		02	05
	Derryarkin Lower and Gortenny	17	Charles Dauenport gent	09	08
	Derryarkin Upper	10		02	08
	Ballygoodin	14		04	10
	Gortegertye Lower	06		06	—
	Gortgertye Upper	09		05	04
	Tully	12		10	02
	Carwoony	07		06	01
(folio 11).	Ardnegoynog	06		—	06
	Campson Upper	12		10	02
	Campson Lower	07		000	07
	Cloghall	11		11	—
	Edingilcoppy	10		07	03
	Aghacarny	12		09	03
Cumbe	Crossebally-Cormick	11		07	04
	Fany	06		06	000
	Killanon	06		06	—

Parrishes	Townelands	Number of People	Tituladoes Names	Eng & Scotts	Irish
	Ballynemure	06		04	02
	Tawnaghmore	04		04	—
	Brackway	12		08	04
	Gortnarade	04		000	04
	Brokac	12		—	12
(folio 12).	Taunerin and Dunguillian	19		—	19
	Taunyreagh	08		02	06
	Oghill	08		—	08
	Ballydroll	008		—	008
	Maloboy	12		—	12
	Lettershaune	10		—	10
	Ervoy	14		—	14
	Listras and Oughtagh	10		—	10
	Lettermoyre	12		—	12
	Gortneraine	08		—	08
	Kilcatton	06		02	04
	Cregg	13		—	13
	Clady	20		—	20
	Bally McClanagon & Dongorton	21		—	21
(folio 13).	Ballyhollow	15		—	15
	Kinculbrack	14		—	14
	Kilcor	13		—	13
	Kincul Mcranold	14		—	14
	Leare	08		—	08
	Tereeghter	16		—	16
	Ballyrory	07	Rory Ô Haron gent	—	07
	Long and Carnanbane	16		—	16
	Stranogolwello	22		—	22
	Carnonreagh	11		—	11
	Altoheny	10		—	10
	Downede	10		—	10
	Salloghwelle	09		—	09
	Lisbuny	09		—	09
	Alla	10		02	08
(folio 14)	Cumbe	08		—	08
	Binkinnera	10		—	10
	Lettermucke	11		—	11
	Ballyarton	011		002	009
	Clonlogh	05		—	05
	Gortneske	05		—	05
	Ballycallaghan	06		02	04
	Lackagh	12		—	12
	Culdoage	18		—	18
	Ardgriffin	08		—	08

Parrishes	Townelands	Number of People	Tituladoes Names	Eng & Scotts	Irish
	Tonduffe	12		08	04
	Legacory	14		—	14
	Gossidon	11		—	11

Principall Irish Names

McConnell, 06 ; Ô Cahan, 06 ; McClosker, 09 ; Ô Doghertye, **38** ; Ô Donaghy, 07 ; Ô Donell, 08 ; O Dowey, 06 ; Ô Gormely, 06 ; O Heggertye, 12 ; Henry & Ô Henry, 10 ; O Kelly, 07 ; O Keile, 07 ; McKnogher, 06 ; McLaughlin, 19 ; Mackey, 07 ; O Mullan, 11 ; Ô Mullfoyle, 07 ; Ô Quigley, 06.

(*folio 14 verso*) : Barrony : Terkerin : Eng & Scotts, 640 ; Irish, 979 ; 1619 tott.

(*folio 15*).   **KENAGHT BARRONY**

Parrishes	Townelands	Number of People	Tituladoes Names	Eng & Scotts	Irish
Tamlaghfinlagan	Largy	015		009	006
	Drumrane	09		09	000
	Mullagh	10		10	—
	Luskeran	05		05	—
	Tullydrum	02		02	—
	Moyghmore	08		03	05
	Ballynarock	03		—	03
	Ballymore	09		07	02
	Machrimore	11		02	09
	Drummore	11		11	—
	Drumgeighlin	10		08	02
	Coralaragh	06		—	06
	Clogan	11		11	
	Shunreagh	04		04	
	Monyranell	09		09	
	Drumakerne	06		06	—
	Cloghfin	07		07	
(*folio 16*)	Tully	06		06	—
	Mulkeragh	14		14	—
	Lomon	14		14	—
	Culmore	11		07	04
	Crinell	026		012	014
	Ballyhenry	08		—	08

Parishes	Townelands	Number of People	Tituladoes Names	Eng & Scotts	Irish
	Carrowmuddle	08		02	06
	Carrynagh	10		07	03
	Tatenekelly	13		05	08
	Drumballydonoghee	09		09	—
	Arnargall	08		04	04
	Corndall	10		08	02
	Barnally	06		06	—
	Carrowreagh	22		18	04
	Corraclare	18		10	08
(folio 17).	Ballynerow	12		10	02
	Back	11		11	—
	Brogheater	09		06	03
	Broglaskert	17		014	03
	Harlogh	07		07	—
	Tonbrock	39		—	39
	Glack	27		02	25
	Ballykelly	72	Nicholas Lane George Downing and Christopher Freeman gents	42	30
	Ballykean	08		08	—
	Dromond	08		06	02
	Ballyspallin	09		06	03
	Broghoreston	10		09	01
	Tullytwo	08		03	05
	Carnan	08		06	02
	Shesracule	11		11	—
	Drumcony	06		06	—
(folio 18). Drumcose	Lematady and Monenglare }	13	Dudly Phillips Esq and Thomas Phillips gent	07	06
	Ardnederogh	014		004	010
	Calesson	09		09	—
	Newtowne Lemavady	116	George Phillips Esq and Thomas Campbell gents	70	46
	Rathbredie	11		06	05
	Killean	04		03	01
	Shrenagh	07		07	
	Derrybegg	09		09	
	Derrymore	10		08	02
	Mollan	05		02	03
	Bolea	11		09	02
	Donmore	02			02
	Donmorebeg	03			03
	Gertkerbribeg	08			08
	Gortkerbrimore	04			04
(folio 19).	Carryduffe	11		05	06
	Ballyriskmore	06		03	03

I

Parishes	Townelands	Number of People	Tituladoes Names	Eng & Scotts	Irish
	Ballyriskbeg	06	John Paton gent	06	—
	Largireagh	11		09	02
	Kedie	07		03	04
	Leck	08		—	08
	Dromramer	10		—	10
	Ballycrom	06		04	02
	Ballyauylan	05		02	03
	Termaquir	06		06	—
	Ruskie	06		06	—
	Clonkaine	08		04	04
	Gortnegarne	08		05	03
	Cahary	06		06	—
	Dromond	20		18	02
	Bovally	06		06	—
(folio 20). Taulatard alius Ardmagilligan	Ye six townes of Bally-morgy	040	John Gage gent	021	019
	½ Ballycarton	02		02	
	Ortaghmoyle and Drumnacagh	19		17	02
	Ballyscullin and Ballymategert	17	George Cooke gent	09	08
	Lenemore and Drumavally	08		08	—
	Ballymagoland	06	Thomas Rowth Elder gent	05	01
	Ballymaholland	19		04	15
	Ortaghmore and Drummacorgan	15		—	15
	The 3 Dromons	17		11	06
	Lower Dowaghs	12		10	02
	Upper Dowaghs	03		02	01
	Bally McLary	09		03	06
(folio 21)	Oghill	02			02
	Umrican and Anis	04			04
	Tircrevin	11			11
	Ballyleghery	18		08	10
	Duncrun	13	John Major gent	13	—
	Taulatard	16		09	07
	Taulatbeg	09		08	01
Anlow	Ballycarton	04		03	01
	Bally McGillir.	07		04	03
	Turcurren	06		06	—
	Ballymony	05		03	02
	Monyrenan & ye 3 towns of Anlow	21		19	02
	Ballycastle, Lisronan, & Crott	15	Sr Robert Maxwell Knt and James Maxwell gent	13	02

Parrishes	Townelands	Number of People	Tituladoes Names	Eng & Scotts	Irish
(*folio* 22).	Drumadery	008		008	—
	Dowling	04		02	02
	Carboylane	08		06	02
	Granagh	06		02	04
	Lisnegrib	08		04	04
	Drumleife	06		06	—
	Killibreedy	07		04	03
	Largentean	08		06	02
	— —	48		26	22
Baltragh	Cloghan	21	Donell McManus Ô Mullan gent	—	21
	Drumsurny & Bovill	16		—	16
	Kilchoyle	08		—	08
	Monygogie	01		—	01
	Drumgauny	10		—	10
	Maine	10		04	06
(*folio* 23).	Balleluckerye	11		03	08
	½ Ballyanlan & Teredowey	20			20
	Aghneshilogh	14		09	05
	Gortinarny	09		07	02
	Derry	07		06	01
	¾ of Drumgasker	03		03	—
	Lislane	09		04	05
	Carnan	08		08	—
	Ardmore and Drumgesse	13		13	—
	Ballymully	13		11	02
	½ Tedenmore	06		01	05
	Teredremont	12		—	12
	Carrick	11		03	08
	Ballyquin	015			015
(*folio* 24).Boveva.	Carrick	14			14
	Templemoyle	16		07	09
	Leecke	08		08	
	Bally McIlduffe	08		08	
	Ardinerin	16			16
	Bouevy	10		10	
	Glanconway	06			06
	Drumdreene & Mulkeragh	09			09
	Drumneece	06		04	02
	Gorticlare	09		09	—
	Carinnish	09		02	07
	Derryard	08		05	03
	Muldony	08			08
	Farclene	04			04
	Ballymony	08			08
(*folio* 25).Boueva.	Drum and Ballycarrygan	13			13

Parrishes	Townelands	Number of People	Tituladoes Names	Eng & Scotts	Irish
	Derryraflagh	08			08
	Killiblught and Banonybuy ⎱	17		04	13
Dungeavan	Ballymulby	39	Edward Carey Esqʳ	18	21
	Lackagh	14		08	06
	Scriggin	07		07	—
	Owen Begg	11		07	04
	Brisse	04			04
	Ballyhillan & Derryduffe	09		02	07
	Gortnagrosse	04		04	
	Clontagary	20			20
	Crewbarky & Lenemore	020		—	020
(folio 26).	Tauny Haron	11			11
	Cashell	10			10
	Carne	17			17
	Bovill	17			17
	Ballynasse & Bally McCallin ⎱	14			14
	Gortgarne	14			14
	Derryorke	17			17
	Tergolan	06		02	04
	Ouill	10			10
	Curraghlane Killerfagh	10			10
Bannagher	Ballydonagan	12			12
	Taunyaghagan	10			10
	Culnemunnan	08			08
(folio 27).	Dreen	13			13
	Taunagh McIlmurry	10			10
	Teredreene	08			08
	Killownaght	08			08
	Ballaghaneden	11			11
	Carnanbane	10			10
	Fincarne	04			04
	Maghremore	12			12
	Tranan	13			13
	Laghteloobe & ½ Altinure	012			012
	Gallanogh & ½ Naghluske	10			10
	Mogrew and ½ Nagluske	14			14
	Clogan Ballywooter	001		—	001
(folio 28)	Tirglasson	10			10
	Knockan	14			14
	Drumconid	08		04	04
	Neefeeny and Umrican	01			01
	Templemoyle & Releagh	20			20
	Derrykreer	16			16
	Monyhoan	04			04
	Straid Bally Haron	12			12

Principall Irish Names [and] their Number

McCloskey, 031 ; O Cahan, 036 ; McCleland, 018 ; McConnell, 006 ; O Doghertye, 034 ; McDonoghy, 008 ; Ô Feeny, 008 ; Ô Heany, 007 ; Ô Haron, 007 ; Henry & McHenry, 009 ; O Hamson, 007 ; McKnogher, 015 ; O Kelly, 006 ; McLaughlin, 036 ; O Mullan, 034 ; Moore, 024 ; Martin, 015 ; McGwyre, 009 ; Smith, 010.

(*folio* 28 *verso*). Barrony : Kenaght ; Eng & Scotts, 1012 ; Irish, 1215 ; 2227 tott.

(*folio* 29).   **LOGHINSHOLIN BARRONY**

Parrishes	Townelands	Number of People	Tituladoes Names	Eng & Scotts	Irish
Kilrea	Monyegne	007		002	005
	Fallahoge	08		02	06
	Listlee	17		11	06
	Moytunke	10		10	—
	Ye 2 Mony Groouse	05			05
	Kilrea	40	Richard Clutterbooke Tho : Church and Charles Church gentlemen	29	11
	Ergina	06		04	02
	Clara	13		09	04
	Mavanahir	07			07
	Lisnegallin and Monelarban	08			08
Tawlat Ichrilly	Lissamoill	12			12
	Ballynanean	14			14
	Toyconey	002		—	002
(*folio* 30)	Bovidy	22			22
	Killimuck	12			12
	Killigullibe	12			12
	Glenen	16		06	10
	Tyonee	24		02	22
	Gortmacrean	17		08	09
	Drumcan	08		02	06
	Teden	08			08
	Monystean	07			07
	Drumard	10	Bryan Mulholland Esqr		10
	Drumlien	06		06	
	Drumchalice	08		08	
	Drumnakena	08		02	06
	Drumsara	06			06
	Monyshalin	07			07

Parishes	Townelands	Number of People	Tituladoes Names	Eng & Scotts	Irish
	Innishcrosse	14		04	10
(*folio* 31)	Swetragh	04			04
Maghara &	Culnegrue	06			06
Turminany	Kedie	04			04
	Mackeinagh	02			02
	Doungladie	06		04	02
	Culknady	10		000	10
	Tergarwell	10			10
	Criue	9			9
	Knockeneill	4			4
	Interregrolagh	7		02	05
	Monymoore	10		10	—
	Craigmoore & Tornymolan	21		15	06
	Largantagher	13		03	10
	Felgertrewey	004		—	004
	Craigadick	06		04	02
(*folio* 32).	Bolinhona	13	Alexand\r Blare gent	13	
	Dernagh	07		07	
	Cabragh	06		04	02
	Bolynecrosse	05		05	—
	Brughinsikeene Larneguese	10			10
	Leamonroye	04			04
	Carrickkeelte	07		06	01
	Slaghvoyland	04			04
	Mullagh	07	John Magomerie	05	02
	Brackagh	04			04
	Keerly	04			04
	Falleglone	06			06
	Bolunackilcar	04			04
	Goleduffe	05			05
	Bolinekrege	05			05
(*folio* 33).	Drumlagh	04			04
	Knockakeelty	10	Hugh Montgomery Esq\r	06	04
	Curragh	06			06
	Drummuck	07			07
	Moygoll	03			03
	Bally M\cPeake	07	Cormuck Ô Mulholland Esq		07
	Drenan	06			06
	Drumarde	06			06
Killelagh	Gortnawee	10			10
	Boloknock	06			06
	Fallalee	08			08
	Carlakie	10			10
	Slatnerll	09			09
	Tirhire	010		—	010

Parrishes	Townelands	Number of People	Tituladoes Names	Eng & Scotts	Irish
	Kermanagh	12		04	08
	Tollokerane	06			06
(folio 34).	Tirkiane	08			08
	Moryseriant	02			02
	Granahan	02			02
Ballyscullin	Ballyscullin	18	Alexandr Cornewell Esqr	02	16
	Tamboughdood	08		04	04
	Drumany	31		25	06
	Ballyagheg	52	Hugh Gawen Esqr and Adam Carie gents	39	13
	Ballydermott	07	Tho : Windsor Esqr	01	06
	Edenreagh	04		—	04
	Killaberry	04		04	—
	Tamimaran	28	Thomas Dawson gent	16	12
	Cullanavea	15		—	15
	Bally McLecombebeg	14		06	08
	Bally McLecombmoore	12		06	06
(folio 35)	Upper Ballyneas	10	Captn John Hardlye Esqr	08	02
	Lower Ballyneas	13		07	06
Maghrafelt	Maghrafelt	71		44	27
	Souldiers & their Wiues in the towne of Magh- rafelt	113	Captn Nicholas Barrington Esqr Francis Rust gent	92	21
	Glenmaquill	06		06	—
	Ayhagaskine	08		06	02
	2 B. Moghans	08		—	08
	Killyfaldy	10		02	08
	Lackagh	02			02
	Mallyboy	06			06
	Anaghmore	10			10
	Taunediese	002		—	002
	Ballyknogher	06			06
	Lishneise	10	Robert Hathorne gent	08	02
(folio 36).	Shane Mullogh	12			12
Magharafelt.	Drinarany	09		03	06
	Dunany	06		04	02
	B : Hener	07		07	
Kilcranaghan	Tolleroan Tauniagher Mirmihellgrany	12			12
	Brackagh Listea	10			10
	Gortikorky	06			06
	Coolesahan	07			07
	Cooleminiber	08		08	
	Ye ½ towne of Clone & ye ½ towne of Ballin- derry	08			08

Parishes	Townelands	Number of People	Tituladoes Names	Eng & Scotts	Irish
(folio 37)	Tonnoghmoore Quarter	02			02
	Molock beg Quarter	02			02
	Ye ½ towne of Drumcroe	04			04
	Monishnare	04			04
	Drumballyhagan	10		02	08
	Tobermoore Qr	03			03
	Calmoore & Cloghfin	08			08
Dissert Lyms	½ Dunroman	04			04
	Monykelwary	09			09
	Bally McElkeny	08		02	06
	Carmean	06		06	
	½ Ternoagh	06		06	
	Mogargy	04		04	
	Colsing	06		06	
(folio 38)	Monymoore	46	Robert Downeing gent	23	23
Dissert Lynn	Dunarnan	08		08	—
	Mowelly	08		04	04
	Lauacormuck	004		—	004
	Morris Scullin	07		05	02
	Caris Doragh	06		06	—
	Tamny Derry	04		—	04
	Crosenervy	03		03	—
	Carudafhin	08		—	08
	Tullymagehy	04		04	—
	½ Colley	04		02	02
	Ballycomlarsy	05		05	—
	Gortagolly	05			05
Dissert Marten	Gortneery	06			06
	Brackagh	10			10
	Enishcarne	06			06
(folio 39).	Cullan	06			06
	½ towne of Boveagh	04			04
	Longfield	06			06
	Rossegarran	08			08
	Derrynoscallan	08			08
	Grange	08			08
	Moyatelly	06			06
	Senany	10		10	
	Ballynegowne	05		05	
	4 townes of Dissert Marten	04		02	02
	Annagh and Culcam	06	John Hatton gent	02	04
	Drumore	08			08
	Roshure	06			06
	Cullabogan	06			06
	Leckonicher	06			06
(folio 40)	Crainy	10			10

Parrishes	Townelands	Number of People	Tituladoes Names	Eng & Scotts	Irish
	Carnto	04			04
	Tirregan	04			04
Ballyniskrean	MoyKiran & ye ½ towne of Makillan	008		—	008
	Tonnagh	08			08
	Straghdrund & Algone	07			07
	Lebby	06			06
	Dissert	08			08
	DunoGilduffe	05			05
	Moydoucaght	06			06
	Donmurry	06			06
	Carnemony	05			05
	Gortaskey	06			06
	Ballynanure	06			06
(folio 41)	Cullnesillagh	06			06
	Moyneegne	06			06
	Drumlierge	04			04
	Brancharan	06			06
	Moghertragh	06			06
	Dunearnan	06			06
	Cavanreagh	06			06
	Moyneconif	06			06
	Onereagh	06			06
	Noynebeg	08			08
	½ Moyneguigye	06			06
	ye other ½ of Moyneguigye	04			04
	½ Moycelan	06	Major James Craford Esqr & Will Springham gent	04	02
Lisson	Banovragy	06			06
	Ballyferlea and Rossemore	05			05
(folio 42).	Caltrien	07		03	04
	Dromrott	05		05	—
	Monahay	04		04	—
	Mooffe	006		—	006
	Killebaskey	04			04
	Tullynarr	08			08
	Moybay	06			06
	Dirry Inan	06			06
	Derrygenard	06			06
	Tentagh	06			06
	Knockduffe	06			06
	Canish	04			04
	Dromard	04			04
	Dromfyn	06			06
	Tyrebrekan	08		04	04

Parishes	Townelands	Number of People	Tituladoes Names	Eng & Scotts	Irish
	Lismony	03		01	02
(folio 43) Taw-lett & Killetra	Ballydally	06		02	04
	Drumnaer	08			08
	Ballymoyell	06			06
	Ricshey	08			08
	Ballygonay	08			08
Ballinderry	Ballinderry	09			09
	Ardteraffe	03			03
	Ballyaghery	07			07
	Ballyronanbeg	05		04	01
	Ballydonell	05			05
	Kinainocke	10			10
	Salterstowne	09		04	05
	Ballylefart	07			07
(folio 44). Arbo & Derryloran	Kilbrarue	04		04	000
	Cloghouge	04		04	
	Tulboy	02			02
	Tawnaghmore	04			04
	½ of Derrycrumny	04			04
	Domoyan	04			04
	Ballyloughan	06			06
	Drumullan	006		—	006
	Ballygonay	10			10
Artra p^t	Ballynoye	08			08
	Ballydally	04		02	02
	Ballneallmoore	06			06
	Ballygurby	08			08
	Ballym^ccuggin	10			10
	Aghrime	06			06
(folio 45).	Dirrigarvy	10			10
	2 townes of Moyola	14		09	05
	Ballynenanagh	06			06
	Ballyneheglis	06			06
	Tannagh	07		07	000
	Raskiestressuagh	02			02
	Ballindromo	04			04
	Lishdonmore	06			06
	Druminagh	04		02	02
	Ballynigrow	08			08
	Ballyronanmore	08			08
	½ Ballyronanbeg	02			02
	Ballymulligan	06			06
	Ballyneallbeg	03			03
	Ballygillanmore	03			03
	Ballygillanbeg	05			05
(folio 46). Artra.	Ballyreffe	06			06
	Myaghedoan	05			05
	Ballygrogly	06			06

Principall Irish Names [and] their Number

Ô Corr (6), Ô Core (4), 010 ; Ô Cahan, 008 ; McConnell, 011 ; McCan, 006 ; McCormuck, 006 ; McConnor, 006 ; McDavitt (8), McDewett (4), 012 ; Ô Donell, 006 ; Ô Dyman, 007 ; Ô Doughertye, 010 ; Ô Graffan, 006 ; Ô Henry, 018 ; Ô Hagan, 017 ; Ô Kenedy, 006 ; O Kenan, 006 ; O Kelly, 006 ; Mullholland, 018 ; McMurrey, 008 ; Ô Mullan, 014 ; Moore, 006 ; O Neale, 30 ; McPeake, 08 ; Ô Quin, 07 ; O Scullin & Ô Scullen, 10 ; Smith, 07 ; McShane, 06.

(*folio* 46 *verso*). Barrony of Loghinsholin : Eng & Scotts, 655 ; Irish, 1431 ; 2086 tott :

(*folio* 47). **COLRAINE[1] BARRONY**

Parrishes	Townelands	Number of People	Tituladoes Names	Eng & Scotts	Irish
Colraine	Colraine towne & Libertys	633	Symon Hillmon, Stephen Cuppage, Nicholas Griffin, Samuell Wilkins, William Godfrey Reinold Berresford Thomas Lance Tho : Reynolds gentlemen Wm Adams & Tristram Beresford Esqr, Richard Brasier and Thomas Hillman Aldermen, Hugh Muller John Browne, John Thomson, Hugh Craige, William Galt John Twadell John Galt Joshua Brookes & William Moore Shopkeepers	467	166
Ballyrashean	Cloghfin	006		006	—
	Ardnecronaght	04		04	
	Irish Ardnecronaght	07		07	
	Kirkstowne	09		06	03
	Upper Ballyversell	06		06	
	Lower Ballyversell	06		06	
(*folio* 48).	Gortocloghan	07		07	
	Lisnagatt	04		04	—
	KnockenKeeragh	10		06	04
	Lissevatick	06		06	
	Upper Ballyknag	008		007	001
	Irish Ballardreen	08		08	
	Scotts Ballardreen	08		08	
	Lower Ballyknag	05		03	02
	Upper Ballyvelton	13		12	01
	Lower Ballyvelton	05		04	01

[1] *Colranie*, folios 50 and 52.

Parishes	Townelands	Number of People	Tituladoes Names	Eng & Scotts	Irish
	Big Ilan Everick	07		07	—
	Little Ilan Everick	06		—	06
	½ Qr of Pollans	04		04	—
	Tournaganock	08		07	01
	½ Culdary	14		—	14
	½ towne of Drumore	08		04	04
	Loughanreagh	16		10	06
(folio 49). Ballymony pte	Pt of Tournagnock	03		03	000
	Upper Ballydonelan	07		07	
	Lower Ballydonelan	03		03	
	Culbrine Eaglesse	07		—	07
Balliwillin	Carneboye	06		04	02
	Cloyfin	06		04	02
	Killgreyne	05		03	02
	Ballylaggan	07		07	—
	Ballylagan	04		04	—
	Ardsmernan	10		10	—
	Bally McKillnena	07		05	02
	Ilanmore	06		—	06
(folio 50). Bally-willin.	Bally McIllwena	09		09	—
	Balleyreagh	04		03	01
	Ilanflakey	05			05
	Lukestowne	02			02
	Magherryboye	05		05	
	Maghremenagh	04			04
	Coristowne	05		04	01
	Killgren	03		01	02
	Cragardavarran	008		—	008
	Carnanrigg	05		03	02
Ballaghran	Drumslead	08		06	02
	Maghretlay	02			02
	Killteny	10		06	04
	Killtenny	06		04	02
	Ballyleace	10			10
(folio 51)	Ballyleace	08		08	
	Gallnolly	04		02	02
	Gallvolley	12		04	08
Killoyne	Ballycarne	12	Captn Richard Bickerstaffe Esqr	10	02
	Killcranny	06		04	02
	Drimaquill	07		05	02
	Castletodry	10		08	02
	Ballymore more	05		05	—
	Maghareby	17		05	12
	Cullerasheskin	16	Lieut Robert Brice gent	09	07
	Knockvernisse	19		10	09

Parishes	Townelands	Number of People	Tituladoes Names	Eng & Scotts	Irish
Macasquy	Macosquy	22	Cornelius Wall & Edward Canning gents	11	11
	Farrenseere	05		05	—
(folio 52).	Advernisse	02		000	02
Macosquy	Dundergg	04			04
	Crossegarr	04		04	
	Cullur	06		06	
	Kilconogher	06		06	
	Clanlary	14		12	02
	Busstowne	06		06	—
	Drumor	06		02	04
	Moyclary	14		14	
	Croaghan	06			06
	Cashell	02			02
	Lactlestrum	012		002	010
	Balteagh	08			08
	Kiltenny	14		06	08
	Ringrashbeg	08		04	04
(folio 53).	Ringrashmoore	06		02	04
	Farrenlestrum	07		06	01
	Liss McMurphy	02		—	02
	Craghan	10	Francis Haward gent	04	06
	Taunemony	11			11
	Killmaconell	04			04
	Castleroe	28	John Rowley Esqr	15	13
	Lower Cumus	19		18	01
	Dunerat	05			05
	Ballyleggan	02		02	—
	Corduggan	05		05	—
	Coole	07		07	—
	Coolleveny	04		04	—
	Glantrull	05		03	02
	Cordram	04		04	—
(folio 54).	Curras	07			07
	Ballyteggert	06		05	01
	Ballyrakanan	10		08	02
	Camm	10		—	10
	Kinnaglass	13		10	03
	Drumreun	09		08	01
	Ballyruntagh	03		03	—
	Derrydorragh	10		10	—
	Litterloan	11		—	11
	Ballywilliam	08		08	—
	Ballenteerebeg	07	James Jackson gent	04	03
	Ballenteeremore	11		03	08
	Ballyvenoxe North	17		13	04

Parrishes	Townelands	Number of People	Tituladoes Names	Eng & Scotts	Irish
Dunboe	Ballystrons	07		05	02
(*folio* 55).	Quillies	010		005	005
	Ballybleeks	05		05	—
	Upper Dartrees	06		—	06
	Fox Dartrees	08		04	04
	Dunallies	14		05	09
	Ballanrees	07		06	01
	Masrigue	15		07	08
	Ballany	07		05	02
	Farran lester	10		03	07
	Mullan	10		08	02
	Grange.·.·e	12		06	06
	Pottoch	14		14	—
	Grangebeg	07		03	04
	Ballywillin	08		06	02
	Beggtowne	06		04	02
	Famullan	04		02	02
(*folio* 56)	Scoutland	05		02	03
	Farmoile	03		—	03
	Brotwall	08		04	04
	Artibryan	05		—	05
	Duinguie	04		02	02
	Ballywillriggmoore	08		06	02
	Ballywilriggbeg	04		04	—
	Knockanther	03		03	—
	Burians	19		04	15
	Beurees	09		—	09
	Drumagullien	02		—	02
	Tertoriane	10		10	—
	Artikirah	05		03	02
	Coxherna	06		06	—
(*folio* 57).	Ballyhacketts Glusuktarnie	05			05
	Ballyhacketts Magillegan	008		006	002
	Ballyhacketts Tabyochis	06		02	04
	Ballyhacketts Glenhonie	05		—	05
	Ballywodoke	07		07	—
	Ballmadukin	16		09	07
	Ballymadukin Freehold	12		06	06
	Luffeg	10		08	02
	Ballymony	06		04	02
	Articleare	34		17	17
Oughill Desert	Coolenoman	12		02	10
(*folio* 58).	Monydregie	24			24

Parrishes	Townelands	Number of People	Tituladoes Names	Eng & Scotts	Irish
	Trenaltenagh	08			08
	Coolaromar	16		11	05
	Ye 2 Moveinryes	24		10	14
	Dullaghey	14			14
	Ballyvory	16		10	06
	Lissacrin	09		07	02
	Edentaine	09			09
	Moletraghtay	06			06
	Drumdemph	10		06	04
	Keering	12		06	06
	Killavally	11		08	03
	Carroreagh	05		05	—
	Ballyagon	14		08	06
	Moletraghkill	10		09	01
(folio 59).	Gorterloughon	04			04
	Duimeringay	07		03	04
	Ballydonaghan	08		03	05
	Greggate	04		04	
	Luragh	04		04	
	Prosclount	11			11
	Poole bane	009		003	006
	Magharemoore	10		06	04
	Deerteerin	12		06	06
	Parballintubber	05		01	04
	Ballymanagh	04		02	02
Aughadowey	Lihomoore	22	Paull Canning Esqr	15	07
	Culleroe & Pee	14		04	10
	Skallter	07		07	—
(folio 60).	Rusky	05		03	02
	Derniecrosse	34	Robert Blaire and Hugh Rowly gentlemen	16	18
	Ballygally	08		05	03
	Lisnemuck	07	William Blaire gent	06	01
	Ballybrittum	04		04	—
	Cullems	05		03	02
	Cruaghstanly	05		05	—
	Ballynaclogh	03		03	—
	Killeagh	17		10	07
	Minibranan	04		04	—
	Manogher	12		08	04
	Knockadon	09		04	05
	Balsenry	19		15	04
	Clagan	06		—	06
	Drumell	04		—	04
	Ballywillen	02		—	02
(folio 61).	Senlongfortt	02		000	02

Parrishes	Townelands	Number of People	Tituladoes Names	Eng & Scotts	Irish
	Ballenakellymore	03		01	02
	Ballenakellybeg	06		06	—
	Mullan	03		—	03
	Killine	03		02	01
	Ballynamintagh	02		—	02
	Creaggalynn	06		04	02
	Clantagh	06		—	06
	Crossmitkerer	008		008	—
	Neameknogher	06		02	04
	Killtest	06		—	06
	Myncregge	08		—	08
	Menogh	02		02	—
	Carusalogh	09		05	04
	Ardriach	09		09	—
	Derinegrosse	03		02	01
(*folio* 62). Augho-dowey.	Lisboy	18		07	11
	Colicapell	05		05	—
	Clankin	04		04	—
	Mallachinch	08		08	—
	Gortine and Kavetatt	08		06	02
	Caruro	04		02	02
	Bovach	11		11	—
	Chaeine	12			12
	Sodagevie	10			10
	Glaskarlt	31		13	18
	Clonbabe	08		05	03
	Clarhilte	09			09
	Killikergen	04			04
	Monitary	05		05	—
	Mulmabrowe	06		02	04
	Gortine	11		—	11
(*folio* 63).	Mirchell	13		06	07
	Sigorrie	08		05	03
Arrygall	Shanlongford	06		—	06
	Curraghnadolke & Mayboy }	12		08	04
	Cogh	06			06
	Taunaghmoore	06			06
	Lisscall	08			08
	Clunkeene	06			06
	Moyettican	006		002	004
	Junisseene	07			07
	Farrentimly	08			08
	Duneveny	08			08
	Brackaghboy	07			07

Parrishes	Townelands	Number of People	Tituladoes Names	Eng & Scotts	Irish
(folio 64)	Culcroskran	08			08
	Lisnaskreghog	06			06
	Brockagh	12			12
	Tingauly	04			04
	Tuibarrean	04			04
	Ballystrade	08			08
	Gortmeah	10			10
	Gortfad	07			07
	Ballyrogan	06			06
	Cullnisillagh	08			08
	Ballysrin	08			08
	Bealragh & Frighidonell	09			09
	Garvagh	47	George Mines gent	22	25

Principall Irish Names [and] their Number

McAllester, 012 ; Allen, 07 ; Browne, 08 ; Black, 07 ; McConnell, 09 ; Ô Cahan, 27 ; McCormick, 07 ; Clearke, 07 ; McCleland, 09 ; McCooke, 06 ; Ô Doughertye, 06 ; Ô Demsie, 13 ; O Henry, 12 ; Moore, 11 ; Ô Mullan, 29 ; McNeale, 06 ; O Quig, 14 ; Reade, 13 ; Smith, 19 ; White, 08.

(folio 64 verso). Barrony [of Coleraine] : Eng & Scotts, 1549 ; Irish, 1201 ; 2750 tottall.

Barronies & ye Citty of	Pages	Eng & Scotts	Irish	Totall of Eng Scotts & Irish
Londonderry Citty	04	572	480	1052
Terkerin Barr :	14	640	979	1619
Kenaght Barr :	28	1012	1215	2227
Loghinsholin	46	0655	1431	2086
Colraine towne & Barrony	64	1549	1201	2750
		4428	5306	9734
		572	480	1052
		3856	4826	8682
			3856	
			8682	

COUNTY OF MONAGHAN
4083

(folio 1.) Parishes	Places	Numbs of People	Tituladoes Names	English	Irish
Monaghan	Monaghan	133	Richard Blaney Esqr Thomas Wyatt gent Nicholas Owen gent Mathew Boyd gent John Thomas gent	32	101
	Tullyard	10			10
	Cormeen	6			6
	Cornemody	4			4
	Sheetrim	12			12
	Rakeeragh	4			4
	Tonerigiban	6			6
	Knokeaghy	6			6
	Skegervie	8			8
	Gartekeghan	11		2	9
	Veblekirke	4			4
	Cornekessagh	12		2	10
	Aghanaved	4			4
	Tawlatt	2			2
	Drumbior	4			4
(folio 2).	Croghery	2			2
	Coolehanagh	8		4	4
	Corvess	2			2
	Aghanaseid	14			14
	Killmoghill	12			12
	Teerflevertye	9			9
	Lisraherke	2			2
	Corduffles	4			4
	Castleshean	13		2	11
	Teerlum	2			2
	Leggnerey	7			7
	Rackwalis	9			9
	Off the Moyles	2		—	2
Teedawnett	Tulaghan	28	John Forster Esqr		28
	Anyerk	11			11
	Anaghgally	10			10
(folio 3).	Kibragrallan	14			14
	Quigalagh	14			14
	Raffman	8		3	5
	Monaghanduff	10	Patrick Roonye gent		10
	Corchill	2		2	
	Tullycruman	9			9
	Cappoge	6		4	2
	Drumgoase	8		8	—
	Drumgarne	4		2	2
	Tubedan	6			6
	Coolkill	10			10

Parishes	Places	Numbs of People	Tituladoes Names	English	Irish
	Drumsillagh	22			22
	Drumslavoge	10	George Scott gent	8	2
	Aghagae	4		2	2
	Ligess	8	Richard Cadie gent		8
	Gola	6	James Wright gent	2	4
	Graffagh	12			12
(folio 4).	Farmogle	4		2	2
	Clomvollye	4	John Forster gent	2	2
	Aghaboy	6	John Burrowes gent	6	—
	Itererye	16			16
	Foremace	12			12
	Aghery	18			18
	Edenbrone	16			16
	Sheskan	6			6
	Skenedowan	8			8
	Bogha	8			8
	Drumbyor	14			14
	Teeravertye	8			8
	Drumlarye	6		2	4
	Teenaskee	6		—	6
Kilmore	Mullmacross	8	Richard Poakrich gent	4	4
	Aghanamalaght	4	Michaell Poekrich gent	2	2
(folio 5).	Druma Conn^r	8	Edward Pockrich gent	6	2
	Anaghcenye	5	Beniamin Rose gent	2	3
	Ballymeaghan	1	John Cole gent	1	—
	Ballyleck	4		3	1
	Kilaleine	8			8
	Lisnart	12			12
	Sranudan	8			8
	Banaghue banc	13			13
	Glenesh	5			5
	Ballingarriagh	3			3
	Losht	13			13
	Doonremon	2			2
	Lisnaber	3			3
	Teetappagh	4			4
	Corr	6			6
	Tulligillan	6			6
	Corneglare	10			10
	Teer McDowan	4			4
(folio 6).	Carcavan	7	Humphrey Sherigley Esqr	4	3
	Cloonlagh	7	William Smyth gent	5	2
	Druminikin	6		3	3
	Skerowan	10		4	6
	Carnebane	8		4	4
	Knaghill	4		4	—

Parishes	Places	Numbs of People	Tituladoes Names	English	Irish
	Coolsillagh	2		2	—
	Knaghill	4		—	4
	Liscatt	2		2	—
	Drumgarrow	15			15
	Ballagh	12			12
	Calcaragh	8		—	8
	Cabragh	6			6
	Cooldarragh	3			3
	Drumguill	6			6
	Skeagh	3	John Wileman gent	3	—
(folio 7). Eriglee	Grange	6	James Hamilton gent	2	4
	Mulaghcore	12			12
	Mullidorragh	2			2
	Erigle	4		4	
	Mullaghnetarne	2		2	
	Derinlossett	4			4
	Deryveagh	2			2
	Killoreen	4			4
	Liskma	10			10
	Kilibragh	4			4
	Kilileckoghtragh	4			4
	Glassmullagh	6			6
	Glanmore	8			8
	Glanbegg	12			12
	Drumfurror	2			2
	Dremdrislen	8			8
	Shanmullagh	8			8
(folio 8). Erigle.	Killnegullan	10			10
	Brackagh	4			4
	Kilbressell	8			8
	Davagheaghtragh	2			2
	Lanagh	6			6
	Lisvargue	4			4
	Aghareske	2			2
	Kilnageere	2			2
	Lanagh	8			8
	Corlattallon	4			4
	Cavan	6		4	2
	Drumconra	6		—	6
	Kilfahawen	8			8
	Kilymurrey	8			8
	Drumtorke	6			6
	Fedilreagh	12			12
	Mullin	6			6
(folio 9).	Corkin	4			4
	Aghaliskeevan	5	Lewis Blaney gent	2	3

Parishes	Places	Numbs of People	Tituladoes Names	English	Irish
	Kessaghmone	8			8
	Austrich	4			4
	Kilidonagh	8			8
	Kilidreen	4			4
	Kileleckeaghtragh	6			6
	Derrylea	6			6
	Aghie McCluny	10		2	8
	Mulaghoaghtragh	6		2	4
	Cloonkin	6			6
	Kilibrane	4			4
	Esker	4			4
	Drumberrin	4		2	2
	Tonagh	6		2	4
	Derinaved	4			4
	Raghcooan	4			4
(folio 10)	Mullaghcask	6		4	2
	Mullaghmore	6		2	4
	Dermamock	4			4
	Davagheaghtragh	6			6
	Derygoledagh	4			4
	Drumconnelly	8			8
	Kilcorran	4			4
	Derykinea	6			6
	Kilyhoman	12		2	10
Donagh	Glasslough	41	Oliver Ankettill Esqr William Johnston gent	24	17
	Mulaghjordan &c	8		—	8
	Clerye	12			12
	Anaghgattin	2			2
	Cavan	8		2	6
	Anaray	9	William Norrice gent	6	3
	Sillis	10			10
(folio 11).	Luart	6		2	4
	Kilibollye	4		2	2
	Tonicumigan	2		2	—
	Rinanye	9			9
	Mullaghbane	6			6
	Bruaghmore	4		4	
	Aghanesklin	6	David Johnston Esqr	6	
	Edanillan	12		10	02
	Cornasrora	6			6
	Drumgarne	5			5
	Kilylaghan	9			9
	Griggie	10			10
	Teernanyneile	4			4
	Mullaghbreak	4			4

Parishes	Places	Numbs of People	Tituladoes Names	English	Irish
	Inagh	10			10
	Toneygarvye	8			8
	Aghagapp	4		2	2
	Tullycalloge	4		2	2
(folio 12).	Dondonagh	8		8	—
	Aghboy	10		—	10
	Clognart	6		4	2
	Kilerean	10			10
	Derylea	8			8
	Imoge	25	Walter Crimble gent	8	17
	Derywish	4			4
	Mulinlisk	4			4
	Monmorey	8		—	8
	Lick	6			6
	Anaghbegg	8			8
	Tiledan	6	William Hollande gent	5	1
	Drumbanchor	14	Nicholas Hollande gent	6	8
	Purtnaghie	4			4
	Tullagh	6			6
	Pallis	6	Thomas Baker gent	3	3
	Derygassan	2		2	
(folio 13).	Skevernakeeragh	10		6	4
	Celvie	4			4
Dartrye all's	Conaghie	7	John Mulhallam gent		7
Galoone	Drumgillye	4	Patr' Mulhallom gent		4
	Rooskie	4			4
	Drumca	4			4
	Shancoagh	8			8
	Carnoyne	5			5
	Lecklevery	4		2	2
	Cornewall	8	Thomas Boyle gent	6	2
	Coaghin	11			11
	Lishtellen	11	Rich : Beard gent	2	9
	Kilcunagh	4			4
	Ballinure	6			6
	Gartgreenca	7			7
	Drumhillagh	6			6
(folio 14). Dartrye all's	Corconalye	7			7
Galloone.	Coolenalonge	2			2
	Drumlume	6			6
	Crossoane	4			4
	Drumsarke	4			4
	Lisabock	6		2	4
	Cloonfadd	4		—	4
	Lisnagorr	3	Rob't Bramston gent	2	1
	Mulnaseno	3		3	

Parishes	Places	Numbs of People	Tituladoes Names	English	Irish
	Drumskett	2			2
	Lishalea	7			7
	Tulyard	6			6
	Kileevan	5			5
	Corhinsagagh	13		09	4
	Creeran	18			18
	Drumboriske	6			6
	Tonentalagh	6			6
(*folio* 15).	Aghareagh	11			11
	Drum	25	Robert Aldrich gent	9	16
	Lisarcark	10			10
	Kilenanye	16			16
	Cabragh	15			15
	Drumgeen	15			15
	Cavan	7			7
	Kilsanlish	17			17
	Mullaghmore	10			10
	Aghanahoula	26	William Scott gent	3	23
	Lisleagh	15			15
	Coolenechart	11			11
	Kilifargee	10			10
	Doonsryin	10		2	8
	Any	6	Tho : Farmor gent	2	4
	Gobduff	4		2	2
	Clonisten	26	Jacob Lerye gent		26
	Clenluer	6		2	4
(*folio* 16). Datrye all's Galloone.	Cloonfadd and Cortuber }	18			18
	Corvackan	20		—	20
	Corgary	16			16
	Corney	12			12
	Kilmore	18			18
	Drumlaghill	8			8
	Dean	6		6	00
	Kilcree	6			6
	Monninton	2		2	
	Druminton	2		2	
	Lysnaspeenan	4			4
	Aitteeduff	6		2	4
	Drynamoyle	4		4	
	Kilmore	6			6
	of ye Island	2		2	
	Drumore	4		2	2
(*folio* 17)	Drumlyna	13			13
	Corlack	12			12
	Carran	10			10

Parishes	Places	Numbs of People	Tituladoes Names	English	Irish
	Drumullan	o6			6
	Tonarry	2			2
	Drumbargach	6			6
	Drumsona	25			25
	Carowglass	6	John Cossens gent	2	4
	Bakeeragh	8			8
	Kilagragh	8			8
	Tonagh	14			14
	Mullagh garran	19			19
	Coragh	14			14
	Crogher	8			8
	Aghareagh	4			4
	Drumheagh	8			8
	Lislaughill	6	Hugh Elott gent	2	4
(folio 18). Dantry all's Galloone.	Kileleagh	2	Joseph Welch gent	—	2
	Curraghastee	2	Richard Ley gent	2	—
	Doohailee	2		—	2
	Cornewall	2		2	
	Corkaleir	6			6
Clownish	Clownish	27	Richard Barrett Esqr	15	12
	Fee	5			5
	Clondraghill	3			3
	Cloonmore	3		1	2
	Cloankeen	5			5
	Anaghill	7			7
	Cloontreal	5			5
	Drumcreue	8			8
	Clankirkue	8			8
	Leggnakelly	3			3
	Cavan	7		002	05
	Lawhill	2			2
	Coraghue	4			4
(folio 19). Clonish.	Crevagh	2			2
	Clooncurin	7			7
	Bologbrene	3		3	
	Ratmoy	7			7
	Shankill	8			8
	Ballintoppan	11			11
	Kilygormlye	3		3	
	Ratgolin	3		2	1
	Cloonily	8			8
	Magheryarne	10			10
	Tonelegee	5		2	3
	Drumard	3			3
	Teernahinch	5		—	5

Parishes	Places	Numbs of People	Tituladoes Names	English	Irish
Macaross	Macaross	150	The Marquess of Hartford and the Viscount his sonn William Barton Esqr	50	100
	Drumgoane	6			6
(folio 20)	Mullaghcroghey	11		000	11
	Cornasaghna	8		—	8
	Tullygarvans	10			10
	Latanalbin	6			6
	Corcreagh	3			3
	Cargehey	10			10
	Corcreen	4			4
	Corentigagh	12			12
	Greagh	6			6
	Lisdrumtirk	6			6
	Rafferagh	4			4
	Ardragh	6			6
	Corvalyes	4			4
	Drumgowan	5			5
	Cormentye	8			8
	Peisl	5			5
	Feaghice	7			7
(folio 21).	Gragnaroge	10			10
	Leckemurrey	8			8
	Magheryboy	6			6
	Lisaniskie	9		4	5
Donomoyne	Donomoyne	12			12
	Larragh	10			10
	Corleck	10			10
	Bockes	10			10
	Skenagin	8		—	8
	Clescluie	12			12
	Lisnamoyle	10			10
	Coriagan	10			10
	Corintiogatt	2			2
	Drumconver	10			10
	Kilmore	8			8
	Corligorin	12			12
	Blittery	10			10
	Aghergin	9			9
(folio 22)	Mullagh in Sinan	12			12
	Black Staffye	02			02
	Creevie	8			8
	Kilibeggie	10			10
	Ramore	08			08
	Petertowne	4		2	2

Parishes	Places	Numbs of People	Tituladoes Names	English	Irish
	Drumhillagh	2		2	oo
	Corderymone	8			o8
	Lisagower	8			8
	Drumgarnes	8			8
	Mulariagh	6			6
	Tullycomett	4			4
	Drumgrittan	4			4
	Drumgoase	6			6
	Macurkill	4			4
	Kednyagutlin	10			10
	Cooldery	6			6
(folio 23)	Srencoagh	8			8
	Cloonagrettan	6			6
Magherecloney	Mulaghcosht	14			14
	Corcreagha	7			7
	Kilnabegg	6		—	6
	Kilark	6			6
	Tomiskie	12			12
	Maghernacley	4			4
	Drumboe	12			12
	Liscarnan	10		2	8
	Derry	3			3
	Newrbegg	18			18
	Ballyloghan	8			8
	Newrmore	6			6
	Doohaite	8			8
	Derinscoab	2			2
	Derinlagh	6			6
(folio 24). Maghereclony.	Corkirin	4			4
	Clooncon	8			8
	Drumgossatt	8			8
	Tulylogherly	6			6
	Corbrackan	6			6
	Comaghie	2			2
	Deryvock	16			16
	Lawgillduff	6			6
	Drumbrackan	4			4
	Graghloan	6			6
	Tonenene	6			6
	Doneltye	7			7
	Mullaghinteer	6			6
	Conterk	10			10
	Coolremoney	4			4
	Drumrevie	6			6
	Sanra	7			7
(folio 25).	Anaghian	12			12

Parishes	Places	Numbs of People	Tituladoes Names	English	Irish
	Leige	8		—	8
	Anaghmerian	8			8
	Drumgenor	6			6
	Ballingarne	13			13
Eniskeene	Ballykelly	7	Arthur Whitehead gent	2	5
	Drumgleragh	9			9
	Cornegarvoge	14			14
	Drumore	10			10
	Aghieglass	11			11
	Drumerill	20			20
	Carraghs	27			27
	Drumass	10			10
	Teernasrullye	4			4
	Keenogess	5			5
	Drumboat	8			8
(folio 26)	Emryes	6		2	4
	Druman	21			21
	Teerdonery	6			6
Aghanamullan	Ballinlogh	8			8
	Baraghie	5			5
	Lutture	5			5
	Tullenahmone	5			5
	Banmore	4			4
	Caragh	14			14
	Corskeagh	6			6
	Mullingour	6			6
	Clossagh	4			4
	Keenoge	2			2
	Corywrann	4			4
	Carrikatee	8			8
	Corwellin	10			10
	Shanvonagh	11		—	11
(folio 27)	Luiny	6			6
	Corlaghert	8			8
	Lorgecumlagh	6			6
	Lisdrum	12			12
	Cloantrym	6			6
	Corlea	5			5
	Derydoonye	6			6
	Drumgor	11			11
	Lisdrumloot	9			9
	Farmoyle	12			12
	Tullybrack	7			7
	Corkeerin	10			10
	Corfaddow	7			7
	Muraghmore	8			8

Parishes	Places	Numbs of People	Tituladoes Names	English	Irish
	Annie	11			11
	Corduvless	6			6
	Liscallanan	8			8
(*folio* 28). Clantibred	Cavan Creevy	15			15
	Faddin	10			10
	Creman	8			8
	Teer	2			2
	Drumboe	8			8
	Dooskeagh	7			7
	Eniss	3			3
	Ballagh	8			8
	Crossey	6			6
	Coolentragh	5			5
	Lemagarr	9			9
	Brynlitter	3			3
	Lisglassen	11			11
	Moyghs	9		—	9
	Lisginy	8			8
	Drumore	6			6
	Crossmore	6			6
	Letnehelly	5			5
(*folio* 29).	Cassill	4			4
	Dorna	5			5
	Creevy	11			11
	Litter	5			5
	Aghycurkry	4			4
	Carickneer	5			5
	Cloyhan	14			14
	Creemartin	2			2
	Corbatt Durgan	2			2
	Drumirrill	5			5
	Mulaghduff	7			7
	Anyalla	4			4
	Anagh	6			6
	Coraghkeen	5			5
	Griggi	14			14
Tulicabett	Corfinlagh	17			17
	Cornacreevy	6			6
(*folio* 30).	Corway	19			19
	Teeramadan	4			4
	Cargagh	16			16
	Corwale	6			6
	Any McNeile	14			14
	Corduvleck	6			6
	Teeryoraghan	6			6
	Glogher	8			8

Parrishes	Places	Numbs of People	Tituladoes Names	English	Irish
	Tony Glassoge	5			5
	Cnappagh	7		—	7
	Carignare	6			6
	Drumhaum	22			22

Principall Irish Names [and] their Numb

McArdell, 20 ; Ô Boyle & Boyle, 9 ; Ô Beggan, 12 ; Ô Boylan, 13 ; Ô Brynan, 9 ; Ô Bryn & Bryn, 11 ; Ô Birne & Birne, 15 ; McClaue, 12 ; O Coogan, 7 ; McCarwell, 10 ; McConoly &c, 9 ; Ô Connoly, 56 ; Ô Cullin and McCullin, 11 ; McCallan & Ô Callan, 32 ; Ô Clerian & Ô Cleregan, 16 ; McCassye, 7 ; Ô Clerkan, 013 ; McCabe, 40 ; Ô Duffie, 69 ; O Dally, 8 ; McEntee, 13 ; Flanagan, 13 ; Ô Finagan, 22 ; McGonnell, 18 ; McGormon, 15 ; McGinnis, 10 ; McGowan, 10 ; Ô Gowan, 16 ; McGough, 10 ; Ô Hugh, 22 ; Ô Hamell, 9 ; Ô Kenan, 9 ; McKenna &c, 91 ; Ô Lowan, 9 ; Ô Murrey, 10 ; Murphy and Ô Murphy, 38 ; McMaghone, 112 ; Ô Muligan, 9 ; McNeny, 15 ; McPhillip, 23 ; Ô Quin & Quin, 16 ; McQuade, 11 ; McRory, 7 ; Ô Sherry &c, 10 ; McTrenor, 30 ; McWard, 15 ; McAward, 15.

(folio 30 verso).   The Number of People in the County of Monaghan : Eng, 0434 ; Irish, 3649 ; totall of Eng & Irish, 4083.

CLARE COUNTY
16914

(*folio* 1).

BARONY OF BUNRATTY

County of Clare

Parishes	Townelands[1]	Numbs of People	Tituladoes Names	Eng	Irish
Bunratty	——	92		00	92
	Ballynock and Clenemony }	67		00	67
Killraghtrish	Cloneskerrine	07	Thomas Butler gent	00	07
	Ballylinebeg	16	Moses Ash gent	02	14
	Bearafinchyne	17	Loghlen Ô Grady gent		17
	Ballyogane	33	Moylen Bruody gent Daniell Kenedy gent Bryan Kenedy gent		33
	Clonekerry	17			17
	Drumglane	07			07
	Dromkeeny	09	John McInerhidny gent		09
	Ballym-Cooney	43	David White gent Thomas White gent Peirce White gent Pierce White Junr gent Philip Ô Towlow gent		43
	Cappagh	29	Charles Ryane gent	—	29
(*folio* 2).	Cloonebeg	07			07
	Knockleskrane	05			05
	Carrowleahanagh	13	Thomas Stack gent		13
	Dromgranagh	16	Anthony Ryane gent		16
	Gortavally	05			05
	Ballymacahill	14			14
	Rosleavane	08	Nicholas Nealan gent		08
Quinhy	Dangen Iviggeene	35	Pierce Creagh gent		35
	Ballymariaghane	11	Nicholas Strich gent	02	09
	Ballyquilty	10	William Creagh Esq	00	10
	Gurteene	28	Patrick Meade gent Robert Meade gent		28
	Ballyroughane	27			27
	Ballyroughane and Rathlubby }	05	Morrogh O Bryen gent		05
	Cullane	10	James Sexton & George Sexten his sonne gent		10
(*folio* 3).	Ballymulcaney	21	Garrett Barry gent		21
	Carhownenuer	08	Morrish Sexten gent		08
	Cornemalla	14	Donnogh McNemara		14
	Cotteene	26	Mahon McNenda gent James Houregan gent		26
	Crevagh	61			61

[1]*Towns and places*, folios 2–4.

Parishes	Townelands	Numbs of People	Tituladoes Names	Eng	Irish
	Quinhy towne	68	John Sexten gent James Nihill gent Peirce Loftus gent Daniell Kelloher gent Thomas Creagh gent Stephen White gent	03	65
	Knoppog	16			16
	Ballyquiltybeg	10			10
	Quinhy Towne continued	14	Jeremy Reeues gent	02	12
	Laccarowbeg	08	Edward Strich gent	02	06
	Kiefeast	04			04
	Polegare	03			03
(folio 4).	Killnacarongirra	16			16
	Knappoge	13	Arthur Smyth gent	02	11
Cloney	Corbally	10			10
	Knockprichane	04	Gibbon Fitzgibbon gent		04
	Maghery West	09	James Butler gent	00	09
	Maghery East	44	John Power gent John Roch gent William Power and Edward Power gent John Condon gent Marcus McGrath gent		44
	Cahirloghane	16	David Stapleton gent		16
	Townaghs more and Beg	15	Teige Ryane, and Daniell Ryane gent William Ryan and Connr Ô glissan gent		15
	Rathclony	18			18
	Ballyvergin	05	Mathew Lawliss gent		05
(folio 5).	Ballyvroghane	17	Edmond Power and Tho : Power gent		17
	Ballyhickie	14			14
	Clony	15	James Fitzgerald gent		15
	Leassana	09	George Roch, and James Roch gent		09
	Cahirgeridon	22	Daniell McMenda gent Donnogh Ô Glissan gent		22
	Craneeyher	03			03
	Cahirshaghnessy and Corroghmoghan	20	Nicholas Bellow gent	02	18
	Castletowne	17	Doctr John Nealan Esq		17
Dowry	Ballyhinane	57	Thomas Hickman Esq George Stamers gent	07	50
	Poulroe	21	Donnogh McNemara gent		21
	Castletowne	37	Mathew McMahon gent		37
	Knokeneane	11			11
	Knockiskibbell	15		00	15

Parishes	Townelands	Numbs of People	Tituladoes Names	Eng	Irish
(folio 6).	Ballaghboy	19			19
	Kilbrickanbeg	07	Edward Cuff gent	02	03
	Noghovall	18			18
	Moinino	24	Sr David Bourke Kt & Bart David oge Bourk, and James Bourke gent		24
	Ballyorla	17			17
	Kilbrickanmore	11	Teige McNemara gent Connor McNemara gent		11
	Ballymulcrehy	29	Daniell McNemara gent James McNemara gent		29
	Moyreash	26	Terlagh McMahon gent		26
Finagh	Rath	25			25
	Ardkeill	21	Oliver Bourk gent		21
	Killnecreevy	16			16
	Rosmanagher	100	John Tompkins gent Edmond Summers gent John Leo gent Michaell Fitzgerrald gent	10	90
(folio 7).	Finagh Towne	29		02	27
Drombine	Drombine	59	Daniell McNemara gent John McNemara his sonn gent		59
	Crossagh	07			07
	Quillin	22			22
	Ballyquineene	10			10
	Ballycassy	08			08
	Ballycassy-Oughtragh	06			06
	Tullaverga	33	Richard Clanchy gent		33
	Smythstowne	18	Morrish Hallurane gent	00	18
	Knockane	04			04
	Cahirteige	20	John Ô Rideene gent		20
	Dromgilly	17	William Sarsfield gent		17
	Cahirteige	18			18
	Ballynacloghy	09			09
(folio 8).Temple-	Ballymally	18	Robert Roch gent		18
mally	Treanaderry	09	David Fitzgibbon gent		09
	Tranrosk	05			05
	Ballycarwell	14			14
	Killyane	11			11
	Cappaghard	22			22
	Ballycorey	22	James England gent		22
	Drumconra	22	Morgan Ryane gent		22
	Ballyally	62	Redmond Keating gent Isreall ô Callaghan gent David Lawlor Esq		62
	Ballyduff	05			05
Killynoane	Bealkellane	01	Thomas Foote gent	01	00

Parishes	Townelands	Numbs of People	Tituladoes Names	Eng	Irish
	Sᵗ Thomas Iland	o8	Edward Gould gent William Strich gent Thomas Poore gent	o4	o4
(folio 9). Kille-noane	Polequine	o4			o4
	Cappangressane	o9			o9
	Parteen	o2	Michaell Arthur gent	o2	
	Glanegross	o4	Laurence Comyne gent Stephen Creagh gent		o4
	Blackwater	o3		o1	o2
	Girrans	o3			o3
	Dermond	o2			o2
	Bealkellan	o6		o2	o4
Sᵗ Munchion	Ditto	204		29	175
	Glanegross	o2		oo	o2
	Ditto	93		o8	85
KillanaSullagh	Dromolland	14	Robert Starkie gent William Starkie and Bryan Starkey gent		14
	Leattoone	18			18
	Carrowmore	19	Mahon McInerny gent		19
(folio 10).	Ballynecragg	46	Daniell McNemara gent Teige McNamara & Donnogh McNemara his sonns gent		46
	Carrowmore continued	19	— — —		19
	Ballygerrin	36	Peter Arthur gent	oo	36
	Balliconella	11	— — —		11
	Dromollane-agnie	16			16
	East Iny	27	Capt. Robert Nightingall gent	o2	25
	Carrigdorane	16	John Papping gent	o2	14
	Killana Sullagh	29	Samuell Burdett gent		29
	Treanahow	o9			o9
	East Bally Sallagh	23			23
	West Bally Sallagh	41			41
	Rathfeolane	32	Henry Coulpys gent		32
	Lisduff	11			11
(folio 11). Kill-maleary	West Ing	19			19
	Island McKnavin	16			16
	Clenagh	17	Sʳ Henry Ingoldesby Kᵗ Barᵗᵗ	o4	13
	Cahirobane	13			13
	Orlen	o5	Capt. William Duckett gent	o3	o2
Thomfinlagh	Ballycarr	69	John Coulpys gent James Loftus gent	o2	67
	Moghane	31	Ferdinardo Weedin gent	o3	28
	Masserelane	o4		oo	o4
	Laccaroweightragh	14		o3	11
	Tomfinlagh	48	Lawrence White gent	oo	48

Parishes	Townelands	Numbs of People	Tituladoes Names	Eng	Irish
	Rathlagheen	28			28
	Corraeathelin	09			09
Cloneloghane	Cloneloghane	54	Roger Hickie gent		54
(folio 12).	Leinneigh	02			02
Clonologhane	Ballynoskny	01			01
	Lisconnor	13			13
	Tullyglass	09			09
	Ballymortagh	08			08
	Tullaverga	20	Pierce Arthur gent		20
	Lennineigh	02			02
Killconnery	Ballynacloghy	14	Thomas Cullen Esq		14
	Ballykelly	42			42
	Garrynemona	90	Pierce Creagh Esq		90
	Finish Island	07			07
	Knockbeagh	38	Daniell Ô Bryen gent		38
Killfentanane	Erebell	57	Thomas Harrold gent William Thompson gent	06	51
	Ballyludanease	05			05
	Ballyrrogherane	21			21
(folio 13).	Ballintlea	39			39
	Ballymorriss	66	Patrick Brett Esq Francis Brett his sonne gent		66
	Garrincurra	24			24
	Portreene	26			26
	Moyhill, Knocknabricky, Ballemotie, and Toreowre	19	Giles Vandelure gent	02	17
	Moyhill	91	Shida MᶜNemara gent	00	91
Killeilly	Turnepicke	21			21
	Knockahelly	04	Edward Rice, gent	02	02
	Ballynaskie	06		00	06
	Gortgerrane	12		11	01
	Knocknaheelly againe	20			20
	Foybogh	06			06
	Derry	14	Andrew Rice gent	03	11
(folio 14).	Clonecoass	11			11
	Cragganaclugin	12			12
	Melicke	76	John Cooper gent William Nealane gent Teige ô Brien gent	02	74
	Crattellaghmoell	44	Leuᵗ Thomas Wyott gent	06	38
	Crattellaghmore	34			34
Inchicronan	Downe Imulvihill	40	John MᶜNemara Esq		40
	Cappanapestie	36	Richard Barry gent		36
	Bonahow	36	Thomas Butler gent		36
	Knockmoell	19			19

Parishes	Townelands	Numbs of People	Tituladoes Names	Eng	Irish
	Ballivany	30			30
	Iskidagh	07			07
	Cannanagh	04			04
	Millicke	52	Godfry Poore gent		52
	Crusheene	39	Shervington Skinner gent John Drew gent Barthlomew Bourke gent	08	31
(folio 15).	Carrayhill	10			10
	Sunnogh	20	Thomas Butler gent		20
	Dromonateuck	24			24
	Drominaknew	08			08
	Corrownacloghy	11			11
	Knocknamucky	19	Teige Ô Brien gent	00	19
	Shraghnagaloone	46	James Butler gent John Butler and Edmond Butler his sonns gents William Butler gent		46
	Gortaphicky	13	John Butler gent		13
	Drumvmna	32			32
	Clogogh	18	Leut Robert Rosdell gent Bryen Stapleton gent	02	16
	Beallnafiervarnen	19	William Roch Esq		19
	Drumbaniff	21	William Denn gent Robert Denn gent		21

(folio 16).   Principall Irish Names [and] their Numbers

Arthur, 11; Bryen & Mc and O Bryen, 26; Butler, 13; Bourke, 23; Barry, 06; McConnor, 23; Creagh, 14; Cunigam, 09; Considin, 09; Conellane, 11; Connell, 12; Casey or Cassy, 08; Cusacke, 11; Conny & Cunny, 13; Cuneen &c, 08; Clanchy, 16; Culane (8), and Culinane (5), 13; Cahill and Ô Cahill, 08; Carmody, 07; McCarthy, 08; McDaniell, 31; Dermody, 08; McDonnogh, 32; Ô Dwyre, 12; Dally & Ô Dally, 08; Donoghow, 07; Ferrilla. Ferilly and Ferilry, 11; Flanigane, 15; Grady and Ô Grady, 19; Gerane or Girane, 12; Fitzgerrold, 10; Ô Gripha &c, 14; Glissane, 10; O Hehir, 10; Ô Hallurane, 36; Hogan, 22; Ô Hashea, 11; Hickie, 25; Ô Hartigan, 09; O Haneen, 09; McInerhny or McInerny, 29; Fitz James (6), & McJames (5), 11; Kenedy, 14; Kelly, 09; McLoghlin, 19; McMorrogh, 13; Murphy, 11; Ô Mighane, 09; O Mullowny & Mullony, 47; McMahon, 27; Mahony, 07; Malloone &c, 12; McMortath, 17; McNemara, 52; Ô Nealane, 08; Ô Neall, 09; Ô Nihill, 12; Power, 12; Ô Quelly, 09; Roch, 07; McRory, 21; Rudane, 09; O Roughane, 12; Ryane & Ô Ryane, 10; McShane, 34; Slattery, 10; Sexten, 11; Strich, 07; McTeige, 47; McThomas, 10; McWilliam, 08; Welsh, 08; White, 16.

(folio 16 verso).   The Number of People in ye Barony of Bunratty : Eng, 144; Irish, 4204; totall Eng & Irish, 4348.

BARONY OF TULLA

Parishes	Townships	Numbs of People	Tituladoes Names	English	Irish
Teakill	Killana	58	Thomas Faning gent	oo	58
	Fahi	38	Donnogh Ô Brien gent Ter-lagh O Brien his sonn gent Owen O Brien gent	oo	38
	Cahirr	15	Thomas Faning gent	oo	15
	Gortadune	13			13
	Leighgort	38	John McNemara gent Daniell McNemara gent	oo	38
	Gortdrinane	18			18
	Mannaghgullen	44	Daniell McNemara gent		44
	Annagh	11	Thomas Thobbin gent		11
	Kilbarron	09	Doctr Patrick Connell gent		09
	Feakill	16	Mahon Rudan gent		16
	Laccarrow	29	John Butler Esq William Fitzwalter gent		29
	Carocloane	16	Theobald Butler gent James Ryan gent		16
	Knockbeagha	37	William Power Esq		37
(*folio* 18).	Feakill	17	Donnogh McNemara gent		17
Kilmurry	Rosscroe	47	William Purfoy Esq	06	41
	Kilkisheene	20	Peter Purfoy Esq	02	18
	Shandagen	13	Patrick Lysaght gent		13
	Kilcornane	10			10
	Shandangane	14		02	12
Killnoe	Ballydonoghane	18	Daniell Connery gent		18
	Lisbarreny	02			02
	Colereaghmore	19	Patrick Creagh gent		19
	Colereaghbeg	23	Dermott Ô Bryen gent		23
	Ballynahenchy	54	Edmond Magrath Esq Gallatius Dwyer gent		54
	Clonemogher	09	Anthony Garvane gent		09
	Cahirhurly	13	Geffry Prendergast gent		13
	Dromudd	08	Dermott Ryane gent		08
(*folio* 19).	West Cahirhurly	12	John Bourke gent		12
	Kilnoe	08			08
Killurane	Tyrovanine	29	Phillip Roch and Lawrence his sonn gents		29
	Killvoy	12		oo	12
	Duine	07	William Bridgeman gent	03	04
	Drominamakry	06			06
	Moneogennigh	50	John Ryane gent		50
	Killurane	23	Edmond Dwyre gent William Dwyre gent John Ô Dwyre gent		23

Parishes	Townships	Numbs of People	Tituladoes Names	English	Irish
	Clonecowle	24			24
	Laccarowgort-Ganniff	19			19
	Bally McDonnell	34	Morrish Fitzgerrold gent		34
(*folio* 20). Tulla	Lissofine	73	John Hart gent Richard Hartt gent		73
	Lahardane	22	Hugh Ô Kiefe gent		22
	Kilbeagon	27			27
	Ballymoilen	12	Arthur Stapleton gent		12
	Clondinagh	02			02
	Poulefory & Cragancroyne	41	Mathew Hally gent Thomas Wolfe gent		41
	Lisscollane	22	Dermott Carthy gent		22
	Rosslary	04			04
	Fertanemore	11			11
	Garrowragh	36	David Nihill gent		36
	Bunatory	19			19
	Formerly	24	Charles Carthy gent Donnogh Carthy gent		24
	Ballyslatery	19	John Fitzgibbon gent		19
(*folio* 21).	Tyredagh	24	David Sutton gent	04	20
	Carrignagnoe	23	William Bennis gent		23
	Killdonelbellagh	42	Teige Ô Mullowny gent		42
	Knockidoone	35	Connor Ô Mullowny gent		35
	Clonelorney	11			11
	Thome	25	Walter Sherlock gent		25
	Cragroe	11			11
	Kiltenane	23			23
	Affugg	38	Thomas Hewett gent Teige McNemarra gent	04	34
	Lismeeghane	11	Theobald Butler gent		11
	Fertanbeg	27	Thomas Magrath gent		27
	Tullagh	27	Phillipp Kelly gent		27
	Glandree	11			11
Moynoe	Coolecultane	42	Richard Strange Esq Paule and James Strange his sonns gents Rich : Butler gent	06	36
(*folio* 22)	Drumarey	42			42
	Minress	21	Edward FitzEdmond gent John Leo gent		21
	Corrowmore	23	Ôliver Keating gent Ôliver FitzArthur Keating gent Thomas Hennessy gent		23
Inishgaltragh	Clonty West	11	The Poore Lord of Killmallock		11
	Dromarty	19	George Thorneton Esq	02	17
Tuoguinla	— — —	51	George Purdon Esq		

Parishes	Townships	Numbs of People	Tituladoes Names	English	Irish
	Cahir Ballymulrona	12			12
	Scalpenore	12			12
	Ballyhurly	11			11
	Ballynagleragh	20			20
	Beallkelly	31	John FitzWilliam gent		31
	Carrowgard	15		00	15
	Beallkelly again	06			06
(*folio* 23).	Ballyvrane	06			06
	Carrowcore	05	Thomas Marnell gent	02	03
	Raheeny	11	Pierce Poore gent William, and Brice his sonns gents	04	07
	Ballyloghnane	15			15
	Ballyheiffy	10			10
Tomgreany	— — —	55	George Magee gent		55
	Ballyvanane	44	John Magee gent		44
	Raheeny	22			22
	Scarriff	11	David Magee gent		11
	Ballyvenoge	26			26
	Fossamore	16	Edmond Prendergast gent		16
	Fossabeg	11			11
	Knockgrady & Agherim	28	Edmond Roch gent John Roch gent		28
(*folio* 24)	Poligowre	09	Thoby Butler gent Thomas Shortall gent		09
	Cappaghroe, and Killderry	11	Thomas Butler gent, John Roch gent		11
	Cappacanon	19	Andrew Barrett gent Teige Ô Crowley gent David Ô Crowley and Fineene Ô Crowle his sons gent, Mathew Ô Cullane gent	02	17
	Derrymore	28	Miles Hiffernane gent James Hiffernane John Hiffernane and Roger Hiffernane his sonns gents		28
	Coologory	49	Donnogh Ô Driscoll Esq	00	49
	Corroqueile	06			06
Kilfenaghta	The Towne of Six Mile Bridge	259	Thomas White gent, Nicholas Harrold apothycary Edward Gould gent	24	235
	Ballymulchasshill	52	George Bennish gent		52
(*folio* 25). Kil- fennaghta	Ardma Clanchy	02			02
	Ballisseenbeg	08			08
	Ballisseenmore	42	Edmond Poore gent John Poore his sonn	04	38
	Cappagh	24			24

Parishes	Townships	Numbs of People	Tituladoes Names	English	Irish
	Pollagh	06			06
	Cloneasshy	19			19
	Lisheene	02			02
	Meohgally	13	Ensigne Mathew Curtis gent	04	09
	Cappanelaght	13			13
	Killnacreghy	10			10
	Beallacullen	07			07
	Ballynavan beg, and more }	25	Marcus Cransborrow gent	02	23
	Ballyarilla	10			10
Killseyly	Clonetrae	71	James Thobin gent Richard Thobin his sonne gent Richard Thobin gent		71
(folio 26).	Shanevogh	40	Francis Sexton gent James Poore gent		40
	Dromsallagh	20	Edmond Power gent		20
	Snatty	36	Patrick Morgan gent	00	36
	Ardskeagh	11			11
	Calluragh	15			15
	Ballykelly	35	James Wall Esq John Butler gent		35
	Killucully	30			30
Clonelea	Montallone	58	Donnogh Ô Callaghane Esq Teige, Donnogh, and Cahir his sonns gent		58
	Tyronea	07			07
	Scartduff	05			05
	Clonebruicke	04	John Stackpoole gent		04
	Derrinavragh	07			07
	Enagh	40	Barthlomew Stackpoole Esq		40
	Killeyne	13			13
(folio 27).	Gortadroma	15			15
	Knockatenty	27			27
	Gortachorky	15	Richard Barry gent Edmond Fitzgerrald gent		15
	Ballyvoyre	31			31
	Ballyverigane	15			15
	Killyvory	16	Pierce Bulger gent	02	14
	Gortacorky	07	Therlagh Ô Bryen gent Morrogh Ô Bryen gent Bryen Ô Bryen gent		07
Killogenedy	Ballyquine	35	Connor Ô Callaghane Esq		35
	Killmore	15			15
	Agheranabeg	20	James Hackett gent Andrew Hackett his sonne gent		20

Parishes	Townelands	Numbs of People	Tituladoes Names	English	Irish
	Farmoyle	23	Phillipp Prendergast gent Richard Butler gent Thomas Thobbin gent	oo	23
	Cloneconerymore	10	Thomas Magrath gent		10
(*folio* 28).	Cloneconorybeg	10			10
	Cloneyrehine	39	Allexander Howendon gent	02	37
	Barbane	20	John Butler gent		20
	Ballymolony	32	Henry Evers gent Edmond Mandowell gent James Evarald gent Walter Wall gent	06	26
	Hillegy	06	Teige Ryane gent		06
	Kilbane	07	Ireall Kenedy gent		07
	Killogennedy	10	Phillipp Dwyre gent		10
Kiltenanleigh	———— ———	18	William Gough Esq William Gough gent	04	14
	Coolishteig	14	Elias Prestwitch gent & his sonn gent	05	09
	Enirigh	17	Richard Vale gent Edmond Ryance gent Walter Bourke gent	02	15
(*folio* 29).	Killine	14	John Stackpooll gent		14
	Clonelary	13			13
	Neadannora	39	Daniell Barry gent Connor Clanchy gent		39
	Clonecollry	20			20
	Clonecarhy	05			05
	Derry Fady	24	William Bourke gent Thomas Bourke gent Edmond Bourke gent		24
	Garrane	07			07
	Sraghvickin	07		oo	07
	Cappavilly	09	Nicholas Wall gent		09
Killalow	Killalow	75			75
	Ballyvollha	15			15
	Cragleigh	17	Thomas Bourke gent John Bourke his sonn gent		17
	Ardcluony	15		04	11
	Ballycorny	14			14
	Clone Fada	16	Nicholas Starkie gent	04	12
(*folio* 30).	Laccarrowreaghmore	16	Henry Ryane gent Edmond Barry gent Gerrald Barry gent		16
	Laccaregh-beg	13	Dermott Ryane gent		13
	Glan Imulloone	08	Teige Ô Bryen gent Terlagh Ô Bryen gent Connor Ô Bryen gent		08

Parishes	Townelands	Numbs of People	Tituladoes Names	English	Irish
	Carrowgare and Carrowkilly }	27	Dermott Ô Bryen gent Marcus Bryen gent		27
	Ballycuggerane	11	Morrish Roch gent		11
	Ballyroe, Ballyknavin, and Killeragher }	53	Daniell McCarthy gent John Barrett gent	02	51
	Ardteigle	11			11
	Bryensbridge	08			08
	Parteencoreny	04		02	02
	Gortmagee	06	Edmond Hackett gent		06
	Glanagallagh	18	Thomas Stritch gent		18
(folio 31).	Ballygerrane	09	Connor Ryane gent John Ryane gent, and Daniell Ryane gent his sonns		09
	Killcridane	30	John Ô Mollane gent		30
	Agherenamore	14			14
	Troughy	12			12
	Ballyn Carrantroome	15	Garrett Barry gent	02	13
	Ballycarenaglogh	14			14
	Glanloyne	13			13

(folio 32)   Principall Irish Names [and] their Numb[er]

Arthur, 07 ; Ô Bryen, 37 ; Bruody, 10 ; Butler, 25 ; Bourke, 24 ; Barry, 18 ; Carmody, 08 ; Mc & Ô Connor, 24 ; Comane &c, 11 ; McCussocke, 21 ; Connell and O Connell, 07 ; McCarthy, 16 ; Ô Cunigane, 08 ; Ô Callaghane &c, 19 ; Callinane, 08 ; Creagh, 06 ; Culleen and Calene, 09 ; Clanchy, 08 ; Ô Carrull, 11 ; Coony, 09 ; McDonnogh, 22 ; McDermott, 07 ; Ô Dwyre, 36 ; McDaniell &c, 26 ; Dally, 09 ; Doogin &c, 09 ; Fox, 06 ; Feolane, 08 ; Fitzgerrald, 10 ; O Glissane &c, 10 ; O Grady, 11 ; Hallurane, 30 ; O Hea, 20 ; O Hehir, 07 ; Harrold, 07 ; Hart & Ô Hart, 06 ; Hogane, 25 ; Henessy, 06 ; Hicky, 27 ; Hiffernane, 08 ; Hally and Ô Hally, 15 ; Kelly, 10 ; Keogh, 12 ; McLoghlen, 12 ; Lynchy, 07 ; O Mullowny, 80 ; Murphy, 15 ; McMahon, 12 ; McNemarra, 38 ; Mahony, 12 ; Magrgh, 09 ; Minighane, 10 ; Meagher, 07 ; Ô Nealane, 08 ; Ô Neall, 06 ; Nash, 08 ; Oge, 09 ; Prendergast, 17 ; Power, 11 ; Stackpool, 07 ; Ô Sullevane &c, 21 ; McShida, 11 ; Swyny, 11 ; McShane, 30 ; McTeige, 32 ; McWilliam, 14 ; White, 07 ; Welsh, 05 ; Wall, 07.

(folio 32 verso).   The number of people in the Barony of Tulla : Eng, 106 ; Irish, 3903 ; Totall Eng & Irish, 4009.

(folio 33).   **BARONY OF INCHIQUINE**

Parishes	Townelands	Numbs of People	Tituladoes Names	Eng	Irish
Kellneboy	Corofiny	92		02	90
	Kilbodane	27		00	27
	Faukill and Ballydavine }	40	Moregh Ferriss gent	00	40

Parishes	Townelands	Numbs of People	Tituladoes Names	Eng	Irish
	Inchiquine	11			11
	BallyMᶜCuff	13			13
	Killneboy	25			25
	Lis McLyne	18			18
	Tullagh beg	02			02
	Pollagh	02			02
	Roughane	13		02	11
	Cahir Fada	05		03	02
	Caherneheely & Cahirblunick	21	Symon Daniell gent		21
	Dromoghir	11			11
	Owen	20	Loghlin Ô Hehir		20
	Cahir McCunna	21	Loghlin Ôge O Hehir gent		21
(folio 34). Kelneboy	Leymmeigh	28		00	28
	Garrucloune	06			06
	Ballynalaccon	06			06
	Munanaleene	09		01	08
	Cahernemadry	20			20
	Glankeene	46			46
	Dangen McKeogh	22			22
	West Carny	04			04
	East Carny	18	John Emerson gent	02	16
	Ballyportrea	31	Beniamin Lucas Esq	08	23
	Cahirvicyteere	09			09
Rath	Dromfinglass	09	Donnogh Ô Bryen gent		09
	Dromassane	09			09
	Cragvogher	04			04
	Lisscollane	04			04
	Craggevullin	07			07
(folio 35).	Carowvanebeg	05			05
	Moreely	14	Garrett Barry gent		14
	Drynagh	13	Redmond Walters gent		13
	West Moreely	04	Therlagh McOwen gent of Garranse		04
	Garranse	08	Owen Ô Connory gent of West Moreely		08
	Poulebane	06			06
	Cahirgall	09			09
	Tir McBran	26	Garrett Fitzmerie Esq	02	24
	Martry	14			14
	CarrowKelly	06	Hugh McEncroe gent		06
	Boghersallagh	18	James McEncroe gent		18
	Cahirnemogher	09			09
	Cregnowrane	09			09
	Ballinkincorra	12			12
	Carrownecrossy	05		00	05

Parishes	Townelands	Numbs of People	Tituladoes Names	Eng	Irish
(folio 36).	Rath	17	John Ô Hogane		17
	Carnanemore	08			08
	Cahirgrinane	02			02
	Moyhill	14	Hugh Ô Hogane gent		14
Kilkeedy	Moyrhy	52	Mortagh Ô Bryen gent		52
	Carrowcrahine	08	William Power gent		08
	Cloneloane	46	Dominick Dorcy gent	02	44
	Clonesellcherny	10	James Lenchy gent, Stephen Lenchy his sonn gent		10
	Poulenacoona	05			05
	Carrownegowle	08			08
	Magheryraghin	09			09
	Kilquidy	39	Andrew Lenchy gent William Lenchy gent		39
	Templebanagh	06	Richard Butler gent		06
	Athyslany	11	Garrett Nugent gent		11
	Derryvaghan	09	Theobald Butler gent		09
	Agherem	22	Derby Ô Bryen gent		22
	Carrowna, Killy & Carrowshaneduff }	15	John Power gent William FitzJohn gent James Fitz-Nicholas gent		15
(folio 37).	Kells	51	James Rowe gent		51
	Torkenagh	05			05
Desert	Corrowportlicky	28	Sʳ Valintin Browne Barᵗ Thomas Curd Esq	04	24
	Cahir McNea	19	John Welsh gent		19
	Tullydea	49	Pierce Rowe gent		49
	Cahirloghae	16			16
	Ballyoganebeg	11	John Ô Sheaghane gent		11
	Tierinch	14			14
	Ranaghane	23	John Fitzgerrald gent		23
	Ballyheige	21	Gerrald Barry gent John Barry gent	00	21
	Tullavecken	07	Morish Agherin gent		07
	Ballyoganemore	08			08
	Loghanafeleene	19	Mortagh Gripheen gent		19
	Killeene	09			09
	Agherem	49	Coll Charles Henessy Esq		49
	Owen	20	Dermott ô Kerine gent		20
(folio 38).	Agherinkilly	08			08
	Dromkerane	12	John Comyne gent		12
	Coogy	08			08
	Rathrahaneast	13	Loghlen McInerny gent		13
	Kilkee	10			10
	Kilkee al's Lisnecreevy	11			11
	Tyernahy	13			13

Parishes	Townelands	Numbs of People	Tituladoes Names	Eng	Irish
	Ballyharighane	02			02
	Rathrahan West	22			22
	Beallnalichy	16	William Sinane gent		16
	Ballygriffa	27	Garrett Prendergast gent		27
	Low Erenagh	14		04	10
	Dromona	16			16
	Drumcurren West	06	Bryen Henessy gent		06
	Drumcurren East	12			12
(folio 39).	Clonemore	15			15
	Dizartt	22			22
	Ballycullinanteig	10			10
	Clonybegg	15			15
	Townagh	12	Mahon Ô Bryen gent		12
	Ballybrody	13	Edmond Fitzgerrold gent		13
	Gleans	32	Teige Ô Kerrin gent		32
	Dromillagh	04			04
	Killenane	50	Flann Ô Kerrin gent	00	50
	Culesegane	35	Morrish Connell gent Jeffry Connell gent		35
	Mocassin	21			21
	Fermoile	35	Charles Carthy gent	02	33
	Clonenaghie and Skeyghvickencrow }	44	Teige Carthy gent		44
	West Ballylea	23	Daniell Sulevane gent		23
(folio 40). Kil-	Shally	06	Symon Wrotham gent	04	02
namona	Cregloskie	16	Michaell ô Dae gent		16
	Ballynealane	23			23
	Ballymungane	13			13
	Moreane	05			05
	Ballyashea	17	William Henessy gent Phillipp Henessy his sonn gent		17
	Kilnemona	12	Patrick Hogane gent		12
	Rushane	06			06
	Raheene	13			13
	Knockardnehenchy	14			14
	Leckane	10	Manus Ô Cahane gent		10

Principall Irish Names [and] their Numb[er]

Bryen & Ô Bryen, 23 ; Bourke, 11 ; Ô Culenane, 13 ; McConnor (11), & Ô Connor (2), 13 ; Conellane (6), & Ô Conellane (8), 14 ; Carthy & McCarthy, 6 ; Ô Donoghow, 5 ; McDonogh, 9 ; McDaniell &c, 13 ; Ô Dae, 11 ; McEncroe, 09 ; Gripha (10), & O Grypha (11), 21 ; Fitzgerrald &c, 10 ; Henessy & O Henessy, 08 ; Ô Heyne, 07; Hogane and O Hogane, 13; O Hehiir, 12; O Huer, 07 ; Hickie, 7 ; Fitzmorrish, 9 ; Nealane &c, 15 ; McOwen, 10 ; Quine & Ô Quine, 10 ; Ryane, 10 ; Roch, 06 ; Rowe, 07 ; McShane, 07 ; Ô Sheghane, 08 ; McTeige, 13 ; White, 07.

(folio 40 verso). The Number of People in the Barony of Inchiqine : Eng, 034 ; Irish, 1961 ; Totall Eng & Irish, 1995

M

(folio 41).   **ISLAND BARONY**

Parishes	Townelands	Numbs of People	Tituladoes Names	Eng	Irish
Clareaby		37	Geoge Huott gent Samuell Burton Esq John Capleman gent	08	29
	Clare Towne	80	Francis Cassy gent	06	74
	Knocknegamanagh	43	John Huleatt gent	06	37
	Bunergragie	66		00	66
	Bernegehy	30	Therlogh Ô Bryen gent		30
	Cloghaneboy	74	William Cuff gent	01	73
	Barneticke	48			48
	Carrowgare	20			20
	Manusbeg	08	Dominick Creagh gent		08
	Ballyhenane	25			25
	Cony Island	03		02	01
	Low Island	05			05
	Cannon Island	06			06
	Inishtubrett Island	04		00	04
(folio 42). Kil-loone	Tir McLane	54	Stephen Woolfe gent		54
	Killerke	15			15
	Clonvuane	26			26
	Killglassy	14			14
	Dromdagrehid	11	Daniell McConsidin gent Mortagh Oge gent		11
	Drominaclogh	21	Owen McConsidan gent		21
	Knockeneary	16			16
	Dorroghs	30			30
	Lissmulbreedy	17			17
	Ballyea	17			17
	Killnacully	13			13
	Killoone	25			25
	Killmoranbeg	10	Daniell Considin gent		10
Dromcliff	Clonroud	79	John Gore gent John Watts gent	04	75
	Liffor	26			26
(folio 43).	Kilmally Division	21	Nicholas Bourke gent William Bourke gent		21
	Killclogher	13			13
	Killmally	14	David White gent		14
	Ballyeyneene	13	Walter Bourke gent		13
	Laccarrow	21			21
	Rathkerry	15			15
	Ballyellane	17			17
	Dromanure	13	Callaghane Ô Calaghane gent		13
	Gortganiff	06	Richard Woolfe gent		06
	Bally McCally	10			10
	Killeene	15	Edward Rice gent Patrick Rice gent		15
	Ballydonogh	14	John Bourke gent		14

Parishes	Townelands	Numbs of People	Tituladoes Names	Eng	Irish
	Cloneleghin	06		00	06
	Killcollum	23	John Rierdan gent		23
	Lisbiggine	09	Mortagh McCae		09
(folio 44).	Tullassie	23	Nicholas Fitzgerrald gent Luke Fitzgerrald & John FitzGerrald his sonns gent		23
	Gortmore	07	Patrick Fitzgerrald gent		07
	Ballylumney	13	Tobias Fitzgerrald gent		13
	Moyownagh	03			03
	Killquane	25	Edmond Forstall gent Pierce Forstall gent		25
	Crenagore	10	Ôliver Walsh gent		10
	Crayleigh	11	Therlagh Magrath gent		11
	Noafe	04			04
	Inishtrahane	06			06
	Inchy	06			06
	Coore	03			03
	Knockinynane	19	James Butler gent		19
	Coore againe	18	John Brickdall gent		18
	Ballylane	17	Dermot ô Meeghane gent Dermott Mighane gent		17
(folio 45).	Knockdrumacedle	19	Andrew Denn gent	03	16
	Sanevogh	18			18
	Cahircally	34			34
	Dromcarran	45	Daniell Ô Hehir gent	06	39
	Dromcliff	15		02	13
	Cahircally beg	04			04
Clonedagad	Lisheen	34	Thomas Hewes gent	02	32
	Cragbrien	116	James Aylmer Esq	06	110
	Lanna	16	Edward Barry gent Francis Barry Phillipp Barry & Anthony Barry his sonns gent		16
	Clandagad	05		00	05
	Clonedemagh	02			02
	Secassy	12			12
	Deaghamead	19			19
	Clonecollmane	14	Christopher Verdon gent	03	11
(folio 46).	Gurtaguigheen	40	Charles Carthy gent	00	40
	Furrowre	34		04	30
	Cahirea	05		00	05
	Ballaghacorig	21	John Stockden gent	05	16

Principall Irish Names [and] their Numb[er.]

Beolane, 07 ; Bourke, 9 ; Connell, 7 ; Corbane, 5 ; Connor Mc & Ô, 17 ; Consdin (7), & McConsidn (5), 12 ; Clanchy, 6 ; McDaniell &c, 16 ; Ô Dally, 14 ; Gormon, 9 ; Ô Grypha, 7 ; Fitzgerrald, 8 ; Hea & O Hea, 7 ; Hallurane, 7 ; O Hehir &c, 14 ; O Hally &c, 12 ; O Hogane &c, 6 ; McIncargy, 09 ; McMahon &c, 15 ; McMahony, 4 ; O Meolane, 7 ; O Mullowny, 8 ; O Mighane, 7 ; Nealane, 9 ; Sexten, 8 ; O Slattery &c, 11 ; Sulevane, 6 ; McTeige, 15 ; Welsh, 10.

(folio 46 verso). The Number of People in Island Barony : Eng, 058 ; Irish, 1593 ; Totall Eng & Irish, 1651.

(folio 47)   **BARONY OF CLANDIRALA**

Parishes	Townelands	Numbs of People	Tituladoes Names	Eng	Irish
Killerisk	——	98	Leu^t George Ross gent Desimy Norton gent William Brigdall gent Hugh Brigdall gent	17	81
	Inishdea	42		00	42
	Clonekelly	8			8
	Inishmore.	16			16
Killdizart	—— ——	30			30
	Cloneowlae	17			17
	Glanecanane	21	Teige McMahon Esq		21
	Ballyncargy	18	Mahon McMahon gent		18
	Lissconillane	04			04
	Cappanafarnoge	02			02
	Liscormacke	04			04
	Cragherry	05			05
	Inish McCoony Iland	04			04
(folio 48). Kill-dizartt	Crovoghane	15			15
	Ballingard	21		02	19
	Ballyleane	39			39
	Coolegore	03			03
	Laccana Shanagh	25	Teige McMahon gent		25
	Lissanafahy	05			05
Killfadane	Clonedrinagh	79	Morrish Fitzgerrald Esq Garrett Fitzgerrold gent Creagh Murphy gent		79
	Cahiraccon	08			08
	Moyfada	33	John Long gent John Long his sonn gent James Long gent	05	28
	Drishane	17	Charles Carthy gent	00	17
	Allroe	12	Francis Meade gent		12
	Erboll	22	Nicholas Fox gent		22
	Coolemeene	27	Teige Carthy gent		27
	Moy	34	Donnogh Oge gent Bryen Swyny gent		34
(folio 49) Kill-murry	Clandirala	67	Henry Lee gent	03	64
	Knocke	16			16
	Tullagherine	02			02
	Laccarrowbane	08	George Roch gent	00	08
	Killmore	08	James Stackpoll gent	01	07
	Cashernagh	11	Francis Creagh gent		11

Parishes	Townelands	Numbs of People	Tituladoes Names	Eng	Irish
	Carrowinsky	25	Thomas Gillenane gent		25
	Ballycarranc	16			16
Killeymur	——	19	Pierce Murrony gent		19
	Carrowdoly	21	Patrick Harrold gent		21
	Dunegorocke	08	Walter Hickman gent	03	05
	Carrowlengard	19			19
	Tarmon	31			31
	Birrane	22	Thomas Clanchy gent		22
Kill Michaell	Killtuncper	59	Dermott Carthy gent Coll Donnogh Carthy Esq		59
	Cahirmore al's ⎫ Cahirmurphy ⎭	09	— Miller gent George FitzHarris gent Lawrence FitzHarris gent		09
(folio 50).	Leatrim	16	Dominick Roch gent		16
	Lissinea	22	James Fitzgerrald gent		22
	Knocklumane	07			07
	Derrycrissane	02			02
	Killmichaell	02			02
	Lake	13			(13
	Shyane	12		00	12
	Ballydinine al's ⎫ Cargraige ⎭	07	Dermott Fitzpatrick gent		07
	Cahir Murphy Castle	04			04
Killofine	Coolenaslee	10			10
	Colemans towne	06	Francis Stritch gent		06
	Clonekerry	27			27
	Ballyogane	25			25
	Sleauedooly	13			13
	Ballymakeary	31	David Barry Esq		31
(folio 51)	Killofine	04			04
	Ballyarme	25	George Metham gent	01	24

Principall Irish Names [and] their Numb[er.]

Bryen, 07 ; Bourke, 07 ; Cullegane, 08 ; Callaghane, 07 ; Carthy, 08 ; McDaniell, 10 ; McDermott, 06 ; McEdmond, 06 ; Fitzgerrald, 16 ; Grypha, 05 ; Kelly, 09 ; McMahon, 17 ; McMorrogh, 06 ; Oge, 06 ; McShane, 12 ; McSwyny, 5.

(folio 51 verso). The Number of People in ye Barony of Clandirala : Eng, 032 ; Irish, 1144 ; Totall Eng & Irish, 1176.

BARONY OF CORCOMROE.

Parishes	Townelands	Numbs of People	Tituladoes Names	Eng	Irish
Killenorath	Ballyshany	44	William Rumsey Esq William Rumsey Junr gent	03	41
	Ballykeill	05	Daniell McDonogh gent	00	05
	Ballygownane	17			17
	Fantae	09			09
	Ballytomulta	22			22
	Carrowkeill	03			03
	Bally Kinverga	14			14
	Ballyroughane	11			11
	Carrowgard	10			10
	Cahir Inenane	04	Boetius Clanchy gent		04
	Lisdoony	12			12
	Cloneomrae	06			06
	Killcarrugh	08			08
	Cragane	05			05
	Ballyurren	14			14
	Bally McDonellane	26	Daniell ô Leary gent Dermott McDaniell		26
(*folio* 53) Killenoragh	Moghermolenane	10			10
	Cloneene	09		02	07
Kiltoroght	Moneene	32	Moylemury McSwyny gent		32
	Inchiveehy	35			35
	Clogher	23	Dermott O Mahony gent		23
	Lissigorane	03			03
	Carrowreagh	19	Manus McSheehy gent		19
	Oughtagh	04			04
	Imleighbeg	05			05
Killshanny	Ballytarsnae	18			18
	Bally McCravane	30			30
	Carrowduff	08		00	08
	Credergane	22			22
Killmachreehy	Dowgh	19	Pierce Butler gent		19
	Tullygarvane	26			26
	Athy Cristorie	09			09
	Craigg	29			29
(*folio* 54) Killmachreehy	Leavally	07	Patricke Comine gent Patricke Oge Comine gent		07
	Liscannor	09			09
	Ballyshyane	08			08
	Carrowduff	05			05
	Ballyeragh	21			21
	Ballyverdagh	13			13
	Leaghchloyne	03			03
	Knockneraha	05			05
	Moymore	21			21

Parishes	Townelands	Numbs of People	Tituladoes Names	Eng	Irish
	Rahanna	10			10
	Killasbuglinane	05			05
	Ballyvrislane	18	Morrogh Ô Bryen gent		18
	Lisclorkane	12			12
	Cahirderry	17			17
Killmanaghen	Inishtimane	58	Edward Fitzgerrald gent		58
	Leahency	30	Teige Carthy gent Charles Carthy his sonn gent		30
(folio 55)	Ballingadie	46	Thomas Magrath gent Donogh Magrath gent		46
Killeilagh	Ballynchuane	25	Daniell Sulevane gent & Daniell Sulevane gent Owen Ô Sulevane gent		25
	Carownebleary	14	Dermott Sulevane gent		14
	Ballinalarme	06	Donogh Ô Bryen gent		06
	Calluragh	15	Teige McCarthy gent Edmond McSwynie gent	00	15
	Cahir McCrossin	10	James McClanchie gent		10
	Carrowgare	09	Sr Therlagh Magrath a poore decayed Bart		09
	Bally McClanchy	05			05
	East Glassie	04			04
	West Glassie	09			09
	Ballybuoe	26			26
	Ballyvary	02			02
	Downe Mcplelim	02			02
	Slappagh	06			06
	Dowline	06			06
(folio 56).	Carrowkeill, and Tergowneen	13	Daniell McGillireadie gent		13
	Corkeiltie	09			09
	Cahirgalteen	09			09
	Toomulony	10	Edmond Fitzgerrald gent		10
	Downeagher	06			06
Cloney	Derrymore	08	Nicholas Canovane gent		08
	Mognagh	16	Teige Hurly gent John Hurly gent		16
	Mullinenagh	06			06
	Terleagheen	07	Donnogh McCarthy gent		07
	Cnocknegagh	10	Teige Ô Bryen gent		10
	Ballybruine	07			07

Principall Irish Names [and] their Numb[ers].

O Bryen, 11 ; Boy, 7 ; Cahill, 8 ; Cussocke, 7 ; Ô Connor, 24 ; Carthy, 8 ; Clanchy, 5 ; McDonogh, 9 ; McDaniell, 7 ; McDermott, 5 ; Fitzgerrald, 5 ; Hogane, 9 ; Ô Hanraghane, 6 ; McIncarigie, 6 ; Lyedie, 6 ; Mahony, 9 ; Murphy, 5 ; Sulevane, 12 ; McTeige, 13.

(folio 56 verso). The Number of People in ye Barony of Corcomroe : Eng, 005 ; Irish, 1034 ; Totall Eng & Irish, 1039.

(folio 57).   **BARONY OF MOYFERTA**

Parrishes	Townelands	Numbs of People	Tituladoes Names	Eng	Irish
Killrush	Killrushtowne	89	Isaack Granier Esq John Arthur gent Peter White gent	05	84
	Leadmore	37		oo	37
	Monemore	24	Therlagh McMahon gent		24
	Carrowne Cally	14			14
	Ballykitt	10	Coll Edmond Fitzmorrice Esq Thomas Fitzmorrice gent		10
	Moyadmore	24	Stephen Stritch gent		24
	Knockeary	03		03	oo
	Ballynode	30	Peter Granier gent Henry Hickman gent		30
	Girrane	17	Daid Mahony gent		17
	Moylagh	19	John Fitzgerrald gent		19
Moyferta	Moyferta	03			03
	Carigaholta	77	Edmond Fitzmorrice gent		77
	Querren	71	Isaack Vanhogarden gent	01	70
	Moveene	04	Leut Coll John Wright Esq	02	02
	Lisheene	43	Daniell Cahane gent John Cahane his sonn gent	oo	43
Killmacduane	Killmacduane	35	Florence Carthy gent William Ronane gent		35
(folio 58).	Cloneruddane	53			53
	Dangananelly	52	Stephen Rice gent Charles Carthy gent		52
	Cahiricfineene	08		02	06
	Cloynae	04			04
	Ballynagon	39	Mortagh McMahon gent and Mortagh Mahon gent Dermott Considin gent		39
	Dromellighy	17	Loglen Gormon gent		17
	Gore Iland	42	Lawrence Rice gent James Rice gent William Rice gent Coll Henry Blackwell Esq	09	33
	Cloghanebeg	04			04
Killforagh	Killforagh	48	James Stack gent James Pierce gent Garrett Fitzmorrish gent Thomas Joy gent	04	44
	Garrandery Croyne	11	Francis Ipslie gent	05	06
	Killnegallagh	06			06
	Tarmon	05			05
(folio 59)	Moasta	14	John Stack gent Stephen Lysaght gent		14
	Ballyonane	16	John Lysaght gent		16
	Killquy	44	Sr Daniell Ô Bryen Knt Connor Ô Bryen Esq		44

Parishes	Townelands	Numbs of People	Tituladoes Names	Eng	Irish
Kilballyhone	Farighie	31		00	31
	Killeillagh	36	John Monarto gent Dermott Monarto his sonn gent Teige McNemara gent, Morrish Fitz-Gerrald gent, Walter Browne gent		36
	Kilballyhone	31	Mar Nicholas Fitzmorrish Esq Thomas Fitzmorrish gent Nicholas Fitzmorrish gent		31
	Tullakelly	25	Richard Creagh gent John Welsh gent		25
	Killclogher	38	Donogh Croghen gent Dermott Croghen gent William Hierly gent Teige Leary gent		38

Principall Irish Names [and] their Numb[er]

Cahane, 14 ; Connor, 14 ; McDaniell, 6 ; McDae & Ô Dae, 7 ; Fitzgerald &c, 8 ; Gorman, 6 ; Hurly &c, 8 ; Lenchy, 5 ; Lyne, 7 ; Mullowny, 6 ; Mahony, 12 ; McMahon &c, 9 ; Fitzmorrice &c, 10 ; Madigane, 05 ; Quelly, 12 ; Sulevane, 7 ; Scanlane, 11 ; McShane, 10 ; McTeige, 06.

(*folio* 59 *verso*).   The Number of People in ye Barony of Moyferta : Eng, 031 ; Irish, 993 ; Totall Eng & Irish, 1024.

(*folio* 60).   **BARONY OF BURREN**

Parishes	Townelands	Numbs ot People	Tituladoes Names	Eng	Irish
Oughtmania	Thurlagh	13	Donagh McFineen Esq Donogh McFineen his sonn gent Daniell McFineen gent	00	13
	Oughmanea	19	Charles McDonogh gent Dermott McFineen gent	00	19
	Duellen	18	Daniell Oge gent		18
	Dulline	05			05
	Finavarra	33	Teige Ô Dally gent Lawrence Bigg gent Lawrence Marcaghane gent	02	31
	Aghavoinane	16	Teige McFineen gent Daniell McTeige gent		16
Dromcreehy	Newtowne	12	Robert Nugent Esq Thomas Nugent gent		12

Parishes	Townelands	Numbs of People	Tituladoes Names	Eng	Irish
	Mucknish	05	John Jully gent John Oge his son gent		05
	Ballyveghon	14			14
	Ballycorey	15			15
	Dangen	07			07
	Ballycahill	07	Oliver Kiervane gent		07
(folio 61).	Croughsouth	12	Morta Oge Ô Davoren gent		12
	Carrowteige	06	Patrick Hackett gent		06
	Finagh	08	Andrew Hallurane gent		08
	Ballytohill	18	Phillipp Coogane gent Richard Coogane		18
	Cruoghnorth	11			11
	Ballyalbone	18	Thomas Blake gent		18
	Graganes	21	George Marten gent		21
	Oughtgellane	10	Morogh Inderme gent of Kelly Killy	00	10
	Kellykilly	13	Francis Falloone gent of Oughtgellane		13
	Cappagh	13	Andrew Marten gent James Bodkin gent	05	08
	Glann	16	James Ô Heine gent Bryen McGillikelly gent		16
	Cappagh Kenedy	17	John O Hehir gent		17
Carne	Creaguill	11	Therlaghlen Esq		11
	Fahy	8	M Loghlin Ô Hehir gent		8
	Tarmon	14			14
(folio 62).	Coskerine	20	Bryen Ô Loghlen gent		20
	Poullvall	23	Donnogh McCarthy gent		23
	Cahir McKnole	11	Bryen O Loghlen gent		11
	Lismorane	13	Bryen Considin gent		13
	Mogownde	10			10
Nohovall	Cahirpollagh	17			17
	Ballygannor	06			06
	Noghovall	42			42
	Cahir McInaghtie	13	Gillerneaf oge ô Davoren gent		13
	Ballyvoragagh	26	Owen Hallurane gent		26
	Ballymahona	18	Cormucke McCarthy gent		18
	Lissy Lisseene	10			10
	Shessimore	03	Owen McCarthy gent		03
	Poulcullickie	06			06
Killcorney	Enagh	10			10
	Poulbane	06			06
(folio 63)	Poulbane	06			06
	Killcornie	07			07
	Glanslead	08		00	08
Glan Innagh	Glan Innagh	17	Teige O Hea gent		17
Killneeny	Ballyconna South	13	Covara McInerny gent		13
	Knockenard	15	Connor Ô Flanigane gent		15
	Carrowkerrily	07	Nicholas Mahony gent		07
	Ballydonoghow	08	Daniell Ô Bryen gent		08

Parishes	Townelands	Numbs of People	Tituladoes Names	Eng	Irish
	Killmone	10	John Creagh gent		10
	Cahir Clegane	23	David Creagh gent		23
	Lisdoone Varnagh	20	James Butler gent		20
	Bally hushen	05			05
	Lismegh	12			12
	Formoyle	15	Connor O Bryen gent		15
	Ballynie	16			16
	Craggagh	17			17
	Cahera cullen	11			11
	Lislarhy	19	Hugh Ô Dovoren gent		19

Principall Irish Names [and] their Numb[er]

Bryen, 07 ; Connor, 5 ; McCarthy, 5 ; McDonogh, 16 ; Dally & Ô Dally, 10 ; O Davoren, 13 ; McDermott, 06 ; McFineene, 06 ; O Hea, 06 ; Hayne & Ô Hayne, 05 ; McLoghlen (07), and Ô Loghlen (06), 13 ; Oge, 09 ; McShane, 06 ; McTeige, 08.

(*folio 63 verso*). The Number of People in the Barony of Burren : Eng, 007 ; Irish, 816 ; Totall Eng & Irish, 823.

(*folio 64*) **BARONY OF IBRICKANE AND BURROUGH OF ENISH** [1]

Parishes	Townelands	Numbs of People	Tituladoes Names	Eng	Irish
Kilferboy	——	24	Morrish Hicky gent	00	24
	Laccamore	05	Michaell Creagh gent		05
	Fyntra	30	Daniell Clanchy gent Mortagh Mahon gent Mortagh Clanchy gent John Clanchy gent Teige McInerny gent Daniell Clanchy gent Moyleene Mulroney gent		30
	Carrowcott	39	Hugh Clanchy gent		39
	Ballyugine	09	Edmond Bourke gent		09
	Powlemillen	20	Teige Line gent		20
	Carhowgare	27			27
	Brighine	37			37
	Cloghanemore	36			36
	Glandine	21			21
Killard	Dunmore	26	John McNemara gent James Fitzgerrald gent		26
	Carrowblough	02			02

[1] *and . . . Enish*, added, folio 65.

Parrishes	Townelands	Numbs of People	Tituladoes Names	Eng	Irish
(*folio* 65).	Dunbeg	32	James Fox gent Morrish Roch gent		32
Killumry	Knockenalbone	18	William Hobson gent	10	08
	Doonegane	08			08
	Sanevogh	38	Daniell Moriarto gent		38
	Craggyknock	11	Edmond Fox gent		11
	Tromery	33			33
	Cahirrush	07	Nicholas Wolfe gent		07
	Knocky Losgirane	14			14
	Enagh	37			37
	Carrowduff	03		00	03
	Rinroe	27	Richard White gent		27
	Cloghane	14			14
	Ballymackea	41	Patrick Pierce gent		41
	Rineroe	03			03
	Moy	20			20
Burrough of	Inish	267	James McNemara gent Laurence Creagh gent	13	254

Principall Irish Names [and] their Numb[er]

Creagh, 6 ; Clanchy, 10 ; Carthy, 9 ; Connor, 11 ; Cassy, 5 ; Clovane, 5 ; Hiernane, 8 ; Hicky, 5 ; Lyne, 7 ; Mahon & MacMahon, 8 ; Moriarto, 8 ; Mullowny, 7 ; McNemara, 11 ; Shea, 5 ; Sulevane, 4 ; McTeige, 5.

(*folio* 64 *verso*).   The Number of People in ye Barony of Ibrickane & Borogh of Inish : Eng, 023 ; Irish, 826 ; Totall Eng & Irish, 849

(*folio* 65 *verso*).   The Number of People in the County of Clare and in each Barony.

Barronyes	Pages	Eng	Irish	Eng and Irish
Bunratty	15	144	4204	4348
Tulla	31	106	3903	4009
Inchiquine	40	034	1961	1995
Island Bar	46	058	1593	1651
Clandirala	51	032	1144	1176
Corcomroe	56	005	1034	1039
Moyferta	59	031	0993	1024
Burren	63	007	0816	0823
Ibrickane &c	65	023	0826	0849
The Totall		440	16474	16914

CORKE CITTY AND LIBERTYES
4826

(folio 1).

CORKE CITTY

Parrishes	Quarters	Number of People	Tituladoes Names	Eng	Irish
Christ Church	South East	216	Walter Cooper Esq Robert Fletcher John Sharpe Richard Priddin John Barrett Thomas Swabby Charles Dayly Josias Walker Junior Edward Webber George Webber John Hamlyn Timothy Tuckey Senior Thomas Fleetwood Thomas Price Richard Lane Stephen Harris and George Wright gents.	124	092
	North East	316	Aron Stiffe, William Wrenne, and Symon Morgan gents, Benjamin Crofts Esq Edmond Crofts Thomas Fennell Edward Masters George Young Samuell Gravenor John Terry John Hawkins Thomas Swallow Charles Kinaston Benjamin Adams John Berry Richard Covett William Dale and Francis Hodder gents	194	122
	South West	170	Richard Sauage Thomas Morley Richard Terry William Bourke Timothey Tuckey Junior George Gamble Charles Conway John Gardner and Jonathan Percy gents Richard Rich Esq and Robert Chaney gent	097	073
(folio 2). St Peters	South West	160	William Allen James Vanderlure Alien Dominick Coppinger Robert Coppinger Edward Phillips Richard Harvey Richard Bassett Michaell Webber Senior Nathaniell Bullocke Edward Goble John Quynall Nicholas King Richard Carby Charles Whitwell Charles Lambert Samuel Tovey Barry Snell John Bayley and Robert Williams gents Barry Foulke Esq and Richard Crispe gent	106	054
	North West	227	Christopher Rye Christopher Cappacke Samuell Hayes Ferdinando Pennigton John Newenham William Allen Mathew Williams John Blanford Thomas Bullocke Richard Brocklesby Tho : Mitchell Alexand[r] Atkins Edward Arberry Richard Aldwarth Thomas Bent Samuell Whislade Phillip Diamond James Coppinger John Vaughan John Flinne John Mosse and Abraham Enocke gents	159	068

(folio 3)   **THE SUBURBS OF CORKE CITTY**

	Suburbs	Number of People	Tituladoes Names	Eng	Irish
Shandon	North Suburbs	733	Jonas Morris and James Peercy Esq^{rs} Nicholas Lee John Harris gents Dr John Messick alien Esq William Delahide Ignatius Goold Thomas Wills Francis Rogers gents and Phillip Mathews Esq Jonas Morris Juni^r John Craine Symon Everson alien Michaell Stanton Thomas Farren Dauid Barry James Skiddy Richard Goold James Tomlin James Finch Patrick Ronane William Meagh George Caple John Morley & John Skiddy gents Noblett Dunscombe Esq Henry Bennett John Johnson Richd Johnson James Barry John Welsh Thomas Combel John Verkers Thomas Ô Herne Phillip Ronane John Guyn William French John Steuens Martin Boohier and Walter Gall- wey gentlemen	223	510
(folio 4). St Johns	South Suburbs	421	Thomas Mills Richard Beare John Sinhouse Lawrance Harrison Dauid Goold Sampson Roberts George Hopson John Bayley Dauid Meskell Richard Meskell Thomas Crooke Christopher Fagan William Field Phillip Hayes William Heydon Francis Goold Edmond Roch and Nicholas Skyddy gentlemen	102	319
St Finbarry	South Suburbs	160	Barthollomew Rice John Meade Zachariah Trauers Walter Trauers William Wheeler and Will: Holmes gentlemen	043	117

SOUTH LIBERTIES OF CORKE

	Townelands				
Carigrohane	Carigrohane	204	John Baker Esq Edward Ingry John Clements John Loue and Edward Rubey Senior gents	059	145
Carigrohane Inskyny	Curreheene	024	Stephen Gillman gent	003	021
(folio 5). St Fin- barries	Inchygagine	009	Edmond French gent	002	007
	Bainaspickmore	034	Daniell Gefferyes and Capt Thomas Harris gents	008	026
	Farren McTeige	005		—	005

Parrishes	Townelands	Number of People	Tituladoes Names	Eng	Irish
Inskyny	Ballygallane	06			06
	Arderostigge	32	John Tovomy gent		32
St Finbarryes	Ballygagine	06			06
Kinalglory	Ballynora	54			54
Inskyny	Inskyny	06			06
	Ballyma	09			09
	Rochfordstowne	35	Phillip Parker gent	08	27
	Ballynvoltigge	38			38
	Ballynvrinshigge	24			24
	Gortgolane	11			11
	Knockmolinoge	22			22
	Knocklesheene	02			02
	Ballycranick	05			05
	Lehenamore	41			41
(folio 6)	Lehanabegge	06			06
	Freagh	02			02
	Clashduffe & Farrendahadore	04			04
	Hagards land	006		—	006
	Ballycurreene	24	Nicodemus Harding gent	03	21
	Ballywooskey	29	John Roch gent		29
	Hospitall land	42	John Gullivant gent		42
	Gilaboy	40	Rickd Scudamore and Richard Savell gents	20	20
	Dough Cloyne and Garanedarragh	27	William Guppy gent	03	24
	Croughtahuske	04			04
	Bally Phehane	11	John Gallway Arthur Gallwey and Andrew Gallwey gents		11
	Grange	19		03	16
	Curcanaway	21			21
	Carrigdiganigg	06			06
Killanally	Rath McUlicke	13	Thomas Benger gents	05	08
(folio 7) Carag-	Ballyndohigge	011	John Coleman gent	04	07
aline	Ballinrea	37	Thomas Russell and Francis Russell gents	04	33
	Ballyorban	16			16
	Munsfieldtowne	102	Richard Newman gent	05	97
	Monygormey	71	Thomas Woodliffe and William Hoare Esqrs	09	62
	Ballynimilogh	07			07
	Castle Treasure	24	Garrott Goold & Will: Goold gents		24
	Ardarrigg	05			05
	Douglas	38		07	31
St Finbarries	Ballincurrigg	34		07	27

Parrishes	Townelands	Number of People	Tituladoes Names	Eng	Irish
Christ Church St Finbarries	Ballinvre	11	Richard Busteed gent	03	08
	Mahon	08			08
	Dondainon	050	John Waters and Peirce Terry gent & Dominick Waters gent	003	047
	Bally Temple	11		—	11
	Ballylogh	30	William Tucker gent	02	28
	Knockrea	04		02	02

(folio 8)   **NORTH LIBERTIES.**

Parrishes	Townelands	Number of People	Tituladoes Names	Eng	Irish
Killcully	Ballynahiney	019		—	019
	Kilcully	006		—	006
	Raghaniskey	14			14
	Killindonell	09	Henry Gerrald **gent**	02	07
White church	White church	12		01	11
	Ballinvarigge	43			43
	Moneard	51			51
	Coole-Owen alias } Farrenrostigge	88	James Lanallyn gent		88
	Rapeakane	22	Samuel Corbett gent	05	17
	Killevalligge	07			07
	Chaharrowe	03			03
	Kilcronane	01			01
Rathcowney	Lowtagh-begg	10	Will : Creagh & Pierce Creagh gent		10
	Poulioury	08		02	06
	Banduffe	08			08
(folio 9). Rathcowney	Rathcowney	17		02	15
	Lowtaghmore	12		03	09
	BallyPhillip	10	Nicholas Pierce & Christo^r Stephens gents and John Gerrald gent	04	06
	Knockcarragane	10	Charles Gay gent	04	06
	Ballencrosigge	09			09
	Ballyhearon	007		003	004
	Gurranboy	010	George Evens gent	005	005
	BallencroRigge	011		—	011
	Lisnekerny	08		02	06
	Coole	38			38
Downe Bollock	Ballyhesty	14			14
Temple Michell	Ballenvriskigg	40	Edward Gallwey gent		40
Currikippand	Curimurohowe	07			07
	Ballincancene	16		06	10
(folio 10)	Kilard	13		05	08
	Cloheene	15		09	06
	Curriemorohow	36	Daniell Healy gent	07	29

Parrishes	Townelands	Number of People	Tituladoes Names	Eng	Irish
	Knockacullen and Knocknahely	64		04	60
	Kilens	52		—	52
	Clogherine	11		—	11
	Granbraher	07		03	04
Shandon	Ballyvollane	26	Christopher Oliuer gent	03	23
	Kilbarye	14		06	08
	Kilknap	02			02
	Ballycollick	08	Will : Copinger gent		08
	Ballypheris	06			06
	Ballycrokebegg	12			12
(folio 11).	Cahirgall	04		04	—
	Glaunkettane	07		—	07
	Verdonsland	08	Robert Verdon gent	03	05
	Farrennyclary	02			02
	BallinnyMough	08			08

SOULDIERS IN YE CITTY OF CORKE

	Ld Broghill's Company	088	Barry Foulke Lieutent Walter Croker Ensigne	080	008
	Captn Courthops company	090	Peter Courthop Esq Captn Robert Russell Lieutent and Henry Cartwright Ensigne Pierce Powell Gouernor of Halbolin Forte	084	006
	Capt Wakehams Company	090	John Wakeham Capt Charles Odell Lieutn and John Browne ensigne	084	006
	Capt Tenches Company	070	John Tench Captn Thomas Flint Lieutn and Thomas Bayley Ensigne	068	002

Principall Irish Names [and] their Number.

Barry, 29 ; Browne, 10 ; Barret, 19 ; O Bryan, 07 ; Brenagh & Brennagh, 15 ; Ô Boghelly, 09 ; Ô Connell, 09 ; McConnor (6), McCnoghor (9), 15 ; Ô Callaghane & Ô Callahane, 10 ; McCarthey, 17 ; Cummane, 10 ; McDonnogh, 20 ; Ô Daly & Ô Dayly, 07 ; McDonell & McDaniell, 23 ; McDauid, 07 ; McDermod, 13 ; McEdmond, 09 ; Ô Flyne & Ô Flynne, 21 ; Ô Fowlow, 11 ; Fleming, 07 ; Gerrald, 11 ; Goold, 11 ; Gallwey, 12 ; Healy & Haly, 12 ; Ô Hogane, 07 ; Neuill, 07 ; Ô Neale, 07 ; O Keeffe, 12 ; Kelly, 10 ; Leehy, 07 ; Ô Line, 11 ; Ô Leaghy, 08 ; Ô Leary, 24 ; Murphy, 45 ; McMorris and Morris, 17 ; Meagh, 07 ; Mahowny, 07 ; Ô Murroghow, 08 ; McOwen, 07 ; Phillips and McPhillip, 11 ; Punch, 09 ; Russell, 10 ; Roch, 10 ; Roe, 10 ; Ô Riordane, 14 ; Smith, 18 ; Ô Skiddy, 08 ; Ô Skannell, 08 ; Ô Sulleuane, 19 ; McShane, 34 ; McSwyny, 08 ; Ô Sheehane & Ô Sheghane, 11 ; Ô Shea, 09 ; McThomas, 10 ; Terry, 9 ; Ô Twomy, 12 ; McTeige, 16 ; White, 7 ; Welsh, 8 ; McWilliam, 9.

(folio 11 verso).   Corke Citty & Lybertyes : Eng, 1607 ; Irish, 3219 ; 4826 total.

CORKE   COUNTY
62032

(folio 1).

THE TOWNE OF KINSALE

Places	Number of People	Tituladoes Names	English	Irish
High Fisherstreet	426	Robert Southwell Esq, William Hovell, Richard Pearcell, Geo Seaward, Jane Courcy, Giles Groves, Wm Dickinson, Christopher Sugars, Nath Tilson, Robert Best, Nicholas Bagnall, John Sunbery, Marg^t Abraham, Wm Gribble, Robt Southwell, Hills Whittingham, Rich : Sturt, Tho Gookin, Edm^d Yeomans, John Hoveden, John Dorrell, Walter Harbert, 22.	212	214
Without the rampier on the West	38		9	29
Without the rampier	18		10	8
Commoge	4		2	2
Low Fisherstreete	271	Hen Hitchmongh, Jo Denn, Sam Smith, Jo Mountford, Ant Stawell, Geo Burcham, Miles Jackson, Frances Whetcomb, Abraham Holcroft, Wm Breadbeard, Humberston Hurst, Martha Chidleigh, Edm^d Curley, Wm Hill, Thos Burroughes, Richd Burroughes, Cornelius Coveney, Phil Butler, Jane Brown, John Lugg, Josias Percivall, Jo Twisden, Geo Piggott, Jo Stepney, Jo Travers, Hugh Hickman, John Willingham, Lancelott Stepney gent.	136	135
Couke Street	265	Wm Milner Esq, Rich : Cozene, Geo Yardo, Wm Wilson, Jane Pennington, Kath Bagley, Wm Finch, Walt Young, Samuell Wright, Mary Stepney, John White, Joseph Elwell, Michaell Hea, Rich : Way, Tho Sanders, John Nicholson.	85	180
Fryer Streete	318	Jonah Parker, Isaack Calfe, Ezek Preist, Geo Deys, Nich Miagh, Ursula Browne, Marg^t Browne, Rich : Hodden Esq, Symon Smith, Geo Nicholson, James Mansery Esq, Richd Norris, Owen Browne.	126	192

(folio 2)

TOWNE OF BANDON BRIDGE

Places	Number of People	Tituladoes Names	English	Irish
Bandonbridge	846	Clement Woodroffe Nathaniell Cleare Abraham Savage Esq Joshua Brookin William Warner Eliz Warner John Poole, Adderley Byrne, John King Robert Blanchett, Gabriell Miles, John Birne Margarett Unett Wm Wright Jonathan Bennett John Landon Esq Michaell Bull Nicholas Withers Wm Withers Edw :	542	304

Places	Number of People	Tituladoes Names	English	Irish
		Turner Daniell Massey John Poulden John Smith John Roe John Braily Tho Dickinson Mary Newce Edw : Newce John Bird Cuthery Dowden Tho Dowden John Watkins John Jackson Matthias Percivale Roger Olliffe John Remnant Tho Walker Charles Wills, John Browne Thomas Beamish Esq Edwd Cooke Richard Dashwood Tho Frinke		

Principall Irish Names
Ô Rogane, 5 ; Solovart, 3 ; Wheite, 3 ; Martine, 3 ; Carthy, 3 ; Browne, 5.

[YOUGHAL]

Youghall	956	Richd Earle of Corke & Eliz his countesse, Charles Visc. Dongarvan, Richd Boyle Esq, Lady Elizabeth, Lady Anne, Leonard Corstellowe, Wm Chettle, Ambrose Willy, Barry Drew, John Langor Ald^er, Sam Blatchford John Handcock Abraham Vaughan Peirce Meagh Joseph Morduck Ald^er, John Fuller, John Farthing Alder^n, Lewis Davie, Nicholas Lucas Thomas Baker Matt Spemer John Luther Ed Greene Peter Goodwin John Nagle Andrew Wandwick Ald^er, John Hazard Willm Baker Richd Gillett Jefford Stoute Hen Davie Owen Silver & John Deacon Thos Blackwell D^r of Phys, Tho Warren Esq.	459	497
Libertyes of Youghall	17	Thomas Unack	—	17
Ballyhubbard & Muckridge	138		10	128

Principall Irish Names
Gerrald, 5 ; McMorris, 4 ; M^cW^m, 6 ; McThomas, 4 ; Field, 4 ; Barry, 4 ; Brenagh, 10 ; Browne, 4 ; Flyng, 4.

(folio 3).   **THE TOWNE OF MOYALLE**

Places	Number of People	Tituladoes Names	Number of Eng^sh	Number of Irish
Moyalle Towne	463	Allicia Jephson Widdow of Wm Jephson Esq, John Jephson Rich Kirle Esq & Mary his wife Randall Clayton Esq Thomas Farely Mrs Eliz Bessworth Jo Jones Robt Williams	114	349

Places	Number of People	Tituladoes Names	Number of Eng^sh	Number of Irish
		Rich Doave Esq Teige Hogane Tho Waits Jo Brookes Phil Brookes Jo Waggoner Thomas Murrough Tho Blakston Stephen Keene Tho Barnard Wm Holmes Francis Bevridge Sam Kirby John Murphy Tho Grant Wm Chartres, Domni Thirry, Rich Hawkins Wm End Tho Latsford Susanna Alder		
Kile, Knockane & Dromesliggah	22		—	22
Kile Ittrigh	4		—	4
Clogh Lucas	29		—	29
Curragh In Early	14	Rich Williamson Esq	1	13
Ballinveinter	49			49
Ballylagh	9			9
Ballyhankine	5			5
Lower Quarter Town	31	John Fowke	2	29
Upper Quarter Towne	33	Anthony Mulshenoge Esq Anthony Mulshenoge gent		33
Gortny Graggy	13		—	13
Gnarrison of Moyello	117	Henry Stratford Phil Harris Mark Weekes Matthew Pennetather John Gennery.	117	—

Principall Irish Names
   Ô Callaghane, 7 ; Ô Callahane, 3 ; McCnougher, 5 ; Hickey, 4 ; Bourke, 4 ; Ô Leanaghane, 6 ; Ô Morroghow, 5 ; Ô Shighane, 9 ; McTeige, 4.

(*folio* 4).   **BARRONY OF KINALEA**[1]

Parishes	Towneland	Number of People	Tituladoes Names	Eng	Irish
Brinny	Brinny P^ld	27		4	23
	Clashnemode	40		0	40
Knockivilly	Garrihaukard	3		0	3
	Two cussine	24		2	22
	Lissiniskey	20	Robert Thirry Francis Thirry his sonn	1	19
	Lissigroome	11		3	8
	Ballyhander	27		2	25
	Ballivorohow	42	Teige Sweeny	—	42
Inishonane	Inishonane	150	Alex Pigott Esqr Rowland Field Richd Roch Edward Roch his	27	123

[1] *Kinelea*, folio 5 ; *Kenalea* folio 6

Parrishes	Towneland	Number of People	Tituladoes Names	Eng	Irish
			sonn Edwd Adderly Cnohor ô Dyeyneene Patrick Gould Robert Chambers James Galwey Catterine Galwey		
	Farrincarrigh	13		6	7
	Coolemorine	34	Henry Jones	12	22
	Cloughrane	9		—	9
	Annaghmore	47		—	47
	Dunkerine	11		—	11
	Killeene	25		2	23
	Currentriseland	18		7	11
	Ballycoughland	22		4	18
(folio 5). Temple Michaell	Fardlestowne	37		0	37
	Killomnioge	26		2	24
	Cloughdwa	26		7	19
	Culecollity	12		0	12
Inishonane	Knocknullane	10		2	8
Downdurrow	Annaghbegg	27		0	27
	Skehanas	35	John Brooks Esq Ann his daugh	8	27
	Island Effinshy	59	Edwarde Riggs gent Daniel Stinchman Esq	2	57
	Leffony Begg	24		0	24
	Knocknagapull	22		0	22
	Ballwin	03	Jeoffrey Gallwey gent	0	03
Ballineboy	Ballyheedy & Jordanstowne	44	John Plover Esqr Robert his son gent Thomas Fitzgerrald gent	2	42
	Knockanlousy	10		3	07
	Ballineboy 41 Ballineboy 56	97	Francis Gould gent	5	92
Leffony	Lisheedy	13	Timothy Stephens John Herrick gent	10	03
	Castlevary	21		3	18
	Ballydonoghy	20		0	20
(folio 6)	Skonagore	20		4	16
	Dirrneygassy & Mifordstowne	27		5	22
	Sleavegillane	16		2	14
	North Leffony	04		0	4
	Tullogebbane	02	Thomas Segrave Esq	2	—
Ballymartell	Curroury	64	Wm Smart gent	3	61
	Arlondstowne	35		0	35
	Ballymartell	100		8	92
	Ballinloughy	68		2	66
	Fahanlouskane	36		2	34
	Ballintubbeoid & Quarter	21	Wm Meade Esq Maurice Roch gent	2	19

Parrishes	Towneland	Number of People	Tituladoes Names	Eng	Irish
	Garraviasoge	21		2	19
Rincorrane	Ballynemaule	15		0	15
Taxaxon	Ballyregane	22		0	22
Cullin	Cullin	33	Edward Kenny gent	0	33
	Ballalime	18		0	18
	Ballinperus	17	Rich Baroy gent	0	17
(folio 7)	Ballincourty	28		0	28
	Glinny	39	John Godsuffe gent	3	36
	Garragen	08		2	6
	Ballywilliam	07		0	7
Killmahonoge	Mountlong	20	Giles Bustead gent	2	18
	Knockcauleamore	15	Thomas Knowles gent	6	9
	Knockauleabegg	8		0	8
	Ballindriniske	18	John Morley Charles James and Thomas James gent Martha & Wilmoth daughters to John Morley	7	11
	Bealquoly	29		6	23
	Killeaheagh	17		2	15
Kinore	Kinure	18	Swithen Walton gent	0	18
	Killeagh	7			7
	Ballinclassy	8			8
	Ballinwoollin	3			3
	Carrugh	2			2
	Ballinrangalauige	18			18
(folio 8) Kinure	Knockcullin & Knocknynaffe {	23		2	21
Bealefiard	East Ballingary	45	Wm Thirry Robert his sonn Edmd Thirry gent	11	34
	Ballyannisane Ballytrydimigg {	27		0	27
	West Ballingary	14	Wm Daunt gent	0	14
	Farty	25		2	23
	Ballinluige	92	Teige Carthy gent	0	92
	Robertstowne	16	Wm Dyer gent	2	14
Noghevall	Corrivaghill	12		0	12
	Ballyvirane	59	Thomas Daunt	2	57
	Noghevall	5		0	5
	Ballincollobardy	4			4
	Downebegehy	29			29
	Downboige	10			10
Bealefoile	Britsfieldstowne	19		3	16
	Bealesoile	24		1	23
(folio 9)	Ballinvilluge	3		—	3
	Ballindeasigg	21		—	21
	Reyney	32		—	32

Parrishes	Towneland	Number of People	Tituladoes Names	Eng	Irish
Kilpatrick	Killone	07		3	4
	Rathgree	28		2	26
	Ballinviny	9		—	9
	Ballinbolvostigh	11			11
	Kilpatrick	14			14
	Knocknisillagh	17		2	15
	Parkenaule	4		—	4
	Fountainstowne	36		8	28
	Gortigrenane	14	Thomas Daunt Esq George Daunt gent	—	14
Tracton Abby	Tracton	131	Wm Daunt Senr Achilles his sonn gent	15	116
	Knocknimanagh	156		5	151
	Ringabelly	22	Wm Hadder Junr gent	2	20
	Downivanigg	12		0	12

Principall Irish Names [and] their Numb[er].

McTeige & Teige oge, 41 ; Murphy, 46 ; McOwen, 13 ; McDaniell, 17 ; McDesmond, 10 ; McCnohor and Cnohor oge, 21 ; Gogan, 14 ; McShane, 28 ; Ô Halihanane, 8 ; Sullivane, 22 ; Riergane, 13 ; McDonagh, 16 ; McDermod, 14 ; Ô Spillane, 10 ; Sheghane, 10 ; Ô Daly, 11 ; Carthy, 23 ; Ô Leaghy, 8 ; Mahowny, 8 ; Cullilane, 8 ; Fowlue, 14 ; Ô Cullane, 9 ; Galwey, 7 ; McEdmond, 7 ; Kelly & Ô Kelly, 7.

(folio 9 verso). Barrony of Kinalea : Eng, 234 ; Irish, 2460 ; 2694, totall

(folio 10).

BARONY OF KIERYCURRIHY

Parishes	Places	Number of People	Tituladoes Names	English	Irish
Cargaline	Ballinrea	18	Francis Visct Shannon and his Lady Jo : Delacourt	8	10
	Ballyknockeme	14		5	9
	Cooleaultane	34		8	26
	Knockmore & Coolemore	41	William Hodder Esq & Margery his Wife	9	32
	Cargaline	118	Katherine Power Richd Power	22	96
	Cuiribiny	37	Peirce Power & Grace his wife	10	27
	Ballygarvane	47		5	42
	Ballydulugg	8			8
	Bunnycleagh & Kinnycleary	20	Anstace Archdeacon James Archdeacon Wm Archdeacon & Jane Archdeacon	4	16

Parishes	Places	Number of People	Tituladoes Names	English	Irish
	Ballmingrassane	11		—	11
	French Fiuse	57	Patrick Roch	4	53
	Boystowne & Offahalea	35		8	27
Bearnhealy	Bearnhealy	97	Richᵈ Hayes Mʳˢ Gosnold	17	74
	Knockaneikirodigge	27	Sʳ Robᵗ Coppinger Knight & his Lady	11	16
Ballmiboy	Tulligh	6		2	4
	Adamstowne	7		2	5
(folio 11) Killinglie	Killingly	22	John Bustead & his Wife Thomas Bustead & Mary Bustead	7	15
	Killynohone	11	John Mead & his Wife	4	7
	Ballinrisigge	17	Morris Roch Wid	0	17
	Kilcoole	44	Lady Coppinger	6	38
	East Kilmighill	28	Thomas Hayes & Anne his sister	5	23
	West Kilmighill	15			15
	Rinebrow	4		2	2
Temple Bridge	Gortnenone	9		2	7
	Aghamarty	10	Geo Fise & Anne his Wife	1	9
	Rinebroe & Monebrinn	23		0	23
	Gortenonebegge	9		6	3
Kilemoney	Kilemoney	73	William Archdeacon & his Wife	3	70
Marmosune	Pembrokestown	33	John Daly Wᵐ Conway	11	22
Lishcleary	Beillinphellick	11		00	11
	Meadstowne	21			21
	South Meadstown	19		1	18
	North Meadstown	21		2	19
(folio 12).	Ballydunane	17		1	16
	Ballea	22		0	22
	Raghmine	26		0	26
	Munkstown	14		2	12

Principall Irish Names.

Murphy, 19 ; Barry, 16 ; Cogane, 22 ; Sullevane, 10 ; Shehane, 12 ; MᶜDaniell, 15 ; Leaghy, 7 ; Linchy, 7 ; O Connell, 7 ; Brenagh, 6 ; O Daly, 6 ; MᶜDonogh, 6 ; O Dorney, 7 ; MᶜMorris, 7 ; Ô Shea, 7 ; MᶜShane, 7.

(folio 12 verso). Barrony of Keirycurrihy : Eng, 168 ; Irish, 852 ; 1020, totall.

(folio 12) **BARONY OF KINALMEAKY**

Parishes	Places	Number	Tituladoes Names	Eng	Irish
Ballymooden	East Gully	118	Francis Barnard Dan Darley Tho Geogan John Upcole Raph Fuller	47	71

Parishes	Places	Number	Tituladoes Names	Eng	Irish
	Middle Gully	12		3	9
	Deresullagh	20	John Abbott	5	15
	Glancoolebegg	10	William Fuller	4	6
	Glancoolemore	9	Thomas Hewett	2	7
	Knockuneatneely	26	Jane Howard Samuell Poole John Freeke Esq & Mary his wife	7	19
	Knockagurane	19	John Draper	7	12
Desert	Knocknegeilagh	34		2	32
(folio 13) Bally- moden	Domgin	16		—	16
Desert	Cashilbegge	23			23
	Cashilmore	103	Gerus Lie Wm Oliver Abiell Nash	8	95
Ballymoodane	Gogan	18			18
	Capacknockane	46	John Vizard Jeremy Whelply	9	37
	Gortnemahown	5		—	5
	West Gully & Brittace	19	John Beamish	3	16
	Currevarehane & Britace	48	Francis Beamish	12	36
Kilbrogan	Kilbegge	16		3	13
	Ginteene	30		4	26
	Curriclogh	11	Wm Glascott	2	9
	Callitrinn	33	Francis Alcock & Francis his sonn	11	22
	West Mishells	20	James Burwell Esq John Langton	8	12
	Midde Mishells	10	Thomas Harrison	2	8
	East Mishells	28	Walter Baldwin Wm Bull Rich : Shute	13	15
(folio 14).	Sheemagh	16		—	16
	Larragh	25		11	14
	Derrycoole	28		7	21
	Coolefadagh	13	Rich : Hobbs gent	3	10
	Caharoone	51	Zachary Brayly	9	42
	Maligeton	13			
	Maligaton	9		2	20
Killrogane	East derregarriffe	16	Masklin Alcock	7	09
	West Derogariffe	10	Tho French & Tho his son George Wright & Tho Wright	7	3
	Lisnabannrer	13			13
	Derrenoghta	6			6
Murragh	Killowen & Gortegrenane	54		2	52
	Tulleglasse	33	Moylemorry McSweeny		33
	Mabegge	18		9	9
	Mumore & Gorte- grenane	55	John Ware Senior John Ware Junior	11	44
(folio 15).	Newcestown	26			26
	Faren Thomas & Coolenagh	42			42

Parishes	Places	Number	Tituladoes Names	Eng	Irish
Murragh	Coreleagh	28			28
	Killeaneere	26		3	23
	Farenganlogh	50			50
	East Bengower	35			35
	Middle Bengower	19			19
	West Bengower	36			36
Temple Martin	Farenevane	34			34
	Curivordy	51			51
Brinny	Island Fenagh	38	Edwd Newman Arthur Brabant	4	34
	Kilmore	19	John Lane	6	13
	Kilnagnady	112			112
	Kilpatrick	98	Thomas Elwell	20	78
	Grane Looney	30	Walter Baldwin James & Rich^d his sonnes.	6	24
	Lisnegatt	16	James Baldwin	5	11
(*folio* 16) Temple Martin	Kilbarry	45			45
	Muskeagh	37			37
	Scartnamuck	24			24
	Castlenalack	27			27
	Garavephilimy	65			65

Principall Irish Names [and] Their Number.

Ô Boigd, 8 ; Conow, 9 ; Crowly, 9 ; Ô Corkerane, 7 ; McCarthy, 6 ; Ô Canniffe, 6 ; O Finine, 6 ; ungerdell, 6 ; Leaue, 6 ; Ô Murry, 6 ; Ô Mahowne, 8 ; McOwen, 8 ; Rierdane, 7 ; Ô Realy, 6 ; Driscoll, 8 ; McDaniel, 8 ; Ô Cullane, 13 ; Canty, 10 ; Ô Leary, 21 ; Mahowny, 14 ; Ô Morohow, 11 ; Murphy, 25 ; Ô Regane, 19 ; Sullivane, 25 ; McShane, 12 ; McTeige, 22 ; McDermod, 16 ; Ô Donovane, 12 ; McDonogh, 20.

(*folio* 16 *verso*). Barony of Kinalmeaky : Eng, 264 ; Irish, 1628 ; 1892, totall.

(*folio* 17). ## BARONY OF IBAWNE & BARYMORE

Parishes	Places	Numbers	Tituladoes Names	English	Irish
	Court McSherry	24	Robert Gookin Esq John Hodges	7	17
	Keile McCunnagg	70		2	68
	Ballycullenane	3		—	3
	Lislee Temple	48	Charles Gookin Eliz Gookin	6	42
	Lislee & Bally-McCrahane	26			26
	Ballylangce	20			20
	Agha	9	John Wood	1	8
	Butlerstowne	17			17

Parishes	Places	Numbers	Tituladoes' Names	English	Irish
Lislee	Tyrmeene & Ballenbrookey	29			29
	Bally McRedmond	35			35
	Bally McShoneen	11			11
	Shanagh	13			13
	Ballylinch	9			9
	Donworley	3			3
	Curreheene	6	John Oge O Crowly & Oge his daughter		6
	Currygeene	16			16
	Lisnecrimine	23	Randall Warner gent	4	19
	Ballincurdy	2			2
	Ballyhegen	3			3
(*folio* 18)	Barreavagh	15			15
	Ballynemone	26	Lady Travers Richd Travers Esq & Sophia his Sister	5	21
Lislee					
	Kilsullagh	28			28
Abbymawne	Abbymawne	34	Anthony Hollyday	5	20
	The Spittle	9		2	7
	Cregheime	14			14
	Aghafore	13			13
	Garmone	21			21
	Grangibegge	10			10
	Grangimore	17			17
	Donnoghmore	4			4
	Grangimore	10			10
	Currogh	4			4
	Lenneigh	2			2
	Donnoghbegge & Lisclevane	27		5	22
Temple McQuinlane	Ballincoursey	4			4
	Moul McRedmond	8	Teige McShane Crowley		8
(*folio* 19)	Richfordstowne	9			9
	Concamemore	14			14
	Bally McGawny	6			6
	Ring	5			5
Temple O Mulis	Lackyduffe	27		2	25
	Bally McWilliam	2			2
	Ballintemple	8		1	7
	Corare	12			12
	Dorily & Cahirgall	22		3	19
	Aghdowne	5		2	3
	Clowenasby	11		3	8
Timuleague	Timoleague Town	141	John Sweete Esq John & Wm Sweete his sonnes Richd Taylor gent, John O Hea, & John O Hea his sonne, John O Hea McMurtagh, Phillip Bodley	16	125

Parishes	Places	Numbers	Tituladoes Names	English	Irish
	Mohoney & Timoleague Town	13			13
	Curhow	49	James Barry		49
Rathbury	West Cames	19	Murtagh McSheehy Owen McSheehy		19
(folio 20). Kilkeranemore	Curvagh	20			20
	Aghamilla	12			12
Keilgarruff	South Carow	7	Phil Madox	3	4
	North Carow & Ballydnane	26		4	22
Kilkerawnemore	Kilkerawnemore	34	Edward Clerke	2	32
	Coorelea Maulbrack Cleanlea & Crearawer	17	Walter Harris	3	14
Ardfield	Pallice Brittace & Garrymore	16	Dom Mc Tho O Hea		16
	Cahir and Manlinmucky	22	Mlaghlin O Hart		22
	East Aghagnilly	9			9
Kilkerawnemore	West Aghagnilly	13			13
	East Camus	12			12
	Muckaris	13	Tho Bodley & Weldon his sonne	3	10
	Corbally	4			4
Rathbarry	Lisduffe	26		2	24
(folio 21) Island	Downeene&Lenagh	12			12
	Caharlarigge	13			13
	Dunowen	4		2	2
	Dunowen	5			5
	Downycohigge	6			6
Ardfeild	Glenonervigher	27			27
	Corbally	5		2	3
	Creaboy	5			5
	Ballyvacky & Ballybragh	29			29
Rathbury	Carrigrow & Killeleine	18	Adam Clerke	2	16
	Croanogh & Gortigrenane	15	Thomas Hungerford	2	13
	Keilkerawnebeg	35	Mathew Hea Tho Hea James Hea	2	33
	Carrigrow	10			10
	Rathburry Island	10			10
(folio 22)	Carigpadine & Miltowne	33			33
Rosse	Knockingeluy & Downdeedy	29		2	27
	Gawniffe	7			7

Parishes	Places	Numbers	Tituladoes Names	English	Irish
Castleventry	Aghaglastea	15			15
Keilkerawnemore	Ballyvackimore, Ballyvackybegg & Garrylucky	32	Thomas Jermin Mary Jermin	6	26
	Tullenasky	11	David Jermin	3	8
	Dirilone and Tullenasky	14			14
	Creaghbegge	18			18
Rathbuny	Knockponery	6			6
	Knock & Curleagh	6			6
Rosse	Keilrnane	18			18
	Byallnd	31			31
	Derryduffe	21			21
	Knockethoge	6			6
(folio 23)	Bohonoghen & Aghagnilley	27	Martin Galvan		27
	Keil MᶜEnelly	3			3
Kilemine	Diriviren	2			2
	Geachy	22	Daniell MᶜTeige		22
Kilkeranemore	Sleveene	26		2	24

Principall Irish Names

Barry, 16 ; Ô Crowley, 18 ; McCarty, 19 ; Ô Cullane, 12 ; Ô Finn, 10 ; MᶜFinne, 12 ; Ô Hea, 45 ; Moyrane, 10 ; Sullevane, 11 ; MᶜTeige, 32 ; White, 17 ; McDaniell, 15 ; McDermod, 14 ; Ô Donovane, 18 ; McDonogh, 10 ; McPhillip, 9 ; Ô Mongane, 9 ; McCnohor, 9 ; Ô Cullenane, 9 ; Ô Hart, 9 ; Ô Leary, 8 ; Ô Mohir, 8 ; Ô Mahowne, 8 ; Ô Malowne, 8 ; O Regane, 8 ; Dacey & Dacy, 9.

(folio 23 verso). Barrony of Ibawne and Barrymore : Eng, 104 ; Irish, 1604 ; 1708, Totall.

(folio 24). **LIBERTYES OF KINSALE**

Parishes	Places	Numbers	Tituladoes Names	English	Irish
Clonteade	Nicholstown	6		—	6
	Lacknaconime	13		—	13
	Ballyvnstick	3			3
	Pallice Town	7	Stephen Towse Thomas Wetherell	7	0
	Michelstowne	6			6
	Thomastowne	5			5
	Ardmartin & Ballincurry	6			6
	Liscahanebeg	2			2

Parishes	Places	Numbers	Tituladoes Names	English	Irish
	Ballymullin	3			3
	Gortnascotty	3			3
	Knocknaheily	15	John Percivale	2	13
	Knockrobbin	19	Hump : Dudley	4	15
	Coolevalinaneboy	4			4
	Mullindoney	4			4
	Lisnacrilly	10	Richd Coursey gent		10
Ballymartell	Coolecarren	38	Garrett Plunkett gent		38
Rynycorrane	Sillypoint & Coolecarren	132		42	90
	Sleveene	17			17
(folio 25).	South Waters Land at ye Conesbo	40	George Somersett	6	34
Ringcorran	Glanbegge	2		—	2
	Ringcorrane	35		4	31
	Prehane	21		2	19
	Ballymaccus	3			3
	Raiphemore	2			2
	Knockduffe	6			6
	Brownsfeild	10		2	8
	New Mills	19			19
	Coolevalmanemore	10		2	8
	Mellefonts Town	40			40
	Coolevalmanemore	4			4
	Mount Owen or Spittle Land	7			7
	Kilcay	7	Dom Galwey		7
	Nort Watersland	5			5
	Raifemore	32			32
Downderrow	Downderrow	41	Maurice Roch Esq John Roch	4	37
(folio 26)	Bally Thomas	3	John Shipward	2	1
	Mellefontstown	13	Martin Farley		13
Tanaxon	Tanaxonmore & Tanaxonbeg	28	Robt Miagh	4	24
	Ardcloyne	13			13
	Bally William	18			18
	Ballinvarrig	8		1	7
	Wintsmill	10		4	6
Ringrane	Castleparke	47	Henry Bathurst Esq	35	12
Kilvoheme	Ballinaboley	14	Henry Hill	5	9
Ringroane	Ardkilly	7	Rowland Oakeley	6	1
	Ballinidoone	9	Armiger Marsh	2	7
	Castle Parke	110	Maior Rich Goodwin Lt Robt Smith Ensigne John Pine	110	—

Principall Irish Names.
    Murphy, 10 ; Regane 8.

(Folio 26 verso).
    Libertyes of Kinsale : Eng, 244 ; Irish, 613 ; 857, totall.

Parrishes	Townelands	Number of People	Tituladoes Names	Numbr of English	Numbr of Irish
Ringroane	Ouldhead	17	Patrick Ld Coursey Barron of Kinsale John Coursey Esq Ed^m Coursey Miles Coursey Ellis Coursey gent	—	17
	Ringroane	58	Amy Thomas, Vincent Marsh gent	10	48
	Coolebane	5		—	5
	Carrigmoilin	14	John Justice gent	3	11
	Ballinspittle	18		6	12
	Killsarane	27	Wm Fentou Ann Fenton gent	4	23
	Bally McRedmond	34		—	34
	Garrilucas	20	John Bellowe Richd Bellowe	2	18
	Enagh & Lisvodick	31		2	29
	Dorros Bracke	14	Siluester Crosse	3	11
	Bally McKeane	17			17
	Killnaclonagh	12	Richd Billkinton	10	02
	Currohoe	20		13	7
	Ballyhundred	4		—	4
P^t of Killroane	Curte Partine	3	Teige McCurtane	—	3
	Killony	38			38
	Crohane	16	John Browne Domk his sonn	2	14
(*folio* 28). P^t of Templetrine	Gortnacrumes North & South }	22	Walter Tresillean gent	2	20
	Kilmoa	29	Wm Bellue Esq, Lt John Bellue, Edmond Carny, Mary Bellue gent	3	26
	Killbegg	17		2	15
	Moonemore	22		0	22
	Ballycotten	06		0	06
	Ballin Garragh	23		0	23

Principall Irish Names [and their number.]

McTeige, 8 ; McShane, 7 ; Sulliuane, 6 ; Regane, 5 ; Ô Cullane, 6 ; Ô Murry, 4 ; McDaniell, **4** ; McDonagh, 4 ; McCormack, 4 ; Coursey, 10.

(*folio* 28 *verso*).   Barrony of Coursies : Eng, 062 ; Irish, 405 ; 467, **tott.**

(*folio 29*). **THE CANTRED OF KIBRITTAINE**

Parishes	Townelands	Number of People	Tituladoes Names	English	Irish
Ballinader	Coolenapishy	58	Wm Holcombe Jeane and Mary his daughters	15	43
	Ballinvallane	23		3	20
	Carrignagoure	07		2	5
	Raharoouemore	38	Dermod Carthy	o	38
	Rathrought	60		o	60
	Raharoouebegg	43		o	43
	Raharoouebegg & P^t of Raharoouemore	14		—	14
	West Raharoouemore	10			10
	Cloghane	36		1	35
	Kildarragh	14		2	12
	Kilm^e Symon	31	John Points Henry Mansfield	5	26
	Tullelane	o6		—	6
	Cnocknacory	20		2	18
	Knocknacorogh	28		5	23
	Kilgobbin	76		4	72
	Cloncouse	17	Edmond Rashleigh & John his sonn	o	17
(*folio* 30) Ringroane	Coolemaine	95	Tho : Harris	6	89
	Coolemaine bane & Ballyvatten	41	Dauid How	2	39
Templetrine	Ballydownize Knockananewee	12	John Burrowes Hester his daughter	3	9
Ringroane	Glanavirane Killeene & Currowrane	27	John How Abigaill his daughter	o	27
Templetrine	Hackettstowne	09	Ben : Bellew	4	5
	Brownstowne	59		2	57
Inishonane	Cnockroe	24	Geo : Smims	4	20
	Dromqueene	30	Dermod Coughlane & John his sonn	o	30
	Currinnre	18			18
	Downedaniell	4			4
	Ballymountaine	24		4	20
(*folio* 31). Ballymoodane	Tullelane	2		—	2
	Curiefriday	5			5
	Knockreagh	5	Wm Cary		5
	Knockanegeagh	3			3
	Cloyhanebaddick	4			4
	Ballinlaughley	17		8	9
	Glassaffree	8		2	6
	Irishtowne	113	Edward Boyle Ye Lady Hull	40	73
	Lishnapooky	28	Tho : Dodgin	4	24
	Knocknamortely	2			2

Parishes	Townelands	Number of People	Tituladoes Names	English	Irish
Rathclarine	Tullelane	18		3	15
	Gortnahorna	29	John Hurly & Florence his sonn gent	4	25
	Clonecallagh	18	Isaack Philpott Isaack & Randall his sonns Jeane his daughter	8	10
	Ballycattine	5			5
	Clondirrine	27		—	27
(folio 32).	Ballycattine & Clonderine	13		—	13
	Garanedringe & Gortaneauigg	36			36
	Barleagh and Knockbrowne	53		0	53
	Glanduffe & Shallahill	7		7	—
	Barleagh & Knockbrowne	7		—	7
	Glanduffe	2		2	—
	Shanahill	17		4	13
	Glanduffe & Shanahill	12			12
	Ardicrow	16			16
	Garanefine	8			8
	Mawlemawne	35	Donogh Carthy		35
	Burnie	43		2	41
	Cloncallabegg	10			10
	Lissnealine	29		3	26
(folio 33). Kilmalody	Kilmalody	21	Rich : Beamish Geo : Beamish Junr Elizabeth his daughter	8	13
	East Skeafe	15	James Draper Joseph his sonn Samuell Kinstone John Kinstone his sonn	6	9
	Burane	4			4
	West Skeafe	35		4	31
	Clogagh	38		—	38
	Mountaine	6	Tho : Owgan Charity his daughter	—	6
	Slogodeene	21		2	19
	Mountaine	2			2
	Slogodeene	5		—	5
Desert	Tullemnorihy	38	Edwd Scuse	2	36
	Maulrame	13			13
	Farenbanagh	12		2	10
	Aghalosky	36	John Lute		36
	Burrane	26	Tho : Teape	6	20
	Ringarvagine & Garragine	14	James Gilman	2	12
Kilbrittaine	Kilbrittaine	34	Rich : Townsend Esq. Hen: Copley	6	28

Parishes	Townelands	Number of People	Tituladoes Names	English	Irish
(folio 34).	Baltineaquine	43			43
	Bellymore	26		3	23
	Kilnamaule & Maulneskemeny	20		4	16
	Kilthihinine	54		2	52
	Cuoppoage	38			38

Principall Irish Names.

Hurly, 27 ; Reagane & O Reagane, 30 ; Cullane & Ô Cullane, 24 ; Cullenane, 10 ; Mahowny, 10 ; Carthy, 23 ; Leary & Ô Leary, 14 ; Donovane & Ô Donovane, 17 ; Ô Hea & Hea, 10 ; McTeige, 18 ; McOwen, 9 ; Coghlane, 18 ; Daly & Ô Daly, 12 ; McDaniell, 18 ; Crowly & Ô Crowly, 29 ; Murphy, 19 ; Ô Scannell, 8.

(folio 34 verso). Barrony of Killbrittaine : Eng, 198 ; Irish, 1699 ; 1897 Totall.

(folio 35). **THE EAST DIVISION OF CARBERY**

Parrishes	Townelands	Number of People	Tituladoes Names	English	Irish
Part of ye Parrish of Morrogh	Morrogh	55	Edward Hagnes James Mullane	10	45
	Drumouene	28	Richard Scotney	7	21
	Scranefiddoge	31		—	31
Kennegh	East Derregra	32	Mary Bramble	15	17
	Inneskene	82	Francis Armitage Robert Gould George Gould and Peter Gould	26	56
	Tedes	90	Anthony Woodly Esq Ralph Woodly John Keary gent Lewis Goddart	12	78
	West Ballywillowen	48		02	26
	East Cappeene	32		0	32
	East Bally Willowen	24		—	24
	West Clonerege	09			9
	Addrenall	29			29
	Slinoge	11	Robert Warren	2	9
	Blaghnure	26			26
	Ardkilleene	27			27
	Clonomera	27			27
	Gurtmeroe	12		3	9

Parrishes	Townelands	Number of People	Tituladoes Names	English	Irish
(*folio* 36). Kinnegh	Aghillinane	7		5	2
	Aghillinane & Coulbane	19		1	18
	Anagherlicke	9		—	9
	Bockeris	21		0	21
	Kinneghbegg	16	Robert Ellis	2	14
	Connagh	21		—	21
	Teenhye	15	Teige Crowly		15
	Drumfreagh	37			37
	Gorteline	12			12
	Affnolarde	11			11
	Lacavasinagh	8			8
	Castletowne	75	Richard Baker John Eatton John Shipton gent	22	53
	East and West Dromedycloth	35	George Woods	4	31
	West Bilrowes	41			41
	Larrarioltie	27			27
	Killincrinagh	9	John Brokett	4	5
	Killenerinagh	30		6	24
	Farren Maren	15			15
(*folio* 37) Kimregh	Lissyrorke	62		1	61
	Aultaghmore	45			45
	Drumleagh	18	Lieut Coll Manneringe Esq	1	17
	Shanlarigh	9			9
	Shanacrane	9			9
Fanlobish	Keeneragh	5			5
	West Mounigaffe	36			36
	East Mounigaffe	20		2	18
	Quartr Namaderry	21			21
	Alteaghreagh	11			11
	Glaune and Gortroe	23			23
Fanlobus	Downe Manway	108	Bryan Wade Esq	16	92
	Jushie	36	Morrish Cullnane	—	36
	Quartr ofowe	50			50
	Togher	57	Edward Hoare Esq	1	56
(*folio* 38).	Dirilahane	19			19
	Gortinure	12			12
	Killerihenne	22			22
	Nedenneghbeg	50			50
	Nedenemore	10			10
	Tome	23		1	22
	Beagh	10		2	8
	Baltinebracke	33			33
	Beaglhy	11		2	9

Parishes	Townelands	Number of People	Tituladoes Names	English	Irish
	Aghciry	19	John Roch		19
	Lissingteagh	13			13
	Gortenimackly	56			56
	Mahony and Kilronane }	60			60
	Gerranes	18			18
	Mahony and Kilronane	26			26
	Beahigullane	27			27
(folio 39).	Knockaghduffe	23			23
	East Knockaghduffe	18			18
	Sinnagh	15			15
	Ardcahane	62			62
	Dramcierke	18			18
	Manshy	61	Timothy Clea	5	56
Ballemoy	Kilnory	3			3
	Corry begg	8			8
	Goranure	21			21
	North Gilnory	10	Peeter Taylor Shedrick his sonne	4	6
Ballemony	West Derregra	35		8	27
	Garry Crouly	11		2.	9
	Ardea and Bunynumery }	22		2	20
	Insy fane	35	Humphry Barroe Esq James Barroe gent Mary Barroe	11	24
	Eduigcurry and Glaune	35			35
(folio 40).	Fiall	25	Samuel Woodruffe	2	23
	Bodermen & Kilcaskane }	26		—	26
	Shanauogh	40	Richard Fepps & John his sonn	16	24
	Grellagh	36		2	34
	Cnockanedy & Currigillegane }	7		2	5
Desert Surges	Farny Shesiry	18	Richard Bayly Esq Ellizabeth Baunister	3	15
	Garranelahane	21	Robert Harris	3	18
	Aghigohelle	10		—	10
	East Maulbrack	14		2	12
	Lissinguny	21			21
	Lissincuny	25	James Hauglin		25
	Croghan	02			2
	Drumbofiny	9			9
	Maulincruohie	5		03	2
	Maulinruogie	33		1	32

Parrishes	Townelands	Number of People	Tituladoes Names	English	Irish
(folio 41)	Ballenard	5			5
	Derrye	18			18
	Cnockes	25		4	21
	Killenne	16	Callahane Carthy	—	16
	Lisbioge	15			15
	Maulrauer	10			10
	Cariualder	34			34
	Dirimillen	26		8	18
	Kilrouilegath	30	Daniell McCnoughor	1	29
	Kildrumlegath	31			31
	Kilmererane	10			10
	Knockecullin	33	Cnougher McDermod		33
	Aghiyoghell	18			18
	Ballenard	23			23
	Carige Roe	16			16
	Kilrusigarry	11			11
	Boultinagh	17			17
	West Malbracke	17			17
	Cnocke	18			18
(folio 42).	Ardkitt	15	Robert Bramble	3	12
	Ballyvoige	25	Donnogh McCarthy		25
	Ardkitt	20		3	17
	Kilbelloge	11		4	7
	Garram	18		—	18
Drenagh	Drenagh	35		4	31
	Lishya Ladye	32			32
	Maulegaffe & Letter Gormane	17			17
	Capagh	4			4
	Tobane	47		1	46
Killmenne	Cnockauaddera	9	Fynyne McDonnogh		9
	Millengon	22			22
	Cnockenarubly	16		3	13
	Cnockacubly	2		—	2
	Killae	34	Wm Cantie	5	29
	Lisnibrinnie	8		4	4
	Clounetreguie	33			33
	Fiarlihanes	24			24
	Knockduffe	25			25
(folio 43) Killmene	Coulincouerty	30			30
	Dirryne	7		2	5
	Cahircirkie	25			25
	Clounecorbane	9			9
	Rossemore	29			29
	Lisgubbye	43		2	41
	Letter	31	Francis Burneham	2	29

Parrishes	Townelands	Number of People	Tituladoes Names	English	Irish
Rosse	Rosse towne	178	Abell Gullams Thomas Mead John Worrell Thomas Taylor Rich : Painter Patrick Wheite	33	145
	Ballimgoringe & Labertidonnell	41	John Connard		41
	Derryland	25			25
	Kennybricke	35		7	28
	Ballringeringh	14	Rich : Lucas	7	7
	Forrowe	40			40
	Glaunbracke	43	Teige Crowly		43
	Freghane & Meanttroggane	51	Dermod Crowly		51
(folio 44).	Cahirmore	26		4	22
	Glanyruby & Killenlea	38			38
	Tralong & Knocknifiny	38		4	34
	Ballyniren & Coulinvaunoge	27		—	27
	Tinelle, ye Gleabe Land of Rosse	8		2	6
	Farencautry & Giranecore	19			19
	Burgetia Crigane & Lackenrobin	54			54
	Bohonagh	16	Ann Browne	1	15
	Giranegreshine Lisard and Ballyolohane	16			16
	Downen & Curragh	16			16
	Rinivignane & Knockheinge	4			4
	Galtrage & Drumgoune	6			6
(folio 45).	Gullane	26		3	23
	Cahirbegg	19			19
Kilgarruffe	Gortagh and South temple briaal	51	Thomas Burnell	12	39
Iland Parrish		27			27
	Kilgarruffe	21			21
	West Tany	05		2	03
Kilgarruffe	East Tany	07	Edward Berry Esq Wm his sonn gent Eliza : his daughter	6	1
	Kinroe	4			4
	East Tawny	18	Patrick Roch Leonard Robinson	10	8
	Knockscagh	14			14

Parrishes	Townelands	Number of People	Tituladoes Names	English	Irish
	East Tauny	40			40
	Forkill	17	Cnohor Oge Crowly Dauid Crowly		17
	Garanecort	32	Cnohor Oge Crowly	—	32
Iland	North Temple Brien	24			24
	Iland	18			18
	Drumbegg	8			8
Kilgarruffe	Lisbarnes	21	Alexander Arundell	5	16
(folio 46).	Miles	2		0	2
	West Yoehells	28		11	17
	East Yoehells	11		4	7
	North Desert	18		—	18
	South Desert	6		2	4
	Corogrenemore	7		—	7
Kilmacabea	Carugaruffe	58		2	56
	Gortruo	11			11
	Drumolickey	14	Marice Callanane		14
	Kilmacabea	51	Don Oge Corm : Carthy Caulau Owen McCormack vno		51
	Knockshaugh	6			6
	Reuauler	9			9
	Ballyorow	12			12
	Kililinny	8			8
	Duneskline	16	Dan : oge Donovane		16
	Cashell	18	Teigh Crowly		18
	Carouglasse	32			32
Kilnegroffe	Croghane	6		1	5
(folio 47). Kilnegroffe	Garanard	26			26
	Gullanes	42		2	40
	Drumgarriffe	4			4
	Lisghellane	2			2
	Knockapouery	9			09
	Grillagh	14		—	14
	Gullanes	7		2	5
Castle Ventry	Scartcolnygehy	44			44
	Clasagoole	10		2	8
	Castleventery	18			18
	Clastarriffe	3			3
Pt of Kilmalody	Tullagh	31	Teigh Carthy	2	29
The broken lands in ye undernamed Pshs of Timoleg & Temple Ô Quinlane Temple Ô Malis & Kilmalody	Ballenvrogh	57	Samuell Browne	5	52
	Bally McOwen & Knockfouncy	18		4	14

Parrishes	Townelands	Number of People	Tituladoes Names	English	Irish
(folio 48).	Kilcorsie	31			31
	Bally McOwen	13		0	13
	Knocknefouncy	6		3	3
	Carrignevoye	30		—	30
	Bally McOwen & Carignevey	30			30
	Kilitrige	34			34
Kilfaghny begg	Aughtobredmore & Aughtobredbegg	37	Samuell Jervois Esq	5	32
	Rishane	12	Isaack Base	4	8
	Dromaticklogh	9	John Southwell	2	7
	Knockredane	6		2	4
	Clounty & Millens	12		2	10
	Malogowne and Kilbegg	14	George Stafford	2	12
	Kilfinnie	26	Wm Morris Esqr Wm Bowles gent	7	19
	Drombegg	15	Richd Cambridge	2	13
(folio 49). Kilfaghna-begg	Browleagh Creg and Cariglaskie	15	Margt May	1	14
	Rinogrena	3			3

Principall Irish Names [and] there Number.

Hurley and Hurley oge, 45 ; Cullenane & Ô Cullenane, 18 ; Sulevane, 27 ; Crowley Oge & Ô Crowley, 70 ; Ô Carthy, Carthy Oge & Carthy, 26 ; McDonovane & Ô Donovane, 49 ; Ô Hea & Hea, 24 ; Regane and Regane Oge, 39 ; Murphy & Murphy Oge, 37 ; McDonogh & Donogh Oge, 65 ; Cullane & Ô Cullane, 92 ; McDermod & Dermod oge, 72 ; Mahowny & Mahowny oge, 26 ; McTeige & Teige Oge, 99 ; McShane, 46 ; Horgan, 12 ; Leagh, 26 ; Leary & Ô Leary, 42 ; McCnoghor & Cnoghor Oge, 66 ; McDaniell & Daniell oge, 93 ; Reagh & Reagh Oge, 14 ; Roughane, 15 ; McDauid, 16 ; McOwen, 31 ; Murreane, 20 ; McFynyne & Fynyne oge, 25 ; McDermody, 18 ; Daly & Ô Dally, 16 ; Coghlane, 18 ; Buoige (16), Dinane (13), Roe (35), 64 ; McCormack, Cormack Oge & Ô Cormack, 19.

(folio 49 verso). The East Diuision of Carbury : Eng, 422 ; Irish, 4999 ; 5421. totall

(folio 50). **THE WEST DIVISION OF CARBERY**

Parishes	Places	Numbers	Tituladoes Names	English	Irish
	Lahanagh	13		—	13
	Killominoge	13		—	13
	Inogh McDermody	16		—	16
	Cusselowly	11			11

Parishes	Places	Numbers	Tituladoes Names	English	Irish
	Droimnidy	9			9
	Part of Droim Inmidy	5			5
	Caplowry	2			2
	Carhilicky	12			12
	Monanes & Diricluogh	30			30
	Part of Tuo M{c}Dermody	6			6
	Carrighlicky	9			9
Dromaleage	Dromaleague	12			12
	Cawnkilly 1 p{ld}	30			30
	Castle donovane one p{ld}	11			11
	Leaghdirry & Loghtrott	4			4
(folio 51).	Part of Lea dirry & Loghtrott	48			48
	Kilscohonaghty 1 pld	17		2	15
	Dromonadna 3 gneeves	4	Matthew Sweetman	2	2
	Bohir ny Mrydig 9 gneeves	6	Nathaniell Evens	2	4
Dromaleage	Rine Ruo ½ pl{d}	6			6
	Mauleniskelly & Kilmore 1 pld ½	17		—	17
	Beareny Hully 2 plds	13			13
	Garran 1 pld	17		4	13
	Knockane 1 pl{d}	13		2	11
	Dromosty 1 pl{d}	34			34
	East Dromaleagh	10			10
	Muyny 1 pld	53			53
Caharagh	Bunglon 1 ꝑl{d}	13			13
	Banem Ianose	22			22
	Cureny Cleghy ½ pld	10			10
(folio 52).	Madorro 3 gneeves	11	Kedagh M{c}Daniell Donovane		11
	Part of Madorro	5			5
	Carriganiffe 3 gneeves	16			16
	Dirriny ½ pl{d}	10			10
	Turine ½ pld	26			26
	West Lishane ½ pl{d}	43	Ellinor Carthy		43
	The West pl{d} of Aghyarde	14			14
	Dirrylahane ½ p{ld}	5			5
	Curry Clogh 1 pld	4		2	2
	Dronmemore 1 pl{d} ½	15		2	13
	Gortnyscryny ½ plougl{d} 4 gneeves	26		4	22
	Curergniller 1 pld	19			19
	Culebane 9 gneeves	9			9
	Currane 1 pld	29			29
	Middle Ballyourane ½ pld	7			7

Parishes	Places	Numbers	Tituladoes Names	English	Irish
	East Ballyourane 1 pld	22			22
(folio 53).	Cloghanes 4 plds	54		——	54
	Lackareagh ½ pld	12			12
	Killineleagh 2 plds	12			12
	Clonecogir 1 pld ½	9			9
	Droum Currihy	10			10
	East Aghagardae 2 plds	21			21
	Caharagh 1 pld	27			27
	Kilnyguspah	26			26
	Keamemore 1 pld	20	Edw\d Townsend	2	18
	Aghell 1 pld	10			10
	Ballyreary 1 pld	6			6
	Shrylane 9 gneeves	6			6
	Capugboghy 1 pld	33			33
	Moultrahane 1 pld	30			30
	Mauleny Girry 1 pld	9			9
Ayrush Parish	Ardagh 1 pld	38			38
	Braenygreny	9			9
	Brae	17		2	15
(folio 54).	Randletown	19		2	17
Myrusse	Banelehane	19		2	17
	Rahin a Culedorriggy	41			41
	Ryne 2 plds	21			21
	Myrns Ballyintony	29			29
	Coase Koveene & Bane Isell	16			16
	Cahirgall	13			13
	Killny Larhagy & Ardra	13			13
	Cahirgall	13			13
	Monyloghy	16			16
	Bealvaedy & Arera	16		—	16
	South Ballincolly	18			18
	North Ballincolly	7			7
	Scohannagh & Carrighillyhy	33			33
	Clonecah	10			10
(folio 55).Castle-	Castlehaven 2 pld	26			26
haven	Bane Isill, Ardgehane Blued 3 plds	42			42
	Scoh Bane 1 pld	16		2	14
	Tough 3 plds	52			52
	Gort Brack	37			37
	Fornaght 2 plds	41			41
	Lettery Linlish 1 pld	14	Lieut. Lock	2	12
	Adergole 1 pld	10			10
	Aghell 2 plds	35		4	31

Parishes	Places	Numbers	Tituladoes Names	English	Irish
	Farren I Choughor	12			12
	Glanny geele 3 gneeves	5			5
	Banelahane 10 gneeves	18			18
	Geogane 1 pld & 8 gneeves	5			5
	Kilcangell 1 pld 7 gneeves	54		2	52
	Castle Towne 1 pld 7 gneeves	28		4	24
(folio 56). Caha-ragh	Part of Castletown	23			23
	Lisheen Ruo 1 pld	10			10
	Killydury 1 pld	12			12
	Laharedane ½ pld	20			20
Castlehaven	Bludd 1 pld	3			3
	Dunnyne	17			17
	Currybegge	13			13
	Monyvohullughane 1 pld	48			48
	Farrenda & Farrenda-lagg 1 pld	28		9	19
	Eynane ½ pld	32		6	26
	Knockan Eyn 1 pld	8		—	8
	Dirrileagh 4 plds	20			20
Aby Strouzy	Reagh 2 plds	24		5	19
	Inchvingittah	11			11
	Lishyloghirigy 3 plds	50			50
	Kilnyclashy 1 pld	27			27
	Maulbrack ½ pld	9		2	7
(folio 57)	Larigoe ½ pld	8			8
	Skubbyrine ½	12		2	10
	Lishipuhige	9			9
	Cury McTeige 1 pld	19			19
	Gortny Muchullige 1 pld	20			20
	Lahirty Daly ½	11			11
	Drowning	13		2	11
	Curronea 1 pld 2 gneeves	23			23
	Malinonea 4 gneeves	12		2	10
	Aby Strouzy ½ Pld	23			23
Creegh	Gortard	17	Amus Bennett Amus Bennett Junr	3	14
	Rinegirrogy	14		2	12
	Inish Bregge	8		1	7
	Bally Island	35		2	33
	Munnige	12		—	12
(folio 58)	Eynane and Laghahane	13		2	11
	Drissanebegge	58			58
	Dunygaule	4	Wm Steyles gent	4	0
	Gortnycloghy	41		3	38

Parishes	Places	Numbers	Tituladoes Names	English	Irish
	Old Court	5		—	5
	Skibberin Town	54	W Prigge Sam Hall W Galway Adam Gold	5	49
	Creegh	16	Marg Rienard	1	15
	Drissanmore	16			16
	Sick	13			13
Tullagh	Ballymore 3 plds	57	Lyonell Beecher John Selby Collect	14	43
	Ballylenchihane 3 plds	26	Frances Bennett	3	23
	Bally McAcrane 3 plds	26			26
	Ballynard 1 pld ½	18			18
	Bareny Bae 1 pld ½	16			16
	Glawnifnyn 1 pld ½	19		4	15
(folio 59).	Ardagh 2 pld	21		02	19
	Rahmore 3 plds	50		07	43
	Inishirkine 9 plds	61		16	45
	Part of Ballylenchighane	2			2
Cape Cleere Par	Cloyne La	27			27
	Killickindary	5			5
	Knockaneny Kuhige	7			7
	Comeline	7			7
	GlaunIrky	6			6
	Crahagh	5			5
	Lishomony	7			7
	Gortygallane	6			6
	Karrunnigh	4			4
	Camullane	3			3
	Kilvarrime	2			2
	Knocknyhoreven	10			10
Part of Dunisse Parish	Collumlimge	6	Lt Coll. John Read	3	3
(folio 60).	Curcollaght	5	Richd Earlsman	2	3
	Dromreage	23		—	23
	Tullagh	9		—	9
	Rossmoye	11			11
	Bracklisse	2			2
	Killounnoge	6			6
P^t Ducusse	Ballycomane	22			22
	Maulbyvard	17			17
	Letterlicky	27			27
	Skart	32			32
	Baregorume	14			14
	Carrig Buvy	51		4	47
	Clonigh	2			2
Affadown	Affadowne 2 plds	44	Henry Beecher Esq Thomas Beecher Susan Beecher John Godfrey Richard Touson Esq	11	33

Parishes	Places	Numbers	Tituladoes Names	English	Irish
	Hare Iland 3 plds	15			15
	Rinekullisky 3 plds	22			22
	Lishyree & Poulenice 1 pld ½	17			17
(folio 61).	Ardagh 1 pld	16		2	14
	Kilsarlight 1 pld	14			14
	Ardvally 1 pld	6			6
	Killkilline	17			17
	Callatrum begge	5			5
	Leagh Clone 1 pld	11			11
Affadown	Lahir Itanavally	3		2	1
	Knock I Killine	4			4
	Monoghnagh	25		2	23
	The ½ pld of Prohonus	6		—	6
	Ring Morrougg	21		2	19
	Inispige	24		—	24
	Letter Scannlane	34			34
	Monnane 1 pld	13			13
	Drisshine and Rossny grosse	17			17
	Knocknyrahy	14			14
Kilcoe Parish	Boghlea	8	John Gifford Esq	4	4
(folio 62).	Ardurra	12			12
	Skeaghmore	12			12
	Knockruo	12		2	10
	The West ploughland of Killoe	15	Daniell Oge Carthy		15
Kilcoe	The East plowland of Kilcoe	21	Honora Carthy Wid Daniell Carthy Ellen Donovane		21
	The plowland of Glanny Killynagh	10	Dermott Donovane Joano Donnovane		10
	Knockruo	4			4
	Ardglasse	17			17
	The Plowland of Lish Clarige	8			8
Kilerogan	Glanloghy	25			25
	Rosmycaharagg	6	Owen McCarthy		6
	Ryneny Gapull	6			6
	Rosse Kerigh	8			8
	Diry Clavane	6			6
	Aghalige	9			9
(folio 63). Kil-	Fane Moore	7			7
crogan	Killeene	10		—	10
	Kilcrogane	8			8
	Pt of Ross Kerigg	4			4
	Cahir	13			13
	East Letter	7			7
	East Ballyvrane	39			39

Parishes	Places	Numbers	Tituladoes Names	English	Irish
	Dunevre	5			5
	Dromnea	2			2
	Maulenyskehy	17			17
	Farren Manigh	8			8
Scool Parish	Bane Knockan 1 pld	26			26
	Banomshanaclogey & Sparograd 1pld ½	20			20
	Droumkeall ½ pᵈ	10			10
	Glaunshallagh 3 pldˢ	33			33
(folio 64)	Skartinnycullen 3 plds	31	Ellen ny Daniell Carthy gent		31
	Cappaghmore 3 plds	11			11
	Cnolligh 3 plds	59	Dermod Mahony Donnogh Mahony		59
Scooll	Gortinenykilly	21	Teige McCnoghor Mahony		21
	Ballydahab	11		7	4
	Fuilmuck 1 pld	16			16
	Stenane 3 gneeves	8	Robbert Supple gent	1	7
	Cappaglass 1 pld	17			17
	Gurtinruo 6 gneeves	03			03
	Ballycomnnish 1 pld & ½	27	Daniel Carthey		27
	Rosse bren 1 pld	5			5
	Leancon 11 plds	119	Capt. Wᵐ Hull Boyle Hull	18	101
	Carrigargane ½ pld	28		8	20
	Reakule	5		—	5
(folio 65).	Skooll 3 plds	7			7
	Ardmennagh 2 plds	27			27
	Meenvane 1 pld	19			19
	Gubbeene 1 pld	22			22
	Callicroe and Long Island 3 plds	48	Adam Roch	2	46
	Fossiviningh	14			14
Scooll	Lackyreagh & Santullagh 3 plds	31			31
	Duneberkane 3 plds	27			27
	Derivouline ½ pld	8			8
	Quosm Poulhy 1 pld	21			21
	Areentenane ½ pld	8	Philip Roch		8
	Gortnymony 1 pld	22			22
	Kilmoronoge 1 pld	35	Connor Mahony Cormack Oge Carthy		35
(folio 66).	Dirrinenitrae 1 pld & ½	14			14
	Dirry Connell 1 pld ½	32	Connor Mahony		32
	Dromneny 1 pld	9			9
	Dunemanus 10 plds	43	Teige McDonnogh		43
	Lishy Clahy 2 plds	21			21
	Ardrivinny 1 pld	23	Finnine Mahony		23
Kilmoe Parish	Crookehaven	36		7	29

Parishes	Places	Numbers	Tituladoes Names	English	Irish
	Mallavoge 1 pld ½	8			8
	pld of Killian	10			10
	Lynane ½ pld	12		2	10
	Castlemeghegane ½ pld	9			9
	Callyriss Itrigh 1 pld ½	11			11
	3 Plds of Dougy	34		—	34
	Kilbarry ½ pld	12		—	12
	Ballyrized 3 plds	28		5	23
(folio 67).	Bealedilline 3 plds	16		7	9
	9 gneeves of Cloghan	8			8
	Carranmore 1 pld ½	5			5
	Currenbegge 1 pld	10			10
	Carrige Catt 1 pld ½	11		4	7
Kilmoe	Ballinvotrigh 1 pld ½	15			15
	Cloghan Ikilline 3 plds	17	Donnogh Mahony		17
	Callyriss Votrigg 1 pld	11	David Mahony		11
	Bolysillagh ½ pld	12		0	12
	Ballyvoye 1 pld ½	11		2	9
	9 gneeves of Lissegriffin	12			12
	Fossy 9 gneeves	04			4
(folio 68).	Duneloghy 3 plds	44			44
Kilmoe	Dunekilly 1 pld ½	11			11
	Innavotrigh 1 pld ½	14			14

Principall Irish Names [and] thiere Number.

McAulife, 11 ; Ô Buoige, 11 ; Bane, 25 ; Ô Buoy, 38 ; Boughane, 14 ; Browne, 10 ; O Cahane, 14 ; McCnoughor, 66 ; Crowly, 19 ; Ô Cullane, 42 ; McCormack, 20 ; Coughlane & Coghlane, 37 ; McCarthy, 24 ; McDonnogh, 96 ; McDermod, 28 ; Donovane, 29 ; McDaniell, 88 ; Ô Dally, 44 ; McDermody, 57 ; Ô Driscoll, 22 ; Fowlue, 12 ; McFinyne, 38 ; Ô Hea, 13 ; Ô Heagerty, 13 ; Ô Harte, 11 ; Keadagane, 16 ; Leah and Leagh, 20 ; Ô Leary, 11 ; Ô Lennane, 11 ; Munighane, 10 ; Ô Mahony & Ô Mahowny, 38 ; Munnyhane, 11 ; Murphy, 32 ; McMortaugh, 14 ; McMlaghlen, 13 ; McOwen, 33 ; McPhillip, 13 ; Ô Regane & Ô Reagane, 58 ; Reagh, 16 ; Ruoe, 43 ; Roe, 8 ; Sisnane, 14 ; Sullivane, 37 ; McShane, 44 ; Ô Shighane, 18 ; Ô Spillane & Ô Spellane, 20 ; McTeige, 82 ; McWm, 20.

(folio 68 verso).   The West Diuision of Carbery : English, 236 ; Irish, 4811 ; 5047 tott :

(folio 69).   **THE BARRONY OF BEERE AND BANTRY**

Parishes	Townelands	Number of People	Tituladoes Names	English	Irish
Kilmacomoge	Whiddy Island	35		9	26
	Rinedonogane	23	Teige Ô Leary Dermod his sonn		23
	Drumadonell	10			10

Parrishes	Townelands	Number of People	Tituladoes Names	English	Irish
	Ballickey	17	Owen McDaniell		17
	Rinidizett	20			20
	Ardnegashill	05	Roger McDaniell		05
	Trinemaderie	42		7	35
	Coorelome	23			23
	Aghilbeg	17			17
	Carriganasse	14	Tho : Dunkin	2	12
	Keate Kill	19			19
	Kilmacomoge	12	Henry Hull	1	11
	Shandrum	05			5
	Breeny	28	Dun : Oge Sullivane		28
	Glaunbanowgh	15			15
	Ards	10			10
	Drumsullivane	15			15
	Inchiclogh	18	James Galwey		18
(folio 70).	Skehanagh	3			3
	Drumadowney	17			17
	Drumbree	29	George Galwey George Gould Mrs Galwey Wid :	1	28
	Drumnafinchin	15		3	12
	Balligobbane	11		4	7
	Cummer	8			8
	Cosane	22	Teige Oge Lader		22
	Cahirfanish	11			11
	Cahirmuckey	21	Owen McTeige Sullivane Owen Oge Sullivane		21
	Gorteeneroe	27		1	26
	Drumnacapull	4			4
	Glasdargane	8		2	6
	Ringraure	19		3	16
	Cahirdonnell	3		—	3
	Newtowne	119	Richd Browne Mary Burrage Wid : James Galwey Henry Houlden	34	85
Durrus	Blackrocke	44	George Walter Esq Ann Harding Rich : Hutchin	9	35
(folio 71)	Beach	6	John Winspeare Robert his sonn	5	1
	Garryduffe	10			10
	Drumclogh	15		6	9
	East Ruskagh	5			5
	Middle Rouskagh	6			6
	West Rouskagh	12	Dermod Suliuane Dan : his sonn Ellen & Ellane his daughters		12
	Gurteene	33	Edw : Trennwith	2	31
	Gurtene	5			5
	Ardolohane	17			17
	Dromleagh	12			12

Parrishes	Townelands	Number of People	Tituladoes Names	English	Irish
Killaghanenagh	Dromlaffe	6			6
	Kilquonine	10			10
	Kilcoinhin	10			10
	Laghanebegg	14			14
	Ladban	12			12
	Cloghfune	39		3	36
	Cahirmihboae	6			6
(folio 72).	Cahirvilibou				
	Rinetruske	9			9
	Beerehaven	82		16	66
	Castledermod	31		—	31
	Derrykivine	44		—	44
	Derenishvie	31			31
	Irhin	26			26
	Inches	4			4
	Ballihoskin	18			18
	West Rosse McOwen	18			18
	Argromne	33		4	29
	West Rosse McOwen	2			2
	East Rosse McOwen	17			17
Kilcascane	Drumlane	41		2	39
	Stought Finnie	23			23
	Carraffadagh	52	Dan : McOwen bwy Dan : his sonn Honor his daughter Teige McDaniell Donogh Sweeny	2	50
(folio 73). Kil-managh	Kilmany	48		4	44
	Ballydonagane	3			3
	Killaghagh	5			5
Kilcaterne	Kilmacowen	24			24
	Crompane	7			7
	Ireris	6			6
Kilmacomoge	Bantry Forte	113	Tho Lewis Wm Strong officers	113	

Principall Irish Names [and] there Number.

McDermod and Dermod oge, 29 ; McTeige and Teige oge, 33 ; McOwen and Owen oge, 22 ; McShane, 30 ; McDaniell and Daniell oge, 35 ; Murphy, 17 ; McDonagh, 12 ; McCnohor, 12 ; Ô Shea & Shea, 11 ; Sullivane, 9 ; McCragh, 8 ; McMurtagh, 8 ; Downey, 7.

(folio 73 verso). Barrony of Beere & Bantry : Eng, 233 ; Irish, 1321 ; 1554 tott :

(folio 74). **THE BARRONY OF BARRETTS.**

Parishes	Townelands	Number of People	Tituladoes Names	Number of English	Number of Irish
Templemihill	Torreene	62		—	62
	Monyparsons	18		—	18

Parishes	Townelands	Number of People	Tituladoes Names	Number of English	Number of Irish
	Farrenvally	49			49
	Placus	53			53
	Castlemore	34	Wm Barrett Hayward St Leger Esq	1	33
	Ballynamony	34		2	32
	Carrigduffe	2			2
	Ballynamony	26			26
Downaghmore	Garane Veare & Rathaneale	61			61
	East Pluckanes	10		4	6
	Ballycraheene	6			6
	Garane Veare & Rathaneale	12		0	12
	West Pluckanes	29	James Barrett		29
Kilcrohanebegg (folio 75).	Coolitubord	9	John Coulthurst	2	7
	Cooleduffe	21			21
	Coolashaneavally	4			4
	Killigrohanebegg	8	John Ouldis	2	6
	Lackenshoneene	20			20
Garraclone	Garraclone	16			16
	Knocknaleyre	32		—	32
Menagh	Ballyvilleene	11		—	11
	Raghduffe	27			27
Grennagh	Leyruddane	33	Robert Barrett		33
	Ballyvilleene	6			6
	Grenagh	47			47
	Kilemoneton	40		2	38
	Garryadeene	40		2	38
	Ballyphadeene & Garranemamaderee	44			44
	Ballymorisheene	9			9
(folio 76.) Grennagh	Knockbunavehy	22			22
	Ballyfereene	8			8
	Ballimurishrene	15			15
	Lissaverragh	9			9
	Newcastle and Dromnahaghilly	51			51
	Ballygragane	11			11
Mattehey	North Ballyshoneene	29			29
	Ballymawoe	4			4
Inishskarra	Mogoalla	28	Simon Bowles Mich: Dawley	6	22
	Garravagh	48			48
	Courte	4			4
	Curriteagh	30		2	28
	Faha	31	John Barrett		31

Parishes	Townelands	Number of People	Tituladoes Names	Number of English	Number of Irish
	Ballyatti	08			8
(folio 77). Iniskarra	Coolebredogie	43			43
	Knocknamarusse	20		4	16
	Callabegg	14			14
	Carrignaveene	11			11
	Inisling	2		—	2
	Currabeky	5		2	3
The South side of the River Lee in ye Barrony of Barretts.					
Kilnaglory	Geaganagh	31		—	31
St Finbarries	East Ballyhonine	28			28
Inskinny	Ballyvacadane	7			7
Aglish	West Ballyneadae	18			18
	Kilnacluony	19			19
Desertmore	Lower Bally Gromuny	26		4	22
Kilgrohanemore	Cooleroe	5			5
(folio 78). Ovens	Grange	9			9
Kilnaglory	Ballyburdonmore & Bally Burdonbegg }	44	Theo : Cary	2	42
St Finbarries	West Ballishoneene	6			6
St Bridgetts	Magulleene	23	Mary Cooper Catherin Heard Will : Barnes	5	18
Kilnaglory	Kilnaglory	20			20
Bridgetts	Magulleene	13		2	11
Carrigrohane	Ballyncolly	31			31
Kilnaglory	Knocknaburden	6			6
Owens	Carrigane	11			11
Carrigrohane	Cooleroe	8			8
Owens	Classhiganiffe	11	Robert Pierce Christian Gallwey	2	09
Aglish	Kilecluony	37			37
Owens	Lisheeny	5			05
(folio 79). Iniskinny	Ballivacadane	17			17
St Finbarries	Corbally	13			13
Kilnaglory	Ballyhank	30			30
	Ballingully	10		—	10
	Maulcosligg	23		—	23
Downaghmore	Dirrie	29			29
	East Pluckanes	8	Charles Carthy		8
Kilcolemane	Disert	8			8
	Meeshill	6			6
	Tullagh	17			17
Downaghmore	Derrie	15	James Ronane		15
Aglish	East Forgus	17			17
Mattehy	Caron	50	Phillip Crosse	5	45
Aglish	Forgus	10			10

Parishes	Townelands	Number of People	Tituladoes Names	Number of English	Number of Irish
Mattehy (*folio* 80).	West Barno & Droumgownah }	8			8
	East Birne	32			32
	Lower Aghreenagh	13			13
	West Birne & Droumgowna }	32			32
	Upper Aghreenagh	35		0	35
	Lower Aghreenagh	42	Charles McOwen Carthy		42
	Lishnashandrum	11			11
	Gortaterea	6			6
	Lisladeene	12			12
	East Birne	20			20
	Both Kibblafurs	22			22
	Raghyrillagh	3			3

Principall Irish Names [and] thiere Number.

Ô Sulevane, 26 ; Murphy, 45 ; Rierdane & Ô Rierdane, 15 ; McTeige & Teige oge, 34 ; McDonogh & Donogh oge, 17 ; McCallaghane, 15 ; McOwen, 17 ; McShane & Shane oge, 24 ; McDaniell & Daniell oge, 28 ; Welsh, 8 ; McCnohor & Ô Cnohor, 8 ; McMahowny, 12 ; Ô Brien & McBrien, 14 ; Ô Twomy, 31 ; Ô Shea, 9 ; Brenagh & Brennagh, 20 ; Carthy, 13.

(*folio* 80 *verso*). Barrony of Barretts : Eng, 049 ; Irish, 1954 ; 2003 tott :

(*folio* 80).

THE BARRONY OF KILNATALLOONE

Parishes	Townelands	Number of People	Tituladoes Names	Number of English	Number of Irish
Knockmorue	Glanatore	34	Bryan Agharne	—	34
	Carragen	36		—	36
	Coolidorihy	29	Francis Rossington	3	26
	Clashnaganiffe	25	Richd Seaward	5	20
	Ballybreed	32		1	31
	Conehy Castle	33	Edward German	5	28
	Kilclare	5		2	3
	Kilvarery	23			23
	Curreeheene	11	Tobias Browne	3	8
	Ould Conehy	10			10
Agharen	Agharen	43	Tho : More ; Thomas & George his sonns	4	39
	Garanetogert	15			15

Parishes	Townelands	Number of People	Tituladoes Names	Number of English	Number of Irish
	Knocknagapull	9	Baptist Lawrence	2	7
	Balluskey	32			32
	Bally McSemon	23		2	21
	Garicaragh	16			16
Ballynoe	Ballyknock	14		2	12
	Ballysurloge	22		2	20
(folio 81)	Ballymouten	28			28
	Ballinatten	30			30
	Garranecibbeene	13			13
Clonmotte	Garriduffe	22		—	22
Ballynoe	Killassaragh	10		2	8
	Killphillipen	23		2	21
	Cullenagh	7			7
	Ballylagane	9			9
	Glanreagh	8			8
	Lougawell	42			42
	Ballydorehy	11	John Carew		11
Mogeely	Mogeely	12	Mich : Pine & Henry his sonn Esqrs	3	9
	Kilmacow	33	— —	5	28
	Curriglasse	32	Boyle Maynard Esq Wm Haddone Francis Cooper	10	22
	Lisnabrinn	62		6	56
	Glangouragh	8			8
	Kilcrouett	17			17
	Ballycolane	8			8
(folio 82).	Shanakill	19	John Russell	2	17
	Glanballycoulane	53			53
	Gortnafyragh	10			10
	Templevally	11			11
	Ballyclogh	8			8
	Ballyerren	2			2
	Lagbracke	2			2
	Glashowse	5			5
Coole	Coole	88		2	86

Principall Irish Names, [and their number]

Brenagh, 18 ; McDermod, 14 ; McDaniell, 9 ; McTeige, 15 ; McShane, 10 ; Ô Gyrie, 9 ; Ô Griffen and Ô Griffin, 10 ; McWilliam, 13.

(folio 82 verso).   Barrony of Killnatalloone : Eng, 063 ; Irish, 922 ; [total], 0985.

THE BARRONY OF CONDON AND CLANGIBBON

Parrishes	Townelands	Number of People	Tituladoes Names	Number of English	Number of Irish
Killurth	Cloghlea	31	Francis Fleetwood George Norton Esq Grace Norton Ann Norton gent	8	23
	Killaly	21			21
	Glanseskin	41	Timothy Rutter Esq	4	37
	Killurth	135	Wᵐ Hutchens Barth Rutter	26	109
Kilcrumper	Ballydiraowne	33	George Prater Esq	1	32
	Ballincarigir	23	Haniball Cone	——	23
	Ballinglauna	9			9
	Ballinrish	2			2
	Fermoy	101	Robert Boyle Esq Wᵐ Babington Robert White Hanibal Horsey Edward Giles John Kingsmell John Blake gent	16	85
	Cullenagh	6			6
	Cooleneboy	11			11
	Curraghiorgen	2			2
	Bally McPhillip	7	Luke Gernon Esq Nich: Brady gent	4	3
	Carrignogrehery	28			28
(folio 84) Kilcrumper	Donetahine	35		5	30
Clondullane	Fermoy	8		—	8
	Rahelly	15		—	15
	Sanacloyne	8			8
	Ballenveduny	34		2	32
	Carigibrick	5			5
	Curraghmore	25			25
	Bally McPhillip	13		2	11
	BallyMcPatrick Garmore and Knockdromclohy }	38	Peter Cary Esq Peter Cary Junr John Jackson gent	4	34
	Clondullane	24	Edward Beale Esq	6	18
	Upper Ballinfana	12	Edward Ashton Wᵐ Ashton	4	8
	Lower Ballinfana	12	Richard Lawrence	2	10
	Carrigturtane	14			14
	Curraghballymorogh	31			31
	Kilbarry	30	Dauid Condon	2	28
(folio 85) Clandullane	Ballydargane	19	Henry Holton	2	17
	Curribehy	35	John Smyth	2	33
	Kilenemagner Coolgowne & Ballyclogh }	9		2	7
	Ballynaglasse	39		2	37
	Modelligo	40		0	40
	Kilcurrane	29			29

Parishes	Townelands	Number of People	Tituladoes Names	Number of English	Number of Irish
	Garringoule	41		4	37
Cariganeady	Cariganeady	66	Arthur Hide Esqr Ellen Hide	4	62
	Cahirdriny	86	Hugh Hide	3	83
	Ballyadocke	38		2	36
	Kilnadruo Carunotta and Ballykindell }	59	Robert Powell George Powell	4	55
	Kilnadruocor	6		0	6
	Ballynaghane	72	Robert Hide Esq	8	64
	Garaveogeny	14		—	14
(folio 86).	Kilveneton	19		—	19
	Manning	14	Robert Fennell	3	11
	Kilfelane and bolle Curriheenes }	73		4	69
Letrim	Letrim	18	Thomas Campion Esq	2	16
	Colliheene and Ballyparkie }	61		2	59
	Ballinlaccenn	35			35
	Kilmorry	12		2	10
	Knockatrasaane	25			25
	Propoge	28			28
	Ballinamodagh	11			11
	Glanacorky	8			8
Mucrony	Mucrony	10	James Manseryhe Esq	4	6
	Currouefeidie	16			16
	Kilcloghy	22			22
	Curoghmore	28			28
	Dungolane	40		17	23
	Culmohane	15			15
(folio 87).	Curaghnalmory	9		—	9
	Bulleragh	42		2	40
	Cornaghlane	14		4	10
	Arglinbridge	4		—	4
	Ballinalacconn	9	John Tethrington	4	5
Michells town & Brigowne }	Michellstowne	39	Maurice Fenton Esq John Gash	39	—
	Michellstowne & Kilcouglane }	251	John Rutter ensigne Sr Wm Fenton Anthony Raymond John Lauder Thomas Cooke	36 sould^rs 50	165
	Brigowne and Tounlough	41		4	37
	Ballinamona & Keilickane }	14			14
	Ballybegg and Torbehey	10		2	8
	Garryleagh	6			6

[*Folios* 88–115 *inclusive are missing. From the page summary given on the endorsement of folio* 122 *it appears that the Census of the Barony of Barrymore commenced on folio* 110.]

(folio 115).   **BARONY OF BARYMORE**

Parishes	Places	Numbers	Tituladoes Names	English	Irish
	Kilsaimshans	12	Michaell Webber	6	6
	Ballyglissane	16		2	14
Caslelion	Caslelion	297	Rich⁴ Earle of Barrymore & his countesse ye Countesse Dowager John Boyle Esq John Masie gent Eliz Flagettor Rich : Peard	86	211
	Glanneruske	41		—	41
	Ballyveorane	40	Ulick Fitzmorrice Esq	6	34
	Kilenycurry	107		3	104
	Bellick	10	Francis Geagh	2	8
	Bally Robert	30		—	30
	Kilrillin	45		7	38
	Ballymurphy	8		0	8
	Ballyhamshry	8		2	6
	Grange	3		—	3
	Tuormore	4			4
	Ballitrasny	3			3
(folio 117). Clone-mell & Temple robin Par.	Ballytrae	6		2	4
	Fannagh	7		2	5
	Ballydonelmore	5		1	4
	Ballyshanervoe	2			2
	Ballydulea	23	Thomas Mead Anthony Houeden Esq	5	18
	Lisinisky	11			11
	P¹ of Garraeffy	6	Anthony Whitcraft gent Henry Whetcraft Esq	5	1
	Tinenock	15		4	11
	Carraghnieffe	11		4	07
	Cove part of, Bally-nilloone	12		2	10
	The Same	4	Richard Escott gent	2	2
	Spike Island	14	Thomas Selby James Harding	4	10
	Kilgarvane	11	John Davy & Wᵐ Gough	3	8
	Coshkinny	10	Alexander Kenedy	—	10
	Ballymcrussy	25		7	18
(folio 118). Clone-mell & Temple-robin	Rinemoen	30		2	28
	Tinelassie	12	Wᵐ Thirry Patr : Thirry Rich : Thirry	1	11
	Ballylearie	15		5	10
	Belevelly	28		8	20
	Fotie	9	Stephen Towse	3	6
	Kilhodnett	20	Thomas Cattle	7	13
	Passage and P¹ of Ballylearie	13	Pierce Powell Esq	4	9
	Halbollin Island	8	William Harding Esq Peter Harding gent	6	2

Parishes	Places	Numbers	Tituladoes Names	English	Irish
	Ballymore	22	Francis Knowle	4	18
	Corvally	11	Richd Walkam	2	9
	Walterstowne	6		—	6
	Kilvokery	33	Richd Plumer Ann Monke	12	21
Lisgole and Bally-crany Par	Ballinvige	25			25
	Lisgoole	7			7
	Corbally	6			6
(*folio* 119).	Ballyniglassy	38	Solomon Wood	3	35
	Downys	19			19
	Leamlary & Glanne-garuff	13			13
	Ballyniglogh	7			7
	Leamlary	37			37
	Ballyvillery	33		4	29
	Diminns[?]	11			11
Ardnegihy	Ballinvige	15			15
	Glanne Iphreane	50			50
	Lackendaragh	17			17
	Corbally	6			6
	Tignageariagy	11			11
	Kilivnton	21			21
	Ballylegane	12			12
	Ardnegihy	8		—	8
	Byshopps Island	7	James Coppinger	1	6
(*folio* 120) Brittwag Par	Coolkindane	49		—	49
	Curraghdermody	14		—	14
	Ballyvolane	18		—	18
	Ardrae	9			9
	Barraphony	13			13
Kilsainaghane	Skarthbarry	53			53
	Culegnane	8			8
	Ballynaltigh	3			3
	Torenoge	2			2
	Skart Inarune	6	Stephen Coppinger	4	2
	Cosane	3			3
Clonemost	Clonemost	61	Wm Power		61
Inchmibacky	Inchmibacky	78		10	68
	Knocknesmuttane	11		2	9
Aghada Par	Aghada	61	John Wakham Capt	10	51
(*folio* 121). Tente-skine Par	Tenteskine	7	Major Farmer Esq	1	6
Garrane Par	Garranes	48			48
Ballynacorra	Banearde	48			48
	Knockane Ireaghy	15	Oliver Parr Henry Parr Junior	9	6
Carigtowill Par	Barris Court	53		5	48
	Ballinsperigge	33	Edm^d Cotter		33
	Woodstock	42		2	40

Parishes	Places	Numbers	Tituladoes Names	English	Irish
	Carriginsky	25		2	23
	Lockenbeaghy	14			14
	Gortinmucky	30			30
	Ballyadam	11			11
	Licestowne	31	Richd Barry gent	1	30
	Keilecleene	8			8
	Curry	58	Wm Goold	—	58
	Clonnie	14			14
	Tibotstowne	19			19
	Ballyregin	7			7
(folio 122)	Carigtowill	158	Stephen Golborne Wm Gole Wm Rumney	28	130
	Garanecleme	14	Thomas Deyer Capt, Ro^bt Smarth	4	10
	Carrigane	7			7
	Ballyshonegaul	30	Ellen Parr		30
	Bristowne	21			21
Mugessy Par	Ballyannin	18	St John Broderick Esq Wm Broderick	8	10
	Carrigmogvane	19			19
	Ballyvodick	8		1	7
	Garryduffe	12	Peter Betsworthy	2	10
	West Ballytuberid	7			7
	East Ballytuberid	35			35
	Rosmore	74	George Dillon Henry Flagetter Edwd Nicholas Cary Roper Esq	70	4

Principall Irish Names [and] their Number.

Barry, 123 ; Ô Bryen, 16 ; Ô Brodir, 13 ; Brennagh, 10 ; Bourke, 12 ; Ô Couglane, 12 ; Ô Cronyne, 12 ; McCnougher, 34 ; Ô Curtaine, 31 ; Ô Cotter, 51 ; Condon, 13 ; Ô Cullane, 28 ; Carthy, 11 ; O Connell, 21 ; McDaniell, 45 ; McDonnogh, 27 ; McDauid, 20 ; Ô Daly, 26 ; O Donovane, 10 ; McEdmond, 11 ; Ô Fowlowe, 38 ; Ô Healy, 14 ; Ô Hea, 11 ; Hogane, 10 ; Ô Hagherine, 20 ; Ô Hegertie, 10 ; McJohn, 11 ; McJames & Fitz James, 12 ; Ô Keefe, 46 ; Ô Leaghy, 30 ; Murphy, 44 ; McMorrish, 18 ; Ô Mulcaha, 13 ; Ô Mahony, 17 ; McOwen, 10 ; McPhillip, 14 ; McDermod, 19 ; McDermody, 6 ; Ô Flyne, 15 ; Ô Rierdane, 18 ; Ô Reagane, 10 ; McRichard, 10 ; Ô Sullivane, 19 ; Ô Shea, 13 ; McShane, 36 ; Welsh & Walsh, 29 ; McWilliam, 27 ; McTeige, 35 ; O Kissane, 9 ; O Donoghow, 9.

(folio 122 verso). Barrony of Barrymore : Eng, 500 ; Irish, 3953 ; 4453 tott

(folio 123). **BARONY OF ORRERY & KILMORE**

Parishes	Places	Numbers	Tituladoes Names	Eng	Irish
Kilbolane	Kilbolane	35	John Nicholas Marcus Weeke L^t	8	27

Parishes	Places	Numbers	Tituladoes Names	Eng	Irish
	Curraghoalae	17		—	17
	Church Land	6		—	6
	Ballynablea	5		3	2
	Old Orchard	5		2	3
	Downye	15		4	11
	One Pokine	21			21
	Coolenegoure	15	Stephen Legerstone	7	8
	Prohish	9		2	7
	Coolycormack	25	John Rowell	9	16
	Ballynall	21	Philip Barry	4	17
	Ballinlea	27			27
	Ballinlarbegg	22			22
	Castle Lishine	81	Morrish O Agherns	4	77
	Theobald	7			7
	Castle Lishine	9			9
	Ballyegane	12			12
(folio 124)	Mannye	62		6	56
	Bunnamona	16			16
	P^{te} of Ballenlar	17		—	17
	Ballaghrea	11		—	11
	Leiragh	26		—	26
	Kinteere	8			8
	Scart	34		11	23
	Milford	27		3	24
Shandron	Shandron	61		4	57
	Glangaruffe	9		4	5
	Cloneliegh	42	John Novis Robert Magner	2	40
	Clidarragh	22			22
	Tonarra	16		4	12
	Curraclonbro	44	Edwd Magner	2	42
	Twinife	21	Richd Gold		21
	Kilneganre	15		3	12
	Coolesmuttane	50			50
	Curriglasse	27			27
(folio 125)	Ballinekilly	72	Edwd Warner Esq	7	65
	Kippane	4		0	4
	Ballydahin	14	John Barry Ja. Barry	1	13
	Listetrum	8			8
	Coolerin & Kilbrahir	88	Daniell Ô Bryan		88
	Newtowne	98		12	86
Coollyney.	Miltowne	36	John Gibbons Esq	5	31
	Cooleyney	5	Henry Bowreman gent	2	3
	Coolniry villadge	39		1	38
	Fedanes	11			11
	Clonequine	15			15
	Coolecan	22			22
	Ballynorran	6			6
	Cahir Cnohor	8		4	4

Parishes	Places	Numbers	Tituladoes Names	Eng	Irish
	Ballyroe	9		—	9
	Ballydiriden	41		5	36
	Ballycosky	23		3	20
	Castledod	17	Wᵐ Fitzgerald	1	16
(folio 126) Parte of Ballyhey Parish	Stapletowne	11		2	9
	Kiltwoge	16	James Penford gent	5	11
	Broghill	66		2	64
Raghgogane	Raghgogane	57		4	53
	Ballysallagh	6		1	5
	Ardvagehy	4		2	2
	Ballyhubbo	3			3
	Ballypeirce	5			5
	Garryvagronoge	24	Thomas Bowreman	2	22
Liscarroll	Liscarrolletowne	78	Richᵈ Beare	20	58
	West Moige	7	Daniell Crone	1	6
	Kilbreedy	4			4
	Rossinarny	12			12
	Ballynalta	10	Richᵈ Bowles Francis his sonne	3	7
Kilbrony	Ballingile	27	Tho : Denny	8	19
	Ballintrill	8			8
	Ballygurdin	8			8
(folio 127)	Temple Connell	23		5	18
	Ballincurrige	19			19
Ballintample	Bally McCowe	34	Sʳ John Percivale Ellinor Brereton	17	17
	Ballenboule	19	Peregrine Bradston	2	17
	Ballintample	16			16
	Bally Adam	13			13
	Annagh	83	Wᵐ Barry		83
	Carrigine	4	James Barry	—	4
	Garraneard	13			13
	Coolemore	13		2	11
	Craganicourty	37	Edmᵈ Magner		37
	Welshestowne	39			39
	Ballygressy	48		2	46
	Imogane	8			8
	Dunebarry	4		2	2
Temple bridge P.	Bragoge	15	Wᵐ Davenport Anne Roberts	4	11
	Tullogh	22		—	22
	Temple Murry	11		2	9
(folio 128)	Lisgriffine	52	John Groves	4	48
	Ard Pryory	24	John Grigge	4	20
	Garranenagivoge	15			15
	Drinagh	15			15
	Grange	33		1	32
	Ballybegge	48		3	45

Q

Parishes	Places	Numbers	Tituladoes Names	Eng	Irish
	Buttevant	274	Anne Muscham Esqs wid	19	255
	Knockanare	12			12
	Rathclare	83			83
	Timuskarty	3			3
	In Buttevant of Maj'r Purdons troope	14	Edw'd Dowty	14	0
Ballyclogh	Balliclogh	126	Nicholas Purdon Esq	8	118
	Scart	13			13
	Lishevohir	20			20
	Kilm'Clevine	26			26
	Corockstowne	33	Leonard Purdon		33
	Kilpatrick	21			21
	Ardohoig	24	John Lisaught Eliz Beats	6	18
(folio 129).	Clarme	10		—	10
	Garryduffe	36			36
	Dromdowny	70		11	59
	Troopers in Ballyclough	47		47	—
Castlemagner	Castlemagner	63	Roger Bretleridge Esq	12	51

Principall Irish Names [and] their Number.

Aulife, 11 ; Barry, 31 ; Brennagh, 10 ; Ô Brien, 17 ; O Connor, 24 ; Carthy, 11 ; Ô Connell, 45 ; Ô Cronine, 10 ; McDonnogh, 19 ; Downegane, 15 ; McDaniell, 22 ; Ô Daly, 26 ; Ô Fline, 12 ; Ô Hogane, 10 ; McDermod, 14 ; Ô Leyne, 18 ; McMahone, 12 ; Murphy, 18 ; Magner, 19 ; Power, 10 ; Rierdane, 10 ; McShane, 35 ; McWm, 9 ; Callaghane, 18 ; Fitzgerrald, 9 ; McTeige, 39 ; McThomas, 15 ; Walsh, 14 ; Ô Hea, 9 ; McMorrish, 9 ; Ô Shea, 22 ; Ô Sullevane, 27 ; Ô Sheghane, 23.

(folio 129 verso). Barrony of Kilmore & Orrery : Eng, 338 ; Irish, 2847 ; 3185, tott :

COUNTY OF KERRY 8390

(*folio* 1).   County of Kerry

BARRONY OF TRUGHANAC

Parrishes	Townelands	Number of People	Tituladoes Names	Eng	Irish
Ballynahagulsy	—	24	Edmond Trant gent	3	21
	Ballyea	4		—	4
	Killynnura	2		—	2
	Listrym	17	John Deatick	3	14
	Barrow	27		—	27
	Clauloght	12		2	10
	Baltogarrane	18		2	16
	Ballymaceagog	20	Edward Healy		20
Clogherbrine	Knockinnis	25			25
	Clogherbrien	24	Rowland Bateman	2	22
	Banebialboy	26			26
	Ballyenaghta	11		1	10
	Weast Kyeryes	13		4	9
	East Kyeryes	23	Phillip Coinyn	2	21
	Traly Burrough	277	Arthur Denny Esq Mr Lutius Denny Symon Rumny	74	203
Traly	—	80	Lt Will. Collis	7	73
Annagh	—	18	James Conway Edmond Conway William Finch	2	16
	Ballyduynleagh	3		2	1
	Ballyarde	8		4	4
	Cluhir				
	Corrigrage	4			4
	Tonevane	31		4	27
	Annagh	11			11
(*folio* 2).	Loghertcannan	22	Peeter White	2	20
	Dyrrymore	10		—	10
Kilgarrenlander	—	39	Lt John Walker	2	37
	Ballyargane	10			10
	Bolteenes	27		4	23
	Ardcanaght	20			20
	Killeene	11		1	10
Kiltollogh	Castlemanig	27	The Spring	4	23
	Ballincrispin	25			25
	Ballingambon	9			9
	Annagh	3			3
Killcolman	—	26		2	24
	Killaha	30		2	28
	Rathpouke	11			11
	Killcloghane	6			6
	Brackell	24	Dennish Styles		24
	Cloinmore	6			6
Killorglin	Killorglin	26	Robert Hassett	4	22

Parrishes	Townelands	Number of People	Tituladoes Names	Eng	Irish
	Gortnaraha	18			18
	Ryne	17	Capt. Owen Sullivan		17
	Droumevally	4		2	2
(folio 3).	Duglassy	6			6
	Tynahally	15		4	11
	Nauntenane	6			6
	Kappamore	2			2
	Duneguile	9		2	7
	Gort Religge	3			3
	Farren Mᶜ Wᵐ	2			2
	Dromin	7			7
	Ballyleadir	12			12
	Ardmoniell & Kilcoulaght	25	Daniell Feris	2	23
	Auenagarry	12		—	12
	Dunemaneheene	5			5
Currens	——	27		1	26
Killenterna	Killalyny	40			40
	Currachore	16			16
	Cloniclogh	6			6
	Bally McDannell	8			8
	Bally McCruttery	4			4
	Killenterna and Rathnalogh	8			8
(folio 4).	Droumaltare	25			25
	Insyancomue	8			8
	Rathnalcon	9			9
Ballycasslane	Knockyly	10			10
	Arniloagh	13		2	11
	Rahindirry	15			15
	Coumannassy	18			18
	Gortglasse	8			8
	Gortacappull	14			14
	Dirveene	11			11
	Killmurry	19			19
	Mullins	16			16
	Killyvinine	30		1	29
	Ballynahally	7		4	3
Island	——	11		2	9
	Caunegully	7			7
	Culicke	12		2	10
	Culliligh	19			19
	Carue	4		2	2
	Kilbanauane	19			19
(folio 5)	Curranes	19		2	17
	Culenagearigh	28		0	28

Parrishes	Townelands	Number of People	Tituladoes Names	Eng	Irish
	Island towne	45	Lord Herbertt Thomas Herbert Esq	9	36
	Cahermare	6		—	6
	Caharagh	10		—	10
	Bohernaballue	15		2	13
	Bally McAdam	4		—	4
	Conenennagh	17		2	15
	Cnocknegassull	25			25
	Tulligibbin	16			16
	Farrennamracke	8			8
	GlauneballySherune	26		4	22
	Fahaduffe	3			3
	West Meanus	20		2	18
Rathasse	Ballybeggane	52	Samuell Morris		52
	Ballybrenagh	9			9
	Lismore	2			2
	Ballingowne	12	John Chambers James Potter	4	8
	New Manner	8	John Loue gentleman in England	2	6
	Little Manner	3		3	0
(folio 6).	Skekanagh	7		0	7
	Ballymullin	11		5	6
	Ballynorigge	36		—	36
Bally McElligott		170	Richard Chute Esq	10	160
	Bally McElligott	56			56
Ô Brenan	——	64		4	60
Balthosidy	——	50	John BlenerHassett Senr John Blenerhassett Junr Esqrs	6	44
Noghauale	——	17			17
Brosnogh	Killmaneeheene	22		—	22
	Carriggeene	21		—	21
	Brosnogh	6			6
Disert	——	24			24
	Annaghbegg	7			7
	Lismebane	3			3
	Clasganiffe	1			1
	Gortnivohir	9		2	7
	Culcow	6			6
	Tyrenagouse	8	William Browne	1	7

Principall Irish Names [and] their Number.

McTeige, 29 ; McMorrish and Fitz Morrice, 13 ; Ô Breene, 10 ; Ô Bryen, 8 ; Barry, 13 ; Brenagh, 8 ; Ô Brenane, 11 ; Ô Connell, 15 ; Ô Cahane, 13 ; McCnoghor, 10 ; Ô Connor, 25 ; McCurtaine & Ô Curtaine, 10 ; McDaniell, 18 ; Ô Daly, 21 ; McDonnogh, 17 ; McDermod, 16 ; McEdmond, 8 ; Ô Fowlue, 12 ; Ô Flyne, 9 ; Ô Griffen, 14 ; Ô Howrane, 12 ; Ô Lyne, 15 ; Ô Lency, 11 ; Ô Murphy, 23 ; McOwen, 14 ; Roch, 11 ; McRichard, 8 ; Ryerdane, 8 ; Stack, 8 ; McWilliam, 15 ; Suvane, 9 ; McShane, 44 ; Ô Shea, 18 ; Ô Sullivane, 24 ; McThomas, 7 ; Ô Healy, 7 ; Ô Leary, 7 ; Gallivan, 8 ; Gerrald, 7 ; Ô Riedy, 7 ; McCormack, 6 ; McDauid, 6 ; Ô Hanafane, 6 ; Mahony, 6 ; Welsh, 6.

(folio 6 verso). Barrony of Trughanac : Eng, 215 ; Irish, 2168 ; 2383 tottall.

(folio 7).   **THE BARRONY OF CLANMORICE**

Parrishes	Townelands	Number of People	Tituladoes Names	Eng	Irish
Kiltomy	Lixnaw	30	Patrick Ld Barron of Kyery Honora Lady Barroness Wm Fitzmaurice Esq	—	30
	Ballynageragh	12		—	12
	Ballincloghir	10		—	10
	Aghebegg	7			7
	Erribegg	4		2	2
	Clohir	12			12
	Toburhine	6			6
	Kiltomy	4		4	0
	Conyger	3			3
	Liscullane	7			7
	Ballinaulort	3			3
	Droumackee	12			12
	Tullacrummyn	2			2
Desert	Ballyhauragane	15		4	11
	Ballingare	6			6
	Curraghcronyn	11			11
Kilfreghna	Kilfreghna	13			13
	Ballirieghans	2		2	
	Cluonduglassie	5		3	2
	Pallice	10			10
	Banemore	13			13
(folio 8).	Bruvadery	6			6
	Ballimessie	6		2	4
	Errimore	17			17
Killshenane & Funug	Buolilienagh	26		1	25
	Behins	9			9
	Gortnycloghane	17			17
	Ballyduhigg & Cuileneline	32			32
	Funuge	20		3	17
	Ballinrudeligg	10		3	7
	Ballygrenane	5		3	2
Ardfertt	Ardfertt Towne	47	Thomas Crosby Edward Shewell Patrick Crosby	7	40
	Tibbridd	10			10
	Rahonyine	9		3	6
	Ardglasse	2		—	2
	Ballinpriora	4			4
	Bally McCoine	3			3
	Caraghane	2			2
	Fienett	7			7
Ô Dorny	Abbey Ô Dorny	12		1	11
(folio 9). Ô Dorny	Rahennye	14			14
	Bally Broman	8			8

Parrishes	Townelands	Number of People	Tituladoes Names	Eng	Irish
	Dromconigge	12		10	11
	Lackabegg	8			8
	Lackamore	9			9
	Bohiruo	12			12
	Binecree	23			23
	Kilgolbin	6			6
Killury	Farrenruoge	8			8
	Ardguonigh	4			4
	Killmore	5	Wᵐ Crosby		5
	Cloghane	8			8
	Ardae	4			4
	Ardoughter	4		2	2
	Clasmelcon	6		1	5
	Mineogalane	17		2	15
	Dramguine	4			4
	Ballinglanny	15			15
	Ballinae	17	John Heerd gent Henry Kinveton in London gent	2	15
	Rahmurrill	11		—	11
(folio 10). Ballyheige	Knockennery	2		—	2
	Tyre Sanaghane	2		—	2
	Cloghan Lysie	2			2
	Balliriogane	12			12
	Ballinclimeasig	7			7
	Ballyheige	6			6
	Ballylongane	3			3
Kilmoily	Bennagh	23			23
	Lerrigg	4		2	2
	Killy Killie	15			15
	Garineskie	20			20
	Banemore	13			13
	Kilmoily	24		2	22
	Toghirbane	17			17
	Ballimickine	28			28
	Clohir	4			4
Killaghine	BallimᶜLuine	19		3	16
	Agha Mᶜcrime	6			6
	Aulane	14			14
	Bally Henry	5			5
	Aghamore	4			4
Kilfloine	Crottoe	24	Henry Ponsonby Esq	6	18
	Knockbreake	10			10
(folio 11).	Kill Bally McSheen-ickine	32			32
	Ballyconnell	4			4

Parrishes	Townelands	Number of People	Tituladoes Names	Eng	Irish
Rathoe	Ardcullin	9		2	7
	Dromartin	12			12
	Corbally	4			4
	Ballincrossig	6		—	6
	Minemore	8			8
	Burgessland	12			12
	Lisnegoinny	11		2	9
	Glannerdallune	9		2	7
	Ballshanragane	9		2	7
	Knoppoge	8			8
	Ayle	4			4
	Ballinbrenagh	3			3
	Knock McIliuin	4		2	2
	Tullaghine	3			3
	Rathoe	6		2	4
Duagh	Dromleggalsh	14		4	10
	Bally Mc Jordan	16		—	16
	Kilcarhae	3		2	1
	Duagh	1			1
	Triemeragh	20			20
(folio 12).	Dirrinduffe	10			10
	Knockouleegane	19			19

Principall Irish Names [and] their Number.

Stack, 17 ; FitzMorrice & MacMorrice, 17 ; McBryen, 6 ; Cahane, 6 ; Ô Connor, 7 ; Crosby, 6 ; Ô Dulinge, 14 ; McDaniell, 8 ; McDermod, 6 ; McEdmond, 10 ; McWilliam, 6 ; Lency, 6 ; Murphy, 8 ; Mahony, 9 ; Piers, 8 ; Roydy, 6 ; McShane, 23 ; McTeige, 12.

(folio 12 verso).   Barrony of Clanmorrice : Eng, 086 ; Irish, 1040 ; 1126 totall

(folio 13).   **BARRONY OF IRAGHT I CONNOR**

Parrishes	Townelands	Number of People	Tituladoes Names	Eng	Irish
Kilnaghtin	Tarbert	61	Ralph Conyers Esq	6	55
	Tynefagh	2		—	2
	Sanavogh	6		2	4
	Killrourally	7		2	5
	Dooneard	22		—	22
	Cahurhuny	5		2	3
	Milcon	24		3	21
	Kilpadoge	12			12

Parrishes	Townelands	Number of People	Tituladoes Names	Eng	Irish
	Pullin	11			11
	Glannesmagh	4		3	1
	Killnaghtin	6			6
	Doonecaha	10			10
	Gort Dromagauna	8			8
	Caru Ieragh	19			19
	Killmena	20		2	18
Murhur	Glaunlap	23		2	21
	Moyvane	26			26
	Murhur	9			9
	Agherim	13			13
	Letrim	25			25
	Killaha and Gort Dromasyllyhy	76	Richard McEllygott		76
(folio 14). Killehenny	Ballyeghna and Ballybonane	71	Edward Allen	8	63
	Rahannagh	6		0	6
	Kilmoholane	2		—	2
Aghavalin	Asdy	23	John Edmond John Hill	5	18
	Carrigafeile	22		8	14
	Aghanagraune	24	Francis Hoskins	9	15
	Ballyloyne	22		—	22
	Lislaghtin and Ballvaccassy	23		2	21
	Tullahivill	19		—	19
	Lisha	2		—	2
	Lettir	34	Thomas Blener Hassett	3	31
Kilconly	——	14			14
Liseltin	Beale	26	Rich : Glanvill		26
	Urlee	39	Jasp : Morrish		39
	Moybilly	8	Wm Justice	2	6
	Ballyconnery	30		2	28
	Laghane	20			20
	Lackacroneene	10			10
	Kilgrauane	11			11
(folio 15).	Corelacka	20			20
	Parte of Urlee	8			8
Listowhell	——	74	John Fitzgerrald Esq Thomas Fitzgerrald John Fitzgerrald Patrick Fitzgerrald & Edmond Fitzgerrald	2	72
	Ross Temple	21		2	19
	Listowhell	72	Ensigne Will : Cony	4	68
Galy	——	35	Thomas Amery Robert Ellyott Thomas Hambery	10	25

Parrishes	Townelands	Number of People	Tituladoes Names	Eng	Irish
	Drombegg	21	Thomas Galleghor		21
	Kiltoan	25			25
	Part of Drombegg	19			19
	Ballyegan	9			9
	Glovry	13			13
	Tullabegg	26			26
	Parte Shrone	11			11
	Culereagh	39			39
	Atrohis	27		2	25
	Tullabegg	5			5

Principall Irish Names [and] their Number.

Ô Bryen & McBryen, 10 ; Barry, 6 ; Brinagh, 6 ; Ô Connor, 13 ; McCnoghor, 7 ; McDonnogh, 22 ; McDaniell, 11 ; McDermod, 10 ; Fitzgerrald, 8 ; Ô Kelly, 8 ; Ô Lency, 8 ; McMorrice & Fitz-Morrish, 14 ; McMahony, 12; Ô Scanlan, 18 ; Sulleuan, 9 ; McShane, 18 ; Stack, 10 ; McTeige, 7 ; McThomas, 7.

(*folio* 15 *verso*).   Barrony of Iraght Iconnor : Eng, 081 ; Irish, 1139 ; 1220, totall.

(*folio* 16)   **CORCAGUINY BARRONY**

Parrishes	Townelands	Number of People	Tituladoes Names	Eng	Irish
Kilgobban	—— ——	7	John Carrick Esqe	—	7
	Cappaclogh	12		—	12
	Ballygarrott	8		—-	8
	Moyge	5			5
	Killeltin	17		2	15
	Tonekilly	3			3
	East Knockelasse	4			4
	Cuile	4			4
	West Knockelasse	12		—	12
StradBally	Carryfioght	18			18
	Killyghran	6			6
	Gowlane	15		2	13
	StradBally	28		4	24
	Duah	17 .		2	15
	Glanlogh	4		—	4
	Killuny	9		2	7
	Castlegregory	10	Anthony Shorttliffe	4	6

Parrishes	Townelands	Number of People	Tituladoes Names	Eng	Irish
	Deehs	4		2	2
	Killshaningge	24		2	22
	Killcomyn	6		—	6
Cloghane and Ballyduffe	—— ——	34		3	31
	Ballycahill	8			8
(folio 17).	Brom	19		5	14
	Murrirrigane	4		4	000
	Lisnakelivey	6			6
	Ballyguine	8		2	6
	Cappagh	8		2	6
	Ballynalaken	10			10
	Ballyduffe	4			4
	Liscarny	4			4
Ballinvohir	Inch	15	James Knight	4	11
	Ballyvauldeir	24			24
	Ballinvohir	6			6
	Ballynahunty	12		2	10
	Logherbegg	8		8	000
	Immelagh	5		1	4
	Ballynecourty	30	Nhillhall Browne		30
	Arres & Gurteens	25			25
Mynard	Doontis	12		2	10
	Weast Mynard	16		—	16
	East Mynard	27		—	27
(folio 18). Kynard	Kynard	22			22
	Cloincorha	30			30
	Garfinagh	19		2	17
	Killarone	17		4	13
	Ballymanuge	17			17
	Ballintaggort	09			9
	Lough	4			4
	Kilnagleriegh	5			5
	The towne and Burrough of Dingle	159	John Chappell Esq William Chappell Thomas Holland gent	26	133
Dingle and Kildrum	Ballymore	14	Edward Trant	2	12
	Cloghane Cahane	4		2	2
	Cahir Boshiny	23			23
	Kilfuntin	4			4
	Ballymorerigh	8			8
	Ballystragh	13			13
	Ballinnasigg	4			4
	Glantis	4			4
	Ballyhea	5		2	3
	Dune Sheane	2			2

Parrishes	Townelands	Number of People	Tituladoes Names	Eng	Irish
(folio 19).	Monaree	6			6
	Ballingowlin	6			6
	Bally McIdoyle	17			17
	Rahen Vegge	4			4
	Carhew	3			3
Ventry	Faun	29			29
	Killdurrihy	13			13
	Rahanane	22		—	22
	Ballyleagh	9			9
	Dunequeene	19			19
	Cahir Bulligge	11		2	09
	Ventry	17			17
	Cahir Trant	24			24
	Ballytrasny	5			5
Marhine and Dunevrlane	Ballinnahigg	13			13
	Marhine	11			11
	Ballyoughtragh	3		2	1
	Teereruane	7			7
	Ballyferritter	29			29
Kilmelcadder & Kilquane	Gurane	9		2	7
	Ballybracke	2			2
	Ballygawnyne	6			6
(folio 20)	Ballyruobucke	8			8
	Kiluane	4			4
	Kilmelcadder	11			11
	Gallaris	3			3
	Rineconnell	4			4
	Ballynaha	9			9
	Cloghane Duffe	5			5
	Ballyfinora	3			3
	Imelagh Padin	9			9

Principall Irish Names [and] Their Number.

McBrien, 6 ; Bowler, 8 ; McCnoghor, 8 ; Ô Cahane, 10 ; Ô Currane, 12 ; McDonogh, 11 ; McDermod, 12 ; McDaniell, 18 ; Ô Griffen, 13 ; Ô Lyne, 7 ; Kenedy, 6 ; Ô Ketighir, 6 ; McKeanan, 12 ; McMorrice & McMorrish, 12 ; Murphy, 18 ; McOwen, 19 ; O Shea, 14 ; McShane, 13 ; McThomas, 10 ; McTeige, 14 ; Trant, 12 ; McWilliam, 8.

(folio 20 *verso).*   Barrony of Corcaguiny : Eng, 097 ; Irish, 1086 ; 1183, totall

(*folio* 21).

BARRONY OF MAQUINIHY.

Parrishes	Townelands	Number of People	Tituladoes Names	Eng	Irish
Kilcomyn	Dromdisart	82	Daniell Leary	2	80
Killarny	Cullie	8		—	8
	Gortdromkiery	8			8
	Muccorus	7			7
	Quilearrymoy	5			5
	East Quilly	8			8
	Gortancunigh	4			4
	Drumhumper	3			3
	Cullybogie	11			11
	Dromiruorke	3			3
	Moynish	4			4
	Fleskebridge	4	Anthony Shakelton	3	1
	Carriganfrieghane	4			4
Killahy	—— ——	28			28
	Curriell	5			5
	Aunemore	6			6
	Dromcarrabane	8			8
	Inshy	7			7
	Killahy	6			6
	Cippagh	2			2
(*folio* 22).	Killarny towne	112	John Gallway	13	99
	Culecasleagh and Billaghcomane	13			13
	Dirrygomligh	5			5
	Direene	6		—	6
	Cnockes	10			10
	Ballyvoige	5			5
	Tulligg	2			2
	West fraction	73		2	71
Kilbonane	Bealamalis	21	Lancelott Sands Esq	2	19
	Listry	14	Arthur Carther		14
	Fagha	10			10
	Rossnacartin	18			18
	Laghard	5			5
	Laugharne	21			21
	Gortnacloghy	14			14
	Colowes	23			23
Molahiffe	——	17	John Plunkett and Thomas Plunkett his sonn gent		17
	Killegh	39			39
	Buollycurrane	20		2	18
	Goulane	8			8
(*folio* 23)	Ballybane	10			10
	Dromore	9			9
	Clounetiburide	2			2

Parishes	Townelands	Number of People	Tituladoes Names	Eng	Irish
	Coolecleiffe	6			6
	Bealafinane	14		2	12
	Garranerouerice	12			12
	Ardglasse	43			43
Killnanea	Gortfadda	6	Ensige Floyd	4	2
	Cnocknymuckully	17			17
	Killanea	14			14
	Clounemelane	11			11
	Dromragh	15			15
	Rah	19	Hugh Faluy	—	19
	Arduonoge	17			17
	Aghadoe and Lisnagaune }	26		2	24
	Knockree	8	William Hall Esq	2	6
	Cahircrohan	3		3	000
	Ballyduny	4		3	1
	Gortroe	9			9
	Lismaghane	6			6
(folio 24) Killnanea	Killilly	5			5
	Ardd	24			24
	Durene	6			6
	Thomies	20			20
	Mauligh	15			15
	Dromon	6			6
	Crohane	9			9
	Gortancollipy	3			3
	Gorteene Ruo	8	Teige Faluy		8
	Clynis	9			9
	Culecurrane	3			3
	Pallice	3	Dermod Mahony		3
	Myniskie	16		2	14
	Annagullymore	6			6
Aglish	Leamnagehy & Kilboune }	21	Brien Swyny		21
	Ballytrasny	18	John Barrett		18
	Aglish	4			4
	Cloune Idonogane	14			14
	Knockanaulgirt	3			3
	Racommane	12			12
(folio 25)	Knockornaghta	25			25
	Ballincurrigh	029		—	029

Principall Irish Names [and] their Number.

McCnoghor, 9 ; Ô Connor, 9 ; Ô Croneene, 6 ; Ô Curnane, 6 ; Ô Connell, 9 ; Cahassy, 9 ; McDaniell, 15 ; McDonogh, 13 ; McDermod, 8 ; Ô Daly & Dally, 10 ; Ô Collaghane, 7 ; McEdmond

& Fitz Edmd, 6 ; Ô Fowlue, 8 ; Faluy, 7 ; McTeige, 20 ; Gallway, 7 ; Ô Hea, 7 ; Ô Lyne, 6 ;
Leaghy, 9 ; Murphy, 16 ; Mahony, 7 ; McOwen, 10 ; Rierdane, 6 ; Rourke, 9 ; O Shea, 12 ;
Sullivane, 8 ; McShane, 9 ; Scannell, 6 ; Ô Spillane, 6.

(*folio* 25 *verso*).   Barrony of Maquinihy : Eng, 042 ; Irish, 1122 ; 1164, totall.

(*folio* 26).   **GLAUNEOROGHTY BARRONY**

Parrishes	Townelands	Number of People	Tituladoes Names	Eng	Irish
Killmackilloge	—— ——	18	George Parsons gent allien	2	16
	Dereeneanvirrige	14			14
	Cryuyne	3			3
Srone Birrane	—— ——	9			9
	Curecrine	4			4
	Glanotrassna	19			19
	Ardea	42			42
	Loughort feramer	19			19
	Killaha	04			04
	Dromoughty	21			21
	Bunnane	7			7
Killgaruane	Ardtinllihy	17		5	12
	Shandrome	47	Ralph Almes	4	43
	Killbunnane	8		1	7
	Barnynstackigg	51			51
	Ardtullyhy Quartr	14			14
	Barnanstockigg Quarter	5			5
Killmare	Currihenmore Or Gearyhudveene	10			10
	Dughill	7			7
(*folio* 27).	Kilgortanny	14		8	6
	Lettir	5			5
	Lacky Roe	12			12
	Lettir	8			8
	Balligriffine	34			34
	Killynny ½ quarter	7		4	3
	Drommatewcke	18			18
	Killowen Quarter	64	Joseph Taylor	2	62
	Neadeene Quarter Kilsara	24		2	22
	The Quarter of Cahir	31		3	28

Principall Irish Names [and their Number.
    McCnoghor, 12 ; Ô Cahesey, 6 ; McDaniell, 14 ; McDonogh, 10 ; Downey, 9 ; McOwen, 6 ;
Sulliuan, 26 ; Ô Shea, 6 ; McShane, 9 ; McTeige, 6.

(*folio* 27 *verso*).   Barrony of Glauneoroghty : Eng, 031 ; Irish, 505 ; 536, totall.

R

(*folio* 28).   **DUNKERRAN BARONY**

Parrishes	Townlands	Number of People	Tituladoes Names	Eng	Irish
Templeno	Doonckerran	58	Doctr Arnalds Allien gent		58
	Claddaneanure	5			5
	Cappana Cossy	20			20
	Droumkenny	21		2	19
Killcroghane	—— ——	10			10
	Ballyrnaghane	8			8
	Durrinane	40			40
	Cahir Doniell	6			6
Knockane	Clunagh	41			41
	Farrennagat	61	Charles Sugherne		61
	Currabegge	8			8
	Killoghane	26			26
	Meanus	23			23
	Culecluhur	17			17
	Culemagort	13			13

Principall Irish Names [and] Their Number.
McCnoghor, 8 ; McOwen, 7 ; McTeige, 11 ; Mahowny, 7 ; McDermod, 7 ; McDaniell, 6.

(*folio* 28 *verso*).   Barony of Dunckerran : Eng, 002 ; Irish, 355 ; [total], 357

(*folio* 29).   **IVERAGH BARONY**

Parrishes	Towneland	Number of People	Tituladoes Names	Eng	Irish
Valentia	Glauntine	21		2	19
	Ballyherny	20		—	20
	Coumbeg	22		2	20
	Corrumore	16			16
Dromod	—— ——	39	Daniell Connell		39
	Tarmon	13			13
	Cahirbearnagh	12	Owen Carthy		12
Ballenskealigg	Arguill	15	Dermod Connell		15
	Killurly	4			4
	Coume	2			2
Killenan	Killurly	27			27
Killimleegh	— — ——	28	Charles Connell		28
	Killtinleagh	11			11
	Aghgort	10			10
	Ballinehan	19	Martine Hussey	2	17

Parrishes	Towneland	Number of People	Tituladoes Names	Eng	Irish
	Leateene	14			14
	Killkeavragh	15			15
	Durie	15		2	13
Glanbehy	——— ———	37			37
(folio 30) Cahir	Ballycarbery	21		02	19
	Killelane ye East	05			05
	Comego	13			13
	Cloghan McQueine	07			07
	Rinard	07		02	05
	Krecoman	05			05
	Aghtoburid	04			04
	Keanburren	09			09
	Letter	02			02
	Carehey	08			08

Principall Irish Names [and] their Number.

Faluey, 07 ; Murphy, 7 ; Ô Shea, 13 ; Ô Connell, 25 ; Shagroe, 6 ; Curran & Curan, 7 ; McShane, 8 ; McDaniell, 7.

(folio 30 verso). Barrony of Iveragh : Eng, 012 ; Irish, 409 ; totall, 421.

Barronies	Pages	Eng	Irish	Totalls
Trughanac	06	215	2168	2383
Clanmorrice	12	086	1040	1126
Iraght I Connor	15	081	1139	1220
Corcaguiny	20	097	1086	1183
Maquinihy	25	042	1122	1164
Glauneoroghty	27	031	0505	0536
Dunekerran	28	002	0355	0357
Iveragh	30	012	0409	0421
		566	7824	8390

LIMERICK CITTY

3105

(folio 1).   **LIMERICKE CITTY**

South Ward : Number of People, 480 ; Eng, 255 ; Irish, 225 ; Tituladoes Names : Christopher Keyes, Will : Thomlinson, Walter Dauies gent, Coll Ralph Willson, and Major Wade Esqrs ; Leut Jess, and Leut Dowdas gent, Thomas Lucas Esqr Capt, Leut Coughlan gent, John Crabb Sheriff, Patrick White, Will Barkell, James Arthur, Christo : Arthur, & James Ash Marchants.

Midle Ward on ye West Side : Number of People, 357 ; Eng, 194 ; Irish, 163 ; Tituladoes Names : Dr Whyte Esq, Lt Heward, William Royall, Capt. Peterson, Mr Peacock and his two Brothers, Mr Perry, Hugh Mongomerie, and Ensigne Benden gents ; Capt Humphrey Hartwell, Esq, Christopher Holmes, Mr Cripps, Mr Hooper, Allderman Bennett, and James Crauen gent, Tho : Poore, Mr Garnet, Thomas Plellps, Tho : Bennis, Peter Rice, Francis Casy, and Mr Houlbert Marchants.

(folio 2). Midle Ward on Ye East Side : Number of People, 370 ; Eng, 183 ; Irish, 187 ; Tituladoes Names : Thomas Sanders, Thomas Phetiplas, Ensigne Thomas Browne, Teige Bryan, Domminick Meagh, Henry Saltfeeld, Henry Price Junor and Leut Will Pope gentlemen ; Thomas Poore, & George Comin Esq, Daniell Hignett Town Clerke, Lt John Comyn, Tho : Martin, Peter Van Hugarden, Robert Collisson, John Cruce, Alderman Boeman, Richard Lennard, Henry Price Senir, Nathaniell Waples, Sherif Pausy, Alderman Warr, Randall Cossens, Robert Shute, Samuell Foxen, James Banting, Antho : Bartless, and Richard Wallis Marchants.

Ye North Ward : Number of People, 160 ; Eng, 88 ; Irish, 72 ; Tituladoes Names : John Hoorst gent, Alderman Will Yarwell, & Will Hartwell Esqrs, George Back, and Alderman Miller, Marchants.

(folio 3).   **THE COUNTY OF YE CITTY OF LIMERICKE**

Parrishes	Townelands	Number of People	Tituladoes Names	Eng	Irish
St Michaels	——	15		2	13
	Belanacurry	26	Captn Bentley Esq	8	18
	Fearanagalleagh	18		—	18
	Wthout Mungrett gate	29		—	29
	Gortskollupp	16			16
Mungrett	Temple Mungrett	56			56
	Bellequen	58			58
	Cnokeard	32			32
	Tirvoe	24	Donnogh ò Mighane gent		24
	Cloghkeaton	27	Arth : Carter gent		27
	Ilanannane	10			10
	Ballicomin	28		2	26
	Cloghicoky	14			14
	Toaradyle	38		—	38
Cruory	Annagh Roch	28			28
Cnocknagaule	Derricknockan	23			23
	Ballinacloghy	04			04
(folio 4). Caher Ivally	Caher Ivally	16	Patrick Creagh gent		16
	Frierstowne	12			12
	Lickidoone	79			79
	Thenakelly	25			25
Carnarry	Skarte	19		2	17

Parrishes	Townelands	Number of People	Tituladoes Names	Eng	Irish
	Carnarry	42	Will Kenn and Jno Ouzzell gent	5	37
Carrigphersoon	Carrigphersoon Towne	23			23
	Tooreen	15			15
Derrigellaneme	Sheadfed	47			47
	Killenenoge Skartirea, and Cluonconny	17		2	15
	Coolehenane	15		2	13
Donoghmore	Drombanny	46			46
Kilmurry	New Castle downe	82			82
	Bellasinon	23			23
(folio 5).	Bellavellen	16	Robert Theoballs gent	04	12
	Kilonane	48	John Mathewes gent	21	27
	Ballinacloghy	13			13
	Castle Troy	54			54
	Balliglissine	17			17
St Laurence	Spittle	46	Lt Jno Carr gent	2	44
	Killeeleen	17			17
	St Johns Acre	24			24
	Ratheurd	18			18
	Ballisheeda	15			15
	Banalisheen	04		02	02
Pt of Stradbally	Upper Garane	09		02	07
	Gransigh towne and lands	14		02	12
	Lower Garrane	15			15
	Cluonclieffe and Ballyvoelane	34		02	32
(folio 6).	Ballingeile	16		06	10
	Lishnegrey and Garrinoe	48	Lt Henry Lee gent	02	46
Killicknegarriff	Ballyvarry	46		02	44
	Cleyduffe	03			03
	Ballinlosky	29			29
	Raheene	13		03	10
St Patricks	—— ——	16	Jno Miller gent	03	13
	Parke	34			34
	Singland	45	William Twayts gent	05	40
	Corbally	11			11
North Liberties of Limerick		06		02	04
	Balligrenane	04			04
	Cluoncanane	16			16
	Shanuolly	04			04
(folio 7).	Cnockardnagalleagh	3			3

Parrishes	Townelands	Number of People	Tituladoes Names	Eng	Irish
	Cluondrenagh	21		2	19
	Coonagh	30	Patrick Sarsfield gent		30
	East Coonagh	8			08
	Cluonmaken	2			02
	Kilrush	4			04
	Castle Blake	4			04
	By ye Strand from ye Bridge West Ward	44			44
	Ye South Side Westward	34		08	26
	Killegly	56	John Collins gent	08	48

Principall Irish Names [and] their Number.

Arthur, 11 ; Ô Bryen & Ô Brian, 27 ; Bourke, 20 ; Creagh, 11 ; McCragh, 06 ; Ô Dule, 09 ; McDoniell, 13 ; McDonogh, 09 ; McConnor, 09 ; Ô Carroll, 08 ; Ô Griphae, 07 ; Fitzgerald, 08 ; Ô Gerrane, 08 ; Ô Hally, 06 ; Ô Hogan & O Hogane, 19 ; Ô Hea, 09 ; McKelly, 14 ; McKeogh, 07 ; Linchy, 07 ; Ô Mulclahy, 06 ; Ô Mullowny, 10 ; Mulrian, 12 ; McNamara (6), McNamarow (6), 12 ; McRory, 6 ; Roe, 7 ; Rice, 6 ; Ryan & Ryane, 17 ; Smith, 6 ; McShane, 29 ; McTeige, 14 ; Whyte, 12 ; McWilliam, 13.

(*folio* 7 *verso*). Limbrick Cittye with ye North Lybertyes & County of Ye Citty : Eng, 819 ; Irish, 2286 ; 3105, totall.

LIMERICKE COUNTY

21872.

(*folio* 1) County of Limerick

SMALL COUNTY BARRONY

Parrishes	Townelands	Number of People	Tituladoes Names	Eng	Irish
	Rathmore	078	John Ferinshaugh Richd Heyne & John Heyne gents	07	71
	Balliea	022	Thomas Carpenter Esq & Wm Carpenter gent	05	17
	Feadmor	82	James Woods & George Woods gents	06	76
	Kildromon	39		—	39
P^t of Glinogry & in P^t of Tullabracky	—— —— ——	58	John Parker gent	02	56
	Crean	53		02	51
	Doone, Creane & Boheregely	88		—	88
	Howardstowne	85	Francis Vincent & Edm : Deane gents	04	81
	Kilbroody	23			23
	Fannings Cluone	40	Richd Thorne & Wm Payne gent	09	31
Killfrush	Carnane	30		05	25
	Ballecarony	45		02	43
	Ballenlany	12		02	10
	Kilfrush	28		—	28
(*folio* 2).	Elton & Briattas	27	Thomas Hurly gent		27
	Ballinloghy	83			83
	Ballyhakish	16			16
	Ballynegalliagh	26	James Browne gent		26
	Hospitall	244	William King & Thomas Browne Esqs Rich : King gent	21	223
Ballenlogh	Ballygearane	07			07
	Ballyneganana	29	Arthur Bleverhassett Esq	02	27
	Ballycahill	25			25
	Kilkellane	38			38
	Ballecolleroe	23	William Ogle gent	02	21
	Gorticline	12	Owen Grady gent	02	10
	Kilgobanemore & Ballyvistellibeg	20	John Bagott & William Bagott gent		20
	Ballincurry	17			17
	Bagottstowne	77			77
	Scoole and Clogh-dullerty	44	Henry Tirrell. John Croker and Michaell Croker gents	06	38
(*folio* 3).	Bulgeden Fox Upper Scoole	23		04	19

Parishes	Townelands	Number of People	Tituladoes Names	Eng	Irish
	Clogdullarty	14			14
Vregare	Bulgedeen Fox	111			111
	Tankardstowne	04			04
	Ballycallowe	19	Henry Verdon gent		19
Athenesie	Gormanstowne & Adamstowne }	28			28
Ballinard		159	Gerrott Fitzgerrald Esq Thomas Fitzgerrald gent	02	157
	Cloghovillow	44			44
P^t of Glinogry & Glinogry Towne		101	William Weeks gent	02	99
	Drombegg	12			12
	Catergullymore	18			18
	Tullybrackin	57			57
	Coscamaddo & Gortemore }	11			11
(folio 4). P^t of Glinogry	Loghguir	46		07	39
	Killilogh	48			48
	Ballyculleene	54			54
	Patricks Well	25			25
	Grange	66			66
	Knockincellor	41			41
	Six Myle Bridge	12			12
	Ballingerly & Rawliestowne }	111			111
	Cromwell & Killeenanaliffbegg }	22			22
Any	Rathany and Kilgobanbegg	47	Edmund Perry gent	10	37
Kilkellane	Harbartstowne & Ballinscooly }	28	Derby Grady & Thomas Grady gents		28
	Harbartstowne	10			10
Any	Ballynamonymore	28	Joseph Ormsby gent	02	26
(folio 5). Kilpecane	Kilpecanetowne	27	John Carew gent		27
	Garry Elline	12			12
Kilteely	Carrig Kettle	38			38
	Knockany	173		08	165
	Oldtowne	106	James Bagott gent	03	103
Feadamor	Eraverstowne	16			16
	Cloghnemanagh	82	Richard Hart Esqr John Hart & Percivall Hart his sons gent	05	77
Any	Kilballyowen	33			33
	Ballyda	09			09
	Ragamusbeg	08			08
	Garryncahery	32			32

Parrishes	Townelands	Number of People	Tituladoes Names	Eng	Irish
	Milltowne	14			14
	Ballenbramy	10			10

Principall Irish Names [and] their Number.

Ô Bryen, 13 ; McBryen, 12 ; Ô Bryne, 15 ; Bourke, 29 ; McConnor, 14 ; Ô Connor, 07 ; Ô Connell & McConnell, 08 ; Ô Cahane, 15 ; Ô Clery, 09 ; Cullane, 10 ; McDauid, 12 ; McDonell, 09 ; McDaniell, 25 ; McDonogh, 17 ; McDermott, 12 ; McEdmund, 09 ; Ô Grady, 26 ; FitzGerrald, 13 ; O Glissane & Ô Glassane, 17 ; Ô Heyne, 06 ; Ô Hogan & Ô Hogane, 18 ; Ô Hea, 31 ; Hurly, 10 ; Hicky, 09 ; Ô Keefe, 13 ; Ô Meary & Ô Mary, 11 ; Ô Mullowny, 21 ; McMorish, 9 ; Ô Mulrian & Ô Mulriane, 9 ; Nugent, 8 ; Ryane & Ryan, 32 ; Ô Ryerdane, 8 ; Rawley, 11 ; McShane, 32 ; McTeige, 23 ; Ô Trassy, 9 ; Wailsh, 15 ; McWm, 16 ; Casy, 8.

(*folio* 5 *verso*). Barrony of Small County : Eng, 120 ; Irish, 2950 ; 3070, totall.

(*folio* 6).

COSTLEA BARONY

Parrishes	Townelands	Number of People	Tituladoes Names	Eng	Irish
Ballingarvey & Lavaghla P'ishes {	Ballinfuntagh	35	John Gibbon gent	—	35
	Ballingarry	26			26
	Knocklary	13		02	11
	Cloghcasty	23	Samuell Bennett & Robert Mease gents	06	17
	Glanlary	8			8
	Glean-ary & pt of Ballingarry }	39		5	34
	Ballynegristoonugh	13	Thomas McTeige gent		13
Ballinlondry	Killeene and Ballinlondry }	44	John Heffernane gent		44
	Spittle	28	Teige McCraith & Edmond Richard gent	03	25
	Cullane	39	Robert Gease gent		39
	Balliduff	14			14
	Ballyfaskeene	16	Teige Ô Liddeene gent		16
	Gleanahagushly	15		04	11
Ballyneskaddane (*folio* 7).	Ballyneskaddane	34	Giles Powell gent	02	32
	Lickelly	12			12
	Scartteene	16			16
Done & Long	Doone Moone Ballynehensy & Pt of Ballinbreeny }	88	Capt. Lewis Griffith Esq Humphery Coleman gent	10	78
	Knocklonge	72	Cornelius Eames & Francis Swayne gents.	07	65

Parishes	Townelands	Number of People	Tituladoes Names	Eng	Irish
	Hamonstowne	08			08
	Michelstowne	24		07	17
	Cnock Torin	13	Cornelius Maddin gent		13
Kilquan	Ballyshonedehy	8	Francis Creed gent	03	05
	BallyMcShaneboy	27	Walter Stephens gent	03	24
	Ballinqrughty	12			12
	Jamestowne	32			32
Pt of Effin	Garrycoonagh & Rathnevitagh	60			60
	Ballinveely Ballycarrownagh & Cleaghah	31			31
(folio 8).	Ballyshonikeene	43	Garrott Gibbons & Garrott Gibbons gent		43
Galbally	Galbally	163	William Hughs gent	14	149
	Killinane	07	John Ward gent	03	04
	Corbally	11	John Petford gent	02	09
	Bohercarrin	15	Edward Moore gent		15
	Lisardconnell	30	William Barraby gent	04	26
	Ballybooba	12		03	09
	Milstowne	08		02	06
	Duntreleage	52	Hugh Massy Esqr & Richd Huthings gent	09	43
	Lakadary	12	John McCragh & Phillip McCragh gents		12
	CastleKrea	18	Robert Cooke & Nicholas Clarke gent	06	12
	Corragharosty	15	Thomas Loyde gent	07	08
	Ballynemoddagh	23			23
	Barnegurrehy	14			14
	Ballylisheene	20			20
(folio 9).	Kilbeheny two pl lands	146			146
	Kilglesse	63	John Condon gent		63
Kilfinane	Cloghmotefoy	70	Robert Oliuer Esq	03	67
	Fannistowne	15			15
	Ballyngreny	15			15
	Ballyorgan	28			28
	Ballynleyny & Ballyngeagoge	86			86
	Ballyroe als Ballynygoseragh	36			36
	Ballynanima	43			43
	Morestowne	30	Dauid Gibbon gent		30
	Balliperode	14			14
	Ballyroskenoge	44	Donnogh Manyhyne Teige Manyhyne & John Welsh & John Shyhane		44

Parrishes	Townelands	Number of People	Tituladoes Names	Eng	Irish
(folio 10).	Ballyna Courty	63	Dauid Touchstone & Henry Touchstone gent	05	58
	Mortellstowne	31			31
	Keale	14			14
	Ballynvoty	32	John Bluett gent	04	28
	Tallow	27	Robert Weilsh gent		27
	Roplagh	31			31
	Kilfinane	102		04	98
	Garrynlacy	08			08
	Dorragh	23	George Vallanne gent and Thomas Vallanne gent	04	19
	Lawrences towne	26			26
	Ballyntobye	18			18
	Garryarture & Kilornoge	25			25
	Spittle Darage	19			19
Kilbridie	Tantstowne	67	Richard Grice gent	05	62
	Ballyidin-Eadin	55		02	53
(folio 11).	Ballyquine	11			11
	Gibbinstowne	53			53
Athenesie	Dorrenstowne	51			51
	Ballynsealy & Stephenstowne	23			23
	Ballycullane	46			46
	Cosse	51			51
	Killmurry	13			13
Ballyngaddy	Ballyngaddymore	91			91
	Ballinnehow	25			25
	Ballingvosy	119		02	117
	Garrikettine	37		02	35
	Glindinnane	22			22
	Mrdovellane	31			31
	Ardpatricke	11			11

Principall Irish Names [and] their Number.

Ô Brine & McBrine, 10 ; Barry, 11 ; Bourke, 12 ; Bryen & Ô Bryen, 17 ; Browne, 09 ; Ô Cormack & McCormack, 09 ; Casy, 15 ; Ô Corbane, 11 ; Ô Cahesy, 23 ; MacCraith, 17 ; Ô Cluvane, 11 ; Ô Connor & McConnor, 11 ; Condon, 10 ; Ô Currane, 12 ; McDauid, 20 ; McDonnogh, 14 ; McDaniell (17), Daniell (2), Ô Daniell (3), 22 ; McEdmond, 11 ; Flemming, 12 ; Gibbon & FitzGibbon, 22 ; Henesy, 16 ; Hiffernane, 12 ; Ô Hogan, 11 ; Ô Hea, 09 ; Ô Keilly, 12 ; Ô Kelly, 10 ; Ô Kenny, 9 ; Ô Keife, 8 ; Langan (6), Lingane (6), 12 ; Murphy, 13 ; McShane, 23 ; McShihy (9), McSheehy (3), 12 ; Mac Teige, 29 ; MacWilliam, 18 ; Walsh & Welsh, 17 ; McDermod, 8 ; Meagh, 8 ; Ô Sullivane & Sullivane, 12 ; Tobbine & Tobin, 08.

(folio 11 verso).   Barrony of Costlea : Eng, 133 ; Irish, 2775 ; 2908, Totall.

S

Parishes	Townelands	Number of People	Tituladoes Names	Eng	Irish
	Robertstowne	46			46
	Ballinroan	04			04
	Rochtowne	17			17
	Ballinloghane	37			37
	Fryarstowne	08			08
	Williamstowne	17	Edward Andrewes gent	04	13
	BallyMcGnard	83	Captn Faithfull Chapman	03	80
	Whytstowne	68	James Casy gent		68
	Kilcooline	36	Wm Cobb & Thymotie Dickson gent	07	29
	Ballymakree	13			13
	Luddenbeg	31	Edmond Bourke & Mortagh Ô Beara gent		31
	Sthrahane	41	John Hale & Wm Clearke gents	06	35
	Knockatanacushland	47	John Friend Esq & Edward Willy gents	13	34
	Cahercourceely	38	Donogh Ô Hea gent	06	32
	Inchy Lawrence	07			07
	Greenarrebegg	44			44
	Knock Ineagh	24	John Loftus gent	04	20
(folio 13).	Boherskeaghaganiffe	17	Richard Willy & Nathalian Watts gents	06	11
	Cloghnadromon	16		02	14
	Kishy Quirke	14	John Syms gent	05	09
	Lismollane	22	Thomas Burton gent	04	18
	Caherkinlish	66	Stephen Towes gent	03	63
	Boskill and Temple Michell }	39	Humphrey Curteois & Edmond Curteois gent	07	32
	Castlevorkine	41	Edward Allen gent	02	39
	Both Greenanes	20		——	20
	Ballyvorneene	39	Wm Ingram gent	01	38
	Killenure and Gortinskeagh }	18	Wm Chapman gent	02	16
	Graingerbegg	17	John Cooke gent	02	15
	Graingmore	33	James Collens gent	05	28
	Brytas & Eque	58	Capt. John Mansell Esq	07	51
	Dromkeene	48			48
(folio 14)	Killinenewearah	14	Theobald Bourke gent		14
	Cohirlish	27	Patricke Whyte gent	——	27
	Breaklone	05	Arthur Brocke gent	05	00
	Caherconreiffy	42			42
	Knockischie	12			12
	Clashbane	26	Robert Thorenborrogh gent	05	21
	Ballyvecode	16	Wm Gabberd gent	03	13
	Caherline and Ballyhobine }	16	Ralph Rusell gent	01	15
	Doonevullen	36			36

Parishes	Townelands	Number of People	Tituladoes Names	Eng	Irish
(folio 15).	Rathjordan	31	Nicholas Hanraghane gent		31
	Cahirelly	64	Robert Wilkinson Esq	05	59
	Caherelly Weast	59		05	54
	Ballybrikine & Ballynebwoly }	73	Major George Ingouldesby Esq	07	66
	Luddenmore	37	Nicholas Jenkins gent	02	35
	Clownekine	06		—	06
	Maddyboy	27	Will Bradford gent	03	24
	Ballygey	23		02	21
	Knockyhursimtah	36	Symon Whyte gent	04	32
	Collinatruimey	02			02
	Gortballyboy	04			04
	Killirknegarriffe	09		02	07
	Ballyluckie	04			04
	Dromenboy	20		03	17
	Gurteene	05			05
	Knockanebane	05	Thomas Turner gent	04	01
	Castle Connell	72	Thomas Wilkinson gent	09	63
	Lower Port Crussy	22			22
	Upper Port Crussy	18			18
	Bohirquiele	11		08	03
	Parke	18	William Giles gent	02	16

Principall Irish Names [and] Their Number.

Ô Bryne, 08 ; Bourke, 29 ; McBryan & Ô Bryan, 11 ; McConnor & Ô Connor, 22 ; Clancy, 08 ; Dwyer, 09 ; McDonnogh, 11 ; McDaniell, 11 ; Ô Heyne, 17 ; Ô Hea, 24 ; Hicky, 08 ; Ô Howrogane, Ô Howrigane & Ô Howregane, 21 ; Hogane, 11 ; Muclahy and Mullclahy, 11 ; Mullowny, 12 ; Ryane, 51 ; McShane, 20 ; McTeige, 20 ; Browne, 07 ; McKeogh, 07.

(folio 15 verso). Barrony of Clanwilliam : Eng, 159 ; Irish, 1590 ; 1749, tott :

(folio 16) **CONNOLOGH BARONY**

Parishes	Townelands	Number of People	Tituladoes Names	Eng	Irish
Rathkeil	Castle Matrickes	26	Edmond Southwell & Thomas Southwell Esqrs	06	20
	Courte Matrickes	45		—	45
	Enish Couch	20		03	17
	Ardbohill	12		02	10
	Ranahan	04			04

Parrishes	Townelands	Number of People	Tituladoes Names	Eng	Irish
	Cloagh	08			08
	Knockan Mc	06			06
	Ileland more	02			02
	Kiltane	08			08
	Inseypostoge	07			07
	BallyWilliams	42		04	38
	Graige	10			10
	Bally Cyea	42	John Massy gent and John Massy his sonn gent	04	38
	Ballydoroug	15			15
	Ballymackey	10			10
	Kilcolmolman	37		04	33
	Ballyallynane	62		02	60
	Loghall	22			22
(folio 17).	Dromard	33	Francis Dowdall gent	06	27
	Ballynalaugh	26		03	23
	Lissadine	29		05	24
	Rathkeiletowne	186	Brooke Bridges Esq	40	146
Cloynagh	Cloynagh	26			26
	Lisnakelly	12			12
	Kilquamc	07			07
	Parte of Ballyegny	43			43
	Rathgownane	27	Eustace Whyte gent	02	25
Rath Ronane	RathRonane & Ballyvohane	42	Lt Copely gent	08	34
	Dromaddy	56			56
	Athy	19		02	17
	Ye ½ Plowland of Dirrynebaymord	10			10
	Temysletlea	17			17
(folio 18).	Ballyegnie Pt	12			12
Downdaniell	Ridbestowne	61	Henry Wendle gent	03	58
	Cloghnarold	30		07	23
Kilskonnell	Coolenorane	20	Thomas Watson gent	02	18
	Clonybroune	11			11
	Kilscanell	11	John Chesterman gent & John Jurin Aduenturer 10li	04	07
	Reenes	26			26
	Clonogulline	34			34
	Ballinlynie	34			34
Croagh	— — —	92	Capt Thomas Walchott gent	06	86
	Amogane	24		01	23
	Ballynimaud	16			16

Parrishes	Townelands	Number of People	Tituladoes Names	Eng	Irish
	Cloagh	23			23
	Croaghnaburgess	62	George Aylmer gent	04	58
	Lisnimuky Ballincurry & Ballynigoole	32			32
(folio 19).	Ballyadocke	04			04
	Ballinweiry	11		06	05
	Ballaghnaguily	12			12
	Kiltenane	02			02
Cappagh	Cappaghtowne	20			20
	Ballindigany	04			04
	Clonoule	05			05
Clonshiere	Clonshieremore	20		04	16
	Gorthne Grewre	11			11
	Clonshiere begg	18			18
	Graige	02			02
Ballingary	Ballingary towne	95	Thomas Boore Esq	02	93
	Knightstreete	83	Nicholas Mouckton gent	05	78
(folio 20).	BallinanLeeny	91			91
	Lisdnane Behernagh & Lisconett	84			84
	Lisconeate	03			03
	Loghdoomeare & Glassemalaffe	52			52
Clouncha	BallyMcRogie	66	Janathan Barron gent	04	62
	Ballebeggane	09		01	08
	The Glibe of Clouncha	08			08
	Gurteenehagherane	20			20
	Bally McEvagie Pt ofBallyMcFranckie belonging to Mr Courtenay	19			19
	Gortnetrehy	41			41
	Ballykennedy	16			16
(folio 21).	Teerenakelly	21			21
	Ballyhahill	13			13
	Ballykeavane	33			33
	Bally McFrancky	20			20
	Ballynoe	70	William Cox gent	06	64
	Kilmacow	70	Thomas Buttler gent		70
	Borneane	22			22
	KillmacanIrly	10	John Feild gent	02	08
	Killbegg and Lismoatty	14		02	12
Killfenny		72	William Piggott Esq	07	65
	Shanaflogh	05			05

Parrishes	Townelands	Number of People	Tituladoes Names	Eng	Irish
	Ballyvolloge	17			17
	Ballygrynane	34			34
	Killatall	31			31
	Graignacurry	21			21
P^t of Ballingarry	Ballynehagh	20			20
(folio 22). Brury	Brury Towne	103			103
& Clouncoragh	Ballyfookine	64			64
& Corchomohir	Forte and Carraghmaddery	56			56
	Garryfoyne	21		03	18
	Clounbanaff & Kilmac Daniell	12			12
	Ballyshalagh	27			27
	Cappinereechane	25			25
	Cappinanta	12			12
	Killcalla and Gortmore	17			17
	Ballyhadiane	20			20
	Castletowne	52	Charles Ô Dee gent		52
	Culegoune	26			26
	Grage	37			37
	Bally Auliffe	05			05
	Clounee	12		02	10
(folio 23).	Gortenegary Keales and Bohonure	58		06	52
	Ahhidaigh	20		02	18
	Clounyneigh	06	Robert Frestone gent	04	02
	Bohard	08		02	06
	Clonenlary	09			09
	Callahow	06			06
	Tulligg	43			43
	Clounpastine	02			02
	Drom Collohir	044		10	34
	Ye Gliab of Drom Collohir	06			06
	Coolobwey	02			02
	Clashnasprelagh	18			18
	Cloun Creaw	15			15
	Mollaghard	18			18
	Kilmurry & Cappaculane	15			15
(folio 24).	Enshyneshedry	16			16
	Rosemarielane & Ballinlangie	26			26
	P^t of Mollaghard	10			10
	Ballymoryhy	34	Robert Fenell gent	02	32
	Moddelly	35	Lt Charles Williams gent	06	29
	Pallice	147	John Odell gent		147

Parrishes	Townelands	Number of People	Tituladoes Names	Eng	Irish
Newcastle	——	154	Captⁿ Nicholas Brumley Capt John Mead and Lt John Williams gents	36	118
	Churchstowne	04			04
	Dualy	23			23
	Glangoune and Bally-pierce	26			26
	Dromonstowne	37			37
	Ballylahiffe	21			21
	Gurraine Keavane	12		02	10
	Dongonwell & Glanstare	28			05 / 28
(folio 25).	Ducateene	05			05
	Ballymany	10			10
	Curraghnomullaght	12			12
Grangie	——	06		02	04
	Carhugare	33		05	28
	Ballyfraty	04			04
	Dromin	03			03
	Gorthrogh	03			03
	Lower Grange	15		03	12
	Dungee	04			04
	Ardrine	04			04
	Cloumsirrihane	08			08
Ardagh	— — —	43		05	38
	Ballyrobine	10			10
	Cahirmoihill	12	Richard Exham & Phillip Exham his sonn gents	04	08
	Liskilleene	06			06
	BallyneBarny	21			21
(folio 26).	North Ballincahane	08			08
	South Ballinlaghane	04			04
	Ballinie	11		03	08
	Kilrudane	30			30
	Eanaghgane	04			04
	Killaghteene	36			36
	Rusgagh	28			28
Abbyfeale	— — —	39			39
	Portthree naud	13			13
	Dromtarsny Killmagh & Bolighbeheene	38			38
	Caherdogafe & Cnockrahidermody	18			18
	Killinlea	10			10
	Cnockbrack	30			30

Parrishes	Townelands	Number of People	Tituladoes Names	Eng	Irish
(folio 27) Mahow- nough	The Towne	56	Richard McGuir William Fitzgerrald and John Fitzgerrald gent		56
	Ballydarta	17			17
	Bally McKelly & Coolly lockey }	24			24
	Ballybrenagh	12			12
	Garryduffe	30	Teige Ô Connell absentee gent		30
	Ihanraught	23		02	21
	Fanelehane & Ballinvulline }	42			42
	Monelany	30			30
	Aherrulke	64			64
	Teteraine	23		03	20
	Inniskin	10			10
	Curraghregeare	17			17
	Gortevonyne	16			16
	Rath	50		16	34
	Coolecormane	12			12
	Clounemore	27			27
	Fohynough	34			34
(folio 28)	Ballygullin	14			14
	Meane	51			51
	Garrandiraugh	06			06
	Coolerahan	02			02
	Ballynusky	02			02
	Gortskar	11			11
Clounelty	Vallynoe	84	Thomas Bramley gent	04	80
	Kilgobun	18			18
	Cahirahanbegg	08			08
	Aheliny	24	Thomas Maguir & Lawrence Maguir gent		24
	Lissunisky	54	John Hankswoorth gent	04	50
	Cnockedirry	19			19
Monegea	Camus	24			24
	Ballynatiborad	29	Anthony Shydy gent	02	27
	Ballymorrogh	69			69
	Rahcahill	50			50
(folio 29).	Glanguem	15			15
	Teampulglatane	14			14
	Thulliguline	29			29
	Mynyloyne	14			14
	Cnockane Icallane	24			24
	Glanduffe	33			33

Parrishes	Townelands	Number of People	Tituladoes Names	Eng	Irish
	Rathneconnerie, FearneWillen and Dromroe	53			53
	Ardnacrohy	10			10
	Killehylem	42			42
	Bally Quirke	08			08
	Ballyclovane	04			04
	Ballygeill	16	George Bruttnell gent	04	12
	Ballyconooe	11		02	09
	Gurteen McGary	06		—	06
	Ballyvogane	12		03	09
	Aranugh	18		02	16
	Ballynehow	10		02	08
(folio 30).	Shannagarry	05			05
	BallymacRannell	04		02	02
	Lisvrelane	02			02
	Garryduffe	04			04
Robertstowne P'ish	— — —	15	Wm Threnchard Esq liuing in England Francis Paluis gent	07	08
	Lyahy	24		03	21
	Robertstowne	15			15
	Ballydonavane	08			08
	Garreenantobur	11			11
	Mineragh	17		03	14
	Cnockpatricke	02			02
Shannagolden	— —	19	Symon Gibbins gent	05	14
	Ballycormacke	17		05	12
	Tooremore	10			10
	Ballynecraggie	21			21
	Shrewlane	15			15
	Ardyneere	20			20
(folio 31)	Ballyantlaba	11			11
Killmoclane	Killcosgrane	09	Capt John Copplen gent	05	04
	Shannett	74			74
	Ballyane	04		04	—
	Ballycnockane	08			08
	Craigg	15			15
	Abby	10			10
	Craiggard	06			06
	Tibberad	02			02
	Carrue	02			02
	Mollagh and Moehraneene	21			21
	Clounety	13			13
	Fynoe	08			08

Parrishes	Townelands	Number of People	Tituladoes Names	Eng	Irish
	Ballyhahill	12			12
	Clounlehard	10			10
	Cnocknegerneagh	13			13
(*folio* 32). Nantenan	— — —	29		03	26
	Curreeheene	19			19
	Scarte	12		02	10
	Shanaclogh	08			08
	Derry	13			13
	Ballymoriseene	04			04
	Grageene	06		02	04
	Ballingaran & Farranree }	40			40
	Ballyhomocke	10			10
	Gragagh	12			12
	Ballyvococke	16		04	12
	Ballytreteady	13			13
	Ballinvirick	10			10
	Collogh	25			25
	Dohellbegg	08		02	06
	Rathnesheare	16			16
Doonmoylen & Killcolmane (*folio* 33). }	Doonemoylen	22	Robert Peacocke gent	04	18
	Lisbane	10	Peeter Midleton gent	04	06
	Ballenloyhand	11			11
	Monymohill	04			04
	Dooneoahy	18		03	15
	Killcolmane	21			21
	Carns	12			12
	Glansarroole	12			12
Loghill	Loghill Towne & lands	57		10	47
	Curry	30	Thomas Chamberline Esq	04	26
	Lis Riedy	06		02	04
	Carrubane	14	Sr Nicholas Crosby Knight	04	10
	Cnocknabuoly	06			06
	Kilteery	21		02	19
	Cappagh	24			24
Askeaton	Askeaton Towne	131			131
	Meogh Nearly	54		02	52
	Ballyhomyne	11	Ensigne Mathew Phillips gent	02	09
(*folio* 34).	Lower Englands towne	10			10
	Bally Noert Ballyne kelly & Gortsheaghane }	18	Nicholas Southcott gent	02	16
	Upper Englands towne	21			21
	Court Browne	28		06	22
	Ballynaish	06			06

Parrishes	Townelands	Number of People	Tituladoes Names	Eng	Irish
	BallynaCarragh	23			23
	Morgans	32			32
	Tomdely	29		04	25
	Aughinsdisert Flaunmore and Craige	30			30
Killaghaliahane	Gortnatiberad	58	Edward ô Dell gent	06	52
	Killmurry	18			18
	Killeans	26			26
	Ryleans	08			08
	Currimore	06			06
(folio 35).	Tulloe	20	John Congreife gent	02	18
	Barnygarrane	11			11
	Killaghaliahane	66			66
Killydy	Lisnafolly Lower Cappagh & Killconroe	21			21
	Killins	08			08
	Killydy	16			16
	Ballyowen	04			04
	Pt of Killydy	10			10
	Bally McKerry	06			06
	Glean Gort	17			17
	Caherlevoile	05			05
	Kill culline	26			26
	Pt of Fyneglassy	40			40
	Pt of Glauncoyner	08			08
	Ballyshane	11			11
	Pt of Clounsericke	04			04
	Clenagh	15			15
	Gleanmore	23			23
(folio 36) Kilbra-	BallinIty	21			21
derane	Gragvre	07			07
	Dromturke	08			08
	Ballyline	17			17
	Arelemane	02			02
	Ballyanes	19			19
	Listotane	02			02
	Killbraderane	18			18
	Tegins	08			08
	Coule Tomyne	25			25
Lismakeery	Lismakeery	16	Capt George Burges gent	03	13
	Ballyneclohy	38	Lt Coll Symon Eaton Esq	06	32
	Tulloe	38	John Purdon gent	02	36
	Conniger	23			23
	Milltowne	04		02	02

Parrishes	Townelands	Number of People	Tituladoes Names	Eng	Irish
	Creave	13			13
	Lefane	09			09
	Ballyculline	13			13
	Ballyttelane	11			11
(*folio* 37) Killfergus	— —	01	Alderman Burker Esq	01	—
	Ballydonoghoo	14			14
	West Meanus	15			15
	East Meanus	10		02	08
	Faran Miller	21		05	16
	Tolloghlash	24			24
	Cooleenecarrgiy	16			16
	Caharagh	69			69
	Killeacalla	23	Alderman Hunt Esq	01	22
	Tulloleige	11			11
	Tullery	03			03
	Killfergus	03			03
Adare	Fineterstowne	56	Coll John Bridges Esq	07	49
Ballyfoline	Killfeny	23	Gerrald McWm gent		23

(*folio* 37 *verso*).   Limbrick County, Barrony of Connologh : Eng, 431 ; Irish, 7545 ; 7976, totall.

(*folio* 37 [*a*])   Limerick County, The Principall Irish Names in the Barrony of Connologh

Allen, 09 ; Bane, 09 ; Barry, 40 ; Browne, 9 ; Bourke, 16 ; Ô Bryne & McBryne, 39 ; Brenagh & Brennagh, 9 ; Ô Cahell, 11 ; Ô Conty, 9 ; Ô Comane, 10 ; Condon, 9 ; Ô Croneene & Ô Cromeene, 15 ; Ô Callaghane & Ô Callahane, 17 ; McConnor & Ô Connor, 59 ; Carty McCarty, 18 ; Ô Connell, 41 ; Ô Casy, 10 ; Ô Curtaine & McCurtane, 13 ; Ô Cullane & O Collane, 35 ; Ô Culleane, 6 ; Ô Cahane, 9 ; Ô Dillane & Ô Dillene, 21 ; Ô Donaghow, 11 ; McDermott, 45 ; McDaniell, 55 ; Ô Connell, 19 ; Ô Dally, 14 ; Ô Daly, 10 ; McDauid, 31 ; McDermody, 16 ; McDonogh, 43 ; McEdmond, 36 ; Ô Flyne, 13 ; Ô Ferally & Ferrally, 13 ; Fitzgerrald, 36 ; McGibbon, 22 ; McGarrett, 19 ; Ô Grady, 31 ; Hely & Ô Healy, 13 ; Ô Haley & Ô Hally, 11 ; Ô Hea, 25 ; Ô Herlyhy & Ô Helyhy, 20 ; Ô Hogane, 21 ; Herbert, 12 ; Ô Hicky, 11 ; Ô Howrogane & Ô Howregane, 11 ; Heeky, 9 ; Ô Hanraghane (19), Ô Hanrahane (3), 22 ; Hurly, 12 ; Halpin, 15 ; McJohn, 12 ; Ô Keife, 11 ; Ô Kelly & O Keilly (31), Ô Kealy (8), 39 ; Ô Kally, 6 ; Ô Kennedy & McKennedy, 24 ; Ô Linchy & Ô Lenchy, 13 ; Ô Lency, 8 ; Ô Lacy, 18 ; Ô Leyne, 23 ; Ô Madigane and Ô Madagane, 38 ; McMorrogh, 12 ; Ô Mullowny, 16 ; McMorris, 40 ; McMurtagh, 21 ; McMahon, 15 ; McMahony, 11 ; Morpheu & Morphy, 30 ; O Mulriane, 11 ; Ô Nonane & Nunane, 12 ; Ô Nea, 11 ; Nash & Naish 21 ; Nagle, 11 ; Ô Neale, 20 ; McOwen, 15 ; McPhillip, 19 ; McRichard, 11 ; Ô Riedy, 15 ; McRory, 15 ; Ô Ryane, 8 ; Russell, 21 ; Ô Regane, 10 ; Ô Rierdane, 13 ; Roch, 20 ; Sheaghinsy (04), Shaughinsy (05), Shagins (05), 14 ; Ô Sheaghane (12), O Sheghane (05), Ô Shyghane (12), 29 ; McSheehy (04), McShyhy (06), 10 ; Ô Sullevane, 33 ; O Skanlane, 29 ; McShane (85), McSheane (06), 91 ; Ô Shea, 11 ; McTeige, 90 ; McThomas, 39 ; McTurlagh, 10 ; Wall, 15 ; Wailsh (24), Welsh (3), 27 ; McWilliam, 50 ; Whyte, 16.

KENRY BARONY.

Parrishes	Townelands	Number of People	Tituladoes Names	Eng	Irish
Irossa	Ballysteene	35	Thomas Donden & Dauid Donden gent	03	32
	Ballyvadicke	08			08
	Ballinvohir	11	Phillip Boyles gent	01	10
	Boah	06			06
	Ballynecourty	20			20
	Milltowne	26			26
	Ballyneheglish	12			12
Kilcernane	Mornane	22	Latimer Sampson gent	04	18
	Digirt	11			11
	Garraneard	16			16
	Teaghnekellie	13	Phillip Fitzgerrald gent		13
	Ballynemony	22			22
	Clonkelly	17			17
	Kilbrydy	15			**15**
	Ardloman	08			08
	Killeene	06			06
	Bally Inickane	10			10
	Ballycahane	09			09
(*folio* 39) Kilcornane	Ballyhetrick	05			05
	Clonogullyne	17			17
	Ballyshersie	15			15
	Moeh	21			21
	Hanmore	40			40
	Ballymartine	24			24
	Dromeherbegg	08			08
	Dromehermore	07			07
	Kilcornane	09			09
	Ballyglahane	21		04	17
	Ballygoage	07			07
	Ballynoe	18			18
	Shanballymor	07			07
Kildemo	Ballycollane & Ballyvarrin }	127		04	123
	Faheyan Ruddery	11			11
	Bealane	26	Garrott McMorris John & James McMorris gents		26
(*folio* 40).	Drominore Ballyvadane and Cahir }	25	John Barry Aduenturer gent	04	21
	Ballygosy	48			48
	Court & Killacollam	31		03	31
	Kildemo	37		04	33
	Cragg McCree Ballyashea and Kilmurry }	26			26
Ardcaham	Pallich and Shannapallice }	20			20

Parishes	Townelands	Number of People	Tituladoes Names	Eng	Irish
	Midle Killashura	11	John McEdd gent		11
	Muckenagh	02	Garrett Fitzgerrald and Morris Fitzgerrald gents		02
	North Killashura	05	John McGarrett gent		05
	Ren Mulleene	14	Garrett Mc James Purcell gent		14
	Ballydoole	19			19
	Ballycharra	15	Morris Gerrald gent		15
	Mullane	07			07
(folio 41). Ardcham	Carheeny	07			07
	FarrenaBryan	08			08
	Ballycarrigg	37			37
Pt of Adare	Currey	08	Veere Hunt Esq	02	06
	Twough	50			50
	Currobridge	30		04	26
	Ballylongford	22			22
	Killcurrelis	17		02	15
	Cloghranes	55			55

Principall Irish Names [and] their Number.

McConnor & O Connor, 16 ; McDonogh, 08 ; McDaniell (11), Ô Donnell (2), 13 ; Ô Dillane, 06 ; McEdmond, 9 ; Fitzgerald, 7 ; Ô Hagane & Ô Hogan, 9 ; O Kelly (4), O Kealy (6), 10 ; Linchy, 09 ; McMoris, 12 ; McPhillip, 8 ; McShane, 22 ; McTeige, 16 ; McThomas, 9 ; McWilliam, 18 ; Walsh, 7.

(folio 41 verso)   Barrony of Kenry : Eng, 035 ; Irish, 1092 ; 1127, Totall.

(folio 42).   **OWHNY BARONY**

Parishes	Townelands	Number of People	Tituladoes Names	Eng	Irish
Duogh	Tone Iterrife	13			13
	Ballybegg	31		04	27
	Killuragh	18		02	16
	Tuogh	66	Thomas Loyde gent	18	48
	Abby Owhny	325	Thomas Jacson & William Groves Esqr & Richard Nay gent Richd Ingrame and Robert Kent	38	287
				062	391
			0453 totall		

Principall Irish Names [and] their Number.

McDonnogh, 07 ; McLoghlen, 05 ;   Ô Ryan, 05 ; Ô Rea, 05 ; Rayne & Ô Raynn, 61.

Parrishes	Townelands	Number of People	Tituladoes Names	Eng	Irish
Doone	Cnocknycarrigg	09	William Whittle gent	02	07
	Killmoglin	22			22
	Coogy	08	Edmond Dwier gent		08
	Mogorough	16			16
	Farnane	22	John Whitchurch gent	04	18
	Ballycausow	10	Thomas Butler & James Butler gent		10
	Castle ne Gaurde	14	Henry Bally & John Bally his sonn gent	03	11
	Gorte Ivalle	19			19
	Gaurt ne Gaurde	10		02	08
Castletowne P'sh	Castletowne	103	Giles Harding & William Harding his sonn gents	20	83
Ulla	Garrishee Rin Garremoragh & Ballyferrin	48			48
	Shannabally	23			23
	Cloaghdaulton	40	Henry Harding & John Harding gent	05	35
Downe	KillmaCoy	04			04
(folio 44) Ulla &	Newtowne	09			09
	Boher ne Gragey	19			19
	Knock Ballyfucon	44	Doonogh McBrien gent		44
	Coollenepesley	37			37
	Pallardstowne	48			48
	Bally lahiff	18			18
	Knock Ullo	23	Connor Hicky gent		23
Clogin	Nue towne	60	John Gebard gent	03	57
	Meeillrath	08			08
	Clogin	20		03	17
	Garey Praskey	06			06
	Garrytowne	12		02	10
Ballynycloghy	Killduffe	40	Mallcome Craford gent & Symon Askin gent	04	36
	Ballynecloghy	13	Jason Whitere gent	02	11
	Killduffe	13			13
	Ballynegatty & Temple Bredane	40			40
(folio 45) Ballyne- cloghy	Garridoolis	16			16
	Cloughkillvarily	24			24
	Dearke	12			12
	Garran	17			17
	Ballincurry	07			07
	Knockare	03			03
	Clohin	05			05
	Killtillee	07			07
	Ballyveden	03			03

Parrishes	Townelands	Number of People	Tituladoes Names	Eng	Irish
	Scart	18			18
	Ballice and Greane	79		15	64
	Ballytorsoy	41	Thomas Marshall gent	03	38
	Grellagh	23	Thomas Lysagert & Garrett Ralagh gent	03	20
	Gartenaleen	15	Thomas Absom gent	02	13
	Ballymoneen	07			07
	Milltowne	16			16
(folio 46).	Ballynegallah	22		02	20
	Ballynewgane	06			06
	Knockare	30			30

Principall Irish Names [and] their Number.

Brian, Ô Brian & McBrian, 24 ; Ô Cato & McCato, 14 ; Ô Casy & Cassey, 8 ; Ô Connor (4), McConnor (4), 8 ; Ô Dyer & Ô Dwier, 10 ; McDonogh, 8 ; McDaniell, 7 ; Ô Donevan, 10 ; Ô Gleasane, 7 ; Ô Hea and Hea, 31 ; Ô Hicky, 8 ; McKenedy, 9 ; Rayne (10), Reigne (5), 15 ; McShane, 9 ; McTeige, 11.

(folio 46 verso).   Barrony of Conagh : Eng, 075 ; Irish, 1034 ; 1109, totall.

(folio 47).   **POBLE BRYEN BARRONY**

Parrishes	Townelands	Number of People	Tituladoes Names	Eng	Irish
Kilkeedy	Carrigogunill	21	Daniell Clancy and James Clancy gents		21
	Boskeagmor	19			19
	Cloghtarky	16			16
	Muckenish	15			15
	Knockrumram	32	Donogh Mahon and Morogh Mahon gent		32
	Upper & Lower Melidee, Ballineveene, Inchy, Ballyeightea, Clogh-anaron, Knockbrack and Cragane.	69	Daniell McTeige and Garrett McMoris gent		69
	Killnykally	20	Daniell McMahowny gent		20
	Tyrvoe	04	John Gullynane gent		04
	Ballybrowny	16	Phillip Fitzgerrald gent		16
	Killboy	13	Robert Wardinge gent		13

Parishes	Townelands	Number of People	Tituladoes Names	Eng	Irish
(*folio* 48) Kill-keedy	Cragbegg	14	Donogh McTherlagh gent		14
	Brostobryenbry	05			05
	Kiltemplane	18	Connor McDermody gent		18
	Faha	08	Phillip McSheane gent		08
Mungrest	Ballyancakan	11	Donogh Ô Bryne gent		11
	Bearnocoyle	11	Roger Bryne gent		11
	Graige	19	William Peacoke gent	06	13
	Dooneene	05			05
	Lower Dooneene	14			14
	KnockBallyglass	12			12
Clounanna	Clounanna	78	Patrick Arthur and Will Casey gent		78
Killonoghten	Dromloghane	46	Richard Newman gent		46
	Ballyvaloge	13	Teige Ô Bryne gent		13
Monasterneny	Monasterneny	14			14
	Caherduff	05			05
Creconry	Bernageehy	27	Thomas Blackhall and Thomas Blackhall his sonn gent	05	22
(*folio* 49)	Ballycahane	28	John Dribson gent	02	26
	Knockgrany	15	Thorloe Oge gent		15
	Lacknegrea	19			19
	Ballybronoge	09	Henry Towner gent		09
Killonoghon	Killonoghon	17	Francis Berkley gent	04	13
	Ballyregan	11			11
	Killcorely	05			05
	Knockdromashell	25	Walter Browne gent	02	23
	Atteflin	25	Edward Lewis gent	05	20

Principall Irish Names [and] their Number.

McBryne and Ô Bryne, 8 ; McConnor & O Connor, 7 ; Casy, 6 ; McDonogh, 9 ; Ô Dea, 7 ; McDermody, 5 ; McDaniell, 8 ; Ô Hea, 6 ; Kenedy, 5 ; McMahon, 6 ; Mollowny, 6 ; McShane & McSheane, 14 ; McTerlagh, 7 ; McTeige, 17.

(*folio* 49 *verso*). Barrony of Poble Bryen : Eng, 24 ; Irish, 655 ; 679 tottall.,

(*folio* 50) **COSMAY BARRONY**

Parishes	Townelands	Number of People	Tituladoes Names	Eng	Irish
Bruffe	—	178	John Standish Will Meagh and Nicholas Meagh gents	03	175

T

Parrishes	Townelands	Number of People	Tituladoes Names	Eng	Irish
Tankardstowne P'sh		140	John Lacye gent	05	135
Killbreedy Minor		103	Will Blakney gent Jeffry Owen gent	06	97
Killpeackon		110	John Carpenter gent	04	106
Pt of Eltin		171	Edmund Spranger Redmund FitzHarris George Aherly gent	03	168
Athlaca		210	Pierce Lane gent Drurie Wiay Esq James Fox gent	015	195
Pt of Vregare		144	John Fitzgergald Richd Condon Donnogh Grady	—	144
Pt of Tullebrackye		116		—	116
Dromin		164	John Rogers gent & Arthur Ormsbey Esq	12	152
Adare		249		04	245
Dummeane		36			36
Drohedtarsny		04			04
(folio 51) Disert and Carriggin		35			35
Monasterneanagh		59	Richard Betsworth gent and John Neunhan gent	04	55
Crom		472	Henry Supple Richard Traghne Robert Ratheram John Cuthbert Marcas Harrison and Edy Lacie gents.	14	458

Principall Irish Names [and] their Number.

Bourk, 8 ; Ô Brine (6), Ô Brien (5), 11 ; Ô Carrull, 13 ; Casie, 07 ; Ô Connor (4), McConnor (11), 15 ; Browne, 8 ; Ô Connell, 8 ; Ô Daly, 9 ; Ô Dannell (10), McDaniell (13), 23 ; McDonnogh, 11 ; McDauid, 10 ; McDermott, 8 ; McEdmond, 7 ; Fitzgerrald, 9 ; Ô Hea, 18 ; Hickie & Ô Hickie, 17 ; Ô Kelly, 7 ; Ô Leyne & Ô Lein, 7 ; Lacye, 9 ; Ô Linchy, 10 ; McMurtagh, 7 ; Ô Mullowny, 12 ; Murphy, 8 ; McMorish, 9 ; Ô Neale, 6 ; McPhillip, 7 ; Ô Rierdan, 9 ; Ô Rergane & Ô Regan, 10 ; Shanoghan and Shannohan, 8 ; Sullevan, 6 ; McShane, 27 ; McTeige, 14 ; McWilliam, 11.

(folio 51 verso).   Barrony of Cosmay : Eng, 070 ; Irish, 2121 ; 2191, totall.

(*folio* 52)	Number of People	Tituladoes Names	Eng	Irish
Killmallock towne & Libertyes	610	Mathew Griffin Esq George Gould George Benson John Holmes Thomas James Edward Harris Jonathan Tilly Thomas Holmes Henry Glouer John Darby Will Hill Beckingham Bentham Richard Cooke Thomas Jubbs and William Bound gents	73	537

Principall Irish Names.

Ô Brine, 6 ; McConnor, 4 ; McDonogh, 6 ; Griffin, 4 ; Kelly, 6 ; Meagh, 6 ; McTeige, 7 ; McShane, 4 ; McWilliam, 4.

(*folio* 52 *verso*).

Barronies	Pages	Eng	Irish	Totalls of Eng & Ir
Smal County	05	0120	2950	3070
Costlea	11	0133	2775	2908
Clonwilliam	15	0159	1590	1749
Connologh	37	0431	7545	7976
Kenry	41	0035	1092	1127
Owhny	42	0062	0391	0453
Conogh	46	0075	1034	1109
Poble Bryen	49	0024	0655	0679
Cosmay	51	0070	2121	2191
Killmallock town & Liberties	52	0073	0537	0610
		1182	20690	21872

COUNTY OF TIPPERARY
26648

(*folio* 1). County of Tipperary

BARONY OF SLEAVORDAGH[1]

Parishes	Places	Numbers of People	Tituladoes Names	English	Irish
Lismalin	Lismaly	156	James Barber gent	33	123
	Gragagh	40		6	34
	Ilands in the said parish	31	John Kevan gent	—	31
	Rosnaharly Pt	25	George Comerford gent James Comerford gent	4	21
	Mohobbur	23		2	21
Ballingarry	Ballingarry	53	Jeffery Fannying Esq William Fannyng gent	5	48
	Glangaull	12		2	10
	Belaghboy	4			4
	Lisnamcock	63	Leut Henry Langley Esq	7	56
	Killeheene	17	George Oliver gent	4	13
	Ballyphillipp	23		4	19
	Gortnany	5		2	3
	Balintagart	31		8	23
	Cappagh	17		2	15
	Kill McKevoge	11			11
	Garinegree	3			3
	Farenncory	40		9	31
	Gorthfree	7			7
(*folio* 2) Modessell Parish	Modessell towne	82	Rich: Read gent	13	69
	Affoly	10		3	7
	Ballyvonyne	13		2	11
	Jamestowne	6		2	4
Fenor Parish	Fenor towne	13		3	10
	Urard	7	William Begett gent	2	5
	Rathbegg	29		—	29
	Garryclohy	12		—	12
	Grage padin	34		5	29
	Domstowne	18		3	15
Mauny Parish	Shangarry	18	Humphg Minchin gent	4	14
	Dundernan	3		1	2
	Knockean Kitt	27		06	21
Booke like parish	Bookelike	38		1	37
	Moylisann	29		5	24
	Clonnilihane	59	John Pennfather Esq	5	54
Killcooly Parish	Killcooly towne	93		—	93
	Glangole	22	Nicholas Bond gent	3	19
(*folio* 3) Killcooly Parish	Lisduff	10			10
	Graghisey	10	Nicholas Ragett gent	2	8
Crohane Parish	Crohane towne	52		8	44
	Knockeane Kitt	8			8

[1] *Slevordagh*, folio 2.

Parishes	Places	Numbers of People	Tituladoes Names	English	Irish
	Ballykirrin	2			2
	Colequile	39		8	31
	Ballyphillipp	3			3
	Clotany	15		3	12
Ballynure Parish	Ballynure towne	32		5	27
Killenule Parish	Killenule Towne	28		2	26
	Caltegans towne	14	Wm Lane gent	9	5
	Bolygreny	39		4	35
	Killeens	22	Thomas Fannynge gent	—	22
	Garrans	10		5	5
	Gragenorhey	16		4	12
	Rooan mooley	8			8
	Moglass	27			27
(folio 4) Killenall P'ish	Knockanglass	28	Edward Pippin gent	5	23
Graistowne Parish	Graistowne	73	Giles Cooke gent	6	67
	Noune	24		5	19
	Ballygreny	6		2	4
	Largoe	5			5
	Ballintahir	14	Edward Markhame gent	4	10
	Ballynanly	12		1	11
	Killbrenill	9			9
Killanunnane	Cloongoe	30	James Tobin gent		30
Parish	West Polcaple	17		2	15
	East Polcaple	20		2	18
	Ballydavid	15			15
	Killatlea	18		4	14
	Clonlaghy	28			28
	Ballyloingane	26	Richard Shea gent		26
	Ballylonaghane	19			19
	Ballywalter	22		2	20
	None Dubred	5	Leut Cleere gent		5
	Killaghye	100	Mary Cleere gent Widd	22	78
Iserkiran and Pte Clonin P'ish	Capagarrane	20			20
(folio 5). Iserkyran & Pt. Clonin p'ish	Capagarran Village	8			8
	Ballyurlea	25			25
	Capamore	30			30
	Gilnegrany	46			46
	Killburry	16			16
Grange Mockler P'ish in Sledeely	Grange Mockeler	43		3	40
	Blenleene	9		2	7
	Mangane	27		3	24
	Corsillagh	36		2	34
	Garry mores	15		—	15
	GlansKagh	24		8	16
	Garrongibon	39		4	35

Parishes	Places	Numbers of People	Tituladoes Names	English	Irish
Newtowne Iannane Pish	Curreheene	22			22
	Clasnasmutt	18			18
	Atty James	18			18
	Castle John	49	Thomas Sheapherd Esq in the said Castle John and and 27 souldiers	29 souldiers	20
Additionall in ye Barony of Slevardagh	Lismalin	6		4	2
Ballingarry Parish (folio 6).	Ballingarry Towne	3			3
	Lissabrake	5			5
	Garrynygree	2			2
	Faran-rory	3			3
	Gortfree	1		0	1
	Ballyboy	4			4
Fenor P'ish	Gragpadid	4			4
	Glangole	2			2
	Poinstowne	1			1
	Moylisane	3			3
Bolike P'ish	Bolike Village	2			2
Mauny P'ish	Shangary	3			3
Crohane P'ish	Colequile	7			7
	Crohane	1			1
	Bally Kirin	4			4
Killmonan Pish	East Pale	1			1
	Capple	2			2
	Balloghane	2		1	1
	Killahea	5			5
	Killaghy	1			1
(folio 7) Grang Mockler Parish	Garrangibon	8			8
	Grang mocler	1			1
	Blenleen	3			3
	Corshillagh	2			2
	Careheene	7			7
	Abby James				
	Castle John				
	East pale				
	Caple				

Principall Irish Names [and] their Number.

Archdeakin, 6 ; Butler, 20 ; Boe, 7 ; Brenane, 10 ; Brohy, 6 ; Bryan & Bryen, 11 ; Bourke, 11 ; Comerford, 16 ; Cormucke, 10 ; Cantwell, 11 ; Crooke, 9 ; Carroll, 14 ; Dungan, 10 ; Dwyre, 11 ; Dugin, 7 ; Fanninge, 31 ; Headen, 11 ; Healy & Haly, 10 ; Heade, 7 ; Henessy, 8 ; Hegan, 9 ; Hackett, 6 ; Kenedy, 11 ; Kelly, 8 ; Kearney, 11 ; Lahy, 12 ; Lonergan, 7 ; Meagher, 40 ; Morres, 13 ; Morissy, 7 ; Murphy, 8 ; Mullowney, 7 ; Purcell, 14 ; Padle, 9 ; Phellane, 6 ; Quiddihy, 6 ; Quirke, 7 ; Ryan, 19 ; Shea, 50 ; St John, 9 ; Tobin, 47 ; Trassy, 12 ; White, 8 ; Welsh, 24 ; McWilliam (6) & FitzWilliam (4), 10.

(folio 7 verso). The Number of People in the Barony of Slevardagh : Eng, 307 ; Irish 2101 ; Totall Eng & Irish, 2408.

(*folio* 8).   **BARONY OF LOWER ORMOND**

Parishes	Places	Number of People	Tituladoes Names	English	Irish
Nenagh P'ish	Nenagh towne	203	John Stoakes gent William Moore gent James Coolman gent	47	156
	Cloune Muckle	72	Seaser Freeman gent Dr Daniell Abott K^t Charles Gilbert gent Edward Hutchinson gent	21	51
Kilbarrane p'ish	Annagh	22	Soloman Cambier Esq	7	15
	Ballycullyton	32		6	26
	Kilbarrone	28		—	28
	Carric Lagowne	19		7	12
	Liskelly beene	6			6
	Kilbellor	10			10
	Castletowne	11	John Brigg Esq Morish Thomas gent	3	8
	Rahine	41			41
	Coolbane	19		5	14
	Clun McGillyduff	33			33
	Cevens towne	11			11
	Bellanagross	9			9
	Ballinderry	39		4	35
	Brocka	12		2	10
	Mala	11		2	9
	Ballyscanlane	7		5	2
	Screboy	11			11
Ḋura Parish	Scruduff	5		3	2
(*folio* 9).	Duffolvoin	17			17
	Gurteene & Pallis	17			17
	Ballyaghter & Clongowny }	7		2	5
	Bonchrum	27			27
	Killin	21			21
	Anagh	44			44
	Rathyobaine	19			19
	Derrynaquillegh	8			8
	Lissine	6			6
	Graigo	8			8
	Carhine	5			5
	Cooleross	15			15
	Killerno	16			16
	Serragh and Ratl.- McKiery }	8			8
	Lielagh	17			17
	Derrylehane	8			8
	Ross	8			8

Parishes	Places	Number of People	Tituladoes Names	English	Irish
	Cuilleagh	16			16
LoghKerne	Killeene	37	Teige Carroll gent		37
	Croghane	5		2	3
	Dakill				
	Amcargy				
(*folio* 10) Loghkeene P'ish	BallyKinass	51			51
	Feddane	29	William Ninsfeide gent	6	23
	Gurtine and Arrigebegg	6			6
	LoghKeene	13			13
	Ballyloghnane	25		6	19
	Castletowne	16			16
	P^te of LoghKeene	33		2	31
	Laskagh	27			27
	P^te of Laskagh	13		1	12
	Glahiskin	4			4
Uskeane P'ish	Keillnelahagh	20	Coll Thomas Sadler Esq	6	14
	Ballyleyney	12		2	10
	P^te of Ballyleyney	11			11
	Uskeane Village	9			9
	Ballynuarkemore	16			16
	Ballynnarkebegg	5			5
	Dromnemehane	17			17
	Derrinvochelly	12			12
	Lisshane	31	Machaell Corroll gent		31
(*folio* 11) Agha Parish	Fyagh	25	Roger Hanely gent	2 [1]	23
	Drominire	25	Capt. Parker gent	6	19
	Killtillocke	6		2	4
	Garranfada	10			10
	Mounsell Mounsea	12		2	10
	Gurtin	9			9
	Belline	9		2	7
	Gourtenonrue	6		4	2
	Carrige	9			9
	Killoshally	4		2	2
	Tomony	9		2	7
	Carrue	11		4	7
	Collane	24			24
	Anaghbegg	7			7
	Cranagh	17		3	14
	Ballyartelly	20			20
	Ballyhymikin	14			14
	Ballycomane	19	George Desney gent	5	14
	Grallagh	16		5	11

[1] *This folio has* Eng *and* Scotts *for this column*

Parishes	Places	Number of People	Tituladoes Names	English	Irish
Modrenhy Parish	Anaghbegg	4			4
	Ballycaple	55	Samuell Clarke gent Paull Grymball gent	18	37
(folio 12)	Cuilnegrowr	12			12
	Barnagule	13			13
	Cowroule	10		3	7
	Gortneally	8		2	6
	Clogh Ioston	28		2	26
	Ballyenavin	22	Donough O Dwyre gent	2	20
	P^{te} of Behagh	3		3	—
	Clogh Jordane	37	John Haryson Esq Joseph Haryson gent	11	26
	Ballisfenan	5			5
	Gurtinnebiest	11			11
	MollenKegh	24	Thomas Corr gent		24
	P^t of Ballicnaum	23			23
	Behaghmare	18	John Jordane Esq Richard Jordane gent	12	06
Tyreglass Parish	Modrenhy Village	27		4	23
	Rorane	24	Archyball O Dwyre gent	2	22
	CappaghneSmeare	10			10
	Slrefeir	15			15
	Carig Corigge	12			12
Lorha Pish	Kilfada	17			17
	Bally McEgane	48	Leut Coll Will Cunningham Esq Andrew Stuard gent	10	38
(folio 13)	Carrone Nottey	8			8
	Kilcarrin	26			26
	Lishirnan	10		2	8
	Ballyturke	13			13
	Porbollaghame	19		9	10
	Lehinsy	38	William Hobbs gent	8	30
	Leackin	35		2	33
	Brekagh	8			8
	Carrighagh	5		2	3
	Ballyquirke	15			15
	Lorha	32			32
	Lehemly	8		2	6
	Dromod	15			15
	Anagh	6			6
	Anagh P^{te}	7			7
	Garryduff	12			12
	Lorha	10			10
Clogh Prior P'ish	Carny	22			22
	Clogh Pryor	61	Wiliam Woodward gent Edmond Card gent	6	55

Parishes	Places	Number of People	Tituladoes Names	English	Irish
(*folio* 14).	Rahone	16	Richard Grace gent		16
	Garranmore	38			38
	Ballycarran	4			4
Kinagh p'ish	Kinagh village	19			19
	Kilard	2			2
	Ballyany	07			07
	Graunge	20			20
	Scaghaneshery	3			3
	Ballyogan	10			10
	Gragenydeale	8			8
Eglish P'ish	Ballyvolveassy	12			12
	Ballinrudery	8			8
	Fodmay	8			8
	Ballyhagh	18	Joseph Walker gent	1	17
Killodernan P'ish	Lisduff	28			28
	Killidanan	19		2	17
	Balygrigane	16		2	14
	P^te of Ballyrigane	17			17
	Criagh	21			21
	Killodernan	15			15
	Ura-ardbally	44			44
(*folio* 15) Ballygarry Pish	Ballygarry towne	39		4	35
	Ballinihensy	10			10
	Carrigh	2			2
	Lisbrier	7		5	2
	Muny	3			3
	Lisneroghy	6			6
	Ballin Vanyne	21			21
	Killiconihinbegg	17		2	15
	Kilconin more	19	Thomas Butler gent	2	17
Finogh pish	Finogh Village	28	Richard Sussers gent	19	9
	Belafin voy	7		7	00
	Clyinkrokey	4		2	2
	Rodine	14	Brashill Kelly gent	1	13
	Killiegh	6			6
	Killrorerane	9			9
	Gruig Illan	2		2	
Porrish P'ish	Tombrecane	21			21
	Killonyermody	6		2	4
	Rathmore	7	Thomas Meara gent		7
	Killine	5		1	4
(*folio* 16) Porris P'ish	Beallaghadin	9			9
	Crotogh	21	John Dwyre gent		21
	Shanbally and Gallross	30			30
	Liscanlane	19	Daniell Carroll gent		19

Parishes	Places	Number of People	Tituladoes Names	English	Irish
Ardowny P'ish	Borres al's Shesiraghmore }	9		3	6
	P^te of Balliloskye	5			5
	Ardownie village	22	Leut John Manson gent	2	20
	Ballinderry	6			6
	Maiheronena P^te Kilroan }	9			9
	BalyyVery	7			7
	Derinasloin	10		2	8
	Cuiliogarran	5			5
	Killowne	10			10
	Tuorboy	6		2	4
	Bellagh losky	28		2	26

Principall Irish Names [and] Their Number

Bryen & McBryen, 11 ; Bane (7), & Banan (4), 13 ; Butler, 9 ; Bourke, 10 ; Conner & McConn^r, 7 ; Cahasy, 8 ; Cleary & Clery, 38 ; Carroll, 19 ; Deane, 18 ; Doogin & Dowgin, 8 ; O Dwyre, 10 ; Daniell (6), & McDaniell, 13 ; McDonnough, 12 ; Donoghow, 7 ; Egane (15), & McEgane (7), 22 ; Glisane, 19 ; Gydagh, 11 ; Galle, 9 ; Hany, 8 ; Hogane, 83 ; Heavane, 6 ; Ingowen, 6 ; Kenedy, 81 ; Kelly, 22 ; Killfoyle, 12 ; Meagher, 12 ; Mara (25), & Meara (30), 55 ; McMarrowe, 7 ; McMorrogh, 8 ; Maddin, 7 ; Murphy, 6 ; Morane, 9 ; Martin, 6 ; Mynoge, 6 ; Morrish & Morris, 7 ; Nollane, 15 ; Quirke, 6 ; Ryan, 24 ; Roe, 7 ; Slattery, 10 ; Scully, 9 ; McTeige, 8.

(*folio* 16 *verso*).   The Number of People in the Barony of Lower Ormond : Eng, 341 ; Irish, 2731 ; total, 3072.

(*folio* 17)   **BARONY OF KILNAMANAGH**

Parishes	Places	Numb's of People	Tituladoes Names	English	Irish
Clogher P'ish	Conyhorpo P'ish	70	Francis Boulton Esq Widd	8	62
	Derrymore	40			40
	Borniduff	7			7
	West Corbally	10			10
	Gortnyskehy	10			10
	East Corbally	7			7
	Tarryhyne	2			2
	Culegort	8			8

Parishes	Places	Numb's of People	Tituladoes Names	English	Irish
	Fana	13			13
	Clonigross	14			14
Pte of Hollycross Parish	Pte of Hollycross Parish				
	Rathkenane	51		3	48
	Poullevarly	37			37
	Milltowne	22		2	20
	Laffordy	4			4
	Gattaghstowne	8	Henry Hebbs gent	3	5
	Graigane	4			4
Moaliffe P'ish	Moaliffe Village	63		3	60
	Bealaoughter	15		4	11
	Coolekeife	16			16
	Farrny bridge	22		2	20
(folio 18).	Drumbane	54			54
	Beallanegry	19		5	14
Tampleoughteragh and Tamplebegg Parishes	Lishin	4			4
	Shea Ury	50		2	48
	Lacknecurry	6			6
	Moughlane	29			29
	Killcomin	3			3
	Rossmult	7			7
	RossKeene	3			3
Bealla Cahill Parish	Lissnesilly	13			13
	Garranro	4			4
Ballintample Parish	Doundrom	97	Sampson Toogood Esq	24	73
	Ballintample Village	51			51
	Gortossy	42			42
Oughterleage	Callynure	36	Christopher Perkins gent	4	32
	Lisnainge	7			7
	Clookelly	11			11
	Morestowne	6		2	4
	Killmore	9			9
	Ballingarran	4			4
	Kilfenan	31			31
(folio 19). Tome and Castle towne P'ishes	Carrow	17			17
	Sandvane al's Shancloone	13			13
	Mahor	18		4	14
	Barnequeill	4			4
	Kappagh	59			59
	Cappagh Allyclogg	13			13
Dounoghill P'ish	Gortnadrum	17			17
	Ballysida	66		8	58
	Aghnecarty	20		2	18
Agherow P'ish	Rossecroe	11		2	9

Parishes	Places	Numb's of People	Tituladoes Names	English	Irish
	Knockegorman	6			6
	Newtowne	15			15
Killpatrick P'ish	Gurtinegoaly	20			20
	Coan	2			2
	Coolecousane	6			6
	Garriora	4			4
	Coole bane	2			2
	Knockeroe	8			8
Clouneoulty Parish	Clouneoulty village	91			91
	Killdomin	5			5
	Ballymore	42		4	38
(folio 20)	Clonebane	7			7
	Bellagh	36			36
	Clone	43			43
	Thory	37			37
Persons to be added P'ish of Tome	to Cappagh in the }	13			13
Glanekeene P'ish	Borres	87	John Cuffe gent	10	77
	Curraghnafarytagh	6			6
	Upper Graige	12			12
	Lissagane	3			3
	Colamaragh	11			11
	Gorttracranagh	15			15
	Corbally	15			15
	Gortiny bearny	10			10
	Cronovoane	14			14
	Fantane	26			26
	Curragh beahy	13			13
	Garrangreny	13			13
	Ballynew	12			12
	Cooline	23			23
	CurraghKeill	12			12
	Carroghill	14			14
	Garrybiss	23			23
(folio 21).	Palline	40			40
	Tuorny	24			24
	Lisse	8	Walter Boorke gent		8
	Lower Graige	20			20
	Rothmoy	29			29
Part of Beallacahill } parish	Barracruory	27			27

Principall Irish Names [and] their Number.

   Boorke, 64 ; Butler, 6 ; Boyle, 7 ; Davorin, 8 ; Dwyre, 138 ; Daniell, McDaniell and O Daniell, 8 ; Fogurty, 6 ; Glyssane, 14 ; Hogane, 8 ; Hally, 6 ; Kenedy, 32 ; Meagher, 9 ; Murphy, 9 ; Quinlin, 7 ; Ryan, 203 ; Ryerdane, 6 ; McShane, 9 ; Shanahane, 19 ; McTeige, 10 ; Thohy & Tohy, 8 ; Walsh, 9.

(folio 21 verso).   The Number [of] People in ye Bar : of Kilnamanagh : Eng, 086 ; Irish, 1749 ; Totall, 1835.

BARONY OF MIDLETHIRD

Parishes	Places	Numbs of People	Tituladoes Names	English	Irish
Drangan P'ish	Drangane	61			61
	Corbally	28			28
	Clonehea	9		3	6
	Ballynenone	31	William Harrison gent	2	29
	Newtowne	46		4	42
	Prestowne	36	Thomas Tobin gent	—	36
	Mogowry	43		3	40
	Bally Loskey	12			12
	St Johns Towne	87		4	83
	Killbidy	10			10
	Lismortagh	25			25
	Meateestowne	40			46
Rathcoole P'ish	Rathvih Sullenuer & Corrignin	18	Richard Comyne gent		18
	Saucestowne	17	Nicholas Sauce gent	2	15
	Comdonstowne	4	John Carran gent		4
	Culemore	23	Bryan Kearny gent		23
	Cunagh Skartyne	18			18
	Killknockane	46		3	43
	Ballybought	5			5
	Ballybought-Shiyces-towne	12			12
	Darryluskine	85	Robt Ward gent Francis Smyth gent	3	82
	Rathcoole	25			25
(*folio* 23) Cloainne P'ish	Ballinard	48	William Baccon gent	2	46
	Milestowne	10		1	9
	Clonone and Quartne	29		2	27
	Ballyhomacke	10			10
	Ballyvadly	32	Edmond Roch gent		32
Clovin P'ish	Garran Luill	5			5
	Banoystowne	44			44
	Strockes	32			32
	Pt Clore	9			9
St Augustines Abby P'ish	Fryars Grange	13		2	11
	Crossyeard	4			4
	Bonetts Grange	11			11
	Peperstowne	24			24
	Laghgorry	7			7
	Rathkeny	26			26
Cromps P'ish	Knockelly	75		4	71
	Killnogh	7			7
	Cromys Castle	6			6
	Cromps graue	8		2	6
Killtynane Parish	Clore	38		3	35
	Sullogh	12	Moris Kerny gent	1	11

U

Parishes	Places	Numbs of People	Tituladoes Names	English	Irish
(*folio* 24)	Clare	14	William Tinohit gent	4	10
	Killosty	32	Edward Sooker gent	2	30
	Loughchapple	24		—	24
	Kiltynane	50	Richard Stapers Esq	5	45
	Grangebegg	29		2	27
St John Baptist Grange P'ish	Milltowne	34	Michaell Kerny gent		34
	Dromdile	7			7
	Gambonstowne	18	James Hackett gent		18
	Corbally	6		2	4
	Carrigine-Shirragh	10			10
	St John Battist Grange	6			6
Red Citty P'ish	red Citty	4			4
	Boredstowne	32			32
	Boredstowne the same	11			11
Knockgraffon P'ish	Knockgroffon village	92	Piers Butler gent	2	90
	Caddles towne	16		2	14
	Cnackanelangnidona	38		6	32
	Dounoguull	04			4
	Knockanenoiuegh	6			6
(*folio* 25).	Carrigin	18			18
	Carrentoberbegg and Carrentobermore	21			21
	Farren Ileyny	7			7
	Roshlogh Kent	33			33
	Cloghbridy	22	George James gent	2	20
	Graignakent	19	David Turnball gent	2	17
	Woodenstowne	39	John Pylle gent	7	32
	Carrenlea	12			12
St Patrickes rocke Parish	St Patrickes Rock Parish				
	Moeldrom	14	Oliver Lathom gent Anne Salli Widdow gent	5	9
	Brickine	27			27
	Georg island	7			7
	Killstobine	3			3
	Thurles begg	17	Giles Gregory Esq	6	11
	Deanes groue	4		2	2
	Hore Abby	18			18
	Roch	21	Thomas Perkins gent	2	19
	Brittas	4			4
	Camus	19		3	16
	Domnicks Abby	28			28
(*folio* 26). St Patricks Rocke P'ish	Gory-Kearny	8			8
	Killbally Fowly	8			8
	St Francis Abby	5			5
	Rathardin	22		2	20

Parishes	Places	Numbs of People	Tituladoes Names	English	Irish
	Gort McEllice	29	Mathew Pennyfether gent	2	27
	Garryard	26			26
	Lynestowne	12		2	10
	Ballydwell	46			46
	halfe Ballineree	7		2	5
Pte of the P'ish of St John Baptist	Stephenstowne	7			7
Mogorbane P'ish	Clonebregone	32	James Kearney gent	2	30
	Mogerbane	31	Derby Dwyer gent		31
	Pookestowne	9			9
	Colreene	4			4
	Curraghtarsny	17			17
	Mobernane	33	Connell Carney gent		33
	Bolyvadyne	22			22
Killconnell p'ish	Killconell towne	35			35
	Ballsallagh	18			18
	Rathbritt	10			10
	Movannogh	20			20
(folio 29. this should haue benne but the 27 page).	Ballydwagh	34	Michaell Kerny gent		34
	Stephanstowne	5			5
	Rathleise	7			7
Ballyshcehane p'ish	Ballyturny	49	Edmond Hackett gent	4	45
Ballysichane p'ish	Ballysichane towne	57		5	52
	Dermott	9		1	8
	Gurrane	26		3	23
	Ballytursny	7		—	7
Pte of Ballyshehane P'ish	Sinnone	36		3	33
	Kilbally herbery	21	Thomas Conin gent	—	21
	Balliherberry	18		—	18
Geall p'ish	Greagenoe	24	Edmond Godwine gent	2	22
	Killogh	40	George Sloughter gent	1	39
	Geale	16			16
	Tibbridory	8			8
	Glanbane	14			14
Ardmoyle P'ish	Ardmoyle	48	Henry Parris Esq	6	42
Pte Ardmoyle Parish	North Clonmoure	5			5
	South Clonmore	11			11
	Nedstowne	55		5	50
(folio 30).	Ardmoyle	106			106
	Caytlemoy	3			3
	North Clonmouer	29			29
Pt of Erry P'ish	Grallogh	24		8	16
Pte of Ballyshehane P'ish	Sherrippstowne	23		2	21
	Ballyowen	46	William Kingsmill Esq	6	40

Parishes	Places	Numbs of People	Tituladoes Names	English	Irish
Colloman P'ish	Rathdron	14			14
	Josinstowne	21			21
	Kylerke	33			33
	Mocklerstowne	40		2	38
Morestowne Kirke P'ish	Ballin Attin	52			52
	Grage ne Brenagh	3			3
	Morestowne Kirke	33			33
	Ouskeigh	10		3	7
	Pt Ballineere	9			9
Dangonergan Parish	Shanballyduff	15			15
	Ballytarsny McCarris	22		2	20
Outragh P'ish	Outragh	62			62
Boyton ragh Parish	Boytonragh	64			64
	Templenoe	14			14
	Boystowne	23			23
(folio 31). Tullachmaine	Tullachmaine	42			42
	Rath McCarty	111			111
	Rathsallagh	28			28
Drangane P'ish	Drangane	10			10
	Corbally	4			4
	Ballynenane	9			9
	Newtowne	7			7
The additionalls of ol upon the revieu	[sic!] Midlethird				
Mogowry P'ish	Mogowry towne	5			5
Sullagh P'ish	Ballylosgy	2			2
	Lismortagh	2			2
	Killbrydy	2			2
Rathcoole P'ish	Saucestowne	4			4
	Colemoore	1			1
	Slaynestowne	5			5
	Killknockane	4			4
	Darrylusgane	4			4
Peppertowne P'ish	Rathkeny	2			2
Cromps P'ish	Crumps castle	3			3
Cloncene P'ish	Ballynard	1			1
	Milestowne	2			2
	Gortnapissy	5			5
Red City P'ish	Red City	4			4
	Barretstowne	2			2
(folio 32) Kiltenane Parrish	Clare	4			4
	Killoshe	14		2	12
	Behalte Collope	4			4
	Killtenane	7		1	6
	Grangbegg	4			4
St John Baptist Grange P'ish	Dromdyle	3			3
	Foulkstowne	3			3

Parishes	Places	Numbs of People	Tituladoes Names	English	Irish
Rylestowne P'ish	Ballydwagh	3			3
St Patricks rock P'ish	Heare-aby	5			5
	Halfe Ballinree	7			7
	Canius	5			5
	Gorryard	4			4
	Rathardin	2			2
Geale P'ish	Killogh	2			2
	Graigenoe and Glanbane	9			9
Erry P'ish	Grellagh	5			5
Bally Sichane P'ish	Ballysichane	4			4
	Garran	14			14
	Ballytarsny	9			9
(folio 33). Boytonrath P'ish	Dogstowne	11			11
Tongondergane	Ballytarsney McOrris	8			8
	Ballinry	4			4
Knockgratton	Cadlestowne	20			20
	Lantorhill	19			19
	Doneagall	3			3
	Logh Kent	3			3
	Knockanenaveigh	7			7
	Graignaveigh	11			11
	Cloghbrydy	18			18
	Rathnecarty	9			9
	Graignemrenagh	5			5
Colman P'ish	Colman	7			7
Ballyclerichan	Mocklerstowne	8			8
	Josinstowne	3			3

Principall Irish Names [and] their Numr.

Bryen, 12 ; O Bryen, 11 ; Brenan, 11 ; Burren, 6 ; Bourke, 40 ; Butler, 56 ; Boyle, 8 ; Britt, 17 ; Brenagh, 07 ; Brytten & Bryttanie, 10 ; Cantwell, 14 ; Coman (18), and Comyne (27), 45 ; Carroll, 13 ; Comerford, 6 ; Carren (8),and Carrane (34), 46 ; Cahill, 12 ; Costello & Costelly, 7 ; Cody & Coddy, 6 ; McDonogh, 14 ; Dwyre, 27 ; O Dwyre, 7 ; Daniell & McDaniell, 18 ; Dwaine, 8 ; Davane or Devane, 15 ; McDermott, 6 ; McEdmond, 6 ; Faninge, 10 ; Fogurty, 22 ; Flemyne, 12 ; Fahy 11 ; Glissane, 12 ; Gredy and Graddy, 10 ; Heany & Henny, 8 ; Hally &c, 8 ; Hiffernane, 24 ; Hogane, 16 ; Hiky or Hicky, 9 ; Hackett, 45 ; Headen, 8 ; O Hea, 5 ; McJohn, 20 ; St John, 7 ; Kelly (10), & Kealy, 25 ; Kearney, 19 ; Kenedy, 24 ; Keatinge, 11 ; Kent, 9 ; Loghnane, 7 ; Lahy, 13 ; Laffane, 9 ; Lonergane, 13 ; Mansell, 6 ; Meagher, 72 ; Maky, 6 ; Morphey, 12 ; Morrish, 10 ; Meara & O Meara, 8 ; Meary & O Meary, 13 ; Morrane & O Morrane, 6 ; Mulryan, 13 ; Morissy, 8; Mockler, 6 ; Neale and O Neale, 12 ; Phellane, 12 ; McPhillip (10), & Fitzphillip (3), 13 ; Quirke, 7 ; Russell, 7 ; Roe, 6 ; Ryen & Ryan, 75 ; Shea, 33 ; Sause, 8 ; McShane, 12 ; Stapleton, 20 ; Smyth, 9 ; Tobin, 12 ; McTeige, 11 ; Walsh & Wailse, 13 ; White, 12 ; McWilliam, 18 ; Walle, 7 ; Woodlocke, 16.

(folio 33 verso). The Number of People in ye Barony of Middlethird · Eng, 134 : Irish. 3778 : Total Eng & Irish, 3912.

Parish	Places	Numbs of People	Tituladoes Names	English	Irish
Carrick	Mononsdihy	15		5	10
	Bealladerry	28	John Neale gent	2	26
Newtowne leman	Richardstowne	25		—	25
	Ballynegananagh	24		6	18
Newtowleman	Cregg	10			10
	Newtowlennan	36		2	34
	Maynstowne	27		—	27
	Ballynory	47			47
Killmorry	Ballyneale	54	John Spillman gent	2	52
	Lissodobbs	22			22
	Mollagh	22			22
	Figglagh	53		4	49
	Ballyneclony	43			43
	Atdoollinn	15			15
Ballinurry	Ballinoreran	8			8
	Ballynemony	13			13
	Curragh dobbin	31	John Hogane gent		31
Killmurry	Muctetybegg	7			7
	Mucretymore	3		2	1
	Garryduff	31			31
(folio 35).	Ballydyne	20	John Mandevile gent	6	14
Killshelane	Maganstowne	5		—	5
	Mynetstowne	9		2	7
	Ballynerahy	34	James White gent	—	34
	Pt of Ballymaul	12	John Elmer gent	3	9
	Poulecherry	23		—	23
	Newtowneanoc	19		1	18
	Ballanahimore	12		—	12
	Ballyglisheene	18		—	18
	Seskin	6	John Ankettle gent	2	4
Killeash	Killeash	81		4	77
	Mylodstowne	21		—	21
	Killnoressy	45	James Comertord gent Lady Frances Butler Sr Redmond Everaid Kt	5	40
Templethny	Graigeloghy	16	Daniell Gwynn gent	2	14
	Ballylin	23	James Butler gent	—	23
	Ballyboe	33	Michell Gwynn gent	2	31
	Killurney	47		4	43
	Ballyboe	5		—	5
	Cooleowneen	14		5	9
	Lisnedobred	2		—	2
(folio 36) Tamplethny	Tamletny	2			2
Killelone	Pryorstowne	7			7

Parish	Places	Numbs of People	Tituladoes Names	English	Irish
	Killfernagh	7			7
Grangmockeer	Beallanamoe	10			10
Cahyr	Cahyr	144	Thomas Tomsson gent	23	121
	Cahir Abby	62	James Tompson gent	3	59
	Loghlongherry	56	Morrish Keatinge gent	4	52
	Bally McAdam	25			25
	Killeen Buttler	15			15
	Grangmore	21			21
	Sottonrath	9			9
	Killemlagh	10			10
	Cnockagh	27			27
	Ballynenonagh	7			7
	Ballyholly	6			6
	Garran Ivelly	36	James and John Tobynn gent		36
	Cloghstany	17			17
	Scart Killcomann	28			28
Derrygrath	Keadragh	41	Francis Bigg Esq	8	33
	Derrygragh or Derrygeath }	32	Peirce Keatinge gent		32
	Killmalloge	13			13
(folio 37).	Ballindonny	31			31
	Bally Thomas	10	Paule Keatinge gent	—	10
	Nichollestowne	74	Richard Keatinge gent	2	72
	Garryroe	23	William Keatinge gent	—	23
Rochestowne	Rochestowne	30		4	26
	Richardstowne	4		—	4
	Ardfinane	106	Capt. William Palmer gent	3	103
	Cloghnecody	25		2	23
Neddans	Neddans	23	Wm Hogane and John Hogane gent		23
	Cloghardine	14			14
	Ballynety	8			8
	Lacke McEorish	8			8
	Rathogally	13			13
	Cloghcully	17			17
Mollagh	Mollagh	13			13
	Garryneha hy	28			28
	Burgessland	8			8
Tullameolane	Knockeen	26			26
	Tullameolane	8			8
	Ballymorris	10			10
	Ballybegg	15			15
	Carrig Iteary	22			22
(folio 38) Tullamelane	Oldgrange	4			4

Parish	Places	Numbs of People	Tituladoes Names	English	Irish
Tubrid or Tubbred	Knocklofty	32		2	30
	Keilroe	32			32
	Burgess	30			30
	Killcorane	17			17
	Whitchurch	12			12
	Reahill	60		5	55
	Whitchurch	21			21
	Reahill	51	George Mathews Esq	6	45
	Rusrath	49	Thomas Aylemer gent	10	39
			Nicholas Ovington gent		
			Robert Ovington gent		
			James Glissane gent		
	Ballydrenane	29			29
	Tubbrid	43			43
	Ballylomasny	23			23
	Dromelomane	6			6
	Knockanecanboy	2			2
	Boullingarrane	19			19
	Currtoure	27			27
Shanrehheene	Shanreheene	49	John Fitzgerrald gent	09	40
	Cloghenmackett	82	Thomas Downeinge gent	04	78
(folio 39) Shanreheene	Flemingstowne	11			11
	Killeating	26		2	24
	Cospoch	44	Sr Redmond Evorard Kt & Bart		44
	Feriglin	19			19
	Cosporth other p'te	17			17
	Grange Silligane	8		4	4
	Carragh Keale	12			12
	Carrigmore	21			21
	Scartachane	27			27
	Ballyshahane	4			4
	Castlegrace	96	Coll John Squibb gent	13	83
			Matthew Bowen, gent		
	Ballyboy	52		2	50
	Garryduff	4			4
	Cullenagh	11			11
	Coolegarranroe	70			70
	Carrygristeell	30			30
	Gortessell	18			18
	Curreleagh	26		9	17
	Ballynemony	14		12	2
	Bally Wm	23		—·	23
	Liefon	27		6	21
	Coolepcevane	26		2	24
(folio 40) Shanaheene or Shanraheene	Glancory	32			32
	Dromcoe	16			16

Parish	Places	Numbs of People	Tituladoes Names	English	Irish
	Coolederry	31			31
	Dangen	23			23
	Listensen	59			59
	Skeheencenky	28			28
	Skehencenky & Cooleroe	30			30
	Killtankeen	4			4
Ballybecan	Gormondstowne	63	Anthony Chearneley gent		63
	Tullagh	30		2	28
	Killdonogh	29		4	25
	Garryroe	27	Garrott Pendergast gent Edmond his sonne		27
	Ballygormon	10			10
	Frehans	19			19
	Killvenen	13			13
	Ballyreety	11			11
	Killfrehane	31			31
	Carhew	10			10
	Killardemer	34			34
Newcastle (folio 41).	Newcastle	73		8	65
	Keillnecarriggyf	25			25
	Croane	15		3	12
	Clashgany	34			34
	Garryduff	13			13
	Curraghetoneen	5	David McCrath and John and Thomas his sonns gent		5
	Boulisallagh	13			13
Abby Inislonnaghty	Morestowne	95	Godfrey Green Esq	3	92
	Killballenemony	46			46
	Glandbane	12			12
	Ballyorley	5			5
	Abby Newtowne	156	Thomas Batty Esq	4	152
	Gortmore and Pat Chapple	11			11
	Monkes grange and Garrytample	35			35
	Monkes grange	53			53
Bally clearahane Newchapple (folio 42).	Ballyclearahane	85			85
	Knockenanama	37	Edward Batty gent	1	36
	Chancellers towne	9			9
	Ballytarnsny	17			17
	Ballyveles	14			14
	Newchapple-orchards-towne	27			27
	Ballyhimikin	20			20

Parish	Places	Numbs of People	Tituladoes Names	English	Irish
Donoghmore	Mollenony	45			45
	Ballygarrane	9			9
	Tubberhany	16			16
	Garryroe	16			16
Rathronane	Rathkevane	23			23
Lisronagh	Court Lisronagh	31			31
	Monemehill	4			4
Killgrante	Glanleemy	15			15
	Powrestowne	15			15
	Redmondtowne	19			19
	Mylodstowne	12	Richard Elly gent	3	9
	Little Lawles towne	3			3
	Rathronan	26			26
	Ballinvohyr	17			17
(folio 43). Rathronane	Croughtamory	2			2
	Ballynemony	44			44
	Orchardstowne	28			28
	Lawlestowne more	6			6
Lisronagh	Cahirclogh	9			9
	Killmore	21			21
	Garrananirle	29			29
	Lisronagh	38	John Shawe gent	1	37

Principall Irish Names [and] their Numb[er].

Butler, 42 ; Bourke, 60 ; Bryon, 30 ; O Bryon, 15 ; Bane, 13 ; Bouhilly, 21 ; Brenagh, 12 ; Cahill, 21 ; Cleary & Cleare, 25 ; Carroll, 16 ; Conner & McConnor, 12 ; Carrane and O Carrane, 22 ; Clanhy and Clanchy, 12 ; Condon, 12 ; Cahasy, 17 ; McCrath, 35 ; Cantwell, 9 ; Connell and McConnell, 9 ; Connelly and O Connelly, 9 ; Donogh and McDonogh, 13 ; Daton, 9 ; Dalton, 9 ; McDaniell, 25 ; and Daniell, 45 ; Dwyre and O Dwyre, 10 ; McDerby, 8 ; McDavid, 11 ; Doody & O Doody, 13 ; Dwayne and O Dwayne, 13 ; McEdmond, 15 ; English, 24 ; Fenosy, 11 ; Flinge and O Flinge, 10 ; Gormon, 12 ; Hogane, 59 ; Hylane and Healane, 21 ; Hackett, 11 ; Hally and Halcy, 13 ; Hicky, 44 ; McJohn (9) & Fitz John (3), 12 ; Kelly & Kealy, 32 ; Keatinge, 48 ; Looby, 12 ; Lonergane, 73 ; McLoghlen & Meloghlen, 10 ; Morrish and McMorris, 13 ; Meara and O Meara, 10 ; Meagher & O Meagher, 26 ; Morphy, 30 ; Meaghan & O Meaghan, 21 ; Morisey, 16 ; Mahowy and McMahowny, 19 ; Mullony, 14 ; Mulryan & Mullrayn, 18 ; Meogand & Meahohan, 12 ; Neale & O Neale, 39 ; McPhillip, 12 ; Prendergast, 62 ; Powre, 21 ; Quin & O Quinne, 19 ; Ryane, 14 ; Roe, 14 ; Reyly, 12 ; Shea, 14 ; O Shea, 12 ; McShane, 28 ; Slattery, 30 ; Tobine, 25 ; McTeige, 27 ; McThomas, 15 ; White, 14 ; Walsh, 51 ; Whelane, 15 ; Wale, 26 ; McWilliam, 23.

(folio 43 verso).   The Number of People in ye Barronyes of Iffay and Offay : Eng, 223 ; Irish, 4729 ;

totall Eng & Irish, 4952.

(*folio* 44) ## BARONY OF ELIOGURTY AND IKERRYN

Parishes	Places	Numbs of People	Tituladoes Names	English	Irish
Thurlus	Thurlus	518	Eliz : Thurlus Lady Viscountesse Dowager, Theobald Mathewes Esq, James Butler gentle, Roger Sturgis gentle, Thomas Fitzgerrold gentle, Patrick Hackett gentle, Luke Ragett gentle, Phillipp Hackett gentle, Peirce Power gentle, Thomas Aske Esq.	72	446
	Ballygynane	13			13
	Cassestowne	35		4	31
	Brittas towne	61	James Grace gent Gerrold Grace his sonne gentle		61
	Killinane	28			28
	Ballygalbert	20	James Shallcross gentle	3	17
	Feartiana	7	Thomas Betts gent	5	2
	Killrush	26			26
	Lenigh	34		2	32
	Cabragh	19	Robert Witherill gent	4	15
	Trucklogh	24			24
	Ballycarrane	9			9
Holly crosse	Holly cross	121	Gryffin Howard Esq Edmond Howard gent Thomas Comerford gentle	9	112
(*folio* 45) Hollycross	Cloghane	14	George Comerford gentle	—.	14
	Grange	9		2	˙7
	Ballycomᵉ	34	Patrick Raggett gent	2	32
	Beakestowne	28	Thomas White gentle Thomas Roberts gent	10	18
	Beallacomuske	32			32
Mokarky	Mokarky	82	James Travers gentle	2	80
	Shanbally	58	Phillipp Grace gentle	1	57
	Foulcherstowne	4		—	4
Corbally	Corbally	16	Laurence Hammon gent	2	14
	Clonyne	31	Edmond Walsh gent		31
	Glanbeagh & Ballegurty	6			6
	Aghsineare	20	James Carroll gent		20
	Cloncreckin	16			16
Ballymurryn	Ballymurryn	28		2	26
	Liskeveene	12			12
	Rathkeinkin	7			7
	Curreheene	4			4
Cullagh begg	Clowne	22		2	20
(*folio* 46). Cullabegg	Killclony	20			20
	Clohoraly	45		2	43

Parishes	Places	Numbs of People	Tituladoes Names	English	Irish
Killfithmone	Barrenstowne	4			4
	Kilffithmone	49	Mathew Shanahane gent		49
	Killfithmone	9			9
	Cloghiny	50			50
Pte of Beallacarhill P'ish }	Bnolynahon	76	Hercules Rogers gentle Joseph Keiche gent John Smallbone gent Humphry Lyons gent	9	67
Templetowhy	Tulloe	53	Walter Aliner gent	2	51
	Crannagh	18			18
	Garrymore	21		2	19
	Loughorchard	4			4
	Barranlishine	10			10
	Drominine	12			12
Aghnameadill	Clonkananane	36			36
	Baresnafearny	16			16
Killoninoge	Clonmore	28	Barthlomew Fowkes Esq Edward Workeman gentl	2	26
(folio 47) Killoninoge	Dromard	33			33
	Ballysarroll	27			27
	Pte of Dromard	12			12
	Agavoy	23			23
	Shannakeill	25			25
	Clonbouch	17		2	15
Pt of Thurlus Parish	Archerstowne	41		3	38
	Corbally	10		2	8
	Gelboyly	10		2	8
Killea	Keillenardy	49			49
	Kilballyhinkin	15			15
	Killkipp	16			16
	Grange	9			9
	Killea	13			13
	Parke	33	Anthony Meagher gent		33
	Coolecoremocke	8			8
Rathelty and Shrane	Rossistowne	39	John Grace Esq		39
	Gortinchry	7		2	5
	Coolegerrane	4			4
	Athinds	14		3	11
	Shyane-mill	5		2	3
(folio 48).	Cloagh bennagh	28	Edmond Morresse gent		28
	Rathelty	39	James Morresse gent		39
	Athlomo	24			24
	Garranroe	23			23
	Shanballyduff	8		2	6
	Peircestowne	4			4
	Lisduff	16			16
Templemore	Templemore	72	Thomas Butler gentle		72

Parishes	Places	Numbs of People	Tituladoes Names	English	Irish
	Lisnafeddoge	39	Richard Conway gentle		39
	Kiltilane	12			12
	Adamstowne	33			33
	Borresbegg	55			55
	Farnedorry	14		4	10
	Kiltullihy	9			9
	Gortroane	26			26
	Bellahy	9			9
	Carraghduff	8			8
	Cloneteife	21			21
	Killoagh	6			6
(folio 49).	Killclehin	17			17
	Ballycahell	28	Richard Ryan gent	4	24
	Mychaell	3			3
	Knockanroe	52			52
Borresliegh	Borrestowne	85	John Collins Esq John Collins his sonne gent	5	80
	Noordtowne	22	Owen Swyny gent	—	22
	Leighmokevoge	17		4	13
	Laghardan	27	Oliver Blanchfield gent	4	23
	Ballydavids	25	Capt Thomas Butler Esq	—	25
	Culcruetowne	18		2	16
	Rathmanagh	25	Daniell Ryan gent	4	21
	Fort Ireton	25		1	24
	Ballybegg	54		3	51
Barnane	Killoskeahane	53	Robert Goff gentle	4	49
	Barnane	100	Joseph Lloyd gentle Owen Lloyd gentle William Heather gent	6	94
Drumspirane	Knockagh	29	Charles Minchin gentle	2	27
	Rorodstowne	31	Richard Purcell gent		31
(folio 50). Dromspirane	Drome	33	Sr John Morres Kt & Bart John Stapleton gent Edmond Morres gent	2	31
	Rathlesty	17			17
	Killwelcorish	10			10
	Killahagane	56			56
	Grages	6			6
Rathmovioge	Ballynakill	108	Joseph Prout gent		108
	Rathmovioge	10			10
	Gurtinnasingua	2			2
	Lackavintane	2			2
	Cappicannurane	4			4
Pte of Castletowne Parish	Lisduff	27			27
	Beallanamoe	1			1
Templerie	Castle Iney	30	Capt John Pecke Esq	9	21

Parishes	Places	Numbs of People	Tituladoes Names	English	Irish
	Castle Lency	7		4	3
	Aghale	14		2	12
	Gurteene	12			12
	Aghalebegg	2			2
(folio 51).	Gortindangane	2			2
Moyne	Lissin Ballyerke	13			13
	Moyne	7			7
	Derryfadda	13		2	11
Loughmoe	Loughmoe	140		4	136
	Clonedotie	13			13
	Ballybristy	15			15
	Garranbane	31	Theobald Stapleton	2	29
	Clonmoge	19			19
	Brownstowne	24			24
	Kilkillaghery	12			12
	Curraghmore	5			5
	Clonmoge begg	13			13
	Killaghery	49			49
Burney al's Burren	Clonkenny	40	Mathew Boage Esq		40
	Curtin	60	Connor Meagher gent	3	57
	Thenekelly	9	John Purcell gent		9
	Duginsallagh	11			11
(folio 52)	Beallany Broghy	13			13
	Glanbehagh	15	Robert Clapham gent	2	13
	Ballyhenty	9	John B. Turnebowle gent	2	7
	Gortanny	5		—	5
	Boelabane	73	Edmond Trohy gent	4	69
	Lorane	9		—	9
	Gortderry	9		—	9
	Coologhill	23		2	21
Roscrea	Roscrea	104		11	93
	Barneny	9		4	5
Souldiers and their Wifes in Roscrea		21		12	9
more souldiers whose name were not retorned in the garrison of Roscrea }		16		16	—
	Roscrea	27		3	24
	Eynane	25		2	23
Inshiofogurty	Gortanny	50	Donogh Fogurty gent	4	46
(folio 53) Insiofogurty	Clequill	12			12
	Bnoclyduff	6			6
	Monerno	8			8
	Liscrea	5			5
	Insye	23			23
	Upper Donea	29	Edmond Fogurty gentle	3	26
	Killimiligh	11			11
	Lower Donea	36			36

Parishes	Places	Numbs of People	Tituladoes Names	English	Irish
	Lissine	13			13
	Patricks towne	3			3
Souldiers in ye towne of	Thurlus	38		33	5

Principall Irish Names [and] their No.

Buttler, 43 ; Bourke, 27 ; Bryen & McBryen, 10 ; Bane, 11 ; Cormocke, 28 ; Carroll, 55 ; Cahell and O Cahell, 39 ; Connell, 12 ; Cleare and Cleary, 10 ; Carrane, 11 ; Cahessy, 8 ; Cantwell, 8 ; Cassin, 8 ; Dwyre and O Dwyre, 25 ; Dullany, 17 ; McDonogh, 13 ; Dermody, 10 ; Doghon and O Doghon, 20 ; Dowly and Dooley, 13 ; Duff, 9 ; Eagan, 13 ; Fogurty, 77 ; Fitzgerrold & Gerrold, 11 ; Gormocke and Gormoge, 15 ; Grace, 14 ; Hackett, 35 ; Haelly and Halley, 14 ; Hicky, 13 ; Heogan & Hogan (6), 17 ; Headen, 20 ; McJohn, 9 ; Kenedy, 28 ; Kelly, 18 ; Lahy, 53 ; Loghlen and McLoghlen, 13 ; Leany, 8 ; Meagher, 193 ; Mullrayn, 11 ; Morres, 15 ; Meara, 12 ; Neale and O Neale, 8 ; Purcell, 52 ; Power, 16 ; Phealan, 12 ; Fitzpatrick, 8 : Quinlin, 15 ; Ryan, 135 ; McRory, 7 ; Russell, 10 ; Shea & O Shea, 8 ; Stapleton, 34 ; McShane, 13 ; Shannahane, 14 ; Swyny, 8 ; Shallowe, 8 ; Trassy, 22 ; McTeige, 18 ; Tierny, 15 ; Trohy, 10 ; Walsh, 16 ; McWilliam, 9.

(folio 53 verso). The Number of People in ye Baronyes of Eliogurty and Ikerim : Eng, 326 ; Irish, 4339 ; totall Eng and Irish, 4665.

(folio 54).

BARONY UPPER ORMOND.

Parishes	Places	Numbs of People	Tituladoes Names	English	Irish
Achnamedill	Coole Tome	24	Edmond Wall gent	2	22
	Bleane	14	Thomas Poe gent	2	12
	Ballinveny	9	Jeffry Morrish		9
	Coologe	27	William Rumball gent	2	25
	Ballybegg	8			8
	Varas	24		2	22
	Parke	12	Teige Mara gent		12
	Tirmaile	19	Walter Cooper gent	2	17
	Currehine	3			3
	Glamyeile	22	Rubb Boorke gent		22
	Killogarny	9			9
	Ballinloghy	2			2
	Lackinvorony	4			4
Ballyngbun	Ballyngbun	33			33
Templedery	Cloghensy	21	Jeffry Boorke gent		21

Parishes	Places	Numbs of People	Tituladoes Names	English	Irish
	Grenan	9			9
	Cloghonyan	12			12
	Gurtinlary	7			7
	Gortingowny	11			11
Ballymacky	Ballymacky	31	Robert Coole Esq	5	26
(folio 55).	Cnockanglass	20			20
	Ballynoe	33			33
	Cappagh	10			10
	Falleny	3			3
	Lislymisky	37	Edward Bandy gent	2	35
	Clasvivyne	4			4
	Coolederry	9		2	7
	Kilbonine	35	Stephen Alin gent	3	32
	Cnocke	15	Emmanuell Roe gent		15
Kilkerry	Grenan	32	Peter Dalton gent		32
	Knockbracke	8			8
	Lissine	25			25
	Ballynemona	14			14
	Killynaffonery	8			8
	Ballycrynett	12		2	10
Lafferragh	Lafferragh	59	John O Howay Esq		59
Pte ot Kilroan P'ish	Raplagh	10	Adonae Morres gent	3	7
	Raththurles	10		2	8
Lisbony	Rathnallin	16	William Ludington gent	4	12
	Tyon	15		5	10
(folio 56)	Gortilegan	7		3	4
	Kilcanon	13		2	11
	Ballintola	17	Nicholas Tyler gentie	2	15
	Ballinnewlan	19			19
	Lisbony	17			17
Bally McCoghny Parish	Ballyneny	26	Dermott Ryan gent		26
	Ballinnarane	13		2	11
	Lisinesalagh	6			6
	Ballinormond	31	Bryen Kenedy gent		31
	Sraghminold	20		2	18
	Kilbalinaghathyna	8	James Wansburgh gent	2	6
	Tyone	4		2	2
	Ballybegg	9		—	9
	Ballynacloghy	50	Alexander Browne gent	4	46
	Ballyquivine	31		3	28
Kilnamisse	Commistowne	34	Hugh Phillipps gentle	5	29
	Killnamiffe	12	Cornett Reed gent	3	9
	Monyquill	22		—	22
(folio 57) Killnamisse	Garryglass	6			6
Dolla	Lisgarryffe	21			21
	Kilnashaldnally	7			7

Parishes	Places	Numbs of People	Tituladoes Names	English	Irish
	Curraghleigh & Barrengowe }	13			13
	Dolla	17			17
	Ballindurry	7			7
	Begintulamylin	19			19
	Kilraflett and Boulmy }	26	James Magrath gentle		26
	Conyny	4			4
Kilmore	Culny	53	Phillipp Kenedy gent Teige Kenedy his sonne		53
	Kilmore	31			31
	Ballycahill	10		3	7
	Lisninarged	12			12
	Errinogh	14			14
	Curraghnyspady	19			19
	Gortboy	7			7
(folio 58)	Lissneclenty	34	Teige Kenedy gent Mathew Kenedy his sonne		34
	Kiltyroma	13			13
	Gortnycleahy	7			7
	Cahue	21			21
	Ballyphillipp	10			10
	Ballyhanrahane	12	Henry Corr gent	2	10
	Clonyagh	6			6
	Gurtindoghy	4		4	—
	Dunnally	13			13
	Ballynoe	12			12
	Dunamona	15			15
	Tyone	10			10
	Bellagragg	7			7
	Baune	23		2	21
	Manes Royall	39	Edward Godwin gent	4	35
Laffragh		5			5
Aghnameddle		8		3	5
Lisbony		9			9
	Ballymollowna	5			5
Dalla	Kilroffett	1			1
(folio 59). Ballymacky	Ballymacky	13		2	11
Dolla	Killrofett	9			9
Templederry	Cloghonane	4			4
Ballynacloghy	Bilbally nagn-ffinagh	2			2
	Ballybegg	2			2
	Bally Ryvine	2			2
Ballymacky	Killonyne	6		2	4
	Ballynoe	3			3
	Cappagh	4	Jndich Andrews gent	2	2

X

Parishes	Places	Numbs of People	Tituladoes Names	English	Irish
Templedonny	Knockaneglass	4			4
	Knockane	5			5
	Bally Phillipp	8			8
	Beallagragy	4			4
	Baune	24			24
	Mayns royall	10			10
	Lisnogally	5			5
	Curryhnowne	8			8
	Tollohedy	11			11
(folio 60). Killmore	Coulin	5			5
	Kilmore	4			4
	Bellacahill	9			9
	Gortboy	2			2
	Ballyanrahane	11			11
	Gurtindowhy	4			4
	Donnally	7			7
	Ballynoe	8			8
	Dounenamona	14			14

Principall Irish Names [and] their Numbs

Bryen, 17 ; Boorke, 14 ; Boy, 8 ; Cleary, 10 ; McDonogh, 19 ; Daniell & McDaniell, 11 ; Flanury, 8 ; Glysane, 85 ; Hogane, 9 ; Kenedy, 72 ; Mara, 41 ; Magrath, 11 ; McMorough, McMorogh, 13 ; McPhillipp, 9 ; Quirke, 8 ; Ryan, 53 ; Roe, 14 ; Tyerny, 11 ; McTeige, 16 ; William & McWilliam, 11.

(folio 60 verso).   The Number of People in ye Barony of Upper Ormond : Eng, 092 ; Irish, 1631 ; Totall Eng & Irish, 1723.

(folio 61)   **BARONY OF OWNY[1] AND ARRA**

Parishes	Places	Numbs of People	Tituladoes Names	Eng	Irish
Castletowne Parish	Castletowne	33	Humphry Dymnock Esq	7	26
	Castleloghe	22	Francis Strongman gent	2	20
	Cornoido	10	John Strongman Esq Edmond Hogane gent	2	8
	Liskelly	15	Henry Feltham gent	5	10
	Ballyvaghan	8		2	6
	Ballycroddock	12		2	10

[1] *Owney*, folio 62.

Parishes	Places	Numbs of People	Tituladoes Names	Eng	Irish
	Curragh	22	Mortagh Bryen gent		22
	Clonny Bryen	10	John Hogane gent		10
	Ballycollreagh	13		3	10
	Tom Quoane	19		2	17
Youghill	Youghill	19		—	19
	Monero	23	James Hutchinson Esq	4	19
	Lisdownedaverne	6			6
	Clayduff	8			8
	Granena Cavane	6		4	2
	Balla Rushine	26		6	20
(folio 62)	Gortnekelle	14			14
	Pallis	40			40
	Killcollman	18	Symon Finch Esq	10	8
	Curragh temple	29		13	16
	Ballygowrage	7		4	3
	Glassabridy	5		2	3
	Combe	3			8
	Barbagh	11			11
Burgess	Clarny	14		4	10
	Carighy toagher	35	John Walker gent	6	29
	Gortmore	20		2	18
	Burgesse	22		7	15
	Sessaraghkeale	4			4
	Cnockanglassny	10		4	6
	Carrick-galle	6			6
Temple hally	Derry	20		12	8
	Caher connor	2		2	—
	Revensey	18	William Fox gent	2	16
(folio 63).	Insymore	6			6
	Bealanaha	35	Samuell Baukley gent	7	28
	Castle Crannath	10		1	9
	Keileneranagh	7		2	5
	Bougher	15			15
	Cnockdromy	11			11
	Insy bigg	6			6
	Ballymullowny	9			9
	Killinstalla	21		6	15
	Coleadorryny	11			11
	Ballycaxrohan	13			13
	Ballytinoe	13		6	7
	Curraghmore	14		2	12
	Gortneskeahy	11			11
Souldiers belonging to The Terrytory ot Owny	Coll Finch	10		10	
Killa Sculla and Comittee Parish	Cnockane	77	William Sheldon gent	18	59

Parishes	Places	Numbs of People	Tituladoes Names	Eng	Irish
(*folio* 64) Killa, Sculla & Committee P'ish }	Craigg	35	John Stumbles gent	5	30
	Bally Kinleagh	14		8	6
	Ballanahensy	19	William Straton Esq	2	17
	Shally	18	Christopher Wiers gent	12	6
	Curreheene	53	Teige Bryen gent	—	53
	Ball Belme	6		—	6
	Downan	17	Richard Day gent	7	10
	Garranbegg	25		6	19
	Cloingh pie	3		3	—
Killneragh	Rossegeyle	10		6	4
	Tullagh	46	Henry Scrimpton Esq	3	43
	Shewer	13		2	11
	Cully	26	Richard Walkes gent and Richard Walkes his sonne	9	17
	Carrickeale	7			7
	Keilenappigh	12			12
	Garriballynen	4			4
	Rossignellin	8			8
	Clonbony	6		2	4
	Bally Keogh	12			12
(*folio* 65).	Clantomer	16	Richard Dingle gent	4	12
	Garrane and Ballyhyley }	14		—	14
	Annaghallty	17		5	12
Killa, Sculla & Kill commitee P'ish }	Cnockane	2			2
	Graigg	2			2
	Ballygowrigan	5			5
	Clonnyloughy	6		2	4
	Shewer	1			1
	Collish & Hirenecapagh }	3			3
	Doonane	3			3
	Consinill	5			5
	Clonbony	8			8
	Bally McKeogh	4			4

Principall Irish Names [and] their Numbs

Bryen, 30; McConnor, 9; McDonogh, 16; Mc & Magrath, 8; Flanora and Flanory &c., 10; Glisane &c, 7; Hogane, 38; Hikye, 8; Kenedy, 9; Mullony, 9; Ryane, 9; Rayne, 13; McShane, 9; Toughie, 9; McTeige, 19; McWilliam, 8.

(*folio* 65 *verso*). The Number of People in ye Baronyes of Owny & Arra : Eng, 235; Irish, 989; Totall Eng & Irish, 1224.

BARONY OF CLANWILLIAM

Parishes	Places	Numbs of People	Tituladoes Names	Eng	Irish
Bruish	Allevellane	43			43
	Ballynyinrosagh	18		2	16
	Ballynyhow	9			9
	Rathmearhill	24			24
	Ballynumenssagh	21			21
Clonpett	Ballinly	27	Redmond Fitzgerald gent Morrish Fitzgerald his sonne		27
	Ballyglassoughterag	9	Walter Boorke gent		9
	Ballyglass Ightragh	37	Peirce Tobyn gent		37
Killcornone	Killcornane & Garriniphibbott	23	Robert Levitt Esq	2	21
	Castlelaghnif	44			44
	Ballyrebbin	47	Wm Armstronge gent Patricke Narbett gent	2	45
Temple Ibridon	Clog Ireda	47	Nicholas Evans gent	2	45
Dumoghill	Lynanestowne	8			8
	Ballyneale	3		2	1
	Shandongan	7		2	5
(*folio* 67).	Risseendermott	22			22
Rathlegny	Dornesreigh	25			25
	Allen	9			9
	Curraghpoore	8		2	6
	Duneiskeigh.	44	Francis Smyth gent	8	36
Donnoghill	Pallice	3			3
	Ballydonnogh	4			4
	Rathnetohy	4			4
	Lyssyne Frankigh	7			7
	Allin	26	Theobald Boorke gent		26
	Lissindermott	7			7
	Garryshane	11			11
	Grange	25			25
	Barryderrige	21	Gyles Ryan gent		21
	Ballintasre	9			9
Killmilbon	Knockanemonygiry	2			2
(*folio* 68). Part of Rathleyne Parish	Laffiny and Drissane	15			15
	Part of DunesKiegh	7			7
Cordagin	Cordagin	22			22
	Fannangowne	23			23
	Ratheyne	6			6
	Killmevomage	3			3
	Cleynkeany	7			7
	Gortknocker	12			12
	Lisnagaull	35			35

Parishes	Places	Numbs of People	Tituladoes Names	Eng	Irish
Killordry and Clonra Ballage P'ish	Dromonckyre	4		2	2
	Cappagh	35			35
	Killmayleher	34		2	32
	Cappagh	6			6
	Dronanebegg	6			6
	Beladagh	7			7
	Ballingortin	9			9
	Grelane	6			6
(folio 69) Killardry and Clen Ballauge Parish	Slarth	12			12
	Clorne	4			4
	Templeharny	10			10
	Rahine	5			5
	Carragh Inea	10			10
P^te of DunIgor and Tramplenoe P'ish	Ballyhasly	21			21
	Part of Grynane Towne	15		2	13
	Coolargan	31	John Courtney gent	2	29
	Graynantowne	42		2	40
Seronill	Sronill	26			26
	Ballycloghy	19			19
	Ballinconry	15	William Stone gent	2	13
	Ballynarde	23			23
	Garrinscotty	21			21
	Serinoll	5			5
	Ballyconry	12	Teige Magrath gent and James Magrath his sonne	1	11
Killshane	Killshane	60	Richard Gerrald gent		60
	Swiffeene	12			12
(folio 70)	Cleibeile	11			11
	Castlecury	8			8
Lattin	Lattin	10			10
	Knockordin	25			25
	Lattin towne	41	Walter Baber gentle	3	38
	Knockordin	19			19
Cullin	Cullin	150	Gamahrill Walter Esq George Warter gentle Gilbert Warter gent William Tubbs gent	25	125
	Clogher	9			9
	Gortnabillin	16			16
	Ballynalta	18			18
	Bnohine	32		3	29
Tampleneyry	Bansigh	64		04	60
	Raghderboy	16			16
	Ballagh Cabcuny	16			16
	Ballyglass	4			4
	Ballybarrane	8			8

Parishes	Places	Numbs of People	Tituladoes Names	Eng	Irish
(*folio* 71).	Bansigh	7			7
	Shartvahhane	10	Mr Brookes gent	4	6
	Gorrane	12		2	10
	Ardane	13			13
	Lish McHugh	31	Robert Knight Esq	5	26
	Ini Ganrigh	8			8
	Rathroe	4			4
	Ballaghbeegg	15			15
	Rossdrohide	14			14
	Barnelahgh	13		2	11
	Ballygormane	8			8
Clonbeegg	Ballynacourty	42	John Darson Esq	5	37
	Lonford	28			28
	Bally creghane	37			37
Pte of Galvally Parish	Ballyveyre	8			8
	Killpatricke	4			4
	Ballycrony	10			10
Imly	Gurteene	15		2	13
(*folio* 72)	Feranacey	4		2	2
	Imly	28		2	26
	Morenore	14	Robert Powell gent Geyles Powell	4	10
	Duncrin	15	Donnogh O Connor gent		15
	Ballyhone	9	Dermott McRory gent William McRory gent		9
	Cnockeare	12			12
	Ballyvecre	6			6
	Ballyvestagh	16	James Grady gent		16
	Ballregruvey	8			8
	Ballyvytene	14	Donnogh Magrath gent		14
	Ballowlone	20			20
Tipp'ary	Tipp'ary	72	Mathew Yeard gent James Bouster gent Robert Slones	17	55
	Carranmore	18			18
	Ballynnelady	10		2	8
	Ballynamoght	2			2
	Bohircrogh	8		2	6
(*folio* 73)	Tobarbaynn	2			2
Currage	Laffally etc	18	John Walsh Esq		18
	Curragmore	4			4
	Klykeyle	3			3
	GarranIbearta	19	Daniell Ryan gent		19
	Spiltleland	6			6
Sollohodmore	Sollohod	63	Mathew Reede gent	10	53
	Killmery	11			11

Parishes	Places	Numbs of People	Tituladoes Names	Eng	Irish
Kilsallagh and pt of the Parish of Castletowne	Ballingduny	10			10
		9			9
	Killsallagh	33			33
Sollohodbegg Parish & Kill		52		2	50
	Phillipstowne	7			7
	Getenstowne	10			10
	Ballychisteen	6			6
Religmory (*folio* 74).	Religmory	63		6	57
	Clogbussell	39			39
	Ouldgrane	42			42
	Ballycloghy	13		2	11
	AbbyeIshell	11		2	9
	Beallourine	18	Nathaniell Lawrence gent	4	14
	Ballyvadey	17		2	15
	Clogleagh	10		---	10
	Ballygriffen	36	George Clarke Esq Gyles Martin gent	6	30
	Parte of Religmory towne	119		20	99
Killfeacle	Killfeacle	41			41
	Part of Ballynekedy	4		2	2
	Granstowne	8			8
	Knockballinoe	6			6
	Dromleyney	4		1	3
	Ballyglassin	10			10
(*folio* 75).	Killfeacle	15			15
	Bally McKeady	28	Jehhep Jegnys Esq	4	24

Principall Irish Names [and] Their Numbs

Bryen, 30 ; Boorke, 48 ; Barry, 11 ; Butler, 11 ; Connor, 12 ; Commyne and Comane, 10 ; Cleary, 10 ; Carrane, 8 ; Daniell, 24 ; McDaniell, 11 ; Dwyer and O Dwyer, 24 ; McDonnogh, 15 ; English, 13 ; Fogurty, 7 ; Fahy, 7 ; Fitzgerrold, 9 ; Gerrold, 7 ; Hiffernane, 28 ; Hicky, 16 ; Hogane, 28 ; Kenedy, 16 ; Kearney, 8 ; McLoghlin, 11 ; Lonnergane, 9 ; Lynsy, 11 ; Murphy, 7 ; Meagher, 14 ; Magrath & McCrath, 17 ; Mullony, 9 ; Morissy, 7 ; McNemara, 7 ; Quirke and O Quirke, 19 ; Ryan, 77 ; Ryardane, 9 ; Shea and O Shea, 14 ; McShane, 15 ; McTeige, 26 ; Tobyn, 9 ; McThomas, 11 ; McWilliam, 17 ; Walsh. 19.

(*folio* 74 *verso*).   The Number of People in the Bary of Clanwilliam : Eng, 180 ; Irish, 2713 ; Totall Eng & Irish, 2893

(*Folio 75 Verso*).

The Number of People in the County of Tipperary and in each Barony.

Baronyes	Pages	Eng	Irish	Eng & Irish
Slevardagh	7	307	2101	2408
Lower Ormond	16	341	2731	3072
Kilnamanagh	21	086	1749	1835
Middlethird	33	134	3778	3912
Iffay & Offay	43	223	4729	4952
Eliogurty & Ikerin	53	326	4339	4665
Upper Ormond	60	092	1631	1723
Owny & Arra	65	235	0989	1224
Clanwilliam	74	180	2713	2893
The Totall		1924	24760	26684

1119   1647
WATERFORD COUNTY AND CITIE
                    1119
                    1647
                    ─────
                    2766

(*folio* 1). County of Waterford

BARONY OF DEACES

Parishes	Townlands	Number of People	Tituladoes Names	Eng	Irish
Rynogonath	Ballyharronane	5		—	5
	Leaghloskey	10		—	10
	Gortnedighey	18			18
	Ballynecourty	35		3	32
	Motey	1			1
	Shannechill	7			7
	Rutnemininene	3			3
	Killneowren	2			2
Aglis	Aglis	30	John Russell gent	2	28
	Ballycallane	19			19
	Monegillagh	20			20
	Shannakile	7		2	5
	Lackensallagh	5		2	3
	Higher Dromere	35	Phillipp McCragh gent	—	35
	Lower Dromere	27		1	26
	Ballingowne	15			15
	Ballynacourt	19	Daniell McMahony gent		19
(*folio* 2).	Ballinreese	3			3
	Ballina Parke	9			9
	Curryheene	6		2	4
	Tenescartye	25			25
	Glanassy	25			25
Kinsalebegg	Pilltowne	58	Thomas Walsh Esq		58
	Kinsalebegg	6		2	4
	Glestonane	14			14
	Dlaghtome	13	Thomas Roayne gent		13
	Killmaloe	19	Thomas Tobin gent		19
	Lachindery	6			6
	Ballyhenny	12	Alexander Roch gent	—	12
	Killgabrell	20			20
	Monastry	40			40
	Killmedy	5			5
	Dromgallan	1			1
Lisgenane	Grange	110	Nicholas Stoute gent	8	102
(*folio* 3).	Knocknegeragh	11			11
	Russins	38	Thomas Butler gent		38
	Ballyshomkins	37			37
	Goolagh	24			24
	Ballylangaden	13			13
	Ballyloan	13			13
	Ardergaull	5			5
	Ballyellynane	10			10
Ardmore	Farrenlonty	20			20
	Loskerane	17			17

Parishes	Townlands	Number of People	Tituladoes Names	Eng	Irish
	Ballycurreene	30			30
	East Ballynomony	30			30
	Hackestowne	35	John Rowe gent	2	33
	Ballentlea	23			23
	Crobly	43	John Mead gent	2	41
	Ballymacart	40			40
	Rathlead	20			20
(*folio* 4).	West Ballenemony	12			12
	Killcolman	24			24
	Moneam	30		2	28
	Duff Carigg	38	Richard Wandrich gent	4	34
	Killknockan	9			9
	Ballynemertinagh	17		2	15
	Croshea	10			10
	Ardogena	15			15
	Ardoscasty	32	Henry Gee gent	3	29
	Mearningesland	7		—	7
Clusmore	Ballynimultinagh	52	Walter Mansfield gent	2	50
	Ballycurrane	9	Arthur Anthony gent	2	7
	Cragges	15	John Power gent		15
	Knockmirish	38	Teige Kelly gent		38
	Rahine	33			33
	Coulbagh	28	Giles Russell gent		28
(*folio* 5).	Clusmore	10		2	8
	BallyniClassy	16			16
	Andsillage	11	John Power gent		11
	Tonnobyny	7			7
	Tonknocke	6			6
	Sannacoole	8			8
White Church	White church	13			13
	Ballynemelagh	20		6	14
	Scart Ballynemellagh	6			6
	Lissgrany	4			4
	Ballynecourt	12			12
	Ballylomen	25			25
	Lisbishell	12			12
	Coolenaffe	2			2
	Laragh	36			36
	Ballin Tayler	21	Sᵣ Rich : Osberne Barᶦᵗ	8	13
(*folio* 6). Whitchurch	Ballymolally	21			21
	Ballygambon	6			6
	Clankerd	13		2	11
	Cappagh	19	Nicholas Osburne Esq	4	15
	Knocknecrohy	52		1	51
	Killcannan	07			7
	Ballyhanbegg	4		1	3

Parishes	Townlands	Number of People	Tituladoes Names	Eng	Irish
	Killclogher	21		5	16
	Knockmone, Knockane Carigo, Carigbea, and Caintag	036		003	033
	Killfarny	12			12
Affane	Affane	104		4	100
	Crannaghtane	16			16
	Clottahinny	28			28
	The Inhabitants of the litle bridge of Affane, next Cappoquen	13			13
(folio 7).	Ballyhanmore	11			11
	Dromanna more	66	Richard Franklin Esq	4	62
Colligan	Knockanpower	16			16
	Knockroe	15			15
	Garryclome	11			11
	Colligan	9			9
	Garryduff	7			7
Modeligo	Curraghnesleady	37			37
	Ballykerin	34			34
	Lisleagh, Lickowran, and Mountaine Castle	39			39
	Upper Garran	22			22
	Lower Garran	5			5
	Scart Modeligo	6			6
(folio 8).	Graigbegg, Graigemore, and Killmony	42			42
	Farnan	23			23
Seskinan	Nyre	56			56
	Inerinmy Cahirnelegy and Bolenventine	24			24
	Bleantisowre	10			10
	Knockboy	20			20
	Lackendarra	19			19
	Killcony and Clonegigiall	9		—	9
	Leskinammill	6		3	3
	Ballynegilky and Curradoone	29			29
(folio 9. Lismolash	Knockelaher, and Clasnedarriff	22	Thomas Farmer gent	04	18
	Killkipp	12		03	9
	Curraroch	07		1	6
	Knocknescagh	32	William Osburne gent	4	28
	Benly	06	William Bagg gent John Farneham gent	5	1

Parishes	Townlands	Number of People	Tituladoes Names	Eng	Irish
	Ballynepky	11		2	9
	Kill McGibboge	7		—	7
	Clogh, and Tinekilly	26	William Hibbart Esq Walter Hibbart his sonn, gent	07	19
Dungarvan	Bally M^cnicholl	11			11
	Ballygery	18			18
	Ballycullane	14			14
	Killelongirt, Shankill, and Brownsland	13			13
(folio 10).	Killmurry	18			18
	Coole Cormucke	5			5
	Ballyduffmore	16			16
	Ballyduffbegg	2			2
	West Bally McMauge	13			13
	East Bally M^cmauge	6			6
	Shandon	1			1
	Ballynemucke	13			13
	Lackfuan	2			2
	Ballynure, Lisnefintly and Cloghrane	2		2	—
	Ballygagin and Mapestowne	5		—	5
(folio 11) Rosmire	Killester, and Glanmore	43			43
	Grenane	10	Pierce Power gent		10
	Ballyhossey	27			27
	Ballyrobert	4			4
	Carrigintnagh	5			5
	Newtowne	4			4
	Ballyshoney	18			18
	Rosmire	25			25
	Ballybracke	9			9
	Ballyboaght	9			9
	Ballywade	4			4
Stradbally	Killminin	16			16
	Curriheene	21			21
	Dromloghan	23			23
	Durrowe	13			13
	Karricke Killy	17	Thomas Fitzgerald gent	02	15
(folio 12)	Knockedromeleagh	8			8
	Karrygeenehahy	7			7
	Ballybegg	29			29
	Ballintallounly	14			14
	Killbarraghan	7			7
	Stradballymore	30			30
	Ballyvony	20		2	18

Parishes	Townlands	Number of People	Tituladoes Names	Eng	Irish
Killgobnett (*folio* 13).	Raghneskilloage	9			9
	Monenekirky	5			5
	Ballyvoile and Iland	19			19
	Argrilline	19			19
	Killbrine	4			4
	Ballynekilly	14			14
	Bohidonne	9		—	9
	Coulnesmiare	6			6
	Curribehy	7		1	6
	Killgobnett	7			7
	Ballynity	11			11
	Killedangin	9			9
	Garranbane	30			30
	Tallacoulmore	4			4
	Dilisse	8			8
	Monemrodde	5			5
	Ballinknocky	7		2	5
	Killnefreechane	20			20
Killrosenty (*folio* 14).	Gliddane	7			7
	Ballykerogemore	38		6	32
	Ballykerogebegg	29		2	27
	Glandallygane	9			9
	Knockhillane	2			2
	Bamakill	34			34
	Lemybryne	13		2	11
	Bollyattine	6			6
	Killrossenty	20			20
	Cottine	26			26
	Killcomorragh	27			27
	Glancurrane	19			19
	Tinescarty	31			31
Phewes	Garran	27			27
	Norrileagh	31			31
	Ballinefinnsogie	9			9
	Ballobay	21			21
	Graigerush	7			7
	Killnegransy	46			46

(*folio* 15). Principall Irish Names [and] Their Number.

Arlant, 6 ; Brennagh & Bernagh, 65 ; Bryne & Ô Bryne, 27 ; Browne, 30 ; Baldon, 8 ; Butler, 13 ; Bryan, 7 ; Curane, Cureene and Currin, 27 ; Cahane, 15 ; Cragh & McCragh, 57 ; Carroll, 18 ; Christopher, 8 ; Clansy, 7 ; Coghan, 25 ; Corbane, 17 ; Crotty, 10 ; Connory and O Connory, 26 ; Connor, 8 ; Dower & Ô Dower, 8 ; Daniell & McDaniell, 17 ; McDavid, 9 ; Daton, 10 ; McDonnogh, 21 ; Dally, 9 ; Donnell & McDonnell, 15 ; Flyne and O Flyne, 40 ; Ô Fling, 31 ; Fowlow & Follon, 70 ; Gerrald and Fitzgerald, 49 ; Hagherin, 25 ; Hogane, 8 ; O Hallaghane, 15 ; O Hea, 9 ; Hubbard

Y

and Hibbard, 9 ; Hanagan, 7 ; Hally &c, 8 ; Hicky, 7 ; Hallenane, 6 ; Henessy, 5 ; Jordan, 8 ; Keating, 16 ; Kelly, 67 ; Kerwicke, 6 ; Kenedy, 16 ; Lander, 6 ; Lendsie, 12 ; Mollone, 6 ; Mansfield, 22 ; Muresie and O Muresie, 62 ; Moreghy &c, 12 ; Mulcaghy, 32 ; Morish & McMorish, 17 ; Mulryan, 7 ; Mogher, 5 ; Mearinge, 13 ; Power, 90 ; Phelane, 17 ; Quine, 10 ; Ronane, 10 ; Raine, 6 ; Ryane &c, 9 ; Roch, 14 ; McRichard, 10 ; McRobert, 8 ; McShane, 36 ; Shea & Ô Shea, 12 ; McThomas, 23 ; McTeige, 15 ; Tobin, 36 ; Veale, 15 ; White, 17 ; Wash, 9 ; Wade, 7 ; McWilliam, 22 ; Whelane, 10.

(*folio* 15 *verso*). Barony : Deaces ; Eng, 129 ; Irish, 3574 ; 3703, Totall.

(*folio* 16).

BARONY OF COSMORE, AND COSBRIDE

Parishes	Townlands	Numb of People	Tituladoes Names	Eng	Irish
Tallow bridge Division					
	Sheane	06		02	04
	Aglis	13		04	09
	Coolowen	19			19
	Killogoody	06			06
	Knocknomucke	34		06	28
	Carroughreagh	31	Capt John Seargeant gent	02	29
	Ballygarren	036		003	033
	Tallow Bridge	49		09	40
	Hanboy	14	John Andrewes gent	03	11
	Ballygally	08		04	04
	Ballyduff	34	Thomas Jackson gent William Jackson gent	06	28
Killwatermoy P'ish	Tercullinbegg	16	Joshua Boyle Esq	02	14
	Tercullinmore	04		—	04
	Ballycleamint	002		—	02
	Ballyhamles	10		04	06
	Ballyfinshoge	12		—	12
(*folio* 17).	Ballymotey	14			14
	Knockinsrath	2			2
	Canmocky	27			27
	Bottadortt	6			6
	Ballymoddogh	9			9
	Killountaine	6			6
	Gloonigeenitaine	12			12
	Bally McShonocke	38		2	36
	Killwatermoy	33		5	28
	Ballynitimore	12			12
	Ballyniteebegg	06			06
	Dunmoone	26	Thomas Carter gent	07	19
Tallough	Killmore	24	Richard Silver gent	01	23

Parishes	Townelands	Numb of People	Tituladoes Names	Eng	Irish
	Killwenhy	14	Francis Drew gent	07	7
	Bogghouse	06			6
	Lower Killbegg	02			2
	Upper Killbegg	19			19
(folio 18).	Killcalfe	19			19
	Carrigroe	07			07
	Barnakelly	100	Richard Burt gent Robert Cooke merchant Edward Rogers gent William Reiues gent Richard Guist gent James Benior gent Pierce Walsh gent	34	66
	Tallough Towne	105	Robert Jones gent Michaell Willson gent John Langley gent Michaell Belleny gent	44	61
	Old Forge	51		28	23
Killcokine	Kill McNicholas	49	Thomas Taylor gent	8	41
	Ballyphillipp	21		2	19
	Ballyphillipelmor	23		2	21
	Strongcally	67			67
	Portonoe	20		8	12
(folio 19). Temple Michaell	Ballynatra	61	Boyle Smith Esqur Pierce Smyth gent William Smith gent John Smith gent	13	48
	Killnegrane	28		02	26
	Coolebeggin	43			43
	Temple Michell	27	John Fitzgerold Esq		27
	Ballycondon	85		05	80
Macollop division	Macollop	70	Thomas Mansell gent Thomas Mansell his sonn gent	06	64
	Eushellemy	35			35
	Arglin	34		6	28
	CoolIshell	48		2	46
	Ballyduff	38			38
	Ballylevane	36			36
	Ballynurrane	06			6
(folio 20). Cappoquen Divission	Cappoquen towne	188	William Mills gent	26	162
	Killbree	51	Edward Nicholas gent	08	43
	Salterbridge	51		--	51
	Balligillane	43		—	43
	New Assane	34	Valentine Greatrakes Esq William Greatrakes gent	08	26
	Tooreene	30	John Nettle gent	06	24
	Ballyanyty	22			22
	Ballyregan	10			10
Lismore Divission	Ballyeene	56	Roger Carew gent	06	50

Parishes	Townlands	Numb of People	Tituladoes Names	Eng	Irish
	Ballyraughter	69			69
	Glanmorish-meeue	14	Richard Browning gent Richard Browning his son gent William Browning gent	04	10
	Rosgreily	27		03	24
	Killohaly	33		03	30
(folio 21)	Camphyre	84	Francis Foulke Esq	13	71
	OKyle	34			34
	Brydane	12			12
	Ballyneraghy	6			6
	Killnecarrigg	3			3
	Monitum	22		2	20
	Ballyvelly	3		3	—
	Ballynaspicke	42	Tobyas Sycamore gent	04	38
	Ballyanker	06	Thomas Croker gent	04	02
	Ballysaggard	74	Richard Downing gent	3	71
	Glanmore	26		5	21
	Lismore	156	Alexander Deane gent	30	126
	Curraheene	16	James Roch gent		16

(folio 22). Principall Irish Names [and] their Number.

Brennagh, 17 ; Bowdran, 10 ; Barry, 6 ; Bryne, 11 ; O Bryen, 13 ; Browne, 17 ; Cleary, 04 ; Corkeran, 8 ; Corban, 4 ; Cahane & O Cahane, 8 ; Carty & McCarty, 7 ; Connell & O Connell, 27 ; Connolay, 6 ; Connohor & O Connohor, 8 ; Crotty, 10 ; Coleman, 15 ; Connory, 7 ; Condon, 6 ; Cassey, 7 ; Deven & Duvin, 8 ; Daniell & McDaniell, 19 ; Doggan & Dugan, 10 ; O Dine, 8 ; Donorty, 8 ; McEdmond, 8 ; Fling (13) & Flin (12), 25 ; O Fowlow, 10.; Farrell, 14 ; Gerald & Fitzgerald, 15 ; O Guyry &c, 10 ; Hogan, 7 ; O Heefie, 12 ; Kerryn & Ô Kerryn, 8 ; Keating &c, 8 ; Lee &c, 8 ; Lucas, 6 ; McMorish, 21 ; Moore, 7 ; Morehey, 19 ; Murfie, 6 ; O Moroghoe, 15 ; Mahony, 6 ; O Nonane, 6 ; O Neo, 6 ; McOwen, 8 ; Oge, 6 ; Power & Poer. 11 ; Roch, 24 ; Ronane, 6 ; Rourke, 5 ; Russell, 8 ; McShane, 38 ; Sulevane, 5 ; Smyth, 7 ; Shanahane, 6 ; McThomas, 11 ; McTeige, 25 ; McWilliam &c, 23 ; McWalter &c, 6.

(folio 22 verso) Barony : Cosmore and Cosbride ; Eng, 355 ; Irish, 2180 ; 2535, totall

(folio 23) ## BARONY OF GLANAHIRY

Parishes	Townlands	Number of People	Tituladoes Names	Eng	Irish
Killronan	Castle conagh	45		02	43
	Clonenaf	23		—	23

Parishes	Townlands	Number of People	Tituladoes Names	Eng	Irish
	Sillehine	16		⸺	16
	Banefoune	7			7
	Coraghteskin	13			13
	Ardepadin	10			10
	Grenan	6		2	4
	Killmaccun	27			27
	Killneman	40			40
	Killmanahin	38		4	34
	Russellstowne	49	James Lee gent	2	47
	Cullenagh	28		4	24
	Gragnengoure	21			21
	Ballydonogh	27			27
	Bally M^cky	06		2	4
(folio 24) Dungar-van & halfe Plowland there unto belonging	Dungarvan Towne	213	Francis Vaughan gent John Dalton gent Richards Williams gent Thomas Swann gent Michaell Hore merc^{tt}	35	178
The eastern P^{te} of Dungarvan P'ish	The Abby Side	44	James Oldfield gent	3	41
	Scart Christopher	4			4
	Ballinle-hissery	10			10
	Ballycourty	6			6
	Ballinrode	4			4
	Garrinageragh	12			12
	Clonroskeran	37		2	35
	Clonyea	35			35

Principall Irish Names [and] their numb.

McCragh, 5 ; Carbery, 5 ; McDonnogh, 5 ; McDaniell, 5 ; Offling &c, 6 ; Fowlow, 12 ; Fitzgerald &c, 4 ; Hagherin, 5 ; Kenedy, 5 ; Kelly, 10 ; Moressy, 10 ; Mullony & Mullany, 5 ; Nagle, 7 ; Power, 12 ; McShane, 8 ; Shearhy, 5 ; McThomas, 6 ; Tobin, 5 ; White, 8.

(folio 24 verso)   Barony : Glanahyry ; Eng, 056 ; Irish, 665 ; 721, totall.

(folio 25).   **BARONY OF UPPERTHIRD**

Parishes &c	Townlands	Number of People	Tituladoes Names	Eng	Irish
Division of........	Gilcagh and Coolfin	46	Walter Power gent John Power gent	⸺	46
	Bealogh	10		⸺	10

Parishes &c	Townlands	Number of People	Tituladoes Names	Eng	Irish
	Curraghtaggirt	4			4
	Coolfin	35		4	31
	Ballyvalkin	21			21
	Killmovee	9			9
	Ballykeahan	25			25
Kilbarrymeaden Parish	Rathanny	2			2
	Rathquage	8			8
	Killmurren	14			14
	Knockandorehy	15			15
	Killbarrymeaden	29		3	26
	Tankardtowne	15			15
	Caherroan	14			14
	Currigeenegillagh	6			6
(folio 26). Kilbarry-	Georgestown	19			19
meaden	Garranmorice	14			14
Ballilanhen	Ballylanhen	10			10
	Brenan	17	Robert Power gent		17
	Killeltin	12			12
	Ballydoan	11	Peter Anthony gent	02	09
	Ballengaran	16			16
	Temple Ibrick	08			08
	Lisnegerigh	14			14
	GarranInogy	22			22
	Carrigkislane	15			15
	Ballynebanoghy	24			24
	Cooletubred	07			07
	Fahafinlagh	08			08
	Graigshonny	11		04	07
	Curbehey	27		02	25
(folio 27). Mothell	Cionea	43			43
	Curraghphillibeene	04		—	4
	Glanfooke	20		02	18
	Falloe	7			7
	Killcannoy	23			23
	Killclony	37			37
	Knocktornora	14			14
	Coolenehorny	8			8
	Monarlargy	26			26
	Rosse, and Clonmoyle	9			9
	Ballygerott	10			10
	Feddan	17			17
	Thomastowne	17			17
	Ballynecurry	13	William Power gent		13
	Ballinkinck	12			12
	Corduff	28	James Power gent		28
(folio 28).	Coolerobegg	11			11

Parishes &c	Townlands	Number of People	Tituladoes Names	Eng	Irish
	Mothell	15			15
	Ballyknaven	13			13
	Whitstone	19			19
	Ballydorren	15			15
Rathgormucke	Upperparke	21	William Power gent		21
	Glanpatricke	4			4
	Glannemore	5			5
	Kilballykelly	43			43
	Knock Lafally	17			17
	Lower Parke	14			14
	Cnondonell	34			34
	Ballycullane	12			12
	Grageevally	32			32
	Rathgormucke	28	Robert Davis gent	04	24
	Shankill	38			38
(*folio* 29).	Killbracke	19			19
	Knockanafferin	18			18
Dysart	Glyn	56			56
	Ballintample	17			17
	Ballycloghy	14			14
	Barnanegeehy	4			4
	Coolenemuicky	63		10	53
	Ballindisert	37		03	34
	Carrigbegg	25		02	23
	Garravone	06			06
	Ballysallagh	15			15
	Tykencor	20	Sr Thomas Stanly Knt	05	15
	Darrenlare	10			10
	Gurteene	14			14
	Coolishill	12			12
	Bagnis	06			06
	Leirnerly	06			06
(*folio* 30). Clonegann	Curraghmore	47	John Power Lo : Barron Richard Power Esq David Power Esq Piers Power Esq	04	43
	Barrencurry	44			44
	Lissessmuttane	37			37
	Killowen	23			23
	Gortardagh-Woodlocke	12			12
	Gortardagh-Strang	36			36
	Cooleeroe	66	Robert Wise gent	2	64
	Knockane	48	Robert Taylor gent	4	44
	Kill McThomas	63		5	58
	Shanchill	06			06
(*folio* 31).	Killamoyleene	16			16

Parishes &c	Townlands	Number of People	Tituladoes Names	Eng	Irish
Tenogh	Ballynevnitigh	09			09
	Crehannagh and Curraghnegarhy }	36	James Butler gent		36
	Tinykally	06			06
	Portonoboe	14			14
	Brownswood	12			12
	Curragh Ballintlea	49		09	40
	Balliquine	11	John Butler		11

Principall Irish Names [and] Their Numbs.

Brennagh, 24; Brassell, 13; Buo, 6; Bryen, 11; Baldin, 6; McCragh, 9; Carroll, 10; Carbery, 13; Coman, 10; Connola, 8; Clery, 6; Donoghoe, 8; Drochan, 8; McDavid, 10; McDaniell, 10; Duogin, 8; McDonogh, 6; FitzEdmond &c, 11; Flin, 30; Floyne, 7; Farhan, 8; Flemming 11; Fowlow, 12; Harny, 10; Hagherin, 11; Hicky, 6; Heany, 6; Hahasie, 13; Heagan, 7; FitzJohn &c, 16; Kelly, 7; Kenedy, 16; Keahane, 10; Kierussy, 5; Kearney, 6; McMorish, 11; FitzMorish, 6; Morissy, 5; Murphy, 11; FitzNicholas, 7; Neale, 6; Power, 130; Phelan, 49; Quillenane, 18; Roe, 10; Rochwell, 6; Shanehan, 9; McShane, 8; Shea, 8; McThomas, 11; Welsh, 8; McWilliam, 9; FitzWilliam, 10; Wale, 8.

(folio 31 verso) Barony: Upperthird; Eng, 065; Irish, 1909; 1974, Totall.

(folio 32).

BARONY OF MIDDLETHIRD

Parishes	Townlands	Numb of People	Tituladoes Names	Eng	Irish
Drumcannon	Castletowne	29	John Briver Esq	02	27
	Ballinkin	13		—	13
	Quilly	10			10
	Ballinknuick	8			8
	Killone	039		—	039
	Ballydrislane	40			40
	Garrcrobally	18		2	16
	Tramore	10			10
	Ballincarnan	14			14
	Newtowne	44			44
	Duagh	13		2	11
	Culneguppocke	8			8
	Gaverus	12			12
Killbreedy	Killbreedy	20		4	16
	Cullen	18			18

Parishes	Townlands	Numb of People	Tituladoes Names	Eng	Irish
	Knockanduff	04			04
(folio 33). Killbreedy	Carrigvrontory	22			22
Kilburren, Killronan,	Lower Butterstowne	10		02	08
Baleashin, & Parte	Banefeowne	8			8
Killoteran	Killronan	17			17
	Knockenatten	35		4	31
	Montohogy	20	James Bryner Esq		20
	Tergate	39			39
Lisnekill	Downyne	18		5	13
	Newtowne	19		5	14
	Whitesfield towne	42			42
	Shanganagh	2			2
	Lisnekitt	2			2
	Pembroxtown	38			38
	Loghdyghin	12	Paul Sherlocke Esq		12
(folio 34) Killmeadan	Killmeadan & Ballyduff	62			62
	Stonehouse	7			7
	Gortvertlade	34			34
	Killmogymog	6			6
	Adamstowne	37			37
	Glannerowrish	34			34
	Dargill	53			53
	Cullenagh	37		2	35
	Rahens	26			26
Newcastle	Rosserudery	4			4
	Ardranloen	10			10
	Lissechan	8			8
	Ballygarran	10			10
	Carrigenure	28			28
	Carrigphillipp	26			26
	Knockderry	17			17
(folio 35)	Hackettstowne	10			10
Donhill	Donhill	23		02	21
	Ballygerigh	22			22
	Ballyrobben	24			24
	Smoore	8			8
	Killowen	11			11
	Knockancorbally	11			11
	Castlecrodocke	7			7
	Ballycrodocke	3			3
	Ballygungagh, Lissevoyran, and Killcannan	43			43
	Shaneclone	16			16
	Ballyunanmore	4			4

Parishes	Townlands	Numb of People	Tituladoes Names	Eng	Irish
Ilan Iken	Ballyleene	12			12
	Ilan Iken	25			25
(*folio* 36).	Illantarnsney	7			7
	Ballycaulan	25			25
	Ballygarran	11			11
	Woodstowne	19			19
	Tynnor	13			13
	Killfarrissey	40			40
Rieske	Ballynecloghy	39			39
	Ballydermott	28			28
	Ballyphillipp	05		01	04
	Ballylygott	13			13
	Ballymahis	17			17
	Rieske	10			10
	Carrigoronghan	17			17
	Ballyadambeg	08			08
(*folio* 37)	Ballymorish	12			12
	Ballybrenocke	04			04
	Killcartan	07			07
	Ballyvillon	02			02
	Clonfady	11			11
Kilburren	Ballycashen	15			15

Principall Irish Names and their Numbers.

Arland, 5 ; Baldon, 8 ; Brennagh, 16 ; McCowman, 5 ; Corkerin, 6 ; Cahane, 6 ; McEdmond (10), FitzEdmond (9), 19 ; Forane, 5 ; Flyne & Flyng, 17 ; Fowlow, 6 ; Flemyng, 5 ; O Fea, 9 ; Gough, 13 ; Gibbon, 7 ; Harny, 9 ; O Hea, 4 ; Hagherin, 14 ; Knaven, 6 ; FitzJohn, 11 ; Kenedy, 11 ; Londay, 6 ; Morphey, 12 ; Moeny and Meany, 12 ; Meaghir, 6 ; Morissy, 15 ; FitzMorish & McMorish, 7 ; FitzNicholas & McNicholas, 7 ; FitzNichas, 6 ; Power, 138 ; Phelane, 44 ; McRichard & FitzRichard, 8 ; McShane, 12 ; Spellane, 5 ; Sulevane, 4 ; McThomas & FitzThomas, 11 ; FitzWilliam & McWilliam, 22 ; Wesh, 17 ; FitzWalter &c, 8 ; Whittle, 8 ; White, 7.

(*folio* 37 *verso*)   Barony : Midlethird ; Eng, 031 ; Irish, 1484 ; 1515, totall

(*folio* 38).   **BARONY OF GALTIRE**

Parishes	Townlands	Number of People	Tituladoes Names	Eng	Irish
Ballymakill	Little Island	06		—	06
	Ballymakill	25		02	23

Parishes	Townlands	Number of People	Tituladoes Names	Eng	Irish
	Grantstowne	10			10
	Farrenshonyne	14			14
	Williamstowne	19	Thomas Coote gent	04	15
	Killcoghan	10			10
Ballygun^r Temple	Ballygun^r Castle	10	Pierce Walsh Esq		10
	Ballygun^r temple	21	Richard Lynn		21
	Knockbwey	02			02
	Ballymaclode	17	Anthony Field gent	02	15
	Ballygunermore	38			38
	Killaghan	23			23
Tathlegg	Tathlegg	32	William Bolton Esq	10	22
			Thomas Bolton gent		
(folio 39)	Passadge	65	Henry Alland Esq	24	41
	Dromroske	16			16
	Parkeswood	19		02	17
	Knockroe	04			04
	Crostowne	18	Nicholas Aylward gent		18
	Killnicolas	22			22
	Ballinglanny	22			22
	Ballycanvan	17			17
	Knocknegapull	17			17
Crooke	Crooke	10	Robert Harding gent	04	06
	Newtowne	29			29
	Dromenagh	45			45
	Cooleteigin	03			03
	Ballydavid	04		02	02
	Kilcop	22		04	18
Killmocum	Woodstowne	22	Henry Kellsall gent	—	22
	Harrystowne	17			17
(folio 40).	Ballinlogh more	28			28
	Ballingeynes	16			16
	Killmocum	12			12
Killea	Credan	25		7	18
	Lepstowne	55			55
	Leckane, and Killahan	12			12
	Fornought	34			34
	Knockeveehy	15			15
	Ballymabin	17			17
	Grageriddy	10			10
	Portalig	5		03	02
	Killaghmore	15			15
	Killaghbeg	6			6
	Glandemus	6		4	2
	Dunmore	5			5
(folio 41). Rathmealan	Brownestowne	07			7
	Ballymaqueill	15			15

Parishes	Townlands	Number of People	Tituladoes Names	Eng	Irish
Kill McLeig	Lissealty	15			15
	Bally McDavid	45		2	43
	Rathmealan	38			38
	Killmoquoagg	7			7
	Ballinloghbegg	9	Abell Hart gent		9
	Corballymore	13			13
	Corballybegg	13			13
	Ballingarre	20			20
	Ballyshonyn	6			6
	Kealeggs	12			12
	Monemantreghmore	4			4
(folio 42).	Ballymonetreagh	23			23
	Kill M^clige more	9		—	9
	Kill McLiegbeg	2			2
	Ballinvelly	15			15
	Monemontraghbeg	4			4
Kill St Lawrence	Killure	25			25
	Kill St Lawrence	20		4	16
	B'pps Court	28	Robert Whittby gent	2	26
	Killcarragh	21			21

Principall Irish Names, & their Numbers.

Aylward, 17 ; Bryen, 6 ; Butler, 9 ; Cahan, 5 ; Droghan, 7 ; FitzEdmond, 9 ; Fling & Flyne, 27 ; Foran, 7 ; Fowlow, 4 ; Ferrell, 4 ; Flemming, 4 ; O Hea, 15 ; FitzJames, 7 ; FitzJohn, 17 ; Kenedy, 9 ; Morish & Fitz & McMorish, 18 ; Morphey, 11 ; Power, 69 ; Phelane, 25 ; FitzRichard, 19 ; McShane, 6 ; Shaneghane, 8 ; M^c & Fitz Thomas, 8 ; Tubbernd, 9 ; Welsh, 9 ; Wise, 9 ; Fitz-William (13), McWilliam (7), 20 ; White, 7.

(folio 42 verso)   Barony : Galtire ; Eng, 76 ; Irish, 1115 ; 1191, totall

(folio 43).   The Number of People in ye County of Waterford and in each Baronye.

Baronyes	Pages	Eng	Irish	Eng & Irish
Deaces	15	129	3574	3703
Cosmore & Cosbride	22	355	2180	2535
Glanahyry	24	056	0665	0721
Upperthird	31	065	1909	1974
Middlethird	37	031	1484	1515
Galtire	42	076	1115	1191
The Totall		712	10927	11639

CITIE OF WATERFORD AND LIBERTYES THEREOF.

(*folio* 1). Westward : Numb of People, 373 ; Eng, 200 ; Irish, 173 ; Tituladoes Names : Thomas Bolton Esq, Peter Rogers Esq, Thomas Grosvenor gent, John Houghton Esq Mayor, Thomas Watts Esq, Will Bainlett Esq, John Williams Esq, Samuell Wade Esq, Robert Lambert Esq, John Gregory Esq, John Cooke ensigne, Richard Wilkinson gent, Wm Leigh Esq, Robert Enith gent, Tho Hickes gent, Edward Marshall gent, Charles Treasley gent, Zech : Clayton mch^t, Rich : Morrice mch^t, Tho : Sparling mch^t, Patrick Grant mcht.

Southward : Numb of People, 246 ; Eng, 161 ; Irish, 085 ; Tituladoes Names : Thomas Dancer Esq, William Hallsey Esq, Richard Maddin Doctr, Edward Butler mch^t, Lodowicke Butler mch^t, Dominick Suniet mch^t, Humphry Deare mch^t, Thomas Weldon town clarke, John Barr gent, Jn Lapp gent, Patrick Maddin gent, Richard Strong mch^t, Tho : Strong mch^t, Tho : Chrismas mch^t, John White mch^t, Nicholas Welch mch^t, Samuell Brinsmeade apothycary.

(*folio* 2). Northward : Numb of People, 331 ; Eng, 177 ; Irish, 154 ; Tituladoes Names : Richard Barrett gent, John Heavens Ald'man, Thomas Eyres mchant, Edward Beacon gent, William Fryth gent, John Dyins Ald'man, Richard Royston gent, Benedict Claybrooke Ald^n, Andrew Lynn Esq, Fradsham Lond gent, Ald'man Jon Tomlinson, Allexsander Mickle Esq, Thomas Noble Ald'man, Capt Arthur Odway, Capt William Baltezar, Thomas Exton Ald'man, Henry Seamor gent, Capt Thomas Wright, William Darwell mcht, Richd Maylard an apothycary, Jn Lewis shopkeeper, Thomas Newman mch^t, Nicholas Lee mch^t, Joseph Parsons mch^t, William Blanch mch^t, John Davis mch^t, Robert Tunbridge mch^t, Rich : Fitzgerrald mct, William Hurt mch^t, Stephen Murphy mcht, Peter Cransborogh mch^t, Symon Sall merctt, Thomas Butler merct, Cnokor Sall merc^t, John Walsh merc^t, Martin Walsh merct, John Davis merct, James Cobleigh merc^t, William Ale merc^t, William Brickain m't, Thomas Eyres m'a^t, William Lone merct, Thomas Lonell merct.

(*folio* 3). Brickenstowne, Cleboy, Lumbardie, Kings Meadow, Bogg Mill, and the 2 bowling greenes and the way leading to Killbarry : Number of People, 202 ; Eng, 027 ; Irish, 175 ; Tituladoes Names : William White m^ct, William Aleward Fact^r in the Barbadoes, William Cooper mercer, —— Starkers Esq.

Kilbarry and Ballynemony, Balliho, Kenenard &c : Number of People, 144 ; Eng, 011 ; Irish, 133.

Johnstowne : Number of People, 119 ; Eng, 014 ; Irish, 105 ; Tituladoes Names : Thomas Lincoln m^ct, Barthlomew Lincoln mc^t, Overington Blundell gent, Michell Lea mc^t, Edward Smyth Esq, Gregory Clemets Esq.

(*folio* 4). Parishes	Places	Number of People	Tituladoes Names	Eng	Irish
Carill Carrick	Killculleheene, Rathclehene, Nurath and Ballyrobin	086	Morris Conway gent, The Heyre of my Lady Calthorpe Esq	032	054
	Killateran, Woodstowne, Knockhouse, Carigferus, & Ballynemony	081		000	081
	Grasedine	020		000	020
	East side of ye passidge within the liberties of the City of Waterford	045		015	030

(folio 5). Principall Irish Names and their Numbs.

Ayleward, 6 ; Butler, 6 ; Brennagh, 5 ; Corkeran, 4 ; Grant, 5 ; Fitz James, 6 ; Fitz John, 8 ; Kelly, 10 ; Morrice, 13 ; Murphy, 13 ; Nugent, 5 ; Poore, 8 ; Power, 8 ; Phelan, 6 ; Quinn, 10 ; Ryan, 5 ; Sulevan, 5 ; Trapnell, 5 ; Welsh, 25 ; Whelann, 10 ; FitzWilliam, 6.

City of Waterford and the liberties thereof : Eng, 637 ; Irish, 1010 ; Totall Numbers of all ye People, 1647.

(folio 5 verso). The Number of People in the County of Waterford Vide page 43.

CATHERLAGH COUNTY
& BOROUGH   2418

(folio 1). Catherlagh County

THE BOROUGH OF CATHERLAGH

Towne-shippes	Number of People	Tituladoes Names	Eng	Irish
Catherlagh Borough	560	Henry Pritty Esqʳ, John Smith Portriue, John Masters gent, Edward Reynolds, marchant, George Rideout gent, Henry Seix Apothecary, Robert Browne gent, and Samuell North Ensigne, Hugh Gough gent.	271	289

Principall Irish Names [and] Their Number.

Browne, 04 ; Ô Bryan, 04 ; Byrne, 08 ; Murphy, 08 ; Nolan, 04 ; Neale, 04 ; Welsh, 04.

Towne[1]	Number of People	Tituladoes Names	Eng	Irish
Vurghlin	053	Robert Mihill Esqʳ	010	043
Johnstowne	017	——	—	017
Ballinakill	073	John Ashton Esqʳ	011	062
Duganstowne	040	Richard Andrewes Esqʳ and William Tyndall gent	019	021
Painstowne	024	Thomas Barry gent	—	024
Ballicroge	015	Walter Bodely Esqʳ	003	012
Stapletowne	014	——	008	006
Clonemulsker	144	The Lady Juliana Butler	004	140
Ballilow	053	Garott Wale gent	—	053
Cloughna	044	Henry Ward Esqʳ	005	039
(folio 2). Ballitrane	027		—	027
Quinnagh	025	John Carpenter gent	005	020
Pollardstowne & Cernanstowne	042	John Clearke gent	006	036
Moyle	028	——	009	019
Killeriske	026	Mathew Shepherd gent	016	010
Graingefort	091	William Huges, William Byrine, Garott Byrne & Will' Smith gent.	003	088
Kellestowne	079	Henry Harman gent	007	072
Bacroge	017	Arthur Harding gent	005	012
Clocristick	038	John Gayson Esqʳ	007	031
Parke	010	Arthur Weldon gent	002	008
Lincardstowne Castletowne & Timlyland	072	James Allen gent	002	070
Ballinecarig	013	— — — —	—	013
Lower Mortestowne	012	Thomas Weathers gent	002	010

[1] *Townshipps*, folio 2.

Z

Principall Irish Names [and] Their Number.

Bane, 06 ; Ô Brenan & Brenan, o6 ; Bolger, o6 ; Byrne, 24 ; Corren & Curren, 07 ; Kinselagh, 08 ; Kelly (11), Kealy (3), 14 ; Ô Doyle & Doyle, 07 ; Doolin, o6 ; Dufie, 07 ; Daniell & O Daniell, 07 ; Dorgan, o6 ; McEdmond, 07 ; McMorish, 07 ; Nolan, 11 ; Roe, 09 ; McWilliam, o6 ; Headon, 08.

(*folio 2 verso*). Barrony & Borough of Catherlagh : Eng, 395 ; Irish, 1122 ; 1517, Totall.

(*folio 3*).   **RATHVILY[1] BARRONY**

Townshippes	Number of People	Tituladoes Names	Eng	Irish
Tulloephelim	211	Richard Burcell, Richd Motly and Richard Fisher gents, James Segnock Esqr, Thristram Thorneton, James Segnock Juno^r, Laudwick Price gents.	071	140
Ballimorphy	018	Hugh Doyne gent	000	018
Downanes	002	--- --- ---	---	002
Butlers Grainge	002	--- --- ---	002	---
Killnagarrocke	004	--- ---	---	004
Croscles and Raglass	058	James Motly gent	---	058
Jancarstowne	034	Mr Papworth gent	004	030
Ralahin	003	--- ---	002	001
Copnagh	020	Thomas White gent	---	020
Clonemore	018	Will : Hudson gent & Eliazor Hudson gent	008	010
Tombay	027		008	019
Hacketstowne	016	Francis Browne gent	008	008
Kilcarton	014	John Rusel gent	012	002
(*folio* 4). Phillips-towne	029	Thomas Flenter Esqr	004	025
Ballyhackett	025	---	---	025
Richardstowne	014	John Flenten gent	004	010
Radonell	016	---	---	016
Rathmore	014	Jeffery Paule gent	008	006
Shrucboe	036	John Pooer gent	---	036
Castlemore and Bankbeg	042	--- ---	---	042
P^{te} of Clonemore	006		---	006
Templeowne and Tulloebogg	057	Mounsieur Seymour gent	006	051
Coolmany	005	--- ---	003	002
Balliduffe	010	--- ---	002	008
Ballinekill	010		005	005
Rathvilie	077	Walter Murry & George Murry Esqr^s and James Atmoty gent	---	077
Walterstowne	013	Edebberd Sponeowes gent	006	007
(*folio* 5) Purtrashin	011	Lieu^t Ashworth gent	004	007

[1] *Rathvilie*, folios 4 & 5.

Townshippes	Number of People	Tituladoes Names	Eng	Irish
Williamstowne	004		—	004
Lisnevagh	014	John Korton gent	005	009
Tobinstowne	014	— —	004	010
Bonecerry				
Busherstowne	051	— —	008	043
Craneskough	020	— —	002	018

Principall Irish Names [and] Their Number.

Byrne & Ô Byrne, 025 ; Conor & McConor, 006 ; Cullen, 005 ; Doyle, 010 ; Duffe, 007 ; McHugh & Ô Hugh, 007 ; Kauenagh, 005 ; Lawler, 006 ; Murphy, 005 ; Nolan & Noland, 013 ; Neale, 009 ; Smith, 005.

(*folio 5 verso*)   Barrony of Rathvily : Eng, 176 ; Irish, 719 ; 895, Totall.

(*folio 6*).   **FORTH BARRONY.**

Townshippes	Number of People	Tituladoes Names	Eng	Irish
Knockbrack	022	Luke Byrne gent	—	022
Aghelare	022	Edmond Noland gent	—	022
Kilmalish	009	Hobbard Cooke gent	003	006
Ballamore	021	Garrott Wale gent	—	021
Capwater	004		—	004
Lisgarvin	006		—	006
Ullard	005		—	005
Rossley	013		—	013
Laragh	025	John Warren gent	002	023
Cappagh	016	—	—	016
Balligarrald	010	John Picton gent	004	006
Shragh	011	—	—	011
Ballour	007		—	007
Balla	002		—	002
Castlegrace	025	James Kauanagh gent	—	025
Ballilean	020	— —	—	020
Ballenvally	009	— —	—	009
Carrignislane	026	Richard Banistor gent	006	020
(*folio 7*) Ahad	004	— —	—	004
Kilbride	003	— —	—	003
Ballmunry	011	— —	—	011
Kilcoole	018	Seymour Wale gent	002	016

Towneshippes	Number of People	Tituladoes Names	Eng	Irish
Ardbyrne	009		—	009
Rathe :	006		—	006
Bondenstowne	019		—	019
Ardristan	036		004	032
Ballitrany	024	George Hartop gent	005	019
Graignespedog	014		004	010
Balliboggnelagh	002		002	—
Kilbracan	026		—	026
Graigenelugg	004		—	004
Ballinoge	012	John Nolan gent	—	012
Kilknock	041		005	036
Ravaren	014		—	014
Newtowne	017	Walter Byrne gent	—	017
(folio 8). Rahera	016	Walter Motley	—	016
Cranemore	006		—	006
Barragh	005		—	005
Kilbride	003		002	001
Newtowne	027	Will : Barnett gent, Emitt Barnett & Captn Graham gents	007	020
Knockiburd	013		—	013
Carrigduffe ⎫ Kilbrany ⎭	021	Charles Kauanagh gent	—	021

Principall Irish Names [and] their Number.

Byrne, 017 ; Bane, 006 ; Curren, 008 ; Doyle, 016 ; Henelan, 011 ; Kauanagh, 007 ; Murphy, 013 ; Nolan & Noland, 033 ; Neale, 007 ; Roe, 005.

(folio 8 verso)   Barrony of Forth : Eng, 046 ; Irish, 558 ; 604. totall.

(folio 9).   **IDRONE & ST. MOLINS BARRONIES**

Towneshippes	Number of People	Tituladoes Names	Eng	Irish
Cloughgrenan	040	Redmond Wale gent	—	040
Rahendoran	023	— —	—	023
Ballinebrana	051	Thomas Fitzgerrald gent	—	051
Crane and Tomard	102	Edward Harman Esqr and Will : Harman gent	004	098
Rathornan	063	— —	—	063
Old Laughlin	139	Thomas Boulton gent	009	130

Towneshippes	Number of People	Tituladoes Names	Eng	Irish
Gurtamore	011	—	—	011
Coolenekissey	060	—	—	060
Siskin	016	—	002	014
Balliknockan	064	—	004	060
Cloughrousk	004	—	—	004
Killinene	014	Ambrose Elton Esqʳ	005	009
Faranefreny				
& Cloughcoyle				
Wells				
Tinegarny	040	— —	002	038
Pheniscourt				
(*folio* 10) Cloughsutton	015	— —	—	015
Garribritt	019	Charles Brenan gent	—	019
Lauglinbridg	118	Miertagh Mora gent	022	096
Inch	012	Thomas Reynolds Tanner & gent	005	007
Ballineboly	025	— —	—	025
Oldtowne	014	Richard Norris gent	002	012
Orchard	021		—	021
Agha	044		—	044
Nurny	048		002	046
Balliryan	022		—	022
Cloneene	009		003	006
Ballidurtane	016	Henry Smithwick Esqʳ	002	014
Fenagh	020		—	020
Ballihubbub	002		—	002
Kilconor	017		008	009
Kilmalin	010		000	010
Ballibromwell	006		002	004
Kilgarran				
(*folio* 11). Lounelone	013		—	013
Rathelin	042	Tho : Burdett Esqʳ and Abraham Highmore gent	007	035
Rawhead	012	— —	—	012
Raduffe	022	Tirlagh Kavanagh gent	—	022
Ratheden	025		—	025
Dunleckney	039	John Corbett Esqʳ	002	037
Kilcarick	052	Morgan Byrne gent	004	048
Labomesrish	002	John Lacary gent	—	002
Garrihill	003		—	003
Knockneran	005	James Evers gent	—	005
Ballidaragh	002		002	—
Siskinraine	053	Thomas Freeman gent	002	051
Ballimone	012		002	010
Bally William Roe	018		—	018
Kildrina	022	Will : Welsh gent	—	022
Boheduffe	011		—	011

Towneshippes	Number of People	Tituladoes Names	Eng	Irish
(*folio* 12) Ballilaughan	044	James Fitzgerrald gent	—	044
Kilmalipoge	016	Morgan Byrne gent	—	016
Donore	025		005	020
Sleguffe	011		—	011
Kilcrott	028		—	028
Rath	030		—	030
Cloughmony	009		003	006
Kilgreny	017		—	017
Balliclontomy	036	John Byrne gent	—	036
Clowater	023	Donagh Doyle gent	002	021
Ballitegleagh	056		002	054
Danganbegg	024		003	021
Tamdarragh	045	Clement Ryan gent	—	045
Ballinehineene	037		—	037
Balliellin	034		2	032
Ballinesallagh	030	— —	—	030
Burres	105	Bryan Kavanagh Esqʳ	—	105
(*folio* 13). Lissalican	043	Symon Kauanagh gent	—	043
Balliline	016		—	016
Ballinegran	011		002	009
Glissane	012		—	012
Balliroan	008		—	008
Corenillane	016	Peirce Butler gent	002	014
Kilcolerem	010		002	008
Rahindoragh	006	Thomas Ewers gent	—	006
Rosdillicke	003	Thomas Eliott gent	—	003
Colnemara	032	Edward Fitzharris gent	---	032
Inchinphora	008	—	—	008
Knockeene	031	—	—	031
Cariglead	030	Garrott Kinselagh gent	—	030
Tinehinch	030	Jonathan Freind gent	004	026
Polmountie	012	Richard Shiner gent	004	008
Ballivan lower	018	Richard Kavanagh gent	---	018
Balliknock Crompane	009	—	—	009
(*folio* 14). Dromine	023		—	023
Dranagh	017		—	017
Timolin	004		—	004
Balliknockviccor	021		—	021
Kildovan	014	Nicholas Deuerax gent	—	014
Clonegan	031	Christopher Fitzgerrald gent	—	031
Coleroe	016		006	010
Monehenum	005		005	—
Leighan	012		—	012
Lean	002		---	002
Kilcarry	005		003	002
Rathnegera	009		—	009

Towneshippes	Number of People	Tituladoes Names	Eng	Irish
Tinecarrig	006		—	006
Bowhermore	010		—	010

Principall Irish Names [and] Their Number.

Bolger, 013 ; Byrne, 064 ; Brenan, 016 ; Bane, 011 ; Butler, 012 ; Curren, 022 ; Ô Clovan, 005 ; Doyle, 040 ; Daniell & McDan^ll, 014 ; Duffe, 012 ; Dillan, 006 ; McEdmond, 006 ; Foly, 010 ; Farrell, 007 ; Gehinn, 006 ; Hogan, 006 ; Ô Headen & Headen, 011 ; Ô Hugh & McHugh, 010 ; Hicky, 005 ; McJames, 005 ; Kenselagh, 014 ; Kauanagh, 039 ; McKeoghe, 005 ; Kelly, 017 ; Lenan, 013 ; Lawler, 011 ; Murry, 005 ; Moore, 010 ; Murphy, 061 ; Magher, 005 ; Nolan & Noland, 034 ; Neale & O Neale, 025 ; Poore, 007 ; Pendergras, 018 ; Roe, 010 ; Ryan, 031 ; McShane, 006 ; Tomin, 011 ; Walsh, 033.

(*folio* 14 *verso*).   Barronyes of Idrone & St Molins : Eng, 136 ; Irish, 2282 ; 2418, totall.

Barronyes	Pages	Eng	Irish	Total
Catherlagh Borough & Barony	2	395	1122	1517
Rathvily	5	176	0719	0895
Forth	8	046	0558	0604
Idrone and St Molins	14	136	2282	2418
		753	4681	5434

DUBLIN CITTY
8780

Parishes	Streets and Lanes &c	Numb's of People	Tituladoes Names	Eng	Irish
St Nicholas P'ish withing the Walls	Skinner Row	402	Ridyly Hatfield, John Preston, Esqrs ; Thomas Kickham, John Pitts, Nicholas Wilcox, Ralph Allen, Francis Harris, James Kelly, gentlemen ; Robert Kenedy, Phillipp Harris, Esqrs ; William Evers, James Steward gent, Sr Thomas Shurlog Kn^t, James his sonn gent Esqr, Theophilus Eton Esqr, Edmond Ramsey, John White, gentlemen ; Richard Kenny Esqr, Leut Henry Wade, Nicholas Knight gent, Thomas Broune, Ralph King, John Pin, Esqrs ; Thomas Floyd gent, Roger Bishopp Esqr, Thomas Storton ; Alderman Tho : Hookes, Esq^{rs}, Thomas Hookes gent, Nathainell Boyle Esqr, James Edkins, Edward Penteny gentle, Silvester Waight, John Bettin, and James Webb, M'chants.	324	078
(*folio* 2). St Andrews P'ish	Swanally	025	John Paine, Capt. Robert Hughs gent, Capt Claypoole, Christopher Palmer gent.	025	000
	Damaske Street	292	John Kithinyman, Robert Candit, Thomas Haydon gent, Mr Samuell Jones lodg^r, Captn Burt Lodger, The Lord Rainllow, Captn John Franklin, John Dodson, Stephen Buston gent, Sr John Temple Kn^t, John Temple Esqr, Henry Temple gent, Maior John Bligh Esqr, William Bligh gent, Capt. Graves, Samuell Drury, Thomas Pooly, John Walsh, William Wesby gentlemen ; Sr George Wenwell Kn^t, Sir Morris Uustice Knt, Mr Elward gent, Tho : Buckarton.	254	038
	St Georges Lane	133	Peter Synyres, Anthony Roe, Ralph Manney, John Crych, gentlemen ; Thomas Maule Esqr, Abraham Muckleborne, Cha : Lemond gent	105	028

Parishes	Streets and Lanes &c	Numb's of People	Tituladoes Names	Eng	Irish
(folio 3).	Trynity lane	018		013	005
	Colledge Greene	087	William Jones, Jeremy Watts, Francis Little Esq[r], Pierce Hast Capt, William Jones, John Boudler, Christopher Blackand, Doct[r] Robert Mould, Henry Jones, Richard Edwards, Cornett Merricke, Quartermas[r] Lloyd, M[r] Cox, Cap[t] Glover, Edward Gutch, gentlemen.	080	007
	Lazy Hill	237	Cap[t] Rich, Cap[t] John Nicholls gent.	180	057
S[t] Patrick P'ish	Francis Street	813	Thomas Whitgrove Esq[r], Robert Arundall gent, William Taylor Esq[r], Capt. Phillpot Esq[r], Alderman John Cranwell Esq, Capt[n] Derbon.	577	236
St Brides P'ish	St Brides &c	286	Leut Coll Warren, Capt[n] Francis Shane, Thomas Foules Esq[rs], Cornett Jefford, Isaack Collier, John Pinson, M[r] Debart gentlemen, Coll Barrow Esq[r], Capt[n] Thomas Poope, M[r] Richard, John Archer gentlemen John Browne M'chant, Richard Ward gent, M[r] Dauson Esq[r], John his sonn gent, Marshall Peake Esq[r], Capt[n] Early, Capt. Shaw Esq[r], M[r] Richt gent, M[r] Markham Esq, Leut W[m] Dason Inkeeper, Robert Seaman gent/George Maxwell, Josias Debart, Capt. Potter, Walter Potter his sonn gentlemen, James Moroly Esq, M[r] Clarke, Leut Lecora.	232	054
(folio 4)	Sheeps Street	116	Salt' Corey, Capt[n] Playford, Robert Broune gentlemen, The Lady Phillipps, Robert hir son, Roger Glascord, Gryffen Borden, gentle-, men; Henry Sancky Esq[r], George King, James Founbaine, Leut Wright, Arthur Padmore, Silvanus Stryny, Arthur Padmore, John Joakes, gentlemen; Robert Hughs, William Seden, John Staughton, Robert Beal-	097	019

Parishes	Streets and Lanes &c	Numb's of People	Tituladoes Names	Eng	Irish
	Golden Lane	078	ing, gentlemen ; Mr Barnes lodger, The Lord Anger, James Cuff Esqr. Capt. Rob't Newman, Patricke Talant gent, Ralph Coleman Bruer, Cornet Roney, Nicholas Combes, gentlemen ; Captⁿ Able Warren Esqr, Leut Robert Newman, Phillipp Alding, Mr Moynes, Captⁿ Pritchet, & Mr Benson, gentlemen.	055	023
(folio 5).	Stevens Street	110	Thomas Ob, Mr Bridges, Thomas Warren, John Warren his son, Thomas Walton, John Thornton, Edmond Gouge, Mr Jeffery, John Guiy gentlemen, John Moore, Esqr, John Avery gent, Thomas Tacker Esqr, Leut Cotton, Richard Bennett gent, Edward Roberts Esqr, Cornett Burton, John Assin gent, Leut Coll. Arnop Esqr.	092	018
Ringsend and the liberties thereof	Chequer Lane	142	Thomas Holford, William Holford, George Dixson, William Dores, Samuell Foxwich, John Harington, John Bryan, John Cliff, Richard Stanton and Robert Hall, gentlemen.	105	037
	Ringsend	080	—	59	021
	Irishtowne	098	Oliver Lord Fitzwilliams, William Fitzwilliams Esq,	023	075
	Simonscourt	022	—	007	015
	Donibrooke	013	—	004	009
	Baggatroth	032	—	003	029
(folio 6). St Johns P'ish	Fishamble Street, parte	300	John Sheapheard gent, James Barlowe M'chant, Richard Blundell gent, Arthur Usher Merchant, Edmond Duff Esqr Lodger, The Lady Crosby, Alderman Weston.	275	025
	Wine Taverne Streete	230	Andrew Lord M'chant, Richard Palfery gent, Jeremiah Berstow Merchant, William Taylor Merchant, John Fitzgerald gent, Adam Gould Merchant, James Gould gent, Alderman Daniell	187	043

Parishes	Streets and Lanes &c	Numb's of People	Tituladoes Name	Eng	Irish
(*folio* 7).	Wood Key Ward	374	Hutchinson, Mathew Farley gent, Leut Coll Hookes Esqr, William Harrison gent, Robert Marshall gent, Henry Markam gent, Francis Dudly gent, Joseph Banks gent, Humphry Withams gent, Tobias Bennell gent a lodger, John Boulton Merchant, Leut Pontoney a lodger. Thomas Summars gent, Thomas Howard Merchant, Nicholas Amansham gent, John Maddin Esqr, William Martin Bruar, William Hill merchant, Vallentine Cooke gent, Alderman William Smyth, Thomas Poole gent, Thomas Fulton Merchant, John Hanway gent, Thomas Kay gent, Thomas Robotham gent, Robert Wade bruar, Doct^r Dudly Loftus Esqr, Thomas Boyd Merchant, Henry Lewis gent, Jeffery Toulson gent, Samuell Bonole gent, William Harborne gent, Christopher Leuett Merchant, Joseph Whitchurch Merchant, Einor Tuinon Merchant, Humphry Jervice Merchant, Edward Aghwell gent, John Price Sheryff, Ezekcell Larkan Merchant.	322	052
(*folio* 8). St Warbroughs P'ish	Castle Street	214	Alderman Daniell Bellingham, John Fletcher gent, Samuell Doughty gent, William Shelton gent, John North gent, Anthony Derry gent, George Stoughton gent, Richard Harvy Esqr, Edward Wallis Esqr, Christophert Hart gent, George St George Esqr, William North gent, Rigmould Wamought gent, Gregory Lambart gent, John Tonstall gent, Horatio Bonoily gent, Joseph Stoakes gent, Tobias Wetherall gent, Andrew Moory gent, Samuell Peepes	202	012

Parishes	Streets and Lanes &c	Numb's of People	Tituladoes Names	Eng	Irish
(folio 9).			Esq, John Hughs Esq, Edward Swan gent, Sr James Ware Kn^t, James Ware Esq, Robert Ware gent, John Brampton gent,/ Richard Phillipps Esqr, Thomas Caulfield gent, John Broun gent, Nicholas Ware gent, John Bushell gent, Robert Bathripp gent, Richard Martin gent, Esqr Robert Woods gent, Doct^r Gerry Esq, Coll Long Esq, Doct^r Waterhouse Esq, John Bisse Esqr, William Tichborne Esq, Samuell Bathurst gentle, Even Vaughan gent, Richard Wilson gent, Robert Cooke Esqr, Robert Symons gent, Richard Butler gent, John Pony Esq.		
(folio 10).	Pte of Copper Alley	034	Thomas Bale gent, Samuell Kett gent, Richard Picknall gent, John Wallis gent, Charles Wainman Esq, Robert Ekin gent, Charles Butler gent, John Flemming gent, Robert Yates gent.	029	005
(folio 11).	Part of St Warbroughs Streete	124	Thomas Sheapherd gent, Thomas Haughton gent, Nicholas Harman gent, Cornet Stanley gent, John Hooker gent, Coll Knight Esq, Thomas Lewis gent, Mathew Forth gent, John Gay gent, James Polexfield Esq, James Polexfield gent, John Polexfield gent, William Robert gent, James Yates gent, Robert Shipcott Esq,/Thomas Harnet gent, Henry Herbert Esq, Wadhine Sands gent, Henry Rawlingson gent, Sr Tho : Herbert Knt, — Alexander Junior gent, Chidly Coote Esq, John Harson gent.	110	014
	Lenthrops Ally	055	William Kenedy gent	040	015
	St John Hoys Ally	019	Jerome Allexander Esq	002	017
	Fishamble Street Pte	015	Mathew Nulty gent. Jn Barker gent.	014	001

Parishes	Streets and Lanes &c	Numb's of People	Tituladoes Names	Eng	Irish
(*folio* 12). St War-broug Parish	St Warbroughs Street	316	Quartermastr Stanly gent, Ralph Whetlock gent, Richard Webb gent, William Lane gent, Edward Burrowes gent, Jonas Lee gent, Richard Crofton gent, Henry Keating gent, William Hill gent, Robert Johnson gent, William Dixson Esq, Doctr Alwoodhouse Esq, Enoch Rider gent, Pp Hasselham gent, Corporall Stiles gent, Jn Norton gent, Sr Charles Coote Kt & Bart, William Sherding gent, Hen : Bollard Esq, Roger Bould gent, Rich : Young gent, Tho : Hooke gent, Isaack John gent, Tho : Reynolds gents, Jn Thornton gent, Sampson Toogood gent, Robert Cadwell gent, Samuel Cotton gent, Nathaniell Fookes gent, Robert Thornton gent, Thomas Parnall gent, Hugh Price Esqr, Robert Theswell gent, John Bush gent, Sr Oliver St George Knt William Hill gent, Cary Dillon Esq, William Bladen Esq, Humphry Poudyhard gent, Hugh Clotworthy Esq, Lewis Fallard Esq, William Stephenson gent, Samuell Nicholas gent, John Branham gent, Richard Haydon gent, Mathew Langdale.	274	042
(*folio* 13) St War-brough Parishes	pte of Corke Hill	021	Garrott Weldon gent	020	001
	Part of Copper Ally	035	Edward Wayman gent, Nicholas Fountaine Esqr, Thomas Dent gent, William Diggs gent.	028	007
	Globe Ally	013	William Butler gent, Dudly Loftus gent, Timothy Grolliax gent, Richard Reeues Esq.	011	002
(*folio* 14). St Audians Parish	Bridge St	257	Alderman John Forrest, Patrick Arthur gent, Thomas Springham M'chant, Alderman George Gilbert, Peter Lesaw gent, Francis Stanford M'chant, Nathaniell Palmer distiller, Symon Caricke	199	058

Parishes	Streets and Lanes &c	Numb's of People	Tituladoes Names	Eng	Irish
			Merchant, James Cleare Merchant, John Cooke Merchant, Peter Travers Merchant, Alderman John Desmineers M'chant Esq', Thomas Freeman Merchant, William Barrow Merchant, Alderman Peter Waybrent Merchant, Lewis Desmineer Merchant, James Ashly Merchant, S' W'" Usher Usher Kt, Mathew Magg gent, David Conly M'chant, Derrick Westinra Marchant, Geo : Dowdall M'chant, Paul Cadmore gent, William Deane gent, Waren Westenra Mc', Robert Goulborne gent, Albertus Crostenton gent, Audly Mervin Esq, M' Morgan Lawyer, John Sergeant M'chant, Robert Dee Esq', Mayor William Summer gent, Allen Jones gent.		
	Sippers lane	005		005	—
	Cooke Street	181	Nicholas Gorman Merchant, Abraham Clemens Merchant, William Hopkins gent, Robert Ardogh gent, Patrick Mapes gent, James White gent, John Hodges gent, John Cardyff gent, William Bragg gent, William Plunket gent, Valentine Savadge gent.	100	81
(folio 15). S' Audians Parish	Corn Markett	215	William Plunkett gent, Richard Ward Distiller, James Ustace gent, Edmond Clere Mchant, John Dutton Mercht, William Fulham Mcht, Paul Delasale Mcht, William Harvy gent, Dominick White Mc', Sam" Saltinsball Merc', Richard Berford Esq, John Salmon Merct, Jn Bollard Apothicary.	134	081
	Pte of High Stret	024	Tho : Johnson Merct, M' Browne gent, Doctor Robert Talbot, Rich : Clarke Apothicary	019	005
	Back Lane P'	014	Rich : Muncke gent	014	
	More of High Street	087	Dot Morgan Smyth, William Kerke Merchant, John Champines	077	010

Parishes	Streets and Lanes &c	Numb's of People	Tituladoes Names	Eng	Irish
	Kysars lane	056	Mchant, Philipp Costleloe Shop Keeper, William Cramby Mct. Regnell Ball gent Ephram Hardy gent	045	011
(*folio* 16). St Michells Parish.	High Streete	274	Mynard Christian Mctt, William Whitihell Mc^tt, Doctr Fennell lodgur, William Brooking Mc^tt, James Wade Apothicary, John Knot clothier, Samuell Chandler Mc^tt, Capt Robert Locke, Thomas Whitmore gent, Sr Robert Ford Knt, John˜ Smyth Merchant, Thomas Kenedy gent, Joshua Rawlinson Mc^tt, Mathew French merchant, Stephen Butler Esq, Alderman Marke Quinn, Geo: Fisher Shopkeeper, Francis Harvy Esq, Alderman Kenedy, Thomas Brett gent, Alderman Cooke, Henry Reynolds gent, Rich: Millinton Merchant, Coll Owens, (*more tituladoes names*), Judge Whaly, Capt Chambers, Capt Chambers, Barnard Wizard, John Foxall Merchant.	220	054
(*folio* 17).	St Michells lane	120	Thomas Hutchinson gent, Mr Mortomer Esq, Henry Martin Attorny	092	028
	Cork Hill pte	027	— — —	024	003
	Christs Church Lane	047	James Galbelly gent James Jones gent	039	008
	Scoole house lane	021	Thomas Richardson Esq	016	005
	Cooke Street	086	Mr Young gent, William Howard M'chant, Edward Barrytt Grocer, Richard Price gent.	068	018
	Rose Mary lane	018	John Sergent Merchant	012	006
	Merchants Key	049	John Hankshaw Merchant, Mathew Barry Esq, Gerrald Fay gent, Daniell Wybrant Merchant, John Beuchamp Merchant, Maior Brighness gent, Mr Lecch Merchant.	043	006
(*folio* 18).	Skippers Lane	036	Mr Bruister gent, Timothy Miller gent, John Kelly gent, John Bygins Phis'.	026	010

Parishes	Streets and Lanes &c	Numb's of People	Tituladoes Names	Eng	Irish
St Kathrines Parish

(folio 19). | | 1356 | Luke Lowther gent, Richard Heynham gent, Owen Jones gent, Ralph Wallis gent, Tobias Creamer gent, John Fryer gent, Tho : Worship Esq, Tristram Thornton gent, Ralph Rosengrane gent, John Workman gent, Ralph Vizard Esq, Edward Earle of Meath, Richard Green gent, Doctr Smyth Esq, Peter Lockard gent, Giles Mee gent, John Eastwood gent, Christopher Bennett gent, William Lecchfield gent, Tho : Clarke gent, Jer Skelton Esqr, Wm Phillipps gent, Aldermant Hunt, Robt Ludlow Esq, Robt Harding Esq, Edw : Brabzon Esq, Jn Hughs Secretary, Tho : Dungan Esq, John Cole gent, Tho : Shaw gent, his sonn Henry, his sonn Thomas, Theophilus Sandford Esq,/Rich : Tyth Esq, Joshua Allen gent, James Mollenex Esq, Patrick Allen gent, Robert Allen his sonn gent, Thomas Powell gent, Thomas Butler gent, William Goragh gent, Henry Spranger gent, Thomas Quirke gent, James Relick gent, Richard Stiles gent, John Pennington Esq, Marke Cheswright gent, Thomas Cooke gent, Thomas Waterhouse Esq, Hugh Roberts gent, Tho : Hoult gent, Robert Wasbery gent, Robert Archer gent, Tho : Dromgold gent, Edward Chambers gent, Tho : Navill gent, John Kelly gent, Sr Robt Newcoment Knt and Bar^t, Robert Wade gent, James Browne gent, Joseph Dobson gent, Hen : Verscoyle gent, Abram Rigg gent. | 970 | 386 |
| (folio 20). St Michans Parish | | 095 | John Kelly Merchant, Thomas Cole M'chant, Robert Mercer | 048 | 047 |

Parishes	Streets and Lanes &c	Numb's of People	Tituladoes Names	Eng	Irish
	Church Street	362	Merchant, Robert Reeues clarke, Ralph Hartney gent, James Stopford Esq, Randall Becket Esq, William Sands Esq, Sr James Barry K^t, Rich: Barry Esq, Stephen Butler Esq, Coll Hen: Flower, Edward Short Esq, William Blackwell Esq, John Southy Esq, William Sands gent.	179	183
(folio 21).	Hangmans Lane	242	Maior William Meredeth Esq, John Brookes Vintner, Tho: Orr Shopkeeper, Henry Orson shopkeeper, Edward Michell Shopkeeper, Tho: Dowding Merchant, William Allen Shopkeeper, Bartholomew Hodser Shop K^r, Robert his sonn, Obediah Bradshaw Shop Keeper, Will' Peachen Merchant, James Boyle Merchant, Rich: Cleabear Merchant, George Clapham gent, Adam Darling, Doct^r Garner, Mr Francis gent, Geo: Prigget Esq, Capt Francis Spence gent.	158	084
	The Abby	258	Alderman Will: Cuff, Felix Birne gent, Bartholomew Lynacar Maulster, Daniell Doyle Merchant, Charles Coote Esq, Charles Meredith Esq, Tho: Doude gent, Wm Thwaits Malster, Wm Hodgkins gent, Ralph Barker gent, Rich: Barret Esqr, Richard Owens gent, Sr Paul Davis Knt, Edward Temple Esq, Sr Robert Meredith Knt, Geo: Carr Esq, Tho: Carre gent, William Carr gent, Tho: Seagrave Esq, Lawrence Thornton gent.	167	091
			Christopher Curren gent, Dan^{ll} Hickson gent, James Barnwall gent, Arthur Chichester Esq, Thomas Taylor gent, William Hatter gent, Edmond Tottericke gent, William Lawles Maulstr, John Bridges Esq, Jo: Doughty		

Parishes	Streets and Lanes &c	Numb's of People	Tituladoes Names	Eng	Irish
(folio 22).			Esq, Sr Arthur Morgan K^t, Sr Hen : Tichborne K^t, John Cole Esq, Edmond Lucas gent, Geo : Crosby Esq, Henry Steele Maulster, Markes Mould Esq.		
	The Greene	031	Thomas Mason Esq	008	023
	Phipps Parke	008		008	000
	Bull Lane	167	Geo : Charlton Esq, Capt Edmond Tomlins Esqr.	033	134
	Little Gaberagh	010	Sr Jeremiah Sankey Knt, Mr Herbert Esq.	006	004

Principall Irish Names [and] Their Numb[er].

Allen & McAllen, 014 ; McAdam &c, 006 ; Boyle, 006 ; Butler, 010 ; Birne, 039 ; Brin, 005 ; Bryan, 013 ; Barry, 008 ; Browne, 019 ; Bourke, 005 ; Casy, 006 ; Cavenagh, 012 ; Carroll, 005 ; Connor, 008 ; Callin & Cullin, 006 ; Clarke, 011 ; Davis, 013 ; Doyle, 020 ; Doly &c, 008 ; Duff, 008 ; McDaniell, 007 ; Flemming, 008 ; Farrell, 005 ; Fullam, 08 ; Fitzgerald, 04 ; Garrett, 05 ; McGloyre, 06 ; Hughs, 09 ; Kernan, 06 ; Kenedy, 09 ; Kelly, 16 ; Martin, 08 ; Mallone, 07 ; Moore, 09 ; Murphy, 10 ; Nowland, 17 ; Neale, 13 ; Roe, 07 ; Reyly, 10 ; Smyth, 23 ; Toole, 06 ; Welsh, 19 ; White, 15.

(folio 22 verso)

The Number of all ye People withing each Parish—Vid	City of Dublin &c People	Eng	Irish
St Nicholas	0402	0324	0078
St Andrewes	0792	0657	0135
St Patricks	0813	0577	0236
St Brides	0732	0581	0151
Ringsend &c	0245	0096	0149
St Johns	0904	0784	0120
St Warbroughs	0846	0730	0116
St Audians	0839	0593	0246
St Michells	0678	0540	0138
St Kathrines	1356	0970	0386
St Michans	1173	0607	0566
Numb. of all	8780	6459	2321

COUNTY OF DUBLIN
17047

(folio 1). **BARONYS OF NEWCASTLE AND UPPERCROSSE**

Parishes	Places	Numb's of People	Tituladoes Names	English	Irish
Tallaght	Tallaght	129	Francis Parsons Esq Thomas Toye gent	40	89
	Ouldtowne	67	Rowland Bulkley gent	6	61
	Newhall	3	—	2	1
	Killeninge or Killenenny	53	Gabriell Briscoe gent Charles Cottle gent	21	32
	Frierstown	7		2	5
	Killenardar	14		5	9
	Glasnamuckye	69		3	66
	Tymen	20	Nicholas Kealy gent	1	19
	Corballyes	58	John Denn gent	6	52
	Newland	9		3	6
	Cookestowne	2		—	2
	Belgard	18		7	11
	Kylnemanagh	33	Robert Hawkins gent	5	28
	Gittons	2		0	2
	Knocklyne	19		9	10
	Ballynescorney	28	Joseph Avory Esqr	9	19
	Ouldcourt	46	Robert Pott gent	7	39
	Temploge	42	Darby Burgoyne gent Roger Brerton Esq	6	36
(folio 2).	Carranstowne	11			11
	Kiltallonen	16		6	10
	Jobstowne	27		4	23
Clandalkan	Dromnagh	56		3	53
	Robinhood	8		7	1
	Fox and geese	8		3	5
	Burnt House	4		2	2
	Ballymount	21		5	16
	Killbride	19	Francis Carbery gent	2	17
	Baldonane	3		0	3
	Ballycheevers	28		2	26
	Corkath	17		—	17
	Clandalkin	89	John Foye gent	8	81
	Nealstowne	11		2	9
	Deane Rath	23		—	23
	Grange	18		3	15
	Collenstowne	10		4	6
	Nangor	7	William Greene gent	2	5
	Blundelstowne	9		2	7
(folio 3). Clandalkan	Clutterland	4			4
	Ballybane	18		3	15
Rathfarnum Whitechurch and Crevah	Rathfarnum	39	Sr Adam Loftus Knt Adam Loftus Esq Robert Loftus gent Mathew Penoyx gent George Hopkins Esq	23	16

Parishes	Places	Numb's of People	Tituladoes Names	English	Irish
	Staughtons fram	10	Daniell Readeinge gent	6	4
	Ballytoudine	6	Edward Gryffith gent	2	4
	Rathgarr	11	Robert Cusack Esq John Cusack gent	4	7
	Tirrenure Cacnadye and Burchersheas	13	Maior Ellott Esq	6	7
	Tirenure	10		2	8
	The long House Pte of Tirenure	9		3	6
	Little Newtown	7	Lawrence Hudson gent	4	3
	Butterfield	17		1	16
	The old orchard	25		2	23
	Schellerstowne	13		7	6
	Harrolds Grang	21		5	16
	Kilmacheoge	22		3	19
(folio 4). Rathfarnum, Whitchurch and Crevah	Crevah, Tibrodan and Jamesland	37		9	28
	James land	2		—	2
	Great Newtowne	28	Samuell Browne gent	13	15
	Woodtowne	27		3	24
	Edmondstowne	11		—	11
	Killakee	21		2	19
Rathcoole	Rathcoole	153	Moses Reyly gent John Robinson gent James Wilson Portreue	30	123
	Ratchedan	29	Richard Harvey gent Symon Harvey his sonn	8	21
Sagard	Calliaghtowne	12	Hermon Miller gent a Foreigner	4	8
	Sagard	76		18	58
	Newtowne	77		7	70
	Colemyne	8		4	4
Ballymore Eustace and Tipperkeavin	Ballymore Eustace	132		22	110
	Dowdenstowne	15		12	3
(folio 5):	Barrettstowne	27	John Graydon gent	7	20
	Tipperkeavan	8		3	5
	Elverstowne	9		3	6
	Killmalumme	5			5
Ballybought	Ballybought	68		9	59
	Silverhill	11		8	3
	Tubber	33		2	31
	Ardinoade	28		7	21
Donlovan	Donlovan	31	Richard Buckley Esq	6	25

Parishes	Places	Numb's of People	Tituladoes Names	English	Irish
	Milltowne	20		8	12
	Logatinnigh	3		0	3
	Tornaat	15		6	9
Newcastle	Tobbar bride	12			12
	Benshee	10		4	6
	Kiltome	3		2	1
	Athgoe	27		—	27
	Colemanstowne	24		—	24
	Newcastle	115	Robert Scarborrough gent Morgan Jones gent	21	94
	Colganstowne	17	John Smyth gent	7	10
(folio 6).	Hasill hast	12		---	12
	Loghtowne	16	William Clinch gent	—	16
Kilmalway	Kilmatalway	17		2	15
	Miltowne	24		2	22
	Galroestowne	10		—	10
	Teddanstowne	18		—	18
	Backestowne	20		6	14
Lucan	Lucan	88	Arthur Usher Esq Sr Theophylus Jones Knt	15	73
	Nespelstowne	31	Edward Harrington gent	12	19
	Larecorr	4		3	1
	St Katherins	7		5	2
Esker	Esker	21		6	15
	Ballydowde	26	Henry Burton Esq	4	22
	Ballyowen	30	Francis Peasley Esq Francis Vaughan gent	5	25
	Tinstowne	18	Edward Cooke gent	6	12
	Rowlagh	25		—	25
	Kishocke	13	Nathaniell Stoughton gent	4	9
(folio 7).	Balgaddy	9		—	9
Palmerstowne	Irishtowne	26	Thomas Vincent Esq	14	12
	Palmerstowne	83		24	59
Ballyfarmott	Ballyfarmott	53	Huibart Adryan Aldr	16	37
	Gallenstowne	27		5	22
	Bolyhouse	10		—	10
Cromlyn	Cromlyn	122	John Blackwell Esq Richard Cowse gent Allexander Usher gent William Purcell gent Ignatius his sonn	18	104
Kilmayneham	Newtowne	16	Captn Roger Beame Esq	6	10
	Inchiguore	8		3	5
	Island Bridge	26		10	16
	Kilmayneham	130	Richard Raynor gent	60	70
	Dolphins barn	31		17	14
Dalkey	Dalkey	44	Capt Richard Newcomen Esq	3	41

Parishes	Places	Numb's of People	Tituladoes Names	Eng- lish	Irish
(*folio* 8). St Keavans	Ballintlea	6			6
		154	Phillipp Fearnely Esq	91	63
	Butterlane	92	John Borr Marchant Esq, Beg- net Borr gent, Jacob Borr gent Forrenner, Cornelius Borr D^r of Physick Esq, Walter Brice gent, Davie Williams gent, Vallentine Dawkins gent, William Williams gent.	63	29
	Milltowne	19		14	5
St Patricks Close	Rathmynes	12	William Shore Esq	6	6
		329	Captⁿ John Smyth Esq, Owen Ellis gent, Walter Clay mar- shall gent, Edmond Bradshaw Merc, John Hughes gent, Jaques Vanderpuer Merchant and Forrenner, Maior Joseph Dean Esq, Robert Brady gent, John Prinn Merchant, Thomas Chabner gent, Adam Foester Merchant, Francis Spring Bruer, Doct^r John Foy Esq, Edward Bryscoe Merchant, John Wyburne gent, Maior Edward Warren Esq.	202	127
(*folio* 9).	Newstreet Ward	390	Thomas Talbott gentl, Edward Bather gent, James Lynsey gent, Peter Ward gent, William Hollaway, John Webber gent, John Rawlinson Marchant, John King gent, John Watson M'chant.	255	135
	The Liberty of Donower	416	William Sterling gent Captⁿ William Cox Esq.	293	123

Principall Irish Names [and] Their Numb[er].

Birne, 86 ; Boorke, 9 ; Bryan, 17 ; Burne, 8 ; Browne Eng & Irish, 24 ; Carroll, 6 ; Connor, 14 ; Doweing, 7 ; Davis English and Irish, 19 ; Doyle, 48 ; Dunn, 18 ; Ennis and Ennos, 16 ; Donell and McDonell, 8 ; Daniell and McDaniell, 13 ; Farrell, 19 ; Gormly, 8 ; Fitzgerrold, 6 ; Kelly, 34 ; Keavanagh or Cavanagh, 24 ; Kearovan and Kearogan. 13 : Kenedy, 8 ; Lawler &c, 16 ; Lawces, 10 ; Malone, 12 ; Murphy, 30 ; Moore, 13 ; Morran, 7 ; Martine, 7 ; Neale and Ô Neale, 20 ; Nowland or Nowlane, 30 ; Plunkett, 8 ; Quinn, 8 ; Roe, 10 ; Realy, 10 ; Smyth, 16 ; Toole, 12 ; Williams E[n]glish and Irish, 12 ; Walsh, 16.

olio 9 *verso*) The Number of People in Ye Baronyes of Newcastle & Uppercross : Eng, 1635 ; Irish, 3043 ; Totall Eng and Irish, 4678.

(folio 10). **BARONY OF RATHDOWNE**

Parishes	Places	Numbs of People	Tituladoes Names	English	Irish
	Shangannagh	74		11	63
	Shankill	40	Evan Vaughan gent	7	33
	Rathmichall	3		2	1
	Mullenestillan	12		—	12
	Promstowne	10		—	10
	BallyForeish	11		6	5
	Connagh	77	Edward Billinsley gent	10	67
	Little Bray	26		11	15
	Ballymon	37	Henry Burnett gent	6	31
	Clunamuck	13		—	13
	Tick Mickie	3		—	3
	Loughanstowne	19		5	14
	Carrickmayne	59		5	54
	Brenanstowne	18	Valentine Wood gent	4	14
	Kilbobban	37	Docr John Harding Esq Anthony Straughton gent William Straughton his sonn	27	10
	Jamestowne	21		18	3
	Glancullan	9		—	9
	Kilternan	14		2	12
(folio 11).	Liapardstowne	21	James Woolverston gent	12	9
	Balacoly	18		7	11
	Dondrom	47	Isaac Dobson Esq	14	33
	Titnocke	15		—	15
	Churchtowne	7		2	5
	Molhyanstowne	18		7	11
	Rabucke and Owens-towne	30	William Manly gent	5	25
	Rabucke	19		2	17
	Symonscourt	10		5	5
	Stillorgan	38	Henry Joanes Esq Owen Joanes gentt	13	25
	Kilmarcadd	13		11	2
	Little Newtowne	2		—	2
	Booterstowne	41			41
	Mounk towne	64	Edmond Lodlowe Esq	11	53
	Newtowne one the Strand	14		2	12
	Rochestowne	5			5
	Ballincley	3			3
(folio 12).	Cornelstowne	32	William Morgan gent	5	27
	Deans graunge	69	Raphell Swinfeild gent	8	61
	Kill of Ye grange	15		3	12
	Bullocke	110		15	95
	Loughlinstowne	72	John Lambart gent	8	64
	Loughanstowne	6			6

Principall Irish Names [and] their Numb[er].

Birne, 28 ; Cavenah, 12 ; Callen and Cullan, 10 ; Doyle, 29 ; Farrall, 8 ; Kelly, 12 ; Moore, 7 ; Morphy, 12 ; Neale, 6 ; Nowland, 6 ; Toole, 11 ; Walsh, 11.

(*folio 12 verso*).   The Number of People in Ye Barony of Rathdowne : Eng, 244 ; Irish, 908 ; totall Eng and Irish, 1152.

(*folio 13*).   **BARONY OF NEITHERCROSS**

Parishes	Places	Numbs of People	Tituladoes Names	English	Irish
Luske	Luske	140	James Woods gent Nicholas Brimingham gent	41	99
	Balmagwire	3	— — —	—	3
	Terrellstowne	5	Thomas St Lawrence gent	1	4
	Collinstowne	12	John Smyth gent	8	4
	Rainconey	21		2	19
	Newhaggard	15		5	10
	Parsonage	7		3	4
	Rahany	10		2	8
	Ballogh	32	Samuell Walshman gent Richard Triar gent	22	10
	Ballakerstowne	10	— —	2	8
	Texmercgin	7		4	3
	Court Duff	15		—	15
	Rogerstowne	23		—	23
	Knockdromyn	6		2	4
	Great Roans	8		6	2
	Little Roans	6		1	5
	Thomond	2		—	2
	Walshtowne	14		—	14
	Newell	16		5	11
	Parnellstowne	8		3	5
(*folio 14*).	Wimbleton	15		—	15
	Murderye	12		2	10
	Knightstowne	12		3	9
	Johnstowne	14		5	9
Portrarne	Portrarne	76	Thomas Jones gent	2	74
	Beverstowne	16		—	16
	Balliske	23		2	21
	Ballileas	11		3	8
	Balmaston	4			4
	Lambay	9			9
Clonmedane	Feildstowne	47		3	44
	Roulestowne	41		—	41
	Clonmeathan	12		5	7
	Killeene	7			7

Parishes	Places	Numbs of People	Tituladoes Names	English	Irish
	Cabragh	5			5
	Oldtowne	28		2	26
	Cottresktowne	9		4	5
	Moorestowne	18		2	16
	Wyanstowne	13	Oliver Barnewall gent	2	11
(*folio* 15).	Newminges	7		—	7
	Jordanstowne	19		3	16
	Worganstowne or Morganstowne }	14			14
Swords	Baldergane	19			19
	Brownstowne	8		4	4
	Little Bealing towne	7		2	5
	Cookestowne	4			4
	Duinstowne	31		3	28
	Magilstowne	18		3	15
	Great Bealings towne	35		2	33
	Gillianstowne	3		2	1
	Balhary	34	Peter Russell gent	2	32
	Skiddowe	49	Thomas White gent	—	49
	Rath	8			8
	Balcurtry	8			8
	Braspott	4			4
	Lispopell	36	John Arthur gent	6	30
	Roganstowne	8			8
	Little Roganston	3		2	1
(*folio* 16).	Tonlegeeth	3		—	3
	Balstibbocke	2		2	—
	Rickenhoare	44		9	35
	Saucerstowne	14		3	11
	Leas	9			9
	Rabeale	16	Walter Plunkett Esq John Wakefield gent	4	12
	Barbistowne	18		—	18
	Balmadraught	32	Andrew Delahoyd gent	5	27
	Great Leffenhall	37		6	31
	Swords	239	Clement Daniell gent, Robert Haward gent, John Locke gent, William Horish gent, Robert Smyth gent, Thomas Dancer Esq.	47	192
	Seatowne	17		—	17
	Newtowne	8		—	8
	Furrowes	34	James Donnellan Esq John Forth Esq	4	30
	Marshallstowne	10		2	8
	Nevenstowne	2		2	0
	Mooretowne	25		4	21

Parishes	Places	Numbs of People	Tituladoes Names	English	Irish
(*folio* 17).	Forsterstowne	11			11
Finglass	Finglas	92	Thomas Springham gent Thomas Taylor gent Nicholas Luttrell gent Thomas Richardson Esq	36	56
	Cabragh	7		3	4
	Finglas Wood	25	John Sedgraue Esq Patrick Sedgraue gent	2	23
	Finglas Bridge	15		2	13
	Jamestowne	18		3	15
	Kilshawe	27		2	25
	Ballygaats	11		5	6
	Skesuble	4			4
	Tobberbarr	10			10
	Braghan	4		2	2
	Balseskin	6		2	4
	Kildonan	4		2	2

Principal Irish Names [and] their Numb[er]

Birne, 13 ; Brimingham, 12 ; Butterly, 8 ; Connor, 10 ; Casey, 10 ; Coleman, 9 ; Doyle, 8 ; Daly, 10 ; Dowdall, 9 ; Daniell & Donell, 12 ; Kelly, 36 ; Lennan, 7 ; Lynch and Lynchy, 10 ; Maccan, 10 ; Murrey, 9 ; Quinne, 11 ; Reyly, 9 ; Ryan, 11 ; Walsh, 19 ; White, 12.

(*folio* 17 *verso*)   The Number of People in the Barony of Neithercross : Eng, 318 ; Irish, 1473 ; Totall Eng and Irish, 1791.

(*folio* 18).   **BARONY OF BALROTHERY.**

Parishes	Places	Numbs of People	Balrothery Tituladoes Names	English	Irish
Balrodery	Knockingen	10		2	8
	Newhaven	34		—	34
	Bremoore	42		3	39
	Tankardstowne	7		2	5
	Cloghrodery	2			2
	Flemingtowne	3			3
	Great Fowkstowne	7		2	5
	Little Fowkestowne	7			7
	Ballemadd	23		5	18
	Ardgillam	2		—	2
	Kilmanham	3		3	—

Parishes	Places	Numbs of People	Balrothery Tituladoes Names	English	Irish
	Balbriggan	30		4	26
	Stephentowne	6		3	3
	Balrothery	68		20	48
	Stephephenstowne	14		3	11
	Knock	7		3	4
	Killelane	13		1	12
	Davistowne	4			4
	Curtlagh	25			25
(*folio* 19). Balscaddan	Tobbertowne	30		3	27
	Balscaddan	50		4	46
	Tobbersoole	22		3	19
	Newtowne of Balscaddan	10			10
	Milestowne	5		2	3
	Whitestowne	6		2	4
	Tubberskeakin	3		1	2
	Haystowne	8		4	4
	Malt	11	John Caddle gent		11
	Ringe	7			7
	The Graunge of Bascaddan	15			15
	Dermottstowne	10			10
	Killogher	13		4	9
East and West Luske Parishes	Kinnure	37	John Coddington gent Francis Walsh gent	6	31
	Loghshinigh and Thomastowne	20	John Aston gent	7	13
	Ballykea	26	Thomas Clarke gent	4	22
(*folio* 20) Parishes of East and West Luske	Hacketstowne	26		6	20
	Ardlawe	2			2
	Haystowne	12	John Flower gent	4	8
	Rush	156	Jeffery Russell gent	40	116
	Corduffe	26		6	20
	Tomingtowne	9		8	1
	Cold Winters	13		6	7
	Ballawlye	18		4	14
	Balconnye	18		2	16
	Heggistowne	8		5	3
	Gracediewe	68	Christopher Barnewall gent	9	59
	Carrickhenhead	9		2	7
	Terrelstowne	20			20
	Effelstowne	13		6	7
	Rathartan	10		2	8
	The Leas	5		4	1
	Newtowne	18			18

Parishes	Places	Numbs of People	Balrothery Tituladoes Names	English	Irish
	Whitestowne	17	Christopher St Lawrence gent	2	15
(folio 21).	Jordanstowne	10			10
	Colcott	4		2	2
	Irishtowne	5			5
	Slafferstowne	12		2	10
	Obriestowne	17		6	11
	Balromyn	6		4	2
Holme Patricke	Holme Patricke	53	Nicholas Coddington Esq	24	29
	Laine	2			2
	Sherryes	56		24	32
	Loghbragh	13		4	9
	Graunge	6			6
	Baltreslon	10			10
	Milverstowne	18		5	13
Baldongan	Baldongan	32	Francis Travers gent William Gibson gent	9	23
	Leatowne	9		8	1
	Little Milverstowne	7		3	4
Donebate	Turvey	63	Nicholas Lord Viscount Barnewall, Henry Barnewall Esq, Francis Barnewall Esq, Mathew Barnewall Esq, Lawrence Dowdall gent	8	55
(folio 22). Donebate	Donebate	28		—	28
	Corballyes	6	Thomas Burton Esq	5	1
	Phillippstowne	5		5	—
	Baltra	22	George Forster gent	10	12
	Kilcreagh	13	Aldr John Carbery Esq	5	8
	Laundistowne	34		8	26
Ballyboughall	Ballyboughall	30		2	28
	Bealingstowne	17		—	17
	Ellistowne	11		2	9
	Drishoye	17		4	13
	Brownestowne	16		3	13
	Gerrardstowne	8			8
	Great Rascall	12		5	7
	Little Rascall	6		6	—
	The Graunge	30		3	27
West Palstowne	West Palstowne	49	John Gyles gent	7	42
	Leestowne	15		6	9
	Morrough	17		5	12
	Newtowne	21		6	15
(foilo 23). Palmerstowne	Jordanstowne	24			24

Parishes	Places	Numbs of People	Balrothery Tituladoes Names	English	Irish
	Cottrelstowne	21			21
	Whitestowne	10			10
	Palmerstowne	29		10	19
Balmadune	Balmadunn	43	James Wickombe gent	12	31
	Wisetowne	13		3	10
	Charlstowne	9		4	5
	Nottstowne	46	Samuell Hall gent	10	36
	Borranstowne	28			28
	Cordanstowne	27			27
Garistowne	Baldwinstowne	51	William Talbot gent	6	45
	Tobbergregan	32		5	27
	Pedanstowne	14			14
	Newtowne ot Garistowne	46		6	40
	Garistowne	126	Richard Talbott gent	17	109
Naall	Naall	51	Robert Whitefield gent Stephen Scarborough gent	16	35
	Haynestowne	8		2	6
(*folio* 24).	Rath	9			9
	Lecklnstowne	14		2	12
	Harandstowne	5			5
	Reinoldstowne	13			13
	Newimings	2			2
	Dowlaght	4		2	2
	Westowne	32			32
Hollywood	Hollywood	6			6
	Grallagh	47		6	41
	Damalstowne	24		1	23
	Little Malahowe	16		6	10
	Great Malahowe	13			13
	Brownestowne	9		2	7
	West Curragh	23		5	18
	Naptowne	6			6
	Trolly	3			3
(*folio* 25).	Little Hollywood	16		9	7
	Great Hollywood	6			6
	Kinaude	6			6
	Kittanstowne	8		4	4
	East Curragh	12			12
	Balgeath	11		4	7
	Balrickard	10			10

Principall Irish Names [and] Their Numb[er].

Birne, 11 ; Browne, 10 ; Brayne, 11 ; Boylan, 7 ; Coleman, 7 ; Callan, 11 ; Connor, 11 ; Corbally, 9 ; Cruise, 10 ; Dowdall, 12 ; Dermott, 10 ; Duff, 9 ; Donn, 7 ; English, 15 ; Fulham, 8 ; Farrall, 12 ; Harford, 17 ; Kelly, 26 ; Laundy, 8 ; Loghlin, 9 ; Lynch, 9 ; Maccan, 10 ; Murphy, 7 ; Murrey, 14 , Martyn, 13 ; Mahowne & Mahon, 9 ; Quinn, 10 ; Russell, 15 ; Realy, 11 ; Walsh, 14 ; White, 17 ; Wade, 10.

(*folio* 25 *verso*) The Number of People in ye Barony of Balrothery : Eng, 518 ; Irish, 1990 ; Totall Eng and Irish, 2508.

Parishes	Places	Numbs of Persons	Tituladoes Names	English	Irish
Kilossery	Kilossery	7	Robert Barnewall gent	—	7
	Rath of Kilossery	7			7
	Grazeele	6		4	2
	Brazeele	22	Nicholas Bolton Esq	8	14
	Surgolls towne	32	James Penteny gent	6	26
	Brecknanstowne	9		3	6
	Knockoeddan	3			3
Killeigh	Killeigh	48	Luke Dillon gent Bonaventure Dillon gent Barthol' Dillon gent	8	40
Swords	Dryneham	37	Jerome Russell gent	5	32
	Raholke	16			16
	Festryne	15	George Lord Barron of Strabane Christopher Fagon Esq	3	12
	Mabestowne	12		4	8
	Kinsaley	67	John Hollywood gent	18	49
P'ish of Cloghran Swords	Corballis	10	Thomas Towers gent	4	6
	Cloghran	25	Lewit' Coll George Smyth Esq	10	15
(folio 27). P'ish of Cloghlan Swords	Baskine	16	Arthur Smyth gent	4	12
	Tobberlonny	8	Edward Bary gent		8
	Stacoole	17	Beniamin Bolton gent	6	11
	Reckinhead	2		—	2
Malahide	Malahide	119	Miles Corbett Esq Richard Cotton Esq Miles Corbett Junior gent	36	83
Portmarnocke	Portmarnocke	32	Roger Bishopp Esq George Usher gent	7	25
	Grainge of Portmarnock	34			34
	Rebs Walls	6		4	2
	Carrickhill	7		2	5
	Connyborrow of Portmarnock	13			13
Howth	In ye House of Howth	27	William Lord Barron of Howth, Peter Wynne gent, William Fitz-Williams gent	14	13
	The Towne of Howth	111	Thomas Lea gent Richard St Lawrance gent	25	86
	The Walls	4	Thomas Ownyan gent	2	2
folio 28).	Sencier	9			9
	Carrstowne	4		1	3
	Sutton	19		3	16

Parishes	Places	Numbs of Persons	Tituladoes Names	English	Irish
	Kilbarrocke	30			30
	Stapolin	8			8
	Balhodge	5		3	2
	Mayme	13		—	13
	Little Mayne	6			6
	Grange of Baldoyle	26			26
	Baldoyle	75		10	65
Balgriffin	Balgriffen	57	Michell Jones Esq	9	48
	St Dowlaght	8			8
Cowlocke	Cowlocke	38		2	36
	Newtowne of Cowlocke	04		—	4
	Donnaghs	2		2	—
	Tonleged	15		2	13
(folio 29).	Kilmoore	28		—	28
	Dernedall	8	John Barker gent	6	2
	Skillinglass	4		2	2
Rathenny	Rathenny	90	Richard Browne gent Michall St Lawrence gent	6	84
Clantarfe	Clantarfe	79	— Mustian Esq Mr Seward gent	45	34
Finglasse	Tartayne	40	Charles Earl of Cavan Oliver Lambert Esq Walter Lambert Esq Edward Taylor gent	8	32
	Killester	32	Coll Chidley Coote Esq	12	20
Santry	Mayock	25	John Baxter Esq Henry Taylor gent	8	17
	Sterminstowne	11	Henry Porter Esq	9	2
	Silloge	24		5	19
	Dubber	30		7	23
	Balleruris	13			13
	Belcamye	4		3	1
(folio 30).	Commons of Santry	9			9
	Collinstowne	9		3	6
	Coultry	11		3	8
	Ballimon	10		4	6
	Santry	57		16	41
	Newtowne	8			8
	Gt Clonshogh	30	Richard Forster gent Richard Gibson gent	8	22
	Little Clonshogh	16		4	12
	Ballistroan	8			8
St Margretts	Donshoghly	22		8	14
	Newtowne of Donshoghly	4			4
	Denbroe	26	Coll Francis Willoughby Esq	5	21

Parishes	Places	Numbs of Persons	Tituladoes Names	English	Irish
(folio 31). Clanturke	Harristowne	35		11	24
	Gt Kingstowne	7			7
	Little Kingstowne	4			4
	Kilreeske	35	Robert Chamberlyn gent Thomas Chamberlyn his sonn	4	31
	Donekernye	14	William Basill Esq Peter Vaughan gent	8	6
	Dromconcagh	113	John Smyth gent	27	86
	Grawngh Clanliffe	4		2	2
	Read Chymny	3			3

Principall Irish Names [and] their Numb[er].

Archbould, 12 ; Bryan, 9 ; Birne, 26 ; Cassy, 8 ; Connor, 10 ; Doyle, 13 ; Farrall, 9 ; Kelly, 23 ; Lawlis, 9 ; Murphy, 10 ; Smyth, 11 ; Walsh, 8 ; White, 11.

(folio 31 verso).   The Number of People in the Barony of Cowlock : Eng, 419 ; Irish, 1425 ; Totall Eng and Irish, 1844.

(folio 32).   **BARONY OF CASTLEKNOCKE**

Parishes	Places	Numbs of People	Tituladoes Names	Eng	Irish
Castleknocke	Churchtowne of Castleknocke	42		12	30
	Castle farme of Castleknocke	32	Mathew Barnewall gent	2	30
	Diswillstowne	45	Nathaniell Leake gent	9	36
	Castigobb	9		4	5
	Pelletstowne	6	John Connell gent	—	6
	Little Cabragh	14		2	12
	Huntstowne	36	James Dillon gent James Barnewall gent	7	29
	Blanchardstowne	31	Henry Rowles Esq, Robert Ball gent, Richard Birford gent, Christopher Plunkett gent, Patricke Plunkett his sonn	5	26
	Great Cabragh	26	Bennet Arthur gent	4	22
	Dunsincke	33			33

Parishes	Places	Numbs of People	Tituladoes Names	Eng	Irish
	Cooleduffe	29	William Warren gent	7	22
	Porterstowne	18	Coll. Richard Lawrence Esq	13	5
	Keppocke	26		4	22
	Abbottstowne	24	James Sweetman gent	2	22
(folio 33).	Abbottstowne	12			12
Izod	Chapple Izod	80	David Edwards gent, John Mason gent, Rouse Davis gent.	20	60
Malahiddart	The Bay	15		3	12
	Kilmartin	36		7	29
	Poocestowne	20	Thomas Lutterell Esq	3	17
	Tobrelstowne & Terrelstowne }	20	John Jordan gent	—	20
	Cruise Rath	2		—	2
	Damastowne	14	Nicholas Cart : gent	3	11
	Little Pace	9		3	6
	Hunstowne	16		2	14
	Buzzards towne	11		5	6
	Pasloestowne	14	Gilbert Kerris gent	3	11
	Holly wood Rath	16			16
	Little Curragh	5			5
Cloghran	Ballycoolan	17			17
(folio 34).	Graunge of Ballycolan	26		2	24
Kilsolachan	Kilsolachan	48	Thomas Bagworth gent	3	45
	Kilcoskan	11			11
	Stradbally	42		9	33
	Corrstowne	20			20
	Collatrath	26			26
	Shallon	20		3	17
	Dunmuskye	2	John Gibson gent	2	—
Warde	Ward	48		5	43
	Sprecklestowne	31		3	28
	Pheopostowne	13			13
Clonsillagh	Clonsillagh	23	Richard Broughall gent	5	18
	Luttrellstowne	31	Sr William Berry Knt	16	15
	Luttrellstowne Mill	6			6
(folio 35).	Barbistowne	15		2	13
	Black Stahenny	10		5	5
	Pheblestowne	4		4	—
	Colemyne	40	James Russell gent	10	30

Principall Irish Names [and] Their Numb[er].

Birne, 5 ; Barnewall, 6 ; Dunne, 6 ; Kelly, 11 ; Murphy, 11 ; Moore, 6 ; Martyn, 6 ; Quinn, 7 ; Ryan, 6.

(folio 34 verso)   The Number of People in the Barony of Castleknock : Eng, 189 ; Irish, 885 ; Totall Eng & Irish, 1074.

(*folio* 35 *verso*)   The Number of People in the County of Dublin and in each Baronye.

Baronyes	Pages	Eng	Irish	Eng & Irish
Newcastle & Uppercross	9	1635	3043	4678
Rathdowne	12	0244	0908	1152
Neithercrosse	17	0318	1473	1791
Balrothery	25	0518	1990	2508
Cowlocke	31	0419	1425	1844
Castleknocke	34	0189	0885	1074
The Totall		3323	9724	13047

KILLDARE   COUNTY

13825

(*folio* 1).   Kildare County

OPHALY BARRONY

Townelands	Number of People	Tituladoes Names	Eng	Irish
Killdare	359	Nicholas Rutledge, Patrick Hanley, and George Staples, gents.	012	347
Rawalkin	007		—	007
Mooretowne	006		—	006
Sillott	007			007
Rahangan	107	Robert Braghall gent	002	105
Bohirquill	006			006
Killtechan	068			068
Kilmuny	037			037
Bolanure	027			027
Elistowne	026			026
Thomas towne	018			018
Ficullan	034	Gerrat Fitzgerrald gent		034
Drinanstowne	034			034
Capenargett	015			015
Cloncconnor	029			029
(*folio* 2). Dunmorie	030	Richard Fitzgerald gent		030
Codlans towne	009	Robert Fitzgerald gent	002	007
Pollards towne	012			012
Knauens towne	017			017
Knocknegallagh	019			019
Lackagh	068	John Evers Esq	004	064
Balliknange	003		002	001
Belakelly	018		002	016
Coolesicken	063			063
Kildengan	035	Teige Walsh gent		035
Walters towne	050	Sr John Crosby Knt Baronet		050
Ballibarnie	004			004
Kineagh	009			009
Nunrie	080			080
Tippenan	017		002	015
Balisonan	079	John Anesley Esq	002	077
(*folio* 3). Martins towne	028	John Sarsfield gent		028
Carne	027			027
Ballisax	089		003	086
Browns towne	022			022
Madins towne	085		005	080
Iron Hill	029			029
Kilrush	066	Maurice Fitzgerrald gent		066
Monestereuen	105	Edward Loftus Ld Viscount of Elye	011	094
Cooleueferah	041			041
Clohene	014			014
Clonyoughell	005			005
Grandgcore	030			030

Townelands	Number of People	Tituladoes Names	Eng	Irish
Grangcorre	016			016
Kill	007			007
Cloukerling	005			005
Clonegah	010			010
(*folio* 4). Youghell	026			026
Grangbegge	013			013
Rathmucke	015			015
Ballygreny	005			005
Duneny	044			044
Geden stowen	023			023
Tullye	098		002	096
Brolisan	012			012
Rathbride	085	Francis Peaslie Esq	002	083
Balliman	023			023
Kilcake	022			022

Principall Irish Names [and] their Number.

Birne, 026 ; Boghan (3), Boaghan (37), 40 ; Boorke, 006 ; Breckan (3), Breackan (9), 12 ; Boy (6) & McEboy (2), 008 ; Conolan & Conlan, 018 ; Connor, 015 ; Carroll, 013 ; Dempsey, 020 ; Doran, 010 ; Doolin, c20 ; Duin, 016 ; Doyle, 007 ; Enose, 015 ; Farrell, 016 ; Fitzgerrald, 014 ; McHuigh, 006 ; Heiren, 006 ; Helan, 006 ; Hinegan, 009 ; Kinselagh, 006 ; Kellie (60), Keely (3), 63; Kegan, 08; Lalor, 21 ; Mooney, 18 ; Moran & Morren, 14 ; Morin, 07 ; Murphy, 20 ; Malone, 08 ; Moore, 11 ; McMorrish, 10 ; Lenan & Lanan, 07 ; Nowlan, 08 ; Roe, 07 ; Samon, 07 ; Smith, 06 ; Toole, 12 ; Walsh, 09.

(*folio* 4 *verso*)   Barony : Ophalye ; Eng, 051 ; Irish, 2187 ; 2238, Totall.

(*folio* 5).   **NAASE BARRONY**

Townelands	Number of People	Tituladoes Names	Eng	Irish
Naase	303	Richard Strecklan, Robert Moore, William Foster, Charles Hall, John Birkett, James Sherlocke, Will Dounebanane, and Tho Tatte, gents ; Will Sands Esq, Rowland Horribon gent, The Right Honoble Earle of Strafford.	030	273
Barronrath	011		002	009

Townelands	Number of People	Tituladoes Names	Eng	Irish
Killen Moore	015	James Slose gent	002	013
Turnings	046	John Burye Esq	010	036
Ladie Castle	014			014
Cloonings	017			017
Boding towne	010	Francis Moore gent		010
Dare	028			028
Rathbogg	005		002	003
Blackhall	035	Anthony Sherlocke gent		035
Sherlocks towne	050	Edward Eustace gent		050
(folio 6). Blackhall	007			007
Athgarrett	007			007
Edstowne	010			010
Little Newton Wast				
Johns towne	025		002	023
Walters towne	012		001	011
Westowne Wast		Isack Sands gent		
Cardifs towne	040	Gerralt Flemminge gent	003	037
Morlings	006			006
Cradocks towne	047	John Smith gent	005	042
Litle Fornogh	016			016
Pauchestowne	017		002	015
Tipper	036		004	032
Osbers towne	080	Charles Reenes Esq Morrish Fitzgerrald, gent	003	077
Rathmoore	059			059
Phillipstowne	006			006
(folio 7). Swadals towne	054			054
Yegogstoun	026			026
Cornaloway	038			038
Killishay	026			026
Flemings towne	030			030
Newland and Newtowne	057	George Clarke gentleman	003	054
Ould towne	012		002	010
Millits towne	015			015
Steuens towne	010			010
Logs towne	042		002	040
Haris towne	055			055
Ballebegge	034			034
Canne court	009	Christopher Doughtie gent	002	007
Grangebogg	097	Henry Warren Esq, Morrice Warren his sonn gents, Edward Soare, and Will Warren, gents.	008	089
(folio 8). Rathargitt	004			004
Cottlands towne	068	Sr John Hoye Knight William Hoye his sonn Esq	009	059
Donando	022			022
Sillagh	007			007

Townelands	Number of People	Tituladoes Names	Eng	Irish
Siggins towne	083	Phillip Carpenter & John Browne gents	012	071
Grangemore	011			011
Walterstowne	004			004
Roches towne	010			010
Giltowne	040		004	036
Westers towne	009			009
L ghbrito	008		002	006

Principall Irish Names [and] their Number.

Birne, 040 ; Beaghan, 006 ; Donnell (7), Dowell (4). 011 ; Doyle, 011 ; Dunne, 010 ; Eustace, 011 ; Fairell, 007 ; Fitzgerrald, 006 ; Kauanagh, 006 ; Kelly, 026 ; Lalor, 009 ; Lannon, 006 ; Moore, 012 ; Murphy, 015 ; Murrey, 006 ; Neale, 011 ; Nowlan, 011 ; Doyne, 006.

(*folio 8 verso*)   Barrony : Naase ; English, 110 ; Irish, 1563 ; 1673, Totall.

(*folio 9*).   **CLANE BARRONY**

Townelands	Number of People	Tituladoes Names	Eng	Irish
Clane	058	Henry Pearce, Patrick Fitzgerrald, and John Warren, gents.	004	054
Keppocke	026	Robert Thornton gent	003	023
Newtown of Slane	043	Humpherie Milles gent	004	039
Beatoghs towne	037	John Emerson, Thomas Wedgwood, Arthur Sheile, Frederick Sheile, and Hercules Sheile, gents.	004	033
Killbeggs	019	Nathaniell Staughton gent	005	014
Curry Hills	006	John Deuenishe gent		006
Longe towne	023	George Carter gent	003	020
Downings	050	Sr Andrew Ailmer Knt & Baronett, James Ailmer his sonn gent, and George Clarke gent	005	045
Graggs	021	Edward Plunkett gent		021
Wood	002			002
Stickens	006			006
New towne	011			011
Ould towne	012			012
(*folio 10*). Donore	035	Peter Holmes gent	002	033
Ballinefagh	012	Oliver Fitzgerrald gent		012
Garvocke	017		002	015
Giltowne	014			014

Townelands	Number of People	Tituladoes Names	Eng	Irish
Stables towne	039	James Fitzgerrald gent		039
Blackwood	030	Francis Eustace gent		030
Landons towne	035	Walter Fiizgerrald gent		035
Castle Keelee	030			030
Yeomans towne	096	Alexand^r Eustace		096
Tymochoe	057	Redmond Fitzgerrald gent		057
Hodges towne	034			034
Coole Caregine	016	John Dongan gent		016
Carduff	019			019
Barrets towne	044	Morrish Eustace gent		044

Principall Irish Names [and] Their Number.

Birne, 06 ; Connor, 12 ; Doyle, 06 ; Dunn, 09 ; Eustace, 08 ; Farrell, 09 ; Felan alias Holan, 06 ; Fitzgerrald, 08 ; Hanlon, 09 ; Hearin (3), Ô Hererin (4), 07 ; Kellie, 07 ; Murphy, 06 ; Nowlan, 05.

(*folio* 10 *verso*)   Barrony : Clane ; Eng, 032 ; Irish, 760 ; 792, Tott :

(*folio* 11).   **CONNELL BARRONY**

Townelands	Number of People	Tituladoes Names	Eng	Irish
Killmaoge	038		003	035
Moylers towne	014			014
Roberts towne	019			019
Loetowne	018			018
Greatwoods	007			007
Grange clare	018			018
Greencroft	012			012
Balliteige	028			028
Barncroh	005			005
Killeagh	020			020
Ballintian	021			021
Pluckres towne	019			019
Carricke	014			014
Barrons towne	031			031
Dunbirn	019			019
(*folio* 12). Granghiggen	021	John Fitzgerrald gent		021
Rahernin	023	James Duin gent		023
Punchards grandy	052	Gerrald Fitzgerrald gent		052

Townelands	Number of People	Tituladoes Names	Eng	Irish
Whylan	005			005
Christins towne	016			016
Miltowne	020			020
Clongony	005			005
Ladie towne	075	Geo : Fitzgerrald & Tho : Moore gents		075
Morristowne	} 030			030
Moynagh				
Newhall	083		003	080
Greenhill	011	William Meridith Esq	007	004
Ballimee	015			015
Corbalis	032		002	030
Great Connell	078	William Talbott gent		078
(folio 13). Clowmins	010			010
Welshes towne	011			011
Aghgarvan	006		002	004
Blackrath	003			003
Ould Connell	046			046
Barrets towne	014			014
Cloongoory	004			004
Peirces towne	013	Walter Whyte gent		013
Rosberrie	026	Walter Weldon gent		026
Moore towne	006			006
Morris towne	} 023			023
Billru				
Giggens towne	021		003	018

Principall Irish Names [and] Their Number.

Beaghan, 08 ; Birne, 13 ; Cullen, 06 ; Duin, 06 ; Doolin, 12 ;   Enose, 10 ; Felan alius Helan, 07 ; Farrell, 06 ; Foran alius Horan, 06 ; Fitzgerrald, 07 ; Hely, 06 ; Kelly, 17 ;   Morin (7), Moran (2), 09 ; Malone, 08 ; Murphy, 06 ; Nowlan, 18 ; Rorque, 10.

(folio 13 verso)   Barrony : Conell ; Eng, 020 ; Irish, 912 ; 932, tott :

(folio 14).   **SALT BARRONY**

Townelands	Number of People	Tituladoes Names	Eng	Irish
Mynowth	289	Francis Nest, John Nelson, Francis Greene, and John Samon, gents.	042	247

Townelands	Number of People	Tituladoes Names	Eng	Irish
Laraghbrian	060	Edward Morgan gent	010	050
Mawes	043	Lawrence Allen gent	003	040
Creeus towne	012		—	012
Cormacks towne	018		002	016
New towne	021		—	021
Cartowne	043	Thomas Newcomen gent	004	039
Rauensdale	012		002	010
Griffinrath	037	George Rutlidge gent	—	037
Walters towne	006			006
Rowins towne	004		004	000
Kellistowne	041	Richard Barry gent		041
Blacks towne	012		004	008
Barrocks towne	017			017
Balligorue	028			028
(folio 15). Tooles towne	010			010
Little Mawes	008			008
Toods towne	019			019
Dorrins towne	010			010
Shian	008			008
Donoghs towne	022		002	020
Mony cooly	020			020
Dowds towne	011		002	009
Teightooe	018			018
Rooske	010			010
Tirnehary	006			006
Couns towne	006			006
Bryans towne	013			013
Windgates	016			016
Corballis	006			006
(folio 16). Smiths towne	017			017
Jobnins towne	006		002	004
Graigsallagh	017			017
Keals towne	022			022
Gragline	014			014
Newtowne Macabb }	015			015
Clonagh	003			003
Bebush	016			016
Straffan	023		004	019
Killadowan	011		006	005
Ballimakely	004			004
Barbis towne	036		002	034
Irish towne	016		004	012
Possecks towne	025		003	022
Ardrasse	011		002	009
(folio 17). Confey	045	Henry Markham Esq. and John Darsy gent.	011	034

2 C

Townelands	Number of People	Tituladoes Names	Eng	Irish
Collins towne	010			010
Leixleipp	100	Nicholas White Esq, James Eustace, & Charles Hooker, gents.	011	089
Kildrought	063		004	059
More towne	005	Humphrey Jones gent	002	003
Castle towne	034	William Smith gent	002	032
Collins hill	002			002
Parsons towne	012			012
Kilmacreedocke	039			039
Rewd and Priors towne	007	Edward Hollins gent	003	004
Colfilch	005			005
Newtowne East	027	Jossua Shippy gent	002	025
Castle Dillon	036	John Gaige gent	005	031
(folio 18). Tippers towne	014		002	012
Laughlins towne	018			018
St Wolstans	018	Sr Bryan Ô Neile Knight and Bryan Ô Neile Esq		018
Simons towne	015			015
Donnoghcomper	005			005
Stackunny	016	Edward Jones gent		016
Lyons	009		003	006
Castlewarning	049		003	046
Oughterard	024			024
Pains towne	035		002	033
Clonaghes	014		002	012
Great Fornaghes	013			013
Hartwell	010		003	007
Kill	092			092
(folio 19). Broges towne and Arthurs towne	025			025
Hains towne	006			006
Hutton Road	020			020
Black Church	007		002	005
Killwarueinge	009		002	007
Killteele	027		003	024
Baths Mill	013		006	007
Bishopps Court	052	Thomas Browne gent	008	044
Allasly	011		004	007
Mynowth	003		002	001

Principall Irish Names [and their Number].

McAnully, 010; Bryan, 09; Birne, 28; Browne, 07; Connor, 08; Dunn, 07; Doyle, 18; Eustace, 07; Enos, 08; Farrell, 06; Kelly, 28; Kauanagh, 06; Keny and Kenny, 07; Lalor, 07; Malone, 15; Murphy, 11; Nowlan, 12; Ô Neale, 09; Smith, 09; Toole, 09; Trasy & Tressy, 07; Walsh, 10.

(folio 19 verso)   Barrony: Salt; Eng, 180; Irish, 1772; 1952, tott:

(*folio* 20) **REBAN[1] AND NARRAGH BARRONIES.**

Parrish	Townelands	Number of People	Tituladoes Names	Eng	Irish
	Athy	273	Robert Preston Esq & Souereign	061	212
St Johns	St Johns in Athy Burrough	093	Robert Weldon Esq and Will: Weldon gent	004	089
	St Dominicks Abey in Athy Burrough	086		006	080
	Fonts towne	031			031
	Rathsillagh	033		003	030
	Bolibegg	040	Daniell Cullen Dr of Phisick		040
	Greengarden	013			013
	Skerris	023	Garrett Nugent gent		023
	Narraghmore	091	Morrish Keating and John Eustace gents		091
	Iuchequire, Moyle Abbey, & Sprats towne	005			005
	Glasellie	050	Bartholmew Hussey Esq	005	045
(*folio* 21).	Blackrath	097	Thomas Cheeke gent	003	094
	Ardincross	014			014
	Youngs towne	014		002	012
	Crooks towne	019	Harmon Wansanton gent	003	016
	Kilmude	019			019
	Timolin	044		002	042
	Ballyfore	009		003	006
	Uske	016		004	012
	Ballimount	037	Will: Eustace gent		037
	Calbins towne	018	John Clearke gent	001	017
	Caluers towne	040	Thomas Eustace gent		040
	Black Halle	055	Edmond Walsh gent		055
	Reban	076	George Halefeild gent	007	069
Churchtowne	Woodestooke	113	Joseph Rea gent	012	101
(*folio* 22).	Rosbren	007		—	007
	Kilcroe	026			026
	Cardens towne	008			008
	Shian	023			023
	Balliroan	017		002	015
	Castle Michell	027		002	025
	Ould Court	004			004
	Kilberrie	049	John Jackson gent	004	045
	Clonye	045			045
	Berte	019		003	016
	Russels towne	013		002	011
	Tullogorie	046	Henry Brynne Esq		046
	Kilcolman	020		004	016
	Ardscoll	036	William Sauadge gent	002	034
	Inch couentrie	004		002	002

[1] *Leban*, tolios 21-22.

Principal Irish Names [and] Their Number.

Burne, 24 ; Brin & Brinne, 5 ; Brenan, 17 ; Carroll, 09 ; Cullen, 07 ; Coneran, 05 ; Dullanie, 05 ; Dunn, 15 ; Dutte, 06 ; Dowling, 14 ; Doran, 05 ; McDermot, 05 ; Daniell, 06 ; Fitzgerrald, 07 ; Farrell, 08 ; Glascock, 05 ; Goine, 05 ; Hylan & Helan, 05 ; Hickie, 06 ; Kelly, 54 ; Keating, 05 ; Keaghoe, 06 ; Kinselagh, 05 ; Lalor, 19 ; Lyon, 05 ; Moore, 07 ; Malone, 05 ; Murphy, 27 ; Neale, 09 ; Toole, 05 ; Walsh, 08.

(*folio 22 verso*)   Barrony : Leban & Narragh ; Eng, 1317 ; Irish, 1516 ; 1653, tott.

(*folio 23*).   **BARRONY OF KILKAE & MOONE**

Townelands	Number of People	Tituladoes Names	Eng	Irish
Kilkae	107	Wentworth Fitzgerald Earl of Kildare, William Hamond gent.	006	101
Becons town	017	Robert Hodges gent	002	015
Moone	109	Edward Dauis Esqr Terrence Fitzpatrick gent	005	104
Breagh	040	John Edworth gent	004	036
Nichols towne	028			028
Grany	065	John Warren gent	002	063
Dollors towne	068	Raphaell Hunt Esq, Raphaell Hunt his sonn, & Charles Richesies, gents.	013	055
Grangerosnoluan	007		002	005
Leuets towne	007			007
Hallaheys	052	Laghlin Leyen gent		052
Carballis	002			002
Phromples towne	033		002	031
Dauids towne	008			008
(*folio 24*). Ballinelarrigg	012			012
Cummins towne	005			005
Boulton	057	George Blount Esq & James Blount gent	008	049
Marshals towne	013	John Hickey gent		013
Morragh bogg	023			023
Simons towne	028			028
Kargin	033			033
Collines	004			004
Both ye Bealans	029	John Westly Esqr	006	023
Molloghmast	032			032
Great Birton	061			061
Litle Birton	042			042
Castlerowe	067	Thomas Harman Esq	004	063
Crookend	031			031
Bellaghmoone	059	Edward Warren gent	004	055
(*folio 25*) Castle dermott	240	Francis Heling, William Hulme, and John Gater, gentlemen.	068	172

Townelands	Number of People	Tituladoes Names	Eng	Irish
Knocknokree	008		000	004
Moore Abby	008			008
St Johns	049			049
Ardrey	024	John Bennett Esq	004	020
Grange Mellon	018	Walter Burrows Barronett	005	013
Bally head and halfe BallyneKill	015		003	012
Ballycollan	020		002	018
Ballybrin	037	Henry Walsh gent		037
DunMonocke	011			011

Principall Irish Names [and] Their Number.

Brenan, 06 ; Birne, 31 ; Bane, 11 ; Bolger, 05 ; Curren (4), Corren (2), Carron (4), 10 ; Dunn, 05 ; McDaniell, 07 ; Dowling, 11 ; Doyle, 11 ; Eustace, 05 ; Fitzgerrald, 06 ; Foaly, 08 ; Hedien, 19 ; Kelly, 21 ; Kealy, 05 ; Keagho, 05 ; Kauanagh, 07 ; Lalor, 20 ; Murphey, 14 ; Moore, 05 ; Murrey, 05 ; Nowland, 32 ; O Neale, 09 ; Phealan, 09 ; Roe, 05 ; Raghter, 05 ; Toole, 07 ; Treuers, 05 ; Welsh, 12.

(*folio 25 verso*) Barrony : Kilkea & Moone ; Eng, 142 ; Ir'sh, 1327 ; 1469, tott :

(*folio 26*). **IKEATHYE BARRONY**

Townelands	Number of People	Tituladoes Names	Eng	Irish
Kilcock Towne	125	Edward Dodleston, Christopher Tirrell, William Leigh, John Person, William Owtton, George Gouldsmith, & Daniell Birne, gentlemen	011	114
Whytes towne and Boys towne	} 012			012
Ports	021	Robert Aylmer, and Christopher Rochfort, gentlemen.		021
Courstowne	016	Meyler Hussey gent	003	013
Laraghes and Roes towne	016	William Rochfort, and Thomas Seax, gents	002	014
Clonsaste	017	Bryen Jones gent		017
Brangans towne	016	Austen Rownyn gent		016
Grragodder	006			006
Belgard	038			038
Doneda	130	Coll Henry Owen Esq	007	123

Townelands	Number of People	Tituladoes Names	Eng	Irish
(*folio* 27). Killmurrye	016		002	014
Cultrime	006	Thomas Rowles gent	002	004
Shurlogs towne	047	Charles Wenman Esq	002	045
Cloancurrye	089	Richard Thomson Esq and Joseph Thomson gent	004	085
Nichols towne	049			049
Pitchers towne	046	Walter Whyte Esq		046
Ballecaghan	016			016
Ballesanon	036	John Aylmer gent		036
Grandgmore	031			031
Newton of Kilbride	017	Thomas Aylmer gent		017
Corckrans towne	053	John Salt Esq	002	051
Kilbride	027			027
Fennaghs	037	John Boorke gent		037
(*folio* 28 Killmacgarrocke	010	Thomas Milborn gent	002	008
Rathcoffy	040	Will : Litchfield gent	002	038
Rahien	008			008
Baltrasey	041			041
Grag pottle	017			017
Clonfert	021			021
Balrahin	007			007
Paynestowne	025	Thomas Brookes gent	003	022
Richards towne	034			034
Maynham	102	Richard Neuill gent	008	094

Principall Irish Names [and their Number].

Aylmer, 05 ; Birne, 10 ; Brannagh, 06 ; Boorke, 07 ; Cartan, 06 ; Dalie (5), Dalli 09 ; Doyne, 11 ; Doyle, 07 ; Dunn, 12 ; Farrell, 09 ; Filan al's Hilan, 09 ; Kenedy. 05 ; Kellye, 11 ; Kenna (5), Kenny (4), 09 ; Mooney, 08 ; Malone, 05 ; Neale, 05 ; Quynn, 08 ; Rochfort, 90 ; Ryan, 06 ; Scully, 05 ; Toole, 05 ; Tagan, 05 ; Walsh, 07.

(*folio* 28 *verso*).   Barrony : Ikeathye ; Eng, 050 ; Irish, 1122 ; 1172, tott :

(*folio* 29).   **CARBERY BARRONY**

Townelands	Number of People	Tituladoes Names	Eng	Irish
Castle carbery	111	Dudly Colly Esq	013	098
Clonkeene	053	John Ash gent	006	047
Killmore	059		—	059

Townelands	Number of People	Tituladoes Names	Eng	Irish
Cassiwany	002			002
Clonmeene and Ranechan }	039			039
Balinane	025			025
Kilrathmory	043			043
Ardkill	019			019
Drihed	002			002
Conagh	034		002	032
Kilraskin	022			022
Drumen	011			011
Dorinany	015			015
Ballinekill	030			030
(folio 30). Kilpatrick	006			006
Ballibrak	024			024
Teekneuan	028	Henry Lyee gent		028
Clonnuff and Tonregee }	018			018
Ballinemallagh	025	Garrot Bermingham gent		025
Clonkeran	012			012
Ballenderry	016			016
Calues towne	003			003
Caddames towne	026	Barnaby Kelly gent		026
Martins towne	026			026
Killmorebranagh	060			060
Clonagh	046	Thomas Lynham and Adam Lynham, gents	002	044
Thomas towne	030	William Bermingham and Redmond Bermingham, gents		030
(folio 31). Ballina	001	Anthony Sambage Esq	001	---
Dunfiert	098	Thomas Bermingham gent	—	098
Disert	023			023
Gurtin Mill	023			023
Mucklon	036	Garett Bermingham and William Bermingham, gents		036
Killian	013	Bartholmew Aylmer gent		013
Killmurry	030	Donogh Connor gent		030
Kilshancboe	024			024
Moyually	060	John Luby gent	002	058
Ballinekill	055		002	053
Ballihenan	016			016
Garisker	025	John Bermingham and James Bermingham, gents		025
Ballindrumny	020			020
Kilglass	017	John Kelly gent		017
Coruenrucklagh	013		002	011
(folio 32). Killagine	023			023
Ballinlugg	014			014
Grange	067	Edward Bermingham and Walter Bermingham his sonn, gents		067

Townelands	Number of People	Tituladoes Names	Eng	Irish
Kinafadd	012			012
Ballindoolen	013			013
Carricke	057			057
Raheen and Rusels wood	049	Edward Waren Esq, and Stephen Waren gent	006	043
Killinagh and Ballicowne	019		002	017
Nurny, Moore towne, & Balrenet	046			046
Dirinlugg	004	Thomas Pallis gent	002	002

Principall Irish Names [and] their number.

Bermingham, 24 ; Boylan, 06 ; Ô Brine, 07 ; Birne, 05 ; Branagh, 07 ; Cormack, 09 ; Comman, 07 ; Calmy, 06 ; Carbery, 05 ; Connor, 10 ; Conelan, 05 ; Dunn, 07 ; McDonagh, 06 ; Ô Donlen, 05 ; Duine, 09 ; Enos, 10 ; Gaffeny, 10 ; Giraghty, 08 ; Healy, 07 ; Kelly, 29 ; Keely, 04 ; Kenedy, 13 ; Leynagh, 06 ; Langan, 05 ; Mooney, 16 ; Moren, 08 ; Malone, 17 ; Maly, 06 ; Moore, 06 ; Martin (5), Gillmartin (4), 09 ; McOwen, 07 ; Scully, 05 ; Trody, 05 ; Wailsh, 10 ; McWard, 07.

(*folio* 32 *verso*)   Barrony : Carbery ; Eng, 040 ; Irish, 1503 ; 1543, tott

(*folio* 33).   **KILLCULLEN ½ BARRONY**

Townelands	Number of People	Tituladoes Names	Eng	Irish
Killcullen	115	Rowland Owens, Thomas Law, Richard Nicholls, Rich[d] Haries, Richard Greene, Ralph Greene, Robert Smith, and Edward Fotterell, gentlemen ; and John Weabb gentleman.	018	097
Haluers towne	002		002	—
Thomas towne	002		—	002
Gallmers towne	064			064
Mors towne	009			009
New Abby and Nichols towne	020	Symon Wessbie gent	002	018
Killeneane	025	L[t] William Willisbie gent	005	020
Toberrogan	007			007
Killgoan	056	Henry Haringtonn & Lodowick Pontin gent	002	054
Castle martin	058		003	055
Killcullen bridge	043	Thomas Bryan gent	002	041

Principall Irish Names [and their Number].

Birne, 22 ; Doran, 06 ; Kelly, 07 ; Murphey, 05.

(*folio* 33 *verso*).

Farronies	Pages	Eng	Irish	Totalls ot Eng & Irish
Ophaly	04	0051	02187	2238
Naase	08	0110	01563	1673
Clane	10	0032	00760	0792
Conell	13	0020	00912	0932
Salt	19	0180	01772	1952
Leban & Narragh	22	0137	01516	1653
Kilkea & Moone	25	0142	01327	1469
Ikeathye	28	0050	01122	1172
Carbery	32	0040	01503	1543
Killcullen ½	33	0034	00367	0401
		0796	13029	13825

KILKENNY COUNTY AND CITTY
                    16217
           CITTY   1722
           CALLAN 451
                  ─────────
                   18390

(folio 1).

Parishes	Townelands	Numbs of People	Tituladoes Names	Eng	Irish
Glashare	Glashare	083	Robert Lloyd gent Thomas Brodston gent	008	075
	Coolenacrutty	031	John Warmand gent	002	029
Raloghane	Kreenekill	017		000	017
Glashare	Shanclogh	021		002	019
Fartagh	Bawnerickin	009		000	009
	Ballilehane	010		000	010
	Mullenemucke	015	Thomas Sharpe gent	002	013
	Lodge	015	Abell Warren Esq	005	010
	Ballikirrin and Fayle	020		000	020
	Whiteswall	074		000	074
	Bawnemore	136	John Bryan Esq	000	136
	Brekannagh	020		000	020
	Rathbane	023		000	023
	Rathreagh	025	John Ryan gent	002	024
	Ballispellane	010		000	010
	Mullenamucke p'te	003		000	003
	Rathpatrick	023		000	023
(folio 2).	Tankardstowne	013		000	013
Quere what P'ishes these be in	Tornamongan	002		000	002
	Waltersland	002		000	002
	Teneslatly	032		000	032
	Durrow	105	William Flower Esq, George Blunt gent, Francis Savadge, William Gray gent	011	094
	Fartagh	073		000	073
	Seaven Sisters	006		000	006
	Knockduff	005		004	001
	Donnoghmore	028		003	025
	Foulkscourt	020		000	020
	Crospatrick	011		000	011
	Ballimis	014		000	014
	Tullovolty	015		000	015
	Urlingford	021	Charles Hawkins gent Thomas Butler gent	004	017
	Burrismore	044	Peter Purcell gent	000	044
	Castletowne She	083	Hugh White gent	007	076
	Ballycanra	041		000	041
(folio 3).	Parkesgrove	048	William Brookes gent	002	046
	Lisdowney	089	Humphry Hurd gent	008	081
	Balleene	088		004	084
	Tefeghiny	039	Lewis Mathews gent	004	035
	Sheskin	054	Walter Butler gent	000	054
	Ballinaslee	045	John Bourden gent of Clone	002	043

Parishes	Townelands	Numbs of People	Tituladoes Names	Eng	Irish
	Clone	124	Theobald Butler gent of Ballinaslee	002	122
	Maior Abell Warrens troope	056	Henry Fleming gent, John Earlsman gent, James Madison gent, John Spoone gent, Edward Butler gent, Henry Baker gent, Thomas Bedborogh gent, Francis Creskitt gent, Thomas Davis gent, Samuell Price gent, Robert Piggott gent, John Spillman gent, Stephen Slaney gent, Gerrard Warren gent.	056	000

[Principall Irish names and their Number].

Boe & O Boe, 009 ; Birne, 05 ; Brohy, 017 ; Butler, 012 ; Bergin, 019 ; Currin, 009 ; Cody, 021 ; Clony, 006 ; Caroll, 006 ; Costigin, 006 ; Dullard, 010 ; Dulany, 030 ; Dowly & Dooly, 007 ; Hicky, 006 ; Hologhane, 008 ; Kelly, 017 ; Kevanagh, 007 ; Kenedy, 05 ; Lawler, 006 ; Mullany, 05 ; Mogher, 023 ; Phelan, 022 ; Purcell, 011 ; Fitzpatrick, 006 ; Quiddihy, 007 ; Ryan, 010 ; Shee & Shea, 007 ; Tenane & Tinane, 012 ; Welsh & Walsh, 013.

(*folio 3 verso*) 　The Number of People in the Barony of Galmoy : Eng, 128 ; Irish, 1446 ; Totall Eng & Irish, 1574

(*folio 4*) 　　　　**BARONY OF GOWRAN**

Parishes	Townelands	Numbs of People	Tituladoes Names	Eng	Irish
	Graige	163	William Cheshire gent	014	149
	Old Grange	019		002	017
	Agh clare	004		002	002
	Ballyogan	069		000	069
	Cooleroe	048		002	046
	Rahin Downore	004		000	004
	Glancoin	001		000	001
Ullard		025		004	021
	Cloghasty	010		000	010
	Miltowne	022		000	022
	Ballygriffin	015		000	015
	Knockbarron	007		000	007
	Killine	008		000	008
Poore Towne P'ish		026		000	026
	Ballicabus and Glasmoling	017		002	015
	Aghuelacke	018		000	018

Parishes	Townelands	Numbs of People	Tituladoes Names	Eng	Irish
	Coolenebrone	005		000	005
	Cournebahelly	016		000	016
	Boherquill	030		000	030
(folio 5). Quere if these	Garrantibbott	014		000	014
be off the aforesd P'ish	Curroghlehane	016		000	016
	Slackally	009		000	009
	Tinekilly	005		000	005
Jerpoynt		036		000	036
	Dissertbegg	016	Alexander Costle Esq Silvester Costle gent	000	016
	Pleberstowne	022		000	022
	Bawneskehy	024		000	024
	Rathduff	004		000	004
	Woollengrange	041		002	039
	Ballylinch	046	Daniell Redman Esq	006	040
	Inesteoge	146	John Johnson gent, George Robbins gent, Francis Lewis gent, Richard Whaley gent	015	131
	Poorewood	035		000	035
	Bohillagh	016		004	012
	Ballyduff	012		000	012
	Killcallan	013		000	013
	Kilkeran	037		000	037
	Bally woole	026		000	026
	Cappagh	014		002	012
(folio 6).	Ballycacksust	026		000	026
	Kilecross	011		000	011
	Killmacshane	012		000	012
	Fedunrahy	008	Christopher Render gent	000	008
	Collumkill	023		005	018
	Ballinary	016		000	016
	Killmurry	046		004	042
	Killfane	024	George St Leger gent	001	023
	Stroan	037		000	037
	Castlegarden	027		000	027
	Cloghstregg	002		000	002
	Dungervan	059		000	059
	Cloghlea	049	John Purcell gent	000	049
	Rahinroch	004		000	004
	Killmonehine	016		000	016
	Bramblestowne	051	Edmond Butler Esq	000	051
	Nehum	030	Richard Butler gent	000	030
	Uppergrange	038		000	038
(folio 7).	Low Grange	058	Richard Stephens Esq	004	054
	Duning	054		000	054

Parishes	Townelands	Numbs of People	Tituladoes Names	Eng	Irish
	Ould Abby	093	Obᵈ Jones Esq	007	086
	Tulloherime	042		000	042
	Ballyneboly	028		003	025
	Newhouse	016		002	014
	Nashtowne	014	Jeffry Pert gent	002	012
	Bishoppslogh	033	Edmond Feake Esq	003	030
	Kilblayne	026	Dudly Mannaring gent	002	024
	Bennetts bridge	022	Henry Fogg gent John Keneslon gent	002	020
	Donbill	030		000	030
	Houlingstowne	018	Nicholas Baygott gent	002	016
	Severstowne	029		005	024
	Kilearny	002		000	002
	Thomastowne	222	Thomas Throgmorton gent, Richard Dobbin Marchant, Simon Smyth gent, Christopher Hewetson gent.	038	184
(folio 8).	Danyin	030	John Norton gent	006	024
	Grenam	062	Anthony Stampe Esq John Stampe gent	002	060
	Shankhill	102	Edward Chilton gent	004	098
	BallimᶜLoghlin	068	Richard Leigh gent	004	064
	Ballytarnsny	065		000	065
	Killderry	016		000	016
	Ballysallagh	032		000	032
	Cantwells court	038	Mʳ Samford Esq John Powell Esq	012	026
	Killkeran	044		000	044
	Carrigeene	045		004	041
	Rathcoole	008		006	002
	Cantwell garran	023		000	023
	Upper Claragh	024	Henry Johnson gent	010	014
	Killmogar	021		000	021
	Brickin claragh	018	Jacob Cormicke Esq	000	018
	Ballyfoyle	053	Walter Archer gent	004	049
	Cloghtooke	030		000	030
(folio 9).	Downemore	151	The Right Honble the Lord Marquess of Ormonde, Thomas Humes Esq, Edmond Ludlo gent, Peter Sᵗ John gent, William Legrond gent, William Hacker gent, William Taylor gent, Luke Archer gent, William Whialon gent.	031	120

Parishes	Townelands	Numbs of People	Tituladoes Names	Eng	Irish
	Gowran	226	Thomas Hossy gent, John Ungly gent, Henry Make- peace	048	178
	Haggard Street	041		004	037
	Bally Shanmore	008		000	008
	Castle Ellis	005		000	005
	Blanchwilds Parke	029		002	027
	Sraghgaddy	003		002	001
	Ballyquirke	016		000	016
	Newhouse	04		002	002
	Butlersgroue	023		002	021
(folio 10).	Paulestowne	052	William Hopkins gent	007	045
	Castle Kelly	022		000	022
	Garryduff	077		000	077
	Ballinvally	022		000	022
	Ratharmore	020	Leut Aggher Honett gent	002	018
	Lavishtowne	007		000	007
	Maddogs towne	022		000	022
	Leigh Rath	002		000	002
	Higginstowne	035		000	035
	High Rath	035		000	035
	Blanch Wilds towne	073	John Collins gent, John Collins his sonn gent, Henry Evans.	011	062
	Ormonds part of Rathcass	012		000	012
	Blanch Wilds pte of Rathcass	010		000	010
	Rathgarvan	022	Thomas Lauson gent	006	016
	Castle Warin	016		007	009
(folio 11).	Grange	022		000	022
	Frenistowne	009		000	009

Principall Irish Names [and] Their Numb[er].

Archer, 06 ; Brin, 05 ; Birne, 048 ; Brohy, 020 ; Butler, 039 ; Blanchvill, 014 ; Bryan, 010 ; Bolger, 010 ; Brenan, 046 ; Bergin, 006 ; O Boe, 07 ; Bane, 08 ; Barron, 09 ; Bourke, 05 ; Brodier, 06 ; Cody, 040 ; Comerford, 015 ; Cullen, 010 ; Coghill, 011 ; Clone & Clony, 010 ; Convoy & Coway, 009 ; Cantwell, 09 ; Cragh, 06 ; Clere & Cleary, 07 ; Carroll, 06 ; Cnogher, 05 ; Cormucke, 016 ; Dulany, 012 ; McDonogh &c, 012 ; O Donell &c, 015 ; Dowling, 016 ; Dobbin, 010 ; McDavid, 07 ; O Drea &c, 08 ; Dowly &c, 06 ; Fanning, 010 ; Farrell &c, 023 ; Flemming 07 ; Fitz- gerald, 011 ; Grace, 020 ; Heiden, 013 ; Hologhon (08) & Halighan (05), 013 ; Healy &c, 011 ; Heban, 08 ; Henessy, 08 ; Joue & Jouie, 010 ; Keating, 012 ; Kelly, 043 ; Kevanagh, 013 ; Kenedy, 05 ; Kearny, 06 ; Keefe, 08 ; McLoghlin, 011 ; Lallor, 017 ; Loghman, 06 ; Laules, 08 ; Morphy, 118 ; Mogher, 015 ; Mulrony, 08 ; Marten, 09 ; Neale, 032 ; Nolan, 030 ; Phelan, 025 ; Purcell, 020 ; Patrick &c, 010 ; Prendergast, 024 ; Power, 08 ; Quin & Quing, 012 ; Quiddihy, 09 ;

Ryan, 089 ; Rock, 012 ; Roch, 06 ; Shortall, 016 ; Shea, 09 ; Tobin, 015 ; Tressy, 08 ; Welsh & Walsh, 095 ; Wall, 012.

(*folio* 11 *verso*) The Number of People in ye Barony of Gowran : Eng, 311 ; Irish, 3543 ; totall Eng and Irish, 3854.

(*folio* 12).   **BARONY OF IVERKE**

Parishes	Townlands	Numbs of People	Tituladoes Names	Eng	Irish
	Ballytarsny	013		000	013
	Agha Tadie	011		000	011
	Kilkregan	034	John Woodcocke gent	010	024
	Barrebehy	011	William Adhow gent	002	009
	Tubrud	005		000	005
	Poulroan	061	John Mason gent	004	057
	Nichas towne	007		002	005
	Grange	011		000	011
	Cloghagh	045		000	045
	Dunenane	034		002	032
	Clonecunny	002		000	002
	Casshell Farrell	009		000	009
	Brahills towne	010		003	007
	Graigo Urne	028	William Frispe gent	003	025
	Ullidtowne	036		000	036
	Tiremore	004		000	004
	Ballynebuohy	039	Robert Hawford gent	003	036
	Mullum	042		000	042
(*folio* 13).	Ballinlogh	003	George Cooke gent	003	000
	Rathkiran	037		000	037
	Filkuckstowne	005		002	003
	Rathcurby	020		000	020
	Ballincurr	009		000	009
	Waddings towne	013		000	013
	Roches towne	011		000	011
	Listroling	004		000	004
	Arderry	017		000	017
	Dunguoly	030		008	022
	Clomemore	032	Humphrey Bridgin gent John Bridgin gent	004	028
	Killinaspug	014		000	014
	Aghlish	021		000	021
	Portneholly	010		000	010
	Ballysallagh	002		002	000
	Portnescolly	016	William Collins gent	002	014
	Lufferry	034		000	034

Parishes	Townlands	Numbs of People	Tituladoes Names	Eng	Irish
	Corloddy	056	Edward Jackson Esq Edward Jackson his sonn gent	005	051
	Lucketts towne	047		000	047
(folio 14).	Fiddowne	047	Robert Frispe gent	009	038
	Ardclaine	005		004	001
	Rogers towne	001		000	001
	Killmanehine	013		000	013
	Tubernebrone	021		000	021
	Pilltowne	005		002	003
	Killmodaly	033	Coll John Porsonby Esq	005	028
	Benagher	013		000	013
	Brenartowne	015		000	015
	Ballynemetagh	021		000	021
	Templeoram	049		006	043
	Ballinge	013		002	011
	Rahine	019		000	019
	Dowlinge	013		000	013
	Corloghon	002		000	002
	Gorcgage	002		000	002
	Part of Cloinemore	005	George Frype gent	002	003
	Fannings towne	011		000	011
(folio 15).	Unninge	023		000	023
	Bally foricke	009		000	009
	Henebryes towne	040		000	040
	Ballynecrony	014		000	014
	Castletowne	067		003	064
	Killonerry	029	John Fennell gent	002	027
	Tibraghny	037		000	037
	Killmacowe	026		002	024
	Flemings towne	003		000	003
	Grennagh	058		000	058
	Danngin	033	John Pratt gent	006	027
	Ballynerloghe	006		000	006
	More Bane	005		001	004
	Clonecasshie	015		000	015
	Gareenerehie	019		000	019

Principall Irish Names [and] their Numb[er].

Aildwood, 007 ; Butler, 014 ; Browne, 06 ; Cody, 006 ; Donell, 009 ; Daton, 022 ; Dullard, 05 ; Dunfy, 05 ; Fitzgerald, 007 ; Grant, 033 ; Haly & Healy, 008 ; Kenedy, 007 ; Kelly, 006 ; Morphey, 006 ; Mogher, 006 ; Phelan, 011 ; Powre & Poore, 008 ; McPhillipp, 007 ; Quin, 020 ; McShane, 009 ; Welsh & Walsh, 087.

(folio 15 verso). The Number of People in the Bar' of Iverke : Eng, 099 ; Irish, 1358 ; Totall Eng & Irish, 1455.

Parishes	Townelands	Numbs of People	Tituladoes Names	Eng	Irish
	Ballilogh	028	Emanuell Palmer Esq	003	025
	Rathsnagaden	012	James Bolger gent	003	009
	Part of Bally logh	022		000	022
	Ballainbarny	024		000	024
	Parte of Coole hill	011		000	011
	Collentroe	012		001	011
	Mungan	014	David Morey gent	000	014
	Ballyvarry	036		000	036
	Coole hill	018	Charles Kavananagh gent	000	018
	Rosenanowle	011	Solamon Bolger gent	000	011
	Part of Cananow	005		000	005
	Carranroe	043	Pierce Cody gent	000	043
	Ballynunre	032		000	032
	Killrundowney	024		000	024
	Grange	008	Thomas Barnes gent	000	008
	Part of Ballycamon	036		003	033
	Carranavally	007		000	007
(folio 17).	Intreyme	007	Daniell Borne gent	000	007
	Bollicumin	015		000	015
	Tinescolly	023		002	021
	Cloyne	047	Edmond Fitzgerald gent Richard Fitz gerald gent	000	047
	Bally gubb	004		000	004
	Collenemucke	003		002	001
	Gurtins	063	Samuell Scrimshaw gent	004	059
	Drumdowny	055	Marcus Bennet gent	002	053
	Rath Patricke	007		000	007
	Luffinny	003		000	003
	Killinurrey	011		003	008
	Knockbrack	021		004	017
	Killogane	015		000	015
	Rathnewre	030		000	030
	Bally hubocke	077	Theobald Fitzgerald gent Nicholas Fitzgerald gent	000	077
	Rochestowne	060	Anthony Denn gent	000	060
	Nichollstowne	027		000	027
	Ballencrea	043		000	043
(folio 18).	Carricknony	006		000	006
Rosbercon	—	110	Edward Raggett gent Morgan Wicken gent	002	108
	Glancensaw	011		000	011
	Rahine	024		000	024
	Garranbehy	009		002	007
	Tinekilley	015		000	015

Parishes	Townlands	Numbs of People	Tituladoes Names	Eng	Irish
Shanbogh	Tinyrany	031	Samuell Goodwin gent	004	027
	—	056		000	056
	Glanelogh	028		000	028
	Bladin	004		000	004
Disertmone	Annagh	036	Henry Peter gent	003	033
	Garrandaragh	039	James Long gent	005	034
	Ballyready	009	Richard Welsh gent	000	009
	Ballyknocke	011	Edmond McShea gent	000	011
	Brownestowne	012		000	012
	Ballyneale	017		000	017
	Glan Ballivale	022	Edmond Fitzgerald gent	000	022
	Tulloghler	049		000	049
(folio 19). Listerling	Broundsford	025	Samuell Bookeley gent	002	023
	Listerling	055		000	055
	Ballicurrin	020		000	020
Ballygurrin	Ballycroney	032	Thomas Forstall gent	000	032
	Forstalls towne	018		000	018
	Busherstowne	020		000	020
Kilbride	Bally Brahey	024		000	024
	Flemings towne	028	Edmond Forstall gent	000	028
	Killbride	019	Walter Forstall gent Redmond Forstall gent	000	019
	Alwards towne	026	James Fanning gent	005	021
	Carrickclony	017	Stephen Devoroux gent	002	015
	Killmakevoge	038		000	038
	Hagard	005		000	005
	Parks towne	004		000	004
	Mullenahone	002		000	002
	Gaules Kill & Lickettstowne }	036	George Bishopp Esq Anthony Bishopp gent Mich : Tempson gent	008	028
(folio 20)	Gawles towne	040	Boyle Mantell Esq	000	040
	Rathnemalogh	002		002	000
	Killcrony	033	Anthony Horsey Esq	003	030
	Bally Keohan	018		000	018
	Killmaskilloge	014		000	014
	Dunkitt	035	William Dowler gent John Adderton gent	004	031
	Ballymountine	020		003	017
	Mullenbrohe	011	Francis Jone gent	002	009
	Ballemekillboy	020		002	018
	Derenemonsy & Ballyhomucke }	011		000	011
	Milltowne	006		000	006

Principall Irish Names [and] their Numb[er]

Aldwood, 008 ; Bolger, 011 ; Birne, 014 ; Brin & Bren, 011 ; Bryan, 007 ; Butler, 008 ; Baron, 010 ; Cody, 014 ; Cullen, 008 ; Carroll, 010 ; Doyle, 013 ; Daton, 006 ; Dalton, 008 ; Denn, 007 ;

Forstall, 012 ; Gerald, 011 ; Fitzgerald, 011 ; Geraldin, 04 ; Grace, 011 ; Grant, 007 ; Gate (7) & Gawle (010), 017 ; Kelly, 016 ; Knock & Knack, 008 ; Laules, 006 ; Morphey, 072 ; Roe, 005 ; Roch, 009 ; Welsh & Walsh, 094.

(*folio* 20 *verso*)   The Number of People in ye Baronyes of Ida, Igrin and Ibercon : Eng, 079 ; Irish, 1867 ; Totall Eng & Irish, 1946.

(*folio* 21).   **BARONY OF KNOKTOPHER**

Parishes	Townelands	Numbs of People	Tituladoes Names	Eng	Irish
Quere what P'ishes these be in	Rossehinon	008		000	008
	Skarte	010		000	010
	Glandoniell	006		002	004
	Ballynekill	012		000	012
	Ballyquinn	005		002	003
	Ballintlea	016		000	016
	Baiogreche	010		000	010
	Garrandarragh and Mullenult	033	Dennis Correy gent	003	030
	Ballilosky	010		000	010
	Ballygonbegg	007		000	007
	Ballyigony	018		000	018
	Smyths towne	031		000	031
	Derbyes towne	004		000	004
	Cappagh Fousy	008		000	008
	Killinmocke	026		000	026
	Dirrilakagh	012		000	012
	Crobally	022		000	022
	Ballytarsny	004		000	004
(*folio* 22).	Castle Ganing	030	John Browne gent	002	028
	Newcastle	057		000	057
	Upper Dirinehinch	021		000	021
	Loer Dirinehinch	031		000	031
	Ballyhoyle	041	Henry Wade Esq, Capt Tomlins Esq, John Johnson gent	013	028
	Kiltockan	015		000	015
	Ballyconway	029	James Howling gent	002	027
	Ballylowry	031		000	031
	Jerpoint	029	Thomas Walton gent	002	027
	Watons groue	041	William Shea gent	000	041
	Cortneboly	049	Robert Knorisborogh gent	002	047
	Rathtuterny towne	020	Patrick Purcell gent	000	020
	Kilkirihill	019		000	019
	Killkrassy	033		000	033

Parishes	Townelands	Numbs of People	Tituladoes Names	Eng	Irish
(folio 23)	Lis Mᶜ Teigue	037		000	037
	Knockmellan	093	Mathew Dermody gent	000	093
	Ballaghbregan	021		000	021
	Ballintober	004		000	004
	Corebehy, Balline, Cowly, and Ballyhowen	038	James Walsh gent	000	038
	Monhenry	015		000	015
	Insencarren	025	Francis Robinson gent	002	023
	Ballyrobogg	003		000	003
	Muckully and Milltowne	007		002	005
	Harristowne	050		000	050
	Ashtowne	010		004	006
	Killmocke	023		000	023
	Ballytesken	005		000	005
	Barnedowne	010		000	010
	Condons towne	009		002	007
	Ballynemaboge	011	Tobias Boyle gent	004	007
(folio 24).	Mylards towne	004		000	004
	Derrilyagh and Croshenoy		Thomas Inmon gent	002	047
	Croan Begg	016		000	016
	Aghy viller	019	Baldwan Ackland gent	002	017
	Knocktopher, Borridstowne, and Sheepstowne	060	George Kempton gent	009	051
	Whites castle	039		003	036
	Mannor of Knocktopher	074	Compton Woogon gent	000	074
	The demeanes of the Abby	045		000	045
	Alt. Ensigne Carren	008	All Souldiers Wifes	003	005

Principall Irish Names [and] Their Numb[er].

Bourke, 005 ; Barron, 09 ; Butler, 16 ; Bolger, 05 ; Brenan, 06 ; Daton, 06 ; McDonogh, 07 ; McEdmond, 06 ; Forstall, 06 ; Howling, 14 ; Kelly, 05 ; Kenedy, 05 ; Morphey, 11 ; Mogher, 07 ; Neale, 06 ; Nolan, 05 ; Power & Poore, 08 ; Ryan, 022 ; Rely, 06 ; Shea, 006 ; Walsh, 111 ; White, 015 ; McWilliam, 005.

(folio 24 verso)   The Number of People in the Bar of Knocktopher : Eng, 061 ; Irish, 1301 ; Totall Eng & Irish, 1362.

(folio 25).   **BARONY OF FASSAGH DEININ**

Parishes	Townelands	Numbs of People	Tituladoes Names	Eng	Irish
	Castlemarkett	040		007	033
	Cooleroe	026		005	21

Parishes	Townelands	Numbs of People	Tituladoes Names	Eng	Irish
	Laughill	052		000	052
	Rosconell	008		000	008
	Wall, parte of Bally uskell, and Barnestoke }	055		000	055
	Nichollstowne	012	John Todd gent	002	010
	Russells towne	004		000	004
	Ballyraggett	127	Nathaniell Williams Esq, Walter Noss gent, Richard Makins gent, Nicholas Shea Merchant, John Roth Merchant, Theobald Purcell gent.	023	104
	Killentane	010		000	010
	Bollinvallagh	002		000	002
	Donoghmore	054	William Cleere gent	000	054
	Conehey	054		000	054
	Old towne	010		000	010
(folio 26).	Fenan and Pte of Ballymartin }	036		000	036
	Ballymartin	005		000	005
	Ballylarkin	035		000	035
	Foulkrath	018		000	018
	Lismain and Knockrowe }	020		000	020
	Christowne	033	James Bryon gent William Stringer gent	001	032
	Tuleglass	011		000	011
	Jenkins towne	067	John Bryan gent Duglass Bryan	000	067
	Gillianstowne	004		000	004
	Esker and Killtollam	018		000	018
	Lisnefansy	020		000	020
	Clasduff	007		000	007
	Disart Maner Land	003		000	003
	Killmocar	030		005	025
	Tillantan	023		000	023
(folio 27).	Part of Raquile	023		000	023
	Coolle Brislan	010		004	006
	Timoheny	022		000	022
	Pte of Raquile	032		000	032
	Glanmacoull	021		000	021
	Damerstowne	046		000	046
	Corbetts towne	025		002	023
	Killmodimoge	036		000	036
	Lubstowne	006		000	006
	Muckully	032		000	032
	Galstowne	008		000	008
	Aghatubred	063		000	063

Parishes	Townelands	Numbs of People	Tituladoes Names	Eng	Irish
	Cloghmoile head	032		000	032
	Cloghrancke	029		000	029
	Ballyhem	025		000	025
	Coolecullanduff	009		000	009
	Confoilan	032		000	032
	John Roth towne	007		000	007
(folio 28).	Burntowne and Toxhill	042		000	042
	Killtowne	061		000	061
	Mihoragh	013		000	013
	Lowen	028		000	028
	Cruill	025		000	025
	Cooleneleene	015		000	015
	Killnebuskehary	010		000	010
	Clowneene	025		000	025
	Gurteene	059		000	059
	Coolebane	027		000	027
	Ardrey	029		000	029
	Moinnerowe	026		000	026
	Aghamuckey	023		000	023
	Croghneclogh	011		000	011
	Castlecumber	040		004	036
	Rathcally	013		000	013
(folio 29).	Rattoom[n]	015		000	015
	Uskert	020		000	020
	Smythstowne	017		000	017

Principall Irish Names [and] their Numb[er].

Brohy, 10 ; Butler, 11 ; Brenan, 116 ; Birne, 31 ; Bergin, 08 ; Blanchvill and Blanchfield, 06 ; Cleere, 06 ; Dulany, 23 ; Duin & Duing, 08 ; Dowling, 09 ; Forstall, 07 ; Ferrell, 06 ; Horoghon (11) & Hologhon (4), 15 ; Henessy, 09 ; Hicky, 09 ; Kenedy, 13 ; Kelly, 20 ; Kevanagh, 10 ; Kehoe, 05 ; Kenny, 05 ; Lallor & Lawlor, 12 ; Murphy, 16 ; Mollowny & Muldowny, 09 ; Mogher, 12 ; Nolan, 08 ; Neale, 06 ; Phelan, 31 ; Fitzpatrick, 08 ; Purcell, 35 ; Ryan, 09 ; Walsh, 12.

(folio 29 verso)   The Number of People in the Barony of Fassagh Deinin : Eng, 053 ; Irish, 1688 ; Totall Eng & Irish, 1741.

(folio 30) **BARONY OF KELLS**

Parishes	Townelands	Numb of People	Tituladoes Names	Eng	Irish
	Towne of Kells	089	Jonas Wheeler Esq John Meagh gent Robert Shea gent	009	080

Parishes	Townelands	Numb of People	Tituladoes Names	Eng	Irish
	Kells grange	024		000	024
	High Street in Kells	083	Beniamin Woodward Esq John Jones Esq	009	074
	Towne of Kilry	012	Morish Morphy Esq	000	012
	Shortalls towne	017		000	017
	Danginbegg	025		000	025
	Hagard	017		000	017
	Growbegg	019		000	019
	Donemagan	022		004	018
	Wingsgroue	013		002	011
	Rahine	011		000	011
	Danginmore	038	Richard Comerford gent	000	038
	Maliards towne	068		000	068
	Rathcubbin & Spruces Hayes	041	Thomas Shea gent	000	041
	Mellaghmore	081		000	081
(folio 31).	Garry Challowes and Lamoge	022		000	022
	Tollohact	008		000	008
	Ballinilinoge	005		000	005
	Kill mc Olliver	033		000	033
	Castle Hoile	045	Elias Pike gent	006	039
	Uny begg	010		000	010
	Lemons towne	010		000	010
	Rosenarrowe	015		000	015
	Cottrells towne	018		000	018
	Killmogany	030		000	030
	New church	011		000	011
	Rogers towne	023	Andrew Manwaring	005	018
	Killrihill	030	Henry Morris Esq	000	030
	Killdromy	026		000	026
	Killamerry	046	Isaack Jackson Esq	003	043
	Garran	014		000	014
(folio 32)	Botlers wood	012	Robert Burchall gent	002	010
	Seskin	040		000	040
	Killtrassy	010	Thomas Butler gent	000	010
	Roscon	031	John Jones Esq	004	027
	Rossonena	021		000	021
	Cooleghmore	055		000	055
	Boelly flagh	010		000	010
	Aghenur	022	William Rooth gent	000	022
	Attetino	022	Richard Mornell gent	000	022
	Bellaghtobin	023	Ralph Hale gent	004	019
	Crotobeg	018		000	018
	Caherlesky	030	John Cussock gent, Robert Shea gent, Michaell Archer gent.	002	028

Principall Irish Names [and] their Numb[er]

Brohy, 05 ; Butler, 23 ; Connor, 05 ; Connell, 05 ; Conway, 07 ; Carroll, 06 ; Fitzdavid, 06 ; Howling, 06 ; Kelly, 12 ; Keefe, 22 ; Millea, 07 ; Morphey, 09 ; Mogher, 17 ; Neile, 08 ; Purcell, 07 ; Power, 09 ; Phelan, 06 ; Quiddihy and Quiddily, 11 ; Ryan, 07 ; Rooth, 05 ; Shee & Shea, 61 ; Tobin, 08 ; Wall, 05 ; Walsh, 031.

(folio 32 verso). The Number of People in ye Barony of Kells : Eng, 050 ; Irish, 1150 ; Totall Eng & Irish, 1200.

(folio 33). **BARONY OF SKILLELLOGHER**

Parishes	Townelands	Number of People	Tituladoes Names	Eng	Irish
	Dunfart	083	Sᵣ Patricke Weymes Knt James Weymes Esq Thomas Weymes gent	008	075
	Rathclough	024		000	024
	Bennetts bridge	014		002	012
	Aghanamolt	051		000	051
	Burnt church	119	William Wordon Esq, Samuell Booth gent, Henry Wassher gent.	022	097
	Cottrells rath	016	Robert Walsh gent	000	016
	Ballymack	024	Mathias Reiligh gent John Groues gent	002	022
	Boley	012	Samuell Sutton gent	004	008
	Castle Eue	042	Henry Baker gent Henry Baker Esq	008	034
	Earlestowne	046	William Boxter gent	002	044
	Garraphilbin	013		000	013
	Ovins towne	022	William Davis gent	002	020
	Tulloghmaine	077	John Campbell Esq	008	069
	Inchiologhan	105	Joseph Cuff Esq	003	102
	Goslings towne	026	George Barton gent Giles King gent	005	021
(folio 34).	Tulleghane	086		000	086
	Dirrin	025		000	025
	Tinehinch	005		003	002
	Kilbricken	017		002	015
	Killinloe	025	Richard Tobin gent James Tobin gent	000	025
	Rossmore	031	Walter Hackett gent	000	031
	Tinekilly	011		000	011
	Tenegarrane	010	Edmond Butler gent	000	010
	Cappohedine	031		000	031
	Balliloue	020	Olt Grace gent	000	020
	Graigooly	027		000	027
	Wasses hayes and Kilfara }	054	Atland Tench gent	002	052
	Outrath	016		000	016
	Garrowoyne	006		000	006
	Killree	028		000	028
	Iniisnage	031		002	029

Parishes	Townelands	Number of People	Tituladoes Names	Eng	Irish
(*folio* 35).	Stamcarty	046	Bryan Moryergh gent	000	046
	Ballyburr	032		000	032
	Grainge	078		000	078
	Earles towne	012		000	012

Principall Irish Names [and] their Number.

Brenon, 09 ; Butler, 08 ; Bane, 07 ; Donell, 10 ; Dulany, 06 ; Fleming, 10 ; Glison, 05 ; Hologhon, 05 ; Kelly, 06 ; Lorkan, 07 ; Morphy, 18 ; Mogher, 17 ; Morish, 07 ; Nolan, 11 ; Phelan, 12 ; Ryan, 09 ; McTeige, 07.

(*folio* 35 *verso*).   The Number of People in ye Barony of Skillellogher : Eng, 075 ; Irish. 1190 ; Totall Eng & Irish, 1265.

(*folio* 36).   **BARONY OF CRANNAGH**

Parishes	Townelands	Numbs of People	Tituladoes Names	Eng	Irish
	Lisballisroote	020		000	020
	Hunts towne	017		000	017
	Oldtowne	015	John Grace gent	000	015
	Ballyquidihy	020		006	014
	Briscallagh	003		000	003
	Failentallure	005		000	005
	Rahealy Rath	012	George Hunter gent	003	009
	Adams towne	013		000	013
	Monemedroole	008		000	008
	Ballyroe Sargt	004		000	004
	Piratts towne and Rahely Lyshe	} 021	Thomas Hunter gent John Smyth gent	005	016
	Courts towne	028	John Grace Esq	000	028
	Lisnelea	006		000	006
	Ballibeaugh	029		000	029
	Trenchers towne	023		000	023
	Brittasmore	048		000	048
(*folio* 37)	Rahine	022		000	022
	Boggane	015		000	015
	Gortenegapp	016		000	016
	Rath Mc Canne	019		000	019
	Ballycanmore	017		000	017

Parishes	Townelands	Numbs of People	Tituladoes Names	Eng	Irish
	Tulloroane	014		000	014
	Bounces towne	018		000	018
	Corestowne	064	Thomes Greene gent George Greene gent	005	059
	Brabstowne	005		000	005
	PobleRagh	070		000	070
	Killeene	013		000	013
	Brittas Dryling	013		000	013
	Shortals grage	017	Redmond Boorke gent	000	017
	Killmanagh Mansland	006		000	006
	Bellaghclonine	009		000	009
	Sheeps towne	009		000	009
	Kilbrehane	045		000	045
(folio 38).	Killmanagh	045	Thomas Knarisborogh gent	004	041
	Ballikeise	046	John Butler gent	000	046
	Killbally Keese	032		000	032
	Damagh	104	John Smyth gent, Luke Smyth gent, Valentine Smyth gent.	008	096
	Ballicallan	033	Nicholas Knarisborough gent	001	032
	Dorath	023		000	023
	Bally fruncke	059		000	059
	Dreilingstowne	006		002	004
	Currogh Kehoe	034		002	032
	Bannanogh	022	George Lodge gent	002	020
	Symonds land	007		000	007
	Leiugh	012		000	012
	Killary	016	Richard Shea gent	000	016
	Bally carrane	001		000	001
	Ballydaniell	024	John Shea gent	000	024
(folio 39).	Darrigine, Boords hayes and Prickes hayes	076	Angelin Grace gent	005	071
	Inch & Crow Hill	028	Robert Grace gent	002	026
	Cloughmantagh	045		000	045
	Balline	004		000	004
Tubred P'ish	Cornefrake	029		000	029
	Tubrid	018	John Dobson gent	004	014
	Garranclonee	003		000	003
	Garry higgin	016		000	016
	Killdreinogh	016		000	016
	Bally lorkane	028	John Hugh gent	004	024
	Uppercourt	031	Willm Portis gent	008	023
	Glaseerowe	030	John Reamon gent	002	028
	Ballydowell	022		004	018
	Clontubrid	037	Michaell Knarisborogh gent	002	035
(folio 40).	Killaghy	028	Walter Harvey gent Gerald Grace	003	025

Parishes	Townlands	Numbs of People	Tituladoes Names	Eng	Irish
	Lughuimg	009		000	009
	Killosullan	030	Edward Butler gent	000	030
	Garrenemanagh	015		000	015
	Killoushee	017	Joseph Wheeler gent	001	016
	Killbealenemoe	014		000	014
	Ballyrone Shortall	018		000	018
	Cooleshell the George	014		000	014
	Sarte	034	Mathew White gent	000	034
	Rahealty	037		000	037
	Gals towne	030		000	030
	Trefford	122	Gregory Marshall gent	006	116

Principall Irish Names [and] Their Numb[er]

Butler, 022 ; Brenogh, 007 ; O Boe &c, 005 ; Brohy, 011 ; Britt, 006 ; Brenon, 008 ; Birne, 013 ; Brin, 005 ; Cormucke, 006 ; Carroll, 007 ; Coghell, 012 ; Cantwell, 005 ; Comerford, 015 ; Coody, 006 ; Crooke, 006 ; Dreiling, 008 ; Dowling, 011 ; Duin & Duing, 011 ; Dulany, 017 ; Dullahunty, 016 ; Fanning, 005 ; Grace, 041 ; Healy, 006 ; Hologhon, 010 ; Hicky, 09 ; Kelly, 14 ; Kenedy, 10 ; Morphy, 12 ; Mogher, 18 ; Pheland, 27 ; Ryane, 10 ; Shea, 10 ; Shortall, 08 ; Tobin, 08 ; Tinan, 06 ; Walsh, 31.

(*folio* 40 *verso*)   The number of People in ye Barony of Crannagh : Eng, 079 ; Irish, 1778 ; Totall Eng & Irish, 1857.

(*folio* 41).   **TOWNE AND LIBERTIES OF CALLAN**

			Tituladoes Names	Eng	Irish
	Towne of Callan	422	James Morphey gent, Derby Doyle gent, John Balfremon gent, Patrick Voice gent, John Warren gent, Roger Boe gent, Ephron Beall gent	083	339
Liberties of Callan	Kilbride	008		000	008
	Folksrath	004		000	004
	Castletobin	002		002	000
	Magstowne	008		000	008
	Balline Banagh	004		000	004
	Westcourt	003		001	002

Principall Irish Names [and] Their Numb[er].

Butler, 06 ; Comerford, 04 ; Lenan, 04 ; Mogher, 08 ; Phelan, 04.

(folio 42).   **CITY AND LIBERTIES OF KILKENNY.**

High towne Ward : Numb of People, 208 ; Eng, 152 ; Irish, 056 ; Tituladoes Names : Hugh
Fox, Thomas Nevill, Richard Baron, Sognez Rigdeway, John Rigdeway, Tho : Taylor, John White,
Tho : Tallbott, Barthlowmew Conor gentlemen ; Thomas Newman Esq, Henry Baker, William
Warring, William Stringer, John Langton, Valentine Reade, Francis Roledge, George Dason, John
Browne, Thomas Smyth, Ralph Scanlan, Bulmer Millcod, Parles Bancks, Thomas Chapman, Walter
Seix, William Floyd, Thomas Honwer, Conlane Donell, Richard Inwood, Nicholas Richards, Jonas
Hadrach gentlemen ; William Burges Esq, John Simes, Nicholas Richards, Robert Robins gentle-
men ; John Jeonor Esq, Robt Joue, Thomas Weatherby, Peter Goodwin, Ralph St Lawrence, Jn
Sines, John Ball, Joh Ball Merchants.

(folio 43). Northward : Numb of People, 227 ; Eng, 068 ; Irish, 159 ; Tituladoes Names :
Peter Blacknell gent, William Bond Esq, Thomas Fogg, Rich : Smyth gentlemen ; Thomas Evans,
Tho : Wilson Esqrs ; William Cuell, Luke Archer, John Bewar, William Wilsby, Samuell Phillipps,
John Goge, John Usher, Thady Corkron, Henry Grewall gentle, Andrew Mannoring Esq, Edmond
Roth, Edmond Fitzgerald, John Archdekin, M'chants ; Charles Empson gent, Thomas Adams gent.

St Patricks inward : Numb of People, 143 ; Eng, 042 ; Irish, 101 ; Tituladoes Names : John
Farrer, Thomas Butler, Esqrs ; Edmond Butler, Richard Donell, Richard Delarahe, Tho Davis,
John Penefaither, Charles Duke, Cornelius Wright, Stephen Slaney, Nathainell Cooper, Edmd
Ardwaher, gentlemen ; Jonas Ash gent.

[MS Blank] : Numb of People, 124 ; Eng, 049 ; Irish, 175 ; Tituladoes Names : William
Pocher gent, Henry Martin Esq, William Davis gent, Thomas Burrill Esq, Edmond Williams gent,
Rice Thomas Esq, Beale Archer gent.

(folio 44).	The Severall Wards &c		Tituladoes Names	Eng	Irish
	St Johns Inward	081	Michaell Bodge, Edmond Hicks, John Phillipps gent.	029	052
	St Kennis Ward	085	Phelim Codon gent	000	085
	St Kennis Butts	140	John Langton gent	010	130
	Bonestowne	033	John Mathewes Esqr	014	019
Belonging to	Cappagh	010		000	010
St Kennis	Lavine lanty	006		000	006
Butts	Bollishee	015		000	015
	Cloran	011	James Sinacke Esq Jonas Sinack his sonn gent	004	007
	Coldgrange	007		000	007
	Grange Parke	011		008	003
	Dunnings towne	014		002	012
	Thorne backe	011		000	011
	Chappell	019		000	019
	Troyeswood	005		000	005
	Talbotts towne	005		003	002
(folio 45).	Pte of Kennis Butts				
	Palmers towne	008		000	008
	New towne	039	William Jewell gent	010	029
	St Patricks outward	147	James Rafter gent	003	444
	Archers towne	014	Robert Tobin gent	000	014
	Drakes land	008		004	004
	Kilkreene	016		000	016
	Baggotts land	006		000	006
	Archers groue	013		000	013

The Severall Wards &c		Tituladoes Names	Eng	Irish
Scales Firrs	005		000	005
Shalloms Rath	008		004	004
Clonmorny	003	Overington Blunden gent	002	001
St Johns Outward	071	Michaell Raggott & Peter Raggott gent	002	069
Maudling Streete	073		004	069
Loghmearan	018		000	018
Rodestowne	028	Henry Brodridge and Richard Pratt gent	004	024
Brounes towne	020		000	020
Garricringe	006		000	006
Ligads Rath	028	Arthur Heilshon Esq	007	021
Purcells Inch	003		000	003
Cellers towne	007		000	007
Green street	012		000	012
Windgate	012		000	012
New Parke	011		000	011
Pte of Cellers towne	003		000	003
New Orchard	008		000	008

(folio 46).

Principall Irish Names [and] Their Number.

Archdekin, 06 ; Archer, 09 ; Birne & Brin, 10 ; Broune, 08 ; Cody, 06 ; Cantwell, 08 ; Corckron, 08 ; Comerford, 07 ; Conway, 06 ; Donell, 12 ; Dowling &c, 17 ; Daton, 06 ; Grace, 06 ; Headen, 08 ; Hologhon, 10 ; Kelly, 13 ; Lalor, 07 ; Lanegan, 05 ; Morphey, 12 ; Mogher, 14 ; Moore, 09 ; Purcell, 07 ; Fitz patrick, 05 ; Phelan, 13 ; Power, 08 ; Ryan, 16 ; Shea, 07 ; Smyth, 09 ; Shortall, 06 ; Tobin, 06 ; Walsh, 05.

(folio 45 verso)   The Number of people in ye City & Liberties of Kilkenny : Eng, 421 ; Irish, 1301 ; Totall Eng & Irish, 1722.

(folio 46 verso)   The Number of people in Ye County of Kilkenny and City of Kilkenny and Towne of Callan &c.

Baronyes & Townes &c	Pages	Eng	Irish	Eng & Irish		
Galmoy Bar	3	128	1446	1574	1442	16948
Gowran Bar	11	311	3543	3854	86	365
Iverke	15	099	1356	1455	421	1301
Ida, Igrin, & Ibercon	20	079	1867	1946	507	1666
Knocktopher	24	061	1301	1362	935	15282
Fassagh Deinin	29	053	1688	1741		935
Kells	32	050	1150	1200	18427	16217
Skillellogher	35	075	1190	1265	451	
Crannagh	40	079	1778	1857	1722	
Towne of Callan &c	41	086	0365	0451	2173	
City of Kilkenny	45	421	1301	1722	16254	
The Totall		1442	16985	18427		

KINGS COUNTY
8310

(*folio* 1).   Kings County

BARRONY OF PHILLIPSTOWNE[1]

Parishes	Places	Numbers	Tituladoes Names	English	Irish
Croghan	Castles towne Croghan	28	John Moore Esq	02	26
	Kilcorky	18	Mr Thomas Cussacke gent	00	18
	Ballibey	23	Mr Adam Cussacke gent	03	20
	Killinkill	06		01	05
	Aughmore	11		2	09
Balliburly	Robins towne	5		—	05
	Bally falogh	16		—	16
	Loghans towne	20			20
	Towher Croghan	15		01	14
	Coole	16			16
Kilclonfarte	Clonaragh	28		01	27
	Mullelogh	13			13
	Mullalogh Idm	12			12
	Killinet	3			03
	ClonIrell	26	Richard Loughlin Esq	3	23
	ClonIrell Idem	20			20
	Baladuffe	5			05
	Barnan	7		1	06
	Bernabey	20		3	17
	O Kilclonfarte	30	Garrot Luther gent	2	28
	Clonen	27		7	20
(*folio* 2). Killadurhy	Killishell	08			08
	Gurtine	09			09
	Castle barnagh	16		02	14
	Bally owen	15		1	14
	Clonadd	13			13
	Phillips towne	129	Richard Lambert, William Coate gent, Charles Lyons Esq	34	95
Bally common	Bally common	25	Walter Bermingham gent	7	18
	Bally teige	18		4	14
	Killmurry	15	Mr Edward Lee gent	4	11
	Bracklone	09		—	09
	Rothdrummon	12			12
Parte of ye P'ish of Ballylean	Raheene	49	William Tate gent	9	40
	Ballinvoher	09			09
	Urney	07		2	05
	Killconey	14			14
	Killcappagh	23		1	22
	Ballykean	26	Richard Hoden Esq Will Hoden gent	5	21
	Clonagowney	59	John Nelson Esq	27	32
	Inohane	06	Laurance Dempsey gent		06
(*folio* 3). Part of Gashell Parish	Bally Cristoll	18		5	13
	Raheenbeg	12		4	8

[1] *Phillipstowne hundred*, folio 2

Parishes	Places	Numbers	Tituladoes Names	English	Irish
	Rathestan	25	Robert Masson gent	5	20
	Raheenna Kerin	21		2	19
	Ballintample	19	Kedah Dempsy gent		19
	Garamoney	08			8
Clonahurke	Ard	32			32
	Cullin	02			02
	Gurtin	12		4	08
	Clonahurke	25		2	23
	Killenagh	15		4	11
	Rathmoore	09		2	7
	Killkerane	08			8
	Cloniquim	09		5	4
	Portahinch	07	Humphry Bromfield gent	7	—
	Gerrahinch	06	Rich : Brickelsby gent	6	—
Haris towne	Richards towne	20		—	20
(folio 4).	Moyler towne	30		2	28
	Haris towne	27			27
Bally brack	Killpatrick	09	Georg Key gent	7	2
	Loughill	04			4
	Gurtin	18		4	14
Part of Lackagh Parish	Ballynagalogh	02		2	—
	Traskan, and Tinne-cranagh	44		3	41

Principall Irish Names [and] Their Number.

Briane, 03 ; Beagham, 12 ; Birne, 08 ; Bracken, 08 ; Burke, 03 ; Beolan, 09 ; Cussack, 03 ; Clary, 10 ; Caroll, 13 ; Duff, 14 ; Dunn, 15 ; Dempsy, 31 ; Flynn, 07 ; Foran, 10 ; Gerold, 03 ; Haverim, 07 ; Keely, 22 ; Moony, 05 ; Murcan, 05 ; Molloy, 10 ; Morrin, 11 ; Murfay, 07; Malloone, 04 ; Moor, 03 ; Neall, 03 ; McShane, 09 ; Quinne, 13 ; Wellahane, 10.

(folio 3 verso). Number of People in the Bary of Phillipptowne according to the severall pages : Eng, 186 ; Irish, 1007 ; Totall Eng & Irish, 1193.

(folio 5).   **BARONY OF COOLIS TOWNE**

Parishes	Places	Numbers	Tituladoes Names	English	Irish
Monesteroris	Edendery	55	Sr George Blundell Barnet Conley Kegan gent	05	50
	Drumcally	17		00	17
	Cloncannon	14			14
	Lyan	18		00	18

Parishes	Places	Numbers	Tituladoes Names	English	Irish
	Codd	09		02	07
	Monesteroris	40		03	37
	Bally colgan	07		01	06
Ballynakill	Ardbas	04		00	04
Monesterroris	Rathmore	08		01	07
Ballynakill	Ballynanny	10	Mr James Sankey gent	01	09
	Bally Killin	03		—	03
	Huminery	01		—	01
	Cappouge	02			02
	Bally moran	04		01	03
	Leitrim	12	Mr Thomas Sankey gent	01	11
	Ballinlea	10		2	8
(folio 6). Part of Bally bogan Parish	Clonmene of Newtowne	22		2	20
Clonsast	Clonbolgue	17	Mr Robt Shallcross gent	2	15
	Clonmeale	09		—	9
	Ballyhemott	02		2	—
	Kiltcumber	03		—	3
	Clonbrone	10		4	6
	Colly gergan	15		4	11
	Clonmore	10			10
	Derringarran	12			12
	Derymullin	07			7
	Brecknaugh	20		4	16
	Kildrumen	08			8
	KillcloncorKery	08		4	4
	Ballyraheene	12	Charles Conner gent		12
	Clonbrine	06		3	3
(folio 7).	Cappagh	09	Charles Dempsy	—	9
	Ballynoltark	11		—	11
Balynahill	Eskerbey	31		7	24
	Drumcage	37		5	32
	Ballynrath	14		6	8
	Eskermore	10		2	8
	Clonkrean	03		—	3

Principall Irish Names [and] their Numb[er].

Beghane, 9 ; Burke, 7 ; Bryane, 2 ; Conner, 19 ; Cassadie, 6 ; Farrell, 5 ; Garre, 5 ; Havarin, 6 ; Kyne, 9 ; Moony, 18 ; Moran, 6 ; Moor, 3.

(folio 7 verso). The Number of People in the Barony of Coolishtowne &c : Eng, 062 ; Irish, 428 ; Totall Eng & Irish, 0490.

(folio 8). ## BARONY OF BALLABOY[1]

Parishes	Places	Numbs	Tituladoes Names	English	Irish
	Rathrobbin	28	John Hollan gent (Thomas Tyly in ras).	6	22

[1] Ballyboy, folio 10.

Parishes	Places	Numbs	Tituladoes Names	English	Irish
	Korlanebeg	8		8	—
	Rothleene	8		3	5
	Gurtacuramore	25		4	21
	Capingolane	10		8	2
	Cappingarren	19		5	14
	Bellingowne	04		2	2
	Bellin kenly	10		6	4
	Killohy	02		—	2
	Newtowne	09		2	7
	Killenany	30		2	28
	Anaghbrack	24		—	24
	Logamorly	08		3	5
(folio 9).	Derridallny	30		—	30
	Gorbelly	11		—	11
	Cully	07			07
	Killmore	08			08
	Killmadonoye,	12			12
	Corcomeala,	19			19
	Belly corne				
Bally boy	Broghelloe	61		9	52
	Killcormack	42		7	35
	Clondaglass	07		2	5
	Capeaneagh	22		2	20
	Lealoghmore	13			13
	Bally collan more	12			12
	Derm boy	15			15
(folio 10).	Coolfin	14			14
	Bally lenan	16		2	14
	Bally boy	45		14	31
	Ballincargy	34		4	30
	Bally William Reagh	08		2	6
	Killeene, & Legnaboly	14			14

Principall Irish Names [and] their Numb[er].

Coghlane, 3 ; Conway, 7 ; Conner, 4 ; Carroll, 2 ; Costigan, 3 ; Dwigine, 7 ; Dun, 9 ; Flanergan, 4 ; Grogane, 4 ; Hogan, 6 ; Keagane, 8 ; Keely, 8 ; Kenane, 4 ; Moloy, 27 ; Mehane, 9 ; Mullerane, 5.

(folio 10 verso). The Number of People in the Bar^y of Ballaboy &c : Eng, 091 ; Irish, 484 ; Totall Eng & Irish, 575.

(folio 11). **BARONY OF BALLYCOWEN**

Parishes	Places	Numbers	Tituladoes Names	English	Irish
Derrone		165	Sr George Herbert K^t & Bar^t, Edward Herbert Esq	30	135
Rahan		216	John Riddinge gent	50	166
Killbride		171		31	140
Lunully		142		21	121

Principall Irish Names [and] Their Numb[er.]

Beolan, 4 ; Bryane, 10 ; Breckan, 8 ; Bohely, 8 ; Conway, 5 ; Carroll, 5 ; Duigen, 5 ; Flynne, 6 ; Keely, 6 ; Kenedy, 4 ; Molley, 24 ; Mury, 10 ; Trassey, 7 ; Spollan, 10.

(*folio* 11 *verso*). The Number of People in the Barrony of Ballycowen : Eng, 132 ; Irish, 562 ; Eng & Irish, 694.

(*folio* 12). **BARONY OF GESHELL**

Parishes	Places	Numbs	Tituladoes Names	English	Irish
Gashell	Gashell	67	John Bauldwine Esq Will : Dunne Mr Thomas Say gent	18	49
	Dallgan	07		2	5
	Ballyrue	02		2	—
	Killeredy	11		3	8
	Ballymoony	30	Robert Cusake gent	—	30
	Anaghorvie	38		2	36
Part of Ballycommon	Cappincurre	48	William Fitzgerrald gent	9	39
P'ish	Clonmore	32	Henry Grenham gent	9	23
Gashell	Cappicoo	15		4	11
	Toberliben	14	Garret Plunket gentle	2	12
	Cappinageragh	19		2	17
	Ballynagarr	16		4	12
(*folio* 13).	Knockbally beg	28	Mr Rober Lloyd Esq	7	21
	Killigh	78	Thomas Johnson Meriell Tarleton gent	36	42
	Ballinshragh	09		0	9
	Ballynvally	12		4	8
	Gurtine	32		8	24
	Killurin	50		4	46
	Aghincush	13		—	13
	Bally laven	29		—	29
	Ballylavill	08			8
	Cloncorey	21			21
	Bally collin	16			16
	Raheeneduff	18		4	14
	Newtowne	18			18
	Killin more	58	William Fitzgerald gent	8	50
	Grage	16	The Lord Digby of Kildare	5	11
Part of P'ish of Bally-kean	Fenleer	25		6	19

Principall Irish Names [and] Their Numb[er.]

Broghane, 7 ; Bryane, 7 ; Conner, 5 ; Clary, 3 ; Conraghy, 4 ; Dempsey, 10 ; McDaniell, 5 ; Doyne, 9 ; Duigen, 3 ; Duff, 3 ; Dun, 3 ; Flynne, 5 ; Flarergan, 4 ; Morrin, 8 ; Mallone, 8 ; Quime, 11.

(*folio* 13 *verso*). The Number of People in the Barrony of Geshell : Eng, 139 ; Irish, 591 ; Eng & Irish, The Total, 730.

(*folio* 14).

BARONY OF WARRENSTOWNE

Parishes	Places	Numbs	Tituladoes Names	English	Irish
Part of Ye P'ish of Ballybarly	Ballybarly	58	John Wakely Esq	07	51
	Shragho	13		—	13
	Coolcorr	26		—	26
	Toullough and Voerr	07			7
	Clonneene	17			17
	Rathmoyle	15		4	11
	Fagh	17		2	15
	Garr	25		5	20
	Killowen	04		2	2
	Guttene	01			1
	Daragh	01		00	1
	Corbets towne	20			20
	Drum	36			36
	Clonmore	40	Robert Dillone gent	14	26
Ballyn William	Ballyeshell	14	Edward Walker gent	09	5
	Ballybrittine	55	George Sankey gent	13	42
(*folio* 15).	Bally mac William	20		8	12
	Lenananearch	42		9	33
Part of Ye P'ish of Ballybogan	Coberdalaugh	19			19

Principall Irish Names [and] their Numb[er.]

Brenagh, 6 ; Brackane, 4 ; Bryane, 2 ; Burk, 2 ; Conallone, 8 ; Doyne, 11 ; Ennis, 8 ; Haverine, 4 ; Mallone, 6.

(*folio* 15 *verso*). The Number of People in ye Barony of Warestowne : Eng, 073 ; Irish, 357 ; Totall Eng & Irish, 0430.

(*folio* 16).

BARONY OF CLONLISK

Parishes	Places	Numbs	Tituladoes Names	English	Irish
Dunkerine	Ballnettolan	18		4	14
	Clonegannagh	8		4	4
	Emell	21	John Rose Esq	4	17
	Castellrohan	17		—	17
	Coologge	22		4	18
	Ballyrehe	30		—	30
	Correclenan	32		6	26
Part of the P'ish of Dunkerine	Cleduff	34		—	34

Parishes	Places	Numbs	Tituladoes Names	English	Irish
Castle towne and Bullerstowne }		36		2	34
Fingelish	Fingelish	13		—	13
	Laughan	5		—	5
Part of ye P'ish of Roscray, and Corkelly and Aghnemadelly of Ye Kings County and Barony of Clonlish P'ish of Roscray and Bally brack }		15			15
(folio 17)	Lisnygeragh	26			26
	Minure	7			7
	Dromikenan	29		2	27
Corbally	Balliskennagh	13			13
The Part of ye Ard-niniadill in the Barony Ronelisk, & Kings County }	Ballinlough	31	John Grice gentle	6	25
	Ballingrottey	23	William Wells gentle	3	20
	Moneygall	9			9
	Raheeney	41	John Andrews gentle	8	33
	Colniwaine	49	John Disbrow Esq	5	44
Shillrone	Shillrone	44	John Holder gentle	6	38
	Camgortt	22	Anthony Adhbenson gentle	8	14
	Rosmend	21		4	17
	Bollinure	71	Ananias Henley Esq	9	62
	Ballinkellin	8		2	6
(folio 18). Kilcommon	Clonlisk	15		4	11
	Ballintoren	35		2	33
	Adrowle	18		—	18
	Keelogs	2		—	2
	Tummangh	19	Margre Arthop Rose Squibbe		19
	Corriolontey	11	Henry Whittell Esq Richard Baucroft gentle	3	8
	Gallbally	2			2
	Tubbride	9			9
	Balloghboy & Fere	12			12
	Berre	8		3	5
	Carrige	6			6
	Kisnybrasny	9		2	7
	Ballynenan	9			9
	Ballymur	13			13
	Gortinalangh	12			12
(folio 19). Emagh	Balliknocan	26	William Candler Esq	4	22
	Aghaduglis	13		2	11
	Glasterybeg	11			11
	Buallaghbeg	16			16
	Glasteymore	18			18
	Ballinloghbeg	4			4
	Knocknamdasd	25	Francis Peasley gentle	6	19

Parishes	Places	Numbs	Tituladoes Names	English	Irish
Killcollman	Coolerod	6			6
	Ballyricord	13		2	11
	Rathmore	42		4	38
	Shanganah	44	Anne Oxbridge Wid	—	44
	Raghbegg	3		—	3
	Lisduff	23			23
	Ballyegan	12			12

Principall Irish Names [and] their Numb[er.]

Bannan, 8 ; Bane, 4 ; Burke, 7 ; Bryane, 7 ; Carroll (36) & Caroll (5), 41 ; Cahell, 7 ; Ciery, 7 ; Coregan, 5 ; Conner, 3 ; Dwaine, 10 ; Duley, 5 ; McDonell, 5 ; Donelan, 4 ; Egan, 4 ; Gillfoyle, 16 ; Hegan, 12 ; Hogan, 6 ; Henan, 5 ; Keenedy, 16 ; Kelan, 8 ; Kelly, 4 ; Mahur, 26 ; Mooney, 2 ; McRedmond, 8 ; Rean, 11 ; Regan, 4 ; Rorey, 2 ; McShane, 6 ; McTeige, 8 ; Trahey, 5 ; Toher, 6 ; Walsh, 15.

(*folio 19 verso*). The Number of people in the Bar of Clonliske : Eng, 109 ; Irish, 972 ; Eng & Irish, 1081.

(*folio 20*).

BARONY OF GARRIECASTELL

Parishes	Places	Numbs	Tituladoes Names	English	Irish
Tissarane	Moys town	12	Henry Lestrange Esq	3	9
	Ardorna	10		—	10
	Lissinisky	6		—	6
	Anaghmore	6			6
	Lisdaly	4			4
	Lisduff	6		2	4
	Camus	8			8
	Cloghill	6			6
	Clonbanny	14		4	10
	Lisdaragh	9	Lewis Jones gentle	5	4
	Lisclonie	24	William Hamilton gentle	5	19
Clomacnall	Clonona	72	William Coghlan gentle	2	70
	Clonfenlogh	34	More Coghlane Widdow	6	28
	Clonderidge	21		6	15
	Clonknaw	9			9
	Clonlyon	8	James Larkin gentle	4	4
	Clonemore	74		4	70
(*folio 21*). Moylane	Corocolane	15	The Lord Weaman, Samuell Rolls Esq Mary Boorke	5	10

Parishes	Places	Numbs	Tituladoes Names	English	Irish
	Carro	6	— Paker Esq Hiber Scot gentle	4	2
	Lachill	9		5	4
	Doone	21		2	19
	Esker	35		6	29
	Capinfotine	4		2	2
	Coledoroghe	9			9
	Ballyard	18	Capt Segray Esq Ensigne Hawkins gentle	13	5
	Cranasallgh	9		4	5
	Bellacomer	16			16
	Castle towne	14	— Darly late of Plattine Esq, Mathew Bellew gentle, Francis Darsy gentle, Mary Plunket Widow.	—	14
(*folio* 22).	Killaghlintober	12		—	12
	Leoghbegg	12			12
	Castlereagh	6			6
	Sraduffe	18	John Coghlan gentle	—	18
	Leaghmanagh	26		—	26
Losmagh	Glaster	85	Phillip Bigoe Esq		85
	Newtowne	10		2	8
	Cloghane	10		4	6
	Gorthnatrynagh	7	Edward Smyth gentle	5	2
	Cartfogh	4			4
	Iniserky	8			8
	Balnnacklogh	14			14
	Corgarane	9			9
	Miltowne	6	Mortagh Bannane Esq — Hensie Esq		6
	Garriecastell	16		5	11
	Beanthar	8		4	4
(*folio* 23). Gallen	Stones towne	9	Edward Armestrong gent	3	6
	Cloghan	14	Francis Page gentle	7	7
	Garnell, and Carick- Bally leir	32		6	26
Rynagh	Streams tonn	29	Hugh Flattery gent	2	27
	Garbally	9			9
	Bellaghanohie	4			4
	Derena Fame	4			4
	Ballycoer	5	Captn John Strongman gentle	2	3
	Atinkie	5		2	3
	Parke	7			7
	Lomclon	13		2	11
	Kilorney	07	Eneas Hensey Esq	3	4

Parishes	Places	Numbs	Tituladoes Names	English	Irish
	Ballyengowne	8			8
	Galrus	12		4	8
	Ballyshane	12		2	10
(*folio* 24).	Ballysheal	10	Robert Harford gentle	5	5
	Knogus	15		4	11
	Gallen	19	Terence Melaghline gentle	2	17
Bellegally	Kilcobgan	39	James Shane Esq, James Walnne gentle, Jean Wixstead gent.	5	34
	Kincorre	28	Richard Warburton Senior gent Richard Warburton Junio[r] gentle	3	25
	Coole	15		—	15
	Derrick	10			10
	Skehanagh	5			5
	Fierbane	18	besides Shropshire adventurers wch p[d] 02*l* ; John Lennan gentle, John Arthur gentle.	4	14
	Bellaclar	2			2
	Endrum	53			53
	Clongawny	4			4

Principall Irish Names [and] Their Numb[er.]

Brassell, 4 ; Bane, 6 ; Branan, 4 ; Bocully, 7 ; Coghlane, 24 ; Connell, 6 ; Durly, 8 ; Dolloghane, 11 ; Dwire, 9 ; Doelane, 9 ; O Dulane, 5 ; Duff, 7 ; Dun, 3 ; Egan, 3 ; Flattery, 6 ; Fox, 4 ; Gennen, 17 ; Gellegan, 4 ; Gilleane, 5 ; Horan, 18 ; Hegan, 10 ; Kenny, 7 ; Keely, 9 ; Lurken, 8 ; Madden, 7 ; Rigny, 10 ; M[c]Redmond, 3 ; M[c]Shane, 4 ; Scot, 6 ; M[c]Teige, 2 ; Tougher, 4.

(*folio* 24 *verso*)   The Number of People in ye Barony of Garriecastle : Eng, 158 ; Irish, 960 ; Totall Eng & Irish, 1118.

(*folio* 25).   **BARONY OF KILCOURCY**

Parishes	Places	Numbs	Tituladoes Names	English	Irish
	Gurteene	47		5	42
	Doughill	46		6	40
	Ballyboghlan	9	John Swinglehurst gentle William Corton gentle	—	9
	Lynamuck	38	Samuell Strongman gentle	7	31
	Belabacklan	8	Gurtham Gurd gentle	5	3

Parishes	Places	Numbs	Tituladoes Names	English	Irish
	Cloragh	29	William Higgin gentle	—	29
	Ballynekill	11		—	11
	Erye	29			29
	Kilmaledy	14			14
	BallyckMoyler and Newtowne	21	Thomas Lawrence gentle, Edmond Nugent gentle, Thomas Kehan gentle, Thomas Kehan gentle.	3	18
	Ballicknahy	14	John Blake gentle	3	11
	Kilfilan	21	Teige Lynon gentle	2	19
	Lehensey	10	Abraham Fuller gentle Neale McCiltry gentle James Geoghegan gentle.		10
(folio 26)	Kilcoursey	28	Samuell Ruth gentle, Teige Dun gentle, Farrell Flattery gentle, Teige Dugine gentle, Teige Daley gentle, John Dillon gentle, Morrough Banane gentle.	4	24
	Moyelly	10		oo	10
	Bellanementan	13	Robert Recubie Esq, Thomas Stroaker gentle, Francis Gurkman gentle	4	9
	Tobber and Kilcilly	8	Henry Fuller gentle John Brenan gentle	1	7

Principall Irish Names [and] Their Numb[er].

Doyne, 4 ; Daley, 11 ; Dillon, 4 ; Flattery, 3; Flanagan, 3 ; Fox, 4 ; Geoghegan, 8 ; Higgin, 4 ; Molloy. 4 ; Mulclyff, 4 ; Muney, 4.

(folio 26 verso). The Number of People in the Bar of Killcourcy : Eng, 040 ; Irish, 316 ; Totall Eng & Irish, 0356.

(folio 27). **BARONY OF EGLISH**

Parishes	Places	Numbs	Tituladoes Names	English	Irish
	Knockbarren	28	Robert Busbridge Esq	2	26
	Killtobired	52	John Dow gentle	7	45
	Killin Martin	10		—	10
	Laghell	11		4	7
	Cnoghes	25		—	25
	Kelline	36		4	32
	Killine	10			10
	Curaghmore	19			19
	Corregearke	8			8
	Cloynebelart	6			6
	Rathingill	14			14
	Collars towne	2			2
	Eglish	50	Tho : Mosse Esq, Mr Grace Smyth	19	31

Parishes	Places	Numbs	Tituladoes Names	English	Irish
	Ballmagully	24	Nicholas Herbert gentle	2	22
	Ballindowne	4		2	2
(folio 28).	Tullchan-Skeagh	10		—	10
	Liffine	8		—	8
	Clonahane	22	John Bery gentle	2	20
	Cloindalla	19			19
	Bwellynan-arge	12	Henry Barton gentle Robert Clerke gentle	12	—
	Ballykeaby	6			6
	Drynagh	8			8
	Shanvaly, and Ardgnoge }	15			15
	Dwinlogh	19			19
	Carrinst	12			12

Principall Irish Names [and] Their Numb[er.]

Beolane, 4 ; Carroll, 6 ; Coghlan, 14 ; Corkerane, 4 ; Durely, 4 ; Egane, 3 ; Flattery, 2 ; Gillmartine, 3 ; Gillduff, 3 ; Horane, 3 ; Kelly, 6 ; Kenedy, 3 ; Molloy, 5.

(folio 28 verso)   The Number of People in the Barony of Eglish : Eng, 054 ; Irish, 376 ; Totall Eng & Irish, 430.

(folio 29).   **BARONY OF BALLYBRITT**

Parishes	Places	Numbs	Tituladoes Names	English	Irish
	Bir	337	Lawrence Persons Esq, John Lawten gentle, William Burke gentle, Thomas Langstone gentle, Michaell Cantwell gentle, Duigen Clery gentle	64	273
	Clonaghill	6		0	6
	Shyftenn	20		—	20
	Crimkill	44	Heward Oxbrugh Esq	3	41
	Fortle	17		2	15
	Crea	18		3	15
	Ghilline Bethan	11	James Lander gentle	—	11
	Dromoyd	41		16	25
	Dranagh	2		2	—
	Castle towne	6		—	6
	Ballininonyn	83	John Weaver Esq	28	55
	Brigemoe	54	Cary Dillon Esq	2	52
	Braghmore	37		2	35
	Clonber	25	Richard Tyler gentle	2	23
(folio 30).	Ballyshane	8		8	—

Parishes	Places	Numbs	Tituladoes Names	English	Irish
	Bally-morogh	3			3
	Ballywillyad	7			7
	Dorekeale	10			10
	Aghagurty	6			6
	Castletowne	32		3	29
	Gleiske	9			9
	Kinetty	8		4	4
	Comer	3			3
	Forlacky	2			2
	Killcloucoff	3		—	3
	Forlacky	9		7	2
	Tully	11		11	—
	Cadams towne	34	William MacEvoy gentle	00	34
	Clonnebegg	21		—	21
	Mooneginene	17		—	17
	Coolerease	17		—	17
	Letter	37			37
(folio 31).	Ballykincalmy	18			8
	Llongfford	34		2	32
	Knockerlea	2			2
	Cooldorcher	9			9
	Roscomroe	23			23
	Newtowne	31		2	29
	Ballyduff	36			36
	Coolfell	19			19
	Ballynoragh	5			5
	Ballybritt	3		00	03
	Ungir	18	Nathaniell Mulleplate gentle	14	4
	Leape	21	Jonathen Derby gentle	4	17
	Cloonneene	3			3
	Aghancon	10			10
	Glancorow	3		2	1
	Aghancon	7			7
	Grageloge	19			19
	Aghancon	6			6
	Curagbegg	8	Mortagh MacEvoy gentle		8

Principall Irish Names [and] their Numb[er].

Brenane, 4 ; **Bryane,** 11 ; **Bane,** 5 ; **Beolane,** 6 ; **Carroll,** 30 ; **Conran,** 6 ; **Cary,** 8 ; **Coghlane,** 7 ; **Clery,** 5 ; **Corkcrane,** 11 ; **Dully,** 8 ; **Dullchanty,** 10 ; **Duff,** 7 ; **McDonough,** 3 ; **Doyne,** 7 ; **Doven,** 11 ; **Dun,** 2 ; **Dugen,** 4 ; **Dowlin,** 5 ; **Dellany,** 4 ; **Evaster,** 4 ; **Evoy,** 9 ; **Egane,** 5 ; **Flanegane,** 5 ; **Fenelly,** 8 ; **Horane,** 3 ; **Heyns,** 5 ; **Kelly,** 8 ; **Kenedy,** 7 ; **Keneshane.** 7 ; **Lurkane,** 4 ; **Morish** 4 ; **Mullreane,** 5 ; **McMorough,** 10 ; **Moor,** 7 ; **Megher,** 7 ; **Redmond,** 5 ; **McShane,** 6 ; **Scully,** 7 ; **Tougher,** 4.

(folio 30 verso). The Number of People in the Barrony of Bally britt : Eng, 181 ; Irish, 1032 ; Totall Eng & Irish, 1213.

(*folio* 31 *verso*).   The Number of People in the Kings County, and in each Barony.

Baronyes	Page	Eng	Irish	Eng & Irish
Phillipptowne	4	0186	1007	1193
Coolishtowne	7	0062	0428	0490
Ballyboy	10	0091	0484	0575
Ballycowen	11	0132	0562	0694
Geshell	13	0139	0591	0730
Warrestowne	15	0073	0357	0430
Clonliske	19	0109	0972	1081
Garriecastle	24	0158	0960	1118
Killcourcy	26	0040	0316	0356
Eglish	28	0054	0376	0430
Ballybritt	30	0181	1032	1213
	The Totall	1225	7085	8310

LONGFORD COUNTY

539^2

(*folio* 1). Longford County

RATHCLEENE BARRONY

Townelands[1]	Number of People	Tituladoes Names	Eng	Irish
Ballimulvee	033	Adam Molineux Esq and Nicholas Dowdall gent	006	027
Ballimaghan	040		002	038
Denian	007		—	007
Moygh	007		—	007
Castlecorr	014			014
Cartronboy	022		002	020
Derrog	017			017
Lackin	021			021
Clonard	004		002	002
Creagh	005		—	005
Tirlikin	017		003	014
Laghill	022		004	018
Clombreny	009			009
Kilcomack	011			011
Foygh	017			017
Kiltafry	023		003	020
Lisneguinog	009		002	007
Shroole	013			013
(*folio* 2) Clogh	027	Thomas Robinson gent and Griffith Jones gent	003	024
Monisillagh	020			020
Clonkeene	002		002	—
Garrincorra	022			022
Ballibronegan	014			014
Derilagh	007			007
Derriadda	009			009
Derimany	004		—	004
Derinagalagh	013		—	013
Derinapantle	011			011
Gortinclarin	009		002	007
Ardoghill	009		002	007
Claris	018	Edward Clarke gent		018
Tonicurry	011			011
Drimnihey	010			010
Ballireagh	006			006
Deriaghanmore	009			009
Clonaghbegg	005			005
(*folio* 3) Cashill	011			011
Carrigg	011			011
Forchill	029			029
Cornedough	015			015
Derinduff	012			012
Derigawney	014		003	011
Portinure	035		002	033

[1] There is a column headed *Parrishes* but it is left blank throughout.

Townelands	Number of People	Tituladoes Names	Eng	Irish
Blenavore	006		002	004
Ilfide	016		002	014
Carroole	006		000	006
St Albens	018			018
Cullintrah	014			014
Fermoyle	014	Robert Mills gent	002	012
Carolurry	012			012
Cashellbegg	013			013
Lisnecosh	030			030
Carrooneskagh	006		o –	006
Rathcleene	016		002	014
Coolecroy	018		o –	018
(*folio* 4). Corry	005			005
Killinure	016		002	014
Killogowullin	012		002	010
Clonbonnah	007		—	007
Killincarra	002		—	002
Lehery	020			020
Ballileag	027		004	023
Clonfore	017		—	017
Souldiers and their⎱ Wiues in Ballileagh⎰	033		029	004

Principall Irish Names [and their Number].

MacBryan, 06 ; Ô Connor, 11 ; Ô Clonine, 07 ; Cormick & Cormack, 07 ; Dowlan, 05 ; Ô Donily, 06 ; Ferrall & Farrell, 51 ; Gill, 12 ; Hobigan, 07 ; Kelly, 09 ; Keegan, 07 ; Mulvihill & Mulvighill, 05 ; Ô Murry. 07 ; Murtagh, 05 ; Scally, 09.

(*folio* 4 *verso*)   Barrony of Rathcleene : Eng 083 ; Irish, 849 ; 0932, totall.

(*folio* 5).   **SHROWELL BARRONY**

Townelands	Number of People	Tituladoes Names	Eng	Irish
Tenelick	021		001	020
Liscormack	032		—	032
Skighan	007		—	007
Killincarroe	007		—	007
Abbyshroole	046			046

Townelands	Number of People	Tituladoes Names	Eng	Irish
Balliglassan	026			026
Carne	005		004	001
Tonelagh	017		—	017
Bellacarro	002		002	—
Lisfarfa	011		—	011
Tully	027			027
Ardanragh	012		006	006
Agharo	008			008
Cliduff	013	Mathew Wilders gent	006	007
Knockagh	010			010
Scribooke	003			003
Lisquill	004			004
Lislom	002		002	—
(folio 6). Knappoge	012		002	010
Barry	011		001	010
Barribegg	012			012
Lisstibbott	026			026
Toome	006		002	004
Kilcurry	007			007
Killinguaican	024			024
Taghshinny	032			032
Doory	018		002	016
Newcastle	036			036
Cloghanbiddy	005	Richard Certaine gent	002	003
Clonkalla	014			014
Rath	021		004	017
Cloncullen	018			018
Cornamuckla	008			008
Forgny	038		002	036
Kildordan	007			007
Pallismore	010			010
(folio 7). Streams towne	043			043
Annagh	013			013
Clonkeene	029	Tibbott Dillon gent	—	029
Rathmore	008		—	008
Tang	014			014
Crevaghbegg	026			026
Crevaghmore	045	Hubbert Ferrall and Symon Sandys gent	006	039

Principall Irish Names [and] Their Number.

Bardon, 06 ; McCormick, 15 ; Cahill, 12 ; Corrigan, 05 ; McDowle, 05 ; Dillon, 05 ; Daly, 05 ; Farrell & Ferrall, 32 ; McJeffey, 09 ; Kene, 07 ; Knowlan & Knowland, 07 ; Kinan, 09 ; Keegan, 11 ; Kenny, 07 ; Quin, 13 ; Mulledy, 05.

(folio 7 verso)   Barrony of Shrowell : Eng, 042 ; Irish, 694 ; 736, Totall.

(folio 8).   **ARDAGH BARRONY**

Townelands	Number of People	Tituladoes Names	Eng	Irish
Newtowne-Longford	039		004	035
Bally McCormick	037		—	037
Glack	011		—	011
Ferahgfadda	009			009
Clonkirin	014			014
Ardagh	018		002	016
Ballinree	018			018
Ballinrodda	015			015
Ravaldrin	021			021
Killinlassie	006			006
Killineghter	017			017
Clooneaughill	011			011
Lower Cooles hill	006			006
Upper Coolees hill	024		002	022
Boghermore	041			041
Ardmiskin	013			013
Lisaghanedin	024			024
Glynn	021	Robert Archbald gent		021
(folio 9). Garriconnell	010			010
Barnloghtikew	004			004
Coolka	005			005
BalliWater	010			010
Crossea	010			010
Rathreagh	020			020
Cargin	014			014
Killeene	014			004[*sic!*]
Slyan	010			010
Cloghiggin	017			017
Ballimac Crifford	012			012
Breana and Lisdrinagh	010	Derby Toole gent		010
Kilfinton	014			014
Blightoge	014			014
Tonilosdy	011			011
Corry	007			007
Motenvally	018			018
(folio 10). Freaghan	015			015
Clonsinnagh	011			011
Lisryan	028			028
Ballow	012			012
Lisduff	007			007
Rinvany	014			014
Cartronreagh	008		004	004
Carriglass	009		—	009
Corriduffy	014		—	014

Townelands	Number of People	Tituladoes Names	Eng	Irish
Cloncoose	011			011
Lisnedaragh	008			008
Clonaghard	007			007
Lissnemuck	017			017
Cloonany	006			006
Gartneskagh	015			015
Coolenehinch	014			014
(*folio* 11). Lisardooly	006			006
Coolineaghtragh	011			011
Coolinoghtragh	011			011
Cranalagh	012	Captn John Edgworth Esq	003	009
Lissard	003			003
Calloge	009		002	007
Laghill	008			008
Monidarah	005			005
Ringawny	012			012
Camma	019		002	017
Mastrim	014			014
Aghafin	017			017
Lisnekeeragh	011			011
Bracklone	020			020
Coolevore	022			022
Tomdooghan	018			018
(*folio* 12). Lisscalmore	015			015
Drumnebarne	008			008
Lissnegriss	011			011
Lackan	017			017

Principall Irish Names [and] their Number.
Cleene, 05 ; Cargy, 05 ; Cormick, 06 ; Conily, 06 ; McConnell, 06 ; Eslenan, 05 ; Ferrall & Farrell, 29 ; McGreene, 06 ; Gwyre, 06 ; Keernan, 08 ; Kenny, 11 ; McLaughlin, 15 ; Leavy, 07 ; Ô Linsy & Lincy, 08 ; Murtagh, 05 ; Mullegan, 05 ; Moore, 09 ; Reily, 29.

(*folio* 12 *verso*) Barrony of Ardagh : Eng, 019 ; Irish, 971 ; 0990, total.

(*folio* 13). **LONGFORD BARRONY**

Townelands	Numbs of People	Tituladoes Names	Eng	Irish
Castle Forbess	015	Sr Arthur Forbess Barronett	006	009
BallimacBryan	022	Arthur Aghmooty gent	002	020

Townelands	Numbs of People	Tituladoes Names	Eng	Irish
Kilmore	010		—	010
Ballikenny	007		002	005
Letrim	010			010
Dulreek	005			005
Clondarah	013			013
Knappog	013			013
Souldiers and their Wiues in Clondarah	030		021	009
Clonellane	008			008
Tully	012			012
Briskill	005			005
Kilterighir	006			006
Carrick	035			035
Cullaghfaddy	016			016
Muinard	016	William Pillsworth gent	004	012
(folio 14). Clontumphir	010			010
Greagh	011		—	011
Bracklagh	007		—	007
Eskirr	008			008
Clanbalty	008			008
Longford	026	Lt Thomas Babington gent	003	023
Cartroones	016			016
Lismore	004		004	
Monilagan	006	Hannibald Seaton gent	003	003
Clagill	015		015	
Corry	003			003
Killeene	012		007	005
Lismoy	010			010
Crinagh	010			010
Cnockan	003			003
Lisbragh	007			007
Clooncart	008			008
(folio 15). Clonigher	007			007
Geig	012			012
Criue	008			008
Foredrumin	011			011
Reine	012			012
Clooneagh	005			005
Mullogh	013			013
Aghareagh	008			008

Principall Irish Names [and] their Number.

McDaniell & Donnell, 010 ; Ferrall & Farrell, 017 ; Ô Hogan, 006 ; McIlleavy, 005 ; Knolan & Knoland, 005 ; Kenedy, 005 ; Quin, 004 ; McRory, 004.

(folio 15 verso). Barrony of Longford : Eng, 067 ; Irish, 396 ; 463, Totall.

(folio 16). **GRANARD BARRONY**

Townelands	Number of People	Tituladoes Names	Eng	Irish
Granard	044		—	044
Rinroe	005		—	005
Killosonna	003			003
Ballinecross	018			018
Robins towne	012			012
Aghbrack	008			008
Ballymorris and Higgins towne	021			021
Killo	004			004
Corboyes	023		002	021
Formulla	004			004
Drumard	002			002
Bauncully	019			019
Corgrany	006			006
Killimihan	006			006
Clonlihy	006			006
Killecon	004			004
Legah	003			003
(folio 17). Annagh	004			004
Cloonemacart	008			008
Farraghio	012		002	010
Lismore	016			016
Castle towne	015		004	011
Kiltecrivagh	015			015
Shanmullagh	005			005
Soarne	030		008	022
Clonfin	012			012
Coolearty	013			013
Killine	012			012
Ballinlagh	025			025
Rathcorr	012			012
Ballimaccroaly	012		—	012
Ballibryan	011		—	011
Aghnegarroon	012			012
(folio 18). Letrim	034			034
Bellamore	013			013
Ballnehowne	009			009
Killosonna	022			022
Granard Kill	028			028
Cartronigiragh	014		005	009
Aghboy	015			015
Aghtoome	002			002
Ardcullein	018			018
Toniwarden	006			006
Tully	022		002	020

Townelands	Number of People	Tituladoes Names	Eng	Irish
Coolegowne	013			013
Esnagh	011			011
Ballinaraghan	011			011
Cartron bower	006			006
Portgurten	020			020
(folio 19). Trumrae	020			020
Gallidd	021			021
Rinnaghan	020		002	018
Cooledonny	005			005
Cammabegg	010			010
Cloncraff	004			004
Diragh	002		002	—
Tonnimore	020			020
Kilbreed-mullaclare, and Clommore	035			035
Ballyboy and Rincooly	028			028
Clogh	021			021
Dalis towne	013		002	011
Balliduffy	010		—	010
Moyne	006		—	006
(folio 20). Fayhora	010			010
Drumhalry	017			017
Krott	012			012
Lisnananagh	019			019
Newtowne	030	Thomas Flood gent	002	028
Kilmore	012			012
Killinmore	014			014
Tinnemuldoone	006			006
Tubber	010			010
Rathbrackan	013			013
Ballinroe	010			010
Killrea	007			007
Drung	018			018
Doricassan	014			014
Clonishog	012			012
Terennis	022			022
Aghreagh	009			009
(folio 21). Gilsagh	022			022
Malla	009			009
Aghkilmore	007			007
Aghkeerin	010			010
Aghneclogh	004			004
Aghkeyne	008			008
Rossduff	011			011
Smeare and Cornedrung	016			016
Clinra	006			006
Dunbeggan	005			005

Townelands	Number of People	Tituladoes Names	Eng	Irish
Rathmore	009			009
Sonnagh and Aghordrinan }	016		—	016
Clonlaughill	017	Richard Kenedy gent	006	011
Drumincross	020		—	020
Mote	006			006
Cnockanbane	010			010
Kilnamodagh	008			008
(folio 22). Lissraghtigan	005			005
Lissmagoonin	020			020
Corbehy	004			004
Clonbrony	003		002	001
Drimmile	013		010	003
Ballinscraghy	015		002	013
Rooe	009			009
Ballinrighan	007			007
Cloncoss	011	William Langford gent	002	009
Killsrully	006		006	—
Ardvexkill	003			003
Lisbeagh	008			008
Corlinan	020			020
Corrigraue	031			031

	Number of People	Tituladoes Names	Scotts	Irish
The Corporation of St Johns towne	047	Andrew Adaire Esq	007	040

Principall Irish Names [and] Their Number.

Biglean, 7 ; Brady, 23 ; McBryan, 5 ; McCabe, 7 ; McConnell, 6 ; Cahill, 6 ; Connillan, 5 ; Derrmott, 11 ; Doncho, 18 ; McDaniell, 8 ; Duffy, 10 ; Ferrall, 25 ; Gaffny, 10 ; McGwyre, 8 ; Ô Hugh, 6 ; Ô Hara, 5 ; Kernan, 34 ; Kelly, 6 ; Linsy & Lincy, 10 ; Mullegan, 16 ; Monegan, 6 ; Mahoone, 5 ; Masterson, 9 ; Ô Mulpatrick, 11 ; Newgent, 8 ; Reily, 67 ; Smith, 5 ; Syridan, 7.

(folio 22 verso)   Barrony of Granard : Eng & Scotts, 066 ; Irish, 1416 ; 1482, totall.

(folio 23).   **MOYDOWE BARONY**

Townelands	Number of People	Tituladoes Names	Eng	Irish
Knoctarrie	010		—	010
Caroomeanagh	019		—	019

Townelands	Number of People	Tituladoes Names	Eng	Irish
Belnamore	026	Thomas Newcomen Esq		026
Ballintanpan	023			023
Clone Ana	010			010
Gowlan	013			013
Trillicks	021			021
Cnocknadaragh	015			015
Aghenkeerin	025		004	021
Clooneoghra	057			057
Leynyn	011			011
Cloonfiegh	005			005
Cloonmore	016			016
Sarvoge	032			032
Dirradda	018			018
Cloonesullin	005			005
Brackagh	029			029
(folio 24)　Baon	017			017
Cloonreene	007			007
Cloone Eved	010			010
Moniskallaghan	004			004
Kilognruble	002			002
Castlereagh	020	Walter Tuite gent		020
Clonkirr	012			012
Aghacnappagh	026		—	026
Cartron	008		—	008
Lisduff	011			011
Abeydergg	060			060
Cartronclogh	021			021
Glinmore	006			006
Lislea	015			015
Lacloonagh	029			029
Keenagh	024			024
(folio 25).　Dromynge	047			047
Keele	007			007
Ballibegg	017			017
CarrigEdmond	021			021
Ballnemanagh	012			012
Cloonkeen	002			002
Killindowde	026			026
Corcreechan	004			004
. . . . . .	006			006
Mornyn	040			040

Principall Irish Names [and] their Number

Casie, 012 ; Cormick, 019 ; Duderan, 009 ; McDonell (4), Donellee (3), 007 ; Dooner, 005 ; Duff, 006 ; McEdmond, 007 ; Farrell, 023 ; Kenny, 016 ; McKwey, 005 ; Keegan, 007 ; Poore, 006 ; McMorogh, 007.

(folio 25 verso)　Barrony of Moydowe : Eng, 004 ; Irish, 785 ; 789, totall.

Barronies	Pages	Eng	Irish	Totall
Rathcleene	04	083	849	932
Shrowell	07	042	694	736
Ardagh	12	019	971	990
Longford	15	067	396	463
Granard	22	066	1416	1482
Moydowe	25	004	0785	0789
		281	5111	5392

LOWTH COUNTY AND CITY OF DROHEDA
```
      8085                    1605
      1605
      ----
      9690
```

(*folio* 1)   County of Lowth.   **BARONY OF LOWTH**

Parishes	Townlands	Numb' of People	Tituladoes Names	Eng	Irish
Dromiskin	Dromiskin	087	Edward Langham	009	078
	Lurgane	002		002	000
	Dundoogin	006		002	004
	Drumlecke	012		004	008
	Newragh	023		002	021
	Walterstowne	002		000	002
	Whiterath	031		003	028
	Miltowne	030	James Smallwood Esq	004	026
Derver	Derver	030		002	028
	Newtowne	053		002	051
Killincoole	Killincoole	055		000	055
	Allers towne	012		000	012
Mandefeild	Bawne	033		000	033
	Mandefeild	026		000	026
(*folio* 2).	Gilbertstowne	028		002	026
	Woottons towne	003		000	003
Lowth	Knocke	023	Richard Bolton gent	007	016
	Grange	029		000	029
	Corballis	023		000	023
	Killcrony	056		000	056
	Balloran	006		000	006
	Horestowne	054		000	054
	Carrickmolan	023		000	023
	Annaghe	006		000	006
	Little Ash	033		000	033
	Dromcath	020		000	020
	Carrickcallan	072		000	072
	Cortall	028		000	028
	Lublogh	051		000	051
(*folio* 3).	Shannonrooke	039		000	039
	Emlogh	022		000	022
	Frendron	015		000	015
	Tullie	035		000	035
	Lowrath	016		000	016
	Rathgarras	019		000	019
	Enniotts towne	008		000	008
	Mallosker	016		000	016
	Ardpatricke	025		000	025
	Corderrie	047		000	047
	Tomms	020		000	020
	Rath brist	043		000	043
	Culcredan	006		000	006

Principall Irish Names [and] Their Numb[er].

Birne, 27 ; Callan, 27 ; Connelan, 11 ; Carwell, 17 ; Cawell, 05 ; McCardell, 08 ; Casy, 08 ; Carroll, 09 ; Cogly, 09 ; Gernon, 09 ; McGormon, 08 ; Hoy, 11 ; McInrilly, 06 ; McIlloy, 07 ; Kelley, 10 ; O Lennan, 10 ; McMahon, 20 ; Murphey, 06 ; Maguyre, 07 ; Plunket 06 ; Roney, 06 ; Rorke, 05 ; Taaffe, 07.

(*folio* 3 *verso*)   Barony : Lowth ; Eng, 039 ; Irish, 1019 ; 1058, Totall.

(folio 4).   **BARONY OF DUNDALKE**

Parishes	Townlands	Numb' of People	Tituladoes Names	Eng	Irish
The Towne and Liberties of Dundalke		072	Edmond Dalton gent	011	061
The mershis of Dundalke		559	Michell Dey gent, John Wilshier gent, Oates Crocother Esq, Jn Bulkelh gent, Robert Mason gent, Samuell Ireland Esq, Josias Fogg gent, George Lambert gent, Christopher Ward gent, John McKnabb gent, Arthur Lloyd gent, John Oldfield gent, Francis Pierce gent, Arthur Bulkely **Esq.**	175	384
(folio 5). Castletown Bellew	Castletown Bellew	084	Wallan Dixey Esq Walter Cox Esq	006	078
	Tankardsrocke	021		000	021
Barrons towne Parish	Barrons towne	019		000	019
	Wardens towne	021		003	018
	Dery mallone	009		000	009
	Lislea	068		000	068
Hayns towne Parish	Raynolds towne	010		003	007
	Hayns towne	053		000	053
	Down maghan	048	Henry Townsly gent	009	039
	Cavan	004		000	004
	Downbin	038		000	038
	Donnoghmore	016		000	016
(folio 6) Haynes towne Parish	Kilcurby or Kilcurley	049		000	049
	Ross	008		005	003
	Gibstowne	013		000	013
Roth Parish	Roth	033		000	033
	Connorstowne	086		000	086
	Shortstone	020		000	020
	Dungooly	010		004	006
	Dungooley in Urny Parish	014		000	014
	Keane	029		000	029
	Killeene	010		000	010
Haggards towne Parish	Haggards towne	078		006	062
Haggard Parish	Balregane	035	Richard Dawson gent	007	028
	Lorgam-Keele	012		000	012
	Rathkrigh	015		000	015
(folio 7). Haggardstowne Parish	Haggards hill	037		002	035
	Ballymony	019		000	019
	Kilcurry	006		000	006
	Part of Balregan	004		002	002
	Monescribagh	016		000	016
Ballyballricke P'ish	Ballybalricke	020		000	020

Parishes	Townlands	Numb' of People	Tituladoes Names	Eng	Irish
	Litle Mill	015		000	015
	The Rath	004		003	001
	Killaly	015		000	015
	Newtowne	008		000	008
Phillipps towne Parish	— — —	032		000	032
	The Tyne townes of the Fewse				
	Lisdrumyer	044		000	044
	Shanmullagh	015		000	015
Ballymaskanlan Parish	Ballymaskanlan	033	John Daniell Esq	010	023
	Feede	006		000	006
(folio 8).	Aghenaskeagh	012		000	012
	Mullyard	014		000	014
	Jenkenstowne	018		000	018
	Aghereverney	018		000	018
	EdenTobber	011		000	011
	Faghard quartr	012		000	012
	Ballynamanan	004		004	000
	Playster	016		004	012
	Proleeke	029		007	022
	Aghenloghan	034		000	034
	Ballylurgan	040		000	040
	Duff-Largy	030		000	030
	Corcarnan	002		002	000
	Balleboyes	023	Thomas Fisher gent	003	020
	Ballemaconelly	119		000	119
(folio 9). Carlinford P'ish	Carlinford Towne	165	Thomas Leech gent	049	156
	Newtowne	052		000	052
	Lemnagh	012		000	012
	Mullaghtee	009		000	009
	Castletowne Cooley	057	Thomas Clarke Esq	004	053
	Cornemuklagh	012		000	012
	Lislea and Dromullagh	026		000	026
	Knockna Gowran	012		000	012
	Corkitt	006		000	006
	Ballymonan	003		000	003
	Bawen, and Ballentesken	014		000	014
	Mullaghbane	007	Peter Turbridge gent	004	003
	Irish Grange	020		000	020
	Ballugg	042	John Slatier gent	004	038
(folio 10).	Bollagan	018		000	018
	Templetowne	023		000	023
	Kenalluske	012		000	012

Parishes	Townlands	Numb' of People	Tituladoes Names	Eng	Irish
	Corballis	020		000	020
	Whits towne	036		000	036
	Ballyinmoney	004		000	004
	Much Grange	019		000	019
	Mill Grange	019		000	019
	Old Grange	018		000	018

Principall Irish Names [and] Their Numb[er.]

McArdell, 33; Boyle & Ô Boyle, 19; McBryan, 05; Birne, 12; Bellew, 10; Brynan, 07; McCourt, 05; Cleryan, 13; Cleary, 11; McCann, 09; Connoly, 15; Connell, 06; Connellan, 11; Cassedy, 06; McCroly, 06; Callan, 22; McCabe, 09; Cawsy, 07; Carwell, 05; McCroley, 07; O Dulleghan, 06; Dowdall, 09; Duffin, 10; Duffie, 04; Dermond, 06; O Donnell &c, 07; McEteggart, 07; Flyn, 07; Fegan, 06; Fenegan, 05; Growder, 06; McGenis &c, 07; Garblany, 06; Gernon, 07; Hanlon, 29; Kelly, 10; Larkan, 10; Lennan, 05; Murphey, 29; Martin, 06; Mathewes, 06; O Mellan &c, 10; Moore, 06; Murtagh, 12; Morgan, 09; McMahon, 10; Mackey, 09; Mulcrevy, 09; O Neile, 08; O Rorke, 08; McShane, 08; Tallon, 05; Taaffe, 05; White, 08.

(*folio* 10 *verso*)   Barony : Dundalke ; Eng, 327 ; Irish, 2209 ; 2536, totall.

(*folio* 11).   **BARONY OF FARRARD**

Parishes	Townlands	Number of People	Tituladoes Names	Eng	Irish
Bully. Parish Terfecan	Bully	052	William Toxtith Esq	016	036
	Baneh towne	008		000	008
	Banke towne	006		000	006
	Balltray	022		000	022
	Terfecan	056		000	056
	Terfecon ps primet	017		000	017
	Mill of Terfecan	004		000	004
	Newtowne Terfecan	005		000	005
	Betauges-towne	011		000	011
	Cananstowne	003		000	003
	Ganders Parke	006		000	006
	Cares towne	046	Leonard Hinks gent	010	036
	Galronstowne	022		000	022
	Milltowne	017		005	012
(*folio* 12) Bully Parish	Curs towne	004		000	004

Parishes	Townelands	Number of People	Tituladoes Names	Eng	Irish
	Dardize Rauth	009		000	009
	Black Hall	009		000	009
	Lawray minze	011		000	011
Killelougher Parish	Killelougher	060		000	060
	Ganders towne	009		002	007
	Aldmonds towne	007		000	007
	Calloughs towne	012		000	012
	Glaspistoll	014		004	010
Maine	Crewes towne	028		000	028
	Reynalds towne	011		000	011
	Maine	023		000	023
	Dalles	011		000	011
Dunaney	Dunaney	042		000	042
(folio 13).	Jones towne	007		000	007
Porte	———	007		000	007
	Nicholas towne	015		000	015
	Porte	024		000	024
Clunmore	Artballan	024		000	024
	Tocher	005		003	002
	Clunmore	030		000	030
	Killalley	016		000	016
	Paines towne	011		000	011
Dizert	Barmeth	018	Henry Wetherell gent	009	009
	Dizert	021		000	021
	Hitchingstowne	009		000	009
	Sine towne	014		000	014
	Grafins towne	009		000	009
Dunleere	Dunleere	076	Robert Peirce gent	004	072
	Burne	023		003	020
	Aclare	022	William Hall gent	004	018
(folio 14). Rauth doumneue	Rauth &c	010		000	010
	Carrick Boggett	042		000	042
	Arbollis	002		000	002
	Weshes towne	028		003	025
Marles towne	Marlestowne	040		000	040
	Glastowne	005		000	005
Drumshallon	Drumshallon	013	Eclston gent	004	009
	Brownestowne	029		002	027
	Hamlins towne	008		000	008
	Cartons towne	010		000	010
	Pipers towne	017		000	017
	Carricke Shannagh	006		002	004
Mullary	Tynure	016		000	016

Parishes	Townelands	Number of People	Tituladoes Names	Eng	Irish
	Radonell	009		000	009
	Ewrles baune	006		003	003
(folio 15).	Caselliminagh	011		002	009
	Priestowne	019		000	019
	Rathwyen	010		002	008
	Stonhouse	011	Tho : Thomlinson gent	002	009
Monesterboye	Monesterboye	006		000	006
	Newtowne-Monesterboy	007		000	007
	Baune taffe	009		000	009
	Sillock	001		000	001
Tallahallan	Salters towne	066		000	066
	Tallahallan	051		000	051
	BeggRauth	025		000	025
	Sheep Graunge	052	Edward Blunt gent	007	045
	Litle Grainge	026		002	024
	Ballynumber	012		000	012
	Culboudy or Culludge }	027		000	027
(folio 16)	Ballgaderen	025		000	025
	Mell	058		002	056
	Dean Rauth	031		000	031
	Greenhills & Newtowne Staleban }	102	Joseph Witter gent Nicholas Conney gent	008	094
Callan, and Mellefont }	Mellefont	068	Henry Lo : Viscount Moore Leut Coll Francis Moore Capt Will : Constable Esq	016	052
	Callan	093		000	093
	BallPatricke	043		000	043

Principall Irish Names [and] their Numb[er.]

Brady, 010 ; Bremegham & Brinegan, 020 ; Birne, 04 ; Berrell, 13 ; Boding, 06 ; Callan, 18 ; Carton, 15 ; Cawell & Carwell, 10 ; McGann, 17 ; Duffey, 09 ; Duffin, 05 ; McEnolly, 06 ; Flanegan, 07 ; Farrell, 13 ; Finegan, 07 ; McGenis, 08 ; McGwyre, 10 ; Gonell, 06 ; Heney, 07 ; Hoy, 11 ; Halgan, 10 ; Kelly, 25 ; Living, 09 ; Lawles, 09 ; Murphey, 13 ; Martin, 08 ; Morgan, 07 ; Markey, 09 ; McMaughon, 05 ; Moore, 08 ; Plunkett, 09 ; Rouney, 08 ; Reyly, 07 ; Rorke, 05 ; Randall, 06 ; Rauth, 07 ; McRory, 06 ; O Sheredon, 05 ; Smyth, 08 ; Tracey, 06.

(folio 16 verso)　Barony : Farrard ; Eng, 115 ; Irish, 1675 ; 1790, Totall.

(folio 17). **BARONY OF ATHERDEE**

Parishes	Townlands	Numbs of People	Tituladoes Names	Eng	Irish
Kilsauran	Germons towne	112	Henry Bellingham Esq Ralph Gibbs gent	016	096

Parishes	Townlands	Numbs of People	Tituladoes Names	Eng	Irish
	Kilsauran	024		002	022
	Mullencrosse	031		000	031
	Boolis	023	Christopher Sibthorpe gent	002	021
	Myles towne	018		000	018
	Wood towne	005		000	005
	Drumcath	013		004	009
	Mayne	024	Roger Gregory gent	003	021
	Williams towne	017		003	014
	Coolis towne	014		000	014
Drumcar	Willis towne	014	Thomas Moore gent	005	009
	Drumcar	032	Richard Holt gent	007	025
	Warrens towne	014	James Hopton Esq	006	008
	Newtowne	027		009	018
	Cargin	005		000	005
(folio 18)	Tullogh Donell	008	Brent Moore Esq Richard Bolton gent		
	Cashells towne	027		002	025
	Verclons towne	025		000	025
Cappocke	Cappocke	042		000	042
	Ardaghs towne	031	Nicholas Moore Esqr	004	027
Drummin	Drummin	000	[sic !]	000	037
	Pains towne	010	William Rutter gent	002	008
	Rathcoole	006		004	002
Mostowne	Rahasker	037	Robt Wynne Esq	016	021
	Phillipps towne	038	William Edwards gent Maurice Edwards gent	004	034
	Marshall rath	03		000	030 [sic !]
	Hamons towne	013	Patrick Fagan gent	000	013
	Mostowne	027		000	027
	Knocke	016	William Savidge gent	000	016
	Listolke	021		000	021
(folio 19). Kildemmocke	Millox towne	027		004	023
	Rose towne	004		000	004
	Haclem	005		004	001
	Hunters towne	003		000	003
	Annagloge	026		000	026
	Blakes towne	010		000	010
	Drakes towne	031		000	031
	Killpatricke	032		004	028
	Pawhans towne	022		006	016
	Funshocke	038		000	038
Smyrmar	Smyrmar	048	Bryan Heron gent Francis Heron gent William Heron gent	000	048
	Purcells towne	02		000	002
Richard towne Parish	Richards towne	078	William Asten Esq	005	073

Parishes	Townlands	Numbs of People	Tituladoes Names	Eng	Irish
(*folio* 20). Richards towne Parish	Irish towne	010		000	010
	Crins towne	010		000	010
	Haris towne	029	John Bernard gent	006	023
	Hoaths towne	002		000	002
	Stickillen	030		003	027
Atherdee	Atherdee	405	Sᵣ Robert Sterling Knt,	157	249
			James Dowglas gent, Henry Neile gent, John Ruxton Esq, Joh : Tooke gent, William Armitage Esq, Thomas Winne gent, John Thomas gent.		
	Gaues land	008		000	008
	Broadlogh	006		001	005
	Mullens towne	025		000	025
	Mullogh cloe	013		000	013
	Guithers towne	021		000	021
	Obris towne	022		003	018 [*sic* !]
(*folio* 21). Charles towne p'ish	Shanlish	044	James Burtsides gent	002	042
	Cookes towne	062	Peter Ashenhurst gent	005	057
	Peppers towne	052	William Pepper gent	008	044
	Charles towne	032		000	032
Clunkeene	Cooles towne	036		000	036
	Stermonds towne	028	John Chambre Esq	002	026
	Rogers towne	015		003	012
	Ballybonny	017		000	017
	Cardis towne	023		000	023
	Rath canory	009		000	009
	Cruemartin	014		000	014
	Lagan	020		002	018
	Tully	025		000	025
	Greatwoode	005		000	005
Killany P'	Tullikeele	019		000	019
	Corcreagh	006		002	004
	Stone town Ye Greater	022		005	017
(*folio* 22).	Stone towne	010	Richard Blomfield gent Richard Blomefield gent	003	007
	Dromard	018		000	018
	Tulligone	010		000	010
	Coolecalan	024		000	024
	Annaermone	021		000	021
Phillipstowne P'ish	Phillippstowne	014		000	014
	Nislrath	042		000	042
	Reagh towne	041		000	041
	Athelint	026		000	026
	Thomas towne	028		000	028
	Clintonrath	015		000	015
	Nicholls towne	010		000	010

Parishes	Townlands	Numbs of People	Tituladoes Names	Eng	Irish
Tallons towne Parish	Tallons towne	051		000	051
	Litle Lisrany	035		006	029
	Great Lisrany	007		002	005
	Litle Rathbody	012		000	012
	Arthurs towne	028		000	028
(folio 23).	Rathory	009		005	004
Mapers towne Parish	Dowds towne	040	George Carfelott Esq	008	032
	Irish towne	010		000	010
Stabanum	Strabanum	028	William Disney Esq	006	022
	Bragans towne	040	James Gastin Esq	009	031
	Roods towne	037		002	035
	Clintons towne	035	John Peirce Esq	004	034 [sic!]
	Drumcashell	032		000	032

Principall Irish Names [and] Their Numb[er.]

O Boyle &c, 13 ; Byrne, 37 ; Boylan, 05 ; Bellew & Bedlow, 06 ; Barran, 06 ; Brady, 08 ; Chamberlin, 05 ; Callan, 16 ; Cullen, 04 ; Clinton, 05 ; Crolly &c, 08 ; Carroll, 07 ; Connolan, 06 ; Connoly, 10 ; Cawell, 11 ; Carwell, 05 ; Carney, 10 ; Cartan, 06 ; Cappocke, 07 ; Dowdall, 10 ; Dowlin, 07 ; Duffie, 10 ; Dermott, 07 ; Fenegan, 13 ; Fedegan, 09 ; Kennon, 06 ; Kelly, 16 ; McLoghlin, 11 ; Lynnan, 06 ; Mullen, 05 ; Murphey, 07 ; McGenis, 08 ; McGrory, 07 ; Gernon, 07 ; McGroyre, 15 ; Hughes, 11 ; Hoy & O Hoy, 18 ; Halfepenny, 09 ; Mathewes, 11 ; Murtagh, 05 ; McMaughon, 16 ; Meghan, 06 ; Ô Mury, 12 ; Neale, 05 ; Reyly, 11 ; Skehan, 06 ; Smyth, 11 ; Taaffe, 08 ; Tath, 07 ; Terty, 07 ; White, 12 ; Wesh, 06.

(folio 23 verso). Barony : Atherdee ; Eng, 356 ; Irish, 2345.

The Number of People in ye County of Lowth & in each Barony.

Baronys	Pages	Eng	Irish	totall
Lowth	3	039	1019	1058
Dundalke	10	327	2209	2536
Farrard	16	115	1675	1790
Atherdee	23	356	2345	2701
Totall		837	7248	8085

(folio 1)   **CITY OF DROHEDA AND LIBERTIES THEROF.**

Quallifications of Persons	Their Numb[er]	Tituladoes Names	Eng	Irish
Esqrs and their wifes &c	044	Maior Edward Martin, John Jeenes Alderman, William Ellwood Alderman, Thomas Stooker Alderman, David Shepheard Alderman, Samuell Osborne Alderman, John Tempest Shieriff, William FytzHerbert Esqr, Robert Bridges Esqr, Worsley Batten Esq, Anthony Nixon Esq, Alderman Sam[ll] Stanbride, Rowland Troly Alderman, Thomas Dixon Alderman, John Midcalfe Alderman, John Towers Alderman, Jonas Ellwood Alderman, Thomas Leigh Sheriff, Moses Hill Esq, Thomas Cobayne Esq, John Bexwick Esq.	044	000
Gentlemen & their wifes &c	113	Richard Orson, Joh Richards, Ignatius Pepper, John Brady, Edmond Graves, Jon Killogh, Francis Poole, Tho: Field, Barthlomew Doyle, Tho: Pepperd, Francis Blacken, Jon Stoker, James Thomas, Richard Lloyd, Gabriell Meade, Jon Tallbott, William Osborne, Tho: Fitzherbore, Sam[ll] Ward, George Richardson, Jasper Dellahoide, Lawrence Jones, Gilbert Jones, Tho: Newton, Josias Ardenton, Fardinado Ross, Andrew Bruerton, Barthlomew Hamtin, Patricke Whitt, Richard Derham, gentlemen ;/ Edward Mastine, William Newton, James Glower, Joseph Whorlloe, Edward Fenterell, Thomas Dellahoide, John Bray, Symon Gaskin, David Dorane, Alexander Plunkett, Edward Harington, Christopher Cheevers, John Lea, James Challenor, John Hardick, Richard Jackson, Edward Nickolls, Thomas Bullin, Alexander Bodington, Patrick Cheneing, Nicholas Hearne, Nicholas Phillps, Thomas Buliner, gentlemen—	087	026
(folio 2).				
Yeomen and their wiues &c	271		159	112
Labourers and their wiues &c	803		312	491
(folio 3). Souldiers and their Wiues.				
Capt[n] Fitzgerald his troope	104	Robert Fitzgerald Capt[n] Hercules Langriss Esq Leut Donwell Protheroe Cornett Henry Fletthery Quart[r]mast[r].	094	010
Leut Coll Smithwicks company	113	Henry Smithwick Capt Esq Henry Buchnan Leutt John Samming Ensigne	112	003
Capt Hoyles Company	113	Edmond Hoyle Capt Esq, John Goter Leut, Peter Tundall Ensigne, John his sonn gent.	111	002
Maior Pepper his Company	042	Maior George Pepperd Thomas Evelin Leutt John Head Ensigne.	039	003

Principall Irish Names [and] their Numb[er.]

Butler, 04 ; Bradigan, 05 ; Chevers, 05 ; Henry, 06 ; Jones, 10 ; Keny, 04 ; Kelly, 09 ; Lea, 04 ; Martin, 09 ; Moore, 08 ; Murphy, 05 ; White, 05.

(*folio* 3 *verso*). The Number of the People in the City of Droheda according to their severall qualliffications

	Their Number	Eng	Irish	
Esquires, and Esquiresses &c	044	044	000	The Number of People in the County of Louth *vide* Page 23
Gentlemen, and Gentlewomen	113	087	026	
Yeomen, and their Wiues &c	271	159	112	
Labourers, and their wiues &c	803	312	491	
Souldiers, and their Wiues	374	356	018	
The totall	1605	958	647	

MEATH

(folio 1).   **DULEEK BARRONY**

Parrishes	Townelands	Number of People	Tituladoes Names	Eng	Irish
Duleeke	Duleeke towne	195	John Hatch and his sonn Esq^{rs}, John Taaff gent.	036	159
	Knockhlan	005		005	—
	Newtowne	011		006	005
	Athcarne	032	Phillip Peake Esq and Francis Parker gent	018	014
	Resk	018		006	012
	Corballagh	028		—	028
	Snyock	014		007	007
	Galestowne	020			020
	Dowans towne	029	Bartholomew Moore and Patrick his sonn gents		029
	Lonford	004		002	002
	Gillingstowne	015		—	015
	Gasking towne	013		—	013
	Deanes	018			018
	Ballepack	007		003	004
	Rahill	004		002	002
	Kellis towne	005			005
(folio 2). Duleek	Malaffin	033		010	023
	Great Hill towne	030		007	023
	Little Hillton	008			008
	Beamon	012			012
	West Gaffny	008			008
	Cales towne	011			011
	West carness	020		005	015
	East carne	017		004	013
	Onges towne	013			013
	Bellews towne	047	Nicholas Darcy Esq	016	031
	Kenock	011		—	011
	Londers towne	012		006	006
	Johns towne	006		—	006
	Great Riuers towne	019		004	015
	Scatternagh	013			013
	Little Riuers towne	017			017
	Little Boolies	009		005	004
	Great Boolies	012			012
(folio 3).	Carrins towne	034	Christopher Darcy Esq	007	027
	Plattin	091	John Watkins gent	023	068
Kilkervan	Gaffny	012			012
	Anegoure	017		005	012
	Kilkervan	005		004	001
	Newhaggard	012			012
	Balgreene	019			019
	Shallon	030		008	022

Parrishes	Townelands	Number of People	Tituladoes Names	Eng	Irish
	Laughan towne	019			019
	Curraghtye	009			009
Ballygart	Balligartt	049	George Pepard Esq	012	037
	Corballyes	033		009	024
Brownstown	Brownstowne	061	Robert Reyner gent	009	052
Abby	Rodder	009		007	002
	Fowlers towne	004		004	—
	Kilnen	006		004	002
(folio 4). Abby	Mill towne	002			002
	Callogh towne	027		006	021
	Corballyes	012			012
	Rough Grang	024		006	018
	Lucher	018			018
Ballemagarvy	Ballemagarvy	030		008	022
	Balrath	036	Garet Almer Esq, Dersomy his sonn Esq, & Andrew Plunkett gent.		036
Dunowre	Burtons towne	045			045
	Staling	054			054
	Ould Bridy	067		006	061
	Sheepe house	033		005	028
	Ramulan	051		003	048
	Crusrath	023	Robert Netreuile Esq		023
Fennor	Fennor towne	032		004	028
	Johns towne	006			006
(folio 5). Pyerc towne	Pyerc towne	036	Leift. Skevington Esq & John Williams gent	010	026
	Hawkings town	017		004	013
Killmoon	Killmoon	018		006	012
	Primats towne	044		008	036
	Ballihack	006			006
	Irish towne	011		008	003
Kentstown	Kentstowne	028	John Burges gent	005	023
	Fleming towne	042	William Gilbert gent	011	031
	Veldons towne	006		002	004
	Knack Erk	022		010	012
	Curraghs towne	013		006	007
	Rathcoon	024		008	016
	Tuthrath	006			006
Knockamon	Resneree	027	John Gennett gent	006	021
	New towne	023		003	020
(folio 6)	Cullin	016	Robert Dillon gent	002	014
	Knockamon	012			012
	Radrynagh	021		001	020
	Gilltown	021		006	015
Clonalvy	Yᵉ Naule	021	Benjamin Perry gent	003	018

Parrishes	Townelands	Number of People	Tituladoes Names	Eng	Irish
	Dardis towne	004		—	004
	Micknans towne	008		001	007
	Heath towne	014			014
	Fleming town	012			012
	Barring town	012			012
	Kenrans towne	009			009
	Yᵉ Mooreside	005			005
	Beashels towne	015			015
	Hamonton	012		003	009
	Cloughtown	009			009
	Dauidstowne	003			003
	Grange	010		002	008
	Rascastowne	003			003
(folio 7). Paynstowne	Paynstowne	068	John Delafyeld gent	016	052
	Dolars towne	052	Math : Aylmer gent		025
	Shenshaelston	018		009	009
	Thirlingston	025			025
	Rowlanstown	014			014
Ardcath	Newtowne	008		003	005
	Balgeeth	049	Edward Keting gent, & Thomas Johnson gent, & his son gent	009	040
	Rath	017		005	012
	Prinstowne	025			025
	Cloghan	021			021
	Ardcath	016		008	008
	Brinnes Parke	009		003	006
	Littlemananton	008			008
	Danams towne	008		006	002
	Roules towne	004			004
	Percly land	002			002
	Moor towne	012		005	007
(folio 8).	Clatterton	017		003	014
	Fennor	009		006	003
	Greatmananton	011			011
	Cluny	011		005	006
	Battrams town	021			021
	Bonrans towne	008			008
	Mooreread	009			009
	Micknans towne	013		003	010
Coulpe	Stameen	024	Thomas Fugill, & John Fugill his sonn Esqʳˢ, Josua Fugill liueing in England Esq.	007	017
	Donaghcarny	041	Derby Dorran gent		041
	Betagh town	017		002	015

Parrishes	Townelands	Number of People	Tituladoes Names	Eng	Irish
	Martinton	080	Patrick Dracoke, Robert Canon, John Hide, & John Peacock gents.	020	060
	Bebegg	030	William Graues gent	008	022
	Bemore	016		004	012
	Coulpe	054	Thomas Doyle & John Bellen gentlemen	009	045
	Piles towne	006			006
	Pains towne	010			010
(folio 9). Julyans towne	Rogers towne	039	Robert Preston gent	009	030
	Nynch	058			058
	Minis towne	018			018
	Julyans towne	064		008	056
	Smyth towne	049		011	038
	Julian town bridge	006		003	003
	Damans towne	008	Henry Osborne gent	001	007
Moorchurch	Irish towne	034		—	034
	Moymoredry	049		008	041
	Morchurch	027		007	020
	Sarsfyelds town	041	George Pepperd gent		041
	Claries town	018			018
	Kenock	018		008	010
	Great Rahallion	011			011
	Little Rahallion	012		005	007
	Laganhale	012			012
	Kents towne	013			013
	Mulaghtylan	021			021
	Lestoraan	068			068
(folio 10).	Dardistowne Tuck Mill	013			013
	Dardistowne	048	Nicholas Frost Freehoulder	008	040
Stramullen	Gormanston	135	Edward Sutton Esq	012	123
	Beltray	026		004	022
	Stamulin towne	075		013	062
	Tulock	018			018
	Damsells towne	008			008
	Giblotts towne	004			004
	Sadls towne	008			008
	Harbers towne	034	Thomas Hill gent	007	207
	Greenans towne	006			006
	Laries towne	006		004	002
	Whitleas	005			005
	Hogers towne	013			013
	Clins towne	008			008
	Kilbers towne	016			016

Parrishes	Townelands	Number of People	Tituladoes Names	Eng	Irish
	Stidalt	037			037
	Buolley	044			044

Principall Irish Names [and their Number].

Allen, 08 ; Andrew, 13 ; Brady, 08 ; Birne, 19 ; Boylan, 10 ; McCanan, 12 ; Coleman, 12 ; Connell, 16 ; Clery, 09 ; Carr (9), Corr (4), 13 ; Claskey, 08 ; Collier, 09 ; Carmick, 09 ; Doran & Dorran, 08 ; Donnell (5), Daniell (5), 10 ; Duffe, 08 ; Fullam, 11 ; Flyn, 09 ; Heily, 08 ; Henry, 08 ; Kelly, 33 ; Kenedy, 08 ; Linan & Lenan, 09 ; Magraue, 25 ; Moore, 11 ; Murphy, 16 ; Martin, 12 ; Morgan, 11 ; Murry, 09 ; Pentony, 08 ; Peppard, 08 ; Quin, 09 ; Russell, 22 ; Realy, 14 ; Roe, 10 ; Sherlock, 10 ; Savage, 13 ; White, 15 ; Welch, 24 ; Weldon, 08.

(*folio* 10 *verso*)   Barrony of Duleek : Eng, 616 ; Irish, 3303 ; 3919, total.

(*folio* 4).   **SCRYNE BARRONY**

Parrishes	Townelands	Number of People	Tituladoes Names	Eng	Irish
Scryne	Cooks towne	038	George Barnewall, John & Robert Barnewall his sonns gents.		038
	Oberis towne	024	— — — —		024
	Scryne	077	Arthur Parefoy Esq and Richard Moorehead gent.	009	068
	Calues towne	008			008
	Prouds towne	040		011	029
	Rosse	023		003	020
Treuett	Treuett	026			026
	Gerrets towne	034			034
	Clowns towne	021	Richard Recroft gent	004	017
	Brick	005		—	005
	Scales towne	008		—	008
	Brants towne	018			018
Killeen	Killeen	105	Tho : Ld Barron of Dunsany	007	098
	Arlans towne	010			010
	Bealiper	045			045
	Ashronan	039	Luke Hussey gent and Christ : Barnewall gent		039

Parrishes	Townelands	Number of People	Tituladoes Names	Eng	Irish
	Smyths towne	038			038
	Clauans towne	015	Edward & Chris : Plunkett gents		015
(*folio* 12). Dunsany	Dunsany	012	Henry Packenham Esq	002	010
	Corballis	012			012
Taragh	Cabragh	032	Sr Robert Forth Knt and Edward Forth gent	010	022
	Calagh towne	021			021
	Castleton Taragh	025		002	023
	Taragh towne	016	Mathew Penteny gent	002	014
	Odder	014	Bartholemew Plunkett gent		014
	Riuers towne	007		003	004
	Jurdans towne	017			017
Athlumny	Athlumny	017	Arthur Hetherington Esq	005	012
	Alexanderead	026	Richd Cusack gent		026
	Johns towne	004			004
	Beauly	011			011
	Fargans towne	010			010
	Ballimulchan	015			015
	Moortown	021			021
Fohes towne	Fohes towne	019	Richard Young gent	002	017
(*folio* 13). Ardmulchan	Ardmulchan	044			044
	Mooresyd in Ardmulchan }	004	George Cusack gent		004
	Haryes towne	006		002	004
	Hayeston and Reask	042			042
	Kings town	018			018
Dowes town	Fillpotts towne	027	Patrick White & Patrick White gents		027
	Dowes town	030	Martin Hangly gents		030
Templekeran	Carballies	037	Henry Woods	006	031
	Gillians towne	018			018
	Blandis towne	003			003
	Lismullin	028	Arthur Dillon Esq		028
Kilcarne	Greate Kilcarne	026		002	024
	Little Kilcarne	015			015
	Garros towne	033	Walter Cusack gent		033
(*folio* 14).	Ould toune	014		002	012
	Branans toune	010	Nicholas Bevans gent	002	008
	Moorell	006			006
Muncks town	Munck towne	035	Edward Dowdall Esq, Henry & Lancelett Dowdall his sonns, and Richard Ganan gents		035
	Walters town	018	Nich : Dowdall gent		018

Parrishes	Townelands	Number of People	Tituladoes Names	Eng	Irish
	Cusacks town	025			025
	Slanduff	018		004	014
Danis towne	Danis towne	071		009	062
Staffords towne	Staffords town	042	Edmond Doyle gent	009	033
Tymoole	Tymoole	043	Robert Caddell gent		043
	Irish towne	018			018
Rath Feagh	Sisly	009			009
	Rathfeagh	056	John Woton & Phillip Carbery gents	010	046
	Great Watersyd	017	Peeter Bath gent	006	011
	Little Watersyd	010			010
	Slanes towne	006		002	004
(folio 15). Rathfeagh	Loghanton	004			004
	Dixiston	021	George Bath gent	002	019
Mace towne	Mace towne	051	Hance Graham & his sonn in Law gents	006	045
	Pains towne	032		005	027
	Curagh towne	017			017
	Portlester	009			009
	Cussings towne	032	Francis Dillon gent		032

Principall Irish Names [and] their Number.

Bryan, 06 ; Brine, 05 ; Birne, 06 ; Cusack, 07 ; Cargan, 05 ; Cary, 07 ; Cormick, 05 ; Carrell, 05 ; Clery, 08 ; Callan & Callin, 06 ; Connell, 06 ; Daniell, 07 ; Duff, 07 ; Doran, 05 ; Daly, 05 ; Doyle, 06 ; Dowdall, 06 ; Dillon, 07 ; Farrell, 12 ; Geogh, 09 ; Kennedy, 08 ; Kelly, 05 ; Lynchy & Lynshy, 14 ; Lawles, 05 ; Lary, 09 ; Moony, 08 ; Martin, 05 ; Muloly, 06 ; Murphy, 08 ; Plunkett, 11 ; Ryan, 05 ; McRory, 05 ; Realy, 09 ; White, 09 ; Ward, 07 ; Welch, 05.

(folio 15 verso). Barrony of Scryne : Eng, 127 ; Irish, 1621 ; 1748, totall.

(folio 16).   **RATOUTH BARRONY**

Parrishes	Townelands	Number of People	Tituladoes Names	Eng	Irish
Donaghmore	Great Flins town	016		002	014
	Muckers towne	020			020
	Little Flins town	027			027
	Wotton	022	Thomas Dillon gent		022
	Arches towne	017	Myles Symner Esq	003	014

Parrishes	Townelands	Number of People	Tituladoes Names	Eng	Irish
	Miltown	027	Richard Aynger gent	004	023
	Dunreagh	004	Edward Bellew gent	002	002
	Donaghmore	031			031
	Roberts towne	023	John Cleark gent	002	021
	Great Buls towne	003			003
Grenock	Rath of Grenock	015	Henry Sorson gent		015
	Grenock towne	080	Thomas Jones and William Webb gents	009	071
Killeglan	Kileglan towne	037		002	035
Cookes towne	Cookes towne	017		002	015
	Ballibin	025			025
	Crickstown Rath	012			012
	More of Ballibin	003			003
Rathregan	Rathregan	032			032
(folio 17).	Belgamston	014	William Robinson gent	010	004
	Crimore	019	Jacob Peartree gent	004	015
	Woodlandton	017			017
	Poores towne	005	Michaell Litterell gent		005
	Ramston	009			009
	Parsonston	012			012
	Ribston	004			004
	Moyleglan	005			005
	Lismachan	002		002	—
Kilbrew	Kilbrew	062	Robert Gorg Esq	004	058
	Cracans towne	014			014
	Bodin	007			007
	Smithston	020			020
	Thomaston	011			011
	Frainckston	016			016
Cruckston	Cricks town	044	Captⁿ John Thompson Esq	008	036
	Soderton	013			013
	Knaningston	008			008
(folio 18). Dunshaughlin	Dunshaughn ⎫ Grange Ende and ⎬ Boyans town ⎭	146	Thomas Cooke, Rowland Cooke, Thomas Barne-wall, John and Patrick his sonns, gents.	009	137
	Derick	031			031
	Peales towne	028		002	026
Rathbeggan	Rathbeggan	016			016
	Warrinton	006			006
	Enis town	004			004
	Porterston	006	Walter Kingham gent	002	004
	Gormanston	004		002	002
	Willington	013			013
	Pouderlogh	012		002	010

Parrishes	Townelands	Number of People	Tituladoes Names	Eng	Irish
	Growton	—	Departed from thence	—	—
	Johns town	008			008
	Roberts town	008			008
	Keshaniston	020			020
	Roes town	023	Thomas Plunkett gent		023
	Thomaston	015			015
Trevett	Gellos towne	021			021
(*folio* 19).	Grange of Trevett	042	George Owens Esqr	004	038
	Halton	010		—	010
Ratouth	Ratouth	166	Roger Streelle, William Barton, John Skoly, Math : Mason gents	019	047
	Ballihack	018	Thomas Bringhurst Esq	003	015
	Mullinham	006			006
	Feyderffe	008		—	008
	Kilrew	016	Robert Piercefield Esq	006	010
	Rayes towne	018		004	014
	Baltrasny	016			016
	Farlockston	014	Mr. Barnewell gent		014
	Feydalfe-Balfeston	007	Steephen Fletcher gent	002	005
	Grange	017	Arthur Spensur gent	002	015
	Ballibin	011			011
	Bigg Glascarne	008			008
	Little Glascorne	006			006
	Peackocks towne	016	Thomas White gent		016
	Little Loghgoure	015			015
	Great Loghgoure	017			017
(*folio* 20).	Moorton	017		004	013
	Loghgoure Mill	002			002
	Ballimoe	002			002
	Flemings towne	025	John Heaster gent	004	021
	Elgers towne	003			003
Ballimaglassan	Wyanston	005	Robt : Sheild Esq & his brother gent	005	—
	Brownston	002			002
	Brown Rath	014			014
	Little Black Hall	016			016
	Growton	013			013
	Cooks towne	006			006
	Pollebane	014		002	012
	Bigg Black hale	023	Allexander Warren gent	002	021

Principall Irish Names [and] their Number.

Andrew, 06 ; Byrne, 13 ; Bryne, 10 ; Bryde, 06 ; Boylan, 07 ; Barnewell, 07 ; Connell, 09 ; Daly, 06 ; Daniell, 07 ; Head, 06 ; Kelly, 16 ; Moran, 07 ; Martin, 06 ; Mouny, 06 ; Fitzpatrick, 06 ; Fagan, 06 ; Welsh, 06 ; White, 07.

(*folio* 20 *verso*). Barrony of Ratouth : Eng, 0128 ; Irish, 1479 ; 1607, totall.

QUEENES COUNTY
11115

(*folio* 1).   Queens County   **BARONY OF OSSERY**

Places[1]	Numbs of Persons	Tituladoes Names	English	Irish
Grenan	21	Oliver Wheeler Esq, Jonas Wheeler gentle	4	17
Oulert-leagh	8		3	5
Crottinamony	7		3	4
Ballinafousen	8		—	8
Aghamock	4		—	4
Farmoyle	37		3	34
Castlewood	16		3	13
Garranconaly	13			13
Water Castle	43	Robert Reeues gent, Thomas Ougle gentle	5	38
Knockanure	12		4	8
Kilballintallin	30		4	26
(*folio* 2). Tentore	9	Thomas Richards Esq, John Neall	2	7
Tentere	32		11	21
Tentore	4		3	1
Eglish	30		3	27
Eglis	6			6
Ballycolla	14		4	10
Coolederry	9			9
Sraghnadredden	3			3
Balligawge	5			5
Culenekeghy	11		3	8
Moyne	8		1	7
Ballygawdanmore	5		5	—
Ballygawdanmore	12		1	11
Ballygaudan Begg	8			8
Margart	6		—	6
Oulglass	8		—	8
Oulglass	8		—	8
Clonkennighunmore	13			13
(*folio* 3). Balligarvin	4		2	2
Gortnaclehy	13	Edward Burrell gentle	5	8
Gortnaclehy	47		4	43
Balligihin	14			14
Ballegihin	33		3	30
Ballegihin	10			10
Coolebally	12		2	10
Palmers-hill	5	Morgan Cashin gentle		5
Boherard	3			3
Knockmullen	9			9
Cross	18			18
Cross	1			1
Carran	13			13
Ahaboe	43		2	41
Magharinaskeagh	4			4

[1] The *Parishes* Column is blank throughout.

Places	Numbs of Persons	Tituladoes Names	English	Irish
Grangebegg	27	John Fennell gentle Phebes Paget gentle-woman	6	21
Ballerilinmore	4		2	2
Ballerylinbegg	14			14
Kilcotten	2			2
(folio 4). Burres	19		2	17
Burres	37		6	31
Burres	26		3	23
Shanboe	5			5
Shanboe	7			7
Downe	46	John Dwigin gentle		46
Monephat	16		3	13
Monephat	22		—	22
Derrinshennagh	10	Bryan Dwigin gentle	—	10
Derrinshenna	31			31
Cappagh	14			14
Ballikivan	5			5
Barnasallagh	8			8
Lissmore	14	Josias Petditd gentle	2	12
Kildelgie	24	John Short gentle	7	17
Kildelig	38		2	36
Balliawly	15			15
Grants towne	12	Gilbert Rawson Esq	4	8
Grants towne	33		6	27
Grants towne	17			17
Courte	39			39
(folio 5). Curraghnenan	14			14
Bordwell	19	Bryan Fitzpatrick gentle		19
Rathenrick	10	Edmond Fitzpatrick gentle		10
Coolfinn	4	Robert Parrott gentle	1	3
Kilbridimore	16		4	12
Kilbridibegg	15			15
Ballemartin	2			2
Graiguenossy	14			14
Coolkerry	50	John Geale gentle	9	41
Monacoghlan	11	Thos Bedborrough gentle	4	7
Ballivoghlin	9			9
Ballemonin	2			2
Cullaghcurry	10			10
Knockfin	22			22
Kilnafeere	10			10
Carrick	13	Thomas Evans gentle	4	9
Culhill	35		5	30
Culhill	32		3	29
Culhill	18		4	14

Places	Numbs of Persons	Tituladoes Names	English	Irish
(*folio* 6). Cannons wood	10		7	3
Aghamackart	23		2	21
Ballidavin	13		—	13
Ballidavin	7		—	7
Shanbally	7		—	7
Meyn begg and Adrigoole	26	Terrence Kelly gentle	2	24
Gurtin	18	John Dwigin gentle	2	16
Gurtin	8			8
Bolybodan	14	Teige Fitzpatrick gentle	3	11
New towne	37	John Tanner gentle	6	31
New towne	5			5
Caher	13	Robert Gough gentle	6	7
Killeny	23		3	20
Knockanagrally	4			4
Graigvoice	2			2
Rahinleagh	14		2	12
Ballinebin	19	Robert Hedges gentle	4	15
Ballirely	40	James Purcell gentle Richard Marshall gentle	6	34
(*folio* 7). Archcherstowne and Tinvair	34	Lettice Basket Widow gentle	8	26
Agharny	14		3	11
Mognoge	12			12
Griagegaran	24			24
Sraghleagh	21		6	15
Sraghnarrow	15	Thomas Lapsty gentle	4	11
Sraghnarrow	10		2	8
Graigard	9		2	7
Sraghvally	3		—	3
Bawnagharry	6		—	6
Graigdrisly	22		2	20
Kilgurtrian	8		2	6
Kilgurtrian	30			30
Resdiragh	16			16
Bawnbolemon	6			6
Cappatenan	4			4
Clonmeen	8			8
Clonmeen	24			24
Templequan	12			12
Clonburren	16		2	14
Castle Fleming	14	John Geyles gentle James Manly gent	6	8
(*folio* 8). Castle Fleming	37		2	35
Tullaghcomin	19			19
Rathneleugh	9			9
Rathneleugh	8			8

Places	Numbs of Persons	Tituladoes Names	English	Irish
Garreduff	11	John Fitzpatrick gentle		11
Clonmore	13			13
Ballimullen	33			33
Rahinshen	5			5
Errell	11			11
Killecae	12			12
Lisduff	11			11
Bellaghrahin	19	John Bryan gentle		19
Ballaghrahin	17			17
Rossmore	21		2	19
Grogan	4			4
Grignegihy	10		2	8
Eglishion	21			21
Rathfarary	9		—	9
(folio 9). Lyrogue	4		—	4
Graigetally	11			11
Rathdowny	31	Thomas Prior Esq, Richard Mendan gentle	3	28
Rathdowny	30		7	23
Cooleowly	11			11
Dunaclegin	4			4
Uppderry	8		3	5
Barnbally Craggh	12			12
Belleddy	4			4
Johns towne	17	Thomas Woods gentle	2	15
Bearchill	5			5
Bally buggy	23			23
Harris towne	11			11
Harris towne	9			9
Kilcoak	31			31
Cloneebe	17		2	15
Pipers rath	4		2	2
Pipers rath	32		2	30
Teneclohy	14			14
Aghkippo	8	Doctor Conly Cashin gentle		8
Castle criffin	10	Charles Watkins gentle	1	9
(folio 10) Castlecriffin	16			16
Balleculede	2			2
Rahindornag	9			9
Donaghmore	25			25
Ballihegadon	7			7
Ballihegadon	7			7
Rahintane	4			4
Tinvonin	7			7
Kilpursett	13		—	13
Rathmore	24		—	24
Killedooly	3		0	3

Places	Numbs of Persons	Tituladoes Names	English	Irish
Killedooly	31		—	31
Gortnalee	10		—	10
Tullaghcommin	15			15
Ballibrohy	5		0	5
Ballebroxy	4			4
Sheirk	44	Abraham May gentle	7	37
Garranconly	12	Peter Buckly gentle		12
Garranettconly	16			16
Tenknock	15			15
Balliguoad	13			13
Upper Erris	9			9
Lower Erris	17			17
(*folio* 11). Killesmisby	8			8
Munnimore	4		4	
Ballinlagartmore	9		4	5
Kilmartin	7		4	3
Ballaghmore	46		31	15
Clonquose	26		15	11
Killballeduff	26		1	25
Clonquose	4		1	3

Principall Irish Names [and] their Numb[er].

Burke, 9 ; Brohy, 36 ; Butler, 8 ; Bergin, 32 ; Byrne, 9 ; Breen, 13 ; O Bryan, 3 ; Bowe, 10 ; O Bowe, 2 ; Brenan, 6 ; Carroll, 5 ; Cashin, 24 ; McConner, 7 ; Cleere, 6 ; Creory, 6 ; Costigan, 12 ; McCoody, 6 ; Campian, 10 ; McDaniell, 7 ; Dullany, 86 ; Dowley, 17 ; Dun, 18 ; Dwigin, 22 ; Dooling, 8 ; Dyvoy, 4 ; McEvoy, 10 ; Felan, 114 ; McFyinn, 6 ; Gormogue, 13 ; Fitzgerrold, 3 ; Haraghan, 12 ; Kelly, 24 ; Kenedy, 8 ; Kegin, 6 ; Kea, 7 ; Loughman, 19 ; Lawler, 8 ; Moore, 6 ; Meagher, 18 ; Murfy, 5 ; Mentan, 5 ; Meolan, 5 ; Purcell, 9 ; FitzPatrick, 99 ; Phelan, 39 ; Quiggly, 10 ; Rafter, 6 ; Shyrin, 9 ; Shiell, 8 ; Tobin, 7 ; Tynan, 23 ; McTeigue, 10 ; Tehan, 8 ; Wailsh, 10.

(*folio* 11 *verso*). The Number of People in the Barony of Ossory according to their severall Pages : Eng, 350 ; Irish, 2663 ; Totall, 3013.

(*folio* 12).

BARONY OF UPP' OSSERY

Places	Numbs	Tituladoes Names	English	Irish
Derrinaserry	41		—	41
The Cantred of Upper Woods :				
Cloynyn	53		—	53

Places	Numbs	Tituladoes Names	English	Irish
Kilbrekan	7			7
Coole	10			10
Camelogue	10			10
Balliclery	9		2	7
Cuddaghmore	32		7	25
Carvigin	4			4
Crannagh	10			10
Castle towne	32	Robert Clerke gentle	10	22
Camhill	4			4
Aghafin	2			2
Clonmore	10			10
Aunatrim	6			6
Cooleroan	7			7
Curnegewer and ye membs	10			10
Rosnadowhy	8	Thomas Paul gentle	6	2
Longford	4			4
Balletarsny	6		2	4
Mannen	9			9
Lowran and Dirrihanen	11		3	8
(folio 13). Rosnaclony	10			10
Moher and Clondaglas	36			36
Killenure	28		4	24
Lackagh and Leaugh	42		17	25
Ballemoy	23	Thos Davis Esq	9	14
Knockbrack	30		12	18
Killogue & Mondrahad	36			36
Clononyne	11			11
Derrilehan & Magharibeg	19	Francis Lovellis gentle	5	14
Cambrosse	13		9	4
Ballenraly	36		2	34
Rossnacryng	23			23
Srahanboy	25			25
Ballicloghlin	12			12
Glandine	10			10
TeneRilley	14			14
Rushin and ye membs	58		4	54

Principall Irish Names [and] their Numb[er.]

Bergin, 5 ; Brohy, 6 ; Byrne, 3 ; Costigin, 12 ; Conner, 4 ; Carroll, 4 ; Dullany, 66 ; Dwigin, 10 ; Dowley, 9 ; Dowling, 4 ; McEvoy, 3 ; Felan, 26 ; Kynin, 11 ; Kelly, 4 ; Lawler, 5 ; FitzPatrick, 14.

(folio 13 verso).   The Number of the People in the Bar of Upper Osory : Eng, 092 ; Irish, 619 ; Eng & Irish, Totall, 711.

(*folio* 14).   **BARONY OF MARYBORROUGH**

Places	Numbs	Tituladoes Names	Eng	Irish
The Towne and liberties of Maryborrough	198	John Partridge gentle, Edward Bolton gentle, Edward Wattkins gentle, William Baker gentle, Edward Nickolls gentle, Bryan Byrne gentle, John Roades gentle.	48	150
Knockmay	12		2	10
Clonruske	6		4	2
Rathleague	25	Thady Dwigin gent	—	25
Cappawley	5			5
Balleknockan	35			35
Eyne	31	Richard Homan gent	8	23
Shaine	32		9	23
Straboes	16	Thomas Wade gentle, Elizabeth Whittny gent.	6	10
Ballidavis	24	John Moor gent		24
Kilnekar	4			4
Kilmensy	38	Henry Gilbert Esq	8	30
Ballinroone	22			22
Coolenemony	31			31
Clonderigmoyle	21			21
Cappagh	11			11
(*folio* 15). Clonreher & Rosslegan	33	Richard Crosby gent		33
Rosslegar	7			7
Togher	23	Josuah George gentle	5	18
Clonadodorane	32		—	32
Clonagowne	19			19
Rosse	24		3	21
Balleroheen	5			5
Ballefin	4			4
Boghlone	7			7
Kilcolmanbane	12		4	8
The Lordship of Dissert	47		8	39
Kilcromine	22	Thomas Fitzgerrald gentle		22
Loughacoe	3			3
Culecrihy	33		2	31
Derry	10			10
Ballemarkin	14			14
(*folio* 16). Balliclidar	6			6
Caricknaparkny	11			11
Kiltete	6			6
Ballecarroll	22			22
Rahinrahan	38	Robert Piggott gent, Charleton Chissell gentle, George Lee gent.	9	29
Ballemonny	8			8
The Lordship of Montrath The forge	36	Phillipp Sergeant gentle, Thomas Peirson gentle	16	20

2 I

Places	Numbs	Tituladoes Names	Eng	Irish
Disertbehagh	10			10
Mountrath	223	Daniell Carroll gent, William Lockington gent, Thomas Lowe gent	49	174
Derrilosgy	11		2	9
Sconce	39			39
Redcastle	30	John Neall gent, James Neall gent	2	28
(folio 17). Clonnagh	35		2	33
Kings towne	21			21
Cappalaghinne	93	Edward Connyn gentle Richard Fitzgerrald gent	9	84
Tromora	32			32
Cromogue	52	Marcus Loffan gentle		52
Rosquittan	51			51
Downe	25	Charles Cooke gent	7	18
Tenekilly	4			4
Killeny	39		4	35
Sroth Rath	12	John Fitzpatrick gent		12
Boelly	44			44
Cappanaclohy	75	Thady Kynin gent	3	72
Rahincullen	13	Morgan Cashin gent		13
Coole	6			6
Coolte	51	Thomas Beard gent	3	48
Clonboyne and Kilmantought }	11		5	6
Clonkeen	22		6	16
Clonadogasy	10		5	5
Closcullane	6			6
Coolenacarton	17		2	15
Arleane	4			4

Principall Irish Names [and] Their Numb[er.]

Byrne, 13 ; Bergin, 23 ; McBryan, 3 ; Bryan, 4 ; Brenan, 10 ; Burke, 4 ; Bryne, 5 ; Brohy, 8 ; Bredan, 11 ; Carroll, 13 ; Conner, 4 ; Conrahy, 13 ; Cashin, 8 ; Costigin, 10 ; Carrolan, 6 ; Cody, 5 ; Crooke, 6 ; Divoy, 14 ; McDaniell, 4 ; Daniell, 4 ; Dullany, 46 ; Dullyne, 8 ; Dun, 25 ; Dooling, 8 ; Dowling, 7 ; Dowley, 5 ; Dowgan, 5 ; McEvoy, 40 ; Felan, 29 ; Fyinn, 7 ; Fitzgerrold, 5 ; McGilfoyle, 4 ; Higgin, 4 ; Keygin, 5 ; Kelly, 29 ; Kynyn, 11 ; Kenedy, 4 ; Lawler, 57 ; Larissy, 5 ; Moore, 11 ; Mulchaell, 6 ; Neale, 5 ; O Neale, 2 ; Piggott, 5 ; Fitzpatrick, 12 ; Roe, 5 ; McShane, 4 ; Tynan, 6 ; Tehan, 4 ; Tobin, 4 ; Wailsh, 15.

(folio 17 verso).   The Number of the People in the Barony of Maryborrogh according to the severall pages : Eng, 231 ; Irish, 1638 ; Eng & Irish, 1869.

(folio 18)   **BARONY OF CULLENAGH**

Places	Numbs	Tituladoes Names	English	Irish
Ballinakill	204	Sr Amos Meredith Bart	51	153
Clohoge	8		—	8

Places	Numbs	Tituladoes Names	English	Irish
Bolibane	16		3	13
Aghnacross	16		2	14
Graighnehown	68		5	63
Moyadd	7			7
Graignesmuttan	33			33
Clarebarcon	11			11
Kilrush	30		3	27
Bolibegg	27			27
Baggetts towne	28		3	25
Samsons Court	41			41
Iron Mill	14		2	12
Lisbigny	14		2	12
The Moate	4			4
Lacknabranagh	9			9
Graigbegg	8			8
Drimsilligg	21			21
Tullore	19			19
Derryfore and Lissogaman	16			16
(folio 19). Lissogamon	39		—	39
Ballypicas	16			16
Abey Leix	52		8	44
Rathmoyle	10			10
Ballimullen	26		7	19
Clonkin or Clonrin	28		2	26
Raylish	21			21
Duary	29	Doctr John Mulhaell gentle		29
Cullenagh	27	Francis Barington Esqr, Allexander Barington gentle	2	25
Ballihelan	13			13
Cullenaghbeg	25			25
Rahinduff	28		12	16
Timohoe	40	Francis Cosby Esq	7	33
Ballentlea	44		5	39
Orchard	23			23
Fossey	15			15
Esquer	31		4	27
Kilballyhoell	20			20
Cremorgan	33	Christopher Barrington gentle	2	31
(folio 20). Balligormull	28			28
Garriglasse	31			31
Ballineclogh	12		4	8
Ballirone	77	John Kiffin gent, Thomas Whittle gentle	31	46
Cashell	23			23
Cloncullan	15		5	10
Crubine	13		—	13
Balligegle	13			13
Cappanaclogh	3			3
Rahinemrougue	2			2
Clontiquos	7	Adam Lofftus Esq, Thomas Lofftus gentle	4	3

Principall Irish Names [and] their Numbers.

Byrne, 12 ; Brohy, 7 ; Brenan, 10 ; Bergin, 7 ; Conner, 10 ; Carroll, 3 ; Cahell, 7 ; Conrahy, 4 ; Dun, 13 ; Dowling, 5 ; Dowley, 5 ; Dullany, 19 ; Dowran, 5 ; Daniell, 6 ; Evoy, 14 ; Felan, 31 ; Forestall, 6 ; Gorinouge, 4 ; Huraghan, 6 ; Holaghan, 4 ; Kelly, 8 ; Kenna, 6 ; Lawler, 27 ; Mulchaell, 6 ; Murfy, 5 ; Moore, 11 ; Muldony, 4 ; Meagher, 5 ; Neale, 3 ; Nowland, 4 ; Fitzpatrick, 9 ; O Shee, 8 ; McTeigue, 5 ; Wailsh, 10.

(*folio* 20 **verso**)   The Number of the People in the Barony of Cullenagh : Eng, 164 ; Irish, 1174 ; Eng & Irish, 1338.

(*folio* 21).   **BARONY OF SLIEMARGEAGH**

Places	Numbs	Tituladoes Names	English	Irish
Castletowne-Omoy	37	Francis Newbolt gentle	7	30
Ballifinnan	3			3
Kilcrue and Clonebegg	33			33
Cloanbegg	4		3	1
Garranes	32			32
Farnans	46			46
Crottentegle	57	Anthony Gayle gentle	6	51
Srule	26	Nathaniell Markes Esq	9	17
Killeny	8	Nicholas Evers gentle farmer	2	6
Leauge	2			2
Ballihormor	11	James Kegan gentle farmer		11
Clona	12	John Vivers gentle	2	10
Cooletexenry	66	David Lea gentle farmer	5	61
Cappinevogue	2		—	2
Cappinlugge	7		—	7
Sraghe	22			22
Cuddy	13			13
Rossnellgan	8			8
Ballinakill and Aghnecros	51		2	49
Slety and Knockbegg	18			18
(*folio* 22). Harris towne	12			12
Graigue	106		10	96
Killishen	21	Stephen Bowen gentle, and Farmer	2	19
Corraghe	15			15
Ballikilleen	10		2	8
Ballehide & Rossmore	32		6	26
Pallimoiler	127		12	115
Toulerton	6			6
Oulteaghe	5	William Padgett gent	2	3
Sradfusseg	21			21
Ballimoyseran	51		9	42

Places	Numbs	Tituladoes Names	English	Irish
Crosnee	11			11
Olderrigg	16		2	14
Rossenagh Ballenrahin and Rathillig	38		10	28
Ballinagawle	54	Christopher Tucke gentle, Joseph Kinder gentle	6	48
(*folio* 23). Tyrernon	17			17
Gurtin	14		5	9
Clonbecan	7			7
Garrindenny	45		10	35

Principall Irish Names [and] Their Numbs.

Bergin, 4 ; Byrne, 11 ; Brenan, 28 ; Branagh, 5 ; Beaghan, 4 ; Conran, 5 ; Cody, 4 ; Comin, 5 ; Dowling, 17 ; Dowley, 6 ; Dun, 4 ; McDaniell, 10 ; Dempsy, 5 ; Dwigin, 4 ; Dunchowe, 5 ; Doyle, 6 ; Devoy, 6 ; McEdmond, 6 ; Flemming, 4 ; Felan, 4 ; Kelly, 17 ; Kingshellogh, 14 ; Keating, 7 ; Lawler, 08 ; Lea, 6 ; Murry, 13 ; Meagher, 4 ; Moore, 11 ; Nowland, 14 ; McShane, 4 ; Wailsh, 4.

(*folio* 23 *verso*)   The Number of People in the Barony of Sliemargeagh : Eng, 112 ; Irish, 954 ; Eng and Irish, 1066.

(*folio* 24).   **BARONY OF BALLYADAMS**

Places	Numbs	Tituladoes Names	English	Irish
Tully	45	Willam Duckingfield Esq	5	40
Ballyadams	43	William Bowen Esq	7	36
Killegavard	12			12
Rathgilbert	31		4	27
Rosbrann	7		4	3
Ballylynan	49	Dame Elizabeth Grahams Lady, Thomas Grahams Esq, John Grahams gentle, Richard Grahams gent.	4	45
Miltowne	51		9	42
Carbally	11		6	5
Ballintubod	24	The Lady Ellis Bowen, George Bowen gent.	3	21
Cronnagh	12			12
Ballintlea	5		4	1
Rahine	47			47
Ballilehane	42		10	32 .
Knockatornor	20			20

Places	Numbs	Tituladoes Names	English	Irish
Classone	16		02	14
Kilfeacle	29	James Dun gent	4	25
Achamacfir	10		2	8
Clonpiers	42	John Bambrick gentle & farmer		42
(folio 25). Curgarron	9			9
Cullenagh	14			14
Shanganaghbegg and Ballinree	} 31	William Scott Esq	19	12
Ballinree	5			5
Skehan	25	Arthur Bambrick gent	3	22
Tankards towne	26	William Walker Esq	10	16
Killebban	24			24
Bellanagaor	11		5	6
Killeene	26			26
Monkes grange	26			26
Ballefoyle	3		3	—

Principall Irish Names [and] their Numbs.

Brenan, 7 ; Byrne, 7 ; Clullen & Cullin, 6 ; Dun, 14 ; Dowling, 12 ; Doyle, 4 ; Doweran, 5 ; McEvoy, 5 ; Felan, 4 ; Grahams, 9 ; Hirly, 6 ; Kenedy, 5 ; Kelly, 10 ; Lawler, 13 ; Mulchaell, 7 ; Murfy, 5 ; Moore, 9.

(folio 25 verso). The Number of People in the Barony of Ballyadams : Eng, 104 ; Irish, 592 ; Eng & Irish, 0696.

(folio 26)   **BARONY OF PORTNYHINCH**

Places	Numbs	Tituladoes Names	English	Irish
Lea	64	William Cruihly gentle	10	54
Dulaght	12		—	12
Kilbride	20		—	20
Loghtowne	11		3	8
Ballinrosh towne	34		00	34
Ballibrittan	30		6	24
Graigue	16			16
Ballicarroll	19	John Quinn gentle		19
Ballintogher	21			21
Cloneene	9			9
Balliteigue	23			23
Cooletederry	13	John Vaghan gent proprietor		13
Ballintogher	13		1	12

Places	Numbs	Tituladoes Names	English	Irish
Balleteigue	29			29
Rathrongy	21		2	19
Brackloune & Terrecoyer	18		2	16
Raleiee	15		2	13
(folio 27). Lower Kilnecourt	20		2	18
Upper Kilnecourt	17		09	8
Kilmullen	30			30
Ballyfubbole & Balleaden	16		5	11
Moritte	42			42
Emoe	53	Henry Sibbaulds gentle	14	39
Ballinderin	21		4	17
Ballimulronow	7			7
Coolebansher	15			15
Carhan	19		2	17
Ballicollan	11		6	5
Killeen Lynagh	19		—	19
Brittas	12			12
Gobbachotty	3		1	2
(folio 28), Kilmanum	25		2	23
Clomosny	11			11
Ballicoliin	13		7	6
Derrygugh	32			32
Derrygugle	3			3
Ballinre Derry	8		4	4
Laraghy	4		4	
Tenekilly	27	James McDaniell gentle		27
Coolaghy	8			8
Clonterry	15	John Fossy gentle	11	4
Dingins	4		4	

Principall Irish Names [and] Their Numb[er.]

Beaghan, 11 ; Byrne, 8 ; Bergin, 4 ; Carroll, 10 ; Conner, 8 ; Conraghy, 5 ; Donellan, 5 ; Dempsy, 9 ; McDaniell, 10 ; McEvoy, 5 ; Foran, 5 ; Felan, 6 ; Farrell, 5 ; Helan, 10 ; Kelly, 16 ; Lawler, 7 ; Murty, 6 ; Moore, 5 ; McShane, 6.

(folio 28 verso). Number of People in ye Barony of Portnyhinch : Eng, 101 ; Irish, 0728 ; Eng and Irish, 0829.

(folio 29).

BARONY OF STRADBALLY

Places	Numbs	Tituladoes Names	English	Irish
Stradbally	54		15	39
Colione	4		2	2

Places	Numbs	Tituladoes Names	English	Irish
Knockany carell	4		—	4
Aghamadock	9		—	9
Oughmale	14			14
Vicars towne and Greate Wood	65			65
Rathcrehy	5		2	3
Rathinsky	4	John Dodd gent	2	2
Ballinspratty	10			10
Rahinchone	17		2	15
Garimadock	14	William Cosby gentle		14
Killeenes	9	John Poordom gentle		9
Kilmurry	15	Francis Brereton gentle	4	11
Balliduff	4			4
Killowe	19			19
Garyduffe	6			6
Kilmarbor	8		5	3
(folio 30). Killpatrick	6			6
Ballimadock	6			6
Ballinowlan	11			11
Bellareader	10	George Williams gent	4	6
Parke	10			10
Toherbavoe	6			6
Kilrory	5	Vincent Kidder gentle	2	3
Rathmore	16			16
Grange	4			4
Ballikilcovan	33	Oliver Wailsh gentle	6	27
Black foord	15		2	13
Ballyduff	12			12
Drumneene	14			14
Bally manus	2			2
Inch	7		2	5
Garrans	21		7	14
Tymogue	43	Beniamin Worsly Esq John Rawlins Esq	8	35
Ballintecken	12		2	10
(folio 31). Ballicubeene	8			8
Guyheene	33			33
Cloghpook	45	William Hetherington gent, Richard Hetherington gent, Walter Butler gent, James Butler gent.	4	41
Fahybegg	26			26
Logg currin	26		10	16
Rahimhohill	23			23
Loghleage	58	Richard Brereton gent	4	54
Muney	45	George Reynolds gent	4	41
Rathimsky	12		2	10
Rahinduff	19	John Pigett gentle		19
Ouldmill	8			8

Principall Irish Names [and] Their Numb[er.]

Bergin, 5 ; Brenan, 9 ; Byrne, 9 ; Brohy, 8 ; Conrahy, 9 ; Donell & McDonell, 9 ; Doyle, 5 ; Dun, 13 ; Fyinn, 8 ; Felan, 10 ; Kelly, 13 ; Lawler, 16 ; Murfy, 7 ; Moghan, 5 ; Mulone, 6 ; Wailsh, 7.

(*folio* 31 *verso*).   The Number of People in the Barony of Stradbally : Eng, 089 ; Irish, 709 ; Eng and Irish, 798.

(*folio* 32).

BARONY OF TYNAHINCH

Places	Numbers	Tituladoes Names	English	Irish
Ballinakell	38	Barnaby Dun Esq, Darby Whitfield gent	3	35
Kappanapingganny	13		—	13
Brittas	39		—	39
Coolbollain	19			19
Ballickneene and Lorgin	19			19
Castle Cuffe	20	William Lestrange gentle		20
Garrihuddet or Garrihunder	28			28
Killinperson	4			4
Castlecuff	4		2	2
Mountmellick	175	Walter Warnford Esq	95	80
Kilkeevan	9	Joseph Hamon gent	2	7
Garimore	4		1	3
Gloraghdow	3			3
Cappolaghan	10			10
Mucklone	4			4
Forreste	7			7
Parke	8			8
(*folio* 33). Monacudde	10			10
Castlebrack	25			25
Roskeene	11	James Barnwall gent	1	10
Clanchill	20	Edmond McShane gentle		20
Sraduillin	8			8
Clonose	8			8
Rerybegg	18			18
Rerimore	11			11
Affoly	3			3
Clonagh	24			24
Tenehinch	25			25
Derry	13			13
Ballinabeg	10			10
Clappard & Cloncannon	46	Thomas Piggott Esq Robert Piggott gentle	5	41
Cloncannon	9			9
Cappaghbegg	11			14
Gurtin	12		5	7
Rossen Allis	26	Godfrey Cantrell gent, William Edmondson gent, William Barcroft gent	19	7

Places	Numbers	Tituladoes Names	English	Irish
(*folio* 34). Dirrinae	16			16
Rossenallis	39		20	19
Clooneheene	20			20
Capolane	18			18
Lucan	5	Mrs Dorothy Dun gent		5

Principall Irish Names [and] their Numb[er.]

Bane, 5 ; Bryan & McBryan, 5 ; Carroll, 6 ; & McCarroll, 4 ; Conner & McConner, 7 ; Conraghy, 17 ; Dun, 18 ; McDonnogh, 8 ; Divoy, 5 ; Daniell & McDaniell, 6 ; McEdmond, 5 ; Kenedy, 5 ; McMortagh, 5 ; Mallone, 5 ; Ogue, 7 ; McRory, 6 ; McShane, 11 ; McTeigue, 9.

(*folio* 33 *verso*).   The Number of People in the Bar of Tynahinch : Eng, 153 ; Irish, 642 ; Eng & Irish, 795.

(*folio* 34 *verso*).   Queens County.   Number of People in this county and in each hundred viz :

	Pages	Eng	Irish	totall of English & Irish.
Ossory	11	0350	2663	3013
Upper Ossory	13	0092	0619	0711
Maryborogh	17	0231	1638	1869
Sliemargeagh	23	0112	0954	1066
Cullenagh	20	0164	1174	1338
Ballyadams	25	0104	0592	0696
Fortnihinch	28	0101	0728	0829
Stradbally	31	0089	0709	0798
Tynahinch	33	0153	0642	795
Totall		1396	9719	11115

WESTMEATH COUNTY

12672

(folio 1). Westmeath County

DEMIFOURE BARRONY

Parrishes	Townelands	Number of People	Tituladoes Names	Eng	Irish
Foyran	Foyran	018	Christopher Fitzsymons gent	—	018
	Rachand	008		—	008
	Ballintullagh	034	Richard Kearnan gent		034
	Ballinskarig	008			008
	Munny	026		002	024
	Togher	018			018
	Williams towne	005			005
	Fynah	094	Nicholas Hoyse gent	018	076
	Tullinally	056	Gabriell Begge & Thomas Louton Esqrs	012	044
Mayne	Carne	019			019
	Williams towne	010			010
	Dyrae	003			003
	Culure	016			016
	Mayne towne	022			022
	Turbotts towne	021	John Clerke, Peter Prench, and John Browne gent	002	019
	Monck towne	006			006
Rathgarrane	Millcastle	027		002	025
	Rahin	003			003
(folio 2).	Balemanus	008			008
	Kinturke and Ballnagross	037		015	022
	Rathgarrane	011			011
	Ballicamcoyle	029	Barthollomew Dardis gent	003	026
	Kinturke and Ballnagross	041			041
	Turme	009		—	009
	Stone towne	005			005
	Bratty	020	Richard Andrewes gent	002	018
	Moor towne of Learchyll	003			003
	Ballany	004			004
	Wind towne	004			004
	Hamons towne	004			004
St Fahins	Rannaghan	053	James Nugent gent	002	051
	Templens towne	012			012
	Hill towne	017		000	017
(folio 3). St Fehin	Lienhill	015		009	006
	Carpinters towne	033	Robert Nugent gent		033
	Corballis	008			008
	Gillards towne	042			042
	Callaghs towne	023			023

Parrishes	Townelands	Number of People	Tituladoes Names	Eng	Irish
Lickblae	Clenegeragh	014	Robert Nugent gent		014
	Castle towne	016			016
	Ardnagross towne	006			006
	Carrollans towne	037		019	018
	Dirracraffe	005			005
	Lickblae	047			047
Killpatrick	Rathcrivagh	013			013
	Gillbers towne	007			007
	Comaim	003			003
	Killpatrick	047			047
	Clondaliner	006			006
	Drumhurlin	002		002	—
(folio 4).	Tuits towne	018		003	015
	Bellanavyne	020			020
	Christons towne	008			008
	Commers towne	034			034
	Martins towne	008		—	008
	Castle martin	007			007
	Foure	036			036
	Glanidan	033			033
Lady Fahaltowne	Foure	027			027
	Derengarran	060	William Markham Esq	009	051
	Gartlans towne	042			042
	Streams towne	027	Richard Nugent gent		027
	Killtume	038		009	029

Principall Irish Names [and] their Number.

Brady, 007 ; Browne, 009 ; O Connor, 009 ; Donoghow, 011 ; Fagan, 057 ; Fay, 007 ; Fox, 007 ; Kearnan, 009 ; Kelly, 009 ; Lency, 010 ; Mullgan & Mulligan, 008 ; Murphy, 009 ; Murtagh, 012 ; Newgent, 022 ; Relye, 013 ; Fitzsymons, 014 ; Symons, 007 ; Terrell, 007.

(folio 4 verso)   Barrony of Demifoure : Eng, 109 ; Irish, 1224 ; 1333, totall.

(folio 5).   **MOYGOISHE BARRONY.**

Parrishes	Townelands	Number of People	Tituladoes Names	Eng	Irish
Killmacknivan	Emper	064	Faustian Collens gent	002	062
	Contanstons	032	Henry Dalton gent	—	032
	Lakinstons	010		—	010

Parrishes	Townelands	Number of People	Tituladoes Names	Eng	Irish
Kilbixy	Ballenlue	042	Richard Dalton & Christopher Fitzgerrald gent		042
	Laragh	021	George Fitzgerrald gent		021
	Tristernagh	049	Sʳ Henry Piers Knt	009	040
	Grange	061	James Fitzgerrald gent	—	061
	Banans towne	014	Walter Tuitte gent	—	014
	Ballacorsley	009	Thomas Hopkins Esq	003	006
	Kilbixy	032	Nicholas Ledwidge & Arthur Nangle gent		032
	Janue	013			013
	Comens towne	034			034
	Ballencargie	022			022
	Ballesallagh	024	Edward Plunkett, Robert Unill, Marcus Bealing and Walter Bealing his sonn gent		024
(folio 6).	Ballroe	018			018
	Kilbalabrigh	012			012
Templeoran	Templeoran	038			038
	Johns towne	041	Henry Fitzgerrald gent		041
	Sandonagh	018			018
	Coulneha	013			013
	Goders towne	016			016
	Sonnaugh	037	John Duckenfield Esq	002	035
	Parcellstone	030	Alexandʳ Hope & Richard his sonn gents	003	027
	Kildollane	008			008
Street	Colamber	025	John Hawkins gent	002	023
	Ballegildivin	006	John Widowes gent	002	004
	Clunmore	022			022
	Colnegan	014			014
	Lisduss	030			030
	Fiermore	017	Bryan Reily gent		017
	Correlly	011			011
(folio 7).	Dunonan	011	Gerrott Delamare gent		011
	Street	069			069
	Rath	019		—	019
	Culoin	014	Tho : Long & Edward Knight Esqrs	007	007
Russagh	Russagh	023	John Patrickeson and Walter Delamare gents	—	023
	Loghanstone	003		003	—
	Corredonellon	019	John Cormick gent	004	015
	Cappagh	045	William Christmas, Abraham Geales, Theobald Ledwidge, Edmond Walsh, and Luke Nangle, gents.	004	041

Parishes	Townelands	Number of People	Tituladoes Names	Eng	Irish
Rathaspick	Conolagh	007			007
	Cockinclar	015			015
	Deriduan	012	Hubert Farrell & Richd Ferrell gents.		012
	Rathowne-Edward	012	Francis Hallingworth gent	002	010
	Killmakahill	002			002
	Rathclittagh	013			013
	Ballmardan	009			009
(folio 8).	Coristin	008			008
	Rathaspick	069	Abraham Michelburn Esqr	005	064

Principall Irish Names [and] Their Number.

Casey & Cassey, 10 ; Conelly & Conally, 07 ; Cormick, 11 ; Dalton, 12 ; Delamare, 06 ; Farrell & Ferell, 16 ; Fagan, 06 ; Fitzgerrald, 07 ; Kegry, 08 ; Kenny, 09 ; Kelly, 06 ; Laughlin, 07 ; Mortagh, 14 ; Moran & Morran, 10 ; Nangle, 06 ; Tuitte, 06 ; Ward, 06 ; Welsh & Walsh, 08.

(folio 8 verso).   Barrony of Moygoishe : Eng, 048 ; Irish, 1086 ; 1134, totall.

(folio 9)   **CORKERIE BARRONY.**

Parishes	Townelands	Number of People	Tituladoes Names	Eng	Irish
Portloman	Portloman	046	John Sallsibery gent	002	044
	Freugin	025		—	025
Portnesangan	Ballard	010		—	010
	Ballaboy	012			012
	Scurlogstowne	002			002
	Loghanstowne	025	John Juyce gent	002	023
	Ballnegall	015	Edward Nugent gent		015
	Black castle	015	Garrett Tuitte & Wa^r Tuitte his sonn gents		015
	Portnesangan	011			011
	Ballenselott	039	Coll. John Clarke Esq & Phillip Teeling gent	005	034
	Mulmoran	021			021
Tifurnan	Tifarnan	022			022
	Killmagliss	013			013
	Doone	008	Will : Bangfield gents	002	006

Parrishes	Townelands	Number of People	Tituladoes Names	Eng	Irish
Taghmon	Taghmon and Farrenkellyn }	057	Will: Disney Esq and Will: Ledwidge gent	008	049
	Munck towne	026	Thomas Delamare and Richard Tuitte gents	—	026
(folio 10).	Tiberquill	018	Piers Tuitte gent		018
Stonehall	Stonehall	018	Rowland Willson Esq		018
	Killington	014	Christopher Nugent and Oliuer Nugent his Sonn gents		014
	Gallmoylston	011			011
	Martynstown	006	James Snow, William Snow, Rubyn Leigh, & Robert Massey, gents.	003	003
Leny	Ballnefedd	038	Phillip Ebzury Esq and John Ebzury gent	007	031
	Kilpatrick	028	James Delamare gent	—	028
	Rathrory	014		—	014
	Bonbrosney	010			010
	Farra and Rathbennett	034			034
	Baleuad	013			013
	Killenhue	017			017
	Ballenalack	010	Brian Mungan gent	002	008
	Knightwood	033	Edmond Nugent, Robert Newgent, and Edward Newgent, gents.		033
Lacken	Lacken	045	Walter Ledwidge gent		045
(folio 11).	Ballaherne	015			015
	Folmortt	012			012
	Carrick	020			020
	Grange	006		003	003
Multifarnan	Multifernan	081	Jonathan Handy, George Madocks, Zephania Smith, George Harrison, and Mathew Allen, gents.	010	071
	Donoer	018	George Talbott Esq		018
	Tober	023			023
	Ballikill	003			003
	Ballenport	020			020
	Ballenredie	005			005
	Monintown	032	Francis Newgent gent		032

Principall Irish Names [and] their Number.

Branan & Brenan, 05 ; Dalie, 08 ; Dalton, 06 ; Delamare, 06 ; Farrell, 08 ; Galcor, 05 ; Hueghs & Hues, 08 ; Kiraghty, 14 ; Ledwidge, 14 ; Martin, 05 ; Mullican, 05 ; Newgent, 25 ; Ward, 10 ; Tuitte, 07.

(folio 11 verso). Barrony of Corkerie : Eng, 044 ; Irish, 847 ; 891, totall.

2 K

(folio 12). **MAJASKELL AND MAGHEREDERNAN BARRONIES**

Parrishes	Townelands	Number of People	Tituladoes Names	Eng	Irish
Mollingar	Cullenmore, Brocke, and Cullenbegg	} 046	James Leigh gent	—	046
	Glaskerne	028		002	026
	Balligarrett	032			032
	Stratens towne	006	Lord Wharton Lord Baron	001	005
	Stokes towne	018			018
	Taylers towne	014			014
	Tulchan	009	Tho : Norwick Advent^r	001	008
	Sersans toune	008			008
	Cloune	019	Richard Sherbroke gent	007	012
	Rathcolman	007			007
	Grange	010			010
	Bellaveniske	009			009
	Sleanmore	024			024
	Baltrasney	029	Will : Pettitt gent and Nicholas Darcy gent.		029
(folio 13).	Kiols towne	020			020
	Ledwids town	013			013
	Hopes towne	027		002	025
	Belena	011			011
	Kilpatrick	040	Richard Fitzgerrald gent		040
	Kanemodagh	032			032
	Welshes towne	039	Ambrose Newgent and Will : Mackanry gent	003	036
	Slayne towne	003	Lauallin Newgent gent	—	003
	Irish toune	055			055
	Robins toune	010			010
	Ballinderry	007	Wm Dodd gent	001	006
	Boards towne	006		005	001
	Clongawney	001			001
Disart	Ballebrine	016			016
	Disert	069	Mr Lucas and Roger Mounrag gents	003	066
	Loagermore	036	Mr Coue Esq	001	035
Roconnell	Killinan	019	Sr John Whitman Knight	003	016
(folio 14).	Lisdullen	007			007
	Clonlostie	027	Thomas Newgent gent		027
	Ballatorr	009			009
	Crosserderry	007			007
	Clun-nec-avant	016			016
	Turin	021			021
	Edmonds towne	006	James Newgent gent		006
	Roconnell	039	John Thomson Esq and Oliuer Newgent gent	001	038
	Monylea	065	Moyses Jenkins Esq	001	064

Parrishes	Townelands	Number of People	Tituladoes Names	Eng	Irish
	Moygullin	039	Captn Robert Cooke Esq	002	037
	Geffris towne	011			011
	Fennor	029	Thomas Swift Esq and Redmond Pettit gents	001	028
	Ballinderry	025	Sr Nicholas Crispp Knt & Bar^{tt}	003	022
	Balbrenogh	035			035
	Clowndaliner	008			008

Principall Irish Names [and] Their Number.

Coffy, 06 ; Cormick, 13 ; Daly, 21 ; Farrell, 07 ; Ô Glynn & Glynn, 09 ; Gaynor & Goynor, 09 ; Gauan & Gauen, 06 ; Hope, 07 ; Hughs & Hues, 11 ; Le Strange, 06 ; Leny, 09 ; Martin, 06 ; Newgent, 12 ; Rorke, 05 ; Skally, 07 ; Sogh, 05 ; Tuitte, 11.

(*folio* 14 *verso*). Barrony of Majaskell : Eng, 37 ; Irish, 970 ; 1007, totall.

(*folio* 15). **FERTULLAGH BARRONY**

Parrishes	Townelands	Number of People	Tituladoes Names	Eng	Irish
Lynn	Lynn	022	Lt Dennis Broune gent	001	021
	Clonmoyle	024	John Tyrrell gent	—	024
	Cathrins towne	018		—	018
	Vilans towne	053			053
	Corbally	021			021
Moylesker	Tyrrells towne	023	Thomas Griffin & James Griffin his sonn gents		023
	Bolybrack	020			020
	Paslogstowne	008	Patrick Darcey gent		008]
Mullingar & Eniscoffy p^t	Raheen & Raduffe	016	John Darcey gent		016
	Redmons towne	015			015
	Symons towne	009			009
	Brenocks towne	010	William Vennor gent, John Humphry Freholder, & Will his sonn	008	002
	Russells toune	022			022
The Pass ot Kilbride	Kilbride Pass	032			032
	Miltowne	018		008	010
	Coorlonagh	008		004	004
Castlelost	Ballymolan	024	Henry Jephson gent	002	022

Parishes	Townelands	Number of People	Tituladoes Names	Eng	Irish
(*folio* 16). Castollost	Rahanyn	012		—	012
	Castellost	042	Thomas Aggas & George Marley gent	003	039
	Farthings towne	029		—	029
	Collins towne	009			009
	Owl towne Geewbane	019			019
	Kilbrenill	013			013
	Piers towne	013			013
New towne	Ragarett	015	Conn Geoghegan and Conly Geoghegan gents		015
	Rahinquill	016			016
	Balligillmore	015		003	012
Clonfadd	Rathnure	013			013
	Ramore	009		002	007
	Dalis towne	011			011
	Gadachanstownebegg	029			029
	Canerstownemore	010			010
(*folio* 17).	Mideene	004			004
	Newcastle	018		006	012
	Dauids towne	006		002	004
	Tirrellspass	033			033
Kilbride	Kilbride	010		002	008
	Tonlegihie	006			006
	Carrigg	010			010
Eniscofty	Robins towne	029	Edward Tyrrill, Lauallin Newgent, and Dominick Newgent his sonn, gents.		029
	Comins towne	005			005

Principall Irish Names [and] Their Number.

Birne, 07 ; Brogan, 05 ; Brynan (5), Brenan (2), 07 ; Coffy, 07 ; Cully, 10 ; Dempsy, 08 ; Duffy (6), Duff (4), 10 ; Darcey, 06 ; Doyne, 05 ; Daly, 05 ; Geoghegan, 07 ; Glanan, 05 ; Griffin, 05 ; Keegan, 06 ; Lenagh, 09 ; Tyrrell, 16 ; Whitechan, 10.

(*folio* 17 *verso*). Barrony of Fertullagh : Eng, 041 ; Irish, 678 ; 0719, totall.

(*folio* 18).　　　**MAY CASHELL BARRONY**

Parishes	Townelands	Number of People	Tituladoes Names	Eng	Irish
Kilbeggan Burrowh		099	Richard Harrison and John Nelson gents	019	080

Parrishes	Townelands	Number of People	Tituladoes Names	Eng	Irish
Castle towne	Managhans towne	026	John Clerke gent	002	024
	Killelin	008	John Roe gent	—	008
	Brenans towne	032		—	032
	Newrey	002			002
	Tulloghaneny	012			012
	Ballanagooe	010		002	008
	Balrath	017	Solloman Griffin gent		017
	Ballyconnell	009	Bryan Sheall gent		009
	Teracrew	007			007
	Twore	018			018
	Derryroe	009			009
	Adams towne	034	Oliuer Brenan gent		034
	Killylee	012			012
	Kile	003			003
	Castle towne	040			040
	Killualard	008		—	008
	Dromore	035		—	035
	Gary	030	Edmond Coffy gent	—	030
(*folio* 19).	Gneue begg & Ballincasky	015			015
	Rathnewgent	024	John Lease gent		024
	Ballyhost	013		004	009
	Kadrishoge	007	John Turbett gent	002	005
	Tulloghan sleeke	022			022
	Benolbett	011			011
	Dromore	004			004
	Tower	002			002
	Gneuebegg	001			001
	Adams towne	003			003
Ardnoroghir	Streams towne	052	George Peyton **Esq**	004	048
	Kilbegg	023			023
	Creine	032	Richard Patience gent	002	030
	Bannanack	017		006	011
	Moycashell	051	Will: Ponntney L^t	015	036
	Donoere	032			032
	Brackagh	017			017
(*folio* 20). Ardnorcher	Killare Capaduff	022			022
	Lissenera	011		003	008
	Monyduffe	007			007
	Syonan	017			017
	Ardnorchir	016			016
	TempleMᶜTyre	020			020
	Corcgaron	016		002	014
	Spittles towne	027			027
	Corecewagh	011			011
	Lismoyne	068	John Johnes Esq	004	004

Parrishes	Townelands	Number of People	Tituladoes Names	Eng	Irish
Newtowne	Newtowne	014	Will : Lowe Esq	004	010
	Loghanlonagh	027	George Lowe gent	002	025
	Rahinmore	005		003	002
	Comins towne	034	John Pearson Esq	007	027
	Kililoghan	012	Thomas Whallop gent	002	010
	Killenallie	017		—	017
	Connehye	008		—	008
(*folio* 21).	Clanecran	003			003
	Cloonekelan	011			011
Killcomrearagh	Ballinlugge	010			010
	Ballinegreny	031	James Geoghegan gent		031
	Derryhall	005	Thomas Ransom gent	002	003
	Lisnegree	003			003
	Ballintober	006			006
	Ballybregoge	014		003	011
	Cappanakirke	008	Huegh Geoghegan gent		008
	Killekuny	006	Huegh Lengly gent		006
	Ballenecrany	013	Henry Hoskins gent	004	009
	Cooletore	018	John Cooke Esq	004	014
	Ballintober	027			027
	Lerha	015		002	013
(*folio* 22). Kilbeggan	Ballinstocan	012			012
	The Grange of Kiltober	019			019
	Shehanagh	011	John Sherlock gent		011
	Cloneglin	014			014
	Killmooneene	013			013
	Muldrom	007			007
	Ballyguigan	014			014
	Grynan	009	Huegh Geoghegan gent		009
	Ballinderye	028			028
	Loghanagore	023	Laurence Sedgraue, gent	003	020
	Shurin	009	Thomas Gibbons gent	—	009
	Tonyfort	028		—	028
	Ballim^cMorish	006			006
Rathue	Monrath	015	Thomas Robinson gent	003	012
	Pallistry	004		004	—
	Garyduffe	007	Mr Edwards proprietor in England, and Thomas Baly gent	002	005
	Capenrush	012		003	009
	Kiltober	015	Thomas Skelson and John Lorde gents	005	010
(*folio* 23).	Attyconner	013		010	003
	Lower towne	003	Edward Loue gent	001	002
	Capataky	009			009
	Pallis	007			007
	Ballybroder	011	Thomas Low gent	001	010
	Freuanagh	011	John Fleetwood gent	002	009

Principall Irish Names [and] Their Number.

Brenan (5), Brynan (5), 10 ; McCarey & McCarrey, 20 ; Crevy, 06 ; Coffy, 06 ; Duffy, 10 ; Duffe, 05 ; Daly, 26 ; Geoghegan, 43 ; Gormely, 06 ; Hackett, 06 ; Keegan, 13 ; King, 06 ; Kelly, 10 ; Lynan, 06 ; Sheery, 09 ; Wyre, 09.

(*folio 23 verso*). Barrony of Moycashell : Eng, 132 ; Irish, 1347 ; 1479, totall.

(*folio 24*).

RATHCONRATH[1] BARRONY

Parrishes	Townelands	Number of People	Tituladoes Names	Eng	Irish
Ballymore	Ballymore	082		010	072
	Bush	011		—	011
	Symnegartagh	022	Cor^{tt} John Tibbs gent	011	011
	Rahin	040			040
	Majvaghlye	057	Henrie Arundell Aduent^r	001	056
	Umoe more	019			019
	Umoe begg	006			006
	Ballimore	004			004
	Symnegartagh	002			002
	Callaghs towne	056	Benjamin Whetcome Advent^r	001	055
	Cloncullan	011	Francis Actery Aduent^r	001	010
	Carricknagnoer and Ballnahiskeragh }	011		005	006
	New towne	002		002	000
	Downsgolmon	005			005
	Ballencarr	007			007
	Ballenlugg	021			021
	Mollimeaghan	027	Lt. Foolk Rokeby gent	002	025
(*folio 25*). Killare	Shenlis	065	Joseph Browne Aduent^r	001	064
	Rathskeagh	018	Boulstered Whitlock Aduent^r	001	017
	Ballenacor	015			015
	Doniell	016			016
	Kynoge	010			010
	Ballemacallin	007			007
	Killinboy	009			009
	Doonegath	010			010
	Gary towne	064			064
	Cloonebanc	020		002	018
	Clare	040			040
	Bishops towne	047		—	047
	Bracknaherly	012		—	012
	KilleRowe	022			022

[1] *Rathcunrath*, folios 25—28.

Parrishes	Townelands	Number of People	Tituladoes Names	Eng	Irish
	Killenagh	011	Roger Nickolds Adventer	001	010
	Balinkeny	029			029
	Killare Church	016			016
	Gibbs towne	035			035
(folio 26).	Huegs towne	008			008
	Killinagrew	012			012
	Killare Church	011			011
	Killare Castle	013			013
	Killinbrake	001	John Perry Adventer	001	
Rathcunrath	Rathcunrath	010			010
	Balliglass	017			017
	Killahee	007			007
	Loghan	018		002	016
	Ballenecarrow	013	Nicholas Lobb gent	002	011
	Symons towne	017			017
	Littell Painstone	011	Daniell Waldo Adventr	001	010
	Great Painstowne	028			028
	Rathduff	010	Martin Aldersee Adventr	001	009
	Irishton	017			017
	Rahinquin	008			008
	Skeamore	016			016
	Skeabegg	026			026
	Mill towne	027		004	023
(folio 27). Rathcon-rath	Rowlands towne	032	John Cropley Aduentr	003	029
	Fardingstone	002			002
	Padingstowne	017			017
	Rathcalled	012			012
	Castlegadry	016	Richard Floyd Aduentr Esq	001	015
Almoritra	Dalistone	038		—	038
	TiberCormick	009		—	009
	Ballemorin	005		003	002
	Newbristie	006	Michell Armin Adventr	001	005
Temple patrick	Mayvoure	092	John Gunning Adventr, Esq, John Edmonds, & Will : Richards, gents.	005	087
	Temple patrick	012			012
	Rathdorish	007			007
	Coolgawney	024			024
	Piers towne	020			020
	Dorisnekilly	010			010
	Williams towne	019			019
(folio 28). Conry	Carne	080			080
	Latis towne	013			013
	Toghers tone	032			032
	Lockards tone	029			029

Parrishes	Townelands	Number of People	Tituladoes Names	Eng	Irish
Churchs tone	Dundonell	026	Albert Widmay gent	002	024
	Monings towne	016			016
	Ballynefearagh	009	Theob : Barlowe gent	003	006
	Churchs tone	006			006
	Ould towne	011	Oliuer Hope gent	002	009
	Kilbelankertt	008			008
	Rogers towne	041	John Sheepherd Advento^r, Mortogh Coffy, John Coffey, & Edmond Coffey his sonnes gents.	001	040
	Coyne	011	Richard Sherberne Advent^r	001	010
	Redmons tone	008			008
	Taboyne	035		001	034
	Conrey	012			012
	Croghoell	036	Miles Corbett Esq, Phillip Pagenham gent	002	034
	Ballrath	033	Dr Worsely Advent^r	001	032

Principall Irish Names [and] Their Number.

Coffy, 029 ; Conally & Conelly, 013 ; Connelan & Connalan, 014 ; Carmick, 017 ; Dalton, 050 ; Dunegan & Donegan, 012 ; Daly, 010 ; Doyle, 012 ; Flanagan, 008 ; Farrell, 010 ; Geoghegan, 010 ; Keny & Kenny, 017 ; Knowlan & Knolan, 013 ; Knally, 014 ; Keegan & Kigan, 014 ; Murrey & Morry, 012 ; Maghan (6), Magan (6), 012 ; Skally & Skelly, 012.

(*folio* 28 *verso*). Barrony of Rathconrath : Eng, 075 ; Irish, 1751 ; 1826, totall.

(*folio* 29). **FARBILL BARRONY**

Parrishes	Townelands	Number of People	Tituladoes Names	Eng	Irish
Killucquin	Ballrone	019	Henry Pardon gent	002	017
	Kerins towne	010		—	010
	Rathwyre	057	John Furlong and Redmond Frayne gents	—	057
	Killucquinn	049	Nicholas Frayne and Michaell Frayne gents		049
	Craddans towne	007			007
	Rathfarne	039	Andrew Darcy gent		039

Parrishes	Townelands	Number of People	Tituladoes Names	Eng	Irish
	Jorgs towne	015	Thomas Fitzgerald gent		015
	Dorimore	014			014
	Boutens towne	009			009
	Aniskean	020		—	020
	Cluncrawe	012			012
	Kinagad	042	Cor George Wilton and William Rowles gents	008	034
	Griffins towne	029			029
	Corrells towne	016			016
	Crossans towne	003			003
	Cnock Symon	013			013
(folio 30).	Ballinlar	015			015
	Riuers towne	018			018
	Cassins towne	008	Edward Cushin gent		008
	Heaths towne	026			026
	Cnockervill	008			008
	Balloghter	009			009
	Balleyghter	015			015
	Clunfadd	015			015
	Ratten	018			018
	Bancher	008			008
	Wooddowne	010			010
	Greatdowne	019	Robert Darcy gent		019
	Newtowne	010			010
	Castledowne	002			002
	Lisnebynn	020			020
	Rathbrack	007			007
	Carbellis	008			008
(folio 31).	Clunicullen	013			013
	Cnackment	007			007
	Porters towne	004			004
	Edmonds towne	009		001	008
	Hodges towne	015			015
	Higgins towne	007			007
	Myles towne	002		—	002
	Preys towne	011		—	011
	Cnockervill	007			007
	Ratten	007			007
	Clunfadd	003			003
	Greatdowne	004			004
	Newtowne	005			005
	Balleyghter	002			002
	Bancher	003			003
	Cnocksymon	006			006
	Balinla	003			003
	Brutens tone	003			003

Parishes	Townelands	Number of People	Tituladoes Names	Eng	Irish
(folio 32).	Griffins towne	012			012
	Cluncrow	003			003
	AnySkenan	010			010
	Kinagad	012			012
	Rathfarne	007			007
	Jorges towne	003			003
	Hodges towne	005			005
	Lysnebin	008			008
	Rathbegg	005			005
	Corbally	007			007
	Cluincullan	004			004
	Lunes towne	002			002
	Knockment	002			002
	Corbeds towne	013	Edmond Darcy gent		013
	Luens towne	005			005
	John Duffs towne	002			002
	Wardens towne	006			006

Principall Irish Names [and] Their Number.

Bardon, 05 ; Brogan, 05 ; Cormick, 06 ; Clery, 08 ; Connor, 05 ; Daly, 12 ; Darcy, 11 ; Duygin, 05 ; Duff, 05 ; Glenan, 06 ; Grogan, 06 ; Heany, 06 ; Keegan, 05 ; Kernan, 05 ; Malone, 05 ; Purcell, 08 ; Slevin, 05 ; Tyrrell, 06 ; Ward, 05.

(folio 32 verso). Barrony of Farbill : Eng, 011 ; Irish, 776 ; 0787, totall.

(folio 33). **CLONLONAN BARRONY**

Parishes	Townelands	Number of People	Tituladoes Names	Eng	Irish
Ballilaughlowe	Ballilaughlowe	061	Lawrence Hyde Esq and Joseph Smith gent	003	058
	Rathduffe	007		—	007
	Laban and Clonmacdude	032	Richard Bestwill gent	003	029
	Twoy	036	George Meverell Esq	008	028
	Donigan	018	Phillip Branthwaite gent	002	016
	Ballidoogan	011		005	006
	Lachiell	008		001	007
	Dunlome	005			005

Parishes	Townelands	Number of People	Tituladoes Names	Eng	Irish
	Knockdoning	011		009	002
	Tulchaingearagh	010		003	007
	Killinlomack	004			004
	Carne	047	Robert Bromwell Esq and Anthony Bromwell gent	004	043
	Creeuebegg	005			005
	Both ye Culvocks	021		—	021
	Quolins	012	John Baal gent	004	008
	Ballinegarbragh	009		004	005
	Tullibane	015	Isaac Walsh gent		015
(folio 34).	Tully	005	Richard Jagiues gent	003	002
	Syoge and Fornought	007		005	002
	Killogmaghan	014		010	004
	Fassagh	015	Gilbert Parker gent	006	009
	Williams tone	016	James Riley gent		016
	Aghavomine	013	Thomas Hodges gent	007	006
	Naghod	012		001	011
	Ballynalack	017			017
	Clonarian	009			009
	Moat : Granoge	023	John Homan gent	005	018
	Tworephelim	007			007
	Legan and Capiatack	023	John Cliburne gent	003	020
	Balliallroe	021	Nicholas Starkey, James Wasley, and William Spike, gents.	010	011
	Kill	014			014
	Aghafine	009			009
	Castle towne	019	Thomas Bradhurst gent	006	013
(folio 35).	Ballinlesca	006			006
	Ballibegg	012			012
	Ballybroder	017			017
	Ballinderry	046	Donnies Sheill gent		046
	Cartron-remoyre and Killomilaghan }	029			029
	Magharemere	009			009
	Killinroan	009			009
	Oldtort	008			008
	Ballinerra	006		—	006
	Banogs	017		—	017
	Ballinemoddagh	009			009
	Boggagh	020			020
	Castle towne Clonlonan	017			017
	Clonidonin	011			011
	Glinn and Capicanron	009		003	006
	Ashsollas	006			006
(folio 36).	Ballmakill	011			011

Parrishes	Townelands	Number of People	Tituladoes Names	Eng	Irish
	Clonlonan Wood	042		002	040
	Kilcleagh	042	John Quelch Esq	004	038
	Clanmore	018			018
	Knockanach	046		006	040
	Ballamock Feogh	011	Richard Legland gent	004	007
	Ballenehowne	048	Godfry Keeler gent	002	046
	Curraghbegg	012			012
	Kilgarvon	043			043

Principall Irish Names [and] their Number.

Coughlane, 007 ; Cloffy, 010 ; Daly, 010 ; Ô Dully, 005 ; Dillon, 005 ; Fury, 015 ; Killeen, 005 ; Kelly, 007 ; McLaughlin, 010 ; Moran & Morran, 006 ; Naughten, 005 ; Riley, 005.

(*folio 36 verso*).   Barrony of Clonlonan : Eng, 123 ; Irish, 917 ; 1040, totall.

(*folio 37*).   **KILKENNY BARRONY**

Parrishes	Townelands	Number of People	Tituladoes Names	Eng	Irish
Dromraney	Killenenen	061	Pilex Brafield Esq	004	057
	Bremore	039		—	039
	Ballenagleduff	033	John Rotherham gent	002	031
	Killendra	014			014
	Lissenoide	021			021
	Ballysallagh	022	Henrie Dillon gent		022
	Doonemony	031	Henrie Dillon gent		031
	Drumraney	042	Morish Dillon and Edmund Dillon gents		042
	Corra	009			009
	Lowe Baskin	029	Christopher Webster and James Dillon gents	002	027
	Ballentrohan	014	Christopher Dillon gent		014
	Ardnegragh	003			003
	Walters towne	012			012
	Skihin	011			011
	High Baskin	038	Thomas Walding gent	002	036
	Ballemollinkle	008		004	004
(*folio 38*).	Ballentrohan	004	James Dillon gent		004
	Kilkenny	052		003	049
	Lisdachon	006			006

Parrishes	Townelands	Number of People	Tituladoes Names	Eng	Irish
	Tobernaguoge	004			004
	Tully	006			006
	Corr	002			002
	Rath	008			008
	Ballaghkirne	013			013
	Caldragh	006			006
	Anagh	024			024
	Tober Clare	010			010
	Ballibegg	011			011
	Killinfaghny	025		003	022
	Ballineclehy	008			008
	Bleanfuttoge	013		003	010
	Ballineclehy	026	Thomas Page gent	002	024
	Killmacaron	043			043
(folio 39).	Ballinekill	003			003
	Wathers towne	049	Peter Sterne gent	003	046
	Mullinglashan	004		002	002
	Killinure	004		000	004
	Killinmore	026	Gerott Dillon and John McShaen gents		026
	Portleeke	025			025
	Fuinn	009			009
	Bunowne	026			026
	Koghovall	040	Gerott Dalton gent		040
	Arnecraney	014			014
	Marara	007	Edmond Dalton gent		007
	Conors towne	022	Capt Henry Baker Esq	004	018
	Creggie	028			028
	Donees	023	Manus Lenan gent		023
	Killcornan	022		004	018
	Muckenagh	024			024
(folio 40).	Cartron Croy	009			009
	Gortmore	020			020
	Lisdossan	010	John Dillon gent		010
Proprietors of High	Baskin and Arnegragh :		Sr Robert Goodwin Knt, John Lisle, Elisha Coysh, —— Shuttleworth, Nathaniell Fines, —— Crossey, and Thomas Needham, Esqrs.		
Mollingar Burrough		334	Richard Sloy, Richard Smith, John Douglas, William Willson, Christopher Gilbert, and John Lord, gentlemen,	037	297

Principall Irish Names of Kilkenny Barrony & Mollingar Burrough [and their number].
Birn, 06 ; Clery, 07 ; Carne & Kearne, 10 ; Dillon, 24 ; Ô Daly, 08 ; McDoyle, 07 ; Duff & Duffie, 11 ; Dalton, 09 ; McGanley, 11 ; Keny & Kenny, 15 ; Keegan, 12 ; Kenedie, 06 ; Moran & Morran, 15 ; Marten, 09 ; Sirey, 09 ; Cormick, 05 ; Knolan, 05 ; Killen, 05 ; Laragh, 05 ; Murrey, 05.

(folio 40 *verso*).   Barrony of Killkenny : Eng, 75 ; Irish, 1272 ; 1347, totall.

(folio 41).   **DELVYN BARRONY**

Parishes	Townelands	Number of People	Tituladoes Names	Eng	Irish
Castle towne	Cronis towne	051	Walter Dowdall gent	002	049
	Little Cronis towne	006			006
	Cloon Capull	010			010
	Mabous towne	008			008
	Ballevally	005	John Skeeper gent	002	003
	Castle towne	080	John Gale Esq	005	075
	Martins towne	022		002	020
	Cloonmaskill	024			024
	New towne & Daruis towne	026	George Barnewell gent	002	024
	Calues towne	011		002	009
	Balrath	036	Edward Fay gent		036
	Balleine	008		000	008
	Lisclogher	041			041
	Clunyne	022			022
	Cloonmanill	009			009
(folio 42).	Scurlocks towne	010		—	010
	Adings towne	037		—	037
	Ballinure	019		004	015
	Billins towne	028	Henry Whissed gent	002	026
	Drugans towne	010	Walter Cussok gent		010
	Arthors towne and Mullgans towne	046			046
	Rossmeed and Robins towne	026	Richard Corkdyale gent	002	024
	Ellins towne	008			008
	Bolans towne	015			015
Kiltumny	Drumcree	057		007	050
	Johns towne	013		002	011
	Cooledoghrane	055		008	047
	Granges towne	005			005
	Kiltumy	008			008
(folio 43). Kiltumy	Robins towne	025			025
	Heaths towne	030	Francis Gibbon Esq		030
Rilluak	Cloghran	021			021
	Magreahan	019			019
	Killcullentro	003			003
	Killuah	061	Benjamin Chapman gent	002	059
	Killrush	011			011

Parrishes	Townelands	Number of People	Tituladoes Names	Eng	Irish
Killologh	Ballinlogh	012			012
	Bracklin	035	Henry Spierms Esq	002	033
	Dreedors towne and Killologh	020			020
	Gigins towne	023		co2	021
	Glacks towne	014			014
	Dardis towne	037	John Britton gent	002	035
	Johns towne	007			007
(folio 44).	Rickors towne	026		002	024
	Hiskins towne	008		—	008
	Dissartally	011	Nick: Ogle gent	002	009
	Ballenecur	012			012
Killagh	Killagh	026			026
	Luens towne	002			002
	Mulchans towne	010			010

Principall Irish Names [and] Their Number.

    Carrell, 06 ; Duff, 10 ; Fagan, 15 ; Farrell, 11 ; Fay, 11 ; Glenan & Glinan, 08 ; McGarr & Garre, 06 ; Lency, 06 ; Murrey, 08 ; Moore, 06 ; Newman, 07 ; Newgent, 15 ; Plunkett, 07.

    (folio 44 verso).   Barrony of Delvin : Eng, 052 ; Irish, 1057 ; 1109, total.

Westmeath County

Barronies	Pages	Eng	Irish	Totalls
Demifoure	04	109	1224	1333
Moygoishe	08	048	1086	1134
Corkerie	11	044	847	891
Majaskell	14	037	970	1007
Fertullagh	17	041	678	719
Moycashell	23	132	1347	1479
Rathconrath	28	075	1751	1826
Farbill	32	011	776	787
Clonlonan	36	123	917	1040
Killkenny	40	075	1272	1347
Delvin	44	052	1057	1109
		747	11925	12672

WEXFORD COUNTY 12778
TOWNE 902
──────
13680

(*folio* 1). County of Wexfford.

WEXFFORD TOWNE AND LIBERTIES.

	Townlands	Number of People	Tituladoes Names	Eng	Irish
Wexford Towne	East ward	143	Thomas Low Esq Mayor of Wexfford, John Cotterell, Paul Wakefield, Robert Phillips, Constantine Neale, William Reynolds, Christopher Dobson, and Anthony Cauldron, gentlemen.	70	073
	West ward	161	Hugh Hobbs, Michaell Lewling, Thomas Pilkington, John Roberts, and Richard Neale, gentlemen.	064	097
	South ward	259	Ambrose Andrews, Valentine Chyttwood, George Linnington, Charles Huddle, and William Barker, gentlemen.	115	144
	North ward	118	James Roe, John Walton, Francis Harvye, Robert Wilkinson, Isaac Freborne, and William Cleburne, gentlemen.	052	066
The Suburbs	Faigh	092		012	080
	Bridstreete	015		002	013
	St John streete	074		016	058
	Weststreete	034		009	025
	Maudlin town	006		000	006

Principall Irish Names [and] Their Number.

Murphy, 14; Synott, 11; Welsh, 07; Codd, 13; Doyle, 06; White, 06; Connors, 05; Furlong, 05; Redmond, 05; Deuereux, 05.

(*folio* 1 *verso*) Towne and Liberties [of] Wexford: Eng, 340; Iris[h], 562; Totall, 902.

(*folio* 2). ## THE TOWNE AND LIBERTIES OF NEW ROSSE

	Townelands	Number of People	Tituladoes Names	Eng	Irish
New Rosse Towne	and Liberties	519	William Ivery, and John Pinkle, Esqrs, Richard Hunt, Lyonell Woodward, John Winkworth, John Rawkines, and Eusebines Cotton, gentlemen, & Walter Davies.	201	318

	Townelands	Number of People	Tituladoes Names	Eng	Irish
	Reylin	018		000	018
	Arnes towne	015		000	015
	Little Island	016		000	016
Souldᵣˢ and their wiues & Seruants belong to Coll Ridgeleys company in Rosse		050		040	010

Principall Irish Names [and] their Number.
Murphy, 10 ; Doyle, 09 ; Kelly, 06 ; Browne, 06 ; Keating, 05.

ENISCORTHY TOWNE & LIBERTYES.

		Number	Tituladoes Names	Eng	Irish
Eniscorthy Towne	& Libertyes	389	Tymothy Stamp Esq, John Stamp, and Tymothy Clint, gentlemen.	067	322

Principall Irish Names [and] their Number.
Redmond, 04 ; Doyle, 04 ; Synnott, 03.

(folio 2 verso). Towne and Liberties [of] Ross : Eng, 241 ; Irish, 377 ; Totall, 618.
Towne and Liberties [of] Eniscorthy : Eng, 067 ; Irish, 322 ; Totall, 387.

(folio 3).   **BARRONY OF FORTH**

Peer[1]	Townelands	Number of People	Tituladoes Names	Eng	Irish
Rathaspok	Johns towne	018	Edward Wythers Esq	005	013
	Kodfinolan	001		001	000
	Weddings land	002			002
	Redmonstowne	004		002	002
	Lares towne	009			009
	Bally Kelly	004		002	002
	Quoans towne	003		000	003
	Peter Street	025		002	023
	Kilelloge	026			026
	Rathaspok	018	Loftus Codd gent		018

[1] Parrishes, folios 9, 10.

Peer	Townelands	Number of People	Tituladoes Names	Eng	Irish
	Little Haies towne	004			004
	Whites towne	005			005
	Peeter Street	008		006	002
	White rock	006			006
	Great Haies town	008	John Arthure Esq John Arthur gent	004	004
	Litle Clonard	012		003	009
	Newbay	005			005
Dreynagh	Whites towne	006			006
	Beggans towne	006		002	004
	Jackets towne	007		001	006
(folio 4).	Roches towne	006		002	004
	Synotts towne	006		000	006
	Kellis toune	06		02	004
	Levetts toune	08			08
	Poulbrean	02		02	
	Great Killian	25		02	23
	Litle Killian	07	Jonas Chamberlyn gent	02	05
	Balle Kelly	12		02	10
	7 acres	02			02
	Great Ballyfenok	15			15
	Litle Ballyfenok	08			08
	Kimkree	07			07
	Dreynagh	35		05	30
	Grange	06			06
	Stevens towne	04			04
	Talbotts towne	04			04
(folio 5) Rath mc Knee	Rath mc Knee	28	Thomas Hart Esq	09	019
	Shortals towne	02			02
	St Mary	03		03	000
	Tynge	06			06
	Hodges mill	04			04
	Peirces towne	05			05
	Knock Eugall	06			06
	Poulsallagh	06			06
	Little Poulsallagh	04			04
	Rathgarvyn	05			05
	Welshes towne	07			07
	Ringe Kerr	04		—	04
	Ballynasse	09		—	09
	Owins towne	04		—	04
	Hobbins towne	07		—	07
	Deans towne	10		000	10
	Ablington	04		—	04
	Gurchinmenock	12		—	12
(folio 6). Rath mc Knee	Rathlouan	08		000	08

Peer	Townelands	Number of People	Tituladoes Names	Eng	Irish
	Miltowne	05		02	03
	Kildeuan	04		000	04
	Stapples towne	01		—	01
	Twenty acres	02		—	02
	Mourrouton	07		02	05
Maglas	Tagonan	14	Thomas Knox Esq	04	10
	Haggar towne	04		000	04
	Loughgonan	07		02	05
	Bushers towne	06		000	06
	Maglas	48		13	35
	Nort Randelstown	15		07	08
	South Randels towne	05		000	05
	Granusk	02		02	000
	Cornels town	02		000	02
	Dampton	04			04
	Cloane	09			09
	Balledoyle	04			04
(folio 7).	Pettits towne	08			08
	Ballycoghy	14	Richard Orrsley	03	11
	Leachis towne	11		02	09
	Couloughter	07			07
	Loughgonan	01			01
Ballymore	Gragelagh	02		02	
	Hil towne	09			09
	Gibbogs towne	02		—	02
	Lynges towne	09		—	09
	Garrehack	08		—	08
	Bally begg	07		—	07
	Johnocks towne	06		—	06
	Balleregan	02		—	02
	Grakerok	04		—	04
	Chappell	06		—	06
	Litle Codds town	05		—	05
	Great Cods town	06		—	06
	Harves town	06		---	06
(folio 8).	Balleboigh	09		000	09
	Bridge barge	09			09
	Church towne	07			07
	Gragin	04			04
	South Gracormuck	05			05
	North Gracormuck	05			05
	Youl towne	08			08
Ballybrenan Parish	Ballybrenan	22	Richard Wilbore	03	19
	Youl towne	10			10
	Ballyran	07			07
	Martyns towne	05			05

Peer	Townelands	Number of People	Tituladoes Names	Eng	Irish
	Rathdowny	06			06
	Lackard	03			03
	Bally Knocan	06		—	06
	Polrankan	11		—	11
	Bush	04		—	04
	Feere & Ballylang	02		000	02
	Bally Knocan	02		02	000
(*folio* 9). Kilinick	Foord Assaly	03		03	
	Assaly	14			14
	Common	06			06
	Bally dusker	06		02	04
	Kilinick	03			03
	Ballisheen	10			10
	Litle Ballimenad	06			06
	Hors towne	06			06
	Great Ballimenad	07			07
	Muchrath	06			06
	Little Ballycorboy	02		02	
	Great Ballycorboy	02			02
	Coulkerran	04			04
Sharmon	Lyngs towne	17	William Thresher gent	02	15
	Graige	07		02	05
	Bally golick	06			06
	Hilbowne	03			03
	Butlers towne	07			07
	Ballybogher	09		02	07
(*folio* 10).	Knockhowlin	09		002	007
	Welsh towne	08			08
Kilsceran Peer	Hill	08	Richard Nunn Esq	03	05
	Sladd	18		02	16
	Synottsbalsee	05			05
	Peirs Balsee	05			05
	Moghrans towne	04			04
	Codds Balsee	06			06
	Baldungan	05			05
	New towne	04			04
	Balmaquishin	14			14
	Molringe	04			04
	Shilmane	02			02
	Ballygarvy	03			03
	Mil towne	08		01	07
	Ballycowan	05			05
	Trommer	08			08
Roslare Peer	White house	12	Edmond Hyegate & John Hyegate gent	05	07
(*folio* 11). Rosclare	The Lake	06		02	04

Peer	Townelands	Number of People	Tituladoes Names	Eng	Irish
	Wood towne	02			02
	Lake	04			04
	Berlagh	15		02	13
	Knocan	09		02	07
	Barris towne	14			14
	Church town	19			19
	Stremton	07			07
	Rowes towne	02			02
	Dromogh	02		—	02
	Ballibree	04		—	04
	Ballydran	06		—	06
	Fiue Acres	04		—	04
	Grange	11		—	11
	Morish towne	02		---	02
	Dromogh	02		—	02
	Hillosed	03		—	03
	Meath towne	08		02	06
	Gracermuck	08		000	08
(*folio* 12). Kilran	Litle Ballyconer	07			07
	Haies land	04			04
	Baldugin	06		—	06
	Ballehore	07	Osborne Edwards gent	03	04
	Bynge	02		000	02
	Fasagh	02			02
	Litle Ballatragh	02			02
	Great Balatragh	04			04
	Bally Knocan	02		02	
	Roscrean	03		—	03
	Drenagh	02		—	02
	Killellen	10			10
	Hil towne	09			09
	Ballytrent	10		03	07
	Bally wich	03		01	02
	Ballyveat	02			02
	Camcornells	02		002	000
	Harris towne	06			06
	Ballygillan	16		03	13
(*folio* 13).	Ballegeary	008			008
	Great Ballyconor	018		002	016
	Church towne	005		—	05
	Ballicronigan	013		01	12
Carne	Castle towne	018	Nicholas Codd Esq		18
	White house	002		02	000
	Castle towne	004			04
	Summer Towne	008		---	08
	Three acres	002		—	02

Peer	Townelands	Number of People	Tituladoes Names	Eng	Irish
	Bonargge	003		—	03
	Castel towne	002		—	02
	Nine acres	004			04
	St Wakes	003		—	03
	Nether towne	008		—	08
	Pullington	002		—	02
	Barneivheel	004		—	04
	Coules	004		—	04
	Hil towne	002		—	02
	Moor towne	002		—	02
(folio 14).	Chowre	04		000	004
	Balvinhan	07		02	05
	Ballytrae	06		—	06
	Clogh East	07	Edmond Waddey gent	02	05
	Churchton	25		02	23
	Carnogh	07		02	05
	Logans herd	06		—	06
	Taghire	05		—	05
	Bollosk	06		—	06
	Ringe	08		—	08
	Balichin	03		—	03
	Balvurhan	03		—	03
	Boucarrigg	04		—	04
	Coksmore	02		—	02
Iland Peer and St ⎱ Margret Parish ⎰	Balicullen	21		—	21
	Ballare	09			09
	Cussins toune	05		02	03
	Summerton	15		000	15
Iland Parish	Eardon	14		04	10
(folio 15). Iland Peer ⎱ & Iland Parish ⎰	Kause End	04		—	04
	Ballycushlan	07		—	07
	Rathdowny	04		—	04
	Balleshite	07		—	07
	Coulbloe	02		—	02
St Iberius Parish in ⎱ ye sd Iland Peer ⎰	Allen towne	08		—	08
	Aghmore	07		—	07
	Ramore	07		—	07
	Kishangh	04		—	04
	St Iberius	05		—	05
	Grange	12		—	12
	Tean	06		—	06
	Butlers towne	07		—	07
Tacumshan	Rochesland	02		—	02
	Youl towne	07		—	07
	Rathshillan	04		02	02
	Ecclis towne	02		—	02

Peer	Townelands	Number of People	Tituladoes Names	Eng	Irish
(*folio* 16).	Hil towne	04		—	04
	Furser towne	04		—	04
	Fene	03		—	03
	Bally McKarn	19		—	19
	Molcloghran	02		—	02
	Ballytory	15		—	15
	Beatin	03		—	03
	Coulbloe	05		02	03
	Racrolan	03		000	03
	Siggins towne	16	Wm Jacob gent	04	12
	Church towne	09		—	09
	Comquiston	06		02	04
	Mucks toune	05		—	05
	Benetts towne	07		—	07
	Couleam	04		—	04
	Bally samson	05		—	05
	Groivgan	09		—	09
	Ballemary	03		—	03
	Rostoustowne	06		—	06
(*folio* 17).	Tacumshan	013		—	13
	Bonaraitt	03		—	03
	Reads towne	13		—	13
	Ringe	07		—	07

Principall Names [and their Number]

Browne, 13 ; Beggan, 11 ; Bolger, 11 ; Codd, 32 ; Conick, 10 ; Cussin, 11 ; Cheuers, 07 ; Ô Doyle, 16 ; Deuereux, 27 ; French, 09 ; Furlong, 22 ; Fertern, 08 ; Hay, 32 ; Howlin, 11 ; Kauanagh, 08 ; Kelly, 11 ; Keating, 11 ; Ô Lary, 18 ; Lamport, 26 ; Murphy, 16 ; Morrogh, 19 ; Meylor, 11 ; Ô Morroe, 27 ; Neuport, 09 ; Rossetor, 10 ; Redmond, 10 ; Roch, 18 ; Rowe, 14 ; Scallan, 10 ; Stafford, 28 ; Skallan, 08 ; Synott, 43 ; Whitty, 22 ; Welsh, 12.

(*folio* 17 *verso*)   Barrony : Forth ; Eng, 178 ; Irish, 1667 ; 1845, tott :

(*folio* 18)   **BARONY OF BERGIE**

Peer	Townelands	Number of People	Tituladoes Names	Eng	Irish and old English
Kilmoore	Balliteige	010	Nicholas Deuereux Esq Richard Deuereux his sonn gent	001	009

Peer	Townelands	Number of People	Tituladoes Names	Eng	Irish and old English
	Crosfernoge	18			18
	Growgan	05			05
	Chapple	03			03
	Mill of Balliteige	01		—	01
	Nunes towne	08		—	08
	Grange	12		—	12
	Sarshile	13		—	13
	Nemis towne	13		—	13
	New towne	08		—	08
	Balleburne	07		—	07
	Sarshill	16		—	16
	Whithall	03		—	03
	Lanaght	12		—	12
	Balliharty	16	Richard Row gent	02	14
	Pullier towne	02		000	02
	Bally crosse	13		—	13
	Castle towne	04		—	04
	Bally crosse	03		03	—
(folio 19).	Balleboght	06		—	06
	Balliceskin	09		—	09
	Windmill	04		01	03
	Bastards towne	13		—	13
	Ballegraugans	18		05	13
	Ballegranga'	08		01	07
	Ranards towne	08		000	08
Kilturke	Bridge Bargy	02		—	02
	Tomhaggar	22		02	20
	Croschall	03		02	01
	Croschill	05		—	05
	Mountpill	03		—	03
	Thillduan	07		02	05
	Jents towne	09		—	09
	Ploudboher	01		—	01
	Hores towne	07		02	05
	Graig Robben	06		—	06
	Littles towne	02		02	—
	Cussens towne	05		—	05
	Ballihaly	49		08	41
(folio 20).	Kilturke	02		—	02
	Clangaddye	07		—	07
	Ballosk Collolste	06		—	06
	Tillabard	06		04	02
	Gallughs	03		—	03
	Soohan	06		02	04
	Polran	03		—	03
	Balliclery	07		—	07

Peer	Townelands	Number of People	Tituladoes Names	Eng	Irish and old English
Malrankan	Ballihaly	07		01	06
	Youl towne	02		—	02
	Kilioghan	17		02	15
	Mush towne	06		—	06
	Russells towne	11		—	11
	Coolcrall	04			04
	Baldens towne	25	John Swan gent	07	18
	Rath towne	14		—	14
	Youl towne	11		—	11
	Brids towne	14		03	11
	Old Hall	03		02	01
	Rathgarke	04		—	04
(folio 21).	Haggards towne	02		02	—
	More towne	04		—	04
	Church towne	15			15
	Bridwell	08			08
	Bally kepoge	08			08
	Arpons towne	04			04
	Church towne	01			01
	Malrannan	20		06	14
	Balleburangh	08		—	08
	Lake	08			08
	Coolecall	02			02
	Graig Scurr	02			02
	New towne	08			08
	Balliluberna	02			02
Duncormuck	Killagg	13			13
	Ballimagir	49	William Jauncy gent & Isaac Gale gent	06	43
	Pembrocks towne	12		—	12
	Rewes	25		01	24
	Redmore	06		—	06
(folio 22).	Gibbe Patrick	09		—	09
	Rathangan	28		—	28
	Iuberivill	12		02	10
	Duncormuck	22	Nicholas King gent	04	18
	Leckan	09		—	09
	Cross of Belgrow	02		—	02
	Fanis towne	07			07
	Scurlocks bush	15			15
	Scarr	21	Rich[d] Wilson gent	04	17
	Knock town	04			04
	Leuetts towne	07			07
	Cooleboy	08			08
Bannow	Dens castle	34		03	31
	Barris towne	05			05

Peer	Townelands	Number of People	Tituladoes Names	Eng	Irish and old English
	Grants towne	03			03
	Graige	17			17
	Grange	18		3	15
	Bannow	32			32
(folio 23).	Longhouse	02			02
	Haggard	05			05
	Fernely	12			12
	Slade	03			03
	New towne	27			27
	Brandon	02			02
	Grange	28		02	26
	Cullins towne	14	Gerrald Wallis gent		14
	Blackhall	10			10
	Kiltra	05			05
	Ballymadder	12		02	10
	Carrig	18			18
	Lough	11			11
	Culholl	33			33
Kilkeanan	Harpers towne	28	Sollomon Richards Esq, Sollomon Richards Senor gent	10	18
	New towne	14			14
	Roches towne	14		—	14
	Ballenegallagh	07			07
	Woodgraig	09			09
(folio 24). Kil-keauan	Halsirath	02		02	—
	Knockbane	04		—	04
	Tallakena	37	Nicholas Gower gent	04	33
	Ambross towne	03		—	03
	Great Mortowne	03		03	—
	Ambross towne	06		02	04
	Gublis towne	04		—	04
	Bushers towne	18		02	16
	Ballyaghtin	22		000	22
	Harris towne	04		02	02
	Kilkeauan	18	John Thompson gent	04	14
	Tree	20		—	20
	Mill	08		000	08
	Maudlin towne	10		—	10
Kilmennan	Sledagh	07		—	07
	Little Gurchins	10		—	10
	Great Gurchins	04	William Radford gent	04	—
	New castle	16	William Russell gent	—	16
(folio 25).	Kilmennan	022			22
	Glanboluge	02			02

Peer	Townelands	Number of People	Tituladoes Names	Eng	Irish and old English
	Clonlinannoge	07			07
	Norris towne	09			09
	Cleris towne	04		02	02
	Heauens towne	02		—	02
Balleconnicke Parrish	Balleconnicke	10		04	06
	St Tennants	09		—	09
	Edwards towne	02		—	02

Principall Names [and their Number].

Byrne, 08 ; Brodie, 07 ; Browne, 12 ; Bryan, 06 ; Cullen, 11 ; Deuereux, 18 ; Doyle, 08 ; Furlong, 22 ; Fardye, 07 ; Farrell, 06 ; Hay, 16 ; Hood, 09 ; Keating, 10 ; Kauanagh, 06 ; Lamport, 06 ; Larcan, 06 ; Ô Morrow, 06 ; & Morrogh, 05 ; Murphy, 20 ; Meyler, 14 ; Ô Murchoe, 07 ; Neuill, 07 ; Prendergass, 07 ; Power, 07 ; Pearle, 19 ; Perce, 06 ; Pursell, 10 ; Roch, 15 ; Redmond, 13 ; Revell, 08 ; Synnott, 17 ; Stafford, 18 ; Whitty, 15 ; Welsh, 11 ; White, 13.

(*folio* 25 *verso*). Barrony : Bargie ; Eng, 126 ; Irish, 1353 ; 1479, tott :

(*folio* 26).   **SHELMALEER BARRONY**

Parrishes	Townelands	Number of People	Tituladoes Names	Eng	Irish
Carrick	Parke	03		02	01
	Ballibogan	24		02	22
	Culcotts	08			08
	New towne	15		04	11
	Cnockan Sheene	06			06
	Cullintragh	02		02	—
	Barns towne	20			20
	Colledge	17		02	15
	Priors towne	18			18
	Colnett	01			01
	Polhore	07		03	04
	Scalgagh	04		03	01
	Ardcanrash	09			09
	Muchwood	11			11
	Bolgers towne	13			13
	Ballinelege	02			02
	Redmagh	05		03	02
	Teigenehely	05			05

Parrishes	Townelands	Number of People	Tituladoes Names	Eng	Irish
(*folio* 27).	Carrigmenane	015			15
	Bollibane	17			17
	Killurin	07			07
	Ballikeoge	64		04	60
	Mackmain	26		01	25
	Kilgibbon	05		02	03
	Bragurteen	06	Thomas Holmes gent	02	04
	Culteene	06			06
	Harris towne	10			10
	Grow towne	41	John Morgan gent	02	39
	Tomcoole	02			02
	Ballinveller	02		02	—
	Furlongs towne	08			08
	Sigginsagard	02			02
	Aghfadd	18			18
	Ballishelan	38		02	36
	Dirr	06		04	02
	Ballinclea	09			09
(*folio* 28).	Cooles	05		05	—
	Rows towne	10			10
	Dauids towne	02			02
	Homes towne	09		07	02
	Kealoge	03			03
	Taghmon	117		06	111
	Dungare	42			42
	Old Booly	12			12
	Coluell	07			07
	Ardnamore	22			22
	Colrahin	05		04	01
	Ardnabegg	14			14
	Traces towne	09		05	04
	Hore towne	28			28
	Shanoyle	12			12
	Balliliswran	24			24
	Arsmeae	08		03	05
	Rahinduffe	12		04	08
(*folio* 29).	Woodhouse	06			06
	Cullings towne	10			10
	Little Horton	07			07
	Rasillagh	09		02	07
	Ballinergin	13			13
	Glonoure	04			04
	Aghaggard	22			22
	Sleuey	20	Edward Gratrix gent	02	18
	Balliknocke	03		02	01
	Hil towne	12		04	08

Parishes	Townelands	Number of People	Tituladoes Names	Eng	Irish
	Ballingly	12			12
	Arnis towne	08			08
	Marshalls towne	08			08
	Rosgarland	19	Wᵐ Skinner gent	04	15
	Ballyduffe	06			06
	Garri Richard	06			06
	Longraige	23	Thomas Scott Esq	02	21
	Keile	09			09
	Clongeene	25			25
(folio 30).	Coleboy	07			07
	Ballinmony	04			04
	Mellendery	23	John Tenck Esq	05	18
	Bryans towne	23	Hutton gent	03	20
	Rospoile	17		04	13
	New castle	39		02	37
	New bane	75			75
	Ballilonan	19			19
	Kilbreny	29	John Graham gent	04	25
	Ballishanon	32			32
	Ballulemock	25		02	23
	Great hortowne	19			19
Synotts land	Ballitroman	08	Roger Lenesay gent	03	05
	Knottan	11		05	06
	Cranegain	24			24
	Ballicarran	08			08
	Balinemaragh	15			15
	Castle bridge	11			11
	Polregan	08			08
(folio 31).	Ballimartin	05			05
	Garigibbon	13			13
	Johns towne	05			05
	Ballilagh	07			07
	Curraghtloe	21	Wᵐ Trevill gent	01	20
	Kilmacoe	08			08
	Balliblak	04		02	02
	Ballina	19			19
	Ballinestra	04			04
	Ballinacooly	10			10
	Ardcollum	13		02	11
	Kilmistin	15			15
	Galbally	24			24
	Cros towne	03			03
Roches land	Poldarge	15			15
	Balledukin	15			15
(folio 32).	Ballenecossy	05		05	—
	Ballewater	06		000	06

Parrishes	Townelands	Number of People	Tituladoes Names	Eng	Irish
	Killowne	23		03	20
	Concarrig	12		01	11
	Balleharinhan	04			04
	New castle	04		04	—
	Garriwill	13			13
	Balleregan	18			18
	Elfockan	04			04
	Dipps	08			08
	Ballinecard	05		02	03
	Dipps	11	Robert Sanders Esq	09	02
			Joshua Sanders gent		
	Monmore	05	Wm Frompton gent	05	—
	Tobernefenog	09			09
	Cassegow	13			13
	Kilcorrely	18			18
(folio 33).	Ballibogan	18		04	14
	Roches Mill	01			01
	Mackwry	10			10
	Artroman	18		02	16
	Kilpatrick	15		05	10

Principall Names [and their Number].

Ô Breene, 09 ; Bane, 07 ; Ô Bryan & McBryan, 15 ; Connor & Connors, 15 ; Ô Cullin, Ô Cullun, and Ô Cullen, 14 ; Brennagh, 07 ; McDonell, 17 ; Duffe, 12 ; McDonogh, 07 ; Doyle, 33 ; McEdmond, 10 ; Furlong, 25 ; Hore, 10 ; McJohn, 09 ; Kelly, 18 ; Lacye, 08 ; McMurtagh, 06 ; McMorrogh, 06 ; Ô Magher, 06 ; Murphy, 42 ; Ô Neale, 08 ; Roch, 28 ; Roe, 15 ; Redmond, 14 ; Ô Ryan, 07 ; Synnott, 23 ; White, 06 ; Welsh, 07 ; McWilliam, 09.

(folio 33 verso). Barrony : Shelmaleer ; Eng, 163 ; Irish, 1650 ; 1813, tott.

(folio 34). **SHELBYRNE BARRONY**

Quarters	Townelands	Number of People	Tituladoes Names	Eng	Irish
Tinterne	Tinterne	028	Sr Caesar Colclough Barronett of Tinterne, Anthony Flood gent	006	022
	Talagh	40			40
	Castleworkhouse	06			06

2 M

Quarters	Townelands	Number of People	Tituladoes Names	Eng	Irish
	Ballihaibeg	11			11
	Kearan	27			27
	Garricullen	17			17
	Saltmill	14		02	12
	Corrowmore	20			20
	Ballis towne	16			16
	Ballicullan	20			20
	Bourks towne	03			03
	Taylors towne	06		02	04
	Ballinroan	17			17
	Kinneigh	15			15
	Rathnegeragh	26			26
	Nash	37			37
(*folio* 35).	St Leonard	19			019
	Clonagh	13			13
	Dunmaine	42		03	39
	Balligaruin	25			25
	Ballitarsny	25			25
	Booly	32			32
	Garriduffe	14		02	12
	Rathumney	52			52
	Yol towne	17			17
Hooke	Temple towne	18			18
	Hewisland	21			21
	Little graigs	12			12
	Lambs towne	09			09
	Great Graigs	13			13
	Haggard	11			11
	Alridge	11		06	05
(*folio* 36).	Booly	03		02	01
	Kilclogan	26		04	22
	Portrines gate	10		04	06
	Galgois towne	24			24
	Galyys towne	09			09
	Flade	13			13
	Church towne	02	Robert Orphye gent		02
	Hall	12			12
	Fetherd	119	Nichs Loftus Senr, and Nicholas Loftus Junr, Esqrs, Henry Loftus, John Loftus, and Thomas Loftus, gents.	09	110
	Rath	11			11
	Conogh	20			20
	Dungulp	14	John Cliffe Esq		14
	Stonehouse	02		000	02
	Balliverodge	05			05

Quarters	Townelands	Number of People	Tituladoes Names	Eng	Irish
(*folio* 37). Dunbrody	Clamine	34			34
	Dunbrody	16		02	14
	Salt Mills	12			12
	Grange	13		04	09
	Ballihack	51		05	46
	Ballivelick	18			18
	Nuge	21			21
	Ramsgrange	36			36
	Balligow	12			12
	Haggard	23			23
	Battles towne	37			37
	Kilbride	26			26
	Morsin	21			21
	Clonserragh	31			31
	Colman	28		02	26
	Tinknocke	06			06
	Boderan	40			40
	Corremore	22			22
	Rowes towne	19			19
(*folio* 38).	Coole	39			39
	Shilbeggan	41			41
	Kilheile	36			36
Slequilter	Ballilerog begg	24			24
	Kilmanoge	17		05	12
	Aclare	43			43
	Ballibrasill	22		04	18
	Ould Court	11		05	06
	Ballinteskin	12		08	04
	Ballisop	12		03	09
	Killeske	18		02	16
	Ballikerognor	39			39
	Knockagh	06			06
	Ballinemony	17		02	15
	Aclamon	08	Michaell Dormer gent		08
	Balliveroge	06	Humphry Smyth gent	02	04
	White church	30		02	28
(*folio* 39).	Polmaloe	32			32
	Ballifernoge	31		03	28
	Tolleraght	55			55
	Great Island	40		04	36
	Prishaggard	16		08	08
	Ballibarny	07			07
	Hors wood	12			12
	Dungans towne	47			47

Principall Names [and their number].

Branagh & Brennagh, 13 ; Byrne, 09 ; Bane, 09 ; Ô Boe, 10 ; Bryan & McBryan, 08 ; Browne, 10 ; Barron, 08 ; Coluer, 09 ; Cullin, 14 ; Chapman, 08 ; McDonnogh, 07 ; Deuereux, 11 ; Doyle,

19 ; McEdmond, 14 ; Forstall, 12 ; Furlong, 08 ; FitzJames & McJames, 09 ; Kauanagh, 09 ; Kenaght, 11 ; Keating, 13 ; Kelly, 15 ; Lacye, 07 ; Loughnan, 08 ; Ogan & Owgan, 07 ; Power, 16 ; Poore, 09 ; Roch, 18 ; McRichard, 07 ; Redmond, 07 ; Sutton, 25 ; McShane, 10 ; Synnott, 08 ; McTeige, 08 ; Walsh, 15 ; Welsh, 11 ; Whelan, 12 ; Murphy, 33.

(*folio* 39 *verso*).   Barrony : Shelbyrne ; Eng, 101 ; Irish, 1893 ; 1994, Tott.

(*folio* 40).   **BANTRIE BARRONY**

Quarters	Townelands	Number of People	Tituladoes Names	Eng	Irish
Clogh	Cloghas	10	Thomas Barrington Esq	01	09
	Clogh	103	Robert Thornhill Esq	10	93
	Clonmore	06			06
	Bree	18	Francis Randell gent		18
	Balliadin	15			15
	Edermyne	13	John Smyth gent	07	06
	Balliadin	12			12
	Templeskoby	22			22
	Balliadin	02			02
	Coolymorihy	10			10
	Dauids towne	13			13
	Ballybretas	10			10
	Moynhore	34			34
	Barenemony	11			11
	St Jones	63		07	56
Adams towne	Adams towne	69		05	64
	Templenecroy	08			08
(*folio* 41). Ould Rosse	Camlin	19	Samuell Shepheard Esq	03	16
	Courteile	21			21
	Ould Rosse	15		04	11
	Cussins towne	42			42
	Killscanlan	21	Thomas Bower		21
	part of Old Rosse	31			31
	Rahinclony	29			29
	Roch towne	49			49
	Carnagh	10			10
	Millers Parke	59			59
	Ballylane	35			35
	Leakan	08			08
	Stokes towne	16			16
Killegny	— —	13			13
	Ferrestalls towne	11			11
	Knocks towne	14			14
	Clonroch	12			12
(*folio* 42).	Bellaborrow	34			34

Quarters	Townelands	Number of People	Tituladoes Names	Eng	Irish
	Rahingrogh	03			03
	Ballymakisey	12			12
	Rathirteene	10			10
	Great Robins towne	29			29
	Coolenecon	02			02
	Little Robins towne	31			31
	Ballyelland	04			04
	Courtnecodihy	10			10
	Monetokry	16			16
	Tomnearly	31			31
Monks land	Pole Caple	09			09
	Ballyane	25	Henry Haughton gent	06	19
	Ballygobane	18			18
	Ballynebanoge	21			21
	Ballynecullagh	13			13
	Downard	14			14
(folio 43).	Mulligary	06			06
	Monemoling	18			18
	Ballindeny	13			13
	Ballygallsugard	02			02
	Templehudigan	34			34
	Tomneyngs	06			06
	Rahenure	03			03
	Ballynluge	04			04
	Monenemogh	11			11
	Ballybane	05			05
	Cooleback	16			16
	Ballyleach	24			24
	Rapadinboy	06			06
	Askenfarny	12			12
Glan	Lambs towne	20	Robert Cuppage Esq	03	17
	Barmony	06			06
	Downoning	20			20
(folio 44)	Ballybrenane	19			19
	Garrinstokole	03			03
	Konott	06			06
	Corleckan	20	Charles Collins gent	03	17
	Ballyntlea	13		01	12
	Ballyanreagh	11		04	07
	Dauids towne	14		02	12
	Wilkins towne	03			03
	Blackhall	02			02

Principall Names [and their number].

Birne, 15 ; Browne, 07 ; Cogely, 11 ; Clouny, 08 ; Doyle, 41 ; Dorane & Doran, 07 ; McEdmond,

07 ; Forestall (6) & Forstall (9), 15 ; Fouly (6), & Fuoly (4), 10 ; Kinsalagh, 08 ; Kelly, 08 ; Murchoe, 18 ; Murphy, 31 ; Power, 11 ; Roch, 16 ; Redmond, 14 ; Welsh, 11 ; McTeige, 08.

(*folio* 44 *verso*).   Barrony : Bantry ; Eng, 056 ; Irish, 1347 ; 1403, tott.

(*folio* 45).   **BALLAGHKEENE BARRONY.**

Parishes	Townelands	Number of People	Tituladoes Names	Eng	Irish
Kiltennell	Prospect	002	Edward Chichester Esq	001	001
	Kildermott	04	Thomas Neile gent	04	—
	Ballimony	05	Robert Pue gent	02	03
	Balliconlone	03		03	000
	Benoge	03		03	00
	Kilbride	45	John Tottie Senr gent John Tottie Junr Esq	05	40
	Murro Castle	26		07	19
	Kittor	18			18
	Ballintagard	03			03
Killenagh	Parkneswell	05		02	03
	Rahin	13			13
	Culluckmore	13			13
	Balliwalton	08		02	06
	Cullockbeg	20			20
Ardmaine	Midleton	34	John Fontaine Esq	07	27
	Ballimakill	05			05
(*folio* 46).	Ballinacur	04			04
	Ballintra	03		02	01
	Boleny	03	Daniell Franke gent	02	01
	Balliduffe	07			07
	Garrina	26		06	20
	Balliduffe	02			02
	Glascarrig	32	Pencer Vincent Esq Thomas Vincent gent	02	30
	Killanyduffe	02		02	—
	Kilmihill	13			13
	Tiggary	04			04
	Balliwatts	03			03
	Tourduffe	10		02	08
	Rahenlosky	02		02	
	Ballimony	02		02	
	Ballimonihy	26			26
	Ballomoone	13		02	11
(*folio* 47).	Garremoile	06			06
	Balleneclogh	06			06
	Kilnoe	13			13

Quarters	Townelands	Number of People	Tituladoes Names	Eng	Irish
	Knocknesillog	07			07
	Kilnoe	29			29
	Knocknesillog	20		04	16
	Ballinemony	39		04	35
	Ballihaske	19			19
	Ballicahin	05		03	02
	Killancoole	29			29
	Sillournogh	05		02	03
	Ballilackin	02			02
	Winchoge	06		06	—
	Balliltraduft	10		09	01
	Ballinehone	10			10
Killelly	Ballinvally	16			16
	Ballimacue	04			04
	Ballnekellob	12			12
(folio 48).	Ballinekelog	10			10
	Inch Mill	04			04
	Kinckan Sherreuill	38			38
Edermine	Edermine	26		01	25
	Garrimske & Tomlane	053		000	053
	Ballineake	01			01
	Balliroe	02			02
	Ballinebanoge	15			15
Ballihuskart	Balliranell	06			06
	Ballinakdonoghfine	09		02	07
	Ballinstra	25			25
	Clonmore	05		02	03
	Mill of Colledin	06			06
	Kilcothy	28			28
(folio 49).	Ballinmole	15			15
	Ballinnodagh	08			08
	Kilbride	03			03
	Kilmalocker	20			20
	Ballisillagh	09			09
	Garrvacon	02			02
	Mullaghdarke	07			07
	Ballekile	20			20
	Ballinae	22		04	18
	Bollenbirgidan	09			09
	Ballikelly	16			16
Templeshan	Templeshan	37			37
	Browns wood	09	John Webb Henry Proud gent	05	04
	Molibegg	02			02
	Tomnifinsoge	18			18

Parrishes	Townelands	Number of People	Tituladoes Names	Eng	Irish
Ballineslany	Rahaile	32			32
	Coolekipp	04			04
(*folio* 50).	Owell	08			08
	Cooleman	24			24
Castle Elis	Ballilucas	17		000	17
	Killeske	19			19
	Bolifarnog	07			07
	Ballintegard	10		04	06
	Garriadin	08			08
	Ballineled	07		04	03
	Ballinegor	05			05
	Asksillagh	04			04
	Ballicrocan	15			15
	Ballinemony	16			16
	Ballinrae	15			15
	Ballymony begg	03			03
	Ballinra	02			02
Mellenagh	Kilgowne	04			04
	Oulord	18		02	16
(*folio* 51).	Monnev	03		03	—
	Killurine	04			04
	Kilnemanagh	04			04
Joreene	Balliteig	28			28
	Ballimore	19			19
St Nich :	Garrilough	09		05	04
	Balliwollire	21		04	17
	Ballinasker	13			13

Principall Irish Names [and their number].

Byrne, 15 ; Bolger, 15 ; Ô Bryan, 13 ; Connor & Connors, 20 ; Dempsy & Demsy, 15 ; Doyle, 21 ; Ô Deoran, 08 ; Kauanagh, 08 ; Lacye, 12 ; Lary, 08 ; Murchoe, 24 ; Murphy, 60 ; Roch, 15 ; Redmond, 44 ; Synnott, 28.

(*folio* 51 *verso*).   Barrony : Ballaghkeene ; Eng, 122 ; Irish, 1219 ; 1341, tott.

(*folio* 52).   **GOARY BARRONY**

Parrishes	Townelands	Number of People	Tituladoes Names	Eng	Irish
Kiltriske	Goary	089	Abell Ram & Richd Fitts gents	015	074
	—	10	Samuel Windowes gent	04	06
	Cooletrondell	04			04

Parishes	Townelands	Number of People	Tituladoes Names	Eng	Irish
	Ballrackny	07		05	02
	Bally cart	33			33
	Limbricke	66	Captn John Sands	11	55
	Tomnahely	06	Morgan Kauanagh gent		06
	Ballim^ccae	10			10
	Toberduffe	06			06
	Correcanane	10	Christopher Goffe gent	04	06
	Ballnastra	02		02	
	Ballaghtegin	04			04
	Clonee	27	Henry Maisterson Esq	02	25
	Castle towne	07			07
	Kilbegnet	05			05
	Moquile	02		02	000
	Kilmacandoge	04		02	02
	Killebegg	02		02	—
Inch	Scarnagh	05		05	
	Ballikelty	06		02	04
(folio 53).	New towne	02		02	—
	Coolegreny	09		09	—
	Fort Chichester	05	Samuell Sheares gent	05	—
	Killebegg	05			05
	Ballilin	04			04
	Ballilarkin	12			12
Cross	Comerduffe	21			21
	Lagan	31	Coole Toole gent		31
	Killinhue	19			19
	Ballingallen	02			02
	Ballintlea	05		03	02
	Ballinegary & Kilmichell	13			13
	Moniseede	04			04
	Ballidoragh	18			18
	Ballineculagh	11			11
	Annagh	30		04	26
	Cranrewer	10			10
	Ballinamony	02			02
(folio 54).	Ballicley	06			06
	Ballileig	19			19
Rosmenog	Clonagh	13			13
	Iland	11			11
	Sralmore	14			14
Kilneauor	Pallish	06		02	04
	Tomquile	03		03	
	Cloghnehissy	20	Phillip Drue gent	15	05
	Ballyagnlin	06			06
	Tomquile	31			31

Parrishes	Townelands	Number of People	Tituladoes Names	Eng	Irish
Arklow	Colleroe	14		03	11
	Balliteig	04	Miles Kensellagh gent		04
Tome	Ballishane	08	Walter Talbott gent		08
	Ballitrasey	16	Bryan Doran gent		16
	Garribritt	05			05
	Balliorlimor	07	Wadkins gent	03	04
	Ballensaryen	14			14
	Cullentragh	47			47
(folio 55).	Annagh	10			10
	Ballinakilly	04		02	02
Kilpipe	———	17			17
	Ballithomas	11			11

Principall Irish Names [and] Their Number.

Birne, 19 ; Connor & Ô Connors, 07 ; Doyle, 27 ; Kauanagh, 15 ; Kensly, 11 ; Murphy, 25 ; Redmond, 13 ; Toole, 09.

(folio 55 verso). Barrony : Goary ; Eng, 107 ; Irish, 687 ; 0794, tott.

(folio 56). **SCARWELSH BARRONY**

Quarters	Townelands	Number of People	Tituladoes Names	Eng	Irish
	Ballearrill	046	Alex : Barrington Esq	008	038
	Kilallegon	05		02	03
	Clonsourdan	18			18
	Knockduffe	11		07	04
	Dauids towne	03			03
	Marshal towne	02			02
	Carregine and Mangan	22			22
Moynart	———	58	Thomas Lee gent	20	38
	Carrig Bruce	04			04
	Ballenemanan	33			33
	Ballebrine	23		02	21
Kilteally	———	66	John Cotterell gent	02	64
	Coolereech	22			22
	Timcurry	01			01

Quarters	Townelands	Number of People	Tituladoes Names	Eng	Irish
	Moycurry	23	Mathew Stotnard Esq	03	20
	Coolerey	03			03
(*folio* 57).	Wheelo-gowre	03			03
Temple Shanbogh	Ballelosky	18			18
	Rossard	21			21
	Bollebegg	23			23
	Degans towne	06			06
Monglasse Mongan and Tincurry qr }	— —	47			47
Cromocke	———	07			07
	Tomnedilly	26			26
	Ballenekilly	11			11
	Ballene Wm Roe	04			04
	Balleduffe	07		05	02
	Coolecleere	14	Wm Lambe gent	04	10
	Tombrick	06		03	03
	Fnogh	02			02
Kilmashill	———	34			34
	Ballephillip	27			27
(*folio* 58) Parrishes					
The Town and Parrish of Fernes		076	John Denison gent	08	68
	Kilborow	10		04	06
	Ballenaspoge	05			05
	Kil Thomas	12			12
	Ballinaspeck	03			03
Kilcome	Balliduffe	19		03	16
	Coolenelyne	23			23
	Carrigleggan	10			10
	Rahin	11	Captn Buttler gent		11
	Tome	03			03
	Carran	17			17
	Owlerdard	07			07
	Tomnefunshope	17			17
	Cloghamon	94		14	80
	Coolmealogh	03			03
(*folio* 59).	Balleshannoge, Johnstowne and Drumderry }	23	Anthony Rudd gent		23
	Balleneparke	07	Captn Richard Woodward gent	05	02
	Ballicarny	43	Coll Francis Wheeler Esq	04	39
	Cloghbemond	22		05	17
	Ballilugh	05		04	01
	Ballirobeg	21			21
	Curraghlahin	10			10

Parrishes	Townelands	Number of People	Tituladoes Names	Eng	Irish
That part of ye P'ish of Toem yt lies in ye Bar : of Scarwelsh	Curraghduffe	04		04	—
	Ballinebarny	03		02	01
	Ballitasny	12			12
	Cranecrinagh	05	Edward Rotheram Esq	05	
	Camolin	41	Walter Lyndan, Roger Lyndon, and John Selling, gents.	17	24

Principall Irish Names [and] Their Number.

Ô Bryne, 17 ; Byrne, 08 ; Ô Bryan, 08 ; Doyle, 25 ; Doran, 10 ; Duffe, 08 ; Ô Fowly, 09 ; Jourdon, 07 ; Murphy, 07 ; Nowlan and Nolan, 10 ; Neale, 07 ; Redmond, 12.

(folio 59 verso).   Barrony [of Scarwelsh] : Eng, 131 ; Irish, 971 ; 1102, tott :

Barronies	Pages	Eng	Irish	Totall of Eng : & Irish		
Wexfford Towne and Liberties	01	0340	0562	0902	1632	12048
					340	562
New Ross towne & Liberties	02	0241	0377	0618	1292	11486
Eniscorthy towne	02	0067	0322	0389 340		1292
Forth Barony	17	0178	1667	1845		12778
Bargie	25	0126	1353	1479		
Shelmaleer	33	0163	1650	1813		
Shelbryne	39	0101	1893	1994		
Bantry	44	0056	1347	1403		
Ballaghkeene	51	0122	1219	1341		
Goary	55	0107	0687	0794		
Scarwelsh	59	0131	0971	1102		
		1632	12048	13680		

LEYTRIM COUNTY
1929

(*folio* 1). County of Leytrim.

BARONIES OF LEITRIM MOHILL AND CARRIGALLAN.

Parishes	Townelands	Numb' of People	Tituladoes Names	Eng	Irish
Killtogher	Carrick, Drumrush	047	Sᵣ George Sᵗ George Knt, Bryan Cunigane gent.	033	014
	James towne	238	William Sᵗ George Esq, Edward Wood gent,	102	136
			Thomas Barrington Esq, John Ellis Senior gent, John Ellis Junior gent, Hugh Gray gent, Bryan Birne Merctᵗ, Stephen Chamberline Mctᵗ		
	Leytrim	014	Owen Ruork gent	—	014
	Carecabone	005		—	005
	Rosconnis	4			4
	Kreeny	6		2	4
	Dromnasirie	2			2
	Dromgarmon	8			8
	Dromkerine	6			6
	Killmaghery	2			2
(*folio* 2	Krey	6			6
	Killoghcrier	9			9
	Brenrim	6			6
	Shrahmore	7			7
	Moherlegath	4			4
	Dromorto	7			7
	Deritegroe	9			9
	Derintobo	5		2	3
	Mogran	20			20
	Meaghavagh	10			10
	Aughagrany	11			11
	Duffcarrick	9			9
	Stukry	4			4
	Shermore	6			6
	Mongue	16			16
	Drumganagh	1			1
	Anaghbrodyan	2			2
(*folio* 3). Kiltogher	Aughkinconell	3			3
	Aghnemadda	4			4
	Lisdrunesie	4			4
	Lisnagea	2			2
	Finaskline	5			5
	Lismakeygan	9			9
	Killiharke	14			14
	Garrologh	2			2
	Aughrewman	7			7
	Kellynanorle	2			2

Parishes	Townelands	Numb' of People	Tituladoes Names	Eng	Irish
	Dromnodober	4			4
	Liscallyrvan	2			2
	Carickeny	7		2	5
	Dromhircle	7			7
	Dromhirkhen	16			16
	Drumore	5			5
	Dromrush	9		4	5
	Auchymony	4			4
	Carsperoge & Cloondayga }	11		2	9
(*folio* 4). Killtibrett	Loghscurr	68	Humphry Reynolds Esq		68
	Seybeg	24			24
	Scrabagh	19			19
	Drumlukill	5			5
	Achillmoreah	8			8
	Leader	5			5
	Cortaskine	3			3
	Carrickport	18			18
	Drombelling	4			4
	Drummod and Curragh	11			11
	Aghgeany	17			17
	Rosconish	8			8
	Drumongroo	4			4
(*folio* 5). Fenagh	Kelltifannane	04			4
	Drummany	09			9
	Macrusse	06			6
	Carrabeg	17			17
	Anaghbeg	03		2	1
	Ardagh	11			11
	Arthrodey	11			11
(*folio* 6). Anaduff	Lismana	13			13
	Cariarde	8			8
	Lismacmoyle	2			2
	Drumdaragh	8			8
	Lisduff	10			10
	Taise	9		4	5
	Dromkerine	4			4
	Rathgobane	5			5
	Dromersnan	22		4	18
	Gartenty	7			7
	Drumcroe	6			6
	Aghamore	12			12
	Fadderoe	12			12
	Derrybracke	10			10
	Derry	4			4
	Mullagh	15			15

Parishes	Townelands	Numb' of People	Tituladoes Names	Eng	Irish
(folio 7).	Fennelagh	4			4
	Killyfaddy	4			4
	Dericastine	6			6
	Derrywily	10			10
	Drumad	18			18
	Carrick	6			6
	Lisnegan	8			8

BAR CARI GALLIN

Parishes	Townelands	Numb' of People	Tituladoes Names	Eng	Irish
Caragallen in ye Barony of Carrigallin	Towmanaghan	46	Edward Alline Esq Thomas Alline gent	32	14
	Snafrallagh	3			3
	Derrinegan	2			2
	Legnegan	7			7
	Longfeill	6			6
	Lechine	5			5
	Drumnisheen	4			4
	Drumergowle	7			7
(folio 8).	Anagh	004		000	004
	Corglass	5		—	5
	Kilbrecken	3		—	3
	Sesiagh	6			6
	Sunagh	5			5
	Aughavore	2			2
	Killagher	4			4
	Aghleagh	7			7
	Clanbecher	8			8
	Drumbernles	4			4
	Dromdarglen	6			6
	Tullagh	10			10
	Gartermony	7			7
	Coranaghy	6		—	6
	Mullynadaragh	4		—	4
	Muchaviline	6		—	6
	Cornefirst	2		—	2
	Clowncarrick	8		—	8
(folio 9).	Sessiagh	6		000	6
	Aughavar	4		—	4
	Drumsillagh	6		—	6
	Killdachorte	3		—	3
	Bridah	6		—	6
	Beagh	8			8
Oughterah	Caregrier	12			12
	Clenan	10			10
	Killrussell	11			11

Parishes	Townelands	Numb' of People	Tituladoes Names	Eng	Irish
	Drumlunane	3			3
	Kenaboe	4			4
	Lissecarny	8			8
	Clenagh	11			11
	Bellynard	6			6
	Lehard	13			13
	Lisnalillagh	11		—	11
(*folio* 10).	Aghillmony	5		000	5
	Ardmynin	14		—	4
	Aughtounyfighterah	3			3
	Aghaloy offalan	20	Bryan Brangh O Connor gent		20
	Dromrane	5			5
	Bellinamore	13	Coll Laurence Parsons Esq	4	9
	Killamodan	6			6
	Cammagher	7			7
	Caraglass	9			9
	Caltlerachy	4			4
	Derinahily	2	Henry Baker Esq	2	—
	Clogher	4			4
	Vachteragh	18			18
	Gorochshally	2			2
	Derinaspellan	2		—	2
(*folio* 11).	Dromrockine	005		000	005
	Mullaghnasallagh	9		—	9
	Carakrockheor	9			9
	Cardrema	9			9
	Mayo	11			11
	Killtipurdon	2			02
	Dargonan	14			14
	Derrikiher	6			6
	Caraboyacher	5			5
	Dromboyle	12			12
	Cornekerrew	9			9
	Listuell-fresh	10			10
	Killnemadore	4		—	4
(*folio* 12). Dromreilly in Carrigallin Barr	Garvoruss & Bociscile	013	Henry Reynolds gent	000	013
	Killcrivy	3	William Tipping gent	2	1
	Cammcarrick	7		—	7
	Radagh	4			4
	Killtiporte	3			3
	Slewcurran	13			13
	Carrickmakegan	9			9
	Dromlea	6			6
	Shiraloghen	14			14
	Longhill	9			9

Parishes	Townelands	Numb' of People	Tituladoes Names	Eng	Irish
	Stradrynan	5			5
	Corrimehane	8			8
	Lislaghy	7		2	5
	Lurga	3			3
	Liscrudy	14			14
	Dromdiffer & Kergoch	9		—	9
(folio 13). Cloone	Leckine	008	Henry Ô Neale gent	00c	008
	Lewelly Biah	11		—	11
	Annagh	6			6
	Catten	12			12
	Farglass	10			10
	Milteran	14			14
	Crenagh	3		3	—
	Tryne	11			11
	Rinne	3			3
	Tubcon	5			5
	Taunaghmore	4			4
	Dromhallagh	5			5
	Sunaghbeg	11			11
	Drumgraney	4			4
	Coillfea	5			5
	Drumuy	2			2
	Anaghbranagh	4		—	4
(folio 14).	Donaunly	004		000	004
	Drumgillry	10		—	10
	Boy	11			11
	Caneaneary	8	William Bray Esq	1	7
	Aughowass	4			4
	Aughologhy Doncory	12			12
	Drumode	4			4
	Suaghgone	5			5
	Clonsarran	6			6
	Dromlayge	4			4
	Tuma	3			3
	Drunhavoe	6			6
	Coilegortine	8			8
	Gortnowels	5			5
	Artdune	4			4
	Drumgolelaw	10		—	10
(folio 15).	Derrinkillvoy	006		000	006
	Mullaghbrake	8		—	8
	Drumshavors	3			3
	Drumhurke	10			10
	Drumdirkine	9			9
	Fernaght	10			10
	Drumosniton	2			2

Parishes	Townelands	Numb' of People	Tituladoes Names	Eng	Irish
	Clownconga	5			5
	Drumkeda	2			2
	Errue	008			005[*sic!*]
	Tumune	3			3
	Clumcomy	6			6
	Drumhirkine	4			4
	Drummine	8	Phelomy Ô Neale	—	8
	Drumconvy	5		—	5
	Leganamine	9		—	9
(*folio* 16). Cloone	Aghoragh	007		000	007
	Shunagh	11		—	11
	Drumcausse	4		—	4
	Gob	7		—	7
	Machmaculline	3			3
	Dromadorne	4			4
Mohell	———	26	Henry Crofton Esq	3	23
	Drumboy	8			8
	Listitudinan	8			8
	Clalankell	9			9
	Gregine	4			4
	Carrick	7		—	7
	Corran	12		—	12
	Gort Fadda	5		—	5
	Aughdrumcarran	8		—	8
(*folio* 17).	Ogekell	019		000	019
	Brendrim	9		—	9
	Loghine	12		—	12
	Dromvahine	3		—	3
	Corbaghell	8		—	8
	Bandynore	13			13
	Drummoly	6			6
	Lisdringevell	4			4
	Drumillaragh	5			5
	Cargen	4			4
	Loghevine	8	Walter Jones gent	1	7
	Corvagh	6			6
	Clunfenan	4			4
	Kilboman	7			7
	Clacklina	7			7
	Esker	10			10
	Clunbonnagh	15			15
(*folio* 18).	Aughnarshan	2		2	—
	Clenmorish	10			10
	Claneagh	6			6
	Rusky	4			4
	Dromarde	18			18

Parishes	Townelands	Numb' of People	Tituladoes Names	Eng	Irish
	Asser	15			15
	Tallaghbeg	4			4
	Drumrachull	8			8
	Drumsaney	12			12
	Talcone	4			4
	Stuck	9			9
	Tallagh	3			3
	Drumdae	3			3
	Mohell	2			2
	Clunine	6			6

Principall Irish Names & their Numb[ers].

Bryan, 10 ; Birrin, 5 ; Brady, 6 ; Birne (4) & Brine (4), 8 ; Bohane, 8 ; Caffery, 6 ; O Cannon, 5 ; Currine, 7 ; Carten, 5 ; McCaba, 10 ; O Duigenan, 20 ; McDermot, 5 ; O Donelly, 20 ; Dolan, 9 ; Farrell, 7 ; Ô Flyne, 10 ; McGwyre, 18 ; McGranell, 12 ; McGarry, 10 ; McGee, 6 ; Gowran, 8 ; Gowan, 13 ; McGleoine, 14 ; McGilleroy, 5 ; McGanna, 2 ; Gillacynny, 8 ; McHugh, 12 ; Kelly, 13 ; McKeone, 27 ; Mulloy, 10 ; Moran &c, 20 ; McMahon, 7 ; McManus, 5 ; Managhan, 5 ; O Neale, 18 ; McNemee, 21 ; Reynolds, 62 ; Riddaghan (6) & Rodaghan, 9 ; Reyly, 38 ; McShanly, 15 ; Shyrydan, 7 ; McTernan, 12 ; Terny, 4 ; McTeigue, 7.

(*folio* 18 *verso*). The Number of the People in the three Baronyes of Leytrim, Mohill, and Carrigallan, according to the severall pages : Eng, 0207 ; Irish, 2139 ; Totall Eng & Irish, 2346.

(*folio* 19). **BARONY OF DROMAGHEIRE**[1]

Parishes	Townlands	Numb	Tituladoes Names	Eng	Irish
Cluneclare	Arduonin	004		000	004
	Loghres	4		—	4
	Monyduft	2		—	2
	Minhirragh	007		—	007
	Kilkloghan	3			3
	Cornaman	3			3
	Mogher	8			8
	Sradrine	6			6
	Cornaghleigh	7			7
	Greaghnagran	9			9
	Leghawnagh	5			5

[1] *Drumagheire*, folios 20-24.

Parishes	Townlands	Numb	Tituladoes Names	Eng	Irish
	Ardvarnagh in Glenboy }	5			5
	Aghloghacon	10			10
	Gortnatubritte	10			10
	Farrow Mᶜ Glanboy	5			5
	Cornastake	13			13
	Tullaghsherney	015		009	006
(*folio* 20)	Rosse	8		2	6
	Ramoney	8		5	3
	Tonewifekrell	8		3	5
	Mannor Hamilton	18		7	11
	Farrow	4			4
	Donoghmore	7			7
Killargand & Clunelagher }	Gortermone	17			17
	Brincoill	5			5
	Bogganlands	46		5	41
	Lemskally	9			9
	Drumderry	5			5
	Annagh	3			3
	Leonagh	4			4
	Gortgaregan	10			10
	Clunequin	2			2
	Clunlogher	9		2	7
(*folio* 21).	Greunnagh	008		000	008
	Tullynamucke	6		—	6
	Altwra	6		—	6
	Knockcuillin	4		—	4
	Drumduly	3			3
	Corgery	2			2
	Lisgormus	14			14
	Sockres	17			17
	Killarga	27			27
	Carrignewna	13			13
Killinumera	———	5			5
	Ardupp	10		5	5
	Derrivrishe	8			8
	Bowne	15		4	11
	Ragbane	9			9
	Carbin	21			21
	Killan	7		—	7
	Kellivoggy	12		—	12
(*folio* 22).	Goulagh	006		000	006
	Killynanna	10		—	10
	Corriosiony	5		—	5
	Arduarnagh	31			31
Drumleas	Drumaheire	56	Sʳ Geo : Villers Barᵗᵗ	7	49
	Fenne	3			3

Parishes	Townlands	Numb	Tituladoes Names	Eng	Irish
	Killiossagh	5			5
	Coola	21			21
	Cornelaghta	7			7
	Corrigulan	17			17
	Conreagh	5			5
	New towne	59	Robert Parker Esq	15	44
	Dulin	5			5
	Monyduff	8		—	8
	Balleneball	20		—	20
	Fanalenie	21		—	21
	Carraghan	19			19
(folio 23).	Connaghell	006		000	006
Inish McRaw	Killnagarne	16	Hugh Ô Rourke gent	—	16
	Floonmeein	22		—	22
	Dromonnaleassa	7		—	7
	Corr Boghelaigh	9		—	9
	Letter	5			5
	Corrlaghachell	17			17
	Termonn	16			16
	Dromonnasewan	16			16
	Corragh	4			4
	Tullymorrey	3			3
	Dromonn	2			2
	Derinwoher	5			5
	Moydoragh	9			9
	Altinie	12			12
	Derinweer	11			11
	Fionvola	5			5
(folio 24).	Cloonemorgett	7			7
	Cloonen	18			18
	Derinnocny	9			9
	Lisdromgranc	3			3
	Corduff	2			2
	Glassdrinonn	12			12
	Corey	17			17
	Derinwollen	6			6
	Greaghnosliue	6			6
	Lintaghwile	5			5
	Dromonnafaghrod	4			4
	Tully corikie	7			7
	Derin	13			13
	Lisnanorish	6		—	6
	Drombrehad	11		—	11
(folio 25).	Tullytohell	010		000	010
	Geoglin	5		—	5
	Greaghnaghogh	14		—	14
	Cornetullagh	16			16

Parishes	Townlands	Numb	Tituladoes Names	Eng	Irish
	Derinwoollen againe	18			18
	Drumonfinolta	26			26
	Claranbegg	5			05
	Claranmore	11			11
	Scaghdreynagh	4			04
	Minenasamer	34			34

BARONY OF ROSSCLOGHER

Parishes	Townlands	Numb	Tituladoes Names	Eng	Irish
Killassnett in Ros-clogher Barony }	Agavoine and Tallincloy	004		—	004
	Carrick Elunagh	18			18
	Corrulones	34			34
	Crollinboy	7			7
	Gortinure	7		—	7
(folio 26). Killassett	Minour	010		000	010
	Lergandowne	6		—	6
	Tragherighon	6	John Ebercrumber gent	02	04
	Legnefagherowe	7		—	7
	Duffrine	19			19
	Mulliane	6			6
	Trumrode	6			6
	Glassedrumin	9	Charles Connor gent		9
	Castlecaragh Togher	8			8
	Lissanabracke	6			6
	Culruskagh & Castlecaragh {	62		13	49
	Fure	6			6
	Larganboy	17	Thomas Abercrumber gent	16	1
	Manner Hamilton	21	John Waldrum gent Owen Wynn Esq	12	9
(folio 27). Rossenver	Ballagh Ô Mehan	128	Neale Ô Neale gent	000	128
	Sesmorish and Burchoide of the forfeited lands {	31		—	31
	Bailemore, Rossilogher, Leaght, and Moineene {	23		—	23
	Aghavoghell	14			14
	Agroderaird	13			13
	Guirteene dairagh	16			16
	Gortnasvillagh	20			20
	Cloone-car	21	William McGlanchy gent		21
	Kinlagh	10		—	10
	Feartagh	6		—	6
(folio 28).	Inshennagh	019		000	019
	Vragh	3		—	3
	Taly	18		—	18
	Boyatinagh	24		—	24

Parishes	Townlands	Numb	Tituladoes Names	Eng	Irish
	Gleinhoda	056		000	056
	Dune Garbry	45	Leut Thomas Ellis gent	02	43
	Sr Henry Tichburnes lands, Aderdaoven	} 26		03	23

Principall Irish Names and their Numbers.

Armstrong, 7 ; McBoyheen, 5 ; Ô Conan, 6 ; O Curmine, 6 ; Ô Cuillen, 7 ; Connelly, 6 ; O Derrogan, 5 ; McElveaine, 8 ; McEnaw, 12 ; O Fline, 15 ; Fellane, 6 ; O Fergussa, 13 ; O Fihily, 5 ; O Gallagher, 15 ; McQuan, 40 ; McGillaholy, 6 ; McGowren, 7 ; McGlanchy, 12 ; McGwyre, 9 ; Gloghlen, 5 ; McGlevine, 14 ; McGilleroy, 5 ; McHugh, 6 ; McKenan, 6 ; Kelly, 28 ; O Keregan, 6 ; Kegan, 8 ; McKilleagher, 6 ; McKeoine, 7 ; McLoghlen, 32 ; McMorrey, 30 ; McMulloghry, 5 ; O Myhan, 12 ; O Mulgohery, 7 ; Parlone, 25 ; O Rourke, 24 ; O Sharry, 17 ; O Trower, 13 ; McTiernan, 26.

(*folio* 28 *verso*). The Number of the People in the Two Baronyes of Drumaheir, and Roscloger according to the severall pages : Eng, 0112 ; Irish, 1817 ; Eng and Irish, 1929.

The Number of the People in County of Leitrim.

Baronyes	Eng	Irish	Totall of Eng & Irish
Leitrim, Mohill, Carrigallan page 18	0207	2139	2346
Drumaheir and Rosclogher	0112	1817	1929
The Totall	0319	3956	4275

ROSCOMMON COUNTY AND   11768
ATHLONE BORROUGH   1075
_____
12843

(*folio* 1).   Roscommon[1] County

ROSCOMON BARRONY

Parrishes	Townelands	Number of People	Tituladoes Names	Eng	Irish
Elphyn	Comoge	028		—	028
	Glanbalettony	37	James Farrell gent		37
	Toberrory	13	William Malone & Phillip Conner gents		13
	Arnegouny	13			13
	Drenan	11	Nicholas Doyle Esq		11
	Killinecher	17	Richard Nugent gent		17
	Lechteaske	8			8
	Rossmore	12			12
	Cluncullan	8			8
	Clunmurre	9	Francis Nugent gent		9
	Grallagch	49			49
	Corthree	30	Sr Thomas Nugent Barronett		30
	Rosbeg	24			24
	Cluniquin	21	Robert Newgent	6	15
	Clummechan	5			5
	Tullintippen	21	Patrick Barnuell gent		21
	Elphin	118	Nicholas Mahon Esq	10	108
(*folio* 2).	Clounibranon	15			15
	Tully	5			5
	Knock	9			9
	Lisgouock	9			9
	Crevevolan	8			8
Shankill	Carefore and Kilboy	14			14
	Lishonardell and Bracloone }	18			18
	Rathroe	4	Peeter Dowell gent		4
	Kelline and Gort mc crannagh }	13			13
	Clonnobioge	30	Allen Dowell gent		30
	Rontivolan	2			2
	Ballioughter	15			15
	Killine Est	4			4
Killmacumsy	Killocomsy	18	Thomas Fitzgerrald and Peter Esmond gents		18
					18
	Lisnebole	2			2
(*folio* 3).	Caroentogher	17			17
	Carronnelagh	10			10
	Lis Mc Dowell	6			6
Lissanulloy	Lismadderell	7			7
	Lisvallerow	2			2
	Lorga	10	Corporall Erasmus Mathews gent	3	7

[1] *Roscoman*, folio 58.

Parrishes	Townelands	Number of People	Tituladoes Names	Eng	Irish
	Clunkeran ½ qr	4			4
	Carginna ½ qr	7			7
	Ballyduffey	13	Nicholas Sutton gent		13
	Lissanuffey	7	Thomas Plunkett gent		7
	Clounikeran	15	Faghny Farrell Esq		15
	Grannacan and Montagh	20			20
	Erry	4			4
	Trevocerrye	12	Robert Leynes and Alexandr his sonn gents	2	10
	Trevevolgan	6			6
	Tolleverran	8			8
(folio 4). Lissa- nuffy	Carowarde	8		4	4
	Tremvolgan	10			10
	Aghadain	4			4
	Kill Mᶜ Eneny	13	Walter Dillon gent		13
	Lispopble	22	Peirs Power & Theo : his sonn gent		22
Aghrinn	Lisedorne	50	Richard Croffton Esq	4	46
	Bryanbegg	2			2
	Clunfade	18			18
	Carrikenagh	7	Robert Ervinge gent	2	5
	Corliss	2			2
	Grange	21			21
	Killinierra	8	Edward Croffton gent	2	6
	Towmore	17	Lucas Dillon Esq		17
	Buanagh	11			11
	Kariskillowe	9	Robert Redmond gent		9
	Caroreaogh	4	Robert Purshell gent		4
	Laskan	14	Robert Plunkett gent		14
(folio 5).	Killnedan	8			8
	Brianmore	5			5
	Killero	10			10
	Killkanneran	8			8
	Crynekirck	10			10
	Ardlogheher	9			9
	Lissennoran	3			3
	Rodine	10			10
	Bellragh	6	George Begg & Mathew Begg		6
	Polemghell	22	Peirse Power & Edmond Power gent		22
	Karrowreagh	2			2
	Karrikellow	3			3
	Laughboy	2			2
Bomlin	——	9	Migheall Scafeeld gent	2	7

Parrishes	Townelands	Number of People	Tituladoes Names	Eng	Irish
	Clunmedane	4			4
	Orny	8	Robert Dillon gent		8
	Furnebege	10	Francis Farsfeeld gent		10
(*folio* 6).	Clorebragan	10	Tho : Pariell gent		10
	Ballefiny	11		2	9
	Ballerauill and Lisroin	18			18
	Ballefiue	3			3
	Balimagenale	11	Lucas Dillon gent		11
	Skrymoge	11			11
Clunfinlagh	Casselsherwood Clunfinlagh	47	Lawrence Netervill, Thomas Butler, and Edward Nugent, gents.		47
	Dughill	25	Patrick Verdon gent		25
	Farne	9			9
	Cloonewany and Cloonfuey	18			18
	Grahoone in Cloonefey Lenaghlaa	25	Cormak Hanly & Richd Dillon gents		25
	Balanacorly	12			12
(*folio* 7). Clounfinlagh	Balanafad	11			11
	Moher	10			10
	Kellevaikan	5			5
Killculey	Cargintulke	14	Edward Scurlog gent		14
	Munyboy	8			8
	Karker	10	ye sonn of Mary Fitzgerrald gent	—	10
	Annaughmore	004	Daniel Gilleclin gent	000	004
	Corslicy	7		—	7
	Carginagapall	7		—	7
	Clouneagh	7	Dudly Connor gent		7
	Clounakilly	18	John Connor gent		18
	Grange	29			29
	Corbally	11			11
	Ardkeanagh	14			14
	Balighbae	11			11
	Tulske	15			15
	Ardkenagh	6			6
(*folio* 8).	Clounculan	20	John Connor and Gerald Barnawell gents		20
	Corbegg	15	William Jussey gent	2	13
	Cloungara	7			7
Clounfinlagh P^t	Clare	10	Bryan Connor gent & John Connor gent		10
	Clouncaugh	23	Edward Mastron gent		23

Parrishes	Townelands	Number of People	Tituladoes Names	Eng	Irish
	Coraghnegole	20	Patricke Plunkett gent		20
	Clouneragh	25	Oliuer Ketin gent		25
Killuckin	Shrue	14			14
	Clanmurry	4			4
	Killuckin	4			4
	Clasininy	5			5
	Ballinydry	3			3
		6			6
	Ardkellin	10			10
Ogula	Killfree	18	Faughna Farrall gent		18
	Ballemocorleffoy	5			5
(*folio* 9).	Carvenashagh	3			3
	Carvegane	12			12
	Bally begg	13			13
	Lisneneane	2	Turlogh Kelly gent		2
	Ogulla	15			15
	Carveincossan	11	Jenecoe Taaffe & John Taaffe gent		11
	Grange in Tulske	10			10
	Ould Castle	17			17
Clancraffe	Clunehily	7			7
	Keey	15		2	13
	Carhukeele	5			5
	Kenard	10	Charles gent		10
	Cluncraffe	10			10
	Clunicatten	13		2	11
	Drumilis more	4			4
	Cullineene	4			4
	Drumullin	6			6
(*folio* 10). Clun-craffe	Clunfee	11	Patricke Boyton gent		11
	Clancosker	4	Nicholas Verdon gent		4
	Drummott	13	Francis Dillon gent		13
	Duntrien	9			9
	Clunglasin	4	Thomas Dillon gent		4
	Clunglasin begg	3			3
	Leiarhu	4			4
	Corry	5			5
Killtrustan	Cnowingallagh	5	James Dowell gent		5
	Corry	4			4
	Letrim	8			8
	Cretagh	8	Charles Ô Donelan gent		8
	Levally	4			4
	Calldragh	4			4
	Lishengrogy	8	Tho : Ledwich gent		8
	Kilvevagh	24	Walter Laly gent		24

Parishes	Townelands	Number of People	Tituladoes Names	Eng	Irish
(*folio* 11). Kil-trustan	Cloonin	9	Jno : Bellew Esq	3	6
	Corskeagh	9			9
	Creaghagh	10	Turlagh Ô Wale gent		10
	Rathmore	14	Jno : Conry gent		14
	Tober	4			4
	Darneard	13			13
	Kildulloge	7	James Nugent & Nicholas Nugent his sonn gents		07
	Carungary	16	Olin Conry gent		16

Principall Irish Names [and] their Number.

Brenan & Branan, 7 ; Ô Bierne, 24 ; Ô Connor, 28 ; McCarroly, 27 ; Daly, 6 ; McDermott, 8 ; Cahane & Cohane, 9 ; Cauanagh, 6 ; Conry, 15 ; McDowell, 13 ; Dillon, 10 ; McEgan, 6 ; Flanagan, 24 ; Farrell & Ferrall, 16 ; Ô Finy, 6 ; Fitzgerrald, 8 ; Gormly & Gormely, 6 ; Hanly, 15 ; Ô Higin & Ô Higgin, 9 ; Kerny, 6 ; Kiernan, 6 ; McKeny & Kenny, 11 ; Kelly, 15 ; Moran, 15 ; Murtagh, 7 ; Nugent, 12 ; Power, 7 ; Plunkett, 6 ; Reylie, 8 ; Smith, 7 ; Verdon, 6.

(*folio* 11 *verso*) Barrony : Roscommon ; Eng, 046 ; Irish, 1974 ; 2020, tott :

(*folio* 12).   **BALLINTOBBER BARRONY**

Parishes	Townelands	Number of People	Tituladoes Names	Eng	Irish
Killalagh	Ballinlagh	036	Feoghra Flin Esq	---	036
	Clooninesglin	006			006
	Clooncalgi	6			6
	Bally bane	16			16
	Cloonefinin	4			4
	Bally garne	29	James Lyach gent		29
	Miltoran	5			5
	Palnalty	17			17
	Gortmecanedle	8			8
	Syarvagh	12			12
	Clooneacrew	5	John Flin gent		5
	Clydagh	8			8
	Kiltulagh	7			7
	Cloonalagh	3			3
Killglass	Moyglass	11		4	7
(*folio* 13).	Giles towne	16			16

Parrishes	Townelands	Number of People	Tituladoes Names	Eng	Irish
	Ballyfiny	8	Allexand.r Hope gent		8
	Begully	7			7
	Bowan	10	Francis Farrall gent		10
	Milleconny	8			8
	Bally morelin	26			26
	Lagan	6			6
	Carowskeing	5			5
	Cargine	14			14
	Ballengillecline	13	Roger Gernon gent		13
	Archenemurley	13	Dermot Hanly gent		13
	Killgarue	14	William Dane gent		14
	Derramas terre	4			4
	Dromnimore	5			5
	Derecle	4			4
	Knockhale	8			8
(folio 14).	Machinach & Ratrinach	13	Thomas Brinan gent		13
	Tower Machinach	7	Bryan Fox gent		7
	Achevanna	10			10
	Lecarrow	3			3
Killgeffin	Clunicashell	27	Garrott Dillon gent		27
	Gortelihan	3	Garrott Dillon gent		3
	Clunshee Tuam and Cawawebonine	32	John Hanly gent, Thomas Terrill Esq, and Christopher Terrill gentleman.		32
	Aghavoryn	18	James Malyan gent		18
	Tuomranill	16	James White gent		16
	Cloonegeragh	11	Patrick Warren gent		11
	Corry	12	Gillernan Hanly gent		12
	Curraghe	15	William Hanly gent		15
	Clogher	12			12
(folio 15).	Shian	6			6
Ros comon	Adsallagh	6			6
	Ballinagowe	2			2
	Lishdorne	7			7
	Caromore	12			12
	Lisbride	12	Gerald Leynes gent		12
	Ballegalde	24			24
	Ballebohane	32			32
	Ballebride	22	Allexand.r Irwing gent	2	20
	Lesagalan	52			52
	Ballinbore	6			6
	Clanmore	6			6
	Clanishert	4			4
	Killerny	2			2
	Carrowree	18	Symon Bomus Esq		18

Parrishes	Townelands	Number of People	Tituladoes Names	Eng	Irish
(*folio* 16). Fuerty	Cloonyne	50	Thomas Louelace Esq	3	47
Killcorrey	Ballanagar	21	Edmond Dillon gent		21
	Killcorey	5			5
	Maghan	27	Patrick Betagh gent		27
	Bellatulcha	27			27
	Tully	5			5
	Killbarry	10			10
	Lacke	15			15
	Ballynegrive	6			6
	Cloonfade	14			14
	Racksikey	12		2	10
	Cloonemore	12			12
Baslick	Drishican	50	Dudley Colelough gent		50
	Lisalwe	65	Thomas Dillon gent		65
	Ballynedolchan	14			14
(*folio* 17).	Evillagh	18			18
	Casselleene	38	James Hill gent	2	36
	Sleuen	17			17
	Lislaghna	15			15
	Rossinn	14			14
	Rafondagh	18			18
	Casheltine	14			14
	Rahardagh	7			7
	Rahardivin	19			19
	Lishmurtagh	18			18
Kilkeevin	Kelmore	7			7
	Clonesuck	21			21
	Clooneraghan	20	Gilternew Flin gent		20
	Ralegg	29		4	25
	Cloonesallagh	31	Dudly Flin gent		31
	Cloonemalice	34			34
(*folio* 18). Killkeevin	Cagher	21		6	15
	Cloonekine	29			29
	Carowdovan	29			29
	Lisleady	20	Mathew Simpson gent	5	15
	Bihagh	62		22	40
	Castlereagh	24			24
Killmore	Charles towne	7	James King Esq	7	—
	Drumclevery	2			2
	Charles towne	8			8
	Cloonawery	4			4
	Laccha	5			5
	Killmore	40	Nathaniell Euanson gent	2	38
	Feraghmore	9			9
	Cloonsellagh	8	Neile Ô Melaghlin gent		8

Parishes	Townelands	Number of People	Tituladoes Names	Eng	Irish
	Rathrovenagh	4			4
	Cartron	10	Edmond McGenis and Glessny McGenis gents		10
(folio 19).	Mulick	4	Thomas Cunegan gent		4
	Killesenoge	5	Daniell McGennis Esq		5
	Row	2	Donnogh Beirn gent		2
	Ballicumin	28			28
	Killbride	10	William Ô Birne gent		10
	Corgollin	10			10
	Carrowmore	10			10
	Knockbreeneen	2			2
	Cloonecouse	6			6
	Dangen	4			4
	Knocknegawnah	12			12
	Ballagh	8			8
Ballintober	Ballintober	56			56
	Cloonekeherny	2			2
	Ballemageher	43	Roger Flin gent		43
(folio 20).	Cleabeg	6			6
	Moyne	8			8
	Rauigg	2			2
	Raneloleigh	10			10
	Knocklaghy	20			20
Cluntoskert	Monyne	20	William Delamar gent	2	18
	Anritibeg	6			6
	Belalege	27			27
	Gortgulla	5	James Veldon gent		5
	Moher	9			9
	Cluntoskert	12	John Farrell gent		12
	Clunadroe	10			10
	Gallagh	10	Ed : Hanly gent		10
Kiltivan	Kiltiuan	13	Thomas Mapother Esq & Richard Mapother gent		13
	Agedriss	13			13
(folio 21). Kil-tiuan	Cloongaher	8			8
	Cloonetenilane	8			8
	New towne	15			15
	Clounshilin	6			6
	Clouncrane	13			13
	Dirinturk	5			5
	Killinvoy	2			2
	Cloonemorly	7		2	5
	Criuiquin	4	John Guidon gent		4
	Dirimacarbery	8			8
	Cloonkeene	19			19

Parrishes	Townelands	Number of People	Tituladoes Names	Eng	Irish
Killbride	Clooneeragh	32			32
	Boyanagh	78			78
	Cooleteige	43			43
	Lower Cooleteige	25			25
	Ballender	24		4	20
(*folio* 22). Kil-bride	Tully	9			9
	Tonergill	33			33
	Derane	33	Mathew Begg gent	4	29
	Carleconnogirrah	6			6
	Kriaghes	36			36
	Karowkile	5			5
	Kinelty	14			14
	Corneshannagh	19			19
	Ramore	9			9
	Cloncorry	8	William Dennish gent		8
	Corresline	8	Teige Donnogher gent		8
	Clonnerry	4			4
	Rathconnor	10			10
	Cashellmoagh	14	Marcus Fitzsymonds gent		14
	Lisgobane	2			2
	Carboe	3			3
	Carucrin	6			6
(*folio* 23). Kil-bride	Clooneirk	4			4
	Dromidafe	1			1
	North Criagh	9			9
	Carowlessiny	3			3
Tarman	Clanmore	2			2
	Ruskhy	2			2
	Clunfada	1			1
	Lack	1			1
	Kilbary	1			1
	Ballmegrine	2			2
Roscomon Towne		94	Robert Bradly Esq, & Rich^d. Dalton gent, Nicholas Fallan, & Richard Giraghty, Marchants.	8	86
Part of Major Tho : Cootes Companie & their wiues	}	56	Richard Izod Ensigne	48	08
Capt Chichesters	Troope	39	Obediah Evanson Leiut	33	06

Principall Irish Names [and their number].

Ô Bierne, 57 ; Bourke, 6 ; Colly, 9 ; Cassy, 6 ; O Connor, 34 ; Connelan, 6 ; McCormack, 9 ; Croghan, 10 ; Duffe, 6 ; McDermott, 14 ; McDonell, 11 ; Dane & Dune, 10 ; Ô Dillon, 14 ; Flanigan, 18 ; Flin, 29 ; Finan & Finane, 9 ; Farrell & Ferrall. 20 ; McGenis, 7 ; O Hanly, 45 ;

Higin & Higgin, 11 ; Kelly, 23 ; Kenedy, 6 ; Ô Melaghlin, 11 ; MacManus, 7 ; Moore, 9 ; Murrey, 8 ;
Moran, 7 ; McTeige, 6 ; McWard, 7.

(*folio* 23 *verso*).   Barony : Ballintobber ; Eng, 160 ; Irish, 2593 ; 2753, tott :

(*folio* 24).   Roscomon County.   **BOYLE BARRONY**

Parrishes	Townelands	Number of People	Tituladoes Names	Eng	Irish
Kilbogan	Keelog	012		—	012
	Kilbreene	012		—	012
	Ballykeeuegan	021		—	021
	Smutternagh	009		—	009
Kilcola	Dunin	19			19
	Knockglass	17			17
	Leackane	7			7
	Rutalin	6			6
	Carrowmongen	4			4
	Tullyboy	13		03	10
	Clogher	13			13
	Knockroe	15			15
	Fass	21			21
	Carrowkeele	9			9
	Grany	11			11
	Carrownegapple	10			10
	Knocknesassog	33			33
(*folio* 25)	Camlin	11			11
	Cloonesaghan	8		2	6
	Cloorey	10			10
	Issersnow	7			7
Killve ½	Cordeighery	4			4
	West Mohiden	11	John Lambert gent	2	9
	Lemgare	12	John Coghlan Esq		12
	Attmongrana	6	Thomas Coghlan gent		6
	Ballevolaghan	3			3
	Gortnecroshy	2			2
	Martry	5			5
	Erblagh	8			8
	Cancly	4	Bryan Mulconry gent		4
	Corbally	5			5
	East Mohiden	14			14
Killconan	Knockrany	8			8
(*folio* 26)	Iron Worke	30		11	19
	Carrownalte	12		2	10
	Tirehowall	4			4
	Derinisky farworke	6			6
	Seltervinny	16			16

Parrishes	Townelands	Number of People	Tituladoes Names	Eng	Irish
	Derevogge fordge	20			20
	Greayth	8			8
	Sorabragan	8			8
	Corgannan	8			8
	Iron Worke	20			20
	Drommore	11			11
	Camagh	11			11
	Coyleagges	9			9
	Tolaghglasse	15			15
Killuemanagh	Callow	17	Robert Druery gent	4	13
	Clunecarow	7			7
(folio 27).	Killuemanagh	3			3
	Creeff	6			6
	Ardmoyle	6			6
Killomode	Croughan	15			15
	Killapoge	26		4	22
	Knockroe	12			12
	Lishidully	12			12
	Bellanamreigh	8			8
	Fenner	2			2
	Lishloghlin	14			14
	Killimoda	9			9
	Collintrine	12			12
	Cartrone	8			8
	Daneclounagh	19			19
	Canboe	11			11
(folio 28). Arde-arny	Carrick	19			19
	Crevist	9			9
	Carrowcashell	6			6
	Carrowmore	16		4	12
	Ardcarne	46			46
	Clunibrine	4			4
	Ardglass	7			7
	Knocknicarry	7			7
	Dorttandarragh	5			5
	Killied	7			7
	Oughterhery	27	William Molloy gent		27
	Cline	7			7
	Aughafinegan	8			8
	Tollyvall	13			13
	Sleuegormaly	9			9
	Rossiny	17			17
	Carrigine	23			23
(folio 29).	Corrobegg	13			13
	Ardlarine and Knockelin	21	Captn Anthony Turner gent	02	19

Parrishes	Townelands	Number of People	Tituladoes Names	Eng	Irish
	Knockvisker	7			7
	Knockidaniell	8			8
	Cloury	5			5
	Crosna	18			18
	Druminy Cormack	8			8
	Slouenbougher	10			10
	Cloonboyher	12			12
Killmakcompsy	Scorrmore	15	Sr Oliuer Tuit Knt & Barronett, Dominick French, & Thomas Bright, gents.	2	13
	Carrowtogher	8			8
	Clineray	12			12
	Corrogh	7			7
	Caldragh	5			5
	Punechaka	7			7
(folio 30). Kill-mackcompsy	Runeradden	11			11
	Carrowcully	4			4
Killuken	Corrotober	25		2	23
	Killuken	9			9
	Mullaghmore	8		2	6
	Skrege	12		2	10
	Legoy	6		2	4
	Castlillinny	9			9
		6			6
	Cnockanhary	15			15
	Croghane	16			16
	Ardmore	11			11
	Knockannma and Tullagh	17		02	15
(folio 31) Kil-lukan	Coredrehitt	5			5
	Cruancas	13			13
	Ballichellin	12			12
Tuamana	Bally clanhugh	13	Will: Tirrell Esq		13
	Tonigane	5			5
	Miry	6			6
	Gortgrasagh	6		6	000
	Avagh Iregain	8			8
	Moigh	10			10
	Annagh Ilanagach	11			11
	Lesty	3			3
	Knocknasana	8			8
	Tulileige	1			1
	Oughterhiry	6			6
(folio 32).	Drumsallagh	10			10
	Osna	02			2

Parrishes	Townelands	Number of People	Tituladoes Names	Eng	Irish
Boyle. Captⁿ Fran & their wiues i	. Kings Foote company } n Boyle Towne	94	Lt Robert Folliott and Ensigne Mathew Curtis gents	89	05
	Boyle Towne	304	Sr John King Knt, John Yeadon gent	53	251
	Grangemore	28			28
	Corbally	27			27
	Grallagh	13			13
	Learne	19			19
	Knockadno begg	13			13
	Knockdow more	04			04
	Irrishe	31			31
	KillM^ckrouc	04			04
(folio 33).	Drumdoe	18			18
	Knockrosse	14			14
	Tanecarine	8			8
	Lislarduca	32			32
	Grange begg	17		2	15
	Knocknoe	18		4	14
	Drome	19	Owen Lloyd Esq	2	17
	Knocknecloy	10			10
	Augh Grange	7		2	5
	Carrownegeuagh	14		2	12
	Brenedrom	18		2	16
Tobohin	Tully artagh	16			16
	Carrownegnuken	22			22
	Clunetowart	23			23
(folio 34). Tobihin	Cauaghsallagh	18			18
	Coletinane	12			12
	Creue	10			10
	Corregell	20			20
	Loghlin	48	Theobald Dillon Esq		48
	Kilcodan	4			4
	Eadon	8			8
	Bally McMurraghy	6		6	
	Feeh	12		4	8
	Lissgoole	4			4
	Leitrim	4			4
	Mullen	4			4
	Taghbohin	12			12
	Ratra	2			2
(folio 35).	Bally Cashell	4			4
	Dunegarr	5			5
	Clunesanmoyle	10	Walter Dauis gent		10
	Sivinane	3	Roger McDermott Esq		3

Principall Irish Names [and] Their Number.

Ô Berne & Ô Birne, 35 ; Ô Brenan & Brennan, 30; Bourke, 6 ; McCallely, 6 ; Ô Connor, 11 ;

McCormack, 8 ; McDermott, 61 ; McDonnogh, 7 ; Ô Flin, 9 ; Ô Flanagan, 7 ; McHugh, 7 ; O Higgin (5), Ô Higgan (3), 8 ; O Kelly, 17 ; McLoghlin, 8 ; Ô Lennaghan, 9 ; MacManus, 8 ; Ô Mulkiran, 8 ; Ô Mullany, 11 ; Ô Moran (5), O Morrane (4), 9 ; McMorrish, 6 ; Ô Regan & Ô Reigan, 11 ; Ô Relly, 6 ; Ô Rory, 6 ; McTeige, 13 ; McWard, 6.

(*folio* 34 *verso*).   Barrony : Boyle ; Eng, 218 ; Irish, 2110 ; 2328, Tott :

(*folio* 36).   **BALLIMOE ½ BARRONY.**

Parrishes	Townelands	Number of People	Tituladoes Names	Eng	Irish
Cloonegormegan	Ballemakcrally	034	Thomas Tyrrell gent	000	034
	Ardlaghan	23		02	21
	Cloonegormegan	21		02	19
	Rathconely	16		04	12
	Ballentorlie	7		02	5
	Carrowdriagh	9	James Barnewell gent		9
	Carrowduffe	21	Thomas Castello Esq		21
	Kiltoltoge	33	Patrick Weldon gent		33
	Carrowbane and Knonemkagh }	18			18
	Clunogormegon	21			21
	Fararagh	13		2	11
	Roomvooth	8			8
Oran	Criue	16			16
	Oran	50			50
(*folio* 37).	Carrownegillod	9			9
	Emblaghmore	21		2	19
	New towne	20			20
	Riuenvaghane	8			8
	Drymill	3			3
	Clooniglelaghane	9			9
	Emlaghbegg	6			6
	Rathmeaeva	3			3
	Ballacagher	12	Richard Gernon gent		12
	Leaghbegg	6		2	4
	Carstono more	10	Antho : Keervan gent		10
	Larragh	13			13
	Sanquah	9			9
	Erstonobegg	9		2	7
	Killire	6			6
	Tobermakee	5			5
(*folio* 38).	Dundermott	2			2
	Cloonimenagh	20			20
	Dunamon	31			31
	Cargons	7			7

Parrishes	Townelands	Number of People	Tituladoes Names	Eng	Irish
Ballenekill	Ilinbaghfodagh	10			10
	Corbally	31			31
	Lyagh more	13			13
	Enlaghglass	16	Nicholas Welsh gent		16

(*folio* 38 *verso*). Barony : Ballimoe ½ ; Eng, o18 ; Irish, 551 ; 569, Tott.

(*folio* 39). **MOYCARNAN ½ BARRONY**

Townelands[1]	Number of People	Tituladoes Names	Eng	Irish
Ballinesloe	036		—	036
Laughill	006		—	006
Ardcarne	17	Daniell Kelly gent		17
Karine	13	Jno : Manyne gent		13
Behagh	28			28
Creagh	12	Owen Kelly gent		12
Drumsillagh	25	Robert Mildrum gent		25
Atiferaie	7	Bryan Kelly gent		7
Viner	2			2
Killinmulruny	15	James Fitzg'r'ld gent		15
Attirory	16	Edward Brabson gent	3	13
Culdiry	6			6
Druoghtagogh	16			16
Cornitepoy	5			5
Tullrisk	23			23
Cluniburrin	28			28
Raghrabegg	12			12
(*folio* 40). Moore	33	Loghlin Kelly gent		33
Dermott	30			30
Raphoky	5			5
Killessill	70			70
Clunerallagh	31	Owen Killy gent		31
Clunefada	17			17
Cullagh	7			7
Felty	7	Jno : Kelly gent		7
Ardighboy	5	William Coghlane gent		5

[1] The *Parishes* column is blank throughout.

Principall Irish Names in these two ½ Barronies [and their Number].

Ô Cahan, 11 ; Dillon, 6 ; Dolane & Dollane, 14 ; Ô Higgin & Ô Higgan, 7 ; Kelly, 32 ; McLoughlin, 5 ; O Teige, 11.

(*folio* 40 *verso*). Barony : Moycarnan ½ ; Eng, oo3 ; Irish, 469 ; 472, Tott.

Parishes	Townelands	Number of People	Tituladoes Names	Eng	Irish
Kiltoome	Mill towne Pass	081	Steeven Fallon & his sonn gent	—	081
	Bellamullallin	019		—	019
	Ballikreggan	12			12
	Gortlussane	8			8
	Hannys and Carromore	12			12
	Barybeg	21			21
	Barymore	19		4	15
	Clyraghlissin	10			10
	Lishgrahan	4			4
	Moyvanan	26			26
		5			5
	Carwinorah	14			14
	Carwindery	13			13
	Carrick	8			8
	Carrwconally	12			12
	— —	12	Murtagh Naghten gent		12
(*folio* 42). Athleig	Athleige	145	Michaell Stanley & Michaell Boyer gents	10	135
	Correbegg and Araghty	59			59
	Knockedagan	14		4	10
	Glanenomer	12			12
	Dirmile	4			4
	Liscoffy	24			24
	Caldragh mor	3			3
	Keylmore	15	Terlagh Bryan gent		15
	Carrowreogh	4			4
	Lissenarin	31		02	29
	Armone	13			13
	Toberkeegh	17			17
	Corrowmore	17			17
		24		08	16
(*folio* 43). Fuerty	Aghegadmore	21		02	19
	Mogh	7		03	4
	Aghegad beg	15			15
	Aghagorr	21			21
	Torromony	12			12
	Tobervady	17	Edmond Ormesby Esq	07	10
	Castlestrange	30		—	30
	Clonyorise	14		04	10
	Carrostellan	17			17
	Ballenturlagh	6	Robert Stanley gent	3	3
	Ballilugg	25		6	19
	Collee	12		2	10
	Collinine	9		—	9

Parishes	Townelands	Number of People	Tituladoes Names	Eng	Irish
	Emlagh	39		5	34
	Lisnebally	12		3	9
	Fuerty Towne	39		9	30
(folio 44).	Castle Coote	30	Cha : Coote Esq	7	23
	Currell	23		2	21
	Moyles	12		4	8
Raharrow	Barincullin	24			24
	Ardrone	21	William Kelly gent		21
	Carrowminah	21			21
	Barnapeak	12			12
	Ranorkelloe	13			13
	Ladkan	29	Keaghda Kelly gent		29
	Killmass	6			6
	Carowkeele	10			10
	Gortnecasagh	20	Edmond Coyle gent		20
	Ballagh	43			43
Killmyhan	Dorttereny	45	John Ferrall gent		45
	Killeagh	7			7
(folio 45).	Togherfin	29			29
	Coolefoble	15			15
	Corry	19	Jno Talbott Esq & his sonn gent		19
	Tobberreog	9		06	3
	Killcoish	54			54
	Moate	38	Edward Crofton Esq & Jno Crofton gent	2	36
	Tulleroe	5			5
	Ballimurry	20			20
	Glannatober	7	James Kelly gent		7
	Carrownymadry	8			8
	Knockbryangarue	14		4	10
	Carginy	9			9
		23			23
(folio 46). Teagboy	Cloghan	30	Edmond Donelan Esq		30
	Teagboy	25			25
	Turrick	34	Edmond Smarte gent	03	31
	Ballinavay	18			18
	Clonagh	4			4
	Carowntheriffe	23	Roger Fallon gent		23
	Farremore	10	William Lea gent		10
	Carrowmore	27	Geo : Plunket gent		27
	Lishfooke	10		02	08
	Tarpan more	2			2
	— — —	8			8
Disert	Milltowne Fallon	53	Law : Dowdall Esq		53
	Savananan	12			12

Parrishes	Townelands	Number of People	Tituladoes Names	Eng	Irish
(*folio* 47).	Disert	04			04
	Balliglass	15			15
	Fivaghbegg	8			8
	Fivaghmore	18			18
	Dirricahell	4			4
	Cronyne	19			19
	— — —	20			20
St Johns	St Johns	67	Allin Pouey Esq	03	64
	Carowpadin	45	Jno Dillon gent		45
	Killincartan	30			30
	Creganclery	21	Donogh Kelly gent		21
	Calldragh	7	Hugh Kelly gent		7
	Lishphelim	28		4	24
	Ballinasegort	17			17
	Calldercuffan	16			16
(*folio* 48).	Benmuck	11			11
	Cargin more	12			12
	Ballibrogan	17			17
	Caher	3			3
	Knocka Connor	33		4	29
	Gallibegg	12			12
	Tobiedon	2			2
Killinvoy	Killinvoy	18			18
	Knockroghery	33			33
	Galy	31			31
	Galy in Knockroghery	9			9
	Carowdrishagh	20			20
	Killoges	19			19
	Skerrigge	12			12
(*folio* 49)	Ballinloghan	9			9
	Corbally	8			8
	Balliglass	11			11
	Lishgarue	7			7
	Killoye	20	Jon : Hinde gent	04	16
	Lishdallon	18			18
	Moylitteragh	17			17
	ye other Moylitteragh	14			14
	Cornemart	8			8
St Peters	Bellnerumly	18	Jno Glass gent & Hubert Bryne gent		18
	Cloonikilly	6			6
	Rooscagh	16			16
	— — —	15			15
Caina	Cornlee	13	William Fallon Esq		13
(*fol.* 50). Cama	New towne	20			20
	Ardmollen	19	Thomas Carr gent	2	17

Parrishes	Townelands	Number of People	Tituladoes Names	Eng	Irish
	Kilclare	26			26
	Caraughboy	25		2	23
	Coulegary	26			26
	Eskerbane	17			17
	Killereeny	7			7
	Lisnafeene	6			6
	Sirananan	6			6
	Carrick	12			12
	Garryenforte	11			11
	Ballylien	9			9
	Liskorr	8			8
	Lismoyle	3			3
	Lisclogh	10			10
	Grange	18	Antho Lister gent	3	15
(folio 51).	Cornagee	39	Donnogh Keogh gent		39
	Corryduffe	21		2	19
	Corrigarrow	12	Jno : Osbaldes gent		12
	Corrilea	9			9
	Culenegeere	28			28
		23			23
Teaghsrara	Attyknockan	33			33
	Funsinnagh	21			21
	Cloone McCegga	22			22
	Kellnony	10			10
	Clooneingly	13			13
	Derryinlorge	7			7
	Dundermott	18	Morish Kavanagh gent		18
	Dubbearny	12		03	09
(folio 52).	Carroward begg	22			22
	Cloghnasead	9			9
	Coolederry	11			11
	Correla	13			13
	Lisduffe	4			4
	Cloonelaghnan	10			10
	Corcotty	12			12
	Carrowentleay	30			30
	Funsinnagh	6			6
	Shangary	16			16
	Cornagatty	6			6
	Cloondaratt	10	Sr Harry Talbott Knt and Theobald Dillon Esq		10
Teage McConell	Killmore	7			7
	Ancoran	5			5
(folio 53). Teagh McConell	Culenecaldry	13			13
	Isker	8			8
	Castlesamson	10			10

Parishes	Townelands	Number of People	Tituladoes Names	Eng	Irish
	Tober McLoghlin	24	Peter Keogh & Hugh Keogh gents		24
	Taunaugh	9	Marcus Carvile gent	02	7
	Skeaghvally	6			6
	Teag McConell	9	Thomas Naghtenn gent		9
	Pte of Castle Samson	16			16
	Knocke	30	Jno : Keogh gent		30
	Skeaghvally	14	Hugh Keogh gent		14
	Clunadron	9			9
	Gorrowkeeren	16			16
	Killegtan	27	Christopher Nugent and Oliuer Dalton gents		27
	Clunebigny	33	Bernard Talbott gent		33
(folio 54). Teag McConell	Clounadrones	10			10
	Cloonaughy	21			21
	Clunbigny	7	Sr Robert Talbot Knt & Baront		7
Drum	Cloonearke	12			12
	Creggan	8			8
	Cornhooly	10			10
	Moynure	6			6
	Cariganny	5			5
	Lisdollor	6	Richard Moore gent		6
	Kill Mc Colme	10			10
	Gortneclay	21	Farnagh Naghten gent		21
	Cranagh	10			10
	Shanvoy	7			7
	Criagh	6			6
	Taghduffe	6	Henry Naghten gent		6
(folio 55).	Curraghlin	13			13
	Cloonrulagh	11			11
	Bealrehy	6			6
	Drum	11			11
	Ardkinan	13			13
	——	14	Edward Read & Xtopher Newton gents	06	08

Principall Irish Names [and] their Number.   The Seruants Names in this Barrony are not set down.

Bryan, 11 ; Birne, 18 ; Brehan, 9 ; Coyle, 7 ; Coffy, 6 ; Duffe, 16 ; Dalton, 6 ; McDowell & McDaniell, 19 ; Donelan, 6 ; Dolan, 11 ; Dunily, 8 ; Dunegan, 7 ; Fallon, 40 ; Flanagan, 6 ; Ferrall, 6 ; Finy & Finny, 7 ; Glenan, 7 ; Gaffey, 8 ; McGattely, 8 ; Galvan, 7 ; McGraghty & McGiraghty, 10 ; McGrorke, 12 ; McGlinn, 7 ; Ô Hevin & Ô Havin, 7 ; Hanin, 9 ; Hely, 6 ; Harny, 9 ; Killin, 6 ; Kelly, 72 ; McKigan, 6 ; Keny & Kenny, 6 ; McKeogh, 23 ; Kerelly, 10 ; Lynch, 6 ; O Lyne, 6 ; Ô Loghnan, 7 ; Lenan, 8 ; McLoghlin, 8 ; Ô Morey & Murry, 32 ; O Moran, 13 ; Mulry, 9; Naghten, 41 ; Rory, 6 ; McShane, 8 ; McTeige, 7 ; Tully, 7 ; McWard, 10 ; Welsh, 7 ; McWilliam, 9.

(folio 55 verso). Barrony : Athlone ; Eng, 160 ; Irish, 3466 ; 3626, tott :

(folio 56). **ATHLONE BORROUGH**

Westmeath County, Athlone Borrough	Number of People	Tituladoes Names	Eng	Irish.
Within ye Borrough of Athlone	185	William Handcocke, Walter Staylehill, & Oliuer Jones, Esqrs ; Barnaby Madden, William Slade, William Hill, Walter Kelly, Robert Cliffe, John Ellice, Henry Morsh, & John Mills, gents.	75	110
Capt Knights company & their Wiues	053	Phillip Bronthropt L^t, and George Glouer Ensigne.	048	005
Capt Fenwickes company and their Wiues	026		019	007
Capt Meredithes company and their Wiues	004		004	—
Capt Longs company and their Wiues	031	Henry Cooke L^t, and James Robinson Ensigne.	029	002
Capt Mollinenxis men & their Wiues	003			003
Capt Askes troope & their Wiues	022		022	—

(folio 57). **ATHLONE BORROUGH** | **ROSCOMON COUNTY**

Westmeath County, Athlone Borrough	Number of People	Tituladoes Names	Eng	Irish.
Within ye Borrough	201		081	120
Out of ye West Gate of Athlone	008		—	008
In the West liberties Bellagh	038		—	038
Collonomanagh	014		—	014
Capt Mullinenxes Troop & their Wiues	018		010	008
Capt Chicesters Troope pt & their Wiues	002		002	—
Capt Longs company and their Wiues	034		029	005
Capt Fenwickes company and their Wiues	031	William Moulton Ensigne	029	002
Capt Knights company and their Wiues	044		036	008
Capt Meredith company and their Wiues	015		013	002
Capt Askes troope and their Wiues	046		040	006
(folio 58). Out of ye East Gate of Athlone	121		006	115
Capt Knights company and their Wiues	006		004	002
The East Liberties of Gorry Castle	018	Enoch Golborne gent	005	013
Kilm^cugh and Banovally	025	William Cloppam gent	012	013
Cornemadie	016		—	016
Souldiers belonging to Capt Knight and their wiues	006		006	—
Cornemagh	006	John Noble gent	002	004
Lisnavolone	004		—	004
Out of the North Gate of Athlone	003		—	003
Officers, Souldiers Wiues and seruants belonging to the Castle of Athlone	095	Richard St George Esq Capt, Arthur St George his sonn L^t, Henry St George his sonn Ensigne.	072	023

2 P

Principall Names [and] their Number
    Bryen, 8 ; Coffie, 5 ; Dillon, 5 ; Griffith, 5 ; Kelly, 5 ; Murrey, 5 ; Moran, 5 ; Smith, 10 ;
Toole, 4 ; Ô Teige, 4 ; Ward, 4 ; Whyte, 4.

(*folio* 58 *verso*).   Athlone Borrough : Eng, 544 ; Irish, 531 ; 1075, tott.

Barronies	Pages	Eng	Irish	Total of Eng & Ir
Roscommon	11	0046	1974	2020
Ballintobber	23	0160	2593	2753
Boyle	34	0218	2110	2328
Ballimoe ½	38	0018	0551	569
Moycarnan ½	40	0003	0469	472
Athlone	55	0160	3466	3626
Athlone Borrough	58	0544	0531	1075
Totall		1149	11694	12843
		544	531	1175
County		605	11163	11768
			605	
			11768	

SLEGOE COUNTY
6877

(*folio* 1).   County of Slegoe

BARONY OF CARBRY

Parishes	Townelands	Number of People	Tituladoes Names	Eng	Irish
	Sligoe Towne	488	Humphry Booth gent, Rowland Thomas gent, Henry Crafford gent.	130	358
Aghamlish	Ballyscannell	008		002	006
	Lislarry	003		—	003
	Shrehidagh	13			13
	Grange	27	Thomas Soden gent	2	25
	Moniduallt	2			2
	Carne	7		2	5
	Cliffney	9			9
	Cryickeele	16			16
	Creenimore	9			9
	Mullagmore	6			6
	Bunduff	24			24
	Mardneglasse	7			7
	Killsard	21			21
(*folio* 2).	Derilihan	16			16
	Cloonergo	4			4
	Drinnfada	6			6
	Inismores	3	Phillipp Sulevane gent		3
Drumclyffe	Dunawna	17			17
	Ballyconnell	8			8
	Ballyknocke	10			10
	Dunfuard	10		4	6
	Ballynagallagh	9			9
	The Rosses	28		2	26
	Ballytemple	10			10
	Ardtermon, and Ballymolury }	023	Charles Collis Esq	—	023
	Cloandelrar	31		6	25
	Coille Ruala	8			8
	Rahaberny	18			18
	Dunally	20			20
(*folio* 3). Drumcliffe	Gortnagrelly	7			7
	Glann	13			13
	Cloonin	6			6
	Court and Tinid	17	Roger Parke gent	2	15
	Drumcliffe	17		4	13
	Ballygillgan	13			13
	Culadruman	6			6
	Castle gavan	8			8
	Monananen	12			12
	Lisnanorus	6			6
	Aghagan	3			3

Parishes	Townelands	Number of People	Tituladoes Names	Eng	Irish
(folio 4).	Bradecolline	55	Thomas Gryffith gent	4	51
	Ballencarthy	24		2	22
	Kantogher	9		—	9
	Mayhergillernew	6		2	4
	Lishadoill	23			23
	Cargin	20	Anthony Ormsby gent	2	18
	Ballintennan	11		2	9
	Lismarkie	16		6	10
	Calgagh	12		2	10
	Faghta qr	12			12
	Shanoon oghter	5		2	3
	Shanoone Iegher	6	Thomas Osborne gent	2	4
	Maghercarncass	16		7	09
	Anagh	214	William Tod gent, Henry Nicholson gent, Thomas Ormsby gent, Manus Lenaghan gent.	26	188

Principall Irish Names [and] their Numb[er].

Bryan, 7 ; O Conor, 17 ; Canughan, 5 ; McDonogh, 6 ; Finy, 11 ; Gillgam, 6 ; Gillin & Gillan, 9 ; McGuan, 11 ; McGwyre, 4 ; Gillagher, 8 ; McGara, 4 ; Gillconnell, 6 ; O Hart, 34 ; O Higgin, 5 ; Kelly, 10 ; Martin, 7.

(folio 4 verso).   Barony : Carbry ; Eng, 211 ; Irish, 1187 ; 1394, Totall.

(folio 5).   **BAR[ONY] OF LEYNIE**

Parishes	Townlands	Numb of People	Tituladoes Names	Eng	Irish
Aghonry	Belary	062	Capt Edmond Wood gent	006	056
	Moineagh	016		004	012
	Coillcaver	008		—	008
	Cloonleaucoill	19			19
	Curryunnane	8			8
	Rahmagorra	19			19
	Rahscanlane	18			18
	Ballencurry	11			11
	Corry and Garyvaine	26			26
	Cashall	35			35

Parishes	Townelands	Numb of People	Tituladoes Names	Eng	Irish
	Dougharne	37			37
	Maclagha	22			22
	Magheranoir	17	Edward Pole gent	2	15
	Ougham	19		3	16
	Aghonry	14			14
	Muckalta	028		—	028
(folio 6).	Carowcarragh	25			25
	Tully Hugh	18	Thomas Rosevill gent	4	14
	Congall	14			14
	Coorte Abby	19			19
	Cashall	8			8
	Carowenedin	10		1	9
	Cloonderar	7			7
	Carowna Crivy	16			16
	Carowcoillue	6			6
	Cloonbanue	14			14
	Leatrim	12			12
	Dromore	10			10
	Carowreagh	26			26
	Molane	28			28
	Talyvelly	13			13
	Sessucomane	14			14
	Sessugarry	19			19
(folio 7).	Sessumas	62		4	58
Kill McTeige	Bennana	22			22
	Colrecoile	12			12
	Binagh	11			11
	Tullanaglogg	12			12
	Gorterslin	13			13
	Knockbreak	16			16
	Cladagh	20			20
	Kill McTeige	32			32
	Tullamoy	4			4
	Kincolly	6			6
	Glenvee	22			22
	Carowreagh	6			6
	Clongunagh	007		—	007
	Castle-caragh	17			17
	Drimine	9			9
	Rooes	21		6	15
Killvarnett	Templehouse	12			12
(folio 8).	Carrowantawa	8		4	4
	Munuossane	8			8
	Plaragh	16			16
	Munuossane	9		2	7
	Anaghmore	7		0	7

Parishes	Townelands	Numb of People	Tituladoes Names	Eng	Irish
	Edernin	11		0	11
	Finlogh	4		2	2
	Anaghbeg	9			9
	Adoreeoghtir	11			11
	Killvarnett	8			8
	Ragraine	4			4
Ballyassadore half parish	Kellylyny	15			15
	Kearownagiragh	19		11	8
	Coanuy	8		4	4
	Aby Towne	16		4	12
	Cortawnagh	8		—	8
	Killnamanagh	23		7	16
Vide page 9	Killinbridge	9			9
(folio 9). Ballyassa-dore half parish	Killinbridge again	5			5
	Billy	16		2	14
	Lognamakin	23		3	20
	Ballyasadore	13		3	10
	Dromdirig	9		4	5

Principall Irish Names [and] their Number.

O Brenane, 17 ; Brenagh, 8 ; Bourke, 6 ; Conellan, 6 ; Corkan, 6 ; Conelly, 6 ; McDonell, 5 ; O Duhy, 5 ; McDonogh, 4 ; Dogherty, 7 ; McEuchae, 8 ; O Finegane, 5 ; O Fahy & Farihy, 6 ; McGwyre, 6 ; Gallaghur, 40 ; Hara & Ô Hara, 15 ; O Higgin, 11 ; McHenry, 5 ; Kelly, 8 ; McLenany, 9 ; O Mullinihilly, 7 ; McManus, 6 ; McMurey, 5 ; Mullarky, 5 ; Roney & Reyney, 8 ; McSwyne, 7 ; McStayne, 8 ; McTeire, 5.

(folio 9 verso).   Barony Leynie ; Eng, 076 ; Irish, 1105 , 1181, Totall.

(folio 10).   **BARONY OF CORRENN**

Parishes	Townelands	Numb of People	Tituladoes Names	Eng	Irish
Imlaghfada	Lishananymore	012		—	012
	Cloonagun	006		004	002
	Emlafadd	004		—	004
	Corhubber	9		3	6
	Cargagh	40		6	34
	Ballymote	112	William Webb Esq	14	98
	Dorin	8			8

Parishes	Townelands	Numb of People	Tituladoes Namos	Eng	Irish
	Ardnaglasse	13			13
	Cloonamanagh	12			12
	Clonyne	6			6
	Carownacloode	24			24
	Rathdowney	28	Francis King Esq	5	23
	Bally-Brenan	24			24
	Ardconnell	10			10
	Portinohy	15		—	15
	Emla Naghtin	10		—	10
Killturrow	Ballyfay	018		00	018
	Knockaylor	006		—	006
(folio 11).	Rabane	8			8
	Killturrow	13			13
	Ogham	15			15
	Ballindow	15			15
Clooneoghill	Bunanadan	30	Timothy Howes gent	4	26
	Ballinvally	19			19
	Collere	17			17
	Clooneoghill	13			13
	Climemeahan	8			8
	Climemeahan againe	6		4	2
	Ballinglogh	13			13
	Carewreagh	7			7
	Knocanurhar	14			14
	Lislea	2			2
Killoshallny	Balenspur	13		6	7
	Ballylonaghan	13	Richard Meredith gent	6	7
	Ballintrohan	13			13
(folio 12).	Runelaghta	11			11
	Killow-shalway	8			8
	Clune Cuny	6			6
	Clunagh	6			6
	Cloonebunagh	12			12
	Clunene	5			5
	Thawnaghmore	3			3
	Collnehary	4			4
Drumratt		14			14
	Rathmolin	10			10
	Knockgrane	9		000	9
	Ardlaherty	3			3
	Cloonenacladry	10			10
	Liscoway	011		003	008
	Clunesanbaly	20			20
	Knockbrack	20			20
Killmurran	Kinchium	20	John Duke gent John Geale gent	6	14

Parishes	Townelands	Numb of People	Tituladoes Names	Eng	Irish
(*folio* 13).	Cnochmonagh	13	Donell Conellane gent		13
	Cloonelargo	8	John Clifford gent	2	6
	Durly	16	Edward Tibb gent	2	14
	Drumfin	4			4
	Ardrea	4	Henry Bierast gent	2	2
	Lacahaky	4			4
	Thomune	10			10
	Killmurin	9			9
	Clunenegallell	14	Robert Duke gent		14
	Dunemigin	16	John Houlder gent	2	14
Tumour	Levally	24			24
	Ballinscaruagh	13		2	11
	Drumnegrangy	40			40
	Thumore	8		2	6
	Roseribb	38		2	36
	Cnockloch	6	Robert King gent	1	5
	Templevany	68			68
	Carowreagh	15			15
	Dloonecahu	8			8
	Lorga	8			8
	Thrinemore	12			12
	Morhy	21			21

Principall Irish Names & their Number.

Brenane, 12 ; O Cunane, 5 ; Conellan, 5 ; Connor, 5 ; McDonogh, 30 ; O Dacy, 5 ; McDier, 5 ; O Fluen, 10 ; Gillelorin, 7 ; McGilltrich, 8 ; O Gara, 6 ; O Heiver, 5 ; O Horchoy, 9 ; O Healy, 13 ; O Kerin, 6 ; Mullronifin, 16 ; McSwyne, 6 ; O Scanlane, 19 ; Trumble, 8 ; Tanist, 6.

(*folio* 13 *verso*).   Barony : Corren ; Eng, 076 ; Irish, 1031 ; 1107, Totall.

(*folio* 14).   **HALFE BAR. OF .CULAVIN**

Parishes	Townlands	Numb of People	Tituladoes Names	Eng	Irish
Killaragh	Rossmoyle	019		—	019
	Lesgalan	031		—	031
	Sexifind	71			71
Killfry	Killfry	16			16
	Cloonlehkeene	31			31

Parishes	Townlands	Numb of People	Tituladoes Names	Eng	Irish
	Ratharmon	15			15
	Carownorclare	5			5
	Ardsorine	7			7
	Killaragh	9	Henry Tifford gent		9
	Clogher	8			8
	Fawnymuckelagh	23			23
	Moygara	38			38
	Mullaghroe	34			34

BARONY OF TIRERAGH

(folio 15).

Parishes	Townlands	Numb of People	Tituladoes Names	Eng	Irish
Castleconnor	Castle Connor and Newtowne	076	John Nicholson gent	010	066
	Killanly	023		003	020
	Carne	015		—	015
	Scormore	37	Lewis Wingfield Esq	2	35
	Carownorlaire	4			4
	Carowcardin	23			23
	Ballevoheny	11			11
	Ballyfinane	19			19
	Ballymonine	23			23
	Cottells towne	57		8	49
	Arnery	18			18
	Browhy	17			17
	Qugumanger	4			4
	Qugunaleike	17			17
	South Cromley	14			14
(folio 16).	North Cromley	15		2	13
	Qugunasher	8			8
Templeboy	Graingebegg	29			29
	Ballyarish	8			8
	Gariduff	38	Christopher Armstrong gent	2	36
	Corraghmore	22			22
	Graingemore	14	Nicholas Rutledge gent		14
	Doneghentrae	13		4	9
	Donechohy	56		13	43
	Aghres	12		5	7
	Templeboy Dunanalt	18			18
Dromard	Longford	19	Henry Craston gent		19
	Drumard	28		000	28
	Clonagh	11			11
	Carow McCarrick	17			17
	Tonregoe	34	John Irving gent	4	30
(folio 17).	Lagbane	24	Edward Erving		24
	Bunany	42		2	40

Parishes	Townlands	Numb of People	Tituladoes Names	Eng	Irish
	Mularee	012		—	012
	Faren Iharpy	22			22
	Dunflyn	8			8
	Larragh	18			18
Skreem	Ardneglass	60	Lewis Jones Esq Jeremy Jones Gent	7	53
	Carowcashell	35			35
	Carowen loghane	10			10
	Carowentihane	10		2	8
	Carowne-Caldny	6			6
	Carow Ioteryne	4		2	2
	Drumnegole	7			7
	Skreene	25			25
Killglass	Eskerowne	31			31
	Leackantleavy	17			17
(folio 18).	Cloonederavally	8			8
	Leackan McHerbisi	26	Thomas Wood gent	7	19
	Polikimy	8	John Moore gent	—	8
	Cabbragh	11		2	9
	Leffony	16		5	11
	Leah-Vale, Nedyne and Killglass }	25			25
	Carewcaller	21			21
	Coyllin	25			25
Kill McSalgan	Duneile	38	John Burke gent		38
	Dowmeyckine	18	Robert Hylla gent		18
	Dunowla	8			8
	Carowruish	29	William Edwards gent	2	27
	Carow mabline and Balle McGillchrisi }	19	John Irwin gent	3	16
	Leah-Carow	25			25
	Kean Conally	031		----	031
(folio 19). Eskagh	Rachly	43	William Ormsby gent		43
	Fynidy	3	William Boswell gent	1	2
	Lissaghan	10			10
	Rosly	17	James Ormsby gent		17
	Killyn	21	George Ormsby gent		21
	Coogylaghlin	16			16
	Castletowne	31			31
	Ballyvony	15			15

Principall Irish Names & their Numb[er] in this Barony & halfe Barony of Culavin.

Albonagh, 5 ; Bourke, 15 ; Beolan, 14 ; O Connor, 7 ; Cassey, 8 ; Conellan, 13 ; Clery, 6 ; Dowde, 17 ; Dowda, 7 ; McDonogh, 9 ; McDermott, 5 ; Dunegan, 6 ; McDonell &c, 14 ; Flanagan, 9 ; Ferbishy, 10 ; McGillaghlen, 6 ; Geraghty, 6 ; O Gara &c, 14 ; Helly, 6 ; Hanraghan, 6 ; O Hara, 6 ; O Hart, 9 ; Kelly, 15 ; Loghlin, 6 ; McMurey, 6 ; Mollany, 6.

(folio 19 verso).   Barony : Tyreragh ; Eng, 86 ; Irish, 1409 ; 1495, Totall.

(folio 20). **BARONY OF TIRERILL**[1]

Parishes	Townlands	Number of People	Tituladoes Names	Eng	Irish
Achanagh	Belanafad	032	Henry Hughs gent	009	023
	Bally mullany	010		—	010
	Mullaghfearna	4			4
	Carricknehorna	22			22
	Ballyhely	16			16
	Drumdony	004		—	004
	Carow Keel	4			4
	Claghog	18			18
	Souldiers and their wifes in Belanafad	24		11	13
Drumcolan	Brickliew	45	Edward Nicholson gent	9	36
	Coolskeagh	7			7
Kill McCulan	Coillmore	13			13
	Coredeynce	6			6
	Cleavry	12			12
	Drumraine	13			13
(folio 21).	Lisbrislean	006		000	006
	Cloonine	007		—	007
	Drumcolam, and Killmacolane Parish				
	Lisconay	18	William Mortimor gent	2	16
Drumcolum & Killmacollane	Cnockanarva	4	Ralph Carter gent	4	—
	Cloghfin	8	John Fergusson gent	2	6
	Clooninclagh	9			9
	Ballyderaowne	18	Charles Cartwright gent	2	16
	Carowsparanagh	9			9
	Achculback	11			11
	Cnockro	7	Archy Naper gent	2	5
	Drumleaghin	9			9
	Coilly	14			14
	Drumvicoill	4			4
	Anaghcarry	10			10
	Drumcolum	3			03
	Ardvarnagh	16			16
(folio 22).	Carowreagh	22			22
	Ross	19			19
	Coiltelacha	008		—	008
	Drumshehin	11			11
	Anagh	4			4
Ballissadara	Ballissadara Parish				
	Cnockbegg	25		5	20
	Killinbridge	39		14	25
	Cooloony Castle	37	Richard Coote Esq	10	27

[1] *Tireill,* folios 21–24.

Parishes	Townelands	Number of People	Tituladoes Names	Eng	Irish
	Clooncorra	19			19
	Balleneboll	19			19
	Cnockmolin	19			19
	Carrickbeanaghan	24	Morgan Farrell gent		24
	Lissrunty	6	John Perchy gent	2	4
	Cloonmahin	15			15
	Toburscanamnane	4		2	2
	Marckrea	17	Edward Cooper gent	3	14
(*folio* 23). Ballysadora	Rathgrany	06			6
	Ballissadar	23			23
Killmatrahny	Givagh	27	Henry Ellis gent		27
	Sraduff	10			10
	Tulanure	8			8
	Balinashia	9			9
	Killkeire	21			21
	Ballinlog	12			12
	Derinclare	8			8
	Ballenay	14			14
	Drumbeg	12			12
	Coolmurly	6			6
	Kill M\(^c\)Trany	14			14
	Killamoy	28			28
Killwogoone	Ballindoone	11			11
	Anagh, and Knock-glass	13			13
	Killwogoone	012		—	012
	Ballaghabo	17			17
(*folio* 24). Shancogh	Shancogh P'ish				
	Carownaquillo	6			6
	Darghny	15			15
	Umarero	10			10
	Carowmore	20			20
	Shancogh	9			9
	Cabragh	9			9
	Gorworck	7			7
Bally somoghan	Gidlane	10			10
	Drumnye	15			15
	Largan	13			13
	Carownuinn	7		4	3
	Knocknagey	18			18
	Lehbully	10			10
	Drumeigh	6			6
	Lowally	8			8
Killrasse	Castleloghdergan	104	Thomas Croston Esq	6	98
	Tobernany	200		2	198

Principall Irish Names & their Number.

McAwly, 10 ; McBrehuny, 15 ; O Benaghan, 7 ; Conillan, 18 ; Connor, 6 ; McDermott, 8 ; McDermott roe, 10 ; McDonogh, 37 ; Ferall, 8 ; O Feeny, 6 ; Flyn, 10 ; Gauna, 9 ; Guan & Gowen, 9 ; O Higgin &c, 13 ; O Hely, 14 ; O Hart, 10 ; Kelly, 11 ; O Keoyne &c, 9 ; O Kerin, 5 ; McLoghlin, 15 ; McMulronifin, 5 ; O Molleany, 12 ; McMorey, 14 ; Milegan, 5 ; O Scanlane, 5 ; McTeige, 5.

(*folio* 24 *verso*). The Number of People in the Barony of Tyrerell : Eng, 089 ; Irish, 1300 ; Totall Eng & Irish, 1389.

(*folio* 23 *verso*). The Number of People in the County of Slegoe and in each Barony.

Baronyes	Page	Eng	Irish	Totall of Eng & Irish
Carbery	4	0211	1187	1398
Leynie	9	0076	1105	1181
Corren	13	0076	1031	1107
Calavin halfe Bar	14	0000	0307	0307
Tireragh	19	0086	1409	1495
Tirerell	24	0089	1300	1389
Totall		538	6339	6877

APPENDIX

THE POLL-MONEY ORDINANCES OF 1660 and 1661.

The volume bearing the Press-mark G 4.3.38 in Marsh's Library is a miscellaneous collection of printed Ordinances covering, with one exception, the period 1654–1661 in Irish history. The full list of titles is given below. The Poll-Money Ordinances here printed form the second and third items of the collection. For a discussion of their possible connection with the 1659 Census see Page .ii. of Introduction. They are now printed with the permission of the Governors of the Library. My warmest thanks are due to the Librarian, Mr. Newport B. White, M.A., who allowed himself to be put to no small amount of personal inconvenience in order that I could be enabled to complete the transcript in the limited time at my disposal.

LIST OF CONTENTS OF VOLUME G 4.3.38, MARSH'S LIBRARY, DUBLIN

1. A Declaration for the Payment of Custom and Excize. By the Commissioners of the Common-wealth of England, for the Affairs of Ireland. (Dublin 1654.)

2. An Ordinance for the speedy raising of Moneys towards the Supply of the Army : and for defraying of other Publick Charges. April the 24. 1660. By the General Convention of Ireland. (Dublin 1660.)

3. An Ordinance for the speedy raising of Moneys for his Majesties Service. March the 1. 1660 [=1661]. (Dublin 1660 [=1661].)

4. A declaration and commission for the Assessment of twelve thousand Pounds by the Month ; For the six ensuing Months, (viz.) from the 24th of September 1656, to the 24th day of March following. (Dublin 1656.)

4 (a). *Duplicate of* 4.

5. An Assessment for Ireland for Six Months, at thirteen thousand pounds per Month ; Commencing the 24th of June 1657, and determining the 24th of December inclusive following. (Dublin 1657.)

6. A declaration and commission for three months Assesment, of Ten thousand Pounds by the Month ; Beginning the 12th of January 1655, [=1656] and ending the 12 of April following. (Dublin 1655.)

7. A declaration of the Lord Deputy & Council, for removing and preventing of some mistakes in Government in Ireland. (Dublin 1655.)

8. An order and declaration of His Highness and the Council, for an Assessment of sixty thousand pounds *per mensem*, for six moneths, from the five and twentieth day of December, 1656. (London 1656.) [*This Item relates to England only.*]

9. An Assesment for Ireland for three months ; at ten thousand pounds by the month. Commencing the 16th day of October, 1654, & Determining the 7th of January following. (Dublin 1654.)

9 (a) *Duplicate of* 9.

10. An Assesment for Ireland, for six months. At nine thousand pounds by the month, commencing the 24th day of March 1658 [=1659] and determining the 24th of September 1659. (Dublin 1658 [=1659].)

10 (a). *Duplicate of* 10.

11. An Act of Assesment. Saturday, June 18, 1659. (Dublin 1659.)

11 (a), 11 (b), 11 (c). *Duplicates of* 11.

1—[POLL-MONEY ORDINANCE OF 1660].

(*Title page*)   AN/ORDIÑANCE/For the speedy raising of/Moneys towards the Supply of the,/ARMY :/and for defraying of other/PUBLICK CHARGES./April the 24. 1660./By the General Convention of Ireland./ORdered, that this Ordinance be forthwith Printed and/Published./Signed by Order,/Ma. Barry Clerk of the General/Convention of Ireland./DUBLIN,/Printed by William Bladen, Anno Dom. 1660/.

(*Page* 1)   AN ORDINANCE For the speedy raising of Moneys towards the Supply of the Army, and for defraying of other publick charges.

The General Convention of *Ireland* taking into their consideration the very great vexations and oppressions which have been occasioned to the people of this Realm, by the illegal and unequal raising, taxing, and leavying of publick Assessments (commonly called Contributions) of late laid on them, contrary to the fundamental Laws of this Realm, and to the usual and accustomed manner for raising of moneys heretofore upon necessary occasions by Parliament in *Ireland* : Do declare, and it is hereby declared by this Convention, that it is and hath been the ancient and undoubted right of the subjects of this Realm that no Subsidie, Custom, Impost, or other charge whatsoever, can or may be laid on them without their consent in Parliament in this Realm ; Nevertheless, this Convention taking into consideration the great necessity of providing of moneys for defraying of the publick charge, and particularly towards the supply of the Army, without which, they will be necessitated to fall upon Free-quarter, and other irregular ways of helping themselves, which may be destructive to the people, and considering that it is most equal that all who partake of the benefit of protection and preservation should contribute to, and bear a part of that burthen

(*Page* 2)   which as things now/stand, cannot be otherwise imposed upon them then by their respresentatives in this Convention assembled. This Convention doth therefore for the reasons aforesaid, ordain, and be it ordained by this Convention and the authority thereof, that all and every person and persons of the several rancks and degrees hereafter mentioned, shall pay the several and respective sums of money particularly in this Ordinance set down and appointed. (*viz.*)

That every person above the age of fifteen years, of either sex, of what degree or quality soever, under the degree or quality of a Yeoman, or Farmer or Yeoman, or Farmers wife, or widdow shall pay twelve pence.

That every other person of either sex, above fifteen years of age, of what degree or quality soever, under the degree or quality of a Gentleman or Gentlewoman, shall pay two shillings.

That every other person of either sex, above fifteen years of age, of what degree or quality soever, under the degree or quality of an Esquire or an Esquires wife or widow shall pay four shillings.

That every other person of either sex, above fifteen years of age, of what degree or quality soever, under the degree or quality of a Knight, or Knights wife or widow, shall pay ten shillings.

That every other person of either sex, above the age of fifteen years, of what degree of quality soever, under the degree or quality of a Baronet, or Baronets wife or widow, shall pay twenty shillings.

That every other person of either sex, above the age of fifteen years, of what degree or quality soever, under the degree or quality of a Baron, or Barons wife or widow, shall pay thirty shillings.

That every other person of either sex, of what degree or quality soever, under the degree or quality of a Viscount, or Viscountess or Viscountess Dowager, shall pay four pounds.

That every other person of either sex, of what degree or quality soever under the degree or quality of an Earl, or Countess or Countess Dowager, shall pay five pounds.

That every other person of either sex, of what degree or quality soever, under the degree or quality of a Marquess, or Marchioness, or Marchioness Dowager, shall pay six pounds.

That every other person of either sex, of the degree or quality of a Marquess, or Marchioness, or Marchioness Dowager, shall pay eight pounds,

And whereas there is very great reason that in Corporations in respect of the *(Page 3)* several degrees and qualities of persons therein residing, there should be a more exact distinction of such persons, than will or can be ascertained under the aforementioned distinctions ; Therefore it is hereby ordained, that the more particular rating, taxing, and assessing the several persons residing within such Corporations as aforesaid, for which Commissioners are named and appointed by this Ordinance, shall be left to the discretion of the Commissioners, or some of them of that county wherein such Corporations are, being not Counties of themselves being joined unto certain other honest and substantial inhabitants of every of the said Cities, Boroughs, and Towns Corporate as are hereafter nominated to be Commissioners for such Cities, Boroughs, and Towns Corporate in this Ordinance ; And the Commissioners hereby appointed for the County wherein such City, Town Corporate, or Borough doth lie, and the Commissioners hereby appointed for such City, Town or Borough, are required within convenient time after notice of this Ordinance to meet together, and they, or any three or more them, (whereof one Inhabitant within such City, Town, or Borough, and one Commissioner for the said County are always to be two,) are to set such rates upon the Inhabitants of such Cities, Towns, or Boroughs as to them shall be thought fit, so as no such rate to be set upon any one person be above the sum of twenty shillings, or under the sum of twelve pence, and the said rates being so set, are to be leavyed in manner as hereafter in this Ordinance for the other sums hereby limited is provided; And where such Cities or Towns are Counties of themselves, then to the discretion of the Commissioners for such Cities and Towns, And also that every alien and stranger born out of the Realms of *England, Ireland* and *Scotland* being Denizens or not Denizens, of what degree or quality soever and being of the age of seaven years or above, shall pay double the sum of money which a free born subject of these Realms being in the same degree or qualification with the said alien, is by this present Ordinance required to pay.

And be it further ordained by the authority aforesaid, That every such person, as well such as be born within *England, Ireland* and *Scotland* as every other person, stranger, born Denizen or not Denizen inhabiting within this Realm, or elsewhere, which at the times of the said ratings or taxations to be had or made shall be out of this Realm, and have Goods, Chattels, Lands or Tenements, Fees or Annuities, or

(*Page* 4) other/profits within this Realm, shall be chargeable and charged for the same where such Goods, Lands, Chattells, Tenements, or other the premises then shall be, or in such other place where such person or persons or his or their Factors, Deputy, Agent or Atturney shall have his or their most resort unto whithin this Realm, in like manner as if the said person were or had been at the time of the said rating or taxing within this Realm.

And the Master or Mistress being sole with whom any servant is, or shall be abiding at the time of the ratings or taxations aforesaid, liable to the payments in this Ordinance, as also every Father, or Mother being a Widow, with whom any child or children are residing at the time of the ratings and taxations aforesaid not being married and liable to the payments in this Ordinance, and also every Husband is and are and shall be charged for such respective payments due by their wives, servants, or children, for lack of payment thereof by such Wives, Servants, or Children, and that it shall and may be lawfull for every Master or Mistress to defaulk such sum or sums of money as he or she shall pay by virtue of this Ordinance for their servants out of such wages as are or shall hereafter grow due to such servants.

And be it further Ordained by the Authority aforesaid, That for the better and more regular ordering of the said Moneys to be rated, taxed and paid, that the several persons hereafter in this Ordinance named, or any three or more of them, be and are appointed Commissioners within the several Counties, Cities and Burroughs in which they are so named and appointed, who hereby have full power and authority to put the same in effectual execution, and that by the authority of this Ordinance after notice thereof given them, they may by their assents and agreements sever themselves for the execution thereof in the several Baronies and other places within the limits of their said County, in such form as shall seem to them expedient to be ordered : And the said Commissioners or any three or more of them, shall direct their several or joynt precept or precepts unto such a number of the able and discreet Protestant Inhabitants if they may be had, to be named by the said Commissioners as aforesaid of and in the Baronies, Parishes, Towns and other places within the limits of their County, straitly by the said precept or precepts charging them to appear in their proper persons before the said Commissioners, or such number of them as they shall divide themselves into at a certain day and place, as by the discretion of the Commissioners (*Page* 5) as aforesaid shall be limited and appointed, regard always to be had where with conveniency it may be that such place appointed be for the most indifferent ease and travail of the Inhabitants of the said County, whose appearance shall be necessary towards the execution of this Ordinance commanding further by every such precept, that he to whose hand such precept shall come, shall shew, and deliver the same to the other Inhabitants named in the same precept, and that none of them fail to accomplish the same upon pain of forty shillings. And it is further ordained by the authority aforesaid, that at the said day and place prefixed and limited in the said precept, every of the said Commissioners then being within this Realm (not having sufficient excuse) shall appear in his proper person, and there the same Commissioners being present, or any three or more of them shall call, or cause to be called before them the said Inhabitants to whom they have directed their precept, and if any person so warned make default, unless he then be letted by sickness or other lawful excuse, or if any appearing, refuse to serve in form following, then every such person so making default or refusing to serve, shall forfeit forty shillings. And upon the same appearance had, they shall be charged before the Commissioners by all convenient ways and means (other than by corporal oath) to enquire of all and every person within the respective places limited to their care of each sex, of and above the age of fifteen years, and of what ranck, quality, or degree he or they are, and of the dwelling and abiding places of such persons within the limits of the places that they shall be charged with, and of all others which shall have his or their most resort unto any of the said places, and chargeable with any sums of moneys by this Ordinance, and of all other things requisite touching the said Ordinance, and according to the intent of the same, And thereupon as near as it may be, or shall come to their knowledg truely to present and certify before the said Commissioners the Names and Sirnames, and the qualification of every person residing within the limits of the places that they shall be charged with, without any concealment, love, favour, or affection, dread or malice, upon pain of forfeiture of five pounds to be taxed, extracted, and leavyed in form as hereafter in this Ordinance shall be limited and appointed, and thereupon the said Commissioners shall openly there read, or cause to be read unto them, the several qualifications of the persons, and the sums by such persons under such qualifications payable as is in this Ordinance mentioned and in what manner and form they ought to make their certificate, and of all manner of persons as well aliens and strangers, Denizens or not *(Page* 6) Denizens inhabiting within this Realm, as of such persons as be born within the said three Realms, and persons being in the parts beyond the seas having Goods and Chattells, Lands or Tenements within this Realm as aforesaid, and of all goods being in the custody of any person or persons to the use of any such absentee : by the which information and shewing the said persons shall have such plain knowledg of the true intent of this present Ordinance, that they shall have no reasonable cause to excuse themselves by ignorance.

And after such charge, and this Ordinance, and the manner of the said Certificate to be made in writing, and every thing requisite and necessary to their said Certificate to them declared, the said Commissioners there being, shall by their discretion appoint and limit unto the said persons another day and place to appear before the said Commissioners, and charging the said persons that they in the mean time shall make diligent inquiry by all wayes and means of the premises, and then and there every of them upon pain and forfeiture of forty shillings to appear at the new prefixed day and place there to certifie unto the said Commissioners in writing according to their said charge and according to the true intent of this Ordinance as to them in manner aforesaid hath been declared and shewed by the Commissioners, at which day and place so to them prefixed if any of the said persons make default, or appear and refuse to make the said certificate, then every of them so offending to forfeit fourty shillings, except there be a reasonable excuse, and of such as appear ready to make the certificate as aforesaid, the said Commissioners there being, shall take and receive the same certificate, and if the Commissioners see cause reasonable, they shall examine the said presenters thereof, and thereupon the said Commissioners at the said days and place by their agreement amongst themselves shall from time to time there openly prefix a day at a certain place or places within the limits of their County by their discretion for the further proceeding in execution of this Ordinance, and thereupon at the said day of the said Certificate, as is aforesaid taken, the said Commissioners shall make their precept or precepts to such persons or Officers as they shall think fit within their jurisdiction, comprising in the said Precepts the Names and Surnames of all such persons presented before them in the said certificate, of whom the said Commissioners shall have vehement cause to suspect to be of a different qualification then under what

(Page 7)

they are in the said Certficates returned, (except the Commissioners upon their own knowledge can ascertain the same, in which case they have/power by this Ordinance to amend the said Certificate) accordingly, to warn such persons whose names shall be comprized in the said precepts at their mansions, or to their persons, that the same persons and every of them shall personally appear before the said Commissioners at the same new prefixed day and place, there to be examined concerning the premisses, at which day and place so prefixed, the said Commissioners then and there being, shall cause to be called the said persons whose names are comprized in the said precept for their examination, and if any of those persons which shall be warned, which at any time after the warning and before the prefixed day shall be within such place where he may have knowledge of his said appearance to be made, make default and appear not, unless upon reasonable cause or excuse shewn, that then every of them so making default, to be taxed and rated according to such qualification as he or they are supposed or suggested to be comprised in, and power and authority is hereby given to the said Commissioners to enlarge or encrease or otherwise to abate or diminish the taxations of such persons as they shall find by due examination, or upon their own knowledge to be falsely returned under any qualification.

And it is further ordained by the authority aforesaid, that every person to be rated and taxed as aforesaid, shall be rated and taxed and the sum on him set, to be leavyed at such place where he and his family were resident for the most part of the year next before the same presentment made and nowhere else ; And if any person chargeable by this Ordinance at the time of the said rating or taxing happen to be out of this Realm, or far from the place where he shall be known, then he to be taxed where he was last abiding within this Realm, or if he were never within this Realm, then at such place where he hath a known, real, or personal estate ; And that every person taxed in any County or place other than where he, her, and his family were resident for the most part of the year then next before, upon Certificate under the hands and seals of two Commissioners in the same County and place where such person and his family were resident for the most part of the year before, testifying such his most residency and his being taxed there shall be a sufficient discharge for the taxation of that person in all other places, and of, and for all other sums of moneys upon such persons so rated and taxed, save onely the taxation made in that County or place from which such Certificate shall be made as aforesaid./

(Page 8)

And if any person or persons that ought to be rated and taxed to any of the payments in this Ordinance mentioned, by reason of his or their resorting and removing from place to place, or by reason of his or their saying that he or they were elsewhere taxed, or by reason of any priviledge of his or their dwelling or abiding in any place not being forprized in this Ordinance, or otherwiise by his or their coven or craft, or by any words or sayings or otherwise ; or if any that is a Commissioner or Presentor, or Assessor of others, happen to escape from the said Taxations, and be not rated and taxed according to the true intent of this Ordinance, and that proved by presentment, or examination or information or otherwise, before the said Commissioners or any three of them, then every such person that by such means or otherwise, willingly by covin or without just cause, shall avoid the payments or taxations aforesaid or any of them, shall be charged upon the knowledge and proofs thereof with and at treble the value of so much as he or they should, might, or ought to have been rated and taxed at by virtue of this Ordinance, and the same treble value to be gathered, leavyed and paid of his or their Goods and Chattels, Lands and Tenements in manner as hereafter is expressed.

And be it further ordained by the authority aforesaid, That the said Commissioners which shall be or inhabit in any County or place within the limit of that County, or the greater part of them, shall have full power and authority by this Ordinance to rate, tax and sess every other Commissioner joyned with them in that County according to their respective qualifications, and the said Commissioners within every division shall also rate and tax every Presentor or Assessor within his or their division according to their respective qualifications : and that as well the sums upon every of the said Commissioners and Presentors so set, rated, and taxed as the sums made and presented by the presentors, shall be written, certified, set and estreated and the estreats thereof to be made with the other Inhabitants of that part and within the limits of the said County or division, so to be gathered and leavyed in like manner as it ought or should have been if the said Commissioners or Presentors had been private persons.

And be it further ordained by the authority aforesaid, That after the said taxes and assesses of the said sums, upon and by the said assessing and Certificate as is aforesaid made, the said Commissioners, or any three of them, shall with all convenient speed by their writing, estreat the said taxes thereof, under their Seals and Signes *(Page* 9) manual, and the same shall deliver unto such sufficient and substantial Inhabitants of the Baronyes, Parishes, or other places aforesaid within their limits, as shall be approved of by the high Collectors hereafter to be appointed, containing as well the particular Names and Surnames as the remembrance of all sums of moneys, not in figures but in writing at large, taxed and set of and upon every person chargable by this Ordinance according to their several qualifications : by authority of which writing and esttreat so delivered, the same persons so named and deputed severally, shall have full power and authority by virtue of this Ordinance immediately after the delivering of the said writing or estreat, to demand, leavy, and gather of every person therein specifyed, the sum or sums in the said writing or estreat comprized, and for non-payment thereof, to destrain the said person or persons so being behind by their Goods and Chattels, and the distresses so taken, to keep by the space of six days at the costs and charges of the owner thereof : And if the said owner or owners do not pay such sum or sums of moneys as shall be rated or taxed upon him or them by authority of this Ordinance within the said six dayes, then the same distress to be appraised by two of the Inhabitants where such distress is taken, and then to be sold by the said Collectors for the payment of the said moneys, and the overplus coming of the sale and keeping thereof, (if any be,) immediately to be restored to the owner or owners of the distress, which said persons so deputed to take, ask, gather and levy the said sums, shall answer and be charged for the portion onely to them assigned and limited to be gathered and levyed, and comprised in the said writing or estreat, so to them (as is aforesaid) delivered, and the said sums in that writing or estreat comprised, to pay unto the high Collector of that County for the collection of the same in manner and form underwritten thereunto to be named and deputed.

And further be it ordained by the said authority, That the said Commissioners which shall be present at their first meeting, or the major part of them, shall then name and appoint one sufficient and able person as by their discretion shall be thought fit residing within the limits of their County to be high Collector, and to have the collection and receipt of the said sums set and leavyable within the said County, and the said Commissioners or any three or more of them, with all convenient speed after the whole

Page 10)

sum be rated and taxed in all the divisions of their County, shall under their Seals and Signes manual deliver unto the said high Collector, one estreat indented, comprising in it/the names of all such persons as were assigned to leavy the said particular sums, and the sums of every Barony, Cantred, Hundred, City, Town, Parish, and other place aforesaid, with the Names and Surnames of the persons so chargeable according to the estreats thereof, made and delivered as aforesaid, and the said high Collectors to be assigned, shall be charged to answer the whole sum comprised in the said estreat limited to his collection.

Provided always and be it ordained, That before the delivery of the aforesaid estreats unto the said high Collector, the said high Collector do enter into bond with sufficient security to the Treasurer hereafter appointed before the said Commissioners or any three or more of them, to be bound in double the sum of his Collection upon condition, That if the said Collector, his Heirs or Executors, do truly content and pay unto *Arthur Annesley Esq* ; his Deputy or Deputies, or to the other persons to be nominated, on his default as hereafter in this Ordinance is mentioned, or his or their order all and every the sum and sums of moneys which he shall receive within the limits of his collection accordingly, as from time to time he shall receive the same, That then the said obligation to be void, or else to remain in full force and virtue, which said obligation so taken, the said Commissioners shall send and cause to be delivered unto the said *Arthur Annesley Esq* ; his Deputy or Deputies, or to the other persons to be nominated, on his default with the several estreats of the said taxations and rates within the limits of their several Jurisdictions, and also duplicates thereof to *Roger* Lord Baron of *Broghill*, Sir *Charles Coote*, Knight and Baronet, Lord President of *Connaught*, and Sir *William Bury*, Knight, or any one of them within convenient time after taking thereof. And the said *Arthur Annesley*, his Deputy or Deputies, or the other persons to be nominated on his default, upon payment of the said several collections at the times therein limited for the payment thereof, being at or before the first day of *July* next at the farthest, shall cancel and deliver the said obligation to the said high Collector without any Fee or reward : And every high Collector so deputed, having the said estreat as is aforesaid, shall have authority by this Ordinance, to appoint days and places within the divisions of that County whereof he is high Collector, for the payment of the said sums to him respectively to be made, and thereof to give notice to all such persons having the charge of the particular Collections within the Baronies, Cantreds, Hundreds, Parishes, Towns, or other places to make payment

(Page 11)

of the particular/Collections of every sum as to them shall appertain, and if at that same day and place so prefixed and limited by the said high Collector, the said persons appointed by the particular collection within such Barony, Cantred, Hundred, City, Town, Parish, or other place, do not pay unto the said high Collector the sum within the several Baronies, Cantreds, Hundreds, Towns, Parishes, and other places due and comprised within the said estreat thereof to them delivered by the said Commissioners, or some of them, or so much thereof as they have by any means received : That then it shall be lawful to the said high Collector and his assignes, to destrain every of the said persons for their said several and particular collection of the said sums comprised in the said estreat to him (as is before expressed) delivered, or for so much of the same sum, as so then shall happen to be gathered and leavied, and to be behind and unpaid, by the Goods and Chattells of every of them so behind and unpaid, and the distresses so taken, to be kept and appraised and sold as aforesaid, and thereof to take and leavy the sums so then being behind and unpaid ; and the overplus coming of the sale of the said distress (if any be) to be restored and delivered to the owner in form above remembred.

And it is also by the said authority ordained, That if any person charged to and for the collection and receipt of any part or portion of the sums comprised in the said estreats according to this Ordinance after all lawful means and endeavours by him used to collect and receive the same, yet if by the dying of any person, or departure of any person from the place where he was so taxed & set or being an absentee, or that his Goods and Chatells be so eloyned or in such privy or covert manner kept, as that the said person or persons charged with the same by estreats or other writing from the Commissioners cannot or may not leavy the sum or sums comprised within the said estreats by distress within the limits of their collection : Then upon relation thereof, and due examination of such person or persons as shall be charged with and for the receipt and collection of the same, before the said Commissioners, or any three of them, where such person or persons were rated and taxed, and upon plain certificate thereof made unto the said *Arthur Annesley*, his Deputy or Deputies, or to the other persons to be nominated on his default, by the same Commissioners of the dwelling place, Names and sums of the said persons of whom the same sums cannot be leavyed and had, then the said persons appointed for the same particular collection against the high Collector, as the high Collector upon his account to be discharged thereof :/And over that the *(Page 12)* same Commissioners to whom all such Declaration of the premises shall be made in form aforesaid from time to time shall have full power and authority to direct their precept or precepts to the said person or persons charged with any sum of, for & upon any such person or persons, or to any other person, or to any Sherif, Steward, Bailif, or other whatsoever Officer, Minister, person or persons of such place or places where any such person or persons so owing any such sum or sums shall have Lands, Tenements, or other Hereditaments, or reall possessions, Goods and Chattels whereby any such persons so indebted his Heirs, Executors, Assigns, or others haveing the custody, governance or disposition of any Goods, Chattels, Lands, Tenements, or other possessions whereof such sum and sums which by any such person and persons may or ought to be Leavied be it within the limit of such County where such person or persons was or were taxed or without in any place in this Realm of *Ireland* by which precept as well such person or persons shall be charged to Leuy such mony as the Officer of the place or places where such distress may be taken shall have full power and Authority to distrein every such person indebted charged and chargable by this Ordinance, or his Executors or Administrators, of his Goods, Chattels, his Guardians, Factors, Deputies, Lessees, Farmors, and Assigns, and all other persons by whose hands or out of whose Lands any such person should have fee, rent, annuity, or other profits, or which at the time of the said rating, or taxing shall have Goods or Chattles or any other thing movable of any such person or persons being indebted or owing such sum, and the distresses so taken cause to be kept appraised and sold in like manner and form as is aforesaid : And if any such distress for Non-payment happen to be taken out of the limits of the said persons charged and assigned to leavy the same, the person so charged for leavying any such sum by distress shall have for the labour of every such person going for the execution thereof, for every mile that any such person so laboureth for the same, two pence, to be leavied upon the party making default by distress, over and above the sum charged on the said party, and every Farmer, Tenant, Guardian, Factor or other whatsoever person, being distreined or otherwise charged for payment of any such sum or sums, or any other sum by reason of this Ordinance, shall be of such sum or sums of him or them so leavied and taken, acquitted and discharged at his next day of payment of the same, or at the delivery of such goods and chattels as he that is so distreined had/in his custody or governance against him or them that shall be so taxed and set, any grant or writing obligatory or other whatsoever matter to the contrary made heretofore notwithstanding.

And be it further Ordained by the Authority aforesaid, That all penalties mentioned in this Ordinance which shall happen to be incurred by any person or persons, shall be set down particularly in the estreat which shall be delivered to any person or persons particularly appointed to collect and receive the several sums in their respective divisions where such person or persons are residing by whom such penalties shall be incurred, and to be leavied and received in such manner and form by the said Sub-collectors, and paid over to the high-collectors, as if such penalties had been imposed upon such persons for the sums rated and taxed upon them for their respective qualifications, and in the same Estreats to be returned to the said *Arthur Annesley* his Deputy or Deputies, or to the other persons to be nominated on his default, that thereby a particular accompt of such penalties may be had ; as also of the sum or sums being behind or unpaid by any person or persons which are to be leavied and gathered by force of the aforesaid process to be made by the said Commissioners that further order may be taken therein ; And if any Collector or other person charged with any receipt of any part of the said several sums, or any other person taxed or otherwise by this Ordinance charged with or for any part of the said several sums, or with any other sum, penalty or other forfeiture happen to die before the Collectors or other whatsoever person or persons have executed, accomplished, satisfied or sufficiently discharged that which to every such person appertain or belong to do according to this Ordinance, then the Executors and Heirs of every such person, and all others seised of any Lands and Tenements, that any such person being charged by this Ordinance and deceasing before he be discharged thereof, or any other to his use onely had of Estate of Inheritance at the time that any such person was named Collector or otherwise charged with or for any manner of thing to be done, satisfied or payd by reason of this Ordinance, and all those that have in their possessions or hands any goods, Chattels, Leases or other things, that were to any person or persons at the time of his death, or any Lands or Tenements that were to the same persons at the time he was (as is aforesaid) charged by this Ordinance, shall be by the same compelled and charged to do and accomplish in every case as the same person being so charged

should have done, or might have been/compelled to do if he had been in plain life, after such rate of the Lands and Goods of the said Collector or other person as abovesaid, as the party shall have in his Lands.

And it is further Ordained by authority aforesaid, That every person of or above the age of fifteen years of each sex under the degree of a Gentleman or Gentlewoman upon payment of the sum upon him or them set and taxed, shall receive a Ticquet or acquittance, expressing his or their Name, Surname and qualification, and his Office, place of abode, and that he or they have paid the sum due and payable by virtue of this Ordinance, which acquittance is to be signed by the Sub-collector of that division or place wherein such person made payment : and in case any such person be found within any County, City or other place of this Realm, without such ticquet or acquittance such person shall be liable to be charged in such County, City or other place where such person shall be so found and accordingly pay to the Sub-collector of that place or division the sum of two shillings, upon payment whereof such person shall receive an acquittance or ticquet from such Sub-collector, receiving the same without fee or reward, and the said Subcollector upon the return of the Certificate for his subdivision shall certifie by way of addition all such sums so received, and the Names and Surnames of the persons so paying the same, all which shall be inserted in the general Estreat of the whole County, and to be returned to the said *Arthur Annesley* his Deputy or Deputies, or to the other persons to be nominated on his default as aforesaid, that no part of the sums intended to be raised by this Ordinance may be concealed or withdrawn from publique accompt.

And it is further Ordained by the authority aforesaid, That the Commissioners hereby appointed in the several Counties, Cities, Towns and Burroughs in this Realm are and shall be hereby authorized out of the moneys that shall be raised by virtue of this Ordinance to make such allowances to the high Collectors and other Collectors and Clerks that shall be by them employed, or for any other charges that shall to them seem requisit for the better leavying and bringing in the several sums of money herein formerly mentioned, as to them shall be thought fit and necessary, so as the allowances so to be made by the said Commissioners, do not exceed the sum of twelve pence in the pound, which said twelve pence in the pound is to be allowed by the said Treasurer unto the several high Collectors upon their respective accompts.

And it is further Ordained by the authority aforesaid, That/*Arthur Annesley Esq.*, *(Page* 15) be and is hereby appointed to be Treasurer for receiving the several sums of moneys that shall be leavied by virtue of this Ordinance, and to execute the said Office by himself, his sufficient Deputy or Deputies by him the said *Arthur Annesley* thereunto lawfully authorized. Provided that if the said *Arthur Annesley* having first notice of his being appointed Treasurer by this Ordinance, do not signifie his acceptance thereof to the said Lord *Broghill*, Sir *Charles Coote* and Sir *William Bury*, and execute the same by himself, his Deputy or Deputies, as aforesaid, before the first of June One thousand six hundred and sixty, that then it is hereby Ordained, That the said Lord *Broghill*, Sir *Charls Coot*, and Sir *William Bury* shall and have hereby full power and authority to nominate and appoint two such able and sufficient persons as they shall approve of to be Treasurers for the receiving and assigning the said moneys, and to execute the said Office to all intents and purposes, as also to observe, execute and perform all things tending to the said office, as the said *Arthur Annesley*, his Deputy or Deputies, by this Ordinance might or ought to have done.

And the high Collectors in the several Counties of this Realm are to pay the said moneys from time to time to the said *Arthur Annesley*, or his Deputy or his Deputies at *Dublin*, or elsewhere by his or their Order, in case of the said *Arthur Annesleys* acceptance as aforesaid, or in default thereof, then to the persons to be appointed by the said Lord *Broghill*, Sir *Charls Coot*, and Sir *William Bury*, and the acquittance or acquittances of the said *Arthur Annesley* or of his Deputy or Deputies under his or their hand or hands, or of the other persons to be nominated on his default as afore-said, shall be their sufficient discharge or discharges for the same. And the said *Arthur Annesley* or his Deputy or Deputies, or the other persons to be nominated on his default as aforesaid, are to issue out and pay the said Moneys for the use of the Army, and defraying of other necessary charges of the Realm, according as by the said Lord *Broghill*, Sir *Charls Coot*, and Sir *William Bury*, or any two of them, they shall be from time to time required, which said Lord *Broghill*, Sir *Charls Coot*, and Sir *William Bury*, or any two of them, are hereby appointed a Committee for managing and issuing out the said moneys to the intents and purposes in this Ordinance formerly declared, as also to call the said *Arthur Annesley*, his Deputy or Deputies, or the other persons to be nominated on his default as aforesaid, from time to time to accompt for the moneys which shall be received by them or any/of them in virtue of this Ordinance and no other ; and the said *Arthur Annesley*, or his Deputy or Deputies, or the other persons to be nominated on his default as aforesaid, shall have also power and authority by virtue cf this Ordinance, to call the high Collectors in the several Counties in this Realm to accompt for the several sums of money that they shall receive by virtue of this Ordinance ; And the said Commissioners and also the high Collectors in the said several Counties, Cities, Towns and Burroughs are (from time to time as there shall be occasion) to certifie the said *Arthur Annesley*, or his Deputy or Deputies, or the other persons to be nominated on his default as aforesaid, at *Dublin*, of their proceedings upon and in execution of this Ordinance.

And it is hereby declared, That whereas several persons have covenanted, contracted, or agreeed either with their Lessors or Lessees to be freed and exonerated from all Contributions, Assesments, or other publick payments, That it is not hereby intended (this being a personal charge, and not arising out of Lands, Tenements and Hereditaments) that such Lessor or Lessees shall be hereby freed and exonerated from paying the several sums chargeable upon them according to their respective qualifications, but that the said Lessor or Lessees shall pay the same notwithstanding any such covenant, contract or agreement to the contrary.

Provided always, That this Ordinance or anything therein contained in any wise extend not to charge the Provost, Fellows and Scholars of the College of the Holy Trinity near *Dublin*, nor to any ordained Ministers, their wives or such children as are resident and living in their families unmarried, nor to any hospitalmen or people living upon alms.

And be it further Ordained by Authority aforesaid, That these persons under written, and no other, be and are nominated and appointed to be Commissioners for putting in execution this Ordinance within the several Counties, Cities and Burroughs of this Rearlm of *Ireland*.   That is to say,

For the City and County of the City of *Dublin*, the Mayor, and Sherifs for the time being, *John Bysse* Recorder of *Dublin*, *Peter Wybrant*, *William Smith*, *William Bladen*, *Richard Tigh*, *Daniel Hutchinson*, *John Preston*, *Thomas Hook*, *Ridgley Hatfield*, *Thomas Waterhouse*, *George Gilbert*, *John Cranwell*, *William Cliffe*, *Richard Cook*, *John Desmoneer*, *Daniel Bellingham*, *Mark Quin*, *Samuel Weston*, *John Forrest*, *Ralph Vizard* Aldermen, Sir *William Usher*, Sir *Robert Newcomen*, Sir *James Barry*,/Sir *Robert Meridith*, Sir *Paul Davis* Knights, *Jerom Alexander*, *William Knight*, *William Dixon*, *Robert Kennedy*, *Richard Kennedy*, Doctor *Ralph King*, *Abraham Clements*, *Thomas Richardson*, Doctor *Dudley Loftus*, *Richard Palfrey*, *Robert Arrundel*, Major *William Merideth*, *William Sands*, *John Doughty*, *John Exham*, *Abraham Yarner*, *Philip Ferneley* Esquires, *Thomas Boyd*, *Nathaniel Foulk*, *Enock Reader*, *Lewis Desmoneer*, *Samuel Saltonstall*, *John Beauchamp*, *John Smith*, *Thomas Howard* Merchants.   Capt. *Thomas Jones*, Capt. *John Nicholas*, Capt. *Taylor*, *Philip Harris*, *Thomas Pooley*, *Robert Hughes* Collector of the Customs, *Patrick Tallant*, *John Pinsent*, *Nathaniel Philpot*, *Thomas Cleark*, *Tobias Creamer*, *John Eastwood*, *Luke Lowther*, *Ralph Wallis* Gentlemen.

For the County of *Dublin*, *Arthur* Lord Viscount *Rannelagh*, Lord of *Howth*, Sir *Henry Titchbourn*, Sir *Paul Davis*, Sir *James Barry*, Sir *William Usher*, Sir *Theophilus*

Jones Knights. *William Tichbourn, Robert Cusack, Iames Donnelan, Thomas Maul,* Mr. Recorder *Bysse,* Col. *Chidley Coot,* Doctor *Dudley Loftus, Robert Kennedy,* Lt. Col. *Philip Ferneley, Thomas Richardson, Walter Pluncket, Francis Peasley,* Col. *Iohn Cole, Richard Kennedy* Esqs ; Alderman *Daniel Hutchinson,* Mr. *Edward Cook,* Mr. *Ralph Wallis,* Mr. *Iohn Baxter,* Alderman *Hubert Adrian,* Alderman *Charles Foster, Richard Cotton, Thomas Vincent, Richard Buckley, Oliver Lambert, Adam Loftus, Richard Barry* Esquires, *Matthew Barry* Gentleman.

For the County of *Wicklow, Edward* Earl of *Meath,* Sir *William Vsher,* Sir *Iohn Hoey,* Sir *Theophilus Iones* Knights. *Richard Kenneday, William Knight, Roger West, Philip Ferneley, William Neave, William Hoey, Robert Hassels* Esqs. Doctor *Abraham Yarner, Samuel Pepys, Iohn Boswell, Thomas Bolles, Cromwell Winkfield, Thomas Kennedy, William Warren, Philip Harris,* Capt. *Farrer,* Cornet *William Pinsen, Iohn Humfreys* Gent. Major *Thomas Brereton, Thomas Waterhouse* Alderman, *Thomas Boyd* Merchant, *Walter Walsh* Gentl.

For the Burrough of *Wicklow,* The Soveraign of the said Burrough for the time being, *Samuel Weston, Richard Lock, Iohn Hacket, Edward Hartshorn.*

For the County of *Kildare,* Sir *George Blundel* Baronet, Sir *Robert Meredith,* Sir *Maurice Eustace,* Sir *Paul Davis,* Sir *Theophilus Iones,* Sir *Iohn Hoey,* Knights, *Iohn Salt* Esq, Sir *Walter Burrows* Baronet, Major *William Meredith, Henry/Warren, Raphael* (Page 18 *Hunt, Thomas Harman, Dudley Colley, George Blunt, William Hoey, Richard Thompson, Henry Owen, Iohn Brown, Richard Tigh, Daniel Hutchinson* Aldermen, *Iohn Annesley, Iohn Ewers, Thomas Gifford, Walter White, Iohn Bury, Henry Sankey, Thomas Brown, Philip Fernely, Charls Ryves* Esqs. Sir *Iohn Percival* Knight, *Francis Peasly* Esq.

For the Town of *Naas,* the Soveraign for the time being, *Charls Ryves* Esq, *Nicolas Stafford.*

For the Town of *Kildare,* the Soveraign for the time being, *Francis Peasly, Nicolas Rutlidg.*

For the Town of *Athie,* the Soveraign for the time being, *William Scot, William Weldon* Esqs.

For the County of *Catherlogh,* Sir *Iohn Percival* Kniuht, *William Temple, Oliver Iones, Henry Warren, Iohn Aston, Henry Sankey, Thomas Burdit, Walter Bodeley, Henry Smithick, Thomas Harman, George Hartop, Iohn Corbet, Robert Mihil, Richard Tighe* Esquires. *Abraham Highmore, Eleazar Hudson, Thomas Bolton, Richard Fisher, Richard Norris, Iohn Warren, William Bernard* Gentlemen.

For the Town of *Catherlogh,* the Portreeve for the time being, *Edward Reynolds, Thomas Reynolds, Iohn Masterson.*

For the County of *Wexford, Nicolas Devereux* Esq., high Sheriff, *Nicolas Loftus* Senior, *Thomas Scot, Thomas Hart, Iohn Tench, Edward Withers, Nicolas Loftus* Junior, *Iohn Fountain, Thomas Barrington, Matthew Stodhard, Thomas Knox, Spencer Vincent,* the Mayor of *Wexford* for the time being, the Soveraign of *Ross* for the time being, the Portriff of *Eniscorthy* for the time being, *Iohn Totty, Samuel Shepheard, Richard Ousley, Iohn Arthur, Henry Masterson, Nathaniel Boyse, Walter Plunket, Iohn Cliff, Francis Harvy, Roger Levesey, Richard Wildboar, Iohn Swan, Richard Row, Edward Rotheram, Edmond Waddy, Richard Kenney, Roger Drake* Esqs.

For the County of *Kilkenny,* Sir *Theophilus Iones* Knight, *William Warden, Ioseph Cuff, Henry Baker, Iohn Ponsonby, Thomas Evans, Thomas Burril, Oliver Wheeler, Humphry Hurd, Abel Warren, William Bond,* Lt. Col. *Iackson, Thomas Butler, Robert*

Floyd, Ioseph Bradshaw, Iohn Ieonar, Oliver Iones, William Palmer, Anthony Horsey
Esquires, *Francis Rolleston, Ionas Wheeler, Iohn Iones, Allen Tench, Iohn Pressick*
Dudley Manwering, Christopher Huetson, Simon Smith, Edward Butler, Edward Chilton
(Page 19) Gent ; *Alexander Castle, Iohn Powel, Harvy Morris, Iohn/Farrer, William Baker, Iohn*
Campbell Esqs. Ensign *Lodg, Philip Sargent* Gent.

For the City and County of the City of *Kilkenny*, the Mayor, Recorder and
Sheriffs for the time being, Sir *Patrick Wemys* Knight, *Iohn Ieonar, Thomas Evans,*
William Warden, Oliver Wheeler, Thomas Burril, Ioseph Cuff, Henry Baker, Thomas
Butler, Iohn Campbell Esquires, *Thomas Davis, Iosias Haydock, William Connel, Peter*
Goodwin, Philip Sarjeant, Gent.

For the Queens County, Sir *Amos Meredith* Knight and Baronet, *Henry Gilbert,*
Walter Warneford, Thomas Burril, Thomas Vincent, Iohn Weaver, Gilbert Rawson,
Thomas Prior, Francis Barrington, Iohn Rawlins, William Scot, Nathaniel Marks,
Henry Sybhals, Adam Loftus Esqs ; *Edward Burril, Richard Smith, Iohn Fanner,*
Robert Gough, Thomas Ogle, Philip Sarjeant Gent.

For the Kings County, Sir *George Blundel* Baronet, *Edward Herbert, Thomas*
Gifford, Henry Sankey, William Hamilton, Henry Lestrange, Iohn Weaver, Charls
Lambert, William Purefay, Robert Lloyd, Charls Lyons, Robert Busbridg,——Candler,
Lawrence Parsons, Iohn Hallam, Philip Bigo, Iohn Michel, Iohn Wakely Esqs. *Richard*
Warburton, Iohn Rose, Robert Chafe, George Sankey, Anthony Atkinson Gentl. *Thomas*
Vincent, Walter Lambert, Peter Purefoy, Iohn Moor, Edward Herbert Esqs.

For the Town of *Philipstown, Robert Lloyd, Charls Lyons* Esquires.

For the County of *Westmeath, Charles* Earl of *Cavan,* Sir *George Blundel* Baronet,
Sir *Theophilus Iones,* Sir *Henry Peirce* Knights. *Charls Lambert, Thomas Long, William*
Handcock, William Markham, Iohn Iones, Laurence Hide, George Payton, George Talbot,
Robert Cook, Iames Leigh, William Moor, Alexander Iephson, Henry Packenham,
Ridgley Hatfield, Henry Baker, Walter Lambert, Thomas Hopkins, Edward Knight,
Iohn Quelsh, Francis Gibson Esquires. *Godfrey Keeler, Hans Albert Widman, Foulk*
Rooksby, William Courtney, Henry Iephson, Dennis Brown, Henry Purdon, —— Wilson,
Francis Gibbons, George Meverall, Benjamin Chapman, Iohn Forrest, Thomas Newcomen,
Richard Harrison, Thomas Nugent, —— Michelburn Gentlemen. Olever *Lambert* Esq.

For the Town of *Athlone, Walter Staplehill, Enock Golburn, Edward Donelan,*
Iames Donelan, Lewis Iones, Oliver Iones Esquires.

For the Town of *Kilbeggan, Richard Harrison, Iohn Fleetwood, Thomas Laurence,*
Esqs. *Iohn Nelson* Gent./

(Page 20) For the County of *Longford, Francis* Lord *Angier,* Sir *Arthur Forbes* Baronet,
Iohn Edgworth, Henry Sankey, Thomas Vincent, Adam Molineux, Henry Packenham,
Thomas Waterhouse Esquires. *Richard Tomson, Iames Grigges, Simon Sands, Iohn*
Ahmonty, Edward Knight, William Kennedy, Thomas Babington, Arthur Ahmonty,
—— Robinson, William Longford Gentlemen, *Iohn Kennedy* Esq.

For the Burrough of *St. Iohnstown, Andrew Adare, Iohn Edgworth* Esquires.

For the County of *Meath, Arthur* Lord Viscount *Rannelagh, Henry* Lord Viscount
of *Mellifont,* Doctor *Henry Iones,* Sir *Theophilus Iones,* Sir *Robert Foord,* Sir *Thomas*
Meredith Knights. *Thomas Gifford, William Cadogan, Philip Fernely, Iohn Franck,*
Iohn Bligh, William Toxteth, Henry Packenham, Thomas Loftus, Thomas Worship,
Ierom Alexander, Ioseph Fox, Thomas Vincent, Iames Napper, George Peppard, Edward
Sutton, Randal Moor, Arthur Purefoy, Robert Franck, Miles Sumner, Arthur Dillon,
Robert Gorges, Thomas Ash, Alexander Iephson, Robert Lill, Iohn Hatch, Thomas Wren,

Roger Pierce, Iames Usher, Philip Peak, Henry Osburn Esqs.   *Iohn Fort, Iohn Dorrel* Gent.

For the Town of *Trym. George Warris* Portrife, *Alexander Iephson, Robert Lill* Esquires.

For the Town of *Navan. William Cadogan* Portriff, *Henry Packenham* Esq. *William Graham* Gent.

For the Town of *Kells.* Sir *Henry Ingoldsby* Knight, *Ierom Alexander, Henry Morton* Esqs.

For the Town of *Athboy, Iohn Bligh* Esq. *Thomas Chillingworth, William Bligh, Iohn Baxter, Iohn Barnes, Thomas Dean, Richard Ieanes, Henry Wade, Henry Guithers, Hans Graham, Iohn Bevins, William Parkinson* Gentlemen.

For the County of *Lowth, Iohn Ruxton* High Sherive of the said County, *Henry* Lord Viscount *Moor, William Aston, Henry Bellingham, William Toxteth, Wolston Dixy, Iames Smallwood, Richard Bolton, Nehemiah Donnelan* Esquires, *Thomas Clerk, Samuel Ireland, William Brickardick, Iohn Tomlinson* Gentlem. *Arthur Buckley, Oates Crowther* Bailifs of *Dundalk, Brent Moor, Robert Wynn, Iohn Howk* Esqs. *Henry Wetherel, Humphrey Barry, Nicolas Ward, Iames Brabazon, Nicolas Combe, Peter Ashenhurst, Brian Horn, Edward Nicolson* Gent. *Rowland Trolly, Ionas Elwood* Esqs.

For the County of the Town of *Drogheda.* The Mayor and Sherifs for the time being, *William Toxteth, Rowland Trolly, Samuel Stanbridge, Moses Hill, Robert Bridges, George Peppard, Edward Harrington, William Elwood, Ionas Elwood, Thomas/Dixon* (Page 21) Esqs. *Gabriel Mead, Francis Pool, Ioseph Whirloe, Thomas Cokain* Gentlemen.

For the County of *Cork* the Earl of *Cork, Roger* Lord Baron of *Broghil, Richard* Earl of *Barrimore,* Sir *William Fenton,* Sir *Iohn King,* Sir *Maurice Fenton,* Sir *Iohn Percival* Knights, *Henry Tyne, Nicolas Purdon, Peter Courthorp, Richard Kyr[.]e, Richard Townsend, St. John Broderick, Henry Bathurst, Randolph Clayton, Alexander Piggot, Garret fitz Gerald* Esquires, The Mayor and Sherifs of the City of *Cork* for the time being, The Mayor of *Youghal* for the time being, The Soveraign of *Kinsale* for the time being, The Provost of *Bandonbridg* for the time being, *William Supple, Iohn Hodder, William Hodder, Francis Foulks, Richard Smith, Redmond Barry, Walter Cooper, Robert Foulks* Esqs. *Samuel Brown* Gent. *Robert Southwell, Iohn St. Leiger, Howard St. Leiger, Robert Gookin, Iohn Baker, Thomas Long, Iohn Wakeham* Esqs. *Henry Pyne* Gent. *Boyl Maynard, William Mead* Esqs. *Edward Kenny, Pierce Power, William Dant* Senior Gent. *Benjamin Crofts* Esq. *Iohn Bellew, William Bellew, Iohn Brocket* Gent. *Abraham Savage, Richard Aldworth, Iohn Gibbons, Richard Gordwin, Walter Daly, William Harmer, Andrew Ruddock, Iohn Iepson, Iohn Gifford, William Hull* Esqs, *Walter Baldwin, William Holdcomb* Gent. *William fitz Gerald, William Thornhill, Roger Bretrage, William Arnold, George Prater* Esqs, *Peter Carew* Gent. *Timothy Rutter, Robert Hide* Esqs. *Iohn Sweet, Edward Townsend, Abel Guillim, George Syms* Gent. *Iohn Read* Esq. *Edward Ingry, Richard Hutchins, Richard Cover, David Iermin, Anthony Woodly, Francis Alcock* Gentlemen.

For the City and County of the City of *Cork,* The Mayor, Recorder and Sherives for the time being, *Peter Courthorp, Iohn Hodder, William Hodder, Philip Matthews, Iohn Baker, Walter Cooper, Thomas Woodliff* Esquires. *Christopher Oliver, Iames Vandelew* Aldermen, *Benjamin Crofts, Edmund Crofts* Esquires, *Richard Scudmore, Theophilus Carew, Philip Parker, Zachary Travers, Giles Bursted, Ionathan Perry* Gent. *Richard Travers* Esq.

For the Town of *Youghal*, The Mayor, Recorder and Bailifs for the time being, *Henry Tynt* Esq., *Richard Meirs, Ioseph Cox, Iohn Farthing, George Giles, Thomas Vaughan, Owen Silver* Gentlemen.

For the Town of *Kinsale*, The Soveraign and Recorder for the time being, *Robert Southwell* Esq, *Iohn Stepney, William Howel, Lancelot Stepney, Iohn Suxbury, William Brodbear, Iohn Willingham, Iohn Mountford, Iohn Martin* gentl./

ige 22) For the Town of *Bandonbridg*, The Provost for the time being, *Samuel Brown, Abraham Savage* Esquires. *William Wright, Iohn Iackson, Thomas Beamish* Gent.

For the County of *Waterford*, *Richard* Earl of *Cork*, Sir *Richard Osbourn* Baronet High Sheriff of the said County, *Francis Foulke, Boyle Maynard, Iohn Fitzgerrald, Thomas Walsh, Nicolas Osbourne, Richard Poer, Pierce Walsh, Iohn Cole, Andrew Lynn, William Halsey, Boyl Smith, Thomas Taylor, William Hubbart, Iosuah Boyl* Esquires. *Philip Harris, Iohn Smith, Nicolas Stout, Iames Oldfield, Iohn Poer, Richard Silver, Edward Rogers, William Bradley, Iames Briver, Robert Taylor, Henry Gee, Alexander Dean, Michael Wilson, Richard Williams* Gentlemen.

For the City of *Waterford*, The Mayor, Recorder and Sheriffs for the being, *Francis Foulk, William Halsey, Thomas Dancer* Esquires. *Thomas Exten, Iohn Heaven, Benedict Claybrook* Aldermen, *Robert Lynn* Gent. *Iohn Lapp, Thomas Christmas* Merchants.

For the County of *Kerry*, *Thomas Herbert* Esq. High Sherif, *William Fitzmorris, Arthur Denny, Redmond Fitzmorris, Iohn Blenerhasset, Thomas Crosby, Iohn Blenerhasset* Junior, *George Dillon, Edward Shewell, Richard Chute, Henry Ponsonby, William Hall, Thomas Amery, Edward Allen, Iohn Love* Esqs. Capt. *Iohn Rose*, Col. *Humfry Barrow*, Lt. —— *Witherston, Robert Blenerhasset, Iohn Steers, Iohn Walker, Thomas Blenerhasset, Ralph Conniers, Iames Conway, Patrick Crosby, Anthony Shertliff, Iames Lloyd* Gentlemen.

For the Town of *Dingle*, *Lancelot Sands* Esq.

For the County of *Limerick*, Sir *Henry Ingoldsby* Baronet, *Ralph Wilson, William Piggot, George Ingoldsby, Thomas Southwell, William King, Robert Oliver, Arthur Ormsby, Brook Bridges, Iohn Frenier, Gerald fitz Gerald, William Hartwell, Iohn Purdon, Richard Hart, Iohn Ormsby, Lewis Griffith, Gamaliel Walter* Esqs. Cornet *Iames Dogherty, Iohn Gileard, Vere Hunt, Richard King, Mark Harrison* Gent. *Drury Wray, Simon Eaton, Humphry Hartwell* Esqs. *Iohn Syms, Arthur Hasset, Giles Powel, Iohn Odel, William Downs, Ionah Lynch, Iohn Croaker, William Weeks* Gentlemen.

For the Town of *Kilmallock*, *Thomas Holms, Henry Glober, Edward Harris* Gentlemen.

ige 23) For the City and County of the City of *Limerick*, the Mayor, Recorder and Sheriffs for the time being, *Henry* Earl of *Thomond*, Sir *Henry Ingoldsby* Baronet, *Ralph Wilson, George/Ingoldsby, William King, William Wade, William Hartwell, Thomas Miller, William Yarwell, Ioshua Bennes* Aldermen, *William Purefoy, Daniel Harrington, Christopher Sexton, Henry Bendon, Iohn Comin, Peter Ash, Christopher Kyes, Daniel Hignes* Esqs. *Samuel Foxon, Iames Banting, Dermot Coghlan, Timothy Steven, Thomas Martin, Iohn Cripps, William Ryal, Henry Saltfield, Bartholomew Garnet, William Pope, Patrick Dowdal, Henry Price* Senior, *Iohn Crewse, Henry Lee, Iohn Matthews, William Ken, William Ioint, William Allen, Iohn Hecker, George Bucks, Iames Philips* Esquires.

For the County of *Clare* : *Iohn Frend* High Sherif of the said County, *Henry* Earl of *Thomomond*, Sir *Henry Ingoldsby* Knight, *William Purefoy, Ralph Wilson, Iohn Cooper, Thomas Cullen, Samuel Burton, George Pourdon, Thomas Hickman, Isaac Graneer, William Rumsey, Peter Purefoy, Thomas Curd, Thomas Bentley, Peirce Butler, Iohn*

Colpoise Esqs. *Neptune Bloud, Iohn Gore, George Ross, Giles Vandelure, Henry Lee, Thomas Hewet, Richard Hart, Peter Graneer, George Norton, William Goff, Patrick Lysat, Nicolas Bourk, Isaac Vanhogarden* Gentlemen.

For the Town of *Inish : William Purefoy* Esq. *William Cuff, Iohn Cruse, William Bridgal, Anthony Bernard, Robert Hone, Iohn Payn, Charls Chafine, Archibald Young* Gentlemen.

For the County of *Tipperary. Iohn Booker* Esq. High Sherif of the said County, *Charls Blunt, Simon Finch, Solomon Camby, Henry Paris, Bartholomew Foulks, Robert Knight, —— Howard, Edward Dinham, Nicolas Everard, Iohn Peck, Arthur Purefoy, Godfrey Green, Humphrey Dimock, Gamaliel Waters, Sampson Towgood, Iohn Harrison, Robert Cole* Esquires. *Iohn Matthews, Giles Martin, Tho. Poe, Nic. Towler, Wil. Heydon, Wil. Palms* Gent. *Iohn Iordan* Esq. Sir *Iohn Percival* Knight. *Francis Peisley, Charls Alcock* Esquires. *Oliver Latham, William Bacon* Gent.

For the Burrough of *Clonmell, Richard Perrot, Robert Lovelace* Gentlemen.

For the Burrough of *Cashel, Peyton Lehunt* Esquire, *Richard Hatton* Gentleman.

For the Burrough of *Fetherd, Robert Powel, Peter Cook* Gentlemen.

For the Burrough of *Carrick, William Sheffield, Michael Lamot* Gentlemen.

For the County of *Roscomon,* Lord President of *Connaught, Arthur* Viscount *Rannelagh,* Sir *Iohn King,* Sir *Oliver S. George* Knights, *Richard Coote, Charls Coote, William Handcock, Edmund Donnelan, Iames King, Richard Crofton, Edward Crofton, Thomas Caulfield, Thomas Lovelace, Iohn Moor, Dominick French, Iames Donnelan, Allen Povey* Esqs. Cornet *Michael Stanley, Owen Lloyd, Nicolas Mahown, Robert Folliot, Thomas Bright* Gent./

For the County of *Leitrim.* Sir *Charls Coot* Knight and Baronet Lord President (*Page 24*) of *Connaught, Richard Coot* Esq. Sir *Arthur Forbes* Baronet, Sir *Oliver St. George* Knight, *Robert Parks* Esq. *Owen Wynn* High Sheriff, *William St. George, Henry Crofton, Iames Bathurst* Esqs. *Bryan Cunningham, Christopher Matthews, Edward Woods,* Gent. *Iames King* Esq. *Thomas Ellis, William Keys, Iohn Akmooth* Gent. *Walter Iones.*

For the County of *Sleigo,* Sir *Iohn King* Knight, *Richard Coote, Robert Park, Robert Morgan, Francis King, Lewis Winckfield, Lewis Iones, Thomas Crofton, William Webb, Charls Gore, Kenie O Hara* Esqs. *Andrew Lindsey, Thomas Hart, William Ormsby, Thomas Griffith, Anthony Ormsby, Gregory Limry, Edward Cooper, Edward Nicolson, Timothy Howes, Dominick French, Henry Tifford, Thomas Wood, Henry Nicolson, Iames Beirn, Thomas Boswel* Gentl. *William Hunter* Merchant, *Iames Bathurst,* Esq.

For the County of *Gallway, Henry Waddington* High Sherif, Lord President of *Connaught,* The Mayor, Recorder and Sherifs of the Town of *Gallway* for the time being, Sir *Oliver S. George, William Edwards, Thomas Caulfield, Iames Cuffe, Henry Greenway, Henry Whally, Richard Bingley, Iohn Whalley,* Esqs. Capt. *Thomas Cuff, Edmund Donelan, Iohn Morgan, Francis Gore, Charles Coot, George S. George* Esquires, *William Brooks, Gilbert Carter, Michael Stanley, Iohn Bullenbrook, Matthew Tubman, Henry Davis, Iarvis Hynd, Richard Walcot* Gent.

For the County of *Mayo,* Sir *Oliver S. George, Arthur Gore, Iames Cuff, Arthur Swanwick, Owen Vaughan, Henry Webb* Esqs. *Edward Hill, Anthony Harrisson, Ioseph Bond, Francis Brent* Gent. *Francis Knight* Esquire ; *Henry Waddington* High Sheriff.

For the County of *Fermanagh,* The High Sherif of the said County for the time being, *Thomas* Lord *Folliot,* Sir *William Gore* Knight and Baronet, Sir *Iohn Humes* Knight and Baronet, Col. *Iohn Cole, William Davis, Nicolas Willoughby, William Cosby, Robert Cole, Henry Blannerhasset, Stephen Butler, William Archdale, Bartholomew Drope,*

Adam Cathcart, Iohn Madden Esqrs. *William Hamilton, Iohn Cormick, Iohn Cheslin, Henry Langford* Gent. The Provost of the Burrough of *Eniskillen* for the time being, *Edward Cook, Hugh Rowley, Roderick Mansel* Esquires.

For the Town and County of the Town of *Carickfergus.* The High Sherive of the said County for the time being, The Mayor for the time being, *Roger Lyndon* Recorder, *Matthew Iohnson, Iohn Orpin* Aldermen, *Iohn Harris, Edmund Davis, Anthony Hall* Merchants, *Iohn Dolloway, Hercules Davis* Esqs./

(Page 25)   For the County of *Monaghan, Iohn Forster* High Sherif of the said County, *Richard Blany, Richard Barret, Thomas Coote, Thomas Vincent, Oliver Ancthill, Arthur Dillon, William Barton, Peter Beaghan, Henry Cope, Nicolas Willoughby,* Esqs. *Tristram Cary, Michael Pockeridg, Simon Richardson, Roger Smith, William Holland, Carew Genelly,* Gent. *William Iohnson, William Davis* Esquires.

For the City and County of the City of *London Derry:* The Mayor of the City of *London Derry* for the time being, *Iohn Godbolt* Esq. *Samuel Hill, Thomas Cole* Esqs. Sherifs of the said City and County, The Mayor of *Colerayn* for the time being, *Michael Berrisford, Tristram Berrisford, Stephen Cuppage, Randolph Berisford, Iohn Rowly* Esqs. Col. *Iohn Gorges, George Philips* Esq. Lt. Col. *Alexander Staples,* Major *Robert Blare, Edward Carey, Hugh Gawen* Esq.

For the County of *Ardmagh,* The high Sherif of the said County for the time being, *William* Lord *Cawfield,* Sir *George Atcheson, Tobias Pointz, Hance Hamilton, Edward Richardson, Thomas Chambers* Esqrs. *Francis Chambers, Edward Rowley, Roger Parish* Gentlemen. *Henry Cope, Foulk Martin,* Esqs. The Soveraign of the Burrough of *Ardmagh, William Draper* Gent. Capt. *William King, Thomas Clerk* Esq.

For the County of *Donnegall,* The high Sherif of the said County for the time being, *Thomas* Lord *Folliot,* The Lord chief Justice *Basil,* Sir *Arthur Forbes,* Sir *William Gore* Baronets, Sir *Paul Davis* Knight, *Henry Brooks, Charls Hamilton, Iohn Folliot, Richard Perkins, George Cary, Henry Vaughan, Thomas Steward, Iames Erskin, William Dutton, William Warren, Thomas Dutton, Andrew Knox, Arthur Newborough, Will. Cuningham* Elder, *Iames Cuningham, Iohn Hamilton* of *Cavan, Thomas Grove, David Mortimer* Esqs.

For the Burrough of *Lifford* the Warden of *Lifford* for the time being, *Edward Tarleton, Peter Benson, George Knox, Archibald Pierson, Andrew Lindsey, Arthur Lening, Iohn Colhown, Iohn Breeding* elder, *Iames Hamilton, Alexander Stewart* Gent. *George Butler, David Stewart, Alexander Montgomery.*

For the County of *Down.* The high Sheriff of the said County for the time being, The Lord *Chichester, Hugh* Lord Viscount *Montgomery, Oliver Cromwell* Esq ; Sir *George Blundell* Baronet, *Arthur Hill, Marcus Trevor, Iames Trayl, George Rawden, Roger West, Edward Muschamp, Bernard Ward, Tobias Norris, Robert Fenwick, Henry Maxwel, Hugh Montgomery* of *Ballimalady, Matthew Harrison* Esquires. *Hugh Magill*
(Page 26)   of *Bellihenny, Richard Price, William Shaw* of *Newtown, Nicolas Ward, William/ Hatfield, Hugh Savage, Thomas Clerk* Gentlem. The Provost of *Newtown* for the time being, *Iohn Reynolds, Patrick Montgomery* of *Creboy, Iohn Swadling, Iohn Savage, William Bear* Gentlemen. Capt. *Collin Maxwel, Michael Smith* Gent, *William Hamilton* Esq. The Provost of *Killeleagh, David Williamson* Esq, *Archibald Hamilton, Alexander Scone* Gent.

For the County of *Antrim,* the high Sherif of the said County for the time being, *Arthur* Lord Viscount *Chichester, Edward* Lord Viscount *Conway,* Sir *Iohn Clotworthy* Knight, Sir *Iohn Skevington* Baronet, Col. *Iohn Gorge, Ralph King, Arthur Hill, George*

Rawden, Dr. *Alexander Colvill, Arthur Upton, Robert Colvill, Roger Lindon, Michael Harrison, William Adayre, Iames Shaw, Peter Beaghan, Richard Dob, Ioseph Strowd, Michael Berisford, Tristram Berisford* Esquires. *Adam Boyd, Iohn Donaldson* Gent. Capt. *Henry Spencer, William Hughson, Iohn Edmundston, Iohn Shaw* Gent. The Mayor of *Carrigfergus* for the time being, *Iohn Davis* Esq. *Hercules Davis* Gent.

For the County of *Tyrone*, the high Sherif of the said County for the time being, *William* Lord *Cawfield*, Sir *Arthur Forbes* Knight, *Audley Mervin, Arthur Chichester, Ferdinando Davis, William Richardson, William Moor, Robert Steward, Henry Mervin* Esqs. *Thomas Golbourn, William Cahoon, Richard Palfrey, Alexander* mac *Castguile, Iohn Young, Iohn Lesley* Junior, Gentl. *Richard Perkins, Ralph King, Edward Cook, Thomas White, Iohn Muns, Robert Lindsey* Esqrs.

For the Burrough of *Strabane : Iohn Modrell, Patrick Hamilton* Esquires.

For the County of *Cavan*, The high Sherif of the said County for the time being, *Charls* Lord *Lambert, Oliver Lambert* Esq. Sir *Francis Hamilton* Knight and Baronet, *Charles Hamilton, Thomas Coote, Tristram Berisford, Edward Philpot, Thomas Richardson, Thomas Coach, William Moor, Edward Cook, Humfrey Perrot, Samuel Townley, Thomas White, Robert Sanderson, Ambrose Beadle, Thomas Guillim, Richard Lewis, Thomas Ash, Lewis Craige, William Cosby* Esqs. *Iohn Madden, Wil.* [...]*n, Thomas Burton, Charls* mac *Fadin, Merrick Hart, Thomas Palmer, Daniel Clement, Iohn Beary, William Lowther, Iohn Blachford, Lancelot Lowther, Faustin Cuppage, James Hamilton, George Atkins, William Pepper*, The Provost of *Belturbet* for the time being, The Soveraign of *Cavan* for the time being, *Stephen Butler, Thomas Burrows* Esqs. *Richard Gibson* Gentl.

April the 24. 1660. Ordered, That this Ordinance be forthwith printed and published.

MA. BARRY
Clerk of the General Convention of Ireland *:*

11—[POLL-MONEY ORDINANCE OF 1661].

itle Page)   AN/ORDINANCE/For the Speedy/Raising of Moneys/FOR HIS/Majesties Service./ March the 1. 1660/Ordered, That this Ordinance be forthwith Printed and Published./ Mat. Barry Clerk of the/General Convention of Ireland./Dublin Printed by William Bladen, by Special Order, Anno Dom. 1660.

---

age 1)   AN ORDINANCE For the speedy raising of Money for his Majesties Service.

The General Convention of *Ireland* being by Proclamation set forth by the right Honourable the Lords Justices and Council, bearing date the seaventh day of *January* last past, and grounded upon his Majesties Letter of the eighteenth of *December* last, required to assemble and meet together, and in obedience thereunto, being accordingly assembled, and taking into consideration his Majesties said gracious Letter directed unto the said Lords Justices, and by them communicated to this Convention, purporting an absolute necessity for the raising of a supply of money for the present support of the Army here, and the preventing of Free-quarter, and other inconveniences which might otherwise arise, until the Parliament shall provide for the same ; And expressing his Majesties desire that some provision might be speedily made accordingly ; And also upon due consideration of the weighty reasons and earnest desires of the said Lords Justices for the speedy doing thereof for some short time until a Parliament shall sit ; And finding upon account taken aswel of the monthly charge of the Army, as of his Majesties Revenue both certain and casual, and his other Incomes to defray the same, that they do fall very much short to discharge the present pay of the Army.   And

age 2)   this Convention/likewise having a deep sence of his Majesties gracious favours and concessions to his Subjects of this his Kingdom, by his late declaration bearing date the thirtyeth day of *November* last past for their establishment and continuance in their possessions, and for the speedy calling of a Parliament as the onely visible and effectual remedy for the settlement of this Kingdom ; And being in all things ready to comply with his Majesties most just and reasonable desires, and in gratitude to his Majesties most gracious said concessions, notwithstanding the present poverty which the Inhabitants of this Kingdom are reduced unto by the late confusions thereof, and also for the satisfaction of so much money of the debt due from divers Members of this Convention, to Alderman *Bellingham* by Statute-staple entred into by Order of this Convention for his Majesties service, as the money already raised, and that hereafter shall be raised by the last Ordinance of this Convention for Pole-money shall fall short to satisfy.   This Convention upon the grounds and reasons aforesaid, doth think fit to Ordain, and it is accordingly by this Convention and the authority thereof Ordained, That all and every person and persons within this Kingdom of *Ireland*, of the several Ranks, Qualities and Degrees hereafter mentioned, shall pay the several and respective sums of money particularly hereafter in and by this Ordinance set down and appointed, (*viz.*)

That every Baronet shall pay six pounds *Sterl.*

That every Knight shall pay four pounds *Sterl.*

That every Esquire shall pay forty shillings *Sterl.*

That every Gentleman shall pay one pound four shillings *Sterl.*

That every Yeoman or chief Farmer shall pay fourteen shillings *Sterl.*

That every Husbandman or petty Farmer shall pay six shillings *Sterl.*

That every Widdow respectively according to her Husbands degree, shall pay the third part rated by this Ordinance upon that degree of which the Husband of each Widdow was in his lifetime ; And that every such Widdow for every Ten pounds she hath *per annum*, shall pay two shillings more, for every Ten pounds she so hath *per annum* as aforesaid.

That every Heir, Male and Female of what age soever, shall pay according to their respective degrees, qualities, and Estates as if he, she, or they were of full age./

That all common Handicrafts-men not residing in Corporations or Sea Towns, (*Page* 3) shall pay equally with the Husbandman and petty Farmer.

That all Car-men and Carriers shall pay equally with the Husbandman and petty Farmer.

That all In-holders and Shop-keepers not in Corporations, shall pay equally with the Yeoman and chief Farmer.

That every person of what degree soever, under the degree of a Baron that can dispend Ten pounds *per annum* in Lands, Tenements, Hereditaments, Beneficial Leases, Offices Civil or Military, or otherwise, shall pay (over and above the sums in the former Qualifications mentioned) two shillings *Sterl.* for every such Ten pounds a year he hath.

That every other person or persons of either sex of what degree or quality soever, as well Souldiers as others being above the age of fifteen years, and not comprised within any of the said Qualifications before mentioned, shall pay two shillings *Sterl.*

And it is further ordained by the authority aforesaid, that all & every person and persons chargeable with any sum of money by this Ordinance, shall be rated and charged for his or her degree and quality in such place onely, where he or she, or his or her Family was resident for the space of three months next before, or where he or she shall be found resident at the time of putting of this Ordinance in execution, and no where else.

And that all and every person before mentioned, and every absentee under the degree of a Baron, that hath neither Family, Stock, or habitation within this Realm shall pay for all and every ten pounds *per annum*, which he or she shall have in Lands, Leases, Tenements, or Offices, the sum of two shillings for each ten pounds in the County or place where the same shall respectively accrew or arise, which said sum every Tennant or Deputy holding the same, shall be liable to pay, and shall and may defaulk the same out of the Rent or sums due to the said Landlord, or other person that shall so be absent as aforesaid, unless by Contract, or Covenant between such Landlord and Tennant it be otherwise agreed or provided for.

And it is further ordained by the authority aforesaid, that all the sums of money due and payable by virtue of this Ordinance, shall be paid unto the high Collectors hereafter named, or to be named by virtue of this Ordinance, at two distinct payments, by even and equal portions, the first moyety/thereof to be paid on or before the tenth (*Page* 4) day of *April* next ensuing ; And the second moyety thereof to be paid to the said high Collectors on the seaventh day of *May* then next following ; And the said high

Collectors within six days after receipt of each of the said several moyeties respectively, are hereby required to pay the same to the Vice-Treasurer and other persons hereafter appointed for the receipt thereof, accordingly as hereby is afterwards limited.

And whereas there is very great reason that in Cities, Burroughs and Towns Corporate in respect of the several degrees and qualities of persons therein residing, there should be a more exact distinction of such persons, then will or can be ascertained under the aforementioned distinctions ; Therefore it is hereby ordained, that the more particular proportioning the sums to be paid by the several persons residing within such Corporations as aforesaid, (for which Commissioners are in and by this Ordinance named and appointed) shall be left to the order and discretion of the said Commissioners, or some of them of that county where the said Corporations respectively are, (being not counties of themselves) being joyned unto certain other honest and substantial Inhabitants of every of the said Cities, Burroughs, and Towns Corporate as are herein named to be Commissioners for such Cities Burroughs and Towns Corporate by this Ordinance. And the Commissioners hereby appointed for the County wherein such City, Burrough, or Town Corporate doth lie, and the Commissioners hereby appointed for such City, Town, or Burrough are required within four days after notice of this Ordinance to meet together, and they or any three or more of them (whereof one Inhabitant within such City, Town, or Burrough, and one Commissioner for the said County are always to be two,) are to set such rates and sums of money upon the Inhabitants of such respective Cities, Towns, or Burroughs as to them shall be thought fit, due and equal regard being had to the profits and advantages arising out of each persons Traffick, Trade, Stock, Profession, or Manufactory, so as no such rate or sum of money to be set upon any person or persons, be under the rate before expressed, for their respective qualities, degrees, offices, and Estates, and as they would have been assessed if he or they did not live in any City, Burrough, or Town Corporate.

Page 5)
Provided that every Baronet, Knight, Esquire, and Gentleman, and every other person or persons, residing in any/City, Burrough, or Town Corporate, not using any Merchandize or Trade, shall pay according to the rates aforementioned and no otherwise ; And the said proportions so set, are to be leavyed and received in manner as hereafter in this Ordinance for the same and the other sums hereby limited is provided, And where such Cities, Towns, or Burroughs are Counties of themselves, then to the discretion of the Commissioners for such Cities, Towns and Burroughs. And also that every Alyen or stranger born out of the Realms of *England*, *Scotland*, and *Ireland*, being Denizens or not Denizens, of what degree or quality soever, and being of the age of seaven years or above, shall pay double the sum of money which a free born Subject of these Realms being in the same degree or qualification which the said Alien is by this present Ordinance to pay.

And be it further ordained by the authority aforesaid, That every such person or persons of the several degrees or qualities aforementioned, as well such as be born within *England*, *Scotland*, or *Ireland*, as every other person, stranger born, Denizen, or not Denizen inhabiting within this Realm or else where, which at the time of the said ratings so to be had or made shall be out of this Realm, and have Goods, Chattels, Lands or Tenements, Fees, or Annuities, or other profits within this Realm shall be chargeable, and charged for the same where such Goods, Chattels, Lands, Tenements, Fees, Annuities, or other profits then shall be, or in such other place where such person or persons, or his or their Factors, Deputie, Agent or Attourney shall have his or their most usual resort unto within this Realm, in like manner as if the said person were or had been at the time of the said rating within this Realm.

And be it further ordained by the Authority aforesaid, That every Master or Mistress being sole with whom any Servant is or shall be abiding at the time of the ratings aforesaid, liable to the payments in this Ordinance, as also every Guardian, Father, or Mother being a Widdow, with whom any Child or Children are residing at the time of the ratings aforesaid, not being marryed, and lyable to the payments in this Ordinance, and also every Husband is, and are, and shall be charged for such respective payments due from their Wives, Children or Servants, for lack of payment thereof by such Wives, Servants, or Children, And that it shall and may be lawful for every Master or Mistress to defaulk such sum or/sums of money as he or she shall *(Page 6)* deposit or lay down for their Servants, out of such wages as are or shall hereafter grow due to such Servants.

And be it further ordained by the authority aforesaid, That for the better and more regular ordering of the said moneys to be rated, charged and paid, that the several persons hereafter in this Ordinance named, or any three or more of them be, and are hereby appointed Commissioners within the several Counties, Cities, Burroughs in which they are so named and appointed, who hereby have full power and Authority to put the same in effectual execution, and that by the authority of this Ordinance after notice thereof given them, they may by their assents and agreements sever themselves for the execution thereof in the several Baronies, and other places within the limits of their said County, in such form as to them shall seem expedient to be ordered ; And the said Commissioners, or any three or more of them shall direct their several or joynt precept or precepts unto such a number of the able and discreet Protestant Inhabitants if they may be had, to be named by the said Commissioners as aforesaid of and in the Baronies, Parrishes, Towns and other places within the limits of their County, straitly by the said precept or precepts, charging them to appear in their proper persons before the said Commissioners, or such number of them as they shall divide themselves into, at a certain day and place as by the discretion of the Commissioners as aforesaid shall be limitted and appointed, regard always to be had where with conveniency it may be that such place appointed be for the most indifferent ease and travail of the Inhabitants of the said County, whose appearance shall be necessary towards the execution of this Ordinance commanding further by every such precept, that he to whose hand such precept shall come, shall shew, and deliver the same to the other Inhabitants named in the same precept, and that none of them fail to accomplish the same upon pain of forty shillings.

And it is further ordained by the Authority aforesaid, That at the said day and place prefixed and limitted in the said precept, every of the said Commissioners then being within this Realm, not having sufficient excuse, shall appear in his proper person, and there the said Commissioners being present, or any three or more of them, shall call, or cause to be called before them the said Inhabitants to whom they have directed their precept, and if any person so warned make default, unless he then be letted by sickness or other lawful excuse, or if any appearing, refuse/to serve in form following, *(Page 7)* then every such person so making default, or refusing to serve, shall forfeit forty shillings, and upon the same appearance had, they shall be charged before the Commissioners by all convenient ways and means to inquire of all and every person within the respective places limited to their care of each sex, of and above the age of fifteen years and of what Rank, Quality, or Degree he or they are, and also of what

Estate he or they have by the year in Lands, Offices or otherwise chargable by virtue of this Ordinance, and of the dwelling and abiding places of such persons with the limits of the places that they shall be charged with, and of all others which shall have his or their most resort unto any of the said places, and chargable with any sums of money by this Ordinance, and of all other things requisite touching the said Ordinance, and according to the intent of the same, and thereupon as near as it may be, or shall come to their knowledge truly to present and certify before the said Commissioners the names, and sir-names, and the qualifications and estates of every person residing within the limits of the places that they shall be charged with, without any concealment, love, favour or affection, dread or malice, upon pain of forfeiture of five pounds, to be taxed, extracted, and leavyed in form as hereafter in this Ordinance shall be limitted and appointed, and thereupon the said Commissioners shall openly there read, or cause to be read unto them, the several qualifications of the persons, and the sums by such persons under such qualifications payable as is in this Ordinance mentioned, and in what manner and form they ought to make their Certificate, and of all manner of persons as well Alyens and strangers, Denizens or not Denizens inhabiting within this Realm, as of such persons as be born within the said three Realms, and of persons being in the parts beyond the Seas, having Goods and Chattels, Lands or Tenements within this Realm as aforesaid ; and of all goods being in the custody of any person or persons to the use of any such absentee : by the which information and shewing the said persons shall have such plain knowledge of the true intent of this present Ordinance, that they shall have no reasonable cause to excuse themselves by ignorance.

(Page 8)

And after such charge, and this Ordinance, and the manner of the said Certificate to be made in writing, and every thing requisite and necessary to their said Certificate to them declared, the said Commissioners there being, shall by their/discretion appoint and limit unto the said persons another day and place to appear before the said Commissioners, and charging the said persons that they in the mean time shall make diligent inquiry by all ways and means of the premisses, and then and there every of them upon pain of forfeiture of fourty shillings to appear at the new prefixed day and place, there to certify unto the said Commissioners in writing according to their said charge, and according to the true intent of this Ordinance, as to them in manner aforesaid hath been declared and shewed by the Commissioners, at which day and place so to them prefixed, if any of the said persons make default, or appear, and refuse to make the said Certificate, then every of them so offending to forfeit forty shillings ; except there be a reasonable excuse, and of such as appear ready to make the Certificate as aforesaid, the said Commissioners there being, shall take and receive the same Certificate, and if the Commissioners see cause reasonable, they shall examine the said presenters thereof, and thereupon the said Commissioners at the said days and place by their agreement amongst themselves, shall from time to time there openly prefix a day at a certain place or places within the limits of their County by their discretion for the further proceeding in the execution of this Ordinance, and thereupon at the said day of the said Certificate, as is aforesaid taken, the said Commissioners shall make their precept or precepts to such persons or Officers as they shall think fit within their jurisdiction, comprising in the said precepts the names and sir-names of all such persons presented before them in the said Certificate, of whom the said Commissioners shall have cause to suspect to be of a different qualification, or value in Lands, Offices or otherwise, then under what they are in the said Certificate returned, (except the Commissioners upon their own knowledge can assertain the same, in which case they have power by this Ordinance to amend the said Certificate) accordingly, to warn such persons whose names shall be comprized in the said precepts at their mansions, or to their persons, that the same persons, and every of them shall personally appear before the said Commissioners at the same new prefixed day and place, there to be examined concerning the premisses, at which day and place so prefixed, the said Commissioners then and there being, shall cause to be called the said persons, whose names are comprized in the said precept for their examination, and if any of those persons which shall be warned, which at any time after the/ warning, and before the prefixed day, shall be within such place where he may *(Page* 9) have knowledge of his said appearance to be made, make default and appeare not, unlesse upon reasonable cause or excuse shown, that then every of them so making default, to be charged and rated according to such Qualification or Value as aforesaid, as he or they are supposed or suggested to be comprized in, and Power and Authority is hereby given to the said Commissioners to inlarge or increase or otherwise to abate or diminish the ratings of such persons, as they shall find by due examination, or upon their own knowledge to be falsely returned under any Qualification.

And if any person or persons that ought to be rated and charged to any of the payments in this Ordinance mentioned, by reason of his or their resorting, and removing from place to place, or by reason of his or their saying that he or they were else where charged, or by reason of any priviledge of his or their dwelling or abiding in any place not being foreprized in this Ordinance, or otherwise by his or their covin or craft, or by any words or sayings, or otherwise, or if any that is a Commissioner, or Presenter, or Assessor of others, happen to escape from the said chargings, and be not rated and charged according to the true intent of this Ordinance, and that proved by presentment, examination, or information, or otherwise, before the said Commissioners, or any three of them ; then every such person that by such means, or otherwise willingly by covin, or without just cause, shall avoid the payments or chargings aforesaid or any of them, shall be charged upon the knowledge and proofs thereof with and at treble the value of so much as he, or they, should, might or ought to have been rated and charged at by virtue of this Ordinance for his or their degree or quality, only a third part of which penalty or treble value, the Commissioners of each County, or any three or more of them, are hereby impowered to allow to any person or persons that shall discover the frauds aforesaid or any of them, and the same treble value to be gathered, leavyed and of his or their Goods, and Chattels, Lands, and Tenements in manner as hereafter is expressed.

And be it further ordained by the Authority aforesaid, that the said Commissioners which shall be or inhabit in any County, or place within the limit of that County, or the greater part of them, shall have full power and authority by this Ordinance, to rate, charge, and sess every other Commissioners joyned with them in that County, according to their respective/qualifications, and the said Commissioners within every *(Page* 10) division, shall also rate and charge every Presenter or Assessor within his or their division according to their respective qualifications and estates as aforesaid, and that as well the sums upon every of the said Commissioners and Presenters so set, rated, and charged as the sums made and presented by the presenters shall be written, certifyed, set and estreated, and the estreats thereof to be made with the other Inhabitants of that part, and within the limits of the said County or division, so to be gathered and leavyed in like manner as it ought or should have been if the said Commissioners or Presenters had been private persons.

And be it further ordained by the Authority aforesaid, that after the said rates and charges of the said sum upon and by the said Assessing, and Certificate as is aforesaid made, the said Commissioners, or any three or more of them shall with all convenient speed by their writing, estreat the said rates and charges thereof under their seals and signes manual, and the same shall deliver unto such sufficient and substantial Inhabitants of the Baronies, Parrishes, and other places aforesaid within their limits, as shall be approved by the high Collectors hereafter to be appointed, containing as well the particular names and sir-names, as the remembrance of all sums of moneys not in Figures but in writing at large, charged and set of and upon every person chargable by this Ordinance according to their several qualifications and estates as aforesaid, by Authority of which writing and estreat so delivered, the same persons so named and deputed severally, shall have full power and authority by virtue of this Ordinance, immediately after the delivering of the said writing or estreat, to demand, leavy, and gather of every person therein specified the sum or sums in the said writing or estreat comprized, and for non-payment thereof, to distrein the said person or persons so being behind by their Goods and Chattels, and the distresses so taken, to keep by the space of six days, at the costs and charges of the owner thereof : and if the said owner or owners do not pay such sum or sums of moneys as shall be rated or charged upon him or them by authority of this Ordinance within the said six days, then the same distress to be apprized by two of the Inhabitants where such distress is taken, and then to be sould by the said Collectors for the payment of the said moneys, and the overplus coming of the sale and keeping thereof (if any be) immediately to be restored to the owner/or owners of the distress, which said persons so deputed to take, ask, gather, and leavy the said sums, shall answer and be charged for the portion onely to them assigned, and limited to be gathered and leavyed, and comprized in the said writing or estreat, so to them (as is aforesaid) delivered, and the said sums in that writing or estreat comprized, to pay unto the high Collector of that County for the collection of the same in manner and form under written thereunto to be named and deputed.

And further be it ordained by the said Authority, that the said Commissioners which shall be present at their first meeting, or the major part of them, shall then name and appoint one sufficient and able person, as by their discretion shall be thought fit, residing within the limits of their County to be high Collector, and to have the collection and receipt of the said sums set and leavyable within the said County, and the said Commissioners, or any three or more of them with all convenient speed, after the whole sum be rated and charged in all the divisions of their County, shall under their Seals and Signes manual, deliver unto the said high Collector, one estreat indented, comprizing in it the names of all such persons as were assigned to leavy the said particular sums, and the sums of every Barony, Cantred, Hundred, City, Town, Parish, and other place aforesaid, with the names and sir-names of the persons so chargable according to the estreats thereof made and delivered as aforesaid, and the said high Collectors to be assigned, shall be charged to answer the whole sum comprized in the said estreat limited in his collection.

Provided always, and be it ordained, that before the delivery of the aforesaid Estreats unto the said high Collector, the said high Collector to enter into Bond with sufficient Security to the use of his Majestie, his Heirs and Successors, before the said Commissioners or any Three or more of them, to be bound in double the Summe of

Page 11)

his Collection upon Condition, that if the said Collector his heires or Executors do truely content and pay unto the Vice-Treasurer, and Treasurer at Warrs for the time being, his Deputy or Deputies, or his or their Order, all and every the summe and summes of Money, which he shall receive within the limits of his Collection accordingly, as from time to time he shall receive the same, That then the said Obligation to be void, or else to remaine in full force and vertue, which/said Obligation so taken, the *(Page* 12) said Commissioners shall send and cause to be delivered unto the said Vice-Treasurer and Treasurer at Warre for the time being, his Deputy or Deputies, with the severall Estreats of the said Chargings and Rates within the Limits of their several Jurisdictions, and also Abstracts thereof, under the hands and seales of the said Commissioners, or any Three, or more of them, to the Lords Justices, or other Chief Governor or Governors for the time being, on or before the fourteenth day of *April* next, and the said Vice-Treasurer, his Deputy or Deputies, upon payment of the said severall Collections at the times herein limitted for the payment thereof, shall cancell and deliver the said Obligation to the said high Collector without any Fee or Reward, and every high Collector so deputed having the said Estreat as is aforesaid, shall have Authority by this Ordinance, to appoint daies and places, within the Divisions of that County, whereof he is high Collector, for the payment of the said Summes to him respectively to be made, and thereof to give Notice to all such persons, having the Charge of the perticular Collections within the Barronies, Cantreds, Hundreds, Parishes, Townes, or other places, to make payment of the perticular Collections of every Sum as to them shall appertaine, and if at that same day and place so prefixed and limitted by the said high Collector, the said persons appointed for the particular Collection, within such Barrony, Cantred, Hundred, Citty, Town, Parish, or other place, do not pay unto the said Collector the sum within the several Barronies, Cantreds, Hundreds, Towns, Parrishes, and other places due and comprized within the said Estreat thereof to them delivered by the said Commissioners, or some of them, or so much thereof, as they have by any meanes received, that then it shall be lawfull to the said high Collector and his Assignes to distrein every of the said persons for their said several and particular Collections, of the said Summes comprized in the said Estreat to him (as is before expressed) delivered, or for so much of the same Summe, as to them shall happen to be gathered and levied, and to be behind and unpaid, by the Goods and Chattels of every of them so behind and unpaid, and the Distresses so taken to be kept and appraised and sould as aforesaid, and thereof to take and levy the Sums so then being behind and unpaid, and the overplus comming of the Sale of the said Distresse (if any be) to be restored/ *(Page* 13) and delivered to the Owner in Forme above remembred.

And it is also by the said Authority Ordained, That if any person charged to and for the Collection and Receipt of any part or portion of the Summes comprized in the said Estreats according to this Ordinance, after all lawfull meanes and endeavours by him used to collect and receive the same, yet if by the dying of any person, or departure of any person from the place where he was so charged, and set or being an Absentee, or that his Goods and Chattels be so eloyned, or in such privy or covert manner kept, as that the said person or persons charged with the same by Estreats, or other Writing from the Commissioners, cannot or may not Levy the Summe or Summes comprized within the said Estreats, by Distresse within the Limitts of their Collection, then upon Relation thereof, and due Examination of such person or persons as shall be charged with and for the Receipt and Collection of the same before the said Commissioners, or any Three of them, where such person or persons were rated and charged, and upon plaine Certificate thereof made unto the said Vice-Treasurer, and Treasurer at Warre for the time being, his Deputy or Deputies by the said Commissioners, of the dwelling place, Names and Summes of the said persons, of whom the same Sums cannot be levyed and had, then the said persons appointed for the same particular Collection against the high Collector, as the high Collector upon his Account to be discharged thereof, And over that the said Commissioners, to whom all such Declaration of the Premisses shall be made in Forme aforesaid, from time to time shall have full Power and Authority to direct their Precept or Precepts to the said person or persons charged with any Sum of, for and upon any such person or persons, or to any other person, or to any Sherriffe, Steward, Bayliffe, or other whatsoever Officer, Minister, person or persons of such place or places where any such person or persons so owing any such Sum or Summes shall have Lands, Tenements, or other Hereditaments, or reall Possess-ions, Goods and Chattels, whereby any such person so Indebted, his Heires, Executors, Assignes, or other having the Custody, Governance or Disposition of any Goods, Chattels, Lands, Tenements or other Possessions, whereof such Summe and Summes which by any such person and persons may or ought to be levyed, be it within the Limit of such (Page 14) County, where/such person or persons was or were charged, or without in any place within this Realme of *Ireland*, by which Precept as well such person or persons shall be charged to Levy such Money, as the Officer of the place or places where such Distresses may be taken, shall have full Power and Authority to distraine every such person indebted, charged, and chargeable by this Ordinance, or his Executors or Ad-ministrators of his Goods, Chattels, his Guardians, Factors, Deputies, Lessees, Farmors and Assignes, and all other persons by whose hands, or out of whose Lands, every such person should have Fee, Rent, Annuity, or other Profits, or which at the time of the said Rating or Charging, shall have Goods or Chattels, or any other thing moveable of any such person or persons being indebted, or owing such Summe, and the Distresses so taken, cause to be kept, appraised and sould in like manner and forme as is aforesaid. And if any such Distresse for non-Payment happen to be taken out of the Limits of the said persons charged and assigned to levy the same, the person so charged for leavying any such Summe by Distresse, shall have for the Labour of every such person going to the execution thereof for every Mile that any such person so laboureth for the same two pence, to be levyed upon the Partie making default by Distresse, over and above the Summe charged on the said Party, every such Farmor, Tennant, Guardian, Factor, or other whatsoever person being distrained, or otherwise charged for Payment of any such Sum or Sums, or any other Summe by reason of this Ordinance, shall be of such Summe or Summes of him or them so leavied and taken, quitted and discharged at his next Day of Payment of the same, or at the Delivery of such Goods and Chattels as he that is so distrained had in his Custody or Governance against him or them that shall be so charged, and set any Grant or Writing Obligatory, or other whatsoever matter to the contrary made heretofore notwithstanding.

And be it further ordained by the authority aforesaid, That all penalties mentioned in this Ordinance which shall happen to be incurred by any person or persons, shall be set down particularly in the estreat which shall be delivered to any person or persons particularly appointed to collect and receive the several sums in their respective divisions where such person or persons are residing, by whom such penalty shall be incurred, (Page 15) and to be leavied and received in such manner and form by the/said Sub-Collectors, and paid over to the High-Collector as if such penalties had been imposed upon such persons for the sums rated and charged upon them for their respective qualifications, and in the same estreats to be returned to the said Vice-Treasurer and Treasurer at War for the time being, his Deputy or Deputies, that thereby a particular account of such penalties may be had, as also the sum or sums being behind or unpaid by any person or persons which are to be leavyed and gathered by virtue of the aforesaid process to be made by the said Commissioners, that further Order may be taken therein ; And if any Collector or other person, charged with any receipt of any part of the said several sums, or any other person rated or otherwise by this Ordinance charged with or for any part of the said several sums, or with any other sum, penalty, or other forfeiture, happen to die before the Collectors, or other whatsoever person or persons have executed, accomplished, satisfyed, or sufficiently discharged, that which to every such person appertain or belong to do according to this Ordinance, then the Executors and Heirs of every such person and all others, seized of any Lands and Tenements that any such person being charged by this Ordinance, and deceasing before he be discharged thereof, or any other to his use, onely had of Estate of Inheritance, at the time that any such person was named, Collector, or otherwise charged with or for any manner of thing to be done, satisfyed or paid, by reason of this Ordinance, and all those that have in their possessions or hands any Goods, Chattels, Leases, or other things that were to any person or persons at the time of his death, or any Lands or Tenements that were to the same persons at the time he was (as is aforesaid) charged by this Ordinance, shall be by the same compelled and charged to do and accomplish in every case as the same person being so charged should have done, or might have been compelled to do if he had been living after such rate, of the Lands and Goods of the said Collector, or other person as abovesaid, as the party shall have in his Lands.

And it is further ordained by the authority aforesaid, That the Commissioners hereby appointed in the several Counties, Cities, Towns and Burroughs in this Realm, are and shall be hereby authorized, out of the moneys that shall be raised by virtue of this Ordinance, to make such allowances to the High-Collectors, and other Collectors, and Clerks that shall be by them imployed, or for any other charges that shall to/ them seem requisite for the better leavying and bringing in the several sums of money *(Page 16)* herein formerly mentioned as to them shall be thought fit and necessary, so as the allowances so to be made by the said Commissioners, do not exceed the sum of Twelve pence in the pound, which said Twelve pence in the pound is to be allowed by the said Treasurer unto the several High-Collectors upon their respective accounts.

Provided always, that this Ordinance, or any thing therein conteined, in any wise extend not to charge the Provost, Fellows and Schollers of the foundation of the Colledge of the Holy Trinity near *Dublin*, nor to any Hospital men, or people living upon Alms.

And whereas it hath been declared to this General Convention, that the insolvencies and deficiencies of the two former Polls hath principally risen from, and been occasioned by the removeal of many of the Under-tennants, and meaner sort of people out of the Towns and Villages wherein they did inhabite at the time of making up the Estreats, or Lists of the Inhabitants of such Townes and Villages, and that purposely to avoid the Payments of the said Pole-monies, so that the Collectors of the severall Counties and Baronies could neither finde them, or their Distresses, to make Payment of the Summe or Summes charged on them in the said Estreats, to the great dis-service of his Majestie, and disappointment of the Expectations of this Generall Convention : And forasmuch as the same could not happen without the Connivance of the Land-Lord, Farmor, or Head-Tennant of such Town or Village. Be it therefore ordained by the authority aforesaid, that where any person or persons inhabiting in any of the

Townes and Villages of this Kingdome at the time of laying in of this present Poll, shall go about to remove him or themselves, out of such Towne or Village as aforesaid, That then it shall and may be lawfull for such Land-Lord, Farmor, or Head-Tenant, residing in any such Towne or Village to distraine, and he is hereby Ordered to distraine on the Goods or Chattels of such person or persons to double the Value of the Pole-money, rated on them by this present Ordinance, and the same to deliver to the Collector of that Barrony, who is to dispose of the same, as by this present Ordinance he is appointed to dispose of other Distresses, And where any Land-Lord, Farmer, or Head-Tennant

(Page 17) of any of the said Townes and Villages, shall neglect or faile to distraine/as aforesaid, That then the Collector nominated and appointed for that Barrony, shall demand the Summe or Summes rated on such person or persons so departed from such Land-Lord, Farmor or Head-Tennant, and upon non Payment, to distraine on the Goods or Chattels of such Land-Lord, Farmor or Head-Tennant, and the same to dispose of, as by Vertue and Authority of this Ordinance in other cases of Distresse he is authorized and appointed.

Provided alwayes, and it is hereby Ordained, That Sir *William Vsher* Knight, and *Thomas Boyd* Merchant, Members of this Convention, shall be, and are hereby impowr'd by this Generall Convention, from time to time to take an Account of what money is, or shall be raised by Vertue of the second Ordinance of this Convention for Pole-money, towards Satisfaction of the said Money due by Statute Staple to Alderman *Daniell Bellingham* from severall Members of this Convention, and of what part thereof, the said Money so raised, and to be raised, shall fall short to satisfie. And the high Collectors of the severall Counties in the Province of *Leinster*, are hereby required within the times above limitted, to pay the severall Summes of Money that shall be raised by vertue of this Ordinance in the severall Counties in the said Province of *Leinster*, to the said Sir *William Vsher* and *Thomas Boyd*, who out of the said Monies are to satisfie and pay to the said Alderman *Bellingham*, what shall remaine due unto him upon the said Statute Staple, by the Dificiency of the money raised, or to be raised by the said second Ordinance for Pole-money. And after Satisfaction of the said Money so due by the said Statute Staple, and the Interest thereof, the said Sir *William Vsher* and *Thomas Boyd* are hereby required to pay the residue of the said Money, that shall be so by them receceived to his Majesties Vice-Treasurer, and Treasurer at Warre, for his Majesties use. And the said Sir *William Vsher* and *Thomas Boyd*, are to make such allowances out of the said moneys to be by them received as by the said Vice-Treasurer, is to be made out of the residue of the moneys to be paid unto him by virtue of this Ordinance.

And be it further ordained by the authority aforesaid, That these persons under written and no other, be, and are nominated and appointed to be Commissioners for putting in execution this Ordinance within the several Counties, Cities, and Buroughs of this Realm of *Ireland*, That is to say, /

Page 18) For the City and County of the City of *Dublin*, the Mayor and Sherifs for the time being, *William Davis* Esq ; Recorder of *Dublin*, *Robert Deey*, *William Smith*, *William Bladen*, *Raphael Hunt*, *Richard Tigh*, *Daniel Hutchinson*, *John Preston*, *Thomas Hook*, *Ridgley Hatfield*, *Thomas Waterhouse*, *Peter Wibrant*, *Daniel Wibrant*, *Robert Mills*, *George Gilbert*, *John Cranwel*, *William Cliff*, *Richard Cook*, *John Desmineer*, *Daniel Bellingham*, *Mark Quin*, *John Forrest*, *Ralph Vizard* Aldermen, Sir *William Vsher*, Sir *Robert Newcomen*, Sir *Robert Meredith*, Sir *Paul Davis*, Sir *Wil. Domvile*, Sir *Hierom Alexander* Knits, *Wil. Knight*, *Philip Fernely*, *Wil. Dixon*, *Rob. Shapcot*, *Rob. Kennedy*,

Esquires, Doctor *Ralph King*, Doctor *Dudley Loftus, Thomas Richardson, Richard Palfrey, William Sands, Abraham Yarner, Thomas Boyd, Abraham Clements, Enoch Reader, Lewis Desmineer, Samuel Salterson, John Beuchamp, John Smith, Thomas Howard, Thomas Pooley, Robert Hughes, John Povey, John Ket, Thomas Maul, Thomas Kennedy, Patrick Tallant, William Cory, Iohn Moor, Iohn Burniston, Ralph Allen, Thomas Worsop* Esq.

For the County of *Dublin*, Lord chief Baron *Bysse*, Sir *Henry Titchborne*, Sir *Theophilus Iones*, Sir *Iohn Hoy*, Sir *William Domvil*, Sir *William Usher*, Sir *Richard Kennedy*, Sir *Iohn Cole*, Sir *Walter Plunket* Knights, Col. *Chidley Coot*, Doctor *Dudley Loftus, Robert Kennedy, Philip Fernely, Edward Cook, Thomas Richardson, Francis Peasly, Daniel Hutchinson, Iohn Baxter, Ralph Wallis, Thomas Vincent, Robert Cusack, Richard Bulkley, Iohn Povey, Thomas Maul, Iohn Burniston* Esquires, *William Dixon* Esq ; *William Davis* Esq ; Recorder of *Dublin, Richard Barry, William Hoy, William Titchborne, Edward Barry, Thomas Kennedy* Esqus.

For the County of *Wicklow*, Sir *Henry Titchborne*, Sir *William Vsher*, Sir *Iohn Hoy*, Sir *Theophilus Iones*, Sir *Richard Kennedy* Knights, *Robert Kennedy, William Knight, Roger West, Philip Fernely, William Hoy, Robert Hassels, William Toxteth, Richard Renal,* — *Whitehead*, Doctor *Abraham Yarner, Edward Harrington, Samuel Pepys, Iohn Boswel, Humphrey Abdy, Thomas Bowls, Cromwel Wigfield, Thomas Kennedy, Edward Billingsley, William Warren, William Matthews, Iohn Povey, Philip Harris, William Pinson, Thomas Brereton, William Rieve* Esquires, *Thomas Waterhouse* Alderman, *Thomas Boyd* Merchant, *Iohn Humphreys, Walter Walsh* Gent. *Robert Stradford* Esq ; /

For the Burrough of *Wicklow*, The Portrif of the Burrough for the time being, *(Page 19)* *Iohn Hacket, Edward Hartshorn, Iohn King, Iames Stanley* Gent.

For the County of *Kildare*, Sir *George Blundel*, Sir *Walter Burroughs*, Sir *William Meredith* Barronets, Sir *Robert Meredith*, Sir *Paul Davis*, Sir *Iohn Hoy*, Sir *Theophilus Iones* Knights. *William Hoy, Iohn Salt, Henry Warren, Raphael Hunt, Thomas Harman, Dudley Cooley, George Blunt, Richard Tompson, Iohn Browne, Richard Teigh, Daniell Hutchinson, Iohn Annesley, Iohn Ewers, Thomas Iefford, Walter White, Henry Sanckey, Thomas Browne, Phillip Ferneley, Charles Reeves, Francis Peasley, William Warren, Edward Bermingham,* Esq. *Will. Davies* Esq. Recorder of *Dublin, Francis Nest*, Gent.

For the Town of *Naas*, the Soveraign for the time being, *Charls Ryves, Nicolas Stafford*, Esq.

For the Town of *Kildare*, the Soveraign for the time being, *Francis Peasly, Nicolas Rutlidg*, Esquires.

For the Town of *Athie*, the Soveraign for the time being, *William Scot, William Weldon* Esqs.

For the County of *Catherlogh*, The Sherriffe for the time being, *William Temple, Henry Warren, Edward Harman, Thomas Burdet, Iohn Aston, Henry Smithick, Abraham Highmore, Rob. Browne, Walter Badley, Robert Michael, Richard Andrews, Iohn Warren, Osborne Edwards, William Hudson, Oliver Iones, Richard Norris, Thomas Harman, Thomas Bolton, Henry Ward, Samuel Bathurst,* Esqs. *George Hartop, William Bernard, Richard Fisher, Peter Flowre, Richard Doys* and *Iohn Corbet*, Esqs.

For the Burrough of *Catherlogh*, The Portrieve for the time being, *Thomas Reynolds, Edward Reynolds, John Clerk, Iohn Smith, Richard Courtess*, Esquires.

For the County of *Wexford, Iohn Fountaine*, Esq high Sheriffe of the said County, *Nicholas Loftus* Senior, *Timothy Stamp, Nicolas Devereux, Thomas Scot, Iohn Brett, Thomas Hart, Iohn Tench, Edward Withers, Nicholas Loftus* Junior, *Henry Masterson*,

Alexander Barrington, Thomas Barrington, Matthew Stoddard, Spencer Vincent, Thomas Knox, Iohn Cliff, Nathaniel Boyse, Richard Ousley, Iohn Totty, Esqs. The Mayor of *Wexford* for the time being, *Constantine Neale, Francis Harvey,* The Portriff of *Enis-corthy* for the time being, *Iohn Sands, Edmund Highgate, Roger Levesey, Richard Wilbore, Iohn Swan, Richard Row,* Esqs. Sir *Richard Clifton,* Sir *Walter Plunket,* / Knights, *Roger West, Iohn Warren, Roger Lyndon, Edward Rotheram, Iohn Kitchingman, Robert Hassells, Nicholas Cod, Samuel Shepheard, Richard Kenny, Osborne Edwards,* Esquires, *Edward Chichister,* Gent.

(Page 20)

    For the County of *Kilkenny,* Sir *Patricke Weymes,* Sir *William Flowre,* Sir *Iohn Ponsonby,* Knights, *Daniel Redman, William Warden, Oliver Wheeler, Thomas Evans, Oliver Iones, Iohn Campel, Henry Baker, Joseph Cuff, James Weyms, Bryan Manswer, Thomas Burrel, John Ieoner, Thomas Sanford, Iohn Powel,* Lt. Col. *Iackson, Anthony Horsey, Abel Warren, Humphrey Hurd, George Bishop, Edward Butler, Thomas Burdet, Henry Martin, Thomas Butler, Robert Lloyd, Henry Slade, Ionas Wheeler* Esqs. *William Baker* Gent. *Henry Fog, George Lodge,* — *Haford, Charls Hawkins, Dudley North, Iohn Iones, Robert Walsh, Francis Rowlston, Thomas Bowers, Emanuel Palmer, Ioseph Wheeler, Simon Blackmore, Iohn Woodcock,* Ensign *Norse, Allen Tentch* Gent. Lt. Col. *Richard Stephens.*

    For the City and County of the said City of *Kilkenny, Thomas Evans* Mayor Esq. the Recorder and the two Sherifs for the time being, Sir *Patrick Weymes,* Knt, *William Warden, Daniel Redman, Thomas Burrill, Henry Baker, Ioseph Cuffe, Thomas Butler, Peter Goodwin, Valentine Read,* Esqs. *Iosias Hadock,* Gent.

    For the Burrogh of *Callen* in the County of *Kilkenny, Iohn Warren* Gent. Soveraigne, *Iohn Campell, Henry Baker* Esqs. *Patrick Vance, Darby Dingle, Iohn Pressick,* Gent.

    For the Burrough of *Thomas-Towne* in the County of *Kilkenny, Christopher Hewetson* Soveraigne, Gent. *Thomas Burrill, Anthony Stamp,* Esqs. *Henry Rogers, Phillip Young, Thomas Hill,* Gent.

    For the Burrough of *Goran* in the County of *Kilkenny, Tho. Hussey* Portriffe, Gent. *William Warden, Iohn Powell,* Esqs. *Charles Eager,* Gent.

    For the Burrough of *Ennisteige,* — *Whaley* Portriff Gent, Sir *Iohn Ponsonby, Alexander Castle,* Esq.

    For the *Queene's County,* The high Sherriffe for the time being, The Burgesse-Master of *Mariborrough* for the time being, Sir *Amos Meredith,* Sir *Oliver St. George,* Knights *and* Barronets, Sir *William Flowre* Knight, *Henry Gilbert, Thomas Coote, Oliver Wheeler, Geo[r]ge St. George, Walter Warnford, Thomas Burrell, Thomas Vincent, Iohn Weaver, Gilbert Rawson, Thomas Prior, Francis Barrington, Iohn Rawlins, William Scot, Nathaniel Marks, Henry Syballs, Adam/Loftus, Edward Bolton, Barnaby Doyne, Thomas Piggot, Francis Cosby, Vincent Kidder, Robert Meredith, Iohn Gilbert, Iohn Whitny, Iohn Piggot, William Weldon, William Bowen, Rich. Warburton,* Esqs. *Edward Burrell, Richard Smith, Iohn Tanner, Robert Gough, Thomas Ogle, Phillip Sergeant, William Lestrange, Iohn Rhoades,* Gent.

(Page 21)

    For the Burrough of *Marriborugh,* the Burgesse Master, *Henry Gilbert, Iohn Weaver,* Esqs.

    For the *Kings County,* The Sherriffe for the time being, *Cary Dillon,* Sir *George Blundell,* Sir *George Herbert, Edward Herbert, Thomas Gifford, Henry Sanckey, William Hamilton, Henry Lestrange, Iohn Weaver, William Purefoy, Robert Lloyd, Iohn Moore, Robert Busbridge, William Candler, Laurence Parsons, Michael Herbert, Iohn Hallom,*

Iohn Nelson, Iohn Mitchell, Iohn Wakely, Samuell Rolls, Richard Warburton, Thomas Vincent, Walter Lambert, Cap. — *Done, Peter Purefoy, Iohn Baldwin, Iohn Rose, Robert Chafe, Anthony Atkinson, Geo. Sanckey, Francis Peasly,* Esqs. *Francis Nest,* Gent.

For the Burrough of *Phillips-Towne,* The Burgesse Master, *Robert Lloyd, Charles Lyons.*

For the County of *Meath, Arthur Dillon* Esq high Sherriffe, Col. *Cary Dillon,* Sir *Robert Forth,* Sir *George Wentworth,* Sir *Thomas Meredith,* Sir *Theophilus Iones,* Sir *Hierome Alexander,* Sir *Edward Sutton, Randle Moore, Thomas Gifford, Thomas Loftus, Iames Napper, Iohn Bramhall, Iames Lesly, Robert Gorges, William Cadogan, Iohn Bligh, William Toxteth, Henry Packenham, Ioseph Fox, Henry Morton, Thomas Worsop, George Peppard, Iohn Forth, Arthur Purefoy, Edward Dowdall, Henry Dowdall, Miles Sumner, Robert Lill, Thomas Wren, Symon Crane, Iohn Bevans, Thomas Ash, Alexander Iephson, Iohn Barnes, Hanse Graham, Iohn Franck, Iohn Hatch, William Bligh, Thomas Chillingsworth, Iames Nangle, Arthur Hethrington, Richard Iannes, Iames Mortimer, Thomas Bringhurst, Roger Pierce, Thomas Vincent, Robert Harrison, Robert Shreld, Iohn Ford, Michael Iones,* Esqs.

For the Corporation of *Trym,* The Portriffe of *Trym, Robert Lill, Alexander Iephson* Esqs. *William Malone,* Gent.

For the Corporation of *Navan,* The present Portriff, *William Cadogan, Henry Packeham* Esq. — *Tynt,* Gent.

For the Corporation of *Kells, Henry Morton* Esq. *Henry Gwither* Gent. Cornet — *Haynes, William Cadogan, Richard Stephens,* Esquires.

For the Corporation of *Athboy,* The present Portriffe, *Iohn Bligh* Esq. *William Bligh,* Gent./

For the County of *Lowth, Iohn Howke,* High Sheriffe, Sir *William Aston* Knight, (*Page* 22) *Marcus Trevers,* Sir *Robert Starling, Garret Moor, Henry Bellingham, William Toxteth, Iohn Ruxton, Wolston Dixy, Brent Moor, Thomas Fortescue, Francis Moor, Iames Hopton, Nicolas Moor, Richard Bolton, Iohn Chambers, Bryan Herne, Edward Brabazon* Esquires, *Iames Brabazon, Iohn Bernard, Nehemiah Donnelan, Humphrey Barry, Robert Wynn, Rowland Trolly, Iohn Tomlinson, William Peppard, Peter Ashenhurst, Thomas Clerk, Samuel Ireland.*

For the Town of *Dundalk,* The Bailifs for the time being, *Iames Smallwood, Richard Price* Esqus, *Walter Cox, Arthur Buckley, Henry Wetherel* Gent.

For the County of the Town of *Drogheda,* The Mayor and Sherifs for the time being, Sir *Iames Graham* Knight, *William Toxteth, Iohn Trevors, Rowland Trolly, Samuel Stanbridge, William Elwood, Edward Martin, Thomas Dixon, Moses Hill, Robert Bridges, George Peppard, Edward Harrington, Samuel Osbourn, Iohn Towers, David Shepheard, Thomas Cockain, Gabriel Mead, Francis Pool, Joseph Whirloe, Thomas Leigh, Edward Graves, Hercules Langaridge* Esqus.

For the County of *Longford, Richard Thomson* Sherif, Sir *Arthur Forbes* Bar. Sir *Rich. Lane, Iohn Edgworth, Henry Sankey, Tho. Vincent, Adam Molineux* Esqs. *Tho. Waterhouse, Iames Grigges, Simon Sands, Ed. Knight, Tho. Robinson, Iohn Kennedy, Andrew Adare, Will. Longford,* Cornet *Tho. Flood, Henry Crofton, Oliver Iones, Iohn Edmonds, Hanibal Seaton, Iohn Aghmonty, Arthur Aghmonty, Mat. Wilder* Gent. Sir *Robert Newcomen* Barronet, *Thomas Newcomen* Esq.

For the Burrough of *St. Iohns-Town, Iohn Edgworth, Andrew Adare* Esqs. Mr. — *Newton.*

2 S

For the County of *Westmeath, Ridgley Hatfield* Esq. High Sherrif of the County of *Westmeath,* Sir *Theophilus Iones,* Sir *George Blundel,* Sir *Henry Pierce* Baronets, *Oliver Lambert, Walter Lambert, Thomas Long, William Handcock, William Markham, Lawrence Hide, George Peyton, Robert Cook, George Neverel, Iames Leigh, Philip Packenham, Fulk Bookby, Dennis Brown, Oliver Iones, Edward Birtles, Iohn Iones, George Talbot, William Moor, Alexander Iephson, Henry Packenham, Henry Baker, Thomas Hopkins, Edward Knight, Iohn Quelsh, Robert Bromwel, Francis Gibbons, Iohn Edmonds, Adam Molineux, Stephen Coyn* Esqs. *William Rowls, Godfrey Keeler, Hansalbert Widman, William Pountney, Henry Iephson, Henry Purdon, William Venner, Benjamin Chapman, Faustian Collins, Thomas Newcomen, Thomas Nugent, Abraham Michaelburn, Iohn Salisbury, Peter Stern, Iohn Brittaine, George Wilton, Richard Bradburn, Philip Brathwait, Thomas Gibbons, Thomas Gilbert* Gent./

(Page 23) For the Burough of *Mullingar, Richard Smith, William Wilson, Christopher Gilbert, Iohn Douglase* Gent.

For the Burrough of *Athlone,* The Soveraign, *Oliver Iones* Esq ; Recorder *and* Bailifs, *Edmond Donnelon, Walter Staplehil, Arthur St. George* Esqs. *Enoch Golbourn, Richard Kelly, Iohn Knox, William Moorhead* Gent.

For the Burrough of *Kilbeggan,* Provost for the time being, *Iohn Fleetwood, Iohn Nelson, Henry Dey.*

For the County of *Cork,* Sir *William Fenton, Maurice Fenton, Iohn Percival,* Sir *Henry Tint, Nicolas Purdon, S. John Broderick, Peter Courthorp, Richard Rise, Richard Townsend, Henry Bathurst, Randolph Clayton, Alexander Piggot, Garret fitz Gerald,* Mayor and Sherifs of the City of *Cork,* Soveraign of *Kinsale,* Mayor of *Youghal,* Provost of *Bandon, William Supple, Iohn Hodder, William Hodder, Francis Foulks, Redmond Barry, Walter Cooper, Richard Smith, Robert Foulks, Robert Southwell, Iohn St. Leiger, Samuel Brown, Howard St. Leiger* Esqus. Sir *Boyl Maynard, Robert Gookin, Iohn Baker, Iohn Wakeham, Henry Pyne, Christopher Oliver, William Mead, Pierce Power, William Dant, Benjamin Crofts* Esq. *Iohn Bellew, William Bellew, Iohn Brocket* Gent, *Abraham Savage, Walter Dawly, Richard Goodwin, Andrew Ruddock, William Harmer, Iohn Iepson, William fitz Gerald, William Thornhill, Roger Bretrage* Esqus. *William Arnold, George Prater* Gent. *Peter Carew, Timothy Rutter, Richard Gething, Robert Hide, Arthur Hide, Iohn Sweet, Peter Petsworth, George Syms, Edward Townsend, Edward Deny, Beverly Usher, Richard Covet, David Iermin, Anthony Woodly, Francis Alcock, Iohn Read, Archilles Daunt, Francis Smith* Esqs.

For the City and County of the City of *Cork,* The Mayor, Recorder and Sherives for the time being, *Peter Courthorp, Iohn Hodder, William Hodder, Philip Matthews, Iohn Baker, Walter Cooper, Thomas Woodlif* Esquires, *Christopher Oliver, Iames Vanderlew* Aldermen, *Benjamin Crofts, Edmond Crofts* Esquires, *Richard Scudmore, Theophilus Carew, Philip Parker, Zachary Travers, Giles Bursted, Ionathan Perry* Gent. *Richard Travers* Esq.

For the Town of *Youghal,* The Mayor, Recorder and Bailifs for the time being, Sir *Henry Tynt, Richard Meirs, Ioseph Cox, Iohn Farthing, George Giles, Thomas Vaughan, Owen Silver* gentlemen.

For the Town of *Kinsale,* The Soveraign and Recorder for the time being, *Robert Southwell* Esq. *Iohn Stepney, William Howel, Lancelot Stepney, Iohn Suxburie, William Broadbeare, Iohn Mountford, Iohn Martin* Gent./

(Page 24) For the Town of *Bandon-bridge,* The Provost for the time being, *Samuel Browne, Abraham Savage* Esqs, *William Wright, Iohn Iackson, Thomas Beamish* Gent.

For the County of *Waterford*, High Sheriff of the County, *Francis Foulk*, Sir *Boyle Maynard*, *Iohn Fitzgerrald*, *Thomas Walsh*, *Nicholas Osbourne*, *Richard Poer*, *Pierce Welsh*, *Iohn Cole*, *Andrew Lynn*, *William Halsey*, *Boyl Smith*, *Thomas Taylor*, *William Hubbart*, *Iosuah Boyl* Esquires. *Philip Harris*, *Iohn Smith*, *Nicholas Stout*, *Iames Old-field*, *Iohn Poer*, *Richard Silver*, *Edward Rogers*, *William Bradley*, *Iames Briver*, *Robert Taylor*, *Henry Gee*, *Alexander Dean*, *Michael Wilson*, *Richard Williams* Gent.

For the City of *Waterford*, The Mayor, Recorder and Sheriffs for the time being, *Francis Foulk*, *William Halsey*, *Thomas Dancer* Esquires, *Thomas Exten*, *Iohn Heaven*, *Benedict Claybrook* Aldermen, *Robert Lynn* Gent. *Iohn Lapp*, *Thomas Christmas* Merchants.

For the County of *Kerry*, The Sherif of the County for the time being, Sir *Arthur Denny* Knit, *Iohn Blenerhasset*, *Thomas Herbert*, *Iohn Blennerhasset* Junior, *Lancelot Sands*, *George Dillon*, *Henry Ponsonby*, *Richard Chute*, *Redmond Fitzmorris*, *Thomas Amery*, *William Collis*, *Iohn Steers*, *Robert Blennerhasset*, *Nicholas Munckten*, *Thomas Hasset*, *Iohn Walker*, *Humfry Barrow*, *Edward Allen*, *Ralph Conyer*, *Walter Langden*, *Iohn Love*, *William Hall*, *Garret Rieves*, Lt. *Witherston*, *Iames Conway*, *Patrick Crosby*, *Edward Shewel*, *Edward Heally* Esqs.

For the Burrough of *Dingle*, *Henry Hussy*, *Samuel Renshaw* Gent.

For the Burrough of *Traly*, Major *Philip Camine*, Provost *William Collis*.

For the Burrough of *Ardfert*, *Thomas Crosby*, *Edward Shewel*.

For the County of *Limerick*, Lt. Col. *Simon Eaton* High Sheriffe, Col. *Ralph Wilson*, Cap. *Thomas Southwell*, Maior *William King*, Maior *George Ingoldsby*, Lieut. Col. *William Piggot*, Cap. *Gerald fitz Gerald*, Cap. *Robert Oliver*, Maior *William Wade*, Cap. *Lewis Griffith*, *Gamaliel Walter* Esq. Cap. *Humphry Hartwell*, Cap. *Iohn Purdon*, Ma. *Richard Hart*, Cap. *Iohn Gileard*, Lieut. *John Odett*, Maior *Richard Magwyre*, Cap. *Thomas Butler*, Cap. *Vere Hunt*, M. *Rebert Taylor*, Cap. *Authur Blenerhasset*, M. *Richard King*, Cap. *Drury Wray*, Cap. *Arthur Ormsby*, M. — *Dixon*, Cap. *William Pope*, M. *Brook Bridges*, M. *Henry Rogers*, Cap. *Maurice Downs*, Col. *Michael Serle*, M. *Marcus Harrison*, Cornet *William/Weeks*, Cap. *Iohn Mansell*, Lieut. *Thomas Lloyd*, Lieut. *Rob. Kent*, (Page 25) Cap. *Iohn Friend*, Cap. *Robert Wilkinson*, Lieut. *Nich. Moncklone*, M. *Iohn Crooker*, Cornet *Giles Powell*, M. *Thomas Holmes*, M. *Ephraim Monell*, M. *Darby Grady*, Cornet *Iames Dogherty*, *George Purdon* Esqs.

For the City and County of the City of *Limerick*, The Mayor, Recorder and Sheriffs for the time being, Col. *Henry Ingoldsby*, Col. *Ralph Wilson*, Maior *William King*, Maior *George Ingoldsby*, Cap. *Garret fitz Gerrald*, *Standish Hartstrong*, Esqs. *William Hartwell*, *William Yarwell*, *William Wade*, *Humphery Hartwell*, *Thomas Miller*, Aldermen, *Iohn Comin*, *Henry Bindon*, *Peter Ash*, *Henry Saltfield*, *Christopher Kyes*, *Dermitius Coghlan*, *Iohn Crabb*, *William Pope*, *Thomas Martin*, *Iames Banting*, *Henry Price*, *Robert Shute*, *Patrick Dowdal*, Burgesses, *Iohn Cripps*, *Thomas Bea[s]ley*, *Zachary Holland*, *Samuel Foxon*, *Iohn Syms*, *Nathaniel Whaples*, *Daniel Hignet*, *Nathaniel Webb*, *William Ioint*, *William Allen*, *Iohn Miller*, *Authur Carter*, *William Ken*, *Henry Lee*, *Iohn Collins*, *Bennet Whittington*, gent. *Iohn Friend* Esquire.

For the County of *Clare* : *Thomas Cullen* High Sherriff of the said County, Col. *Henry Ingoldsby*, Col. *Ralph Wilson*, Lieut. Col. *William Purefoy*, *Iohn Cooper*, *Samuel Burton*, *George Pourdon*, *Thomas Hickman*, Lievt. Col. *Benjamin Lucas*, *Isaac Graniers*, *William Rumsey* Senior, *Thomas Curd*, *Iohn Colpoise*, *Richard Hart*, *Neptune Bloud*, *Iohn Gore*, *George Ross*, *Giles Vandelure*, *Henry Lee*, *Thomas Hewet*, *Peter Graniers*, *George Norton*, *William Goff*, *Patrick Lysagh*, *Nicholas Bourk*, *Isaac Vanbogarden*,

Robert Nightingale, William Hobson, Esqs. Walter Hickman, Henry Colpoyse, Arthur Smith, Henry Eveers, Robert Peacock, Gentlemen.

For the Burrough of *Inish*: *William Cuff*, Provost, *William Purefoy, Anthony Bernard, Robert Hord, Iohn Pyne, Charles Chattin, Archibald Young*, Gentlemen.

For the County of *Tipperary, Gamaliel Water*, Esq. high Sheriff, *Iohn Booker, Charles Blunt, Simon Finch, Solomon Camby, Henry Paris, Bartholomew Fowke, Robert Knight, Griffith Howard, Nicolas Everard, Edward Dinham, Iohn Peck, Arthur Purefoy, Sampson Towgood, Iohn Harrison, Robert Cole, Iohn Iordan, Daniell Abbot, Iohn Godfrey, Iohn Ewers, Henry Shrimpton, Richard Lehunt, Eliah Green, Thomas Sadlier, Giles Gregory, Samuel Clark, William Woodward, Mathew Iacob, Henry Legg, Charles Alcock, Iohn Dawson, Francis Peisley, Anthony Stamp* Esquires. *Iohn Matthews, Giles Martin, Iohn Pike, Tho. Poe, Iohn Otway, Nicholas Toller, Wil. Heydon, Archiball Adare, Michael Gwinn, Wil. Palmes, Oliver Latham, William Bacon,/Richard Hamerton, Francis Legg, Thomas Manby, Richard Moore, Walter Baker, William Brooks, Christopher Perkins, Iohn Cuffe, Mathew Pennifeather, Thomas Cotton, Godfrey Greene, Humphrey Minchin, Iames Barker, Anthony Atkinson*, gent.

(Page 26)

For the Citty of *Cashel, Peyton Lehunt* Esq., *Humphrey Wray, Richard Hatton* gentlemen.

For the Burrough of *Clonmell, Samuel Foley*, Esq. *Robert Lovelace, Richard Perrot*, gent.

For the Burrough of *Fetherd, Peter Cook, Robert Powel*, gentlemen.

For the Burrough of *Carrick, Michael Lamor, William Sheffield, Nicholas Towler*, Gentlemen.

For the County of *Roscomon*, Lord of *Castle Coot*, the High Sherif for the time being, Sir *Oliver St. George* Barronet, Sir *Richard Lane*, Barronet, *Richard Iones, William Handcock, William St. George, Oliver Iones, Edmund Donnelan, Edward Crofton, Iames King, Richard Crofton, Thomas Caulfield, Thomas Lovelace, Iohn Moore, Allen Povey, Richard St. George, Michael Stanley, Arthur St. George, Owen Lloyd, Nicolas Mahown, Robert Folliot, Ellis Goodwin, Walter Iones, Alexander Atkins, Henry Crofton* Esqs, *Edward Crofton, Charles Crofton, Robert Drury, Christopher Matthews, Iohn Crofton, Brian Cunningham, Nathaniel Evanton*, gent.

For the County of *Leitrim*, The Sherif for the time being, Sir *Oliver St. George*, Sir *Arthur Forbes, Robert Parks, Owen Wynn, William St. George, Bryan Cunningham, Iames Bathurst, Walter Iones* Esqs, *Christopher Matthews, Edward Woods, Thomas Ellis, Iohn Akmooth, Alexander Atkins* gent. *Humphrey Reynolds, Bryan Iones* Esqs.

For the County of *Sleigo*, The Sherif for the time being, *Robert Park, Arthur Gore, Francis King, Lewis Winckfield, Lewis Iones, Robert Morgan, William Webb, Charls Gore, Keyan O Hara, Thomas Hart, William Ormsby, Thomas Griffith, Edward Cooper, Henry Tifford, Thomas Wood, Iames Beirn, Anthony Ormsby, Francis Gore, Thomas Crofton* Esqs.

For the County of *Gallway*, The High Sherif for the time being, the Lord of *Castle Coot*, Sir *Oliver S. George, Thomas Caulfield, Henry Waddington, William Edwards, Iames Cuffe, Henry Greenway, Henry Whaley, Richard Bingley, Thomas Cuff, Edmund Donelan, Francis Gore, George S. George, Gilbert Carter, Iohn Morgan, Iohn Whalley, Iohn Bullenbrook, Matthew Tubman, William Brooks, Michael Stanley, Henry Davis, Richard Walcot, William Spencer, Gabriel King, Iohn Groom* Esqs./

(Page 27)

For the County of the Town of *Galway*, the Mayor, Recorder and Sherifs for the time being.

For the County of *Mayo*, the High Sherif, Sir *Oliver S. George*, Lt. Col. *Arthur Gore*, Cap. *Arthur Swanwick*, Sir *Francis Iackson*, Cap. *Lewis Winkfield*, Cornet *Iohn Crofton*, Mr. *Francis Knight*, Mr. *Robert Palmer*, Cap. *Ioseph Bond*, Cap. *Henry Waddington*, *Philip Gallature*, *Thomas Knight*, *Iames Cuff*, Esqs. *Francis Brent*, Cornet *Robert Miller*, *Foulk Hughes*, Cor. *Philip Ormsby*, *Iohn Ormsby*.

For the County of *Fermanagh*, Sir *Iohn Cole*, *William Gore*, Sir *Iohn Humes* Barronets. *Michael Cole*, *Stephen Butler*, *Henry Blannerhasset*, *Nicolas Willoughby*, *William Davis*, *William Cosby*, *Robert Cole*, *William Archdale*, *Hugh Rowley*, *Humphrey Shingly*, *Iohn Madden*, *Adam Cathcart*, *Henry Horsdenel*, *Roderick Mansel* Esqurs. Doctor *Edward Cook*, *Bartholomew Droope*, *William Hamilton*, *Iohn Cheslin*, *Iohn Carleton* Gent. *Iohn Curry*, *Gilbert Eccles* Merchants. *Edward Rowley*, *Iames Galbrith* Esquires.

For the Burrough of *Eniskillen*, the Provost of the said Burrough for the time being, *Iason Hassard*, *Thomas Picken*, *Iohn Chelling* Gent.

For the Town and County of the Town of *Carickfergus*, the Mayor and Sherifs for the time being, *George Rawden* Esqs. *Roger Lyndon* Recorder, *Iohn Davis*, *Richard Dob* Esqs. *Hercules Davis*, *Iohn Orpin*, *Iohn Harris*, *Edmund Davis*, *Iohn Dolway*, *Henry Davis*, *Gilbert Wye* Gent.

For the County of *Monoghan*, The High Sherif for the time being, *Richard Blaney*, *Richard Barret*, *Thomas Coot*, *Oliver Aucketil*, *Arthur Dillon*, *Iohn Foster*, *William Borston*, *Nicolas Willoughby*, *Tristram Carey*, *Michael Pockerish*, *Simon Richardson*, *Roger Smith*, *William Davis*, *Peter Beaghan* Esqs.

For the town of *Monoghan*, The Provost for the time being, Mr. *Wade*, Cap. *Richard Blaney*, Mr. — *Owens*.

For the Citty and County of *London derry*, The Mayor of *London-derry*, The Maior of *Colraine*, The Sherriffes for the time being, *Tristram Beresford*, *Iohn Rowley*, *Iohn Godbold*, *Stephen Cuppage*, *Dudley Phillips*, *George Phillips*, *Richard Clutterbooke*, *Ralph King*, *Alexender Staples*, *Iohn Gorges*, *Edwad Cary*, *Randle Beresford ; Samuell Hill*, *Paul Canning*, *Robert Blair*, *Richard Brazier*, *Francis Howard*, Esqs. *Thomas Bourk*, *Thomas Moncriefe*, *Iohn Plunkett* Gen. Sir *Robert Stuart*, *Edward Rowley*, *Hugh Rowley*, *Mathew Draper*, *William Godfrey*, Esquires./

For the County of *Ardmagh*, The Sherriffe for the time being, Sir *George Atcheson*, (*Page* 28) *Toby Pointz*, *Hance Hameltcn*, *Roger West*, *Edward Richardson*, *Thomas Chambers*, *Francis Chambers*, *Edw. Rowley*, *Henry Cope*, *Foulke Martin*, *Walter Cope*, *William Draper*, *Thomas Clerk*, *Edward May*, *Robert Gray*, *Iames Maxwell*, Esqs.

For the County of *Donegall*, the high Sherriff for the said County for the time being, Sir *Arthur Fourbes*, Sir *William Gore*, Barronets, Sir *Paul Davies* Knight, *Charles Hamilton*, *Richard Perkins*, *Henry Brooks*, *William Cuningham*, *Iohn Folliot*, *George Cary*, *Thomas Stewart*, *Iames Erskin*, *William Dutton*, *Thomas Dutton*, *Andrew Knox*, *Iohn Hamilton* of Cavan, *Tho. Groves*, *Albert Conningham*, *Andrew Linsey*, *Peter Benson*, *Iames Collun*, *Iames Coningham*, *Iohn Collun*, *Iohn Nisbit*, *Iames Hamilton*, *George Butler*, *Andrew Nisbit*, *David Stewart*, *David Mortimer*, The Warden of *Lifford* for the time being, Capt. *William Stewart*, *Henry Vaughan*, *Bassill Brooks*, *Tho. Golborne*, Esqs. *Robert Murray*, Knight, *William Davies*, *Archibald Pierson* Esqs.

For the County of *Downe*, The high Sherriffe for the time being, *Vere Essex Cromwell*, *Oliver Cromwell*, Sir *George Blundell* Barronet, *Arthur Hill*, *Marcus Trevers*, *Nich. Bagnall*, *William Montgomery*, *George Rawden*, *Hugh Savage*, *Bernard Ward*, *Moses Hill*, *William Hill*, Esqs. *Henry Maxwell* Clerk, *Iohn Weaver*, *Iames Triall*, *Roger West*, *Tobias Norris*, *Archibald Hamilton*, *Nicholas Ward*, *Charles Bolton*, *Edward Muschamp*,

Iames Lesly, William Hamilton, William Lesby, Iohn Magill, Richard Pierce, Iohn Savage, Iohn Reynolds, Esqs. *Hugh Shaw, Nicholas Fitz Symons, Iames Hamilton, Iames Magill, Iohn Swadling, Nicholas Trurk, Bernard Magenis, Michael Smith, Collen Maxwell,* Gent. The Provost of *Newton,* The Provost of *Killeleagh.*

For the County of *Antrim,* the high Sherriffe for the time being, Sir *Iohn Skevington* Barronet, *Arthur Hill, George Rawdon* Esqs. Doctor *Alexander Colvill,* Doctor *Kalph King,* The Maior of *Carrigfergus, William Adare, Iohn Davies, Tristram Beresford, Archibald Stewart, Moses Hill, Robert Calvill, Archibald Upton, Roger Lyndon, Iames Shaw, Iohn Shaw, Michael Harrison, Henry Spencer, Peter Beaghan,* Esqs. *Henry Davies, William Huston,* Maior *mac Awly, Daniel O Neale, Thomas Dobbins, Adam Boyd, Daniel mac Kay, Gilbert Wye, Simon Hilmon,* Gent.

(*Page* 29) For the County of *Tyrone ;* The high Sherriffe ; Sir *Wil. Usher,* Sir *Arthur Forbes,* Sir *Audley Mervin,* Sir *Arthur/Chichester, Ferdinando Davis, William Richardson, William Moor,* Lt. Col. *Robert Stewart, Henry Mervin, Iames Stewart* Esquires, *Thomas Golborne, Matthew Combes, William Cahoon, Iames Shaw, Richard Palfrey, Alexander* mac *Castlan,* Quarter Mr. *Douglas, Iohn Young, Iohn Lesley* Junior Gent. *David Michael, Patrick Hambleton, Kichard Adams, Richard Perkins, Ralph King, Edward Cook, Thomas White, Robert Lindsey, Iohn Morris, Thomas Morris, — Wallis* Esquires. *Nathaniel Boyl, Iohn Gladston, Iohn Fixer* Gent.

For the County of *Cavan,* The high sherif of the County for the time being, *Oliver Lambert, Walter Lambert* Esquires, Sir *Francis Hamilton* Knight and Barronet, *Charles Hamilton, Thomas Cook, Edward Philpot, Thomas Cooch, Stephen Butler, Tho. Waldron, Rob. Sanderson, Tristram Berrisford, Lewis Crag, Thomas Whine, William Moor, Humphrey Perrot, Thomas Richardson, Samuel Townley, Ambrose Bradle, Thomas Guillim, Richard Lewis, Thomas Ash, William Cosby, Thomas Newburgh, Thomas Burton, Hance Hamilton, William Hamilton, Iames Hamilton, Abraham Clements, Thomas Burrows* Esqs. The Soveraign of *Cavan* for the time being, the Provost of *Belturbat* for the time being, *Hugh Culme, Henry Palmer, Richard Burrows, Richard Gibson, Daniel Clements, Thomas White,* Esqs.

March the 1, 1660.

Ordered that this Ordinance be forthwith Printed and Published.

Matt. Barry Clerk of the General Convention of *Ireland.*

Imprinted at *Dublin* by *William Bladen,* by special Order, *Anno Dom.* 1660.

INDEX.

I.—PERSONS.

II.—PLACES.

THE Index has been arranged in two divisions—Persons and Places. It covers the Poll-money Ordinances as well as the Census. References in the Index to the Ordinances are not distinguished from references to the Census; as the text of the Ordinances commences at page 610, and ends at page 646, it will easily be understood that Persons or Places denoted as occurring on or after page 610 are to be found in the Ordinances, whilst those denoted as occurring on or before page 607 belong to the Census.

The monotonously mechanical task of arranging the many thousands of index slips was lightened in no inconsiderable manner by the friendly advice and suggestions of Professor Eóin MacNeill and of my colleague Professor James Hogan. I cannot adequately express my sense of gratitude to my friend R. C. Simington for the time and labour he has ungrudgingly given towards the preparation of the Index for press.

INDEX OF PERSONS.

[The following abbreviations have been used : ald=alderman, jun=junior, pn=principal name, sen=senior.

In the Index of Persons an attempt has been made to give cross references to the variant spellings of particular names. As the prefixes Mc, O and Fitz appear to have been adopted or disregarded according to the humour of each particular enumerator, it has been thought advisable to give, also, cross references from, for example, Dowell to McDowell, Doyle to McDoyle and O Doyle, Gibbon to McGibbon and Fitzgibbon, and so on. Those wishing to pursue the study of the variant forms in which an Irish personal name can be made appear in English will find much help and useful information in R. E. Matheson's *Varieties and Synonymes of Surnames and Christian Names in Ireland* (1901), and Rev. P. Woulfe's *Sloinnte Gaedheal is Gall, Irish Names and Surnames* (1923).

The list of names appearing on page 220 of the Text as " Don Oge Corm : Carthy Caulau Owen McCormack vno " has been read by me as follows for indexing purposes :—Don Oge Carthy, Corm Carthy, Caulau Carthy, Owen McCormack Carthy ; Corm = Cormac, Don = ? ; the late Rev. Dr. Paul Walsh suggested to me that Caulau = Caulan = Ceallachán, a forename common in the McCarthy family. As regards " vno," the meaning is uncertain ; Professor Eóin MacNeill agreed with Dr. Walsh in suggesting that it may possibly stand for Latin *una*, meaning ' together, jointly ' ; it could then denote that we have here an instance of joint-ownership].

ABBOT, Daniell, 644.
ABBOTT, John, 206.
——, Mordykay, Leut, 119.
See also Abott.
ABDY, Humphrey, 639.
ABERCRUMBER, Thomas, 568.
See also Ebercrumber.
ABOTT, Daniell, Dr, Kt, 298.
See also Abbot(t).
ABRAHAM, Margt, 199.
ABSOM, Thomas, 288.
ACHYSON, Sir George, 35.
See also Atcheson.
ACKLAND, Baldwan, 423.
ACTERY, Francis, Aduentr, 519.
ADAIRE, Andrew, 459.
——, James, 3.
——, William, 7.
See also Adare, Adayre, Adire.
ADAMS, Benjamin, 191.
——, Kichard, 646.
——, Thomas, 431.
——, Wm, 139.
ADARE, Andrew, 622, 641 (bis).
——, Archiball, 644.
——, William, 646.
ADAYRE, William, 627.
See also Adaire.
ADDERLY, Edwd, 202.
ADDERTON, John, 421.
ADHBENSON, Anthony, 441.
ADHOW, William, 418.

ADIRE, pn, 3.
See also Adaire.
ADRIAN, Hubert, ald, 621.
ADRYAN, Huibart, ald, 379.
AGGAS, Thomas, 516.
AGHARNE, Bryan, 233.
AGHERIN, Morish, 176.
See also Hagherin.
AGHMONTY, Arthur, 641.
——, John, 641.
AGHMOOTY, Arthur, 455.
See also Ahmonty, Atmoty, Akmooth.
AGHWELL, Edward, 366.
AGNEW, pn, 5, 9.
AHERLY, George, 290.
AHMONTY, Arthur, 622.
——, John, 622.
See Aghmooty.
AILDWOOD, pn, 419.
See also Aldwood.
AILMER, Sir Andrew, 398.
——, ——, James his sonn, *ibid*.
See also Aylmer.
AKMOOTH, John, 625, 644.
See Aghmooty.
ALBONAGH, pn, 604.
ALCOCK, Charles, 644.
——, Charls, 625.
——, Francis, 206, 623, 642.
——, ——, his sonn Francis, 206.
——, Masklin, 206.
ALDER, Susanna, 201.

ALDERSEE, Martin, Adventr, 520.
ALDING, Phillipp, 365.
ALDRICH, Robert, 154.
ALDWARTH, Richard, 191.
   See also Aldworth.
ALDWOOD, pn, 421.
   See also Aildwood.
ALDWORTH, Richard, 623.
   See also Aldwarth.
ALE, William, merct, 349.
ALEWARD, William, Factr in the Barbadoes, 349.
   See also Aylward.
ALEXANDER, ——, jun, 367.
——, Sir Hierom, 638.
——, Sir Hierome, 641.
——, Jerom, 620, 622, 623.
   See also Allexander.
ALGOE, Robert, 57.
ALIN, Stephen, 320.
   See also Allen.
ALINER, Walter, 316.
ALLAND, Henry, 347.
ALLEN, pn, 145, 284, 373, 483.
——, Edward, 251, 274, 624, 643.
——, James, 353.
——, Joshua, 371.
——, Lawrence, 401.
——, Mathew, 513.
——, Patrick, 371.
——, ——, Robert his sonn, *ibid.*
——, Ralph, 363, 639.
——, Robert, 371.
——, William, 191 (bis), 624, 643.
——, ——, Shopkeeper, 372.
   See also Alin, McAllen.
ALLEXANDER, Jerome, 367.
   See also Alexander.
ALLINE, Edward, 561.
——, Thomas, 561.
ALMER, Garet, 480.
——, ——, Dersomy his sonn, *ibid.*
   See also Aylmer.
ALMES, Ralph, 257.
ALWOODHOUSE, ——, Doctr, 368.
AMANSHAM, Nicholas, 366.
AMERY, Thomas, 251, 624, 643.
ANCTHILL, Oliver, 626.
   See also Ankettle, Auckctil.
ANDERSONE, Will, 54.
ANDREW, pn, 483, 487.
ANDREWES, Edward, 274.
——, John, 113, 338.

ANDREWES, Richard, 353, 509.
ANDREWS, Ambrose, 531.
——, Jndich, 321.
——, John, 441.
——, Richard, 639.
ANESLEY, John, 395.
   See also Annesley.
ANGER, The Lord, 365.
ANGIER, Francis Lord, 622.
   See also Aynger.
ANKETTILL, Oliver, 152.
ANKETTLE, John, 310.
   See also Ancthill.
ANNESLEY, Arthur, 616 (ter), 617, 618, 619 (novies), 620 (ter).
——, John, 621, 639.
   See also Anesley.
ANTHONY, Arthur, 334.
——, Peter, 342.
ANTRIM, The Marquess of, 8.
APPELLWHITE, John, 8.
ARBERRY, Edward, 191.
ARCHBALD, Robert, 454.
ARCHBOULD, pn, 390.
ARCHDALE, William, 625, 645.
ARCHDALL, Francis, 116.
——, William, 114.
ARCHDEACON, Anstace, 204.
——, James, 204.
——, Jane, 204.
——, William, 205.
——, ——, his wife, *ibid.*
——, Wm, 204.
ARCHDEAKIN, pn, 297.
ARCHDEKIN, pn, 432.
——, John, merchant, 431.
ARCHER, pn, 417, 432.
——, Beale, 431.
——, John, 364.
——, Luke, 416, 431.
——, Michaell, 426.
——, Robert, 371.
——, Walter, 416.
——, William, 35.
ARDENTON, Josias, 474.
ARDGLASSE, Earl of, 69.
ARDOGH, Robert, 369.
ARDWAHER, Edmd, 431.
ARLAND, pn, 346.
ARLANT, pn, 337.
ARMESTRONG, Edward, 443.
   See Armstrong.
ARMIN, Michell, adventr, 520.

BELLOW, Nicholas, 164.
BELLOWE, John, 212.
——, Richd, 212.
BELLUE, John, Lt, 212.
——, Mary, 212.
——, Wm, 212.
See Bellew.
BENDEN, ——, Ensigne, 263.
BENDON, Henry, 624.
See also Bindon.
BENGER, Thomas, 193.
BENIOR, James, 339.
BENNELL, Tobias, a lodger, 366.
BENNES, Joshua, ald, 624.
See also Bennis.
BENNET, Marcus, 420.
BENNETT, ——, ald, 263.
——, Amus, 224.
——, ——, jun, 224.
——, Christopher, 371.
——, Frances, 225.
——, Henry, 192.
——, John, 405.
——, Jonathan, 199.
——, Richard, 365.
——, Samuell, 271.
BENNIS, Tho, marchant, 263.
——, William, 170.
See also Bennes.
BENNISH, George, 171.
BENSON, ——, Mr, 365.
——, George, 291.
——, Peter, 124, 626, 645.
BENSONE, Peter, 49.
BENT, Thomas, 191.
BENTHAM, Beckingham, 291.
BENTLEY, ——, Captn, 263.
——, Thomas, 624.
BEOLAN, pn, 436, 439, 604.
BEOLANE, pn, 179, 446, 447.
BERESFORD, Randle, 645.
——, Tristram, 139, 645, 646.
See also Berisford, Berresford, Berrisford.
BERFORD, Richard, 369.
BERGIN, pn, 414, 417, 425, 495, 496, 498, 500, 501, 503, 505.
BERISFORD, Michael, 627.
——, Randolph, 626.
——, Tristram, 627 (bis).
See Beresford.
BERKLEY, Francis, 289.
See also Barclay.

BERMINGHAM, pn, 408.
——, Edward, 407, 639.
——, ——, Walter his sonn, 407.
——, Garett, 407.
——, Garrot, 407.
——, James, 407.
——, John, 407.
——, Redmond, 407.
——, Thomas, 407.
——, Walter, 407, 435.
——, William, 407 (bis).
See also Bremegham, Brimingham.
BERNAGH, pn, 337, [and see Brenagh note].
BERNARD, Anthony, 625, 644.
——, John, 472, 641.
——, William, 621, 639.
See also Barnard.
BERRELL, pn, 470.
BERRESFORD, Reinold, 139.
BERRISFORD, Michael, 626.
——, Tristram, 626, 646.
See Beresford.
BERRY, Edward, 219.
——, ——, Eliza his daughter, *ibid*
——, ——, Wm his sonn, *ibid*.
——, Eliza, 219.
——, John, 191.
——, Wm, 219.
——, Sir William, 391.
BERSTOW, Jeremiah, merchant, 365.
BERY, John, 446.
BESSWORTH, Mrs Eliz, 200.
BEST, Robert, 199.
BESTWILL, Richard, 523.
BETAGH, Patrick, 579.
BETSWORTH, Richard, 290
BETSWORTHY, Peter, 239.
BETTIN, John, m'chant, 363.
BETTS, Mathew, 6.
——, Thomas, 315.
——, William, 6.
BEUCHAMP, John, 639.
——, ——, merchant, 370.
See also Beauchamp.
BEVANS, John, 641.
——, Nicholas, 484.
BEVINS, John, 623.
BEVRIDGE, Francis, 201.
BEWAR, John, 431.
BEXWICK, John, 474.
BICKERSTAFFE, Richard, 7.
——, ——, Captn, 140.
BICKERTON, ——, Mr, 38.

BRAILY, John, 200.
See Brayly.
BRAMBLE, Mary, 215.
——, Robert, 218.
BRAMHALL, John, 641.
BRAMLEY, Thomas, 280.
BRAMPTON, John, 367.
BRAMSTON, Robt, 153.
BRANAGH, pn, 408, 501, 547.
See Brenagh.
BRANAN, pn, 444, 513, 577.
See Brenan.
BRANHAM, John, 368.
BRANNAGH, pn, 406.
See Brenagh.
BRANTHWAITE, Phillip, 523.
See Brathwait.
BRASIER, Paul, 126.
——, Richard, ald, 139.
See also Brazier.
BRASSELL, pn, 344, 444.
BRATHWAIT, Philip, 642.
See Branthwaite.
BRAY, John, 474.
——, William, 563.
BRAYLY, Zachary, 206.
See also Braily.
BRAYNE, pn, 387.
BRAZIER, Richard, 645.
See Brasier.
BREACKAN, pn, 396.
See also Breckan, Bracken, Brackane.
BREADBEARD, Wm, 199.
See Brodbear, Broadbeare.
BREARELY, Robert, 93.
BRECKAN, pn, 396, 439.
See Breackan.
BREDAN, pn, 498.
BREEDING, John, elder, 626.
See also Braedin.
BREEN, pn, 495.
BREERS, Edward, 6.
BREERTON, William, Ensigne, 20.
See Brereton.
BREHAN, pn, 592.
BREMEGHAM, pn, 470.
See Bermingham.
BREN, pn, 421.

BRENAGH, pn, 195, 200, 205, 233, 234, 247, 284, 309, 314, 440, 600.
See also Branagh, Brannagh, Brennagh, Brenogh, Brinagh, Bernagh. [This latter form, which occurs among the list of Principal Names in the barony of Decies, co. Waterford, on p. 337 of Text, is still the local pronunciation of ᵇreaᵗⁿaċ]. ·
BRENAN, pn, 309, 354, 359, 404, 405, 417, 423, 425, 495, 498, 500, 501, 502, 505, 513, 516, 519, 577.
——, Charles, 357.
——, John, 445.
——, Oliuer, 517.
BRENANE, pn, 297, 447, 602.
See also Branan, Brennan, Brenon, OBrenan, OBrenane.
BRENNAGH, pn, 195, 233, 239, 242, 284, 337, 340, 344, 346, 350, 545, 547.
See Brenagh.
BRENNAN, pn, 585.
See Brenan.
BRENOGH, pn, 430.
See Brenagh.
BRENON, pn, 428, 430.
See Brenan.
BRENT, Francis, 625, 645.
BRERETON, Ellinor, 241.
——, Francis, 504.
——, Richard, 504.
——, Thomas, 639.
——, ——, Major, 621.
BRERTON, Roger, 377.
See also Breerton.
BRETLERIDGE, Roger, 242.
BRETRAGE, Roger, 623, 642.
BRETT, Francis, 167.
——, John, 639.
——, Patrick, 167.
——, ——, Francis his sonne, *ibid*.
——, Thomas, 370.
See Britt.
BRIAN, pn, 288.
BRIANE, pn, 436.
See Bryan, McBrian, O Brian.
BRICE, Robert, Lieut, 140.
——, Walter, 380.
BRICKAIN, William, mt, 349.
BRICKARDICK, William, 623.
BRICKDALL, John, 179.
See Brigdall.
BRICKELSBY, Rich, 436.

CAWFIELD, William Lord, 626, 627.
   See Canfeild, Caulfield.
CAWSY, pn, 468.
CEREIGHTON, Abraham, 111.
CERTAINE, Richard, 453.
CHABNER, Thomas, 380.
CHAFE, Robert, 622, 641.
CHAFINE, Charls, 625.
CHALLENOR, James, 474.
CHAMBERLIN, pn, 473.
CHAMBERLINE, Stephen, mctt, 559.
——, Thomas, 282.
CHAMBERLYN, Jonas, 533.
——, Robert, 390.
——, ——, Thomas his sonn, *ibid.*
——, Thomas, 390.
CHAMBERS, ——, Capt, 370 (bis).
——, Edward, 371.
——, Francis, 38, 626, 645.
——, John, 247, 641.
——, Robert, 202.
——, Thomas, 25, 626, 645.
CHAMBRE, John, 472.
CHAMPINES, John, mchant, 369-370.
CHANDLER, Samuell, mctt, 370.
CHANEY, Robert, 191.
CHAPMAN, pn, 547.
——, Benjamin, 527, 622, 642.
——, Faithfull, Captn, 274.
——, Thomas, 431.
——, Wm, 274.
CHAPPELL, Charles, 25.
——, John, 253.
——, William, 253.
CHARLTON, Geo, 373.
CHARTRES, Wm, 201.
CHATTIN, Charles, 644.
CHEARNELEY, Anthony, 313.
CHEEKE, Thomas, 403.
CHEEVERS, Christopher, 474.
   See Cheuers, Chevers.
CHELLING, John, 645.
CHENEING, Patrick, 474.
CHESHIRE, William, 414.
CHESLIN, John, 626, 645.
CHESTERMAN, John, 276.
CHESWRIGHT, Marke, 371.
CHETTLE, Wm, 200.
CHEUERS, pn, 538.
CHEVERS, pn, 474.
   See Cheevers.
CHICESTER, ——, Capt, 593.

CHICESTER, ——, ——, pt ot his Troope and
   their Wiues, *ibid.*
CHICHESTER, ——, Capt, 581.
——, ——, ——, his Troope, *ibid.*
——, The Lord, 626.
——, Arthur, 372, 627.
——, ——, Lord Viscount, 626.
——, Sir Arthur, 646.
——, Edward, 550.
CHICHISTER, Edward, 640.
CHIDLEIGH, Martha, 199.
CHILLINGSWORTH, Thomas, 641.
CHILLINGWORTH, Thomas, 623.
CHILTON, Edward, 416, 622.
CHISSELL, Charleton, 497.
CHRISMAS, Tho, mcht, 349.
CHRISTIAN, pn, 9.
——, Mynard, mctt, 370.
CHRISTMAS, Thomas, merchant, 624, 643.
——, William, 511.
CHRISTOPHER, pn, 337.
CHURCH, Charles, 133.
——, Tho, 133.
CHUTE, Richard, 247, 624, 643.
CHYTTWOOD, Valentine, 531.
CLANCHY, pn, 168, 174, 179, 183, 188, 314.
——, Boetius, 182.
——, Connor, 173.
——, Daniell, 187 (bis).
——, Hugh, 187.
——, John, 187.
——, Mortagh, 187.
——, Richard, 165.
——, Thomas, 181.
CLANCY, pn, 275.
——, Daniell, 288.
——, James, 288.
CLANHY, pn, 314.
CLANSY, pn, 337.
   See McClanchie.
CLAPHAM, George, 372.
——, Robert, 318.
CLARK, Samuel, 644.
CLARKE, pn, 373.
——, ——, Mr, 364.
——, Edward, 451.
——, George, 328, 397, 398.
——, John, Coll, 512.
——, Nicholas, 272.
——, Rich, apothicary, 369.
——, Samuell, 300.
——, Tho, 371.

COMINE, Patricke, 182.
——, Patricke Oge, 182.
COMMAN, pn, 408.
COMMUNE, James, 14.
COMMYNE, pn, 328.
COMYN, John, Lt, 263.
COMYNE, pn, 309.
——, John, 176.
——, Laurence, 166.
——, Richard, 305.
CONALLONE, pn, 440.
See Connellan.
CONALLY, pn, 512, 521.
See Connelly, O Connally.
CONDON, pn, 239, 273, 284, 314, 340.
——, Dauid, 235.
——, John, 164, 272.
——, Richd, 290.
CONE, Haniball, 235.
CONELAN, pn, 408.
CONELLAN, pn, 600, 602, 604.
CONELLANE, pn, 168, 177.
——, Donell, 602.
See Connellan, O Conellane.
CONELLY, pn, 512, 521, 600.
See Connelly.
CONERAN, pn, 404.
See Conran.
CONGREIFE, John, 283.
CONICK, pn, 538.
CONILLAN, pn, 607.
See Connellan.
CONILY, pn, 455.
See Connelly.
CONIN, Thomas, 307.
CONINGHAM, James, 645.
See Cunningham.
CONLAN, pn, 396.
See Connellan.
CONLY, David, mchant, 369.
CONNALAN, pn, 521.
See Connellan.
CONNARD, John, 219.
CONNEL, William, 622.
CONNELAN, pn, 465, 521, 581.
See Connellan.
CONNELL, pn, 168, 174, 179, 314, 319, 340, 427, 444, 468, 483, 485, 487.
——, Charles, 258.
——, Daniell, 258.
——, Dermod, 258.
——, Jeffry, 177.
——, John, 390.

CONNELL, Morrish, 177.
——, Patrick, Doctr, 169.
See McConnell, O Connell.
CONNELLAN, pn, 468.
See also Conallone, Conelan, Conellan, Conellane, Conillan, Conlan, Connalan, Connelan, Connillan, Connolan, Conolan.
CONNELLY, pn, 314, 569.
See also Conally, Conelly, Conily, Connola, Connolay, Connoly, McConoly, O Connelly.
CONNER, pn, 302, 314, 437, 438, 439, 442, 496, 498, 500, 503, 506.
——, Charles, 437.
——, Phillip, 573.
See Connor, McConner.
CONNERY, Daniell, 169.
See Connory.
CONNEY, Nicholas, 470.
CONNIERS, Ralph, 624.
See Conyers.
CONNILLAN, pn, 459.
See Connellan.
CONNINGHAM, Albert, 645.
See Cunningham.
CONNOHOR, pn, 340.
See Connor, O Connohor.
CONNOLA, pn, 344.
See Connelly.
CONNOLAN, pn, 473.
See Connellan.
CONNOLAY, pn, 340.
CONNOLY, pn, 468, 473.
See Connelly, O Connoly.
CONNOR, pn, 185, 187, 188, 328, 337, 373, 380, 384, 387, 390, 396, 399, 402, 408, 427, 523, 545, 552, 554, 602, 607.
——, Bryan, 575.
——, Charles, 568.
——, Donogh, 407.
——, Dudly, 575.
——, John, 575 (ter).
See also Cnogher, Cnoghor, Cnohor, Conner, Connohor, Conor, McConnor, O Connor.
CONNORS, pn, 531, 545, 552.
See O Connors.
CONNORY, pn, 337, 340.
See also Connery, O Connory.
CONNY, pn, 168.
CONNYN, Edward, 498
CONOGHYE, pn, 19.
CONOLAN, pn, 396.
See Connellan.

GOWER, Nicholas, 541.
GOWNE, pn, 95.
——, Daniell, alius Smith, 71.
GOWRAN, pn, 565.
See also McGowren.
GOYNOR, pn, 515.
GRACE, pn, 319, 417, 422, 430, 432.
——, Angelin, 429.
——, Gerald, 429.
——, Gerrold, 315.
——, James, 315.
——, ——, Gerrold his sonne, ibid.
——, John, 316, 428 (bis).
——, Olt, 427.
——, Phillipp, 315.
——, Richard, 301.
——, Robert, 429.
GRADDY, pn, 309.
GRADY, pn, 168.
——, Darby, M, 643.
——, Derby, 270.
——, Donnogh, 290.
——, James, 327.
——, Owen, 269.
——, Thomas, 270.
See also O Grady.
GRAHAM, pn, 3, 9, 120.
——, ——, Capt, 356.
——, Arthur, 113.
——, Hance, 485.
——, ——, his sonn in Law, ibid.
——, Hans, 623.
——, Hanse, 641.
——, Sir James, 641.
——, John, 544.
——, William, 623.
GRAHAMS, pn, 502.
——, Dame Elizabeth Lady, 501.
——, John, 501.
——, Richard, 501.
——, Thomas, 501.
GRAHINE, Andrew, 72.
GRANEER, Isaac, 624.
——, Peter, 625.
GRANIER, Isaack, 184.
——, Peter, 184.
GRANIERS, Isaac, 643.
——, Peter, 643.
GRANT, pn, 350, 419, 422.
——, Patrick, mcht, 349.
——, Tho, 201.
See also Graunt.
GRATRIX, Edward, 543.

GRAUES, William, 482.
See Graves.
GRAUNT, Edward, 20.
See Grant.
GRAVENOR, Samuell, 191.
GRAVES, ——, Capt, 363.
——, Edmond, 474.
——, Edward, 641.
See also Graues.
GRAY, Hugh, 559.
——, Robert, 645.
——, William, 413.
GRAYDON, John, 378.
GREATRAKES, Valentine, 339.
——, William, 339.
GREDY, pn, 309.
GREEG, John, 46.
GREEN, Eliah, 644.
——, Godfrey, 313, 625.
——, Richard, 371.
GREENE, Ed, 200.
——, Francis, 400.
——, George, 429.
——, Godfrey, 644.
——, Ralph, 408.
——, Richard, 408.
——, Thomas, 429.
——, William, 377.
GREENWAY, Henry, 625, 644.
GREGORY, Giles, 306, 644.
——, John, 349.
——, Roger, 471.
GREIA, Robert, 39.
GRENHAM, Henry, 439.
GREWALL, Henry, 431.
GRIBBLE, Wm, 199.
GRICE, John, 441.
——, Richard, 273.
GRIFFIN, pn, 291, 516.
——, James, 515.
——, Mathew, 291.
——, Nicholas, 139.
——, Solloman, 517.
——, Thomas, 515.
——, ——, James his sonn, ibid.
See O Griffin.
GRIFFITH, pn, 594.
——, Jerimiah, 62.
——, John, 86.
——, Lewis, 624.
——, ——, Capt, 271, 643.
——, Thomas, 625, 644.

HALLAM, John, 622.
  See Hallom.
HALLENANE, pn, 338.
HALLEY, pn, 319.
  See Hally.
HALLINGWORTH, Francis, 512.
HALLOM, John, 640.
  See Hallam.
HALLSEY, William, 349.
  See also Halsey.
HALLURANE, pn, 174, 179.
——, Andrew, 186.
——, Morrish, 165.
——, Owen, 186.
  See also O Hallurane.
HALLY, pn, 174, 304, 309, 314, 338.
——, Mathew, 170.
  See also Halley, Haley, Haelly, Haly, Healy,
  O Hally.
HALPIN, pn, 284.
HALSEY, William, 624 (bis), 643 (bis).
  See also Hallsey.
HALY, pn, 195, 297, 419.
  See Hally.
HAMBERY, Thomas, 251.
HAMBILTON, John, 101.
HAMBLETON, Francis, 100.
——, Patrick, 646.
——, William, 101.
HAMELTON, Francis, 34.
——, Hance, 34, 645.
  See Hamilton.
HAMERTON, Richard, 644.
HAMILTON, Archibald, 626, 645.
——, Charles, 627, 645, 646.
——, Charls, 626.
——, Francis, Captn, 52.
——, Sir Francis, 627, 646.
——, Gustavus, 53.
——, Hance, 626, 646.
——, James, 7, 46, 69, 84, 90, 151, 626, 627,
  645, 646 (bis).
——, John, 52, 53, 92.
——, ——, of Cavan, 626, 645.
——, Lodewick, 102.
——, Patrick, 627.
——, Robert, 52, 94, 107.
——, William, 70, 92, 442, 622, 626 (bis), 640,
  645, 646 (bis).
  See also Hammilton, Hamiltone, Hamelton,
  Hambleton, Hambilton.
HAMILTONE, Archbalid, 84.
——, James, 84.

HAMLYN, John, 191.
HAMMILTON, Gawen, 90.
——, James, 14.
HAMMON, Laurence, 315.
HAMON, Joseph, 505.
HAMOND, William, 404.
HAMPIN, Barthlomew, 474.
HANAGAN, pn, 338.
HANDCOCK, John, 200.
——, William, 622, 625, 642, 644.
HANDCOCKE, William, 593.
HANDY, Jonathan, 513.
HANELY, Roger, 299.
HANFORD, John, 123.
HANGLY, Martin, 484.
HANIN, pn, 592.
HANKSHAW, John, merchant, 370.
HANKSWOORTH, John, 280.
HANLEY, Patrick, 395.
HANLON, pn, 399, 468.
  See also O Hanlon.
HANLY, pn, 577.
——, Cormak, 575.
——, Dermot, 578.
——, Ed, 580.
——, Gillernan, 578.
——, John, 578.
——, William, 578.
  See also Hanley, O Hanly.
HANNY, William, 34.
HANON, pn, 7.
HANRAGHAN, pn, 604.
HANRAGHANE, Nicholas, 275.
  See also O Hanraghane.
HANWAY, John, 366.
HANY, pn, 302.
HARA, pn, 600.
  See also O Hara.
HARAGHAN, pn, 495.
HARBERT, Walter, 199.
  See also Herbert.
HARBORNE, William, 366.
HARDICK, John, 474.
HARDING, Ann, 229.
——, Arthur, 353.
——, Giles, 287.
——, ——, William his sonn, *ibid.*
——, Henry, 287.
——, John, 287.
——, ——, Docr, 381.
——, Nicodemus, 193.
——, Peter, 237.
——, Robert, 347

HIDE, Robert, 236, 623, 642.
  See also Hyde.
HIERLY, William, 185.
HIERNANE, pn, 188.
HIFFERNANE, pn, 174, 273, 309, 328.
——, James, 171.
——, ——, John and Roger his sonns, *ibid.*
——, John, 171.
——, Miles, 171.
——, Roger, 171.
  See Heffernane.
HIGGIN, pn, 445, 498, 582.
——, William, 445.
  See Higin, O Higgin.
HIGHGATE, Edmond, 640.
  See also Hyegate.
HIGHMORE, Abraham, 357, 621, 639.
HIGIN, pn, 582.
  See Higgin, O Higin.
HIGNES, Daniel, 624.
HIGNET, Daniel, 643.
HIGNETT, Daniell, Town Clerke of Limerick,
  263.
HIKY, pn, 309.
HIKYE, pn, 324.
  See Hickey.
HILAN, Filan al's Hilan, pn, 406.
  See also Hylan.
HILL, pn, 9.
——, Arthur, 80, 626 (bis), 645, 646.
——, ——, William and Conway his sonns, 80.
——, Conway, 80.
——, Edward, 625.
——, Henry, 211.
——, James, 579.
——, John, 251.
——, Moses, 474, 623, 641, 645, 646.
——, Phillip, 64.
——, Samuel, Sherif of London Derry, 626.
——, Samuell, 123, 645.
——, Thomas, 482, 640.
——, Will, 291.
——, William, 20, 80, 368 (bis), 593, 645.
——, ——, merchant, 366.
——, Wm, 199.
HILLMAN, Ralph, gent decayed, 21.
——, Thomas, ald, 139.
HILLMON, Symon, 139.
HILMON, Simon, 646.
HINDE, Jon, 590.
  See also Hynd.
HINEGAN, pn, 396.
HINKS, Leonard, 468.

HIRLY, pn, 502.
HITCHMONGH, Hen, 199.
HOARE, Edward, 216.
——, William, 193.
  See Hore.
HOBBS, Hugh, 531.
——, Rich, 206.
——, William, 300.
HOBIGAN, pn, 452.
HOBSON, James, 123.
——, William, 188, 644.
  See also Hopson.
HODDEN, Rich, 199.
HODDER, Francis, 191.
——, John, 623 (bis), 642 (bis).
——, Margery, wife of William, 204.
——, William, 204, 623 (bis), 642 (bis).
——, ——, his wife Margery, 204.
HODEN, Richard, 435.
——, Will, 435.
HODGES, John, 207, 369.
——, Robert, 404.
——, Thomas, 524.
HODGKINS, Wm, 372.
HODSER, Bartholomew, Shop Kr, 372.
——, ——, ——, Robert his sonn, *ibid.*
——, Robert, 372.
HOEY, Sir John, 621 (bis).
——, William, 621.
——, ——, ald, *ibid.*
  See Hoy.
HOGAN, pn, 168, 319, 340, 359, 438, 442.
HOGANE, pn, 174, 177, 183, 239, 275, 302, 304,
  309, 314, 322, 324, 328, 337.
——, Edmond, 322.
——, John, 310, 311, 323.
——, Patrick, 177.
——, Teige, 201.
——, Wm, 311.
  See also Heogan, O Hogan, O Hogane.
HOLAGHAN, pn, 500.
  See Hologhon.
HOLAN, Felan alias Holan, pn, 399.
HOLCOMBE, Jeane, 213.
——, Mary, 213.
——, Wm, 213.
——, ——, Jeane and Mary his daughters,
  ibid.
HOLCROFT, Abraham, 199.
HOLDCOMB, William, 623.
HOLDER, John, 441.
HOLFORD, Thomas, 365.
——, William, 365.

2 Y

K

KAUANAGH, pn, 356, 359, 398, 402, 405, 538, 542, 548, 552, 554.
——, Charles, 356.
——, James, 355.
——, Morgan, 553.
——, Symon, 358.
KAUENAGH, pn, 355.
KAVANAGH, Bryan, 358.
——, Morish, 591.
——, Richard, 358.
——, Tirlagh, 357.
See also Keavanagh, Kevanagh, Cavanagh.
KAVANANAGH, Charles, 420.
KAY, Thomas, 366.
KEA, pn, 495.
KEADAGANE, pn, 228.
KEAGANE, pn, 438.
See Keegan.
KEAGHO, pn, 405.
KEAGHOE, pn, 404.
See Keogh.
KEAHANE, pn, 344.
KEALY, pn, 309, 314, 354, 405.
——, Nicholas, 377.
See also Keely, O Kealy.
KEARNAN, pn, 510.
——, Richard, 509.
See Kiernan.
KEARNE, pn, 526.
KEARNEY, pn, 297, 309, 328, 344.
——, James, 307.
KEARNY, pn, 417.
——, Bryan, 305.
See also Kerny.
KEAROGAN, pn, 380.
KEAROVAN, pn, 380.
KEARY, John, 215.
KEATING, pn, 338, 340, 404, 417, 501, 532, 538, 542, 548.
——, Henry, 368.
——, Morrish, 403.
——, Oliver, 170.
——, Oliver FitzArthur, 170.
——, Redmond, 165.
KEATINGE, pn, 309, 314.
——, Morrish, 311.
——, Paule, 311.
——, Peirce, 311.
——, Richard, 311.
——, William, 311.
See also Ketin, Keting.

KEAVANAGH, pn, 380.
See Kavanagh.
KEEFE, pn, 417, 427.
See also O Keefe.
KEEGAN, pn, 452, 453, 460, 516, 519, 521, 523, 526.
See also Keagane, Kegan, Kegin, Keygin, Kigan.
KEELER, Godfrey, 622, 642.
——, Godfry, 525.
KEELY, pn, 396, 408, 436, 438, 439, 444.
See Kealy.
KEENE, Stephen, 201.
See McKeene.
KEENEDY, pn, 442.
See Kennedy.
KEERNAN, pn, 455.
See Kiernan.
KEERVAN, Antho, 586.
KEGAN, pn, 396, 569.
——, Conley, 436.
——, James, 500.
KEGIN, pn, 495.
See Keegan.
KEGRY, pn, 512.
KEHAN, Thomas, 445 (bis).
KEHOE, pn, 425.
See Keogh.
KEICHE, Joseph, 316.
KEISH, John, 87.
KELAN, pn, 442.
KELLEY, pn, 465.
KELLIE, pn, 396, 399.
See Kelly.
KELLOHER, Daniell, 164.
KELLSALL, Henry, 347.
KELLY, pn, 19, 168, 174, 181, 195, 204, 291, 297, 302, 309, 314, 319, 338, 341, 344, 350, 354, 359, 373, 380, 382, 384, 387, 390, 391, 398, 400, 402, 404, 405, 408, 409, 414, 417, 419, 422, 423, 425, 427, 428, 430, 432, 442, 446, 447, 452, 459, 468, 470, 473, 474, 483, 485, 487, 495, 496, 498, 500, 501, 502, 503, 505, 510, 512, 519, 525, 532, 538, 545, 548, 550, 565, 569, 577, 582, 587, 592, 594, 598, 600, 604, 607.
——, Barnaby, 407.
——, Brashill, 301.
——, Bryan, 587.
——, Daniell, 587.
——, Donogh, 590.
——, Hugh, 590.

KELLY, James, 363, 589.
——, Jno, 587.
——, John, 370, 371, 407.
——, ——, merchant, 371.
——, Keaghda, 589.
——, Loghlin, 587.
——, Owen, 587.
——, Phillipp, 170.
——, Richard, 642.
——, Teige, 334.
——, Terrence, 493.
——, Turlogh, 576.
——, Walter, 593.
——, William, 589.
KELLYE, pn, 406.
  See also Kelley, Kellie, McKelly, O Kelly.
KEMPTON, George, 423.
KEN, William, 624, 643.
  See Kenn
KENADY, pn, 53.
——, Anthony, 48.
  See Kennedy, O Kenady.
KENAGHT, pn, 548.
KENANE, pn, 438.
KENE, pn, 453.
KENEDIE, pn, 526.
KENEDY, pn, 3, 9, 19, 27, 168, 254, 289, 297, 302, 304, 309, 319, 322, 324, 328, 338, 341, 344, 346, 348, 373, 380, 406, 408, 414, 417, 419, 423, 425, 430, 439, 446, 447, 456, 483, 495, 498, 502, 506, 582.
——, ——, ald, 370.
——, Alexander, 237.
——, Bryan, 163.
——, Bryen, 320.
——, Daniell, 163.
——, Dauid, 90.
——, Ireall, 173.
——, Mathew, 321.
——, Phillipp, 321.
——, ——, Teige his sonne, *ibid.*
——, Richard, 459.
——, Robert, 19, 363.
——, Teige, 321 (bis).
——, ——, Mathew his sonne, *ibid.*
——, Thomas, 370.
——, William, 367.
  See Kennedy, McKenedy, O Kenedy.
KENESHANE, pn, 447.
KENESLON, John, 416.
KENN, Will, 264.
  See Ken.

KENNA, pn, 406, 500.
  See also McKenna.
KENNEDAY, Richard, 621.
KENNEDY, pn, 485.
——, Dauid, 94.
——, Fergus, 87.
——, John, 622, 641.
——, Richard, 620, 621.
——, Sir Richard, 639 (bis).
——, Rob, 638.
——, Robert, 620, 621, 639 (bis).
——, Thomas, 621, 639 (ter).
——, William, 622.
  See also Keenedy, Kenady, Kenedie, Kenedy, Kenneday, McKennedy, O Kennedy.
KENNEY, Richard, 621.
KENNON, pn, 473.
KENNY, pn, 402, 406, 425, 444, 453, 455, 460, 512, 521, 526, 577, 592.
——, Edward, 203, 623.
——, Richard, 363, 640.
  See also Kenney, Keny, McKenny, O Kenny.
KENSELAGH, pn, 359.
KENSELLAGH, Miles, 554.
KENSLY, pn, 554.
  See Kinselagh.
KENT, pn, 309.
——, Rob, Lieut, 643.
——, Robert, 286.
KENY, pn, 402, 474, 521, 526, 592.
  See Kenny, McKeny, O Keny.
KEOGH, pn, 174.
——, Donnogh, 591.
——, Hugh, 592 (bis).
——, Jno, 592.
——, Peter, 592.
  See also Keagho, Keaghoe, Kehoe, McKeogh.
KERELLY, pn, 592.
KERKE, William, merchant, 369.
KERNAN, pn, 373, 459, 523.
  See Kiernan, McKernan, O Kernan.
KERNY, pn, 577.
——, Michaell, 306, 307.
——, Moris, 305.
  See also Kearney.
KERR, Michaell, 20.
KERRIS, Gilbert, 391.
KERRYN, pn, 340.
  See also O Kerryn.
KERWICKE, pn, 338.
KET, John, 639.
KETIN, Oliuer, 576.

INDEX OF PERSONS.

MACKANRY, Will, 514.
MAC KAY, Daniel, 646.
McKAY, pn, 64.
——, or McCAY, pn, 19.
McKEANAN, pn, 254.
See McKenan.
McKEE, pn, 7, 29, 45, 48, 53, 86.
See also McKie, McKye.
McKEENE, pn, 35.
See McKeyne, Keene.
McKEGHAN, pn, 19.
McKELLY, pn, 40, 120, 265.
See Kelly, O Kelly.
McKENAN, pn, 569.
See also McKeanan, O Kenan.
McKENEDY, pn, 288.
See also Kenedy, McKennedy, O Kenedy.
McKENNA, pn, 160.
See Kenna.
McKENNEDY, pn, 284.
See also Kennedy, McKenedy, O Kennedy.
McKENNY, pn, 119.
——, John, marchant, 123.
McKENY, pn, 577.
See also Ken(n)y, O Ken(n)y.
McKEOGH, pn, 265, 275, 592.
See also Keogh.
McKEOGHE, pn, 359.
McKEOINE, pn, 569.
McKEONE, pn, 565. *See* O Keoyne.
McKERNAN, pn, 119.
See also Kernan, O Kernan.
McKERRAN, pn, 59.
MACKEY, pn, 128, 468.
McKEYNE, pn, 35.
McKIE, pn, 90, 95.
See McKee.
McKIGAN, pn, 592.
See Kigan.
McKILLEAGHER, pn, 569.
McKILLKER, pn, 48.
McKILLOP, pn, 5.
McKILMARTIN, pn, 119.
See McGillmartin.
McKILROY, pn, 119.
See McIlroy.
McKINLAY, pn, 19, 53.
McKINSTRY, pn, 3.
McKNABB, John, 466.
McKNOGHER, pn, 128, 133.
McKWEY, pn, 460.
McKYE, pn, 3.
See McKie.
McLAUGHLIN, pn, 64, 124, 128, 133, 455, 525.
——, Edmond Moder, 62.
——, ——, Hugh his sonn, *ibid.*
See Laughlin.
McLENANY, pn, 600.
McLOGHLEN, pn, 174, 187, 286, 314, 319, 569.
McLOGHLIN, pn, 168, 328, 417, 473, 586, 592, 607.
McLOUGHLIN, pn, 587.
See also Loghlin, McGlaghlin, McGloughlen, O Loghlen, Melaghline.
McLYNNAN, pn, 119.
See Lynnan, O Lynnan.
McMAGHONE, pn, 160.
McMAHON, pn, 119, 120, 168, 174, 179, 181, 185, 188, 284, 289, 465, 468, 565.
——, Art, 101.
——, Con McColl, 99.
——, Hugh, 100.
——, Mahon, 180.
——, Mathew, 164.
——, Mortagh, 184.
——, Teige, 180 (bis).
——, Terlagh, 165.
——, Therlagh, 184.
——, Tirlogh, 113.
See also Mahon.
McMAHONE, pn, 242.
McMAHONY, pn, 179, 252, 284.
——, Daniell, 333.
McMAHOWNY, pn, 233, 314.
——, Daniell, 288.
See Maho(w)ny, O Maho(w)ny.
MACMANUS, pn, 119, 582, 586.
McMANUS, pn, 119, 120 (ter), 565, 600.
McMARROWE, pn, 302.
McMARTEN, pn, 120.
See Marten, Gillmartin.
McMARYNE, pn, 119.
McMAUGHON, pn, 470, 473.
McMELLEN, pn, 72. *See* O Mellan.
McMENDA, Daniell, 164.
McMICHELL, pn, 19.
McMLAGHLEN, pn, 228. *See* O Melaghlin.
McMORCHEY, pn, 120.
See McMurphy.
McMOREY, pn, 607.
See Morey, McMurray, O Morey.
McMORIS, pn, 286.
——, Garrett, 288.
McMORISH, pn, 271, 290, 338, 340, 344, 346, 348, 354.
See also FitzMorish, Morish.

NOVIS, John, 240.
NOWLAN, pn, 396, 398, 399, 400, 402, 556.
NOWLAND, pn, 373, 380, 382, 405, 500, 501.
NOWLANE, pn, 380.
See Nolan.
NUGENT, pn, 271, 350, 577.
——, Christopher, 513, 592.
——, ——, Oliuer his sonn, 513.
——, Edmond, 445, 513.
——, Edward, 512, 575.
——, Francis, 573.
——, Garrett, 176, 403.
——, James, 509, 577.
——, ——, Nicholas his sonn, 577.
——, Nicholas, 577.
——, Oliuer, 513.
——, Richard, 510, 573.
——, Robert, 185, 509, 510.
——, Thomas, 185, 622, 642.
——, Sir Thomas, 573.
See also Newgent.
NULTY, Mathew, 367.
NUNANE, pn, 284.
See O Nonane.
NUNN, Richard, 535.

O

O AGHERNS, Morrish, 240.
See O Hagherine.
OAKELEY, Rowland, 211.
OB, Thomas, 365.
O BANAN, pn, 119, 120.
See Banan.
O BARR, pn, 64.
See Barr.
O BEARA, Mortagh, 274.
O BEGGAN, pn, 160.
See Beggan.
O BENAGHAN, pn, 607.
O BERN, pn, 86.
O BERNE, pn, 585.
See Beirn.
O BIERNE, pn, 577, 581.
O BIRNE, pn, 48, 160, 585.
——, William, 580.
See O Byrne, Birne.
O BOE, pn, 414, 417, 430, 547.
See Boe.
O BOGHELLY, pn, 195.
O BOIGD, pn, 207.

O BOWE, pn, 495.
See Bowe.
O BOYD, pn, 19.
See Boyd.
O BOYLAN, pn, 160.
See Boylan.
O BOYLE, pn, 19, 45, 48, 53, 59, 64, 160, 468, 473.
——, Teage, 47.
——, Torlagh, 47.
See Boyle.
O BOYNS, Mr Amlett, 36.
O BRADY, pn, 119.
See Brady.
O BREENAN, pn, 45.
O BREENE, pn, 247, 545.
O BREIN, pn, 119.
See O Brien.
O BRENAN, pn, 354, 585.
O BRENANE, pn, 247, 600.
See Brenan(e).
O BRIAN, pn, 265, 288.
See O Brien, Brian, McBrian.
O BRIEN, pn, 233, 242, 290.
——, Donnogh, 169.
——, ——, Terlagh his sonn, *ibid.*
——, Owen, 169.
——, Teige, 167, 168.
——, Terlagh, 169.
See also O Brein, O Brian, O Brine, O Bryan, O Bryen, O Bryn, O Bryne, O Bryon, McBrien.
O BRILLAGHAN, pn, 59, 64.
O BRINE, pn, 273, 290, 291, 408.
See O Brien, Brine, McBrine.
O BRISLAN, pn, 119.
O BRISLANE, pn, 48.
O BRODIR, pn, 239.
O BRYAN, pn, 119, 195, 275, 353, 495, 545, 552, 556.
——, Daniell, 240.
See O Brien, Bryan, McBryan.
O BRYEN, pn, 168, 174, 177, 183, 239, 247, 252, 265, 271, 273, 309, 340.
——, Bryen, 172.
——, Connor, 173, 184, 187.
——, Daniell, 167, 186.
——, Sir Daniell, 184.
——, Derby, 176.
——, Dermott, 169, 174.
——, Donnogh, 175.
——, Donogh, 183.
——, Mahon, 177.

O Dorney, pn, 205.
O Dougherty, Cahair, 108.
O Doughertye, pn, 139, 145.
    See O Dogherty.
O Dovoren, Hugh, 187.
    See O Davoren.
O Dower, pn, 337.
    See Dower.
O Dowey, pn, 128.
O Dowy, pn, 59.
O Doy, pn, 64.
O Doyle, pn, 354, 538.
    See Doyle, McDoyle.
O Drea, pn, 417.
O Driscoll, pn, 228.
——, Donnogh, 171.
    See Driscoll.
O Dromma, pn, 120.
    See McDromma.
O Drum, pn, 120.
O Duffie, pn, 160.
    See Duffy.
O Duhy, pn, 600.
O Duigenan, pn, 565.
O Dulane, pn, 444.
O Dule, pn, 265.
O Dulinge, pn, 250.
O Dulleghan, pn, 468.
O Dully, pn, 525.
    See also Dully.
O Duringg, pn, 120.
O Duyne, pn, 40.
Odway, Arthur, Capt, 349.
O Dwayne, pn, 314.
    See also Dwayne.
O Dwier, pn, 288.
    See Dwier.
O Dwyer, pn, 328.
O Dwyre, pn, 168, 174, 302, 309, 314, 319.
——, Archyball, 300.
——, Donough, 300.
——, John, 169.
    See also O Dwier, Dwyer, Dwyre.
O Dyer, pn, 288.
    See Dyer.
O Dyeyneene, Cnohor, 202.
O Dyman, pn, 139.
O Dyoddan, pn, 119.
O Fahy, pn, 600.
    See Fahy.
O Farran, pn, 64.
O Fary, pn, 59.

O Fea, pn, 346.
O Fee, pn, 119, 120.
O Feeny, pn, 133, 607.
    See O Finy.
O Fegan, pn, 77.
    See Fegan.
O Feggan, pn, 83.
O Fenighan, pn, 27.
O Ferally, pn, 284.
    See Ferrally.
O Fergussa, pn, 569.
O Ferill, pn, 59.
O Ferrall, pn, 40.
    See Ferrall.
O Ferry, pn, 59.
Offling, pn, 341.
    See O Flynne.
O Fihily, pn, 569.
O Finagan, pn, 160.
O Finaghan, pn, 27.
O Finan, pn, 32.
    See Finan.
O Finegane, pn, 600.
    See Finegan.
O Finine, pn, 207.
    See also McFineen.
O Finn, pn, 210.
    See McFinne.
O Finy, pn, 577.
    See Finy, O Feeny.
O Flanagan, pn, 120, 586.
O Flanigane, Connor, 186.
O Flannagan, pn, 119.
    See Flanagan.
O Flin, pn, 586.
O Fline, pn, 242, 569.
O Fling, pn, 337.
O Flinge, pn, 314.
O Fluen, pn, 602.
O Flyne, pn, 195, 239, 247, 284, 337, 565.
O Flynne, pn, 195.
    See Flynn, Offling.
O Fowlow, pn, 195, 341.
O Fowlowe, pn, 239.
O Fowlue, pn, 247, 257.
O Fowly, pn, 556.
    See Fowlow, Fowlue.
O Friell, pn, 59.
O Gallagher, pn, 569.
O Gallogher, pn, 48.
    See Gallaghur, O Gollogher.
Ogan, pn, 548.
    See Owgan.

PLELLPS, Thomas, marchant, 263.
PLOVER, John, 202.
——, ——, Robert his son, *ibid*.
PLUKENET, Charles, 20.
PLUMER, Richd, 238.
PLUNCKET, Walter, 621.
PLUNKET, pn, 465.
——, Garret, 439.
——, Geo, 589.
——, Mary, Widow, 443.
——, Walter, 621.
——, Sir Walter, 639, 640.
——, William, 369.
PLUNKETT, pn, 380, 470, 485, 528, 577.
——, Alexander, 474.
——, Andrew, 480.
——, Bartholemew, 484.
——, Chris, 484.
——, Christopher, 390.
——, ——, Patricke his sonn, *ibid*.
——, Edward, 398, 484, 511.
——, Garrett, 211.
——, John, 123, 255, 645.
——, ——, Thomas his sonn, 255.
——, Patricke, 390, 576.
——, Robert, 574.
——, Thomas, 255, 487, 574.
——, Walter, 383.
——, William, 369.
POAKRICH, Richard, 150.
POCHER, William, 431.
POCKERIDG, Michael, 626.
POCKERISH, Michael, 645.
POCKRICH, Edward, 150.
POE, Tho, 625, 644.
——, Thomas, 319.
POEKRICH, Michaell, 150.
POER, pn, 340.
——, John, 624, 643.
——, Richard, 624, 643.
See Power.
POINTS, John, 213.
——, Toby, 29.
POINTZ, Tobias, 626.
——, Toby, 645.
POLE, Edward, 599.
POLEWHEELE, Peter, 8.
POLEXFIELD, James, 367 (bis).
——, John, 367.
POLLOCK, Dauid, 84.
PONNTNEY, Will, Lt, 517.
See Pountney.

PONSONBY, Henry, 249, 624, 643.
——, John, 621.
——, Sir John, 640 (bis).
PONTIN, Lodowick, 408.
PONTONEY, ——, Leut, a lodger, 366.
PONY, John, 367.
POOER, John, 354.
See Power.
POOL, Francis, 623, 641.
POOLE, Francis, 474.
——, John, 199.
——, Samuell, 206.
——, Thomas, 366.
POOLEY, Thomas, 620, 639.
POOLY, Thomas, 363.
POOPE, Thomas, Captn, 364.
POORDOM, John, 504.
POORE, pn, 350, 359, 419, 423, 460, 548.
——, Brice, 171.
——, Edmond, 171.
——, ——, John his sonn, *ibid*.
——, Godfry, 168.
——, James, 172.
——, John, 171.
——, Pierce, 171.
——, ——, William and Brice his sonns, *ibid*.
——, Tho, marchant, 263.
——, Thomas, 166, 263.
——, William, 171.
See Power.
POPE, Will, Leut, 263.
——, William, 624.
——, ——, Burgess, 643.
——, ——, Cap, 643.
PORSONBY, John, Coll, 419.
PORTER, pn, 53, 64.
——, Henry, 389.
PORTIS, Willm, 429.
POTT, Robert, 377.
POTTER, ——, Capt, 364.
——, ——, ——, Walter his sonn, *ibid*.
——, James, 247.
——, Walter, 364.
POUDYHARD, Humphry, 368.
POUEY, Allin, 590.
See Povey.
POULDEN, John, 200.
POUNTNEY, William, 642.
See Ponntney.
POURDON, George, 624, 643.
See Purdon.
POVEY, Allen, 625, 644.

VAS, William, 59.
VAUGHAN, Abraham, 200
——, Evan, 381.
——, Even, 367.
——, Francis, 341, 379.
——, Henry, 64, 626, 645.
——, John, 191.
——, Owen, 625.
——, Peter, 390.
——, Thomas, 624, 642.
    See also Vaghan.
VEALE, pn, 338.
VELDON, James, 580.
VENNER, William, 642.
VENNOR, William, 515.
VERDON, pn, 577.
——, Christopher, 179.
——, Henry, 270.
——, Nicholas, 576.
——, Patrick, 575.
——, Robert, 195.
VERKERS, John, 192.
VERNER, John, 78.
VERSCOYLE, Hen, 371.
VILLERS, Sir Geo, 566.
VINCENT, Francis, 269.
——, Pencer, 550.
——, Spencer, 621, 640.
——, Thomas, 379, 550, 621, 622 (quat), 626,
    639, 640, 641 (bis).
——, Tho, 641.
VIVERS, John, 500.
VIZARD, John, 206.
——, Ralph, 371.
——, ——, ald, 620, 638.
VOICE, Patrick, 430.

W

WADDELL, Allexr, 78.
WADDEY, Edmond, 537.
WADDINGTON, Henry, 644.
——, ——, Cap, 645.
——, ——, High Sheriff, 625 (bis).
WADDY, Edmond, 621.
WADE, pn, 338, 387.
——, ——, Major, 263.
——, ——, Mr, 645.
——, Bryan, 216.
——, Henry, 422, 623.
——, ——, Leut, 363.

WADE, James, apothecary, 370.
——, Robert, 371.
——, ——, bruar, 366
——, Samuell, 349.
——, Thomas, 497.
——, William, ald, 624, 643.
——, ——, Maior, 643.
WADKINS, ——, 554.
WADMAN, John, 20.
WAGGONER, Jo, 201.
WAGH, James, 99.
——, Walter, 99.
WAIGHT, Silvester, mchant, 363.
WAILE, James, 84.
WAILSE, pn, 309.
WAILSH, pn, 271, 284, 408, 495, 498, 500, 501,
    505.
——, Oliver, 504.
    See Walsh.
WAINMAN, Charles, 367.
WAITS, Tho, 201.
WAKEFIELD, John, 383.
——, Paul, 531.
WAKEHAM, John, 623, 642.
——, ——, Capt, 195.
——, ——, ——, his Company, *ibid.*
WAKELY, John, 440, 622, 641.
WAKHAM, John, Capt, 238.
WALCHOTT, Thomas, Capt, 276.
WALCOT, Richard, 625, 644.
WALCOTT, Thomas, 9.
WALDING, Thomas, 525.
WALDO, Daniell, Adventr, 520.
WALDRON, Tho, 646.
WALDRONN, ——, Mr, 37.
WALDRUM, John, 568.
WALE, pn, 314, 344.
——, Garott, 353.
——, Garrott, 355.
——, Redmond, 356.
——, Seymour, 355.
    See Wall, O Wale.
WALKAM, Richd, 238.
WALKER, Edward, 440.
——, John, 323, 624, 643.
——, ——, Lt, 245.
——, Joseph, 301.
——, Josias, jun, 191.
——, Tho, 200.
——, William, 502.
WALKES, Richard, 324.
——, his sonne Richard, *ibid.*

WRIGHT, Thomas, Capt, 349.
——, William, 624, 642.
——, Wm, 199.
WROTHAM, Symon, 177.
WYATT, Thomas, 149.
WYBRANT, Daniell, merchant, 370.
——, Peter, ald, 620.
See also Waybrent, Wibrant.
WYBRUNE, Olphert, 56.
WYBURNE, John, 380.
WYE, Gilbert, 8, 645, 646.
WYKE, Andrew, 81.
WYNN, Owen, 568, 644.
——, ——, High Sheriff of Leitrim, 625.
——, Robert, 623, 641.
WYNNE, Peter, 388.
——, Robt, 471.
See Winne.
WYOTT, Thomas, Leut, 167.
WYRE, pn, 519.
WYTHERS, Edward, 532.
See Withers.

Y

YARDO, Geo, 199.
YARNER, Abraham, 620, 639.
——, ——, Doctor, 621, 639.
YARWELL, Will, ald, 263.
——, William, ald, 624, 643.

YATES, James, 367.
——, Robert, 367.
YEADON, John, 585.
YEARD, Mathew, 327.
YEO, Edmond, 20.
YEOMANS, Edmd, 199.
YOUNG, pn, 5.
——, ——, Mr, 370.
——, Archibald, 625, 644.
——, George, 191.
——, Jo, 28.
——, John, 627, 646.
——, Phillip, 640.
——, Rich, 368.
——, Richard, 484.
——, Walt, 199.
YOUNGE, William, 52.

——, Charles, 576.
——, Daniell Oge, 185.
——, Donnogh Oge, 180.
——, Luke, maior of Derry, 124.
——, Mortagh Oge, 178.
——, Teige Oge Lader, 229.
——, Therlaghlen, 186.
——, Thorloe Oge, 289.
—— n, Wil, 627.

3 D

INDEX OF PLACES.

The following abbreviations have been used :—

bar	=	barony.	Arm	=	Armagh.	Leit	=	Leitrim.
bor	=	borough.	Car	=	Carlow.	Lim	=	Limerick.
c	=	city.	Cav	=	Cavan.	Long	=	Longford.
co	=	county.	Ck	=	Cork.	Lou	=	Louth.
div	=	division.	Cl	=	Clare.	Mea	=	Meath.
lib	=	liberty.	D	=	Down.	Mon	=	Monaghan.
par(s)	=	parish(es).	Don	=	Donegal.	Qco	=	Queen's County.
pl	=	place.	Dub	=	Dublin.	Rosc	=	Roscommon.
pt	=	part.	Fer	=	Fermanagh.	Sli	=	Sligo.
qr(s)	=	quarter(s).	Gal	=	Galway.	Tipp	=	Tipperary.
t(s)	=	town(s).	Kco	=	King's County.	Tyr	=	Tyrone.
tl(s)	=	townland(s).	Kd	=	Kildare.	Wat	=	Waterford.
tp	=	township.	Ker	=	Kerry.	Wex	=	Wexford.
vill	=	village.	Kk	=	Kilkenny.	Wmea	=	Westmeath.
Ant	=	Antrim.	LD	=	Londonderry.			

References in the Index of Places are to county and page of Text only. The omission of references to barony and parish is due to the fact that their inclusion would have increased the size of the Index to a considerable extent. Counties and cities have been entered separately from baronies, parishes, or townlands of similar name, e.g., *Corke.* Otherwise, all denominations have been grouped together under the one heading :—

> Moycashell, bar, Wmea, 519, 528 ; tl, 517.
> Moyferta, bar, Cl, 184, 185, 188 ; par, 184 ; tl, *ibid.*

The order in which references are arranged within each heading follows the pagination of the Text :—

> Mullaghmore, pl, Fer, 110 ; Mon, 152, 154 ; tl, Rosc, 584.

At the same time, where two or more references to a particular denomination occur, they have been grouped together :—

> Ballymore, pl, Ant, 19 ; Ck, 238 ; Tipp, 304 ; tl, LD, 128 ; Ker, 253 ;
> Wmea, 519 ; 3 plds, Ck, 225 ; par, Wmea, 519 ; peer, Wex, 534.

That is to say, the references ' Ck, 238 ; Tipp, 304,' being to the denomination ' Place,' follow ' Ant, 19,' which is the earliest ' Place ' reference ; in like manner, the ' Townland ' references are grouped together.

Place Names occurring in the Text with the prefix ' B :,' e.g., *B : Nebrean* are placed in the Index as if spelt ' Bally-.'

While no attempt has been made at identification of place names, cross-references have been provided to the variant spellings of frequently recurring prefixes, such as *Ard-, Bally-, Mullagh-,* etc.   As a further help towards the easier handling of the Index the following list has been drawn up.   It gives the modern city, county, and baronial spelling followed by the Census spelling. There are no baronies returned by the Census for the counties of Fermanagh and Monaghan, and in both these cases the parishes have been adopted as identificatory items. It is to be noted that the Index takes no account of the modern spelling of place names ; it is based solely on the spelling as given in the Text of the Census.

Modern Spelling	Census Spelling	Modern Spelling	Census Spelling
ULSTER :		Maghera-culmoney	Magherycoolmony, Maghery-coolemony
ANTRIM	Antrim	Drummully	Drumully, Dumully
Carrickfergus	Carickfergus, Carrikfergus, Carikfergus	Derrybrusk	Derribruske, Terribruske
		Derryvullan	Derrivollan, Derryvollan
Glenarm	Glenarme, Glencarne	Magheracross	Magherycross
Massereene	Masareene	Inishmac-saint	Ennis McSaint
Toome	Toome		
Dunluce	Dunluce, Donluce	Templecarn	Templecarne
Cary	Carry, Carie, Carey	Kinawley	Kilnawly, Kilmawly
Kilconway	Kilconrie, Kilconrye, Kilconway	Enniskillen	Enniskillen
Belfast	Bellfast	LONDON-DERRY	Londonderry, Derry
ARMAGH	Ardmagh	Tirkeeran	Terkerin
Tiranny	Tarranney, Tarranny	Keenaght	Kenaght
Orior	Oryer, Orryer	Loughin-sholin	Loghinsholin
Fews	Fewes		
Oneilland	ONeyland	Coleraine	Colraine, Colranie
Oneilland East	Clanbrassell	MONAGHAN	Monaghan
Charlemont	Charlemount	Tedavnet	Teedawnett
		Kilmore	Kilmore
DONEGAL	Donegall	Errigal	Eriglee, Erigle
Tirhugh	Tirhugh	Donagh	Donagh
Boylagh	Boylagh	Dartree	Dartrye, Datrye, Dantry, *all's*
Banagh	Banagh	Galloon	Galoone, Galloone
Raphoe	Rapho	Clones	Clownish, Clonish
Kilmacrenan	Kill McCrenan, KillMcCrennan	Magheross	Macaross
Inishowen	Enishowen	Donagh-moyne	Donomoyne
DOWN	Downe	Maghera-cloone	Maghereclony, Magherecloney
Lecale	Lecale	Inishkeen	Eniskeene
Iveagh	Iveagh, Evagh, Eveagh	Aghnamullen	Aghanamullan
Newry	Newry	Clontibret	Clantibred
Kinelarty	Kinalerty, Kinallerty, Kinalertye	Tullycorbet	Tulicabett
Dufferin	Duffrane	*MUNSTER :*	
Castlereagh	Castellreagh, Castlereagh		
Ards	Ards	CLARE	Clare
FERMAN-AGH	Farmanagh, Fermannagh	Bunratty	Bunratty
Clones	Clownish	Tulla	Tulla
Aghavee	Aghaveigh	Inchiquin	Inchiquine, Inchiqine
Devenish	Devonish	Islands	Island
Boho	Bohue	Clonderalaw	Clandirala
Rossory	Rossory	Corcomroe	Corcomroe
Cleenish	Cleenish, Clenish	Moyarta	Moyferta
Killasser	Killasher	Burren	Burren
Aghalurcher	Aghahurcher, Aghahurchur, Aghaharcher	Ibrickan	Ibrickane
Enniskeen	Enniskeane	Ennis	Enish, Inish

Modern Spelling	Census Spelling	Modern Spelling	Census Spelling
CORK	Corke	WATER-FORD	Waterford
Kinsale	Kinsale	Decies	Deaces
Bandon	Bandon Bridge, Bandonbridge	Coshmore	Cosmore
Youghal	Youghall	Coshbride	Cosbride
Mallow	Moyalle, Moyello	Glenahiry	Glanahiry, Glanahyry
Kinalea	Kinalea, Kinelea, Kenalea	Upperthird	Upperthird
Kerrycurrihy	Kierycurrihy, Keirycurrihy	Middlethird	Middlethird, Midlethird
Kinalmeaky	Kinalmeaky	Gaultier	Galtire
Ibane	Ibawne		
Barrymore	Barymore, Barrymore		
Courceys	Coursies	LEINSTER :	
Kilbrittain	Kibrittaine, Killbrittaine		
Carbery	Carbery, Carbury	CARLOW	Catherlagh
Bear	Beere	Rathvilly	Rathvily, Rathvilie
Bantry	Bantry	Forth	Forth
Barretts	Barretts	Idrone	Idrone
Kinnatalloon	Kilnatalloone, Killnatalloone	St. Mullin	St. Molins
Condons	Condon		
Clangibbon	Clangibbon	DUBLIN	Dublin
Orrery	Orrery	Newcastle	Newcastle
Kilmore	Kilmore	Uppercross	Uppercrosse, Uppercross
		Rathdown	Rathdowne
KERRY	Kerry	Nethercross	Neithercross, Neithercrosse
Trughanacmy	Trughanac	Balrothery	Balrothery
Clanmaurice	Clanmorice, Clanmorrice	Coolock	Cowlocke, Cowlock
Iraghticonnor	Iraght I Connor, Iraght Iconnor	Castleknock	Castleknocke, Castleknock
Corkaguiny	Corcaguiny	KILDARE	Killdare, Kildare
Magunihy	Maquinihy	Offaly	Ophaly, Ophalye
Glanarought	Glauneoroghty	Naas	Naase
Dunkerron	Dunkerran, Dunekerran	Clane	Clane
Iveragh	Iveragh	Connell	Connell, Conell
		Salt	Salt
LIMERICK	Limerick, Limericke, Limbrick	Reban	Reban, Leban
Smallcounty	Small County, Smal County	Narragh	Narragh
Coshlea	Costlea	Kilkea	Kilkae, Kilkea
Clanwilliam	Clanwilliam, Clonwilliam	Moone	Moone
Connello	Connologh	Ikeathy	Ikeathye
Kenry	Kenry	Carbury	Carbery
Owneybeg	Owhny	Kilcullen	Killcullen
Coonagh	Conagh, Conogh		
Pubblebrien	Poble Bryen	KILKENNY	Kilkenny
Coshma	Cosmay	Callan	Callan
Kilmallock	Killmallock	Galmoy	Galmoy,
		Gowran	Gowran
TIPPERARY	Tipperary	Iverk	Iverke
Slievardagh	Sleavordagh, Slevordagh, Slevardagh	Ida	Ida
		Knocktopher	Knoktopher, Knocktopher
Ormond	Ormond	Fassadinin	Fassagh Deinin
Kilnamanagh	Kilnamanagh	Kells	Kells
Middlethird	Middlethird, Midlethird	Shillelogher	Skillellogher
Iffa	Iffay	Crannagh	Crannagh
Offa	Offay		
Eliogarty	Eliogurty	KING'S COUNTY	Kings County
Ikerrin	Ikerryn, Ikerim, Ikerin		
Owney	Owny, Owney	Philipstown	Phillipstowne, Phillipptowne
Arra	Arra	Coolestown	Coolis Towne, Coolishtowne
Clanwilliam	Clanwilliam	Ballyboy	Ballaboy, Ballyboy
		Ballycowan	Ballycowen

Modern Spelling	Census Spelling	Modern Spelling	Census Spelling
Geashill	Geshell	Rathconrath	Rathconrath, Rathcunrath
Warrenstown	Warrenstowne, Warestowne, Warrestowne	Farbill	Farbill
		Clonlonan	Clonlonan
Clonlisk	Clonlisk, Clonliske	Kilkenny	Kilkenny, Killkenny
Garrycastle	Garriecastell, Garriecastle	Mullingar	Mollingar
Kilcoursey	Kilcourcy, Killcourcy	Delvin	Delvyn, Delvin
Eglish	Eglish		
Ballybritt	Ballybritt, Bally britt	WEXFORD	Wexford, Wexfford
		New Ross	New Rosse, Rosse, New Ross
LONGFORD	Longford	Enniscorthy	Eniscorthy
Rathcline	Rathcleene	Forth	Forth
Shrule	Shrowell	Bargy	Bergie, Bargie
Ardagh	Ardagh	Shelmaliere	Shelmaleer
Granard	Granard	Shelburne	Shelbyrne, Shelbryne
Moydow	Moydowe	Bantry	Bantrie, Bantry
		Ballaghkeen	Ballaghkeene
LOUTH	Lowth	Gorey	Goary
Drogheda	Droheda	Scarawalsh	Scarwelsh
Dundalk	Dundalke		
Ferrard	Farrard		
Ardee	Atherdee	CONNACHT :	
MEATH	Meath	LEITRIM	Leytrim, Leitrim
Duleek	Duleek	Mohill	Mohill
Skreen	Scryne	Carrigallen	Carrigallan, Carigallin, Carrigallin
Ratoath	Ratoath		
		Drumahaire	Dromagheire, Drumagheire, Drumaheir
QUEEN'S COUNTY	Queenes County, Queens County		
Ossory	Ossery, Ossory, Osory	Rosclogher	Rossclogher, Roscloger, Rosclogher
Maryborough	Maryborrough, Maryborrogh, Maryborogh		
		ROS- COMMON	Roscommon, Roscoman, Roscomon
Cullenagh	Cullenagh	Athlone	Athlone
Slievemargy	Sliemargeagh	Ballintober	Ballintobber
Ballyadams	Ballyadams	Boyle	Boyle
Portnahinch	Portnyhinch, Portnihinch	Ballymoe	Ballimoe
Stradbally	Stradbally	Moycarn	Moycarnan
Tinnahinch	Tynahinch		
		SLIGO	Slegoe
WEST- MEATH	Westmeath	Carbury	Carbry, Carbery
Fore	Demifoure	Leyny	Leynie
Moygoish	Moygoishe	Corran	Correnn, Corren
Corkaree	Corkerie	Coolavin	Culavin, Calavin
Moyashel	Majaskell	Tireragh	Tireragh
Maghera- dernon	Magheredernan	Tirerrill	Tirerill, Tireill, Tyrerell, Tirerell
Fartullagh	Fertullagh		
Moycashell	May Cashell, Moycashell		

BALLINAKELL, pl, Qco, 505.
BALLINAKILL, t, Car, 353 ; pl, Qco, 498, 500.
BALLINAKILLY, tl, Wex, 554.
BALLINALACCONN, tl, Ck, 236.
BALLINALARME, tl, Cl, 183.
BALLINAMANAGH, 3 qrs, Don, 43.
BALLINAMODAGH, tl, Ck, 236.
BALLINAMONA, tl, Ck, 236.
BALLINAMONY, tl, Wex, 553.
BALLINANLEENY, tl, Lim, 277.
BALLINA PARKE, tl, Wat, 333.
BALLINARAGHAN, tl, Long, 458.
BALLINARD, par, Lim, 270 ; pl, Tipp, 305.
BALLINARY, tl, Kk, 415.
BALLINASEGORT, tl, Rosc, 590.
BALLINASKER, tl, Wex, 552.
BALLINASLEE, tl, Kk, 413, 414.
BALLINASPECK, tl, Wex, 555.
BALLINATTEN, tl, Ck, 234.
BALLIN ATTIN, pl, Tipp, 308.
BALLINAULORT, tl, Ker, 248.
BALLINAVAY, tl, Rosc, 589.
BALLINBOLVOSTIGH, tl, Ck, 204.
BALLINBORE, tl, Rosc, 578.
BALLINBREENY, tl, pt of, Lim, 271.
BALLINBRENAGH, tl, Ker, 250.
BALLINCAHANE, North, tl, Lim, 279.
BALLINCANCENE, tl, Ck, 194.
BALLINCARGY, pl, Kco, 438.
BALLINCARIGIR, tl, Ck, 235.
BALLINCARNAN, tl, Wat, 344.
BALLINCASKY, tl, Wmea, 517.
BALLINCLASSY, tl, Ck, 203.
BALLINCLEA, tl, Wex, 543.
BALLINCLEY, pl, Dub, 381.
BALLINCLIMEASIG, tl, Ker, 249.
BALLINCLOGHIR, tl, Ker, 248.
BALLINCOLLOBARDY, tl, Ck, 203.
BALLINCOLLY, North, pl, Ck, 223 ; South, *ibid.*
BALLINCONRY, pl, Tipp, 326.
BALLINCOURSEY, pl, Ck, 208.
BALLINCOURTY, tl, Ck, 203.
BALLINCRAG, tl, D, 82.
BALLINCRISPIN, tl, Ker, 245.
BALLINCROSSIG, tl, Ker, 250.
BALLINCURDY, pl, Ck, 208.
BALLINCURR, tl, Kk, 418.
BALLINCURRIGE, pl, Ck, 241.
BALLINCURRIGG, tl, Ck, 193.
BALLINCURRIGH, tl, Ker, 256.
BALLINCURRY, pl, Ck, 210 ; tl, Lim, 269, 277, 287.
BALLINDEASIGG, tl, Ck, 203.

BALLINDENY, tl, Wex, 549.
BALLINDERIN, pl, Qco, 503.
BALLINDERRY, par, Ant, 6 ; LD, 138 ; ye ½ t of, LD, 135 ; tl, 138 ; Wmea, 514, 515, 524 ; pl, Tipp, 298, 302.
BALLINDERYE, tl, Wmea, 518.
BALLINDIGANY, tl, Lim, 277.
BALLINDISERT, tl, Wat, 343.
BALLINDONNY, pl, Tipp, 311.
BALLINDOOLEN, tl, Kd, 408.
BALLINDOONE, tl, Sli, 606.
BALLINDOW, tl, Sli, 601.
BALLINDOWNE, pl, Kco, 446.
BALLINDRINISKE, tl, Ck, 203.
BALLINDROMO, tl, LD, 138.
BALLINDRUMNY, tl, Kd, 407.
BALLINDURRY, pl, Tipp, 321.
BALLINE, tl, Kk, 423, 429.
BALLINEAKE, tl, Wex, 551.
BALLINE BANAGH, in libs of Callan, Kk, 430.
BALLINEBANOGE, tl, Wex, 551.
BALLINEBARNY, tl, Wex, 556.
BALLINEBIN, pl, Qco, 493.
BALLINEBOLY, tp, Car, 357.
BALLINEBOY, par, Ck, 202 ; tl, *ibid* (bis).
BALLINEBRANA, tp, Car, 356.
BALLINECARD, tl, Wex, 545.
BALLINECARIG, tp, Car, 353.
BALLINECHAN, qr, Don, 43.
BALLINECLEHY, tl, Wmea, 526 (bis).
BALLINECLOGH, pl, Qco, 499.
BALLINECROSS, tl, Long, 457.
BALLINECULAGH, tl, Wex, 553.
BALLINEERE, pl, pt of, Tipp, 308.
BALLINEFAGH, tl, Kd, 398.
BALLINEFINNSOGIE, tl, Wat, 337.
BALLINEGAPKE, tl, D, 76.
BALLINEGARBRAGH, tl, Wmea, 524.
BALLINEGARY, tl, Wex, 553.
BALLINEGOR, tl, Wex, 552.
BALLINEGRAN, tp, Car, 358.
BALLINEGRENY, tl, Wmea, 518.
BALLINEHAN, tl, Ker, 258.
BALLINEHINEENE, tp, Car, 358.
BALLINEHONE, tl, Wex, 551.
BALLINEKELOG, tl, Wex, 551.
BALLINEKILL, tp, Car, 354 ; tl, Kd, 407 (bis) ; Wmea, 526.
BALLINEKILLY, pl, Ck, 240.
BALLINELARRIGG, tl, Kd, 404.
BALLINELED, tl, Wex, 552.
BALLINELEGE, tl, Wex, 542.
BALLINEMALLAGH, tl, Kd, 407.

BALLYMAGOLAND, tl, LD, 130.
BALLYMAGONE, tl, Arm, 37.
BALLYMAGROTY, qr, LD, 124.
BALLYMAGRUE, tl, Arm, 38.
BALLYMAGWOGHAN, tl, D, 95.
BALLYMAHIS, tl, Wat, 346.
BALLYMAHOLLAND, tl, LD, 130.
BALLYMAHONA, tl, Cl, 186.
BALLYMAIRE, tl, D, 70.
BALLYMAKEALLY, tl, Arm, 34.
BALLYMAKEARY, tl, Cl, 181.
BALLYMAKERMOTT, tl, Arm, 31.
BALLYMAKILL, par, Wat, 346 ; tl, *ibid.*
BALLYMAKISEY, tl, Wex, 549.
BALLYMAKREE, tl, Lim, 274.
BALLYMALADY, tl, D, 87.
BALLYMALLY, tl, Cl, 165.
B : MANAGH, tl, D, 87.
BALLYMANAGH, tl, LD, 143.
BALLYMANAN ITRAGH, tl, D, 93.
BALLYMANAN UTRAGH, tl, D, 93 (bis).
BALLYMANUGE, tl, Ker, 253.
BALLY MANUS, pl, Qco, 504.
BALLYMANY, tl, Lim, 279.
BALLYMAQUEILL, tl, Wat, 347.
BALLYMARAN-ITRAGH, tl, D, 85 (bis).
BALLYMARIAGHANE, tl, Cl, 163.
B : MARRAN, tl, D, 84.
BALLYMARTELL, par, Ck, 202, 211 ; tl, 202.
BALLYMARTIN, tl, Kk, 424 ; pt of, *ibid.*
BALLYMARTINE, tl, D, 88 ; Lim, 285.
BALLYMARTIRE, tl, D, 92.
BALLYMASKANLAN, par, Lou, 467 ; tl, *ibid.*
BALLYMATEGERT, tl, LD, 130.
BALLYMATTY, pl, Ant, 6.
BALLYMAUL, pl, pt of, Tipp, 310.
BALLYMAWOE, tl, Ck, 231.
BALLYM-COONEY, tl, Cl, 163.
BALLYMCRUSSY, pl, Ck, 237.
B : MEAGHAN, tl, D, 88.
BALLYMEAGHAN, pl, Mon, 150.
BALLYMENAGH, pl, Ant, 7.
BALLYMILL, ½ t, D, 76.
B : MILLTON, tl, D, 88.
BALLYMINIMOR, pl, Ant, 6.
BALLYMODDOGH, tl, Wat, 338.
BALLYMODEN, par, Ck, 206.
B : MOGHAN, 2, tl, LD, 135.
BALLYMOILEN, tp, Cl, 170.
BALLYMOLALLY, tl, Wat, 334.
BALLYMOLAN, tl, Wmea, 515.
BALLYMOLLOWNA, pl, Tipp, 321.
BALLYMOLONY, tl, Cl, 173.

BALLYMOLURY, tl, Sli, 597.
BALLYMON, pl, Dub, 381.
BALLYMONAN, tl, Lou, 467.
BALLYMONEEN, tl, Lim, 288.
B : MONESTROGH, tl, D, 89.
BALLYMONETREAGH, tl, Wat, 348.
BALLYMONEY, tl, D, 93, 94.
BALLYMONINE, tl, Sli, 603.
BALLYMONY, tl, D, 78 ; LD, 130, 131, 142 ;
    Lou, 466 ; qr, D, 79 ; par, pt of, LD, 140.
BALLYMONY BEGG, tl, Wex, 552.
BALLYMOODANE, par, Ck, 206, 213.
BALLYMOODEN, par, Ck, 205.
BALLYMOONY, pl, Kco, 439.
BALLYMOORE, tl, Arm, 29.
BALLY MORAN, pl, Kco, 437.
BALLYMORE, pl, Ant, 19 ; Ck, 238 ; Tipp, 304 ;
    tl, LD, 128 ; Ker, 253 ; Wmea, 519 ;
    3 plds, Ck, 225 ; par, Wmea, 519 ; peer,
    Wex, 534.
BALLYMORE EUSTACE, par, Dub, 378 ; pl, *ibid.*
BALLY MORELIN, tl, Rosc, 578.
BALLYMORE MORE, tl, LD, 140.
BALLYMORERIGH, tl, Ker, 253.
BALLYMORGY, ye six ts of, LD, 130.
BALLYMORISEENE, tl, Lim, 282.
BALLYMORISH, tl, Wat, 346.
BALLYMORISHEENE, tl, Ck, 231.
BALLY-MOROGH, pl, Kco, 447.
BALLYMORRIS, pl, Tipp, 311 ; tl, Long, 457.
BALLYMORRISS, tl, Cl, 167.
BALLYMORROGH, tl, Lim, 280.
BALLYMORTAGH, tl, Cl, 167.
BALLYMORYHY, tl, Lim, 278.
BALLYMOTE, tl, Sli, 600.
BALLYMOTEY, tl, Wat, 338.
BALLYMOTTS, tl, D, 69.
BALLYMOUNT, pl, Dub, 377.
BALLYMOUNTAINE, tl, Ck. 213.
BALLYMOUNTINE, tl, Kk, 421.
BALLYMOUTEN, tl, Ck, 234.
BALLYMOY, pl, Ant, 12.
BALLYMOYELL, tl, LD, 138.
BALLYMUCRAGAN, tl, Arm, 31.
BALLYMUKFIN, pl, Ant, 12.
BALLYMULBY, tl, LD, 132.
BALLYMULCANEY, tl, Cl, 163.
BALLYMULCHASSHILL, tp, Cl, 171.
BALLYMULCREHY, tl, Cl, 165.
BALLY MULLANY, tl, Sli, 605.
BALLYMULLEN, tl, D, 92.
BALLYMULLIGAN, tl, LD, 138.
BALLYMULLIN, pl, Ck, 211 ; tl, Ker, 247.

BALLYNECREIGG, tl, D, 71.
BALLYNECRONY, tl, Kk, 419.
BALLYNECULLAGH, tl, Wex, 549.
BALLYNECURRY, tl, Wat, 342.
BALLYNEDAN, tl, D, 73.
BALLYNEDOLCHAN, tl, Rosc, 579.
BALLYNEFEARAGH, tl, Wmea, 521.
BALLYNEFEARN, a qr of, D, 75.
BALLYNEFOY, tl, D, 75.
BALLYNEGALLAGH, qr, LD, 124.
BALLYNEGALLAH, tl, Lim, 288.
BALLYNEGALLIAGH, tl, Lim, 269.
BALLYNEGANANA, tl, Lim, 269.
BALLYNEGANANAGH, pl, Tipp, 310.
BALLYNEGARRICK, tl, D, 89.
BALLYNEGARRICKE, tl, D, 69.
BALLYNEGATTY, tl, Lim, 287.
BALLY NEGHEE, tl, D, 94.
BALLYNEGILKY, tl, Wat, 335.
BALLYNEGOWNE, tl, LD, 136.
BALLYNEGRISTOONUGH, tl, Lim, 271.
BALLYNEGRIVE, tl, Rosc, 579.
BALLYNEGROSS, tl, a qr of, D, 75 (ter).
BALLYNEHAGH, tl, Lim, 278.
B : NEHATTY, tl, D, 89.
BALLYNEHEGLIS, tl, LD, 138.
BALLYNEHEGLISH, tl, Lim, 285.
BALLYNEHENSY, tl, Lim, 271.
BALLYNEHERICK, tl, D, 88.
BALLYNEHINCH, tl, Arm, 35 ; D, 86.
BALLYNEHOW, tl, Lim, 281.
BALLYNEHUANE, tl, Cl, 183.
BALLYNEIBOE, tl, D, 71.
BALLYNEKEDY, pl, pt of, Tipp, 328.
BALLYNE KELLY, tl, Lim, 282.
BALLYNEKILL, (BallyneKill), tl, Kk, 422 ; ½ of, Kd, 405 ; pl, Kco, 445.
BALLYNEKILLY, tl, Wat, 337.
BALLYNEMABOGE, tl, Kk, 423.
BALLYNEMAULE, tl, Ck, 203.
BALLYNEMELAGH, tl, Wat, 334.
BALLYNEMERTINAGH, tl, Wat, 334.
BALLYNEMETAGH, tl, Kk, 419.
BALLYNEMODDAGH, tl, Lim, 272.
BALLYNEMOGNAGH, tl, D, 75.
BALLYNEMONA, pl, Tipp, 320.
BALLYNEMONE, pl, Ck, 208.
BALLYNEMONEY, tl, D, 77.
BALLYNEMONY, tl, Lim, 285 ; pl, Tipp, 310, 312, 314 ; Wat, 349.
——, in lib of Wat, 349.
BALLYNEMUCKE, tl, Wat, 336.
BALLYNEMURE, tl, LD, 127.

BALLYNENAN, pl, Kco, 441.
BALLYNENANAGH, tl, LD, 138.
BALLYNENANE, pl, Tipp, 308.
BALLYNENONAGH, pl, Tipp, 311.
BALLYNENONE, pl, Tipp, 305.
BALLYNENY, pl, Tipp, 320.
BALLYNEPKY, tl, Wat, 336.
BALLYNERAGHY, tl, Wat, 340.
BALLYNERAHY, pl, Tipp, 310.
BALLYNERLOGHE, tl, Kk, 419.
BALLYNEROW, tl, LD, 129.
BALLYNESCORNEY, pl, Dub, 377.
BALLYNESHELLOGE, qr land, LD, 124.
BALLYNESKADDANE, par, Lim, 271 ; tl, ibid.
BALLYNESSE, pl, Ant, 10, 12.
BALLYNETY, pl, Tipp, 311.
BALLYNEVNITIGH, tl, Wat, 344.
BALLYNEW, pl, Tipp, 304.
BALLYNEWGANE, tl, Lim, 288.
BALLYNGADDY, par, Lim, 273.
BALLYNGADDYMORE, tl, Lim, 273.
BALLYNGBUN, par, Tipp, 319 ; pl, ibid.
BALLYNGEAGOGE, tl, Lim, 272.
BALLYNGRENY, tl, Lim, 272.
BALLYNICLASSY, tl, Wat, 334.
BALLYNICOLL, tl, D, 92.
BALLYNIE, tl, Cl, 187.
BALLYNIGLASSY, pl, Ck, 238.
BALLYNIGLOGH, pl, Ck, 238.
BALLYNIGOOLE, tl, Lim, 277.
BALLYNIGROW, tl, LD, 138.
BALLYNILLOONE, pl, Ck, 237.
BALLYNIMAUD, tl, Lim, 276.
BALLYNIMILOGH, tl, Ck, 193.
BALLYNIMULTINAGH, tl, Wat, 334.
BALLYNIREN, tl, Ck, 219.
BALLYNISKREAN, par, LD, 137.
BALLYNITEEBEGG, tl, Wat, 338.
BALLYNITIMORE, tl, Wat, 338.
BALLYNITY, tl, Wat, 337.
BALLYNKEA, pl, Ant, 13.
BALLYNLEYNY, tl, Lim, 272.
BALLYNLUGE, tl, Wex, 549.
BALLYNNARKEBEGG, pl, Tipp, 299.
BALLYNNELADY, pl, Tipp, 327.
BALLYNOCK, tl, Cl, 163.
BALLYNODE, tl, Cl, 184.
BALLYNOE, par, Ck, 234 (bis) ; tl, Lim, 277, 285 ; pl, Tipp, 320, 321 (bis), 322.
BALLY NOERT, tl, Lim, 282.
BALLYNOLTARK, pl, Kco, 437.
BALLYNOMONY, East, tl, Wat, 334.
BALLYNORA, tl, Ck, 193.

CAPPOQUEN, the litle bridge of Affane next, Wat, 335 ; div, 339 ; t, *ibid.*
CAPPOUGE, pl, Kco, 437.
CAPPY, tl, D, 75.
CAPRIETRAME, tl, Don, 49.
CAPUGBOGHY, 1 pld, Ck, 223.
CAPWATER, tp, Car, 355.
CARABOYACHER, tl, Leit, 562.
CARAG-, *see* Carrick-.
CARAGALINE, par, Ck, 193.
CARAGALLEN, par, Leit, 561.
CARAGH, pl, Mon, 158.
CARAGHANE, tl, Ker, 248.
CARAGLASS, tl, Leit, 562.
CARAKROCKHEOR, tl, Leit, 562.
CARANAGH, tl, Arm, 28.
CARAUGHBOY, tl, Rosc, 591.
CARBALLIES, tl, Mea, 484.
CARBALLIS, tl, Kd, 404.
CARBALLY, pl, Qco, 501.
CARBELLIS, tl, Wmea, 522.
CARBERY, east div of, Ck, 215 ; west div of, 221, 228 ; bar, Kd, 406, 408, 409 ; Sli, 607.
CARBIN, tl, Leit, 566.
CARBOE, tl, Rosc, 581.
CARBOYLANE, tl, LD, 131.
CARBRY, qr, Don, 55 ; bar, Sli, 597, 598.
CARBURY, east div of, Ck, 221.
CARCAROW, qr, Don, 59.
CARCAVAN, pl, Mon, 150.
CARCOUM, tl, Arm, 30.
CARDENS TOWNE, tl, Kd, 403.
CARDIFS TOWNE, tl, Kd, 397.
CARDIS TOWNE, tl, Lou, 472.
CARDONAGH, pl, Fer, 105.
CARDREMA, tl, Leit, 562.
CARDUFF, tl, Kd, 399.
CARECABONE, tl, Leit, 559.
CAREFORE, tl, Rosc, 573.
CAREGRIER, tl, Leit, 561.
CAREHEENE, pl, Tipp, 297.
CAREHEY, tl, Ker, 259.
CARES TOWNE, tl, Lou, 468.
CAREW-, *see* Carrow-.
CAREWCALLER, tl, Sli, 604.
CAREWREAGH, tl, Sli, 601.
CAREY, bar, Ant, 19, 20.
CARGAGH, pl, Mon, 159 ; tl, Sli, 600.
CARGAGHBAN, tl, D, 75.
CARGAGHLATERGANE, tl, Arm, 25.
CARGAGHNOBREGG, tl, D, 69.
CARGAGHY, halfe t, D, 74.

CARGALINE, par, Ck, 204 ; pl, *ibid.*
CARGAN, tl, LD, 126.
CARGANS, tl, Arm, 30.
CARGEHEY, pl, Mon, 156.
CARGEN, tl, Leit, 564.
CARGICRAY, tl, D, 89.
CARGICREVY, tl, D, 80.
CARGIN, tl, Arm, 30 ; Long, 454 ; Lou, 471 ; Sli, 598.
CARGINAGAPALL, tl, Rosc, 575.
CARGINE, tl, Rosc, 578.
CARGIN MORE, tl, Rosc, 590.
CARGINNA, ½ qr, Rosc, 574.
CARGINTULKE, tl, Rosc, 575.
CARGINY, tl, Rosc, 589.
CARGNEE, pl, Ant, 16.
CARGONS, tl, Rosc, 586.
CARGRAIGE, Ballydinine al's, tl, Cl, 181.
CARHAN, pl, Qco, 503.
CARHEENY, tl, Lim, 286.
CARHEW, tl, Ker, 254 ; pl, Tipp, 313.
CARHILICKY, pl, Ck, 222.
CARHINE, pl, Tipp, 298.
CARHOWGARE, tl, Cl, 187.
CARHOWNENUER, tl, Cl, 163.
CARHUGARE, tl, Lim, 279.
CARHUKEELE, tl, Rosc, 576.
CARIARDE, tl, Leit, 560.
CARICK-, *see* Carrick-.
CARICKBALLY LEIR, pl, Kco, 443.
CARICKBRACK, half t, Arm, 30.
CARICKBRADAGH, tl, Arm, 30.
CARICKCORKE, tl, Arm, 30.
CARICKENY, tl, Leit, 560.
CARICKFERGUS, t, Ant, 1 ; Fer (*sic !*), 626 ; t and co of t, 626, 645 ; High Sherive of, 626 ; Mayor of, *ibid* ; Mayor and Sherifs of, 645 ; Recorder of, 626, 645.
CARICKLANE, tl, Arm, 28.
CARICKLEANE, tl, Arm, 35.
CARICKNAPARKNY, pl, Qco, 497.
CARICKNEER, pl, Mon, 159.
CARICKNESSE, tl, Arm, 29.
CARICK RUSKY, tl, D, 84.
CARIE, bar, Ant, 10.
CARIG-, *see* Carrick-.
CARIGAHOLTA, tl, Cl, 184.
CARIGALLIN, bar, Leit, 561.
CARIGANEADY, par, Ck, 236 ; tl, *ibid.*
CARIGANNY, tl, Rosc, 592.
CARIGBEA, tl, Wat, 335.
CARIG CORIGGE, pl, Tipp, 300.
CARIGE, pl, Fer, 102.

3 G

CASTLEGORY, qr, Don, 46.

CASTLEGRACE, pl, Tipp, 312 ; tp, Car, 355.

CASTLEGREGORY, tl, Ker, 252.

CASTLEHAVEN, par, Ck, 223, 224 ; 2 pld, 223.

CASTLE HILL, qr, Don, 61.

CASTLE HOILE, tl, Kk, 426.

CASTLE INEY, pl, Tipp, 317.

CASTLE JOHN, pl, Tipp, 297 (bis).

——, souldiers in, *ibid*.

CASTLE KEELEE, tl, Kd, 399.

CASTLE KELLY, tl, Kk, 417.

CASTLEKNOCK, bar, Dub, 391.

CASTLEKNOCKE, bar, Dub, 390, 392 ; par, 390 ; Churchtowne of, *ibid* ; Castle farme of, *ibid*.

CASTLEKREA, tl, Lim, 272.

CASTLELAGHNIF, pl, Tipp, 325.

CASTLE LENCY, pl, Tipp, 318.

CASTLE LISHINE, pl, Ck, 240 (bis).

CASTLELOGHDERGAN, tl, Sli, 606.

CASTLELOGHE, pl, Tipp, 322.

CASTLELOST, par, Wmea, 515.

CASTLEMAGNER, par, Ck, 242 ; pl, *ibid*.

CASTLEMANIG, tl, Ker, 245.

CASTLEMARKETT, tl, Kk, 423.

CASTLE MARTIN, tl, Kd, 408 ; Wmea, 510.

CASTLE MATRICKES, tl, Lim, 275.

CASTLEMEGHEGANE, ½ pld, Ck, 228.

CASTLE MICHELL, tl, Kd, 403.

CASTLEMOGHAN, tl, D, 72.

CASTLEMORE, tl, Ck, 231 ; tp, Car, 354.

CASTLE MURAY, qr, Don, 46.

CASTLENALACK, pl, Ck, 207.

CASTLENAVAN, tl, D, 85.

CASTLE NE GAURDE, tl, Lim, 287.

CASTLENEGGAN, tl, D, 82.

CASTLENEVARY, tl, D, 87.

CASTLE NORTON, div, Ant, 9.

CASTLE PARKE, (Castleparke), pl, Ck, 211 (bis).

CASTLEREAGH, tl, D, 86 ; Long, 460 ; Rosc, 579 ; bar, D, 90, 95 ; pl, Kco, 443.

CASTLEROBIN, pl, Ant, 9.

CASTLEROE, tl, LD, 141.

CASTLEROWE, tl, Kd, 404.

CASTLESAMSON, (Castle Samson), tl, Rosc, 591 ; pt of, 592.

CASTLESHANAGHAN, qr, Don, 55.

CASTLESHEAN, pl, Mon, 149.

CASTLESHENACHAN, ½ qr, Don, 55.

CASTLES TOWNE CROGHAN, pl, Kco, 435.

CASTLESTRANGE, tl, Rosc, 588.

CASTLE STREET, Dub, 366.

CASTLETOBIN, in libs of Callan, Kk, 430.

CASTLETODRY, tl, LD, 140.

CASTLETON TARAGH, tl, Mea, 484.

CASTLETORRIS, tl, Don, 51.

CASTLETOWN, pt of, pl, Ck, 224.

CASTLETOWN BELLEW, par, Lou, 466 ; tl, *ibid*.

CASTLETOWNE, (Castle towne), 3 belliboes, Don, 46 ; tl, D, 76 ; Cl, 164 (bis) ; Ck, 216 ; Lim, 278, 287 ; Wat, 344 ; Kd, 402 ; Kk, 419 ; Long, 457 ; Wmea, 510, 517, 524, 527 ; Wex, 536 (bis), 539, 553 ; Sli, 604 ; 1 pld 7 gneeves, Ck, 224 ; par, Lim, 287 ; Tipp, 303, 322 ; Kco, 441 ; Wmea, 517, 527 ; pt of, Tipp, 317, 328 ; pl, Tipp, 298, 299, 322 ; Kco, 443, 446, 447 ; Qco, 496 ; tp, Car, 353.

CASTLE TOWNE CLONLONAN, tl, Wmea, 524.

CASTLETOWNE COOLEY, tl, Lou, 467.

CASTLETOWNE-OMOY, pl, Qco, 500.

CASTLETOWNE SHE, tl, Kk, 413.

CASTLE TREASURE, tl, Ck, 193.

CASTLE TROY, tl, Lim, 264.

CASTLEVARY, tl, Ck, 202.

CASTLEVENAN, tl, D, 75.

CASTLEVENTERY, tl, Ck, 220.

CASTLEVENTRY, (Castle Ventry), par, Ck, 210, 220.

CASTLEVORKINE, tl, Lim, 274.

CASTLEWARD, tl, D, 71.

CASTLE WARIN, tl, Kk, 417.

CASTLEWARNING, tl, Kd, 402.

CASTLE WELLDEN, tl, D, 77.

CASTLEWOOD, pl, Qco, 491.

CASTLEWORKHOUSE, tl, Wex, 545.

CASTLI-, *see* Castle-.

CASTLILLINNY, tl, Rosc, 584.

CASTOLL-, *see* Castle-.

CASTOLLOST, par, Wmea, 516.

CATERGULLYMORE, tl, Lim, 270.

CATHERLAGH, co, 351, 353.

CATHERLAGH, bor, Car, 351, 353 (bis), 354, 359 ; Portriue of, 353 ; bar, Car, 354, 359.

CATHERLOGH, co, 621, 639.

——, Sherriffe of, 639.

CATHERLOGH, t, Car, 621 ; Portreeve of, *ibid* ; bor, Car, 639 ; Portrieve of, *ibid*.

CATHRINS TOWNE, tl, Wmea, 515.

CATTEN, tl, Leit, 563.

CAUAGHSALLAGH, tl, Rosc, 585.

CAUAN, halfe t, D, 76.

CAUNEGULLY, tl, Ker, 246.

CAUNNDARACH, tl, D, 85.

CAUSEY, pl, Ant, 6.

CAVAN, co, 627, 646 ; high Sherif of, *ibid*.

CNOCKE, tl, Ck, 218 ; pl, Tipp, 320.
CNOCKEARE, pl, Tipp, 327.
CNOCKEDIRRY, tl, Lim, 280.
CNOCKENARUBLY, tl, Ck, 218.
CNOCKERVILL, tl, Wmea, 522 (bis).
CNOCKES, tl, Ck, 218 ; Ker, 255.
CNOCKEVANANE, tl, Arm, 33.
CNOCKIGIHIN, pl, Fer, 105.
CNOCKLOCH, tl, Sli, 602.
CNOCKMOLIN, tl, Sli, 606.
CNOCKNABUOLY, tl, Lim, 282.
CNOCKNACORY, tl, Ck, 213.
CNOCKNADARAGH, tl, Long, 460.
CNOCKNAGAULE, par, Lim, 263.
CNOCKNEGAGH, tl, Cl, 183.
CNOCKNEGASSULL, tl, Ker, 247.
CNOCKNEGERNEAGH, tl, Lim, 282.
CNOCKNYCARRIGG, tl, Lim, 287.
CNOCKNYMUCKULLY, tl, Ker, 256.
CNOCKPATRICKE, tl, Lim, 281.
CNOCKRAHIDERMODY, tl, Lim, 279.
CNOCKRO, tl, Sli, 605.
CNOCKROE, tl, Ck, 213.
CNOCK SYMON, (Cnocksymon), tl, Wmea, 522
    (bis).
CNOCK TORIN, tl, Lim, 272.
CNOGHES, pl, Kco, 445.
CNOKEARD, tl, Lim, 263.
CNOLLIGH, 3 plds, Ck, 227.
CNONDONELL, tl, Wat, 343.
CNOWINGALLAGH, tl, Rosc, 576.
COAGHIN, pl, Mon, 153.
COAN, pl, Tipp, 304.
COANUY, tl, Sli, 600.
COASE KOVEENE, pl, Ck, 223.
COBERDALAUGH, pl, Kco, 440.
COBRAGH, tl, D, 80.
COCKERMAINE, pl, Ant, 4.
COCKINCLAR, tl, Wmea, 512.
CODD, pl, Kco, 437.
CODDS BALSEE, tl, Wex, 535.
CODDS TOWN, Litle, tl, Wex, 534.
CODLANS TOWNE, tl, Kd, 395.
CODS TOWN, Great, tl, Wex, 534.
COE, pl, Fer, 115.
COGH, tl, LD, 144.
COHIRLISH, tl, Lim, 274.
COILEGORTINE, tl, Leit, 563.
COILLCAVER, tl, Sli, 598.
COILLE RUALA, tl, Sli, 597.
COILLFEA, tl, Leit, 563.
COILLMORE, tl, Sli, 605.
COILLY, tl, Sli, 605.

COILTELACHA, tl, Sli, 605.
COKROME, pl, Ant, 14.
COKSMORE, tl, Wex, 537.
COL-, see Cul-.
COLAFENY, tl, LD, 126.
COLAGHTY, pl, Fer, 110.
COLAMARAGH, pl, Tipp, 304.
COLAMBER, tl, Wmea, 511.
COLCOTT, pl, Dub, 386.
COLDACH, pl, Ant, 14.
COLDGRANGE, libs of Kk, 431.
COLDOW, pl, Ant, 14.
COLD WINTERS, pl, Dub, 385.
COLE-, see Cool-.
COLEADORRYNY, pl, Tipp, 323.
COLEBOY, tl, Wex, 544.
COLEDOROGHE, pl, Kco, 443.
COLEKENAGHT, tl, LD, 126.
COLEMANSTOWNE, (Colemans towne), tl, Cl,
    181 ; pl, Dub, 379.
COLEMOORE, pl, Tipp, 308.
COLEMYNE, pl, Dub, 378, 391.
COLEQUILE, pl, Tipp, 296, 297.
[COLERAINE], bar, LD, 145.
COLERAYN, LD, 626 ; Mayor of, ibid.
COLEREAGHBEG, tp, Cl, 169.
COLEREAGHMORE, tp, Cl, 169.
COLEROE, tp, Car, 358.
COLESONA, pl, Fer, 99.
COLETINANE, tl, Rosc, 585.
COLFILCH, tl, Kd, 402.
COLGANSTOWNE, pl, Dub, 379.
COLICAPELL, tl, LD, 144.
COLITEE, pl, Fer, 105.
COLKERAGH, tl, LD, 124.
COLLANE, pl, Tipp, 299.
COLLARONE, pl, Fer, 106.
COLLARS TOWNE, pl, Kco, 445.
COLLATRATH, pl, Dub, 391.
COLLDRAGH, pl, Fer, 118.
COLLEDGE, tl, Wex, 542.
COLLEDGE OF THE HOLY TRINITY, near Dublin,
    637.
COLLEDGE GREENE, Dub, 364.
COLLEDIN, Mill of, Wex, 551.
COLLEE, tl, Rosc, 588.
COLLEGE LANDS, Arm, 40.
COLLEGE OF THE HOLY TRINITY, near Dublin,.
    620.
COLLEMGRANGE, tl, D, 71.
COLLENEMUCKE, tl, Kk, 420.
COLLENSTOWNE, pl, Dub, 377.
COLLENTROE, tl, Kk, 420.

3 H

CORHULLAGH, pl, Fer, 102.
CORIAGAN, pl, Mon, 156.
CORINANCLEA, pl, Fer, 113.
CORIN BELLAGH, ½ qr, Don, 58.
CORINGREAGH, pl, Fer, 102.
CORINTIOGATT, pl, Mon, 156.
CORISTIN, tl, Wmea, 512.
CORISTOWNE, tl, LD, 140.
CORK, co, 623, 642.
——, c, 623.
——, Mayor and Sherifs of, 623, 642.
——, c and co of c, 623, 642.
——, Mayor, Recorder and Sherives of, 623, 642.
See also Corke.
CORKALEIR, pl, Mon, 155.
CORKATH, pl, Dub, 377.
CORKE, c and lib, 189, 195.
——, c, 191.
——, ——, pars : Christ Church, St. Peters, 191.
——, ——, qrs : South East, North East, South West, North West, 191.
——, ——, suburbs : North Suburbs, South Suburbs, 192.
——, ——, lib : South Liberties, 192 ; North Liberties, 194.
——, ——, souldiers in, 195.
——, co, 197.
See also Cork.
CORKE, pl, Ant, 15.
CORKEERIN, pl, Mon, 158.
CORKE HILL, Dub, 368.
CORKEILTIE, tl, Cl, 183.
CORKELLY, par, Kco, 441.
CORKERIE, bar, Wmea, 512, 513, 528.
CORK HILL, Dub, 370.
CORKIN, pl, Mon, 151.
CORKIRIN, pl, Mon, 157.
CORKITT, tl, Lou, 467.
CORKLEA, tl, Arm, 25.
CORKRERY, tl, D, 79.
CORKY, qr, Don, 49.
CORLACK, pl, Mon, 154.
CORLAGHERT, pl, Mon, 158.
CORLATTALLON, pl, Mon, 151.
CORLEA, qr, Don, 43 : pl, Mon, 158.
CORLECK, pl, Mon, 156.
CORLECKAN, tl, Wex, 549.
CORLECKY, tl, Don, 49.
CORLIGORIN, pl, Mon, 156.
CORLINAN, tl, Long, 459.
CORLISS, tl, Arm, 32 : Rosc, 574.

CORLODDY, tl, Kk, 419.
CORLOGHON, tl, Kk, 419.
CORMACKS TOWNE, tl, Kd, 401.
CORMAGRATH, 3 sessioghes, Don, 53.
CORMECKE, pl, Fer, 116.
CORMEEN, pl, Mon, 149.
CORMEENE, tl, Arm, 26.
CORMENTYE, pl, Mon, 156.
CORMINE, ½ t, D, 82.
CORMYN, ½ t, D, 82.
CORNACARY, tl, Arm, 32.
CORNACREEVY, pl, Mon, 159.
CORNAGATTY, tl, Rosc, 591.
CORNAGEE, tl, Rosc, 591.
CORNAGHLANE, tl, Ck, 236.
CORNAGHLEIGH, tl, Leit, 565.
CORNALAHAN, pl, Fer, 112.
CORNALOWAY, tl, Kd, 397.
CORNAMAN, tl, Leit, 565.
CORNAMUCKLA, tl, Long, 453.
CORNASAGHNA, pl, Mon, 156.
CORNASRORA, pl, Mon, 152.
CORNASTAKE, tl, Leit, 566.
CORNDALL, tl, LD, 129.
CORNEARE, tl, Arm, 30.
CORNE CREE, pl, Fer, 118.
CORNEDOUGH, tl, Long, 451.
CORNEDRUNG, tl, Long, 458.
CORNEFIRST, tl, Leit, 561.
CORNEFRAKE, tl, Kk, 429.
CORNEGARVOGE, pl, Mon, 158.
CORNEGEYE, pl, Fer, 100.
CORNEGLARE, pl, Mon, 150.
CORNEGRAD, pl, Fer, 109.
CORNEHOUGH, tl, D, 82.
CORNEKERREW, tl, Leit, 562.
CORNEKESSAGH, pl, Mon, 149.
CORNELAGHTA, tl, Leit, 567.
CORNELECKE, pl, Fer, 118.
CORNELS TOWN, tl, Wex, 534.
CORNELSTOWNE, pl, Dub, 381.
CORNEMADIE, tl, Rosc, 593.
CORNEMAGH, tl, Rosc, 593.
CORNEMALLA, tl, Cl, 163.
CORNEMART, tl, Rosc, 590.
CORNEMODY, pl, Mon, 149.
CORNEMUKLAGH, tl, Lou, 467.
CORNESHANNAGH, tl, Rosc, 581.
CORNETTSRILL, tl, Arm, 30.
CORNETULLAGH, tl, Leit, 567.
CORNEWALL, pl, Mon, 153, 155.
CORNEY, pl, Mon, 154.
CORNGERAGH, pl, Ant, 15.

F

FAHI, tp, Cl, 169.

FAHY, tl, Cl, 186.

FAHYBEGG, pl, Qco, 504.

FAIGH, tl, Wex, 531.

FAILENTALLURE, tl, Kk, 428.

FALA, pl, Fer, 109.

FALL, the, pl, Ant, 9.

FALLAHOGE, tl, LD, 133.

FALLALEE, tl, LD, 134.

FALLANES, third, Don, 58.

FALLEGLONE, tl, LD, 134.

FALLENY, pl, Tipp, 320.

FALL McRELLY, pl, Ant, 5.

FALLOE, tl, Wat, 342.

FAMULLAN, tl, LD, 142.

FAMULLY, tl, LD, 125.

FANA, pl, Tipp, 303.

FANAGRAIN, pl, Fer, 101.

FANALENIE, tl, Leit, 567.

FANE, ½ qr, Don, 59.

FANE BROAGE, tl, D, 71.

FANELEHANE, tl, Lim, 280.

FANE MOORE, pl, Ck, 226.

FANIS TOWNE, tl, Wex, 540.

FANLOBISH, par, Ck, 216.

FANLOBUS, par, Ck, 216.

FANNAGH, pl, Ck, 237.

FANNANGOWNE, pl, Tipp, 325.

FANNINGS CLUONE, tl, Lim, 269.

FANNINGS TOWNE, tl, Kk, 419.

FANNISTOWNE, tl, Lim, 272.

FANTAE, tl, Cl, 182.

FANTANE, pl, Tipp, 304.

FANULTY, ye ½ of, tl, Don, 58.

FANWALLY, ye ½ qr of, Don, 58.

FANY, pl, Fer, 106 ; tl, LD, 126.

FARAN-, see Farren-.

FARANEFRENY, tp, Car, 357.

FARAN MILLER, tl, Lim, 284.

FARAN-RORY, pl, Tipp, 297.

FARARAGH, tl, Rosc, 586.

FARARALL, pl, Fer, 109.

FARBILL, bar, Wmea, 521, 523, 528.

FARCLENE, tl, LD, 131.

FARDINGSTONE, tl, Wmea, 520.

FARDLESTOWNE, tl, Ck, 202.

FARDRUM, and Bellichan, 7 belliboes of, Don, 60.

FAREN-, see Farren-.

FARENBANAGH, tl, Ck, 214.

FARENCAUTRY, tl, Ck, 219.

FARENEVANE, pl, Ck, 207.

FARENGANLOGH, pl, Ck, 207.

FAREN IHARPY, tl, Sli, 604.

FARENNCORY, pl, Tipp, 295.

FAREN THOMAS, pl, Ck, 206.

FARGANS TOWNE, tl, Mea, 484.

FARGLASS, tl, Leit, 563.

FARGRUM, pl, Fer, 110.

FARIGHIE, tl, Cl, 185.

FARIN McKAUGHLY, tl, Arm, 26.

FARLOCKSTON, tl, Mea, 487.

FARMANAGH, co, 97.

See Fermanagh.

FARME GUSOK, pl, Ant, 16.

FARMOGLE, pl, Mon, 150.

FARMOILE, tl, LD, 142.

FARMOYLE, pl, Mon, 158 ; Qco, 491 ; tl, Cl, 173.

FARNAN, pl, Fer, 115 ; tl, Wat, 335

FARNANE, tl, Lim, 287.

FARNANS, pl, Qco, 500.

FARNAUGH, pl, Fer, 113.

FARNE, tl, Rosc, 575.

FARNEDORRY, pl, Tipp, 317.

FARNELESRE, pl, Ant, 14.

FARNFADE, tl, D, 85.

FARNY SHESIRY, tl, Ck, 217.

FARRA, tl, Wmea, 513.

FARRAGHRO, tl, Long, 457.

FARRAN-, see Farren-.

FARRAN LESTER, tl, LD, 142.

FARRANREE, tl, Lim, 282.

FARRARD, bar, Lou, 468, 470, 473.

FARREMORE, tl, Rosc, 589.

FARREN-, see also Faran-, Faren-, Farran-, Fearana-, Fearne-.

FARRENABRYAN, tl, Lim, 286.

FARRENDA, and Farrendalagg, 1 pld, Ck, 224.

FARRENDAHADORE, tl, Ck, 193.

FARRENDALAGG, and Farrenda, 1 pld, Ck, 224.

FARREN I CNOUGHOR, pl, Ck, 224.

FARREN ILEYNY, pl, Tipp, 306.

FARRENKELLYN, tl, Wmea, 513.

FARRENLESTRUM, tl, LD, 141.

FARRENLONTY, tl, Wat, 333.

FARREN McTEIGE, tl, Ck, 192.

FARREN Mc Wm, tl, Ker, 246.

FARREN MANIGH, pl, Ck, 227.

FARREN MAREN, tl, Ck, 216.

FARRENNAGAT, tl, Ker, 258.

FARRENNAMRACKE, tl, Ker, 247.

FARRENNYCLARY, tl, Ck, 195.

FARRENROSTIGGE, Coole-Owen alias, tl, Ck, 194.

FARRENRUOGE, tl, Ker, 249.

3 K

GASHELL, par, Kco, 439 (bis) ; pt of, 435 ; pl, 439.
GASKING TOWNE,' tl, Mea, 479.
GATOLAGHAN, pl, Fer, 115.
GATTAGHSTOWNE, pl, Tipp, 303.
GAUES LAND, tl, Lou, 472.
GAULES KILL, tl, Kk, 421.
GAURT NE GAURDE, tl, Lim, 287.
GAVERUS, tl, Wat, 344.
GAWLES TOWNE, tl, Kk, 421.
GAWNIFFE, pl, Ck, 209.
GEACHY, pl, Ck, 210.
GEAGANAGH, tl, Ck, 232.
GEAGRELAGH, tl, D, 81.
GEALE, pl, Tipp, 307 ; par, 309.
GEALL, par, Tipp, 307.
GEARYHUDVEENE, tl, Ker, 257.
GEDEN STOWEN, tl, Kd, 396.
GEFFRIS TOWNE, tl, Wmea, 515.
GEIG, tl, Long, 456.
GELBOYLY, pl, Tipp, 316.
GELLOS TOWNE, tl, Mea, 487.
GENVISE, tl, D, 86.
GEOGANE, 1 pld 8 gneeves, Ck, 224.
GEOGLIN, tl, Leit, 567.
GEORGESTOWN, tl, Wat, 342.
GEORG ISLAND, pl, Tipp, 306.
GERMONS TOWNE, tl, Lou, 470.
GERRAHINCH, pl, Kco, 436.
GERRANES, tl, Ck, 217.
GERRARDSTOWNE, pl, Dub, 386.
GERRETS TOWNE, tl, Mea, 483.
GERTKERBRIBEG, tl, LD, 129.
GESHELL, bar, Kco, 439 (bis), 448.
GETENSTOWNE, pl, Tipp, 328.
GHILLINE BETHAN, pl, Kco, 446.
GIBBE PATRICK, tl, Wex, 540.
GIBBINSTOWNE, tl, Lim, 273.
GIBBOGS TOWNE, tl, Wex, 534.
GIBBS TOWNE, tl, Wmea, 520.
GIBLOTTS TOWNE, tl, Mea, 482.
GIBSTOWNE, tl, Lou, 466.
GIDLANE, tl, Sli, 606.
GIGGENS TOWNE, tl, Kd, 400.
GIGINS TOWNE, tl, Wmea, 528.
GILABOY, tl, Ck, 193.
GILBERTSTOWNE, tl, Lou, 465.
GILCAGH, and Coolfin, div, Wat, 341.
GILES TOWNE, tl, Rosc, 577.
GILEVANNER, pl, Ant, 13.
GILLARDS TOWNE, tl, Wmea, 509.
GILLBERS TOWNE, tl, Wmea, 510.
GILLEREE, pl, Ant, 15.

GILLIANSTOWNE, (Gillians towne), pl, Dub, 383 ; tl, Kk, 424 ; Mea, 484.
GILLINGSTOWNE, tl, Mea, 479.
GILLNAMADOOE, tl, Arm, 29.
GILLTOWN, tl, Mea, 480.
GILNEGRANY, pl, Tipp, 296.
GILNORY, North, tl, Ck, 217.
GILSAGH, tl, Long, 458.
GILTOWNE, tl, Kd, 398 (bis).
GINTEENE, pl, Ck, 206.
GIRANECORE, tl, Ck, 219.
GIRANEGRESHINE, tl, Ck, 219.
GIRRANE, tl, Cl, 184.
GIRRANS, tl, Cl, 166.
GITTONS, pl, Dub, 377.
GIVAGH, tl, Sli, 606.
GLABE, The, tl, D, 75.
GLACK, tl, LD, 129 ; Long, 454.
GLACKE, 3 bell', Moriss qr with, Don, 61.
GLACKS TOWNE, tl, Wmea, 528.
GLAHISKIN, pl, Tipp, 299.
GLAMYEILE, pl, Tipp, 319.
GLAN, qr, Wex, 549.
GLAN-, see Glen-.
GLANACORKY, tl, Ck, 236.
GLANAGALLAGH, tl, Cl, 174.
GLANAHIRY, bar, Wat, 340.
GLANAHYRY, bar, Wat, 341, 348.
GLANASSY, tl, Wat, 333.
GLANATORE, tl, Ck, 233.
GLANAVIRANE, tl, Ck, 213.
GLANBALETTONY, tl, Rosc, 573.
GLAN BALLIVALE, tl, Kk, 421.
GLANBALLYCOULANE, tl, Ck, 234.
GLANBANE, pl, Tipp, 307, 309.
GLANBEAGH, pl, Tipp, 315.
GLANBEGG, pl, Mon, 151.
GLANBEGGE, pl, Ck, 211.
GLANBEHAGH, pl, Tipp, 318.
GLANBEHY, par, Ker, 259.
GLANBOLUGE, tl, Wex, 541.
GLANCENSAW, tl, Kk, 420.
GLANCOIN, tl, Kk, 414.
GLANCONCURK, tl, Arm, 38.
GLANCONWAY, tl, LD, 131.
GLANCOOLEBEGG, pl, Ck, 206.
GLANCOOLEMORE, pl, Ck, 206.
GLANCOROW, pl, Kco, 447.
GLANCORY, pl, Tipp, 312.
GLANCULLAN, pl, Dub, 381.
GLANCURRANE, tl, Wat, 337.
GLANDALLYGANE, tl, Wat, 337.
GLANDBANE, pl, Tipp, 313.

GLAUNEBALLYSHERUNE, tl, Ker, 247.
GLAUNEOROGHTY, bar, Ker, 257 (bis), 259.
GLAUNIRKY, pl, Ck, 225.
GLAUNKETTANE, tl, Ck, 195.
GLAUNLAP, tl, Ker, 251.
GLAUNSHALLAGH, 3 plds, Ck, 227.
GLAUNTINE, tl, Ker, 258.
GLAWNIFNYN, 1½ pld, Ck, 225.
GLEANAHAGUSHLY, tl, Lim, 271.
GLEAN-ARY, tl, Lim, 271.
GLEAN GORT, tl, Lim, 283.
GLEANMORE, tl, Lim, 283.
GLEANS, tl, Cl, 177.
GLEINHODA, tl, Leit, 569.
GLEISKE, pl, Kco, 447.
GLEN-, see also Glan-, Glann-, Glaun-, Glin-.
GLENALA, ½ qr, Don, 55.
GLENARIFF, pl, Ant, 5.
GLENARM, Ant, soldiers in, 5.
GLENARME, bar, Ant, 3 ; pl, 4.
GLENAVIE, par, Ant, 6 ; tl, ibid.
GLENBEG, qr, Don, 57.
GLENBOY, Ardvarnagh in, Leit, 566.
GLENBUK, pl, Ant, 17.
GLENCARNE, bar, Ant, 5, 20.
GLENCARRE, qr, Don, 54.
GLENCLIVES, pl, Ant, 4.
GLENCOLMIKILL, 5 qrs, Don, 47.
GLENCORPE, pl, Ant, 5.
GLENCRAGH, ½ qr, Don, 54.
GLENCROSS, qr, Don, 55.
GLENDON, qr, Don, 55.
GLENDUNE, pl, Ant, 5.
GLENEN, tl, LD, 133.
GLENESH, pl, Mon, 150.
GLEN FANET, qr, Don, 58.
GLENGESKE, tl, Don, 47.
GLENGRILLGRENNY, ½ qr, Don, 54.
GLENLARY, qr, Don, 55.
GLENLEE, belleboe, Don, 46.
GLENLESLE, pl, Ant, 15.
GLENLOAGH, pl, Ant, 13.
GLENLYLL, pl, Ant, 16.
GLEN McQUIN, tl, Don, 52.
GLENMAKIN, pl, Ant, 18.
GLENMANAGH, ½ qr, Don, 54.
GLENMAQUILL, tl, LD, 135.
GLENMIR, Don, 46.
GLENMORE, qr, Don, 57.
GLENONERVIGHER, pl, Ck, 209.
GLENREE, qr, Don, 54.
GLENTASKE, pl, Ant, 10.
GLENVARAGORAHAN, tl, D, 76.

GLENVEE, tl, Sli, 599.
GLESDALL, pl, Ant, 14.
GLESTONANE, tl, Wat, 333.
GLIDDANE, tl, Wat, 337.
GLIN-, see Glen-.
GLINDINNANE, tl, Lim, 273.
GLINELL, tl, D, 71.
GLINMORE, tl, Long, 460.
GLINOGRY, par, pt of, Lim, 269, 270 (bis) ; t, 270.
GLINN, tl, Wmea, 524.
GLINNY, tl, Ck, 203.
GLINSH, qr, Don, 58.
GLISSANE, tp, Car, 358.
GLISSMULLAGH, pl, Fer, 114.
GLOBE ALLY, Dub, 368.
GLOGHER, pl, Mon, 159.
GLONOURE, tl, Wex, 543.
GLOONIGEENITAINE, tl, Wat, 338.
GLORAGHDOW, pl, Qco, 505.
GLOVRY, tl, Ker, 252.
GLUNTIOLOGAN, tl, Arm, 36.
GLYB, pl, Ant, 12.
GLYBB LAND, Don, 49.
GLYN, tl, Wat, 343.
GLYNN, tl, Long, 454.
GNEUE BEGG, (Gneuebegg), tl, Wmea, 517 (bis).
GNOGH, pl, Ant, 14.
GNONEGRANES, tl, D, 94.
GOARY, bar, Wex, 552, 554, 556 ; tl, 552.
GOB, pl, Fer, 112 ; tl, Leit, 564.
GOBBACHOTTY, pl, Qco, 503.
GOBDUFF, pl, Mon, 154.
GOBLISK, pl, Fer, 102.
GOBMASKEALE, Cloune and, 4 tls of, LD, 124.
GODERS TOWNE, tl, Wmea, 511.
GOGAN, pl, Ck, 206.
GOLA, pl, Mon, 150.
GOLDEN LANE, Dub, 365.
GOLEDUFFE, tl, LD, 134.
GOLLAGH, pl, Fer, 113.
GOLLAN, qr, Don, 59.
GONDIDALLY, qr, Don, 57.
GOOLAGH, tl, Wat, 333.
GORAN, bor, Kk, 640 ; Portriffe of, ibid.
GORANURE, tl, Ck, 217.
GORBELLY, pl, Kco, 438.
GORCGAGE, tl, Kk, 419.
GORE ILAND, tl, Cl, 184.
GORMANSTON, tl, Mea, 482, 486.
GORMANSTOWNE, tl, Lim, 270.
GORMONDSTOWNE, pl, Tipp. 313.

HARROLDS GRANG, pl, Dub, 378.
HARRYSTOWNE, tl, Wat, 347.
HARTWELL, tl, Kd, 402.
HARVES TOWN, tl, Wex, 534.
HARYES TOWNE, tl, Mea, 484.
HASILL HAST, pl, Dub, 379.
HAWKINGS TOWN, tl, Mea, 480.
HAYESTON, tl, Mea, 484.
HAYNESTOWNE, (Haynes towne), pl, Dub, 387 ; par, Lou, 466.
HAYNS TOWNE, par, Lou, 466 ; tl, *ibid.*
HAYSTOWNE, pl, Dub, 385 (bis).
HEARE-ABY, pl, Tipp, 309.
HEATHS TOWNE, tl, Wmea, 522, 527.
HEATH TOWNE, tl, Mea, 481.
HEAUENS TOWNE, tl, Wex, 542.
HEFFOGORY, pl, Fer, 113.
HEGGISTOWNE, pl, Dub, 385.
HELLENES, pl, Ant, 17.
HENEBRYES TOWNE, tl, Kk, 419.
HEWISLAND, tl, Wex, 546.
HIGGINSTOWNE, (Higgins towne), tl, Kk, 417 ; Long, 457 ; Wmea, 522.
HIGHER DROMERE, etc., *see* Dromere, Higher, etc.
HIGH FISHERSTREET, Kinsale, Ck, 199.
HIGH RATH, tl, Kk, 417.
HIGH STREET, Dub, 369,370 ; in Kells, Kk, 426.
HIGH STRET, Dub, 369.
HIGH TOWNE WARD, Kk, 431.
HILBOWNE, tl, Wex, 535.
HILL, tl, Wex, 535.
HILLEGY, tl, Cl, 173.
HILLOSED, tl, Wex, 536.
HILLTON, Little, tl, Mea, 479.
HILL TOWNE, tl, Wmea, 509.
HILL TOWNE, Great, tl, Mea, 479.
HILNAGEEVE, pl, Ant, 15.
HILS BORROW, t, D, 80.
HIL TOWNE, tl, Wex, 534, 536, 537, 538, 543.
HINFLA, pl, Ant, 16.
HIRENECAPAGH, pl, Tipp, 324.
HISKINS TOWNE, tl, Wmea, 528.
HITCHINGSTOWNE, tl, Lou, 469.
HOATHS TOWNE, tl, Lou, 472.
HOBBINS TOWNE, tl, Wex, 533.
HODGES MILL, tl, Wex, 533.
HODGES TOWNE, tl, Kd, 399 ; Wmea, 522, 523.
HOGERS TOWNE, tl, Mea, 482.
HOLLYCROSS, (Holly cross), par, Tipp, 315 ; pt of, 303 ; pl, 315.

HOLLY CROSSE, par, Tipp, 315.
HOLLYWOOD, par, D, 87 ; Dub, 387 ; pl, *ibid.*
HOLLYWOOD, Great, pl, Dub, 387 ; Little, *ibid.*
HOLLY WOOD RATH, pl, Dub, 391.
HOLME PATRICKE, par, Dub, 386 ; pl, *ibid.*
HOLMGER, pl, Ant, 4.
HOLYWOOD, par, D, 87 ; tl, 87, 88.
HOMES TOWNE, tl, Wex, 543.
HOOKE, qr, Wex, 546.
HOPES TOWNE, tl, Wmea, 514.
HORE ABBY, pl, Tipp, 306.
HORESTOWNE, (Hores towne), tl, Lou, 465 ; Wex, 539.
HORE TOWNE, tl, Wex, 543.
HORS TOWNE, tl, Wex, 535.
HORS WOOD, tl, Wex, 547.
HORTON, Little, tl, Wex, 543.
HORTOWNE, Great, tl, Wex, 544.
HOSPITALL, tl, Lim, 269.
HOSPITALL LAND, tl, Ck, 193.
HOULINGSTOWNE, tl, Kk, 416.
HOWARDSTOWNE, tl, Lim, 269.
HOWTH, par, Dub, 388 ; t, *ibid* ; ye House of, *ibid.*
HUEGS TOWNE, tl, Wmea, 520.
HUMINERY, pl, Kco, 437.
HUNSTOWNE, pl, Dub, 391.
HUNTERS TOWNE, tl, Lou, 471.
HUNTSTOWNE, (Hunts towne), pl, Dub, 390 ; tl, Kk, 428.
HUTTON ROAD, tl, Kd, 402.

I

IBAWNE AND BARYMORE, bar, Ck, 207.
—— Barrymore, 210.
IBERCON, Ida and Igrin, bar, Kk, 420 ; bars, 422, 432.
IBRICKANE, bar, Cl, 187, 188 (bis).
IDA, Igrin and Ibercon, bar, Kk, 420 ; bars, 422, 432.
IDRONE, and St Molins, bars, Car, 356, 359 (bis).
IFFAY, and Offay, bar, Tipp, 310, 314, 329.
IGRIN, Ibercon and Ida, bar, Kk, 420 ; bars, 422, 432.
IHANRAUGHT, tl, Lim, 280.
IKEATHYE, bar, Kd, 405, 406, 409.

J.

3 L

3 M

MODOGE, tl, Arm, 30.
MODRENHY, par, Tipp, 300 ; vill, *ibid.*
MOEH, tl, Lim, 285.
MOEHRANEENE, tl, Lim, 281.
MOELDROM, pl, Tipp, 306.
MOG-, *see* Magh-.
MOGARGY, tl, LD, 136.
MOGAVER, pl, Ant, 19.
MOGEELY, par, Ck, 234 ; tl, *ibid.*
MOGELNEGNE, pl, Fer, 116.
MOGERBANE, pl, Tipp, 307.
MOGH-, *see* Magh-.
MOGH, tl, Rosc, 588.
MOGHANE, tl, Cl, 166.
MOGHER, tl, Leit, 565.
MOGHEREMORNE, pl, Ant, 6.
MOGHERLISRIRKE, pl, Ant, 6.
MOGHERMOLENANE, tl, Cl, 182.
MOGHERTRAGH, tl, LD, 137.
MOGHERYMONAGH, pl, Fer, 117.
MOGHRANS TOWNE, tl, Wex, 535.
MOG-, *see* Magh-.
MOGLASS, pl, Tipp, 296.
MOGNAGH, tl, Cl, 183.
MOGNOGE, pl, Qco, 493.
MOGOALLA, tl, Ck, 231.
MOGORA, qr, Don, 56.
MOGORBANE, par, Tipp, 307.
MOGOROUGH, tl, Lim, 287.
MOGOWNDE, tl, Cl, 186.
MOGOWRY, pl, Tipp, 305 ; par, 308 ; t, *ibid.*
MOGRAN, tl, Leit, 559.
MOGREW, tl, LD, 132.
MOHELL, par, Leit, 564 ; tl, 565.
MOHER, pl, Qco, 496 ; tl, Rosc, 575, 580.
MOHERLEGATH, tl, Leit, 559.
MOHIDEN, East, tl, Rosc, 582 ; West, *ibid.*
MOHILL, bar, Leit, 559, 565, 569.
MOHOBBUR, pl, Tipp, 295.
MOHONEY, pl, Ck, 209.
MOIGE, West, pl, Ck, 241.
MOIGH, tl, LD, 126 ; Rosc, 584.
MOINEAGH, tl, Sli, 598.
MOINEENE, tl, Leit, 568.
MOININO, tl, Cl, 165.
MOINNEROWE, tl, Kk, 425.
MOKARKY, par, Tipp, 315 ; pl, *ibid.*
MOLAGHNAKILLA, tl, Arm, 39.
MOLAGHNASYBY, tl, Arm, 38.
 See Mullagh-.
MOLAHIFFE, par, Ker, 255.
MOLANE, tl, Sli, 599.
MOLCLOGHRAN, tl, Wex, 538.

MOLETRAGHKILL, tl, LD, 143.
MOLETRAGHTAY, tl, LD, 143.
MOLEVEE, qr, Don, 61.
MOLHYANSTOWNE, pl, Dub, 381.
MOLIBEGG, tl, Wex, 551.
MOLLAGH, tl, Lim, 281 ; pl, Tipp, 310, 311 ;
 par, 311.
MOLLAGHARD, tl, Lim, 278 ; pt of, *ibid.*
 See Mullagh-.
MOLLAN, tl, LD, 129.
MOLLEN KEGH, pl, Tipp, 300.
MOLLENONY, pl, Tipp, 314.
MOLLIMEAGHAN, tl, Wmea, 519.
MOLLINDIUME, pl, Ant, 18.
MOLLINGAR, par, Wmea, 514 ; bor, 526 (bis).
MOLLIS, pl, Fer, 114.
MOLLOGHMAST, tl, Kd, 404.
 See Mullagh-.
MOLOCK BEG, qr, LD, 136.
MOLRINGE, tl, Wex, 535.
MOMEIN, qr, Don, 50.
MONACOGHLAN, pl, Qco, 492.
MONACUDDE, pl, Qco, 505.
MONAGH, qr, Don, 61.
MONAGHAN, co, 147, 160, 626.
——, High Sherif of, 626.
 See Monoghan.
MONAGHAN, par, Mon, 149 ; pl, *ibid.*
MONAGHANDUFF, pl, Mon, 149.
MONAGHBEGG, tl, LD, 125.
MONAGHMORE, tl, LD, 125.
MONAHAN, pl, Fer, 103, 115.
MONAHAY, tl, LD, 137.
MONAHIE, pl, Fer, 114.
MONALAN, tl, Arm, 34.
MONALORANE, pl, Ant, 4.
MONANANEN, tl, Sli, 597.
MONANES, pl, Ck, 222.
MONAREE, tl, Ker, 254.
MONARLARGY, tl, Wat, 342.
MONASTERNEANAGH, par, Lim, 290.
MONASTERNENY, par, Lim, 289 ; tl, *ibid.*
MONASTRY, tl, Wat, 333.
MONCK TOWNE, tl, Wmea, 509.
MONCLOYNT, qr, Don, 48.
MONDOWY, qr, Don, 48.
MONDRAHAD, pl, Qco, 496.
MONE-, *see* Money-.
MONEALEAN, tl, D, 70.
MONEAM, tl, Wat, 334.
MONEARD, tl, Ck, 194.
MONEBRINN, pl, Ck, 205.
MONECLOYNE, qr, Don, 63.

3 N

MONEENE, tl, Cl, 182.
MONEFF, qr, Don, 61.
MONEGEA, par, Lim, 280.
MONEGILLAGH, tl, Wat, 333.
MONEHENUM, tp, Car, 358.
MONEK, Upper, pl, Ant, 16.
MONELANY, tl, Lim, 280.
MONELARBAN, tl, LD, 133.
MONELL, ye other third of, Don, 57.
MONELUBANE, qr, Don, 60.
MONEMANTREGHMORE, tl, Wat, 348.
MONEMEDROOLE, tl, Kk, 428.
MONEMEHILL, pl, Tipp, 314.
MONEMOLING, tl, Wex, 549.
MONEMONTRAGHBEG, tl, Wat, 348.
MONEMORE, tl, Cl, 184.
MONEMRODDE, tl, Wat, 337.
MONENEKIRKY, tl, Wat, 337.
MONENEMOGH, tl, Wex, 549.
MONENGLARE, tl, LD, 129.
MONEOGENNIGH, tp, Cl, 169.
MONEPHAT, pl, Qco, 492 (bis).
MONERAR, tl, D, 87.
MONERNO, pl, Tipp, 318.
MONERO, pl, Tipp, 323.
MONESCRIBAGH, tl, Lou, 466.
MONESS, qr land, Don, 50.
MONESTERBOYE, par, Lou, 470 ; tl, ibid..
MONESTEREUEN, tl, Kd, 395.
MONESTERORIS, par, Kco, 436 ; pl, 437.
MONESTERRORIS, par, Kco, 437.
MONETEIK, pl, Ant, 17.
MONETOKRY, tl, Wex, 549.
MONEY-, see also Mone-, Moni-, Mony-, Mune-.
MONEYCARAGH, tl, D, 70.
MONEYDROMBRIST, tl, D, 74.
MONEYGALL, pl, Kco, 441.
MONEY McKYN, pl, Fer, 106.
MONEYNEBAN, tl, D, 75.
MONFAD, qr land, Don, 51.
MONGAN, qr, Wex, 555.
MONGARLIN, mannor, Don, 50 ; qr, ibid.
MONGLASSE, qr, Wex, 555.
MONGUE, tl, Leit, 559.
MONHENRY, tl, Kk, 423.
MONI-, see Money-.
MONIDARAH, tl, Long, 455.
MONIDUALLT, tl, Sli, 597.
MONILAGAN, tl, Long, 456.
MONINALEGH, pl, Ant, 19.
MONINGS TOWNE, tl, Wmea, 521.
MONINTOWN, tl, Wmea, 513.
MONISEEDE, tl, Wex, 553.

MONISHNARE, tl, LD, 136.
MONISILLAGH, tl, Long, 451.
MONISKALLAGHAN, tl, Long, 460.
MONITARY, tl, LD, 144.
MONITUM, tl, Wat, 340.
MONKES GRANGE, pl, Tipp, 313 (bis) ; Kco, 502.
MONKS LAND, qr, Wex, 549.
MONMORE, tl, Wex, 545.
MONMOREY, pl, Mon, 153.
MONNANE, 1 pld, Ck, 226.
MONNEV, tl, Wex, 552.
MONNEY, tl, Arm, 36.
MONNINTON, pl, Mon, 154.
MONOGHAN, co, 645.
——, High Sherif of, ibid.
  See MONAGHAN.
MONOGHAN, t, Mon, 645.
——, Provost of, ibid.
MONOGHNAGH, pl, Ck, 226.
MONONSDIHY, pl, Tipp, 310.
MONPOTOG, Ennisslare alius, tl, Arm, 33.
MONRATH, tl, Wmea, 518.
MONTAGH, tl, Rosc, 574.
MONTALLONE, tp, Cl, 172.
MONTGLASS, and clum, ye qr land called, Don, 51.
MONTOHOGY, tl, Wat, 345.
MONTRATH, the Lordship of, Qco, 497.
MONY-, see Money-.
MONYALLAGHER, bellboe, Don, 46.
MONY COOLY, tl, Kd, 401.
MONYDOROGHBEGG, Monydoroghmore and, 1 t and qr, D, 82.
MONYDOROGHMORE, and Monydoroghbegg, 1 t and qr, D, 82.
MONYDREGIE, tl, LD, 142.
MONYDUFF, tl, Leit, 565, 567.
MONYDUFFE, tl, Wmea, 517.
MONYEGNE, tl, LD, 133.
MONYGEBAGHAM, pl, Fer, 108.
MONYGOGIE, tl, LD, 131.
MONYGORMEY, tl, Ck, 193.
MONY GROOUSE, ye 2, tl, LD, 133.
MONYHAGHLY, qr, Don, 49.
MONYHOAN, tl, LD, 132.
MONYKELWARY, tl, LD, 136.
MONYLEA, tl, Wmea, 514.
MONYLOGHY, pl, Ck, 223.
MONYMOHILL, tl, Lim, 282.
MONYMOORE, tl, LD, 134, 136.
MONYNE, tl, Rosc, 580.
MONYPARSONS, tl, Ck, 230.
MONYQUILL, pl, Tipp, 320.

MULLIDORRAGH, pl, Mon, 151.
MULLIGARRY, pl, Fer, 104.
MULLIGARY, tl, Wex, 549.
MULLIGILLYHOLME, pl, Fer, 101.
MULLIMANE, pl, Fer, 99.
MULLIN, pl, Mon, 151.
MULLINARY, tl, Arm, 27.
MULLINASKARTEY, pl, Fer, 107.
MULLINDEBER, pl, Ant, 12.
MULLINDONEY, pl, Ck, 211.
MULLINEMANE, pl, Fer, 99.
MULLINENAGH, tl, Cl, 183.
MULLINEYNY, pl, Fer, 118.
MULLINGAR, par, Wmea, 515 ; bor, 642.
MULLINGLASHAN, tl, Wmea, 526.
MULLINGOUR, pl, Mon, 158.
MULLINHAM, tl, Mea, 487.
MULLINS, tl, Ker, 246.
MULLINTRA, tl, Arm, 26.
MULLISLOGH, pl, Fer, 118.
MULLITURMALY, tl, Arm, 29.
MULLITY-THOMAS, pl, Fer, 113.
MULLMACROSS, pl, Mon, 150.
MULLOGH, tl, Long, 456.
MULLOGH CLOE, tl, Lou, 472.
MULLOGH UPP, 2 belliboes, Don, 57.
    See Mullagh-.
MULLRO, qr, Don, 55.
MULLUM, tl, Kk, 418.
MULLURTAN, ½, tl, D, 82.
——, ye other ½ waste, ibid.
MULLY-, see Mullagh-.
MULLYARD, tl, Lou, 467.
MULLY KNOCHOW, pl, Fer, 109.
MULLYLANE, tl, LD, 125.
MULLYLETRA, tl, Arm, 35.
MULLYNADARAGH, tl, Leit, 561.
MULLYNESKEGH, pl, Fer, 109.
MULMABROWE, tl, LD, 144.
MULMORAN, tl, Wmea, 512.
MULNASENO, pl, Mon, 153.
MULOGHLOGRANGH, tl, Arm, 39.
MULONE, pl, Ant, 16.
MULS, qr, two thirds of, Don, 57.
MULTIFARNAN, par, Wmea, 513.
MULTIFERNAN, tl, Wmea, 513.
MULVAGH, qr, Don, 47.
MUMIMORE, qr, Don, 49.
MUMORE, pl, Ck, 206.
MUNANALEENE, tl, Cl, 175.
MUNCKS TOWN, par, Mea, 484.
MUNCK TOWNE, tl, Mea, 484 ; Wmea, 513.

MUNE-, see Money-.
MUNEGREVAN, qr land, Don, 51.
MUNEKEMAN, Loer, pl, Ant, 16.
MUNE MORE, ½ t, D, 74.
MUNEY, pl, Kco, 504.
MUNGAN, tl, Kk, 420.
MUNGREST, par, Lim, 289.
MUNGRETT, par, Lim, 263.
MUNGRETT GATE, without, tl, Lim, 263.
MUNIDARAGH, qr, Don, 61.
MUNKSTOWN, pl, Ck, 205.
MUNLAGHGLAS, pl, Fer, 112.
MUNNENOE, pl, Fer, 109.
MUNNIGE, pl, Ck, 224.
MUNNIMORE, pl, Qco, 495.
MUNNY, tl, Wmea, 509.
MUNSFIELDTOWNE, tl, Ck, 193.
MUNTERMILAN, tl, Don, 56.
MUNUOSSANE, tl, Sli, 599 (bis).
MUNY, pl, Tipp, 301.
MUNYBOY, tl, Rosc, 575.
MURAGHMORE, pl, Mon, 158.
MURDERYE, pl, Dub, 382.
MURHUR, par, Ker, 251 ; tl, ibid.
MURLAGH, ½ t, D, 73.
MURLEAGH, tl, D, 70.
MURORKAN, tl, Arm, 36.
MURRAGH, par, Ck, 206, 207.
MURRIRRIGANE, tl, Ker, 253.
MURRO CASTLE, tl, Wex, 550.
MURUSK, pl, Ant, 6.
MURVAGH, tl, D, 85.
MUSH TOWNE, tl, Wex, 540.
MUSKEAGH, pl, Ck, 207.
MUYNY, 1 pld, Ck, 222.
MY-, see Magh-.
MYAGHEDOAN, tl, LD, 138.
MYCHAELL, pl, Tipp, 317.
MYLARDS TOWNE, tl, Kk, 423.
MYLES TOWNE, tl, Lou, 471 ; Wmea, 522.
MYLODSTOWNE, pl, Tipp, 310, 314.
MYLONE, pl, Ant, 9.
MYNARD, par, Ker, 253 ; East, tl, ibid ; Weast, ibid.
MYNCREGGE, tl, LD, 144.
MYNES, pl, Ant, 4.
MYNETSTOWNE, pl, Tipp, 310.
MYNISKIE, tl, Ker, 256.
MYNOWTH, tl, Kd, 400, 402.
MYNYLOYNE, tl, Lim, 280.
MYRNS, pl, Ck, 223.
MYRUSSE, par, Ck, 223.

PALMERS TOWNE, libs of Kk, 431.

PALNALTY, tl, Rosc, 577.

PALSTOWNE, West, par, Dub, 386 ; pl, *ibid.*

PARBALLINTUBBER, tl, LD, 143.

PARCELLSTONE, tl, Wmea, 511.

PARKE, pl, Ant, 12, 19 ; Tipp, 316, 319 ; Kco, 443 ; Qco, 504, 505 ; tl, Arm, 30 ; Lim, 264, 275 ; Wex, 542 ; tp, Car, 353.

PARKE, Lower, tl, Wat, 343 ; Upper, *ibid.*

PARKE, Mr Brinfs, tl, D, 88.

PARKENAULE, tl, Ck, 204.

PARKESGROVE, tl, Kk, 413.

PARKESWOOD, tl, Wat, 347.

PARKNESWELL, tl, Wex, 550.

PARKS TOWNE, tl, Kk, 421.

PARNELLSTOWNE, pl, Dub, 382.

PARSONAGE, pl, Dub, 382.

PARSONSTON, tl, Mea, 486.

PARSONS TOWNE, tl, Kd, 402.

PARTEEN, tl, Cl, 166.

PARTEENCORENY, tl, Cl, 174.

PARTNECLODUFFE, pl, Fer, 116.

PASLOESTOWNE, pl, Dub, 391.

PASLOGSTOWNE, tl, Wmea, 515.

PASSADGE, tl, Wat, 347.

PASSAGE, pl, Ck, 237.

PAT CHAPPLE, pl, Tipp, 313.

PATECALE, tl, Fer, 118.

PATEGARE, pl, Fer, 113.

PATEGEW, pl, Fer, 113.

PATRELISKE, tl, Arm, 27.

PATRICKS TOWNE, pl, Tipp, 319.

PATRICKS WELL, tl, Lim, 270.

PATT MAVE, pl, Ant, 6.

PAUGHESTOWNE, tl, Kd, 397.

PAULESTOWNE, tl, Kk, 417.

PAWHANS TOWNE, tl, Lou, 471.

PAYNESTOWNE, tl, Kd, 406.

PAYNSTOWNE, par, Mea, 481 ; tl, *ibid.*

PEACOCKS TOWNE, tl, Mea, 487.

PEALES TOWNE, tl, Mea, 486.

PEDANSTOWNE, pl, Dub, 387.

PEE, tl, LD, 143.

PEETER STREET, Wex, 533.

PEIRCESTOWNE, (Peirces towne), pl, Tipp, 316 ; tl, Kd, 400 ; Wex, 533.

PEIRS BALSEE, tl, Wex, 535.

PEISL, pl, Mon, 156.

PELLETSTOWNE, pl, Dub, 390.

PEMBROCKS TOWNE, tl, Wex, 540.

PEMBROKESTOWN, pl, Ck, 205.

PEMBROXTOWN, tl, Wat, 345.

PEPERSTOWNE, pl, Tipp, 305.

PEPPERS TOWNE, tl, Lou, 472.

PEPPERTOWNE, par, Tipp, 308.

PERCLY LAND, tl, Mea, 481.

PETER STREET, Wex, 532.

PETERTOWNE, pl, Mon, 156.

PETIGOE, 3 sessioghes, Don, 44.

PETTITS TOWNE, tl, Wex, 534.

PHEBLESTOWNE, pl, Dub, 391.

PHE MORE, pl, Ant, 6.

PHENANNY, tl, D, 79.

PHENISCOURT, tp, Car, 357.

PHEOPOSTOWNE, pl, Dub, 391.

PHEWES, par, Wat, 337.

PHILIPSTOWN, Kco, 622.

PHILLIPPSTOWNE, (Phillipps towne), pl, Dub, 386 ; par, Lou, 467 ; tl, 471, 472.

PHILLIPPTOWNE, bar, Kco, 436, 448.

PHILLIPSTOWNE, (Phillips towne, Phillips Towne), pl, Tipp, 328 ; Kco, 435 ; tp, Car, 354 ; tl, Kd, 397 ; bar, Kco, 435 ; hundred, *ibid* ; par, Lou, 472 ; bor, Kco, 641 ; Burgesse Master of, *ibid.*

PHIPPS PARKE, Dub, 373.

PHROMPLES TOWNE, tl, Kd, 404.

PIERS TOWNE, tl, Wmea, 516, 520.

PILES TOWNE, tl, Mea, 482.

PILLTOWNE, tl, Wat, 333 ; Kk, 419.

PIPERS RATH, pl, Qco, 494 (bis).

PIPERS TOWNE, tl, Lou, 469.

PIRATTS TOWNE, tl, Kk, 428.

PITCHERS TOWNE, tl, Kd, 406.

PLACUS, tl, Ck, 231.

PLAISTER, qr land, Don, 51.

PLANTASION, tl, D, 88.

PLARAGH, tl, Sli, 599.

PLATTIN, tl, Mea, 479.

PLATTINE, Kco, 443.

PLAYSTER, tl, Lou, 467.

PLEBERSTOWNE, tl, Kk, 415.

PLOUDBOHER, tl, Wex, 539.

PLUCKANES, East, tl, Ck, 231, 232 ; West, 231.

PLUCKRES TOWNE, tl, Kd, 399.

POBLE BRYEN, bar, Lim, 288, 289, 291.

POBLERAGH, tl, Kk, 429.

POINSTOWNE, pl, Tipp, 297.

POL-, *see* Poul-.

POLCAPLE, East, pl, Tipp, 296 ; West, *ibid.*

POLDARGE, tl, Wex, 544.

POLE CAPLE, tl, Wex, 549.

POLEGARE, tl, Cl, 164.

POLEMGHELL, tl, Rosc, 574.

POLEQUINE, tl, Cl, 166.

POLHORE, tl, Wex, 542.

POLIGOWRE, tp, Cl, 171.

POLIKIMY, tl, Sli, 604.

POLLAGH, tp, Cl, 172 ; tl, 175.

POLLAND, 6 belliboes, Don, 55.

POLLANS, ½ qr of, LD, 140.

POLLARDSTOWNE, (Pollards towne), tp, Car, 353 ; tl, Kd, 395.

POLLEBANE, tl, Mea, 487.

POLLEGILL, qr, Don, 56.

POLLENTNUE, pl, Ant, 14.

POLMALOE, tl, Wex, 547.

POLMOUNTIE, tp, Car, 358.

POLRAN, tl, Wex, 539.

POLRANKAN, tl, Wex, 535.

POLREGAN, tl, Wex, 544.

POMP STREETE, pt of, LD, 124.

POOCESTOWNE, pl, Dub, 391.

POOKESTOWNE, pl, Tipp, 307.

POOLE BANE, tl, LD, 143.

POOLNOSONI, two balliboes, Don, 43.

POORES TOWNE, tl, Mea, 486.

POORE TOWNE, par, Kk, 414.

POOREWOOD, tl, Kk, 415.

PORBOLLAGHAME, pl, Tipp, 300.

PORRIS, par, Tipp, 301.

PORRISH, par, Tipp, 301.

PORT, pl, Fer, 111.

PORTAHINCH, pl, Kco, 436.

PORTAINLIAN, qr, Don, 56.

PORTALIG, tl, Wat, 347.

PORTAVO, tl, D, 93.

PORT CRUSSY, Lower, tl, Lim, 275 ; Upper, ibid.

PORTE, par, Lou, 469 ; tl, ibid.

PORTEFERRY, tl, D, 91.

PORTERSTON, tl, Mea, 486.

PORTERSTOWNE, (Porters towne), pl, Dub, 391 ; tl, Wmea, 522.

PORTEVOGGY, tl, D, 92.

PORTGRIB, tl, D, 88.

PORTGURTEN, tl, Long, 458.

PORTINOHY, tl, Sli, 601.

PORTINURE, tl, Long, 451.

PORTLEEKE, tl, Wmea, 526.

PORTLESTER, tl, Mea, 485.

PORTLINE, qr, Don, 59.

PORTLOGH, qr land, Don, 51.

PORTLOMAN, par, Wmea, 512 ; tl, ibid.

PORTMARNOCK, Connyborrow of, Dub, 388 ; Grainge of, ibid.

PORTMARNOCKE, par, Dub, 388 ; pl, ibid.

PORTMUSH, pl, Fer, 103.

PORTNEHOLLY, tl, Kk, 418.

PORTNELEGAN, tl, Arm, 28.

PORTNESANGAN, par, Wmea, 512 ; tl, ibid.

PORTNESCOLLY, tl, Kk, 418.

PORTNIHINCH, bar, Qco, 506.

PORTNYHINCH, bar, Kco, 502, 503.

PORTONOBOE, tl, Wat, 344.

PORTONOE, tl, Wat, 339.

PORTORAN, pl, Fer, 118.

PORTPIER, pl, Ant, 4.

PORTRARNE, par, Dub, 382 : pl, ibid.

PORTREENE, tl, Cl, 167.

PORTRINES GATE, tl, Wex, 546.

PORTRUSH, pl, Ant, 10.

PORTS, tl, Kd, 405.

PORTTHREE NAUD, tl, Lim, 279.

POSSECKS TOWNE, tl, Kd, 401.

POTTOCH, tl, LD, 142.

POUDERLOGH, tl, Mea, 486.

POUL-, see Pol-.

POULBANE, tl, Cl, 186 (bis).

POULBREAN, tl, Wex, 533.

POULCULLICKIE, tl, Cl, 186.

POULEBANE, tl, Cl, 175.

POULECHERRY, pl, Tipp, 310.

POULEFORY, tp, Cl, 170.

POULENACOONA, tl, Cl, 176.

POULENICC, and Lishyree, 1½ pld, Ck, 226.

POULIOURY, tl, Ck, 194.

POULLEVARLY, pl, Tipp, 303.

POULLVALL, tl, Cl, 186.

POULROAN, tl, Kk, 418.

POULROE, tl, Cl, 164.

POULSALLAGH, tl, Wex, 533 ; Little, ibid.

POWLEMILLEN, tl, Cl, 187.

POWRESTOWNE, pl, Tipp, 314.

POYTEIGHAGH, pl, Fer, 100.

PRASNA, pl, Fer, 117.

PREHANE, pl, Ck, 211.

PREHEN, tl, LD, 125.

PRESTOWNE, pl, Tipp, 305.

PREYS TOWNE, tl, Wmea, 522.

PRICKES HAYES, tl, Kk, 429.

PRIESTLAND, pl, Ant, 10.

PRIESTOWNE, tl, Lou, 470.

PRIMATS TOWNE, tl, Mea, 480.

PRINSTOWNE, tl, Mea, 481.

PRIORS TOWNE, tl, Kd, 402 ; Wex, 542.

PRISHAGGARD, tl, Wex, 547.

PRISTLAND, pl, Ant, 10.

PROHISH, pl, Ck, 240.

PROHONUS, ½ pld, Ck, 226.

PROLEEKE, tl, Lou, 467.

PROMSTOWNE, pl, Dub, 381.

3 O

WOODHOUSE, tl, Wex, 543.
WOOD KEY, Ward, Dub, 366.
WOODLANDTON, tl, Mea, 486.
WOODS, Upper, the cantred of, Qco, 495.
WOODSTOCK, pl, Ck, 238.
WOODSTOWNE, tl, Wat, 346, 347 ; pl, 349.
WOODTOWNE, (Wood towne), pl, Dub, 378 ;
    tl, Lou, 471 ; Wex, 536.
WOOLLENGRANGE, tl, Kk, 415.
WOOTTONS TOWNE, tl, Lou, 465.
WORGANSTOWNE, or Morganstowne, pl, Dub,
    383.
WORTH, 3 belliboes of, Don, 61.
——, 5 belliboes of, *ibid.*
WOTTON, tl, Mea, 485.
WYANSTON, tl, Mea, 487.
WYANSTOWNE, pl, Dub, 383.

Y

YEGOGSTOUN, tl, Kd, 397.
YEOMANS TOWNE, tl, Kd, 399.
YOEHELLS, East, tl, Ck, 220 ; West, *ibid.*
YOL TOWNE, tl, Wex, 546.
YOUGHAL, t, Ck, 200, 624, 642.
——, Mayor, Recorder and Bailifs of, 623,
    624, 642.
YOUGHALL, t, Ck, 200 ; lib of, *ibid.*
YOUGHELL, tl, Kd, 396.
YOUGHILL, par, Tipp, 323 ; pl, *ibid.*
YOUL TOWNE, tl, Wex, 534 (bis), 537, 540
    (bis).
YOUNGS TOWNE, tl, Kd, 403.

Alex. Thom & Co., Ltd.